For Reference

Not to be taken from this room

Gale Encyclopedia of
World History: Governments

Gale Encyclopedia of World History: Governments

VOLUME 2

GALE
CENGAGE Learning

Detroit • New York • San Francisco • New Haven, Conn • Waterville, Maine • London

Gale Encyclopedia of World History: Governments

Paula Kepos and Derek Jacques

Project Editors: Anne Marie Hacht and Dwayne D. Hayes

Editorial: Ira Mark Milne

Rights Acquisition and Management: Scott Bragg, Margaret Chamberlain-Gaston, Jackie Jones, Jhanay Williams, and Robyn Young

Composition: Evi Abou-El-Seoud

Manufacturing: Wendy Blurton

Imaging: Lezlie Light

Product Design: Jennifer Wahi

For product information and technology assistance, contact us at
Gale Customer Support, 1-800-877-4253.
For permission to use material from this text or product,
submit all requests online at **www.cengage.com/permissions.**
Further permissions questions can be emailed to
permissionrequest@cengage.com

Cover photographs reproduced by permission of Bettmann/Corbis (image of a session of the Roman Senate) and Getty Images (image of the inside of the United Nations building in New York).

While every effort has been made to ensure the reliability of the information presented in this publication, Gale, a part of Cengage Learning does not guarantee the accuracy of the data contained herein. Gale, a part of Cengage Learning accepts no payment for listing; and inclusion in the publication of any organization, agency, institution, publication, service, or individual does not imply endorsement of the editors or publisher. Errors brought to the attention of the publisher and verified to the satisfaction of the publisher will be corrected in future editions.

Library of Congress Cataloging-in-Publication Data

Gale encyclopedia of world history : governments / editorial, Anne Marie Hacht, Dwayne D. Hayes.
   p. cm. --
Includes bibliographical references and index.
   ISBN 978-1-4144-3152-9 (set) -- ISBN 978-1-4144-3153-6 (vol. 1) --
ISBN 978-1-4144-3154-3 (vol. 2)
   1. World politics--Encyclopedias. 2. World history--Encyclopedias. 3. Political science--Encyclopedias. I. Hacht, Anne Marie. II. Hayes, Dwayne D. III. Gale Group. IV. Title: Encyclopedia of world history : governments.

D31.G35 2008
327.003--dc22   2007034403

Gale
27500 Drake Rd.
Farmington Hills, MI, 48331-3535

978-1-4144-3152-9 (set)   1-4144-3152-X (set)
978-1-4144-3153-6 (vol. 1)   1-4144-3153-8 (vol. 1)
978-1-4144-3154-3 (vol. 2)   1-4144-3154-6 (vol. 2)

This title is also available as an e-book.
ISBN-13: 978-1-4144-3155-0 ISBN-10: 1-4144-3155-4
Contact your Gale, a part of Cengage Learning sales representative for ordering information.

Printed in the United States of America
1 2 3 4 5 6 7 11 10 09 08

Contents

VOLUME 1

Introduction xiv

Chronology xvi

Glossary xxvii

Introduction to Early Societies through Classical Civilizations
(4000 BC–AD 300) 1

Early Societies through Classical Civilizations (4000 BC–AD 300)

Ur 2

Empire of Akkad 3

Babylonian Empire 5

Ancient Egypt 6

Hittite Empire 9

Shang Dynasty 10

Kingdom of Israel 12

Chou Dynasty 14

Cush 16

Assyrian Empire 17

Mede Empire 19

Carthage 20

Persian Empire 21

Etruscan Civilization 23

Athens 24

Sparta 26

Scythia 29

Thebes 30

Macedon 31

Magadha 33

Roman Republic 35

Parthian Empire 37

Han Dynasty 40

Roman Empire 42

Aksumite Kingdom 45

Mayan Civilization 47

Introduction to Expanding Cultural Exchange (300–1000) 49

Expanding Cultural Exchange (300–1000)

Teotihuacán 50

Byzantine Empire 51

Visigoths 54

Goguryeo 56

Gupta Empire 58

Hunnic Empire 60

Sassanid Empire 61

Umayyad Empire 63

Khazars 65

'Abbāsid Empire 67

Holy Roman Empire 69

Empire of Ghana 71

Khmer Empire 73

Great Moravia 75

Kievan Rus' 77

Fāṭimid Dynasty 78

Introduction to The Premodern World (1000–1500) 81

The Premodern World (1000–1500)

Republic of Venice 82

Republic of Genoa 85

Sung Dynasty 87

Florence 89

Milan 91

Mongol Empire 93

Mali Empire 95

San Marino 97

Tibet 98

Novgorod Republic 100

Aztec Empire 101

Great Zimbabwe 103

Introduction to The Rise of the Colonial Empires (1450–1770) 107

The Rise of the Colonial Empires (1450–1770)

Inca Empire 108

Portuguese Empire 110

Songhai Empire 113

Spanish Empire 114

Ottoman Empire 119

Mughal Empire 122

Iroquois Confederation 124

Tokugawa Shogunate 127

Chippewa 130

Qing Dynasty 132

Ashanti Empire 134

Kingdom of Prussia 137

The United Kingdom 140

Principality of Liechtenstein 145

Russian Empire 147

Introduction to Revolutions and the Emergence of
Nation-States (1750–1914) 151

Revolutions and the Emergence of Nation-States (1750–1914)

Nepal 152

United States of America 154

France 159

Haiti 163

Sweden 167

Paraguay 169

Netherlands 172

Chile 174

Zulu Empire 178

Peru 180

Mexico 183

Federative Republic of Brazil 187

Bolivia 190

Cherokee 192

Uruguay 195

Ecuador 197

Venezuela 200

Belgium 203

Greece 206

Colombia 208

Costa Rica 211

Nicaragua 214

Guatemala 215

Honduras 217

El Salvador 220

Dominican Republic 222

Liberia 226

Swiss Confederation 227

Denmark 230

Argentine Republic 232

Austro-Hungarian Empire 236

Grand Duchy of Luxembourg 238

Canada 240

Italy 242

Ethiopia 246

Commonwealth of Australia 249

Panama 253

Norway 256

Republic of Bulgaria 258

Portugal 262

Monaco 265

Introduction to World Wars and the Rise of Modern
Autocracies (1900–1945) 269

World Wars and the Rise of Modern Autocracies (1900–1945)

Republic of Albania 270

Republic of Azerbaijan 273

Austria 275

Finland 278

Afghanistan 282

Republic of Kazakhstan 286

Ireland 287

Arab Republic of Egypt 291

Union of Soviet Socialist Republics 293

Turkey 297

Mongolia 299

Vatican City 301

Thailand 304

Kingdom of Saudi Arabia 307

Iraq 310

Nazi Germany 313

Republic of South Africa 317

Iceland 321

Republic of Indonesia 323

VOLUME 2

Introduction to The Postwar Era (1945–1960) 327

The Postwar Era (1945–1960)

Lebanon 328

United Nations 332

Syrian Arab Republic 335

Hashemite Kingdom of Jordan 339

Republic of the Philippines 341

New Zealand 344

Japan 346

Republic of India 349

Islamic Republic of Pakistan 354

Myanmar 358

Sri Lanka 361

State of Israel 365

Republic of Korea 369

Democratic People's Republic of Korea ... 372

Bhutan 375

People's Republic of China 378

Taiwan 382

Oman 386

Great Socialist People's Libyan Arab Jamahiriya 388

Cambodia 390

Republic of the Sudan 393

Morocco 397

Tunisia 399

Ghana 401

Malaysia 403

Guinea 406

Republic of Cuba 408

Antarctic Treaty Summary 411

Introduction to The End of Colonialism (1960–1988) 415

The End of Colonialism (1960–1988)

Republic of Cameroon 416

Togo 419

Madagascar 421

Democratic Republic of the Congo 423

Somalia 426

Benin 428

Niger 430

Burkina Faso 432

Republic of Côte d'Ivoire 434

Chad 437

Central African Republic 439

Republic of the Congo 442

Gabonese Republic 445

Cyprus 447

Senegal 451

Mali 454

Federal Republic of Nigeria 456

Islamic Republic of Mauritania 459

Sierra Leone 462

Kuwait 464

Samoa 467

Rwanda 468

Burundi 472

Democratic and Popular Republic of Algeria 475

Jamaica 478

Trinidad and Tobago 481

Uganda 482

Kenya 485

United Republic of Tanzania 488

Malawi 491

Malta 493

Zambia 495

Republic of the Gambia 498

Maldives 500

Singapore 502

Guyana 505

Botswana 507

Lesotho 509

Barbados 511

Nauru 513

Republic of Mauritius 516

Swaziland 518

Equatorial Guinea 521

Tonga 523

Fiji 525

Bahrain 527

Qatar 530

United Arab Emirates 532

Bangladesh 535

Commonwealth of the Bahamas 538

Grenada 541

Guinea-Bissau 543

Palestine 545

Mozambique 549

Cape Verde 552

Union of Comoros 553

São Tomé and Príncipe 556

Papua New Guinea 559

Angola.. 561

Spain 564

Suriname 567

Lao People's Democratic Republic............... 569

Seychelles... 572

Socialist Republic of Vietnam 574

Djibouti... 578

Solomon Islands 580

Tuvalu.. 582

Dominica 584

Iran... 586

Saint Lucia.. 590

Kiribati 592

Saint Vincent and the Grenadines 594

Zimbabwe... 596

Vanuatu 598

Belize 601

Antigua and Barbuda 603

Saint Kitts and Nevis.............................. 605

State of Brunei Darussalam 608

Federated States of Micronesia.................... 611

Republic of the Marshall Islands 612

Introduction to The Post-Communist World (1988–Present)........... 617

The Post-Communist World (1988-Present)

Republic of Hungary.............................. 618

Poland.. 621

Namibia 624

Czech Republic 626

Republic of Yemen................................ 630

Germany 631

Republic of Georgia 635

Somaliland 637

Croatia.. 640

Slovenia 643

Estonia 645

Latvia 648

Ukraine 651

Belarus 653

Moldova 656

Kyrgyzstan 658

Uzbekistan 661

Lithuania 663

Tajikistan 666

Armenia 668

Turkmenistan 671

Republic of Macedonia 673

Romania 676

Bosnia and Herzegovina 679

Serbia 682

Slovak Republic 685

Eritrea 688

Principality of Andorra 690

European Union 692

Russian Federation 696

Palau 700

Hong Kong 702

Macao 705

East Timor 706

Montenegro 709

Further Reading xxxi

Index xxxiii

Introduction

For millenia, human beings have organized themselves into social structures of increasing complexity and sophistication. From the loosely organized city-states of the Fertile Crescent to the superpowers and supra-national governments of the twenty-first century, the *Gale Encyclopedia of World History: Governments* traces the development of systems of government through the ages. In nine chronological chapters spanning the period from 4,000 BC to the present day, the *Gale Encyclopedia of World History: Governments* tells the stories of 270 governments spanning every major government type in world history.

Structure of Entries

Each entry includes the following subsections:

Type of Government: A brief description of the dominant form of governance practiced by the entry's subject, ranging from the unilateral control of absolute hereditary monarchies and dictatorships to popular democratic and parliamentary rule.

Background: A detailed description of the major historical trends, social transformations, events, and influences leading to the formation of the government.

Government Structure: A detailed description of the government's organization and function during the dominant period represented in the entry (for historical governments), or in the present day (for existing governments). This section describes how leaders are selected, the division of authority across the various branches of government, and the hierarchies and decision-making processes within those branches.

Political Parties and Factions: A description of factions—including castes, dynastic families, religious or ethnic groups, and formal political parties—that influenced the government's operation or development.

Major Events: A description of historical crises and developments, particularly those requiring government intervention or altering the way in which the government conducted its business.

Aftermath (for historical governments) or **Twenty-First Century** (for existing governments). For historical governments, the Aftermath section recounts the government's decline and legacy, emphasizing how the government influenced societies that followed. For existing governments, the Twenty-First Century section outlines current issues that may affect the government's future.

Organization of This Volume

In addition to the individual government entries, each chapter contains an introduction providing a historical overview of the period covered. The chapter structure of the *Gale Encyclopedia of World History: Governments* is designed to be compatible with the National Council for Social Studies High School World History Curriculum Standards, covering the same historical eras and exploring key themes as they relate to the development of governments throughout history. Within each chapter, entries are organized chronologically by the date the government was established.

Criteria for Inclusion in This Volume

The 270 entries in the *Gale Encyclopedia of World History: Governments* were selected for their importance in world history, the uniqueness of their form of government, their recognition by international bodies, or their current status as independent states. Because this is a historical encyclopedia, many distinct governments from different time periods are included, even if they occupied the same or overlapping geographical areas. For example, modern Italy is distinct from the Roman Empire and from the city-states of Venice and Florence, each of which receives its own entry; similarly, Nazi Germany is addressed separately from modern Germany. All 192 current member states of the United Nations are included, along with several other areas of special sovereignty, such as Hong Kong, Macao, Palestine, Somaliland, Taiwan, and Vatican City, as well as international governmental bodies such as the United Nations and the European Union. Historical civilizations without a unifying government structure have been excluded.

The editors hope that this volume helps the reader achieve a greater understanding of the historical forces and influences that have molded the governments of the present, and perhaps the future.

Chronology

c. 2300 BC:
>Akkad invades and conquers the city-states of Sumer.

c. 2100 BC:
>Ur-Nammu orders the construction of the Ziggurat of Ur.

c. 2004 BC:
>Ur is overrun by the Elamites and Amorites, ending the Ur III Dynasty.

c. 1780 BC:
>King Hammurabi of Babylon creates the Code of Hammurabi.

c. 1503 BC:
>Queen Hatshepsut of Egypt declares herself Pharaoh.

c. 1380 BC:
>The reign of Hittite King Suppiluliumas I begins.

c. 1350 BC:
>King Pageng of the Shang Dynasty relocates his capital to the city of Yin, commencing the dynasty's prosperous Yin period.

c. 1122 BC:
>Chou Hsin, the final king of China's Shang Dynasty, is deposed by Wu Wang, first king of the Chou Dynasty.

c. 957 BC:
>The Temple of Solomon in Jerusalem is completed.

c. 771 BC:
>The Chou Dynasty's western capital at Hao is destroyed, ending a period of prosperity and stability.

c. 701 BC:
>The Assyrians lay siege to Jerusalem.

680 BC:
>The Spartans defeat Persia at the battle of Thermopylae.

670 BC:
>The Cushites are driven out of Egypt by the Assyrians.

613 BC:
>Persian King Darius I unsuccessfully invades Scythia.

612 BC:
>The Assyrians are defeated by an alliance between the Babylonians and the Medes.

594 BC:
>Democracy is first introduced and codified in Athens.

586 BC:
>Jerusalem falls to the armies of Nebuchadnezzar II of Babylon.

c. 550 BC:
>Thebes establishes the Boeotian league, a confederacy of Greek city-states.
>
>Cyrus II leads a successful Persian revolt against the Mede Empire.

522 BC:
>Darius I becomes king of Persia.

510 BC:
>The Etruscans are expelled from Rome, marking the decline of their power in Italy.

509 BC:
>Republican government is established in Rome.

494 BC:

The Persians quell the Ionic Revolt orchestrated by an alliance of Greek city-states.

479 BC:

The philosopher Confucius dies.

404 BC:

Sparta defeats Athens in the Second Peloponnesian War.

371 BC:

Thebes defeats Sparta at the battle of Leuctra, ending the Spartan hegemony.

c. 343 BC:

Ptolemy seizes power in Egypt.

323 BC:

The Macedonian King Alexander the Great dies.

c. 297 BC:

Candragupta, under whose leadership Magadha conquered almost all of the Indian subcontinent, dies.

264 BC:

The First Punic War between Carthage and Rome begins.

206 BC:

The Han Dynasty is founded by Emperor Liu Pang in China.

185 BC:

The Mauryan Dynasty in Magadha ends.

146 BC:

Carthage falls before Rome's armies, ending the Third Punic War.

133 BC:

A series of civil wars begin in Rome that last for more than one hundred years and ultimately lead to the end of the Republic.

53 BC:

The Parthians defeat the Roman army at Carrhae.

27 BC:

Augustus is named the first emperor of Rome.

AD 220:

The Han Dynasty officially ends, with its lands divided into three kingdoms.

325: Aksum defeats the Cushites at Meroë.

395: The Roman Empire is divided into Western and Eastern empires after the death of Emperor Theodosius I.

410: Visigoth forces, under Alaric I, capture Rome.

413: The reign of Jangsu, the king of Goguryeo, begins.

445: Attila becomes the undisputed ruler of the Huns.

531: Khosrow I becomes king of the Sassanid Empire.

550: The reign of the Gupta Empire comes to an end.

680: Death of the first Umayyad Caliph, Mu'āwiyah.

727: The first Doge of Venice is selected.

c. 750: The city-state of Teotihuacán collapses.

Abū al-'Abbās as-Saffāḥ founds the 'Abbāsid caliphate.

The Umayyad caliphate ends with the death of Marwān II in Egypt.

800: Charlemagne is crowned Holy Roman Emperor.

802: Jayavarman II founds the Khmer Empire.

830: Mojmir conquers various Slovak lands and becomes king of Great Moravia.

863: Byzantine clerics Cyril and Methodius come to Great Moravia. They go on to create the Cyrillic alphabet.

909: Al-Mu'izz establishes the Shia Fāṭimid caliphate, based in Egypt.

965: The Khazars are conquered by the armies of Sviatoslav I of Kievan Rus'.

976: Basil II claims the throne of the Byzantine Empire.

1019: Yaroslav the Wise becomes grand prince of Kievan Rus'.

1038: The Fāṭimid Dynasty and Byzantine Empire reach a peace accord after decades of hostilities.

1054: The Great Schism divides Christianity into eastern and western churches, based in Constantinople and Rome, respectively.

1066: England is invaded by William the Conqueror of Normandy.

1076: Almoravids conquer Kumbi Saleh, initiating the final decline of the Empire of Ghana.

1099: Genoa becomes a self-governing commune.

1100: The Bantu tribe dominates the region that later becomes Gabon.

1138: The Treaty of Constance ensures the right of Milan and other Italian city-states to self-governance and broad autonomy within the Holy Roman Empire.

1190: Khmer Emperor Jayavarman VII conquers Champa (Vietnam).

1206: Genghis Khan founds the Mongol Empire.

1235: Mandinka chieftain Sundiata founds the Mali Empire.

1236: Alexander Nevsky becomes prince of Novgorod.

1238: The first Thai kingdom is established in Southeast Asia.

1246: Mikhail Vsevolodovich, the last grand prince of Kievan Rus', is captured and killed by Mongol invaders.

1277: Ottone Visconti becomes lord of Milan, establishing a dynasty that rules the city-state for more than a century.

1278: By agreement between Spain and France, the Bishop of La Seu d'Urgell and the Count of Foix are declared co-princes of Andorra.

1282: Danish King Eric V signs the Great Charter, Denmark's first constitution.

1297: The House of Grimaldi comes to power in Monaco.

1324: Mali Emperor Mansa Mūsā commences his pilgrimage to the Muslim holy city of Mecca.

1325: Aztecs found the city of Tenochtitlán in central Mexico.

1339: Simon Boccanegra is elected the first Doge of Genoa.

1348: The Black Plague sweeps through northern Italy.

1355: Montenegro emerges as an independent state.

1405: Timur, the last great Mongol ruler, dies, leaving the Mongol Empire to decline.

1418: The Portuguese Empire begins exploration of the islands off the west coast of Africa, beginning an era of expansion.

1420: Nyatsimba Mutota comes to power in Great Zimbabwe.

1434: Cosimo de' Medici becomes the first Medici ruler of Florence.

1452: Frederick III, the first Habsburg Holy Roman emperor, takes the throne.

1464: The Songhai Empire under Sonni 'Ali begins its expansion throughout western Africa.

1469: The marriage of Ferdinand I of Aragon and Isabela I of Castile unites Spain under one crown.

1471: Defeat by the princes of Moscow in the battle of Shelon marks the end of the Novgorod Republic's independence.

1482: Portuguese explorer Diogo Cão is the first European to visit the region that later becomes the Republic of the Congo.

1492: Spanish explorer Christopher Columbus lands on an island in what is now the Bahamas, in the first landfall of his voyage to the New World.

1520: Süleyman I becomes sultan of the Ottoman Empire, bringing the empire to the zenith of its power.

1521: The Spanish capture the Aztec capital of Tenochtitlán, leading to the demise of the Aztec Empire.

1523: Sweden overthrows Danish rule to establish its own monarchy.

1526: Ẓahīr-ud-Dīn Muḥammad founds the Mughal Empire in India.

1532: Inca Emperor Atahualpa is kidnapped and killed by the conquistador Francisco Pizarro.

1565: The Philippine Islands are claimed as colonies of the Spanish Empire.

1572: The Venetian navy defeats the Ottomans at the Battle of Lepanto.

1581: Northern provinces of the Netherlands sign the Union of Utrecht, forming the Dutch Republic.

1598: Tokugawa Ieyasu becomes the first Tokugawa shogun, seizing control of feudal Japan.

1614: The British open the East India Trading Company in Mumbai, beginning an era of British control in India.

1630: Portugal establishes a colonial administration for the territory of Portuguese Guinea.

1642: Tibet is unified under the theocratic rule of the Dalai Lama.

1644: Qing armies take Beijing, marking the beginning of the end of the Ming Dynasty's dominance in China.

1665: The Act of Royalty overturns Denmark's Great Charter, making the country an absolute monarchy.

1680: The Ashanti Empire is established in Africa by Osei Tutu.

1701: Frederick I becomes the first king of Prussia.

1707: England and Scotland are united under the Act of Union, and a single parliament of Great Britain is formed.

1719: Liechtenstein is granted independence within the Holy Roman Empire.

1721: Czar Peter I founds the Russian Empire.

1744: Ahmad bin Said expels Persians from Oman.

1754: The French and Indian War begins, and the Iroquois Confederation allies itself with the British against the French.

1769: Prithvi Narayan Shah becomes the first king of Nepal.

1776: Thirteen British colonies in North America declare independence from the United Kingdom.

1788: The first British expedition, led by Captain Arthur Phillip, arrives in Australia.

1789: The government of the United States is established.

French revolutionaries storm the Bastille, beginning the overthrow of the French monarchy and France's first republic.

1792: The British firm Sierra Leone Company settles freed slaves in Freetown, Sierra Leone.

1799: Napoléon Bonaparte overthrows the republican government of France, installing himself as an autocratic First Consul.

1804: In the culmination of the most successful slave rebellion in world history, Haiti gains its independence from France.

1809: Sweden becomes a constitutional monarchy.

1811: Uruguay and Paraguay secure their independence from Spain.

1812: The Chippewa Native American tribe allies itself with its longtime enemies, the British, against the United States in the War of 1812.

1814: The Treaty of Kiel transfers control of Norway from Denmark to Sweden.

1815: The Kingdom of the Netherlands is established in the aftermath of the Napoleonic Wars.

1816: Thousands are killed in a slave revolt on Barbados.

1818: Chile secures its independence from Spain.

1819: Gran Colombia, a state occupying the area of Colombia, Venezuela, and Ecuador, declares its independence from Spain under the leadership of Simón Bolívar.

1821: Peru is liberated from Spanish control by General José de San Martín.

The Treaty of Córdoba grants Mexico independence from Spain.

1822: Dom Pedro I, son of the Portuguese king and regent of Brazil, declares the independence of the Empire of Brazil.

1823: Costa Rica, El Salvador, Guatemala, Honduras, and Nicaragua join to form the United Provinces of Central America.

1825: Bolivia proclaims its independence from Spain as the Republic of Bolívar.

Uruguay liberates itself from Brazil.

1827: The Cherokee Nation adopts a constitution modeled on the constitution of the United States.

1828: Shaka, founder of the Zulu Empire, is assassinated.

1830: The London Protocol of 1830 declares Greek independence.

Belgium declares independence from the Netherlands.

Venezuela and Ecuador separate from Gran Colombia to become independent nations.

1838: Costa Rica declares its independence from the United Provinces of Central America.

1840: British warships bombard the coast of China, seeking to protect the right of British traders to sell opium. The Qing government is ultimately forced to capitulate to British demands.

New Zealand becomes a British possession, and the British colonists make peace with the Maori natives under the terms of the Treaty of Waitangi.

1841: El Salvador declares its independence after the collapse of the United Provinces of Central America.

1842: Hong Kong is ceded to the British by China at the end of the First Opium War.

1844: The Dominican Republic obtains its independence from Haiti.

1845: A potato blight strikes Europe, resulting in the Irish Famine. Over the next decade a mass exodus from Ireland ensues, spurring economic depression and political unrest for those who remain.

Tongan King George Tupou I establishes the dynasty that will continue to rule Tonga into the twenty-first century.

1847: Liberia, Africa's oldest republic, declares independence from the United States.

1848: Mexico loses several northern territories to the United States in the aftermath of the Mexican American War.

The Swiss Confederation enacts its first constitution.

1853: Argentina adopts a new constitution after the dissolution of the United Provinces of South America.

A United States naval force under the command of Commodore Matthew Perry arrives in Japan to negotiate a treaty that would open Japan to foreign trade.

1856: American soldier of fortune William Walker becomes president of Nicaragua.

1857: The last Mughal emperor, Bahādur Shāh II, rebels against British control of India and is exiled to Rangoon.

1860: Civil war breaks out between the northern and southern United States. At the end of the four-year conflict, slavery is abolished in the country.

1861: The Italian peninsula is unified as the Kingdom of Italy.

1862: Otto von Bismarck is appointed Prussia's prime minister.

During the national unification of Italy, San Marino's sovereignty is assured by treaty.

1864: Cambodia becomes a French protectorate.

1867: Emperor Meiji takes the throne of Japan, ending the Tokugawa shogunate.

Luxembourg gains independence from the Netherlands.

The Austrian Empire and the Kingdom of Hungary unite under Franz Josef I as the Austro-Hungarian Empire.

Canada achieves self-government as a dominion of the United Kingdom.

1870: The War of the Triple Alliance between Paraguay and the allied nations of Argentina, Brazil, and Uruguay ends.

The Kingdom of Italy seizes Rome from the papacy, confining the pope to the Vatican and Lateran palaces.

1878: Conflicts over trade and coastal territorial rights lead to the War of the Pacific, in which Chile fights against the combined forces of Peru and Bolivia.

1888: Slavery is abolished in Brazil.

1893: Côte d'Ivoire becomes a French colony.

1894: The West African kingdom of Dahomey, now Benin, is subdued by the French, who establish a colony there.

1896: Ethiopia gains independence from Italy under the terms of the Treaty of Addis Ababa.

1898: In the aftermath of the Spanish American war, Spain cedes the Philippines, Guam, and Puerto Rico to the United States.

1899: Russia begins a campaign of Russification in all the autonomous states within its empire to suppress nationalist movements in states such as Finland.

Kuwaiti ruler Sheikh Mubarak al-Sabah signs a treaty with Britain to promote British interests in the region in return for British protection.

1901: The Commonwealth of Australia is founded.

1902: Prince 'Abd al-'Azīz ibn 'Abd ar-Raḥman captures Riyahd for the Saud family.

1903: Panama, under United States sponsorship, declares its independence from Colombia.

1904: José Batlle y Ordoñez becomes president of Uruguay on a platform of modernization.

1905: Norway declares independence from Sweden.

The Maji Maji uprising against German rule in Tanzania becomes one of the first anticolonial rebellions in Africa.

1907: The British establish a monarchy in Bhutan.

1908: The Young Turk rebellion ends with the power of the Ottoman sultan being supplanted by the parliament.

Bulgaria declares its independence from the Ottoman Empire.

1910: Japan annexes Korea and establishes a colonial government.

Portugal abolishes its monarchy, becoming a republic.

The French territories of Chad, the Central African Republic, the Congo, and Gabon are joined into a single administrative unit called French Equatorial Africa.

1911: Monaco becomes a constitutional democracy.

1912: Albania proclaims its independence after the First Balkan War.

1914: Archduke Franz Ferdinand, heir to the Austro-Hungarian throne, is assassinated in Bosnia, triggering World War I.

1915: The genocide of Armenians by Ottoman Turks begins.

South Africa invades Namibia, wresting control from the German colonial government.

Finland gains its independence from Russia.

1917: The short-lived Kazakh state of Alash Orda is established. It is annexed by the Soviet Union in 1920.

1918: The independent state of Lithuania is declared.

The short-lived Azerbaijan Democratic Republic is established. It is annexed by the Soviet Union two years later.

The Russian Empire ends with the execution of Czar Nicholas II by Bolshevik rebels.

With the collapse of the Austro-Hungarian Empire after World War I, Austria becomes an independent republic.

1919: Upper Volta, now Burkina Faso, becomes a French colony.

1921: The Anglo-Irish Treaty establishes the Irish Free State as part of the British Commonwealth.

A short-lived constitutional monarchy is established in Mongolia, under the leadership of Bogdo Khan.

1922: Fascist leader Benito Mussolini takes power in Italy.

Britain grants Egypt independence as a constitutional monarchy.

At the conclusion of the Russian civil war, the Union of Soviet Socialist Republics, composed of Armenia, Azerbaijan, Belarus, Georgia, Russia, and Ukraine, comes into existence.

Niger becomes a French colony.

1923: After the dissolution of the Ottoman Empire, Turkey proclaims itself a republic under the leadership of Mustafa Kemal Atatürk.

1924: After the death of Mongolian King Bogdo Khan, the Mongolian People's Republic is established, existing as a satellite of the Soviet Union and becoming the world's second Communist country after the Soviet Union.

1925: Reza Shah Pahlavi takes power in Iran with British support.

1929: Italy recognizes the sovereignty of the Holy See, creating the independent state of Vatican City.

1932: The Kingdom of Siam (Thailand) becomes a constitutional monarchy after a bloodless coup.

The Kingdom of Saudi Arabia is officially founded.

The Kingdom of Iraq becomes independent from Britain.

Bahrain becomes the first Arab Gulf state to discover large supplies of oil and to prosper from its extraction and sale.

1933: Adolf Hitler is appointed chancellor of Germany.

1935: Juan Vicente Gómez, the longtime dictator of Venezuela, dies.

1936: The Italo-Ethiopian War results in Italian occupation of Ethiopia.

1938: Germany annexes Austria in the military invasion known as the Anschluss.

1939: The Spanish Civil War ends in victory for the Nationalists; a right-wing dictatorship under General Francisco Franco is established.

Lithuania, Estonia, and Latvia are invaded and annexed by the Soviet Union.

1941: Japan attacks the United States naval base at Pearl Harbor, Hawaii, bringing the United States into World War II.

Peru invades Ecuador over a territorial dispute.

Nazi Germany begins the mass extermination in concentration camps of Jews, gypsies, homosexuals, and political undesirables.

1943: Lebanon declares independence from France.

1944: Germany surrenders to Allied forces, ending World War II in Europe.

During occupation by the Allies during World War II, Iceland declares its independence from Denmark.

1945: The United Nations is established after a majority of its members ratify the Charter of the United Nations.

1946: The Republic of the Philippines obtains its independence from the United States.

Bulgaria abolishes its monarchy and becomes a republic.

The Kingdom of Jordan achieves independence from England.

The Roman Catholic priest Barthélemy Boganda becomes the first African elected to the French National Assembly.

1947: French forces put down a nationalist uprising in Madagascar; approximately eleven thousand people are killed in the battle.

New Zealand obtains independence from Britain.

As part of the agreement to end British rule, India is partitioned into two independent states, Muslim Pakistan and Hindu India.

1948: Myanmar is granted independence from England.

Mohandas Gandhi, father of Indian independence, is murdered.

A United Nations mandate creates Israel in former Palestinian territory.

The former Japanese colony of Korea is divided into two separate states, the northern Democratic People's Republic of Korea, and the southern Republic of Korea.

Belgium, the Netherlands, and Luxembourg enter the Benelux Customs Union, allowing free trade and reciprocal rights among the three countries.

The Nationalist Party takes power in South Africa and immediately pursues a policy of legal measures—called apartheid—to suppress South Africa's black population.

1949: Indonesia's war of independence against the Dutch ends with Indonesia's independence.

India and Bhutan conclude an agreement whereby India protects Bhutan and represents Bhutan internationally.

Leaders of the Kuomintang faction, after losing a civil war with Communists in China, flee the mainland for the island of Taiwan, establishing the Republic of China there, while the Communists establish the People's Republic of China on the mainland.

Germany is divided into the German Democratic Republic (East Germany), which is dominated by the Soviet Union, and the democratic Federal Republic of Germany (West Germany).

1951: The European Coal and Steel Community, an international group unifying the European markets for making resources essential to war, is formed under the terms of the Treaty of Paris.

1953: Armistice is achieved in the Korean War.

After a military coup, Egypt's king is exiled and an Egyptian republic is established.

1954: Algerian nationalists launch a revolution against French rule under the name National Liberation Front .

A United States-supported coup in Guatemala installs Colonel Castillo Armas as the new president.

1956: Sudan obtains its independence from England and Egypt.

Morocco reaches accords with both France and Spain to obtain its independence.

Tunisia gains independence from France.

French Cameroon declares itself the independent Republic of Cameroon.

Thousands are killed in a Hungarian uprising against the country's Communist dictatorship.

1957: Dictator François "Papa Doc" Duvalier takes control of Haiti.

Ghana gains independence from Britain.

1958: Guinea obtains independence from France.

The Batista administration abdicates power in Cuba, leaving revolutionaries under the command of Fidel Castro in control.

Mao Tse-tung, leader of the People's Republic of China, initiates a modernization program known as the Great Leap Forward.

1959: Tibetan rebellion against the Chinese military fails, and the Dalai Lama goes into exile in India.

Twelve countries sign the Antarctic Treaty, which calls for peaceful, nonmilitary use of Antarctica and cooperation in research between signatories.

1960: Togo becomes a sovereign nation.

The Democratic Republic of the Congo gains full independence from Belgium.

The former Sudanese Republic declares itself the independent Republic of Mali, dissolving the short-lived Federation of Mali in which it was united with Senegal.

Nigeria gains its independence from Britain.

Madagascar, Benin, Niger, Burkina Fasso, Côte d'Ivoire, Chad, the Central African Republic, the Republic of the Congo, Gabon, Senegal, and the Islamic Republic of Mauritania gain their independence from France.

1961: Dominican dictator Rafael Leonidas Trujillo is assassinated.

A plebiscite splits British Cameroon into two parts: The northern region joins Nigeria and the southern region becomes part of the Republic of Cameroon.

Sierra Leone gains its independence from Britain.

1962: The United States and Soviet Union come to the brink of war over the issue of Soviet nuclear missiles in Cuba.

Samoa becomes the first of the Pacific microstates to achieve independence.

Algeria attains independence from France.

Jamaica attains independence from Britain, as does Trinidad and Tobago.

The Sultan of Brunei, whose dynastic line has ruled the country since the fifteenth century, declares a state of emergency that allows him to suspend most provisions of the constitution. The state of emergency is still in effect in 2007.

1963: Kenya attains its independence from Britain.

1964: Malta gains its independence from Britain.

Nyasaland and Northern Rhodesia gain their independence from Britain, with Nyasaland becoming the nation of Malawi and Northern Rhodesia becoming the nation of Zambia.

The Arab League unites various Palestinian groups into the Palestine Liberation Organization.

The Romanian Communist Party, under the leadership of Nicolae Ceausescu, declares itself independent from the Soviet Communist Party.

1965: Singapore withdraws from the Federation of Malaysia to become an independent state.

Maldives and The Gambia gain their independence from Britain.

White settlers in Southern Rhodesia (now Zimbabwe) declare independence from Britain without regard to the black majority, setting off a protracted guerrilla war.

1966: Guyana, Botswana, Lesotho, and Barbados gain their independence from Britain.

In China Mao Tse-tung initiates the Cultural Revolution as a means of purging dissent through violence and forcible reeducation.

Nauru becomes an independent nation.

1967: Israel defeats Egypt, Jordan, and Syria in the Six Days' War.

Singapore, Malaysia, Indonesia, the Philippines, and Thailand form the Association of Southeast Asian Nations (ASEAN).

1968: Swaziland gains independence from Britain.

The forty-year reign of Portuguese ruler António de Oliveira Salazar comes to an end.

Equatorial Guinea gains its independence from Spain.

A military junta led by General Juan Velasco Alvarado takes control of Peru.

The Communist Khmer Rouge launches an insurgency against the Cambodian government from bases in Vietnam.

Mauritius gains independence from Britain.

Czechoslovakia enjoys a period of political liberalization under Communist rule in a period called the Prague Spring.

1969: The so-called "Soccer War" breaks out between Honduras and El Salvador. Although the fighting only lasts four days, there are thousands of casualties.

1970: Jordan initiates military action against Palestinian guerillas using Jordan as a base to attack Israel.

Qabus bin Said deposes his father to become Sultan of Oman.

1971: Idi Amin stages a successful coup in Uganda, initiating a brutal dictatorship that persists until 1979.

Bahrain, Qatar, and the United Arab Emirates gain their independence from Britain.

Bangladesh declares its independence from Pakistan.

1973: A military junta led by Agusto Pinochet deposes Chilean president Salvador Allende.

The Bahamas gain independence from Britain.

1974: The Greek monarchy is abolished.

Cyprus is divided into Greek and Turkish zones after an invasion by the Turkish military.

Guinea-Bissau gains its independence from Portugal.

Residents of the Ellice Islands elect to break away from the Gilbert Islands to form a separate colony, Tuvalu.

1975: São Tomé and Príncipe, Cape Verde, and Portuguese East Africa gain their independence from Portugal; the latter becomes the nation of Mozambique.

The Union of Comoros declares its independence from France.

Formerly under Australian control as a United Nations trust, Papua New Guinea gains its independence.

Indonesia invades East Timor ten days after the Timorese declare independence.

Angola gains its independence from Portugal, initiating a civil war that lasts for nearly thirty years and results in an estimated one million killed.

Suriname attains full independence from the Netherlands.

The Pathet Lao movement in Laos establishes the Communist Lao People's Democratic Republic.

The Vietnam War ends in victory for North Vietnam; United States troops withdraw.

1976:   The Sahrawi Arab Democratic Republic is established in Western Sahara, but not recognized by Morocco, which claims sovereignty over the territory.

Seychelles gains its independence from Britain.

North Vietnam conquers South Vietnam, and the two are unified under a single government as the Socialist Republic of Vietnam.

1977:   Djibouti gains its independence from France.

Civil war begins in Mozambique. By the time a peace accord is signed in 1992, more than one hundred thousand have been killed and one million wounded.

1978:   Dominica, the Solomon Islands, and Tuvalu gain complete independence from Britain.

1979:   Saint Lucia, Saint Vincent and the Grenadines, and Kiribati achieve full independence from Britain.

Under pressure from the Sandinistas, Anastasio Somoza Debayle flees Nicaragua, ending forty-three years of Somoza family rule.

The Iranian Pahlavi dynasty is overthrown by the Islamic Revolution, led by Ayatollah Ruhollah Khomeini, who returns from exile to lead Iran.

1980:   Dominica prime minister Dame Mary Eugenia Charles becomes the first female head of government in the Caribbean.

The international community recognizes the independent state of Zimbabwe under majority black leadership.

The independent republic of Vanuatu is established.

Protests by shipyard workers in Gdańsk, Poland, lead to the formation of Solidarity, a nationwide trade union, which begins to extract concessions from the Communist government.

1981:   Belize and Antigua and Barbuda gain full independence from Britain.

1982:   After nearly thirty years of military rule, free elections are held in Honduras.

Argentina's failed invasion of the Falkland Islands leads to the downfall of its military government.

Canada achieves true independence from the United Kingdom, with a new constitution called the 1982 Canada Act.

1983:   Civil war begins in Sri Lanka between government forces and the Tamil Tigers rebel group.

The United States invades Grenada to restore order and rid the country of Cuban troops after a Marxist coup.

Saint Kitts and Nevis gains full independence from Britain.

1984:   Brunei gains full independence from Britain, after assurances from Malaysia and Indonesia that they will respect Brunei's sovereignty.

1985:   Communist Albanian premier Enver Hoxha dies, after more than forty years in office.

1986:   Both the Federated States of Micronesia and the Republic of the Marshall Islands enter Compacts of Free Association with the United States. The treaties grant independence to the two countries and pledge military defense and financial assistance from the United States. In 2003 both compacts are renegotiated for an additional twenty years.

The worst nuclear accident in history, at the Chernobyl nuclear power plant in Ukraine, intensifies the Ukrainian movement for independence from the Soviet Union.

1987:   Forty years of martial law ends in Taiwan.

Zine El Abidine Ben Ali deposes Habib Bourguiba, who spent more than thirty years in office as president of Tunisia.

1988: Soviet leader Mikhail Gorbachev announces the withdrawal of troops from Afghanistan and an end to the Soviet Union's policy of intervention in the internal affairs of Eastern Bloc countries.

Myanmar's military takes over the government.

1989: Hungary's ruling Communist Party announces that it is abandoning Communism for democracy.

Romanian dictator Nicolae Ceausescu is executed, ending his twenty-four-year reign.

Communist rule collapses peacefully in Czechoslovakia in the Velvet Revolution.

Lebanon's fourteen-year civil war ends with the Taif Accord.

Free elections are held in Poland for the first time since the start of Communist rule in 1945.

1990: Namibia gains independence from South Africa.

The Yemen Arab Republic and the People's Democratic Republic of Yemen are united under a single government as the Republic of Yemen.

East Germany and West Germany are reunited as the Federal Republic of Germany.

Liberian dictator Samuel K. Doe is assassinated, sparking a decade-long civil war.

1991: Croatia, Slovenia, and Macedonia declare their independence from Yugoslavia.

The leaders of Russia, Belarus, and Ukraine sign the Belavezha Accords, resulting in the formal dissolution of the Soviet Union.

With the collapse of the Soviet Union, the Soviet republics Azerbaijan, Georgia, Armenia, Turkmenistan, Estonia, Latvia, Lithuania, Moldova, Kyrgyzstan, Tajikistan, Uzbekistan, and Kazakhstan declare independence.

An assemblage of clan-based militias, disaffected soldiers, and ordinary citizens drive the Somali dictator Mohammed Siad Barre into exile. Chaos and civil war follow.

Iraq invades Kuwait and is repelled the following year by international forces led by the United States.

Somaliland declares its independence from Somalia but is not granted international recognition.

1992: Rakhman Nabiyev is kidnapped and forced to resign after allegations of electoral fraud in Tajikistan's first presidential elections.

El Salvador's twelve-year civil war comes to an end.

A civil war in Transnistria, a Moldovan territory, ends in a stalemate after the area is occupied by Russian troops.

The newly independent state of Bosnia is torn apart by civil war.

Serbia and Montenegro declare their independence as a joint state under the name Federal Republic of Yugoslavia.

1993: Czechoslovakia dissolves into separate Czech and Slovak republics.

After a thirty-year rebellion, Eritrea becomes a sovereign nation.

The Maastricht Treaty, which formally establishes the European Union, goes into effect.

Andorra approves a constitution, becoming a parliamentary democracy.

1994: Palau becomes an independent state after more than a century of foreign rule and administration.

After decades of international protest, the apartheid system is abandoned in South Africa, and free elections are held with universal suffrage.

North Korea's premier, Kim Il Sung, dies, ending a forty-six-year reign. His son, Kim Jong Il, becomes North Korea's new leader.

The death of Rwandan President Juvénal Habyarimana in a plane crash provokes one of the century's worst episodes of ethnic violence as Hutu extremists murder more than eight hundred thousand Tutsis and moderate Hutus.

The Palestinian Authority is created in 1994 with the approval of Israel.

United States President Bill Clinton helps negotiate the withdrawal of Russian troops from Latvia.

1995: The Dayton Peace Accords end wars between Serbia and Croatia and civil war in Bosnia.

Austria, Finland, and Sweden join the European Union.

1996: Civil war breaks out in Nepal between Maoist rebels and the monarchist government.

Guatemala's thirty-six-year civil war ends.

1997: The treaty allowing a century of British rule in Hong Kong expires; the territory is returned to Chinese rule and named the Hong Kong Special Administrative Region.

1998: General Suharto, Indonesia's autocratic ruler since 1965, resigns amid public demonstrations against his regime.

1999: War breaks out between India and Pakistan over the disputed Kashmir region. In the aftermath of the conflict, the military assumes command of Pakistan's government.

Control of the Panama Canal, held by the United States since its opening in 1914, reverts to Panama.

The Serbian war against the Kosovo independence movement ends after intervention by NATO forces.

2002: East Timor is recognized as an independent state.

2003: Iraq is invaded by the United States, ending the reign of dictator Saddam Hussein.

Arab militias initiate genocide in the Darfur region of Sudan.

Mass demonstrations in the Republic of Georgia bring down the authoritarian government of Eduard Shevardnadze in the peaceful Rose Revolution.

2004: More than four hundred people are killed when Chechen rebels take hostages at a school in Beslan, heightening hostilities in the decade-old Chechen rebellion against Russian rule.

Cyprus, the Czech Republic, Estonia, Hungary, Latvia, Lithuania, Malta, Poland, Slovakia, and Slovenia join the European Union.

2005: Mass demonstrations in Kyrgyzstan bring down the authoritarian government of Askar Akayev.

2006: Montenegro declares independence from Serbia.

Sapamurad Niyazov, Turkmenistan's dictator since 1985, dies, ending a notorious period of dictatorial rule and cult of personality; his deputy prime minister and personal dentist, Gurbanguly Berdymukhammedov, is named to succeed him.

Fijian military commander Frank Bainimarama ousts the country's democratically elected government in a military coup.

A cease-fire agreement is signed in the Burundi civil war.

2007: Bulgaria and Romania join the European Union.

Glossary

ABSOLUTE MONARCHY: A form of government in which a king or queen rules without constitutional or other restrictions.

ANARCHISM: A political philosophy maintaining that government is unnecessary.

ANARCHY: Lawlessness due to the absence of government.

APARTHEID: Literally "separateness"; the system of institutionalized racism that existed in South Africa from 1948 to 1994.

APPELLATE COURT: A superior court that reviews the decision of a lower court at the request of the losing party.

AUTOCRACY: A government in which one person holds absolute power.

BICAMERAL: Having two chambers; used to describe a legislature.

CABINET: A body of government officials most often comprising the heads of the departments making up the executive branch. Under different systems of government cabinet members may determine policy or serve primarily as advisors to the head of state.

CALIPH: The supreme ruler of all Muslim lands. The state ruled by a caliph is called a caliphate.

CAPITALISM: An economic system based on private ownership of goods and the idea that prices and production should be set by the workings of a "free market" rather than by centralized planning.

CASTE SYSTEM: A system of social stratification based on hereditary rank, wealth, race, occupation, or other criteria.

CAUDILLO: An autocratic leader in Spain or Latin America.

CITY-STATE: A sovereign state comprising a city and surrounding regions.

CIVIL LAW: A legal system based on laws enacted by a legislature.

COLD WAR: An ideological conflict between the United States and the Soviet Union that spanned the years 1945 to 1991.

COLLECTIVIZATION: A system of agricultural production in which workers share control of a farm and receive a portion of the harvest as compensation for their labor. Collectivization has often been implemented by communist governments.

COMMON LAW: A legal system based on decisions made by judges, rather than on laws enacted by a legislature.

COMMUNISM: A political and economic system intended to foster a classless society through communal ownership of property and shared rewards. Much of the ideology of communism derives from the writings of the German political philosopher Karl Marx and is also referred to as Marxism.

CONSTITUTIONAL MONARCHY: A form of government that operates according to a constitution but recognizes a monarch as head of state.

COUP D'ÉTAT: The sudden, violent overthrow of a government.

CULT OF PERSONALITY: Public adulation of a political leader who is glorified through propaganda.

DEMOCRACY: A government ruled by the majority.

DIASPORA: The scattering of a group that has emigrated or been forced from their traditional homeland; this term refers in particular to the settlement of Jews exiled from Palestine by the Babylonians in 586 BC.

DIET: The name for the legislature in some countries.

DIRECT DEMOCRACY: A democratic system in which citizens participate in government decisions directly rather than electing representatives to govern on their behalf.

DIVINE RIGHT OF KINGS: The idea that monarchs receive their mandate to rule directly from God.

DOGE: The head of government in city-states of Renaissance Italy.

DUUMVIRATE: A government in which rule is shared between two people.

ECONOMIC SANCTIONS: Economic actions taken by one government to exert pressure on another; examples include halting financial or military aid, instituting trade embargoes, or increasing tariffs.

EGALITARIANISM: A social and political philosophy based on the idea that all people are equal.

ELECTORAL COLLEGE: A group of electors; this term is used in particular to describe the body of representatives that elects the president and vice president in the United States.

EMERGING DEMOCRACY: A country in the process of moving from an authoritarian to a democratic government.

EMIR: An Islamic ruler. The state ruled by an emir is called an emirate.

EXECUTIVE: The branch of government responsible for executing the laws and managing the operations of the state.

FASCISM: An authoritarian political ideology characterized by a centralized government headed by a dictator, strong national unity (often based on the celebration of national ethnicity or culture), and the suppression of opposition.

FEDERATION: A union of smaller political entities.

FEUDALISM: A system of political organization in which land was owned by lords who granted the use of the land to vassals; in return, the vassals were obligated to serve as soldiers for the lord.

FREE MARKET: An economy operating on principles of supply and demand, not controlled by the government.

GENOCIDE: The systematic extermination of an ethnic or cultural group.

HEAD OF GOVERNMENT: The chief of the executive branch of government, such as the president or prime minister.

HEAD OF STATE: The chief public representative of a government, such as the monarch in a constitutional monarchy. Head of state is often a ceremonial role with little decision-making power. Under the presidential system of government, the president is usually both head of state and head of government.

IMPEACHMENT: The trial of a public official for misconduct.

INSURGENCY: An anti-government revolt that is not centrally organized.

JUDICIAL PRECEDENT: The body of principles established in earlier cases that are referred to when deciding a new case.

JUDICIARY: The court system.

JUNTA: A ruling group, particularly after a political coup.

KHAN: A ruler or chieftain on the Central Asian steppe and in other Asian countries. A khan rules over a khanate.

LEGISLATURE: A body responsible for enacting laws.

MARTIAL LAW: Law administered by the military.

MONARCHY: Rule by a sovereign.

MULTIPARTY SYSTEM: A system in which three or more political parties participate in government.

MUNICIPAL GOVERNMENT: A local governing body, as in a county, city, or village.

NATIONALISM: A strong sense of patriotism or a movement in favor of a nation's independence. Also, an extreme form of patriotism that leads to the exclusion of perceived outsiders.

NATIONALIZE: To transfer from private ownership to government control.

OLIGARCHY: A government ruled by a small group.

ONE-PARTY SYSTEM: A system in which a single political party dominates the government.

PARLIAMENTARY SYSTEM: A system in which the head of government is selected from the members of the legislative branch and may be dismissed at the will of the legislature.

PLUTOCRACY: A government controlled by the wealthy.

PRESIDENTIAL SYSTEM: A system in which the head of government is elected separately from the legislature and is not accountable to the legislature.

PRIME MINISTER: The chief executive under a parliamentary system of government.

PRINCIPALITY: A country or territory ruled by a prince.

PROTECTORATE: A sovereign state granted the protection of a stronger country in exchange for political and economic allegiance.

REFERENDUM: Direct vote by the people on a legislative initiative.

REPUBLIC: A government in which citizens and elected representatives make governing decisions.

SHARIA: Islamic law derived from the Muslim holy book, the Koran.

SHOGUN: A Japanese military ruler. The shogun's territory was called a shogunate.

SOVEREIGNTY: The authority to rule or independence from outside control.

SUFFRAGE: The right to vote. The term "universal suffrage" is used when the right to vote is extended to all adult citizens of a country.

TERM LIMITS: A limit on the number of terms a person may serve in a particular office.

THEOCRACY: A government ruled by religious leaders or officials claiming divine guidance.

TWO-PARTY SYSTEM: A system in which political power is divided between two strong political parties.

UNICAMERAL: Having a single chamber; used to describe a legislature.

Introduction to The Postwar Era (1945–1960)

World War II (1939–1945) set the stage for deep transformations in the world order. The war devastated European society, bringing the era of European global dominance to a close as the United States emerged as the preeminent global power. The United States had suffered far fewer losses than the other combatants, and wartime production had lifted its economy out of the Depression.

The United States and the Soviet Union had been allies against Nazi Germany, but an extended period of hostilities between the two nations—referred to as the Cold War—dominated the politics of the postwar years. Between 1945 and 1948, Communist governments subservient to the Soviet Union were installed throughout Eastern Europe. Germany was divided into four occupation zones by the victorious Allies; the northeast quadrant became a Soviet satellite state called the German Democratic Republic. The Soviets tested an atomic bomb in 1949, and the ensuing nuclear arms race heightened the Cold War standoff.

When the full extent of the Nazi Holocaust against European Jews became clear after the war's end, the revelations generated worldwide sympathy for the idea of a Jewish homeland in the Middle East. The United Nations approved a plan for creating a Jewish nation alongside an Arab one in Palestine, and although the population of that country opposed partition, the state of Israel was established in 1948. An Arab coalition immediately declared war on the Jewish state, but was unable to defeat Israel. Nearly one million Palestinians became refugees, setting in motion the central dispute of the Middle East into the twenty-first century.

India's long struggle for independence, led by Mohandas Gandhi (1869–1948), finally succeeded in 1947 as Great Britain handed over sovereignty. However, Gandhi's dream of a united India did not come true, due to persistent conflict between Hindus and Muslims. The British departure split the subcontinent into two nations—India, with a majority Hindu population, and Pakistan, with a Muslim majority. The two South Asian powers went to war several times over the contested province of Kashmir.

In China, the nationalist Kuomintang government and their Communist rivals had suspended their civil war to join forces against Japanese occupation, but their struggle resumed in 1945. The Communists, led by Mao Tse-tung (1893–1976), triumphed in 1949 and founded the People's Republic of China. The nationalists took over the island of Taiwan, insisting that they remained China's sovereign rulers.

The army of the Soviet Union had entered the Pacific theater of World War II in August 1945, mere days before Japan's surrender. Soviet troops rapidly crossed into the Korean peninsula from the north. The victorious Allies temporarily split the peninsula in two, with the northern zone administered by the Soviets and the southern zone controlled by the United States. However, reunification efforts collapsed in the face of the animosity between the superpowers, and two separate Korean states arose. The Korean War of 1950–1953, the first major military engagement of the Cold War, killed roughly three million people and completely failed to resolve the political conflict. The border between North and South Korea remains among the world's most heavily militarized sites.

Cuba's revolution of 1959, and the Communist state constructed by Fidel Castro (1927–) on an island ninety miles off Florida's coast, enraged American leaders and magnified Cold War tensions. The Soviet Union brought on a crisis by surreptitiously shipping nuclear missiles to Cuba. For several days in October 1962, the world dangled on the brink of nuclear war. The crisis was resolved peacefully, but it revealed the precarious nature of global security in the nuclear age.

The Postwar Era (1945–1960)

🌐 Lebanon

Type of Government

The small Middle Eastern nation of Lebanon is a constitutional republic with a unique structure designed to allocate power fairly among a wide variety of religious and ethnic groups.

Background

Lebanon's roughly four million inhabitants occupy an attractive territory on the eastern coast of the Mediterranean Sea. Only slightly larger than the state of Delaware, it shares borders with Israel and the disputed Israeli-occupied territory of the Golan Heights to the south, and Syria to the east and north. Both neighbors have a long history of intervention in Lebanese politics.

Before World War I, Lebanon was a territory of the Ottoman Empire. Following the dissolution of that empire as a result of the war, the French ruled the area for several years under a military administration. In 1923 the League of Nations, forerunner of the United Nations (UN), acknowledged the status quo by granting France a formal mandate over both Lebanon and Syria. The region the French called Greater Lebanon, a narrow southern strip between the Mediterranean coast and the Bekaa Valley, became a constitutional republic in 1926 but remained firmly under French control until independence was declared in 1943. Wartime upheavals, however, delayed full disengagement from France until 1946.

The Levant, as the east end of the Mediterranean basin is sometimes known, has had a mixed population since antiquity. Nowhere, however, is the situation more complicated than in Lebanon, where a wide variety of ethnic, religious, and political groups have retained a strong sense of identity. The single most divisive factor in Lebanese society is probably religion. Of every ten Lebanese, roughly six will be Muslim and four Christian. Within those two groups, however, there are a large number of sects, some of which have closer ties to the other faith than to their own coreligionists. Among the Muslims, for example, there are Sunnis, Shiites, Ismailites (a splinter group of Shiites), Druze (a splinter group of Ismailites), and Nusayri (or Alawites, another Shiite splinter group). Among the Christians, there are Maronite Catholic, Greek Orthodox, and Armenian Orthodox congregations, among others. The Lebanese government officially recognizes seventeen faiths.

Government Structure

The basis of Lebanon's governmental structure remains the 1926 constitution, with several major changes. The most important of these changes is the Taif Accord (also known as the Charter of Lebanese National Reconciliation) of 1989 (signed into law in 1990), which brought an end to a bitter civil war that had begun in 1975, and outlined a series of structural reforms aimed at preventing further violence. In brief, the agreement acknowledged the need to modify traditional power-sharing arrangements in light of longstanding inequalities and the nation's rapidly changing demographics. The general result of these reforms has been a substantial increase in Muslim, particularly Shiite, influence at the expense of the Maronite Catholic community, which had held a disproportionate share of power since the days of the French mandate.

Under the current, post–Taif system, the heads of the executive branch are the president, by tradition a Maronite Catholic, and the prime minister, by tradition a Sunni Muslim. The stipulations regarding religion are not legally mandated, but they reflect an arrangement that predates independence, and the drafters of the Taif agreement left them in place. A third stipulation places a Shiite in the office of speaker for the country's National Assembly.

The president, who serves as head of state, is elected by the National Assembly for a six-year term. He or she is eligible to serve more than one term, but not consecutively. In special circumstances, however, the Assembly can extend a president's term if the consecutive-term rule would otherwise force his removal from office. The precedent for such extensions occurred in 2004, when rising tensions throughout the country persuaded

French fighters assisting the Christian militia in the Lebanese civil war. © *Patrick Chauvel/ Sygma/Corbis*

Assembly members to extend the term of President Émile Lahoud (1936–) for three years.

After election, the president's first task is to consult with the Assembly regarding the selection of a prime minister and deputy prime minister. The final choice rests with the president, but a president who wholly disregarded the wishes of the Assembly would soon find his choices dismissed from office in a vote of no confidence. The prime minister, in turn, consults with the president and Assembly before appointing the members of his cabinet.

Legislative functions are vested in a unicameral National Assembly. The Taif agreement mandated important changes in the number and allocation of Assembly seats; as of 2007 the total stands at 128, half of which go to Muslims and half to Christians. Within each of these blocs, seats are reserved for particular sects. Voting in Assembly elections is mandatory for men aged twenty-one and over and voluntary for women in the same age group who have at least an elementary education. Other women and all active members of the military are ineligible. Seats are awarded to the various parties on the basis of their share of the popular vote and in accordance with the requirements for religious balance. Members serve four-year terms. In the 2005 elections, voting took place in stages, with each of four regions voting a week apart.

The structure of the judicial branch reflects a variety of influences, including Ottoman, French, and Muslim legal traditions. The nation's highest courts are the four Courts of Cassation, three for civil cases and one for criminal cases. Unlike the U.S. Supreme Court, the Courts of Cassation are not empowered to rule on the constitutionality of legislation. Instead, the Taif Accord assigns this function to a Constitutional Council, the precise structure of which remains the subject of debate.

The secular tone of the Lebanese legal system distinguishes it from several other Middle Eastern systems. In particular, Lebanon has no provisions for the enforcement of traditional Islamic law, or sharia. This situation may change, however, with the growing influence of young, socially conservative Muslims, and some observers argue that a swing toward conservatism is already evident in some areas of law. In 2004, for example, Lebanon executed three convicted murderers in its first use of the death penalty in more than five years.

Local affairs are managed by the appointed governors of the nation's eight administrative districts. In addition, towns and cities elect municipal councils, which in turn elect mayors. In villages and rural areas, traditional leaders—usually a village chief and an informal council of elders—retain significant authority.

Political Parties and Factions

Usually, but not always, religious differences coincide with ethnic and political divisions. Christian communities, for example, tend to be pro-Western in their outlook. The Shiites, meanwhile, form the backbone of the Hezbollah movement, which combines increasingly prominent political activity with social programs and militant campaigns against Israel and the West. Most Druze, meanwhile, remain loyal to their longtime leader, Walid Junblatt, head of the Progressive Socialist Party and a vocal opponent of Syria. Junblatt's position illustrates three of the most important forces driving Lebanese politics: religion, personal and familial loyalties, and Syria.

In 2005 Syria withdrew the thousands of troops it had stationed in Lebanon since the early days of the civil war. Nevertheless Syria's influence over its much smaller neighbor remains enormous. Many Syrians, and some

Leader of the pro-Syrian Lebanese Hezbollah movement Sheikh Hassan Nasrallah speaking in Beirut during a memorial ceremony in 2005, marking Israel's assassination of the spiritual leader of Hamas, Sheikh Ahmed. © *epa/Corbis*

Lebanese, believe that Lebanon is an integral part of the larger nation of Syria and must be reattached to it. Even Syrians who are skeptical of this idea tend to place Lebanon within Syria's legitimate sphere of influence. Lebanese politicians, meanwhile, react in a variety of ways. Some, like Junblatt, reject Syrian involvement. Others, like President Lahoud, are much more flexible. Of the three major coalitions in the Assembly, one (the March 14 Coalition) is dominated by Junblatt and the Future Movement bloc of Saad Hariri, whose father, former Prime Minister Rafiq Hariri (1944–2005), died in an assassination widely attributed to Syria. The Future Movement bloc has the largest number of seats (thirty-six) of any single bloc in the Assembly. The second coalition, the Change and Reform Alliance, takes a more pragmatic approach to Syria; dominant here is the Free Patriotic Movement of former general Michel Aoun (1935–). The third coalition, the Hezbollah and Amal Alliance, is a predominately Shiite group relatively open to Syrian assistance. The primary interest of Hezbollah, however, is not Syria but Israel.

Palestinian refugees, now estimated to number more than four hundred thousand, have lived in Lebanon since the creation of Israel in 1948. Their presence—and the relative weakness of the Lebanese central government, particularly during the civil war—has facilitated the use of Lebanon as a launching pad for guerilla attacks against Israel. Israel has responded with three major invasions, in 1978, 1982, and 2006. In the first of these, Israel unilaterally established a security perimeter in Lebanese territory north of the border. Patrolling this region were Israeli troops and their allies, known as the South Lebanon Army (SLA). The withdrawal of Israeli troops from the security zone in 2000 brought an end to the SLA, the most openly pro-Israeli group in Lebanese history. Many of its members have since been tried for collaboration with the enemy. The Palestinians, meanwhile, are increasingly drawn to Hezbollah and other radical movements amid the enduring poverty and unemployment of the refugee camps.

Major Events

In July 2006 the kidnapping of two Israeli soldiers by Hezbollah militants sparked a full-scale, month-long Israeli assault on Hezbollah targets in southern Lebanon. Israeli bombers destroyed a number of bridges and highways in an effort to stop the shipment of arms to Hezbollah from Syria and Iran. Hezbollah strongholds in the suburbs south of Beirut, Lebanon's capital, were also targeted. Hezbollah responded by firing hundreds of rockets daily into northern Israel. There were civilian casualties in both countries, but Lebanese civilians bore the brunt of the fighting, with more than a thousand dead and thousands injured. Their plight generated much criticism of Israeli tactics, both internationally and among Israelis themselves. The government of Israeli Prime Minister Ehud Olmert (1945–) responded that Lebanese casualties, while regrettable, were primarily the result of Hezbollah's use of civilians as shields against attack. Debate on this point continues. What is clear, however, is that Israel did not succeed in its goal of destroying Hezbollah. Despite heavy losses, in fact, Hezbollah emerged from the fighting stronger than ever, with an enhanced reputation and burgeoning support throughout Lebanon. This newfound strength has enabled it to resist persistent calls, backed by a resolution of the UN Security Council, for its disarmament.

Twenty-First Century

Less than twenty years after the end of its devastating civil war, Lebanon once again appears on the brink of disaster. Its economy and infrastructure, both rebuilt with astounding speed after 1990, are again in shambles after the Israeli assault of 2006. The most pressing issue, however, is probably the status of Hezbollah. Despite its participation in the National Assembly, it functions in many respects as a government within a government, with its own schools, social services, and armed militia.

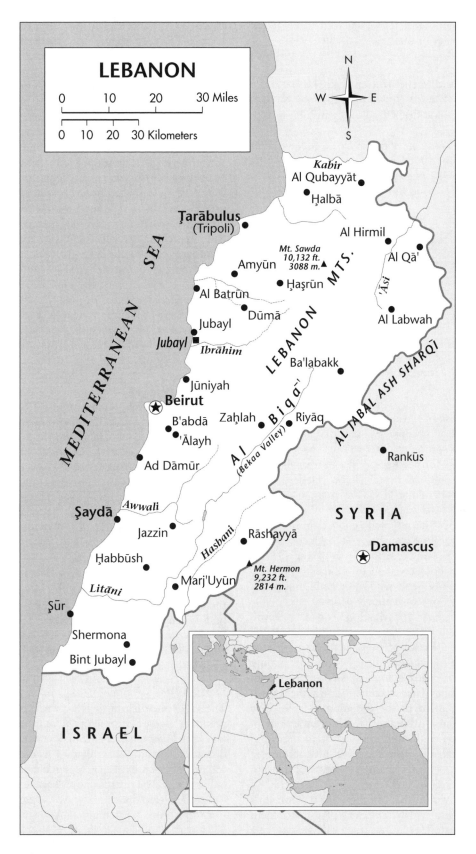

LEBANON

0   10   20   30 Miles

0   10   20   30 Kilometers

N
W   E
S

MEDITERRANEAN SEA

Kabir
Al Qubayyāt
Ḥalbā

Ṭarābulus
(Tripoli)

Al Hirmil

Mt. Sawda
10,132 ft.
3088 m. ▲

Amyūn
Ḥaṣrūn

Al Qā'

'Āsi

Al Batrūn
Dūmā

Al Labwah

Jubayl
Jubayl
Ibrāhim

Ba'labakk

Jūniyah

Beirut ✪

B'abdā
'Ālayh

Zaḥlah
Riyāq

Rankūs

Ad Dāmūr

AL JABAL ASH SHARQĪ

LEBANON MTS.

A l   B i q ā'
(Bekaa Valley)

S Y R I A

Şaydā
Awwali

Damascus ✪

Jazzin

Rāshayyā

Ḥabbūsh

Hasbani

Litāni

Marj'Uyūn

Mt. Hermon
9,232 ft.
2814 m.

Şūr

Shermona

Bint Jubayl

Lebanon

I S R A E L

Lebanon.   *Maryland Cartographics*

As such, it represents a real, if unspoken, challenge to the continued legitimacy of the Lebanese state.

BIBLIOGRAPHY

Achcar, Gilbert, and Michel Warschawski. *The 33-Day War: Israel's War on Hezbollah in Lebanon and its Consequences.* Boulder, CO: Paradigm Publishers, 2007.

Mackey, Sandra. *Lebanon: A House Divided.* New York: W. W. Norton, 2006.

Norton, Augustus R. *Hezbollah: A Short History.* Princeton, NJ: Princeton University Press, 2007.

⊕ United Nations

Type of Government

The United Nations (UN) is the world's primary agency for the promotion of peace, global development, and international cooperation. A voluntary association of 191 nations, the UN is not itself a government; it does not make laws but coordinates the joint efforts of its members, providing assistance as needed in the development or implementation of policy.

Background

The increasing ease of travel and communication in the nineteenth century encouraged the development of organizations to promote international cooperation. Most of these were formed for specific, ad hoc purposes; the goal of the Universal Postal Union (established in 1874 and now part of the UN), for example, was the facilitation of international mail delivery. Wars around the world further necessitated cooperation among nations, as the enormous casualties of the American Civil War (1861–1865), the Franco-Prussian War (1870–1871), and other conflicts soon prompted the growth of international movements with more ambitious goals: the establishment of conventions defining acceptable wartime behavior and the development of effective means for the peaceful resolution of conflict. In 1864, for example, a conference of European powers drafted the first of the so-called Geneva Conventions governing the treatment of civilians and enemy soldiers in time of war. Several decades later a conference in the Dutch city of The Hague led to the founding in 1899 of a Permanent Court of Arbitration for the settlement of international disputes. Despite the success of these and subsequent conferences, there was as yet little interest in the establishment of a permanent association of nations.

The devastation of the World War I (1914–1918), however, sparked a dramatic shift in public opinion. In a series of speeches, widely esteemed U.S. President Woodrow Wilson (1856–1924) urged the creation of a permanent body for the nonviolent resolution of international conflict. The result was the League of Nations, established by the 1919 Treaty of Versailles. A covenant attached to the treaty laid out the means by which the League aimed to reduce the frequency and impact of armed conflict; these included the arbitration of disputes, multilateral arms reduction agreements, and joint action by League members against aggressor nations. Its structure foreshadowed many of the most familiar features of the UN, including a general assembly of all members and an executive council with both permanent and rotating members. Despite the hopeful, enthusiastic atmosphere of its founding, the League faced serious obstacles from the outset. Its legitimacy and credibility were severely damaged by the refusal of several powerful nations, notably the United States, to participate. The greatest obstacle, however, may have been its association with Versailles, a treaty widely viewed in Germany and elsewhere as a vindictive and unfair demonstration of power by the victors of World War I. Versailles thus deprived the League of the neutrality required for the successful mediation of disputes. The final blow to its credibility was its failure to stop or even delay the growing aggression of German dictator Adolf Hitler (1889–1945) in the 1930s. Nearing the end of World War II in the 1940s, the League had ceased to function altogether.

The need for a permanent assembly of nations remained, however, and in August 1944 representatives from four of the major Allied powers—the United States, the United Kingdom, China, and the Soviet Union—met at Dumbarton Oaks, in the Georgetown section of Washington, D.C., to draft possible charters for a stronger, more credible organization, one that focused on the basic needs of the world's growing population as well as on the increasingly complex geopolitical situation. At a subsequent meeting in June 1945 in San Francisco, the representatives of fifty nations finalized and signed the charter of an organization to be known as the United Nations. Poland, whose post–World War II government was not established in time for the San Francisco meeting, signed the charter later that summer, thus bringing the number of founding members to fifty-one. The UN officially began work on October 24, 1945, following the charter's ratification by a majority of members.

Government Structure

The UN's membership has grown enormously since its founding, in part because of the number of former colonies that became sovereign, independent nations in the decades following World War II. As of 2007, there were 191 members, a total that represents nearly every nation in the world. The organization's basic structure, however, has not changed dramatically. At its heart remains the all-member General Assembly (GA), which meets at UN headquarters in New York City. GA sessions usually begin in September and end in December, though special sessions can be called if circumstances warrant. Each member has a single vote, a policy designed to neutralize the often enormous disparities in power that color most intergovernmental relations. Theoretically, at least, the tiny Pacific nation of Palau wields as much influence in the GA as the United States or China. Whether this remains true in practice is the subject of some debate. Topics under discussion vary widely from session to session; in recent years the GA has discussed the humanitarian crisis in the Darfur region of the Sudan, the consequences of global climate change, and the Israeli-Palestinian conflict. The last of these has been a staple of meetings since 1945. Though votes on most matters are decided by simple majority, certain topics, notably budget questions, require a two-thirds majority. Votes on international matters (as opposed to internal UN business) are nonbinding, but they provide policy makers with a clear sense of international opinion.

More prominent than the General Assembly is the United Nations Security Council (UNSC), the UN's principal mechanism for the preservation of peace. Five of the UNSC's fifteen members hold permanent seats: the United States, the United Kingdom, France, China, and the Russian Federation (formerly the Soviet Union). The other ten members are elected by the General Assembly for two-year terms. This mixture of permanent and rotating members, a legacy of the League of Nations' executive council, is intended to balance the interests of the world's most powerful nations against the right of smaller members to have a voice in Security Council deliberations. The Security Council meets in New York whenever events demand it, or at a member's request. Measures need nine of fifteen votes to pass, though each of the five permanent members holds veto power. The UN's founding charter requires all members to adhere to Security Council decisions, often known as resolutions. In practice, however, enforcing resolutions can be difficult, and several from decades past remain unfulfilled. One of the most famous of these is UN Security Council Resolution (UNSCR) 242, passed in November 1967 at the end of the so-called Six Day War between Israel and an alliance of Arab armies. The resolution mandated Israel's withdrawal from territories it had seized during the war and the recognition by all parties that both Israelis and Palestinians had the right to live within safe, secure, and internationally recognized boundaries. "Two Four Two," as it is often known, was intended to be the foundation for negotiations aimed at a lasting peace. Despite occasional progress, however, the regional situation remains much the same forty years later.

Unlike the League of Nations, however, the UNSC does have some ability to enforce its decisions. The question of when and where to exercise this ability is probably the Security Council's single greatest preoccupation. The most common enforcement method involves a range of economic sanctions, some relatively minor and some quite severe. By restricting trade with a noncompliant state, the Security Council tries to persuade, or force, the state's leaders to obey. In 2001, for example, UNSCR 1343 barred all member nations from receiving exports of diamonds from the African nation of Liberia, then engulfed in a civil war largely funded by diamond sales. This resolution is widely credited with speeding the end of the war and restoring a stable, democratically elected government, and the sanctions it imposed were removed in 2007.

If sanctions fail, the UNSC is authorized under the terms of the charter to consider the use of joint military force. In practice, however, nearly all of the military forces dispatched by the UN have been peacekeepers, whose use of arms is strictly limited. Peacekeepers monitor cease-fires, patrol disputed borders, establish demilitarized zones and safe havens for civilians, and facilitate the delivery of humanitarian aid. Since its founding, the UN has dispatched peacekeeping forces more than sixty times. One of the earliest operations, on the disputed border between India and Pakistan, began in 1949 and is still in place.

Though the Security Council and, to a lesser extent, the General Assembly are the most visible units of the UN, they are only two of the organization's six divisions. The other four are the Secretariat, the Economic and Social Council, the Trusteeship Council, and the International Court of Justice. The last of these is located in The Hague; the other five are based in New York. The Secretariat handles most administrative and logistical matters. At its head is the secretary general, who is elected by the General Assembly after a recommendation from the Security Council. By exercising its veto, any of the five permanent members of the Security Council can exclude a candidate from further consideration. The term of office is five years, with no limit to the number of terms. Typically, UN secretaries have spent much of their time on personal diplomatic missions, meeting with heads of state and making media appearances to raise awareness of current issues. Ban Ki-moon (1944–) of South Korea succeeded Ghana's Kofi Annan (1938–) as secretary general on January 1, 2007.

The Economic and Social Council (ESC) is essentially a subcommittee of the General Assembly, which elects fifty-four of its own members to the smaller body for three-year terms. The ESC acts as a clearinghouse for the research and policy recommendations of various UN offices (including the UN Environment Programme, the UN Development Programme, and the UN Office on Drugs and Crime), summarizing and disseminating this information to the General Assembly and the public. The ESC meets year-round, in addition to holding a special month-long series of high-profile discussions every summer.

The Trusteeship Council, the fifth of the UN's six divisions, is effectively defunct. Its mission—to protect the interests of eleven so-called Trust Territories as they prepared for autonomy or independence—came to an end when the last remaining territory became the

A United Nations Security Council hearing on weapons inspections in Iraq, March 2003.   © *Reuters/CORBIS*

independent nation of Palau in 1994. Established in 1945 in accordance with the UN charter, the Trustee-ship Council provided oversight only for territories that met one of the three following conditions: ruled by a foreign power under a mandate from the League of Nations; detached from Germany, Japan, or their allies as a result of the war; or placed under UN trusteeship voluntarily by the ruling power. Technically, the Council is still in existence, with the five permanent members of the Security Council as its members, but it is unlikely to be called back to work.

The last division of the UN is the International Court of Justice (ICJ) in The Hague. Also known as the World Court, it is not to be confused with the Interna-tional Criminal Court (ICC), also located in The Hague. The ICJ handles disputes between governments, while the ICC is concerned with the prosecution of individuals charged with grievous offenses, chiefly war crimes, and is independent of the UN. The fifteen judges of the ICJ are elected by majority votes in the General Assembly and Security Council. No two judges may be citizens of the same country. Each serves a repeatable term of nine years, and elections are staggered, with five seats open every three years. The court can hear cases only with the con-sent of both parties, and that consent can be withdrawn at any time before the verdict. Once the verdict has been read, however, both parties must obey it. Unanimous decisions are uncommon; as in the U.S. Supreme Court,

judges who disagree with the majority of their colleagues may file dissenting opinions. The majority's decision stands, however, and there is no appeal.

The six divisions, large as they are, represent only part of the UN's global reach—a vast array of affiliated organizations exists outside the central framework. The closeness of their affiliations varies widely. Some, like the Universal Postal Union, are formerly independent organizations that have been incorporated into the UN, though they may retain some autonomy in policy or administration. Many others, notably humanitarian groups and other nongovernmental organizations, sim-ply have a close working relationship with UN staff. Finally, there are more than thirty specialized agencies, founded by the UN but independent of it. These include the World Health Organization (WHO), the Interna-tional Monetary Fund (IMF), the UN Educational, Sci-entific, and Cultural Organization (UNESCO), and the World Food Programme (WFP); the latter agency feeds roughly ninety million people per year.

Political Parties and Factions

For the first forty-five years of the UN's existence, the principal division between members was the split between the Communist bloc, led by the Soviet Union, and the non-Communist, or Western, bloc, led by the United States. The enmity between these rivals tended to overshadow other rivalries based on religion, geography, or economic development. These latter, long latent divisions, however, have grown more prominent with the fall of the Soviet Union in 1991. One of these divisions is the split between highly conservative Islamic states like Iran and more secular ones like Jordan. Another split, which is very real but often oversimplified, divides the Islamic and non-Islamic worlds, while a third divides the generally underdeveloped Southern Hemisphere from the wealthier Northern Hemisphere.

Amid this growing fragmentation, several nations have formed influential alliances. The most significant of these ties are probably those linking the United States with Israel. The relationship between these two nations is a complex one; within the context of the Security Council, the United States tends to act as Israel's protector, often exercising its veto to prevent the passage of resolutions that criticize Israeli policy. Another influential bond links the United States to the United Kingdom. Though strong for decades, this relationship grew even closer with the support from U.K. Prime Minister Tony Blair (1953–) of the U.S.-led war in Iraq. The fact that both the United States and the United Kingdom have permanent seats on the Security Council is seen as unfair by several members opposed to the war in Iraq. Internal frustrations and disagreements are inevitable in an organization as enormous and diverse as the UN. These disagreements must be addressed, and the UN is constantly reevaluating its policies, organizational structure, and procedures in light of that necessity.

Major Events

On August 19, 2003, a truck bomb exploded outside Baghdad's Canal Hotel, headquarters of the UN mission to Iraq. Twenty-two people, most of whom were UN staff, died, and more than 150 people were injured; among the dead was then Secretary General Annan's special representative in the war-torn nation. Annan withdrew all staff pending the findings of an independent panel he commissioned to study security procedures. The panel's report, released in October 2003, found a general disregard of security protocols and poor management of security forces. After reforms, a smaller mission returned to Iraq the following year. Meanwhile, a terrorist organization associated with Jordanian-born Abu Musab al-Zarqawi (1966–2006) claimed responsibility for the attack, denouncing the UN as "the friends of the oppressors and aggressors." The incident illustrated both the UN's vulnerability and its willingness to acknowledge its own mistakes.

Twenty-First Century

The changing nature of conflict poses a major challenge to the UN in the twenty-first century. The UN exemplifies the diplomatic tradition of peaceful negotiation between established, sovereign states. Many of the world's conflicts, however, are no longer amenable to

that tradition. The East African nation of Somalia, for example, has lacked an effective central government since 1993. The nominal government has very little power, and many regions of the country are essentially lawless, dominated only by a constantly shifting group of warlords, terrorists, and common criminals. Traditional diplomacy does not work in Somalia, for the simple reason that there is no government with which to negotiate. New methods of handling violent, anarchic situations are desperately needed. If the past is any indication, the burden of developing and using those methods will fall on the United Nations.

BIBLIOGRAPHY

Kennedy, Paul M. *The Parliament of Man: The Past, Present, and Future of the United Nations.* New York: Random House, 2006.

Smith, Courtney B. *Politics and Process at the United Nations: The Global Dance.* Boulder, CO: Lyznne Rienner, 2006.

United Nations. "About the United Nations: Introduction to the Structure & Work of the UN." http://www.un.org/aboutun/ (accessed June 10, 2007).

⊕ Syrian Arab Republic

Type of Government

Syria's 1973 constitution established a republic; however, Syria has been under a state of emergency since 1963, which has enabled authoritarian rule through martial law by the Arab Ba'ath Socialist Party. Elections have been held, but opposition to the government in power is largely restricted, so a republic exists only in a constrained form. Although Islam is not officially designated as the state religion, Islamic law is an inherent part of the legal system and a main source of legislation.

Background

Syria is in Southwest Asia at the eastern end of the Mediterranean Sea. It occupies 71,498 square miles, slightly more than the state of North Dakota. This includes 1,176 square miles of the Golan Heights region, which Israel captured in 1967 and annexed in 1981 despite UN condemnation.

Evidence of human presence in the region that is Syria dates to at least 2500 BC. The current capitol of Damascus is one of the world's oldest cities. Various empires and dynasties controlled the region over time, including the Canaanites, Phoenicians, Hebrews, Arameans, Assyrians, Babylonians, Persians, Greeks, Romans, Byzantines, and the Crusaders. Syria is significant in Christian history, as Saint Paul was converted to that faith on the road to Damascus and organized the first Christian church at Antioch. Muslim invaders later established Islam in the region in 637 AD, and Damascus became the capital of the Islamic world and a base for Arab

Crowd outside the presidential palace in Cairo, Egypt, awaiting the signing of the merger between Syria and Egypt in 1958. After the signing, both President Gamal Abdel Nasser of Egypt and President Shukri al-Kuwatly of Syria addressed the crowd from the balcony. © *Bettmann/CORBIS*

conquests. In 1517 it fell under the control of Ottoman Turks. Syria remained part of the Ottoman Empire until the end of World War I in 1918.

An independent Arab Kingdom of Syria was established briefly in 1920, but it ended after only a few months when French forces occupied the country. The League of Nations put Syria under French mandate, but Syrian resistance and unrest persisted until the French fell to the Germans in 1940 during World War II. By 1941 British and French forces had taken control of Syria again. France permitted elections and the formation of a nationalist government in 1943, but the last French troops did not leave until 1946.

Syria declared independence on April 17, 1946. For the next quarter century Syrian politics were marked by upheaval and regime changes. In the first decade alone, Syria had twenty different cabinets and four separate constitutions. Military coups starting in 1949 continually undermined stability.

In 1958 Syria joined Egypt to form the United Arab Republic, but seceded in 1961. Following further military coups, Syria considered a union with both Egypt and Ba'ath-controlled Iraq in 1963 after the Ba'ath Party established control in Syria. The union failed to happen as serious disagreements developed, and coups created instability in both Syria and Iraq. In 1967 Syria was weakened by war with Israel, to which it lost the territory of the Golan Heights. Stability did not return until the ascension of Hafiz al-Assad (1930–2000) to the role of prime minister in 1970. He worked quickly to organize the government and to consolidate control. In 1973 the current Syrian constitution went into effect.

Government Structure

As a republic, the Syrian government contains three branches led by the head of state, who is an elected president. The president appoints the prime minister and cabinet members. The legislative branch is the unicameral People's Council. A complex system of secular and religious courts comprises the judiciary.

The president is elected for a term of seven years through nomination of one candidate by the People's

Council and confirmation by popular referendum. If the candidate fails to capture a majority of votes in the referendum, the process is repeated with a new nomination. The president serves as commander in chief of the armed forces. The president may issue laws for ratification to the People's Council and may veto laws approved by the Council. Presidential appointments include the prime minister and cabinet ministers, particular civil service posts, and military personnel. The president serves as Secretary General of the Ba'ath Party and leader of the National Progressive Front (NPF), a coalition of political parties allowed by the current regime. Under the constitution, the president must be Muslim and at least thirty-four years old.

Legislative powers are largely the responsibility of the People's Council, a unicameral parliament. Its 250 members are elected to four-year terms. One hundred sixty-seven seats are reserved for candidates from the National Progressive Front, and the remaining eighty-three are reserved for independent candidates. Laws may be initiated by the president or by a group of ten parliamentarians. Although legislative duties under the constitution are largely the responsibility of the People's Council, the current state of emergency allows the president to assert legislative leadership as well.

The constitution guarantees an independent judiciary. The principles of Syrian law derive from a combination of Islamic, French, and Ottoman influence. The judicial branch is overseen by the Minister of Justice, who is appointed by the president, and by the Supreme Judicial Council. Their administrative authority includes the power to appoint, promote, and transfer judges. The judiciary provides for separate secular and religious courts. The secular courts hear both civil and criminal matters and are divided into three levels: courts of first instance, courts of appeals, and the Supreme Constitutional Court. The Supreme Constitutional Court makes decisions on the constitutionality of laws, election disputes, and presidential crimes. Its five members are appointed by the president for renewable four-year terms.

The country is divided locally into fourteen provinces (*muhafazat*). Each province has a presidentially appointed governor who is assisted by an elected provincial council. Local governance is further centralized through districts (*manatiq*) and subdistricts (*nawahi*).

Syria provides universal suffrage to nationals over the age of eighteen.

Political Parties and Factions

Although Syria is a republic, the Arab Ba'ath Socialist Party has maintained dominant power since 1963, when it engineered a military coup that established the party's leadership. Political disagreement challenged that stability until 1970, when al-Assad assumed power as president. Under his leadership, the Ba'ath Party established firm control and expelled opposition parties. In 1982 the government crushed the active opposition forces of the Muslim Brotherhood, resulting in thousands of dead and wounded. Since then, public expression of anti-regime sentiment has been limited.

A small number of alternative political parties are sanctioned by the government to operate in Syria. A multi-party system, however, exists only in appearance. All sanctioned parties are members of the political coalition of the National Progressive Front, which is dominated by the Ba'ath Party. As a result, all NPF members must conform to Ba'ath ideals and government policies.

The Ba'ath Party was founded in 1943 and espouses "Unity, Freedom, Socialism." Its motto refers to the desire for Arab unity, freedom from foreign interference or control, and a society built without regard to class or social hierarchy.

Major Events

In 1976 the Ba'ath Party's authoritarian regime was challenged by a group of fundamentalist Sunni Muslims. The Muslim Brotherhood led an armed insurgency against the government that lasted until its suppression through force in 1982. Thousands died or were wounded, and the event has effectively suppressed public expression of discontent with the government.

Syria has participated actively in international Arab politics, especially concerning Israel. During an armed conflict with Israel in 1967, Syria lost part of its territory, the Golan Heights. Israel officially annexed the region in 1981 despite UN disapproval. Syria considers the territory Syrian and strives to recover it from Israel.

Further conflict with Israel has come through Syria's relationship with Lebanon, which was part of Syria until 1926. In 1982 Israel invaded Lebanon, and Syria sent forces to assist the Lebanese. In 1989 Syria endorsed the Taif Accord that negotiated the end of the conflict and also signed a treaty of brotherhood with Lebanon. Disagreement over implementation of the Taif Accord has strained relations in the region, and Syria has resisted complete withdrawal from Lebanon. Syrian relations with the United Nations, Israel, the United States, and other nations have suffered as a result.

In 1990 Syria participated in the Persian Gulf War (1990–1991) on behalf of the U.S.-led multinational coalition. Though it began limited cooperation with the United States after the September 11, 2001, terrorist attacks, it has not supported the 2003 invasion of Iraq by the United States and multinational forces. Syria has been accused of allowing insurgents access to Iraq through its borders. As a result of this and Syria's refusal to leave Lebanon, the United States imposed economic sanctions on Syria in 2004.

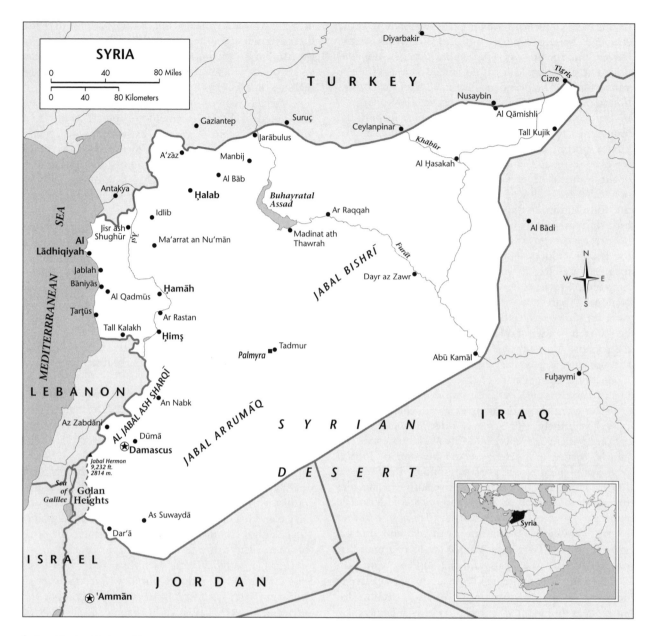

Syria. *Maryland Cartographics*

Twenty-First Century

Syria has established a fairly solid economy built on agriculture, oil, industry, and tourism, but it also faces serious challenges. Oil production has decreased steadily. Syria's growing population with high rates of unemployment, wide-scale corruption, and weak financial markets pose threats to the country's stability. The government has begun to implement reforms, but generally they have been slow to produce effective results.

Syria's foreign policy includes maintaining an active stance in Arab interests. As a result, Syria has played an important role in striving toward an Arab-Israeli peace settlement. How it has chosen to do so has created strained relations with other countries and the United Nations. Concern that the Syrian government is harboring terrorist organizations and that it is assisting rebel forces in Iraq have severely hampered international relationships. The United States has imposed severe sanctions, including freezing Syrian assets in U.S. financial institutions, and has recalled its Syrian ambassador to Washington, D.C.

BIBLIOGRAPHY

Ma'oz, Moshe. *Modern Syria: From Ottoman Rule to Pivotal Role in the Middle East.* East Sussex, UK: Sussex Academic Press, 1999.

State and Society in Syria and Lebanon. Edited by Youssef M. Choueiri. New York: St. Martin's Press, 1994.

United Nations Development Programme-Programme on Governance in the Arab Region. "Democratic Governance, Arab Country Profiles, Syria." http://www.undp-pogar.org/countries/country.asp?cid=19 (accessed August 21, 2007).

⊕ Hashemite Kingdom of Jordan

Type of Government

The Middle Eastern nation of Jordan is a constitutional, hereditary monarchy. The figure of the king dominates Jordanian politics, notably through his appointment of the prime minister. Some constitutional restraints on royal power do exist, including the Parliament's ability to override a royal veto and to dismiss the prime minister and the cabinet through a vote of no confidence. Ultimate authority, however, rests squarely with the king.

Background

Jordan shares borders with Israel and the West Bank to the west; Syria and the disputed Israeli-occupied territory of the Golan Heights to the north; Iraq to the northeast; and Saudi Arabia to the south and east. Access to maritime shipping is available via port facilities and a few miles of coastline on the Gulf of Aqaba, in the extreme southwest. Roughly the size of Maine, Jordan has a rapidly growing population that was estimated in 2007 at just over six million. Most of the land is infertile desert, and petroleum resources are meager.

The Hashemite Kingdom of Jordan, as the nation is officially known, achieved independence from the British in 1946. Britain's administration of the region had begun after World War I, when the League of Nations, forerunner of today's United Nations, granted Britain a mandate over the defeated Ottoman Empire's Middle Eastern possessions. The British soon separated Palestine from the region then called Transjordan, granting limited autonomy over the latter to King Abdullah I (1882–1951), who ruled the region from 1921 to 1951. Abdullah II (1962–) was crowned in 1999 and is the great grandson of the first. The royal family is known as the Hashemites. Like several other Middle Eastern dynasties, the Hashemites trace their ancestry to the Prophet Mohammed.

Government Structure

Jordan's first constitution was drafted in 1947, shortly after the nation gained independence. A new constitution replaced it in 1952; with extensive revisions, it remained in force as of 2007. In addition to defining the structure and function of government, the current version explicitly guarantees freedom of speech, freedom of the press, freedom of association, and freedom of religion.

Within the executive branch, most of the king's authority is delegated to a prime minister and a cabinet; the latter is also known as the Council of Ministers. The process of cabinet formation is distinctive. After the king appoints a prime minister, the two meet to choose individuals for the remaining cabinet posts. The entire slate of appointees is then sent to the Chamber of Deputies, as the lower house of the bicameral (two-house) Parliament is known, for approval. If the deputies fail to approve the prime minister, the proposed cabinet is disbanded, and the process begins again. If the prime minister wins approval, however, the deputies then vote on each of the remaining ministers. One or more of these may be voted down without compromising the cabinet as a whole. Once approved, the cabinet has no more than a month to present its agenda to both houses of Parliament for a vote. If the agenda is rejected, the cabinet resigns, and the king chooses a new prime minister.

While the cabinet is responsible for most of the government's day-to-day operations, the king retains the right to appoint judges, the twelve regional governors, and the mayor of Amman, the nation's capital (other mayors are elected). His signature is required before bills passed by Parliament become law, and he can veto bills he dislikes. This veto power is not unlimited, however, for a two-thirds majority in both houses is sufficient to override it.

Alongside the Chamber of Deputies in Parliament is the upper house, also known as the Senate or the House of Notables. There are currently 110 seats in the lower house and 55 in the upper. The total number of seats may change, but the proportion of lower- to upper-house seats is fixed at a minimum of two to one. Members of the upper house are appointed directly by the king. The lower house, however, is filled by popular vote, with six seats reserved for women. If no women are elected, a special electoral board appoints them. Small blocs of seats are also reserved for ethnic and religious minorities, including Christians and Muslim Circassians. Members of both houses serve four-year terms, though the king can dismiss Parliament at any time. For twenty-two years (1967 to 1989), in fact, there were no parliamentary elections at all, and the country was ruled by martial law and royal decree.

The Jordanian judicial system has three components: civil courts, religious courts, and security courts. The civil system is based upon French legal codes, with certain British influences from the period of the mandate granted by the League of Nations. The civil courts have jurisdiction over most personal and criminal matters; at the top is the Court of Cassation, or Supreme Court. This is usually the court of last appeal, though Jordan's kings have occasionally exercised their right to issue pardons. The constitution guarantees the right to counsel, and a High Administrative Court is empowered to

Jordan's King Hussein at a press conference. © *The Library of Congress*

review the constitutionality of legislation. The religious system includes sharia courts (which adhere to traditional Islamic law) and the tribunals of certain Christian denominations. Most cases heard in the religious courts involve issues of family law, notably divorce. If the parties in a case differ in their religious beliefs, the civil courts assume jurisdiction. Finally, a State Security Court (SSC) hears cases involving alleged threats to domestic and international security, including espionage, terrorism, and drug trafficking. Both military and civilian judges sit on the SSC. The death penalty is occasionally imposed (at least four executions were performed in 2006), and international human rights organizations have expressed concern over the treatment of prisoners, particularly those suspected of involvement in Islamic extremism.

Political Parties and Factions

Though several political parties exist in Jordan, only one has a significant presence in Parliament. This is the Islamic Action Front (IAF), the political wing of the Muslim Brotherhood, an international fundamentalist group. Though members of the Brotherhood have been implicated in acts of terrorism elsewhere, notably the assassination of Egyptian President Anwar as-Sadat

(1918–1981), in Jordan the organization seems to be working through purely political channels. In the 2003 elections to the Chamber of Deputies, the IAF won sixteen seats. Many analysts believe, however, that it would have won many more seats if Jordan's Palestinian citizens had gone to the polls in greater numbers. Voter turnout as a whole was relatively low at 58 percent; in Palestinian areas, however, the percentage was much lower.

The disparity in voting numbers points to a deep rift between the Palestinians, many of whom have lived in Jordan for decades, and other Jordanians. Many Palestinians are unhappy with the Hashemite dynasty's continued reliance on the tribal leaders who have traditionally constituted its primary support. As a result, the Palestinians have had difficulty obtaining political power to match their economic prominence. Another source of conflict is the government's moderate stance toward Israel, expressed in the Israel-Jordan Treaty of Peace signed in 1994.

Growing economic differences also threaten domestic stability. The nation's lack of natural resources continues to hinder economic development, and unofficial unemployment rates hover around 30 percent. Three out of ten Jordanians live below the poverty line, while the wealthiest 10 percent receive nearly 30 percent of the nation's income. These inequalities are likely to widen as Jordan's population continues to grow at one of the fastest rates in the world. Increasingly visible crowds of unemployed, disillusioned young men, who are often susceptible to the rhetoric of antigovernment extremists, are especially worrisome. In January 2002 serious riots erupted in the town of Ma'ān. The immediate cause of the riot was the death of a teenager in police custody, but larger social and economic frustrations undoubtedly played a role as well.

Major Events

The first fifty years of Jordanian independence were dominated by the towering figure of King Hussein (1935–1999), who ruled from 1952 to 1999 and is father of the present leader, King Abdullah II. Hussein earned praise around the world for his moderate, centrist policies. At the same time, however, he did not hesitate to move decisively, even ruthlessly, against domestic enemies. In September 1970, for example, he used air strikes and infantry assaults to expel hundreds of Palestinian guerillas who had been using Jordan as a base for attacking Israel. Among Palestinians, these events quickly became known as "Black September."

King Abdullah II has generally followed his father's moderate, pro-Western policies, a stance that has earned him enemies in some segments of the Arab world. A violent expression of this disdain occurred in November 2005, when suicide bombers attacked three prominent international hotels in Amman, killing about sixty and injuring hundreds more. As the Jordanian-born terrorist Abu Musab al-Zarqawi (1966–2006) made clear in his claim of responsibility, the decision to strike Jordanian targets was intended in part as a pointed rebuke of the king for his support of the U.S.-led invasion of Iraq. Ironically, however, the attacks solidified the king's domestic support, at least temporarily, and tens of thousands took to the streets of Amman to protest the bloodshed.

Twenty-First Century

The war in Iraq has presented special problems for Jordan. Iraqis who have fled the fighting and come to Jordan, many in need of extensive social services, have strained an already overburdened infrastructure. An influx of financial aid from the United States has helped to stabilize the situation. Continued U.S. assistance at the same level, however, is far from assured, and there is a significant risk that the country may become overly dependent on foreign aid. Economic development and family planning projects are urgently needed. The greatest danger, however, may be the feeling of estrangement that some observers have begun to notice between the people and their king. Abdullah II has been energetic and creative in his efforts to strengthen his ties to the people, reportedly visiting hospitals and other public facilities in disguise to monitor performance. But the war in Iraq is a major obstacle. If instability there continues, and particularly if the Shiite majority continues to dominate the Sunni minority in the U.S.-backed government, the appeal of anti-Western extremist groups may grow among the Jordanian people, 92 percent of whom are Sunnis. King Hussein was astute in his management of domestic unrest; it remains to be seen whether his son has the same ability.

BIBLIOGRAPHY

Eilon, Joab B. *The Making of Jordan: Tribes, Colonialism and the Modern State*. London: I. B. Tauris, 2007.

"The Hashemite Kingdom of Jordan." http://www.kinghussein.gov.jo/jordan.html (accessed May 29, 2007).

Schwedler, Jillian. *Faith in Moderation: Islamist Parties in Jordan and Yemen*. Cambridge: Cambridge University Press, 2006.

⊕ Republic of the Philippines

Type of Government

The Philippine government is a representative republic. The president leads the executive branch as chief of state, head of the government, and commander of the armed forces. The legislative branch consists of a bicameral Kongreso (Congress), made up of the Senate and the House of Representatives. The judicial branch consists of the Supreme Court, the Court of Appeals, and the tax courts.

Background

The Republic of the Philippines is an island nation in the western Pacific Ocean, south of Taiwan and northeast of Malaysia. The archipelago contains 7,107 islands, generally divided into three groups: Visayas, Luzon, and Mindanao. Approximately 90 percent of the people live on the nine largest islands.

The islands were first occupied between 40,000 BC and 30,000 BC by Australo-Melanesian tribes. From antiquity to the fifteenth century waves of Indonesian and Malayan immigrants added their racial and cultural characteristics to the developing Philippine culture.

Explorer Ferdinand Magellan (1480?–1521) brought the first Europeans to the islands in March 1521 while he was attempting to circumnavigate the globe for the Spanish monarchy. In 1565 Philip II (1527–1598) formally claimed the islands, then called Filipina, as Spanish territory and appointed Miguel Lopez de Legazpi (1510–1572) as the first governor general. Legazpi chose Manila as the most suitable site for the capital city.

Before the Spanish occupation, the islands were divided into *barangays* (villages), each of which was run by a chief. Residential and agricultural lands were communally distributed. The Spanish colonial government imposed a system of control based on land ownership and religious authority, with led to a hierarchy of wealth that dominated Philippine politics until the modern era.

By 1863 popular protests had become common, especially against the educational system. The Spanish government instituted reforms and allowed natives to travel to Europe for higher education. Filipino émigrés living in Spain fueled the independence movement during the 1870s by publishing books and pamphlets that detailed the injustices of Spanish rule.

Writer and political leader Jose Rizal (1861–1896) founded the Philippine League—the nation's first organization to seek independence—in 1892. He was arrested that same year as a political agitator. Rizal's arrest and exile inspired the formation of an underground revolutionary organization, Katipuneros, under the leadership of Andres Bonifacio (1863–1897) and Emilio Aguinaldo (1869–1964). In 1896 the Katipuneros organized an armed uprising against the Spanish, which became known as the Cry of Balintawak. Aguinaldo controlled small parts of several islands and declared the establishment of an independent government. However, in 1897 Aguinaldo accepted an amnesty agreement and moved his faction to exile in Hong Kong.

During the Spanish-American War (1898), U.S. forces severely weakened the Spanish military in the Philippines. Aguinaldo seized the opportunity to return

Philippine President Ferdinand Marcos and his wife Imelda at an Independence Day celebration in 1981.   © *Bettmann/CORBIS*

to the Philippines and take command of rebel forces. By June 1898 Aguinaldo's rebels had seized control of Manila.

Following the 1898 Treaty of Paris, Spain ceded the Philippines to the United States. Filipino revolutionaries refused to submit to U.S. rule and began, in 1899, the Philippine War of Independence. The war lasted almost two years and resulted in widespread damage to most of the nation's major cities. U.S. forces captured Aguinaldo in 1901.

The United States turned the Philippines into a commonwealth—a territory with which it had a special, insular relationship—that was administered by a combination of locally elected leaders and appointed U.S. officials. In 1902 the U.S. Bill of Rights was extended to include the commonwealth, and the legislative and executive branches of the Philippine government were established. In 1907 the country held its first national elections, which were dominated by the newly formed Nacionalista Party.

In 1934 the U.S. Congress passed the Tydings-Duffie Act, which promised that the Philippines would remain a U.S. commonwealth until July 4, 1946, when it would be recognized as a fully independent republic.

Japanese forces bombed and then occupied the Philippines in 1942. Until the end of World War II the Philippines were under the control of the Japanese army, and thousands of Filipinos were confined to internment camps. During the occupation guerrilla forces organized the Hukbalahap (the People's Anti-Japanese Army) and mounted an effective resistance. When the Japanese surrendered, however, U.S. forces imprisoned many of the Hukbalahap's leaders because of their communist and socialist ties.

As the date for independence approached, the Nacionalista Party—which was seen as closely aligned to the U.S. government—began to lose support. When the elections were held in April 1946, the newly formed Liberal Party won a clear majority, and Manuel Roxas (1892–1948) became the first president of the Republic of the Philippines.

Government Structure

The 1987 constitution established the Philippines as a republic run by a government with executive, legislative, and judicial branches. In the executive branch, the president serves as head of state, head of the government, and the leader of the nation's armed forces. After being elected to a six-year term, the president appoints an eighteen-member cabinet with approval of the legislature. The president is limited to a single term unless he or she was appointed for a term of fewer than four years. The vice president is also elected by popular vote and is usually a former member of the legislature.

The legislature consists of an upper chamber, the Senate, and a lower chamber, the House of Representatives. The exact number of senators and representatives is determined by the distribution and size of the population. Congressional districts are reapportioned within three years of each national census.

The Senate is composed of up to twenty-four senators elected for six-year terms, with half elected every three years. They are chosen by the entire electorate and do not represent specific geographical areas. In the House, district congressmen represent 212 specific geographical areas. In addition, sectoral representatives, who speak for minority interests, make up a small percentage of the total body. Representatives are elected for three-year terms.

The judicial branch consists of the Supreme Court and the Court of Appeals. The Supreme Court is the nation's highest judicial body and has administrative control over the nation's lower courts. It consists of one chief justice and fourteen associate justices whose length of service is limited only by the mandatory retirement age of seventy. Vacancies are filled by presidential appointment from three nominees chosen by a judicial commission.

The second-highest judicial body is the Court of Appeals, which consists of a chief justice and sixty-eight associate justices. The Court of Appeals reviews the decisions of the regional courts and oversees the tax courts.

Political Parties and Factions

The Philippines maintains a multiparty system in which no single political party can independently fill a majority of seats in the legislature and executive offices. Political parties form coalitions, which cooperate to win at each election cycle.

The Nacionalista Party, the nation's first independent political party, was formed in 1901 by Manuel Quezon (1878–1944) and Sergio Osmeña (1878–1961). The major opposition party was the Liberal Party, founded in 1945 by politicians who defected from the Nacionalista Party. They included Roxas, the first president of the republic.

During the presidency of Ferdinand Marcos (1917–1989), most political parties were abolished or severely curtailed. In 1978 he formed the Kilusang Bagong Lipunan, also known as the KBL or the New Society Movement, which functioned as a dictatorial regime.

In 1984 Senator Salvador Laurel (1928–2004) formed the United Nationalists Democratic Organizations (UNIDO), a new coalition of major and minor parties to oppose the Marcos administration. President Corazon Aquino (1933–) was later elected president as a representative of UNIDO, while Laurel served as vice president.

Between 1984 and the elections of 2007, a number of additional political parties surfaced, and two coalitions were organized. One of them, the TEAM (Together Everyone Achieves More) Unity coalition, includes the Kabalikat ng Malayang Pilipino Party (KAMPI), founded by President Gloria Macapagal-Arroyo (1947–) in 2007, and the closely aligned Lakas-Christian Muslim Democrats (Lakas-CMD), founded in 1991 by Fidel Ramos (1928–) and Emilio Osmeña (1938–).

The TEAM Unity coalition is generally associated with conservative social and fiscal policies, but it was also joined by members of the Liberal Party and the Democratic Socialist Party of the Philippines, both considered among the most liberal of the major political parties.

The major opposition is gathered into what is called the Grand Coalition (GC), formerly known as the United Opposition (UNO) and the Genuine Opposition (GO). The coalition was founded in 2005 by Jejomar Binay (1942–), the mayor of Makati, which is part of metropolitan Manila, and is generally considered the most socially liberal of the major coalitions. The GC includes remnants of the Nacionalista Party as well as supporters of the modern Liberal Party. In addition, the GC is backed by a number of smaller parties, including the Nationalist People's Coalition (NPC) and the Force of the Filipino Masses.

A number of minor factions also compete in general elections but are not aligned with the major coalitions. For example, the communist party, Partido Komunista ng Pilipinas, or PKP, is an offshoot of the country's first organized communist movement, which appeared in the 1930s. During the Marcos dictatorship, communism was severely suppressed, but in the 1990s, during the Ramos presidency, it was granted political status.

A militant communist faction known as the New People's Army (NPA), which has been active since the 1960s, has been accused of attempting to overthrow the government and of executing political activists. In 2006 President Macapagal-Arroyo signed legislation that gave the military a two-year deadline to find and imprison the leaders of the NPA.

Major Events

Since achieving independence in 1946, the Philippine government has twice ousted political leaders because of corruption and election fraud. The first such incident occurred at the end of the Marcos presidency. He had been elected in 1965 as a member of the Nacionalista Party and was popular during his first term, although the country was plagued by violence between radical political factions. In 1972, during his second term, Marcos used the growth of the communist faction and several terrorist-bombing incidents as justification for declaring martial law. Hundreds of opposition political leaders, journalists, and activists were detained and arrested. A year later Marcos created a new constitution that abolished the bicameral legislature and the term limit for president. Though some viewed Marcos as a dictator, some foreign governments—most notably the United States—gave military support to Marcos's efforts to eliminate communist factions.

Marcos's most serious political contender, Senator Benigno Aquino Jr. (1932–1983), was arrested in 1972 and spent several years in exile in the United States. Aquino returned to the Philippines to seek office in 1983 and was assassinated shortly after exiting the airplane. Following the assassination, Marcos lost the majority of his domestic and international support. Further compromised by growing economic difficulties, he declared a "snap election" to reaffirm the legitimacy of his government.

Allegations of widespread election fraud led to a popular uprising against Marcos. In February 1986 thousands of rebels and protesters gathered on the main thoroughfare of Manila, the Epifanio de los Santos Avenue (EDSA), in what became known as the EDSA Revolution (or People Power Revolution). It marked the end of the Marcos regime; he was forced into exile in the United States.

Corazon Aquino (1933–), the widow of Benigno Aquino, became the nation's next president. She restored the freedoms restricted under the Marcos administration and also removed most of the provincial governors and military leaders who had been loyal to Marcos. In 1987 a new constitution, which reformed and restored the state as a representative republic, was adopted.

In November 2000 the House of Representatives called for the impeachment of President Joseph Estrada (1937–) after allegations of corruption and bribery appeared in the media. During the trial a group of senators voted to block a crucial piece of evidence relating to the corruption charges. People from across Manila gathered at the EDSA site to protest the trial; the crowd eventually grew to more than one hundred thousand people—the media began to refer to the event as EDSA II or the Second People Power Revolution. Estrada stepped down on February 20, 2001, and was succeeded by Vice President Macapagal-Arroyo.

Twenty-First Century

Though the Philippines has shifted toward a functional republican system, popular opinion of the government is a perennial problem. The Philippines faces high poverty and has had little success with economic reform. In addition, armed struggles with some radical political factions continue to threaten government stability.

In February 2006 Macapagal-Arroyo declared a state of emergency, claiming that her administration had uncovered a coup attempt by communists, soldiers, and members of opposition political parties. The state of emergency was lifted after a month; however, some citizens groups alleged that the president's actions were unconstitutional. In May 2006 Amnesty International issued a statement expressing concern about a rise in vigilante killings and abductions of political activists and workers.

BIBLIOGRAPHY

Schirmer, Daniel B., and Stephen Rosskamm Shalom, eds. *The Philippines Reader: A History of Colonialism, Neocolonialism, Dictatorship, and Resistance.* Boston: South End Press, 1987.

Hedman, Eva-Lotta E., and John T. Sidel. *Philippine Politics and Society in the Twentieth Century: Colonial Legacies, Post-Colonial Trajectories.* London: Routledge, 2000.

Zaide, Gregorio F., and Sonya M. Zaide. *Philippine History and Government*, 5th ed. Manila: All Nations Publishing Company, 2002.

⊕ New Zealand

Type of Government

The Pacific nation of New Zealand is a constitutional, parliamentary monarchy and an independent member of the Commonwealth (formerly the British Commonwealth), a voluntary association of fifty-three former British possessions. New Zealand's head of state remains Queen Elizabeth II (1926–) of the United Kingdom, whose authority in New Zealand is vested in an appointed governor general. Though the structure and functions of New Zealand's government are based closely on those of the United Kingdom, the former colony has added several innovative features. The most significant of these is probably the legally mandated practice of setting aside seats in Parliament for the Maori, the nation's first inhabitants and a long-neglected minority.

Background

Roughly the size of Nevada, New Zealand consists primarily of two large islands (North Island and South Island), though its authority also extends to several smaller island groups scattered across a large swath of the southern Pacific. The nation's nearest neighbor is Australia, another Commonwealth member and an important trade partner.

The first Maoris, of Polynesian origin, arrived on South Island about AD 800. European settlement began about a thousand years later, after the famous expeditions of Britain's Captain James Cook. Though New Zealand became a British possession in 1840 and a

Crown colony (under the monarch's direct control) the following year, its remote location ensured the settlers a significant degree of autonomy from the outset. By 1856 its status had changed officially from Crown colony to self-governing colony, and by 1907 it had ceased to be a colony altogether, instead becoming an autonomous dominion of the British Empire. It retained this status until full independence in 1947.

Immediate conflict with the Maori resulted in the Treaty of Waitangi (1840), many provisions of which are still in force. Despite the agreement, tensions remained high, with the Maori subject to severe discrimination and institutionalized racism. The result was the endemic poverty still visible in many native settlements today.

Government Structure

New Zealand's governmental structure is still evolving. A new Constitution Act was passed in 1986, for example, but the details of its implementation remain the subject of debate. Possible reorganization as a republic is also under discussion, with Prime Minister Helen Clark (1950–) expressing support for the proposal. But the most significant change of the past twenty years has probably been the establishment by referendum (1993) of a new electoral system for Parliament. Called Mixed Member Proportional (MMP), it is a combination of two different systems. Under its guidelines, 69 of the 120 parliamentary seats are to represent single-member constituencies; these are filled by direct, popular vote in a manner akin to gubernatorial elections in the United States. Seven of the constituencies must be Maori, thus ensuring the native community at least that many seats. The remaining fifty-one seats are filled by candidates from lists compiled by each party, with the number of seats awarded to each dependent on its share of the popular vote. The aim of this mixed system is to give smaller parties and minorities a stronger presence in Parliament. All members serve three-year terms, though elections may be called earlier if a ruling coalition collapses.

The structure and legitimacy of the executive branch rest upon the largely formal duties of the governor general, who is appointed by the British monarch to represent royal authority. After every parliamentary election, the governor general legitimizes the new government by a formal display of the monarch's approval. This is done through his or her appointment of the parliamentary majority leader as Prime Minister. This act of appointment is largely symbolic, for longstanding precedent effectively prevents the governor general from choosing an alternative. The same process is used in the selection of Parliament members to serve in the prime minister's cabinet, also known as the Executive Council. These appointments, too, are largely symbolic—the governor general works closely with the prime minister before announcing the selections and, because a cabinet

at odds with its chief is in no one's interest, the Crown's representative has an overwhelming motive for heeding the prime minister's preferences.

The Ministry of Justice administers the nation's judicial system, the structure of which is based on the British system. At the bottom are District Courts, previously known as Magistrates' Courts, with jurisdiction over minor civil matters and some criminal cases. The next level is the High Court (known until 1980 as the Supreme Court), which handles major civil and criminal cases. Above the High Court is the Court of Appeal, which hears appeals in cases initially adjudicated at one of the lower levels. Finally, a Supreme Court serves as the court of final appeal. Previously, appeals in cases decided by the Court of Appeal were sent to London for adjudication by the Judicial Committee of the Privy Council, an arm of Her Majesty's government. Though other Commonwealth nations (Belize, for example) continue to use the Privy Council for this purpose, there was a growing sense among New Zealanders that its decisions did not always take the nation's unique history and culture into adequate account. Parliament agreed, and the Supreme Court Act of 2003 established the new system.

The basic unit of local government is the municipal or district council. All council members are directly elected by popular vote, as are the council chairs in some cases. In many urban districts, for example, an elected city official (usually the mayor) chairs the council. Elsewhere, however, council members, not the voters, choose the chair.

Political Parties and Factions

Two parties have dominated the political scene in New Zealand since its 1947 independence: the left-center Labour Party and the center-right National Party. The influence of both has declined somewhat in recent years, partly because of the changes in the electoral system that happened in 1993 (see above). Though the Labour and National parties remain the largest in Parliament, neither party has been able recently to win a majority by itself. A coalition with smaller parties is therefore required. In theory, any party in Parliament can win the right to form a government if it organizes enough alliances to control the sixty-one seats necessary for a majority. As a rule, however, only the party with the most seats of its own will be able to do so. The more seats a party needs from its partners, the more difficult it is to balance the competing interests of those partners long enough to form a sustainable coalition.

In the wake of the 2005 elections, the Labour Party formed a coalition that put Labour leader Helen Clark back in the prime minister's office for a third straight term. Joining the alliance were two center-left parties, the Progressive Party and the Green Party, and two center-right parties, United Future and New Zealand First. The remaining parties in Parliament—the National

Party, the right-wing group ACT New Zealand, and the Maori Party—constitute the parliamentary opposition.

Major Events

World War I had a profound impact on New Zealand, which suffered one of the highest casualty rates of any nation in the conflict. As a dominion of the British Empire, New Zealand immediately joined the Allies at the outbreak of hostilities in 1914. One hundred and twenty thousand New Zealanders, or more than 10 percent of the country's population, enlisted. Of the 103,000 who served overseas, well over half were killed or wounded. Nearly a century later, ANZAC Day (ANZAC is an acronym for Australia and New Zealand Army Corps) remains a somber occasion throughout the nation.

In July 1985 the city of Auckland was the site of a major international incident. A ship belonging to the environmental group Greenpeace was anchored in Auckland Harbor when two explosions destroyed it, killing one crewmember. Investigations soon revealed the involvement of the French intelligence service, which wanted the ship destroyed to prevent it from sailing to Mururoa Atoll, a small, isolated island where the French planned to test nuclear weapons. Amid an international furor, New Zealanders strengthened their longstanding opposition to nuclear weapons and gained new confidence in international affairs. Vehement protests to the United Nations resulted in an apology and financial settlement from France, but the premature release of the two bombers from a French prison damaged the prospects for further reconciliation.

Twenty-First Century

Immigration and the treatment of minority communities are pressing issues. New Zealand's high standard of living, well-regarded social programs, and natural beauty make it a destination of choice for immigrants from all over the world. It is also one of the relatively few nations that accept a substantial number of petitions for political asylum. As a result, the nation's demographics are changing rapidly, particularly in urban areas. More than two hundred thousand Asians, for example, have arrived within the past twenty years. Throughout that period, the economy has generally been strong enough to accommodate the new arrivals. A sudden economic downturn, however, may stir resentment among more established groups. Several human rights organizations have already reported a substantial increase in anti-Asian discrimination.

Of all the nation's minority groups, the native Maoris have the most obstacles to overcome. In some respects, their situation has improved markedly since New Zealand's independence. Discrimination in education and employment is no longer legal, and their culture is recognized and widely celebrated. The government has apologized for decades of discrimination and injustice and in 1993 began payments to Maori communities as partial compensation for the loss of their ancestral land. The legacy of discrimination is still apparent, however. Decades of inadequate health care, for example, are a major cause of the dramatic disparity in life expectancy between Maoris and non-Maoris. A white New Zealander, on average, will live more than eight years longer than his Maori neighbor. Crime is also a major issue for native communities; an official government study found that Maoris were four to five times more likely than whites to be convicted of a crime. The reasons for that difference are complex, but decades of poverty, lack of opportunity, and continuing prejudice within the justice system all play a role. These disparities must be addressed if New Zealand is to fulfill its full potential as a regional leader.

BIBLIOGRAPHY

Mein Smith, Philippa. *A Concise History of New Zealand.* Cambridge: Cambridge University Press, 2005.

Mulholland, Malcolm. *State of the Maori Nation: Twenty-First Century Issues in Aotearoa.* Auckland, New Zealand: Reed Publishing, 2006.

"Your Front Door to New Zealand Government Online." http://newzealand.govt.nz/ (accessed June 7, 2007).

⊕ Japan

Type of Government

Japan is a constitutional monarchy with a parliamentary government. The emperor serves as the nation's head of state, while the prime minister is the head of government and the commander of the armed forces. The prime minister is designated by the legislature and must command the majority party. The legislative branch is a bicameral parliament, called the Diet, with an upper house called the Sangi-in (House of Councilors) and a lower house called the Shugi-in (House of Representatives). The independent judicial branch is led by the Supreme Court.

Background

Japan is an island archipelago in the western Pacific Ocean, east of China and the Korean peninsula. The nation consists of four main islands—Hokkaido, Honshu, Kyushu, and Shikoku—and more than three thousand smaller islands.

The earliest period in Japanese history is known as the Jomon Period (13,000–300 BC), during which Japanese society developed from hunter-gatherer tribes to an agrarian society, focused on rice cultivation. From 300 BC to AD 538 Japan gradually developed into an empire. The Chinese writing system and the Buddhist religion were imported to Japan and helped to stimulate the formation of an educated elite, which gave rise to a central bureaucracy. Japan's first capital city, Nara, built in 710, was designed in imitation of Chinese cities. In 794, during internal struggles between the imperial government and feudal clans of wealthy warlords, the capital was moved to Heian (now Kyoto).

During the Heian Period (794–1185) families of *bushi* (samurai) took control of Japan as military leaders and turned the imperial government into a symbolic body that represented the ruling clan's policies. The Fujiwara, Minamoto, and Taira families were the most powerful families and competed for control of the nation; the Minamoto clan finally won in the Gempei War (1180–1185). In 1197 Minamoto Yoritomo was appointed shogun, the country's highest military officer, and was thereafter the effective leader of Japan. During the next century the shogunate, called a *bakufu*—meaning "tent government," because the soldiers lived in tents—ruled the country.

In 1333 Emperor Go-Daigo (1288–1339) organized forces and deposed the bakufu. The imperial government lasted until 1336, when a new shogunate took control under Ashikaga Takauji (1305–1358). In the following two centuries leadership split into small governments, each headed by a warlord clan. When Europeans arrived in Japan in 1542, they brought along firearms and modern military techniques, which transformed the struggles between the warlords.

In 1590 Japan was united under Shogun Toyotomi Hideyosi (1536–1598), who eventually relinquished power to the Tokugawa clan under Tokugawa Ieyasu (1543–1616). That clan's rise to power marked the beginning of the Edo period, during which the government established isolationist policies—it prohibited trade with all nations except China, for example—and claimed ownership of all land and property. The capital was moved to what is now Tokyo; authority in other areas was vested in territorial regents who had links to the ruling family. Despite the cultural isolation, the Edo period, which lasted for more than two hundred and fifty years, led to a renaissance of art, music, literature, architecture, and theater.

During the eighteenth and nineteenth centuries, European nations attempted, through negotiation and military force, to get Japan to trade with the outside world. In 1853 Commodore Matthew C. Perry (1794–1858) brought U.S. war ships to the coast in the hopes of persuading Edo to open its ports. Growing public sentiment and foreign influence led to the Meiji Restoration, in which the imperial government overthrew the bakufu and opened the country.

By 1889 Japan had adopted a European parliamentary system with a constitution that vested executive power in the emperor. The first war between Japan and China (1894–1895) and the 1904 war between Japan and Russia, which were fought over disputed territories, allowed an oligarchy of generals and politicians to take effective control of the nation. Japan became a colonial power, as well: During its second war with China (1937–1945), Japan occupied the Chinese capital, Nanjing, and then increased its territory by occupying Vietnam, despite widespread international criticism.

In 1941, after it had formed an alliance with Germany and Italy, the Japanese government sent squadrons to attack the U.S. naval base at Pearl Harbor, Hawaii. That attack turned what had been largely a war in Europe into World War II. Allied forces retaliated and by 1944 had forced Japan to relinquish most of its colonial territories. In 1945 the United States dropped atomic bombs on two Japanese cities, Hiroshima and Nagasaki, which led to hundreds of thousands of deaths. In August 1945 Japan formally surrendered to allied forces.

Following the war, Japanese territory was occupied by U.S., Russian, and Chinese forces for several years. U.S. representatives supervised the development of a new constitution in 1947 that vested all governmental power in the prime minister and the legislature and prohibited the emperor from serving in any capacity other than symbolic head of state. In addition, the document stipulated that the Japanese government would never again create a "projective" military force. In the decades that followed, Japan's government became one of the most stable in Asia.

Government Structure

The emperor—the symbolic and ceremonial head of the Japanese government—addresses the public, meets with foreign dignitaries and, with the consultation of the prime minister and the cabinet, appoints government staff, signs treaties, and awards honors for service. The imperial throne is passed from father to son in dynastic tradition.

Japan's constitution, which provides universal suffrage for persons twenty years of age and older, vests the majority of power in the democratically elected Diet. Its members are chosen in a parallel voting system, which requires each voter to cast two votes. One vote is for a candidate in a single-seat constituency; the other is for a list of candidates created by political parties. Each party is allocated some seats in proportion to the total number of votes the party gets.

The upper house of the Diet, the House of Councilors, has 242 members; 146 are elected from forty-seven single-seat constituencies, known as prefectures, and ninety-six by proportional representation from a single national party list. Councilors serve six-year terms, with half reelected every three years. The lower house, the House of Representatives, has 480 members, 300 of whom are elected from single-seat constituencies and 180 from eleven separate electoral blocks under the party-list system of proportional representation. House members serve four-year terms unless the house is dissolved prior to regularly scheduled elections.

Though both houses have similar powers, the House of Representatives is considered more powerful because it can dissolve the government in times of deadlock; a resolution to dissolve the government must have the support of at least 50 percent of its members. In addition, the House of Representatives can, by a two-thirds majority, overturn any legislation blocked by the House of Councilors. If the lower house seems to be failing its constitutional function, the prime minister can dissolve the house with a no-confidence vote.

The prime minister, who serves as the head of government and commander of the nation's defense forces, is chosen from among the members of the Diet and represents the majority political party. Following appointment, the prime minister chooses as many as seventeen ministers to serve in the cabinet. With the advice of the cabinet, the prime minister submits legislation to the Diet and advises the legislature on foreign relations and administrative matters. The prime minister or the House of Representatives may choose to dissolve the cabinet before the prime minister's term has ended. The prime minister and the cabinet have executive power, but all executive decisions require the approval of the Diet.

The Supreme Court has appellate jurisdiction as the court of last resort and exercises authority over all of the nation's courts. The chief justice is appointed by the emperor with the consensus of the cabinet; the fourteen other justices are appointed directly by the cabinet. All must retire at age seventy. The Supreme Court nominates and the Cabinet appoints justices of the lower courts.

Policy changes in Japan are dictated not only by the Diet and the cabinet but also by the involvement of informal councils representing industrial and special-interest groups. These "deliberation councils" produce proposals for legislation that filter into subcommittees of the Diet and eventually to the legislative floor.

Political Parties and Factions

Japan has a multiparty system, with new political parties and coalitions of major parties appearing in every election cycle. However, several major political parties have dominated the country since the establishment of the current constitution.

The Jiyu Minshuto (Liberal Democratic Party, or LDP) is the nation's largest political party. Formed in 1955, it grew out of a coalition of the Liberal Party and the Japan Democratic Party. The LDP rose to prominence under the leadership of its first president, Shigeru Yoshida (1878–1967), and controlled the Diet until 1993, when the party was weakened by allegations of corruption and was ousted by a new coalition government. In 2001 the administration of Prime Minister Junichiro Koizumi (1942–) reestablished LDP author-

ity. During two terms as prime minister, Koizuimi achieved a level of popularity usually reserved for pop-culture celebrities. The LDP is known as an economically and socially conservative party and generally focuses on economic reform.

The New Komeito (New Clean Government Party) was founded in 1964 as the political arm of the country's powerful Buddhist community. Since then the New Komeito has distanced itself from its religious roots in favor of a moderately conservative platform. In 1998 the New Komeito merged with the New Peace Party. In 2001 it formed a coalition with the LDP. Though the New Komeito has never dominated the central government, party members have considerable clout in regional governments.

The Minshuto (Democratic Party of Japan, or DPJ), the second-largest political party, joined the coalition that led the first government following World War II. The party was dissolved in 1950 when Prime Minister Ashida Hitoshi resigned amid allegations of bribery and corruption. In 1996 the party was reformed under the leadership of Naoto Kan (1947–) as a coalition of several smaller parties and factions opposed to the LDP. The DJP is a socially liberal party.

The Shakai Minshuto (Social Democratic Party of Japan, or SDPJ) was formed in 1946 as a coalition of minor socialist parties. Internal conflicts have led to a constant shifting of membership and have prevented the party from achieving significant support. It was part of a coalition that led the government from 1993 to 1996.

The Nihon Kyosanto (Japanese Communist Party, or JCP) formed around 1922 but remained an underground movement until Japan legalized communism. The JCP supports a peaceful and slow transition to socialism and a foreign policy based on pacifism. Because of its moderate stance, the JCP enjoys a low level of support in regional governments and retains some representation in the Diet.

Major Events

As the only nation to experience a nuclear assault, Japan has been a world leader in promoting nuclear disarmament and an important center for the study of the effects of nuclear radiation. In 1956 the parliament adopted the Atomic Energy Basic Law, which restricted all research on atomic energy to nonmilitary applications. In 1971 the parliament passed a resolution generally known as the "Three Non-Nuclear Principles," which stated that the Japanese government would not create, possess, or allow nuclear weapons to pass through its territory. The principles were first outlined by Prime Minister Eisaku Sato (1901–1975), who was awarded the Nobel Peace Prize in 1974 for his campaigns against nuclear proliferation.

When allied forces began to leave Japan in 1950— they were being transferred to the conflict in Korea—

The Japanese economy experienced its first recession during the oil crisis of 1973, when the Organization of Petroleum Exporting Countries restricted oil exports to nations that had supported Israel during its war with Syria and Egypt. Japan was heavily dependent upon foreign oil; the effects of the crisis lingered for more than a decade. Still, Japan's industrial and manufacturing sectors continued to grow, and by the 1980s Japan had the second-largest economy in the world. In the 1990s, however, the nation experienced a major recession, marked by high unemployment and stock market instability.

Twenty-First Century

Economic recovery has been a dominant issue in Japanese politics since the financial crisis of the 1990s. The Koizumi administration focused on reducing government debt and privatizing the country's postal service as primary measures to ensure economic recovery. Eventually, the nation returned to moderate growth.

In 2006 Shinzo Abe (1954–) was elected prime minister with expectations that he would continue the economic reforms of his predecessor, while making better efforts in foreign relations, especially with China and North Korea. His administration also must deal with such challenges as population growth and the loss of natural resources.

BIBLIOGRAPHY

Karan, Pradyumna P. and Dick Gilbreath. *Japan in the Twenty-First Century: Environment, Economy, and Society.* Lexington: University Press of Kentucky, 2005.

Henshall, Kenneth G. *A History of Japan: From Stone Age to Superpower.* 2nd ed. London: Palgrave Macmillan, 2004.

Pyle, Kenneth B. *Japan Rising: The Resurgence of Japanese Power and Purpose.* New York: PublicAffairs Press, 2007.

U.S. General Douglas MacArthur with Japan's Emperor Hirohito in a famous photograph of their first meeting.   © *Bettmann/CORBIS*

many in the Japanese government became concerned that the nation would be left vulnerable to invasion or internal rebellion. Under the 1947 constitution, the government's ability to develop military capability was restricted. In fact, during the occupation all military training organizations had been abolished.

In 1954 parliament authorized the creation of the Japan Self-Defense Forces (JDSF), a defensive military divided into land, air, and naval divisions. The government explicitly defined the functions of the JDSF as defensive and created an administrative system that placed the forces under nonmilitary control. The antimilitary contingent of the government opposed the establishment of the JDSF, and debates over the constitutionality of the defense forces continued into the 1980s. Since the JDSF was formed it has engaged only in defensive operations at home and provided humanitarian aid internationally. When Japan supported the U.S.-led invasion of Iraq in 2003, members of the JDSF were sent to Iraq to provide aid but not to engage in combat.

From the 1950s to the 1990s the principal goal of the government was economic growth and development. Japan supplied industrial materials to allied forces during the Korean War and, because of its pacifist stance, was not burdened by military obligations during the Cold War. Japan experienced rapid economic growth, becoming one of the world's leading suppliers of technology and industrial machinery.

⊕ Republic of India

Type of Government

India is a socialist, democratic republic with a parliamentary form of government. The executive branch consists of the president, whose role is largely symbolic, and the prime minister, who is the head of the government. The prime minister guides and advises all presidential decisions and forms a Council of Ministers to lead the executive offices. India has a bicameral legislature consisting of the Rajya Sabha (Council of States) and the Lok Sabha (House of the People). The judicial branch consists of a Supreme Court, which has both appellate and original jurisdiction, with special authority to enforce fundamental rights; the high courts, which have jurisdiction over one or more states; and the district courts.

Background

The first Indian culture known to archaeologists was the Indus Valley society, which existed in seclusion from approximately 3000 BC to 1500 BC. Numerous artifacts and other archaeological evidence indicate that the Indus society had a well-developed agricultural system, large settlements that show distinct evidence of urban planning, and complex religious, social, and cultural traditions.

In 1500 BC Aryan tribes invaded from the west, bringing with them the Sanskrit language and the caste system that dominated Indian society until the modern era. The Aryans first settled the northern regions and then moved south and east, where they established additional kingdoms. The Indo-Aryan society produced the Vedas, which are considered among the earliest religious texts.

By 500 BC India had been divided into sixteen Mahajanapadas (Great Kingdoms), which were complex societies with agricultural economies and sophisticated military structures. Most important, the Mahajanapadas developed Hinduism, a combination of native and imported religious traditions. Hindu texts played a major role in the development of Indian society.

The Achaemenid Empire, which originated in Persia, conquered India around 500 BC and ruled for a century before it, in turn, was conquered by Alexander the Great (356–323 BC) of Macedon. The Grecian armies did not remain in India, but they left behind military settlements to ensure that trade routes stayed open. In time the Mahajanapada kings reclaimed most of India and established a native imperial society known as the Maurya Dynasty. Beginning with the reign of King Asoka (c. 304–c. 233 BC), the dynasty ruled through a combination of innovative economic policies and military superiority. Asoka also popularized Buddhism as a major competitor to Hinduism.

When the Maurya Dynasty collapsed, India fragmented into a number of small kingdoms. The region was invaded several times by Chinese and Grecian armies, who were interested in the region's natural resources. Chandragupta II (c. 350–415) then conquered vast portions of India, from the Ganges to the Indus rivers, and founded the imperial Gupta Dynasty, which is considered by some to be a golden age. Although it had a rigid caste system, it did not employ capital punishment and poets and other artists flourished. However, the imperial government was frustrated by frequent military engagements between minor kingdoms.

Arab and Turkish Muslims first began visiting India in the sixth century AD. During the late twelfth and early thirteenth centuries, Muslim armies conquered the northern portions of the country and established what were later called the Islamic Sultanates. Turkish kings remained in control of the country until 1397–98, when Turkic-Mongol general Timur (1336–1405), also known as Tamerlane, invaded and ransacked the city of Dehli.

A chaotic period ensued, leading to the establishment of the Mughal Dynasty in 1527. Its founder, King Zahir-ud-Din Muhammad Babur (1483–1530), was a descendant of Timur. Six emperors followed as leaders of the Mughal Dynasty, each leaving distinct cultural legacies. Emperor Akbar (1542–1605), the grandson of Babur, brought a temporary end to the wars between the Mughals and the Hindus and established each province of India as a self-governing structure with a high degree of religious freedom. Akbar's grandson Shahjahan (1592–1666) began another wave of expansion and conquered most of the remaining Hindu kings. Shahjahan's greatest legacy is the architecture of his rule, including the Taj Mahal in Agra, originally constructed as a tomb for his favorite wife.

In the 1600s Hindu kings in western and central India staged an armed resistance. Although they were never able to conquer the nation, they did precipitate the downfall of the Mughal Dynasty, which by 1674 had fragmented into smaller groups.

The British first entered India in 1583 during the reign of Queen Elizabeth I (1533–1603). They negotiated trade rights with the Mughal government and opened the East India Trading Company in Bombay (now Mumbai) in 1614. It marked the beginning of a long British presence in the region.

During the 1600s the British, French, and Portuguese competed for military and economic presence in India. The British insinuated themselves into local politics through trade and economic incentives. By 1769 the British East India Company held a trade monopoly in the region, and Britain had begun to increase its military presence.

Because of infighting among local leaders, the British slowly took control of India. By 1857, after they quelled a rebellion in the eastern region of Bengal, they had gained almost total authority. Although some native princes remained in power, they were subject to the will of the British government.

An independence movement was a continuous undercurrent, however; its ability to coalesce was hampered by religious tensions. Specifically, the Muslim minority feared that independence would lead to a Hindu-dominated state. In 1915 the independence movement gained strength from the activities of Mohandas Gandhi (1869–1948), a Hindu spiritual and political leader who saw unification of Hindus and Muslims as a necessity if they were to liberate the nation. He pushed independence through nonviolent resistance.

Gandhi succeeded in inspiring nonviolent mass protests, including boycotts—Indians stopped shopping in stores that sold British goods, for example—and various parliamentary actions. The British responded by banning large gatherings and protests. That led to a

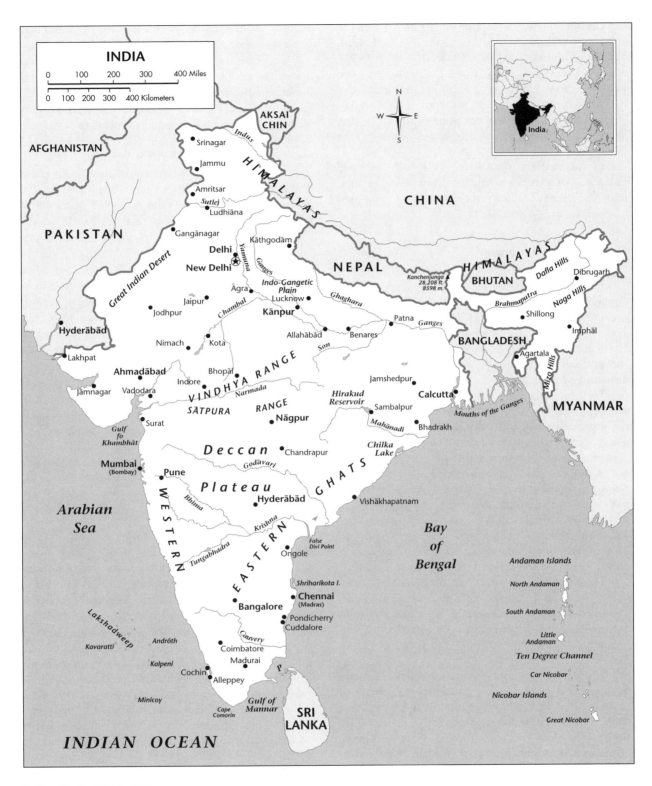

India. *Maryland Cartographics*

massacre in Amritsar, Punjab: When ten thousand people arrived to celebrate a Hindu festival, British troops opened fire, killing some four hundred and wounding twelve hundred more, and then left without caring for the wounded. The incident damaged Britain's credibility as a colonial power. Eventually, with their administration hampered, the British saw that the economic benefits of the colony were dwindling and agreed to leave.

Disputes between the Indian National Congress, under the leadership of Gandhi, and the Muslim League, under the leadership of Aga Khan III (1877–1957), prompted the British to partition the region into two separate nations. On August 14, 1947, the Dominion of Pakistan was established; India was created the next day. During the following months, some fourteen million Muslims and Hindus migrated from one country to the other. Violence frequently erupted.

By the time the British left, India had developed native political parties and held its first national elections. Indian politicians finished work on the first constitution in 1950, creating a democratic republic.

Government Structure

India's central government is controlled by a bicameral parliament and administered by a president, a prime minister, and a cabinet of ministers. Each of the twenty-five Indian states maintains its own government. The country also has seven territories designated as "unions," which do not have their own governments and are administered directly by the central government through union ministries.

The lower house of parliament, the Lok Sabha, consists of as many as 545 members, with 530 elected from the twenty-five states and 13 elected from the seven unions. The president nominates two additional members to represent the interests of the country's Anglo-Indian population. Members of the Lok Sabha are elected by popular vote—India maintains universal suffrage for all persons older than eighteen years of age. In the event that the Lok Sabha fails to carry out its constitutional functions, the president has the power to dissolve it and call for new elections. Unless the house is dissolved, each house member serves a five-year term.

The upper house of parliament, the Rajya Sabha, consists of not more than 250 members, of whom twelve are appointed directly by the president. The remaining members are elected by state legislatures. One-third of its members are elected every two years. The president cannot dissolve the Rajya Sabha.

The president, the prime minister, and other executive branch officials answer to the parliament concerning all actions. As a largely symbolic figure, the president must confer with the prime minister regarding all decisions. He or she is the head of state, the commander in chief of the armed forces, and the designated guardian of the constitution. The president is elected to a five-year term by a special electoral college composed of members from parliament and the state legislatures.

The prime minister, who is nominated by the members of the Lok Sabha and appointed by the president, must represent the party or coalition of parties that has majority support in the parliament. He or she may remain in office so long as the party or coalition maintains that majority. As head of the government, the prime minister generally advises the president on all executive actions.

The Council of Ministers, whose members are nominated by the prime minister and appointed by the president, fall into three basic categories, according to seniority: cabinet ministers, ministers of state, and deputy ministers. All nominees must be members of parliament before they may serve on the council. Additional ministries and departments handle affairs of the unions.

Legislation originates in the parliament. The president has limited powers to suggest changes to legislative proposals and does so with the agreement of the prime minister. The prime minister may suggest legislation independently but generally responds to legislation that originates in the parliament.

The Supreme Court of India, which is independent from the other branches, has original and appellate jurisdiction over any dispute between the central government and any state or between states within the republic. A chief justice and twenty-five associate justices are appointed by the president with the advice of the prime minister. The justices remain in office until retirement, which is mandatory at age sixty-five, unless they are removed by parliament for misbehavior. The remaining judicial power is distributed among twenty-one high courts in the states and a number of district courts for regional and local issues.

India is a socialist republic. To that end, the country has a socialized medical system and provides for the welfare of individuals unable to care for themselves.

Political Parties and Factions

India has a multiparty system with two basic types of political parties. National parties are recognized in four or more states by the Election Commission of India. Regional parties represent a single state or district and generally compete for elections to the state legislatures. Regional parties may also join in alliances or coalitions with national parties during the major election cycles.

The Indian National Congress (INC), formed in 1845, is the country's oldest political party. It played a major role in the independence movement. Jawaharlal Nehru (1889–1964), India's first prime minister, was a member of the INC, as was his daughter, Indira Gandhi (1917–1984), who was one of the first female prime ministers in the world. INC candidates held a majority in parliament from independence in 1947 until the 1990s; the rise of political leader Sonia Gandhi (1946–)—the widow of Indira Gandhi's son, Rajiv—brought the INC back to prominence in 1999. During the 2004 election cycle, the INC became a member of the United Progressive Alliance (UPA), a coalition of left-wing political parties that also includes the Communist Party of India (CPI) and the Revolutionary Socialist Party. In 2007 UPA candidate Pratibha Patil (1935–) was elected the first female president of India.

The Bharatiya Janata Party (BJP), which was founded in 1980, grew out of the Bharatiya Jana Sangh (BJS), the political arm of the Hindu movement in India. In 1998 the BJP became part of the National Democratic Alliance (NDA), a coalition of Hindu-rights organizations and political factions. From 1998 to 2004 the BJP held a majority in the parliament under Prime Minister Atal Bihari Vajpayee (1924–). Since the BJP lost majority power in 2004, Vajpayee has served as the opposition leader in parliament.

The Communist Party of India (CPI) was founded in the 1920s as a conglomeration of smaller communist factions. The CPI, which has never enjoyed majority control in the parliament, supports the United Progressive Alliance, headed by the INC. In 1964 ideological differences led to a split in the party; a group of Marxist communists formed the Communist Party of India (Marxist), usually denoted as CPIM or CPM. Both the CPI and CPIM maintain significant influence at the state and regional levels and are therefore able to affect the policies of the central government.

Major Events

Territorial disputes between Pakistan and India have played a role in four military conflicts, beginning with the Indo-Pakistani War (First Kashmir War) in 1947. Gandhi—in India he is considered the father of the nation—never accepted the partition and continued working for an alliance between Muslims and Hindus. He was assassinated in 1948 by two Hindu extremists who believed that his policies weakened Hindu control of the government.

Nehru, who was Gandhi's close friend and protégé, served as the country's first prime minister. He saw India as a socialistic nation, with equal opportunity, education, and living standards for all. He sought to remove differences caused by religion, caste—he pushed the Untouchability Act of 1955, which outlawed the concept of an untouchable class—and language, by moving the country toward making Hindi the official language. He sought peaceful coexistence with other nations but, significantly, favored a policy of nonalignment with any world power.

In 1967 his daughter, Indira Gandhi, became prime minister. (She was no relation to Mohandas Gandhi.) Her administration was successful in accelerating economic growth and in forging stronger alliances with the Union of Soviet Socialist Republics and the People's Republic of China; however, she was also a controversial politician, often accused of having authoritarian tendencies.

India first began developing a nuclear technology program during the Nehru years, although the nation outwardly assisted efforts by the United Nations to promote nuclear disarmament. Under Indira Gandhi, however, the country's nuclear program was accelerated; she authorized the "peaceful explosion" of a nuclear device in 1974.

Despite high popularity at the beginning of her administration, by 1975 she was losing popular support.

India's spiritual leader Mohandas Gandhi at a protest march in 1930. *Hulton Archive/Getty Images*

Several policies—a voluntary sterilization program to reduce overpopulation, for example, and aggressive control of extremist religious factions—led to widespread protests. When her administration was charged with violating election laws and other acts of corruption, violence erupted. She declared a state of emergency and established a de facto dictatorship.

During the nineteen-month national emergency, Gandhi's administration arrested and detained opposition leaders and political activists, censored the media, and suspended all actions by the state legislatures. Public protests continued, becoming so impassioned that Gandhi agreed to hold elections in 1977. She was removed from office by popular vote. She remained active in politics, however. Aggressive tactics from the opposition resulted in her regaining support from the populace. The government was dissolved because of deadlock in 1979, and Gandhi again became prime minister. Her second administration was troubled by disturbances among the nation's militant religious groups. In 1984, shortly after she launched an aggressive campaign to combat the growth of a militant Sikh faction, she was assassinated by two of her Sikh bodyguards. Although she is often maligned as authoritarian, willing to manipulate state and federal powers, she is just as often credited with transforming the nation through innovative agricultural, economic, and foreign policies.

Gandhi was succeeded by her son, Rajiv (1944–1991), who had been a member of parliament. He fostered new managerial techniques and encouraged economic development and foreign investment. In 1987 he involved India in Sri Lanka's civil war, in which government forces were fighting the separatist Tamil ethnic group. India sent military, medical, and food aid to the Tamil group, partly, many observers say, to appease India's own Tamil minority. In 1989 the INC lost its majority, and Gandhi was forced to resign. He began a campaign for reelection in 1991, but it was cut short by a suicide bomber. Militants claimed the assassination was an act of revenge for India's intervention in the Sri Lankan civil war.

India resumed its nuclear-weapons program in the 1990s in response to Pakistan's efforts to build a nuclear arsenal. In 1998 India conducted a series of nuclear tests. Estimates indicate that India may have developed enough nuclear material for fifty to ninety weapons. India is one of three U.N. members—Pakistan and Israel are the others—that have not ratified the Nuclear Non-Proliferation Treaty. Indian leaders have stated that the country's nuclear weapons would only be used in response to attack by a foreign power.

Twenty-First Century

India, the world's second most populous nation, experiences continual problems related to poverty. However, its economy has grown considerably during the past twenty-five years, largely because the government has invested in the industrial sector, both to ease unemployment and as a way to modernize the nation.

The country continues to face criticism from the international community because of the status of women in society. Traditional Hindi and Islamic customs impede women from seeking the rights guaranteed by the constitution. Some observers believe additional legal reform may be necessary.

Perhaps India's most pressing challenge is to solve its territorial disputes with Pakistan, which date back to the partition of 1947. The countries have fought four wars over territory; all ended in uneasy political agreements or stalemate. Because both nations command nuclear arsenals, the ongoing disputes raise significant international concern.

BIBLIOGRAPHY

Daniélou, Alain. *A Brief History of India*. Translated by Kenneth F. Hurry. Rochester, VT: Inner Traditions, 2003.

Kochanek, Stanley A., and Robert L. Hardgrave. *India: Government and Politics in a Developing Nation*. 7th ed. Boston: Wadsworth Publishing, 2007.

Cohen, Steven Philip. *India: Emerging Power*. Washington, DC: Brookings Institution Press, 2001.

⊕ Islamic Republic of Pakistan

Type of Government

Pakistan is a parliamentary republic with a dual executive office consisting of a president, who serves as head of state and commander in chief of the armed forces, and a prime minister, who serves as head of government. The Majlis-e-shoora (Council of Advisors) has two houses, the Senate and the National Assembly. The judicial branch consists of the Supreme Court and the Federal Shariat Court, a special court that hears cases involving Islamic law. The Pakistani state is Islamic by constitution and grants special status to Islamic law at all levels of government.

Background

Pakistan is a South Asian country bordered by India on the east, Afghanistan and Iran on the west, and China on the northeast. Its southern coast is washed by the Arabian Sea. Before 1947, Pakistan and India were part of what is often called the Indian Subcontinent. When the British partitioned the region, Pakistan consisted of two regions divided geographically by India. In 1971 the eastern region of Pakistan, after a war of independence, became Bangladesh.

Pakistan's history diverges from that of its neighbor, India, in the mid-twentieth century, during the movement for independence from Britain. Islam, which arrived in the subcontinent in the eighth century, was the religion of the Mughal Empire, the dominant force in the region from the sixteenth century until the British gained control in the 1850s. However, the majority of India was Hindu, as was the leadership of the independence movement led by Mohandas Gandhi (1869–1948). While many Muslims participated in Gandhi's strategy of nonviolent protests against British authority from 1920 until the independence movement's ultimate victory in 1947, Muslim leaders feared that they would be an ignored minority in a Hindu-dominated independent state of India.

In 1940 the Muslim League, under the leadership of Muhammed Ali Jinnah (1876–1948), endorsed a two-nation independence policy, insisting that any resolution of the conflict with the British involve a partition of India, with separate countries for Hindus and Muslims. Initially, the British were dubious about the Muslim League's demands, considering them a negotiation ploy aimed at obtaining a better power-sharing arrangement within a united India. However, Muslim support for the partition of India became evident on Direct Action Day, August 16, 1946, when what was planned as a nonviolent protest by the Muslim League degenerated into riots in Calcutta that claimed more than four thousand lives.

Afterward, the intense acrimony between the Hindu and Muslim factions led to a partition plan with borders imposed by the British to break the impasse. On August 14, 1947, the Dominion of Pakistan was formed and immediately became the largest Muslim country in the world. There was tremendous upheaval as Muslims and

Pakistan. *Maryland Cartographic*

Hindus caught on the wrong side of these new borders uprooted themselves to immigrate to Pakistan and India, respectively. Jinnah became Pakistan's first governor general.

A centuries-long history of military insurgency has led to several reformulations of the government since then, including constitutional revisions in 2003. It has been the Islamic Republic of Pakistan since 1956.

Government Structure

Pakistan is divided into four provinces, a federally administered tribal territory, and a capital territory. It has a parliamentary government that acknowledges the primacy of Islamic law. However, since independence in 1947, the government has been interrupted by periods of military control. Parliamentary government was restored in 2001.

The president is required by the constitution to be Muslim and functions as the head of state and commander in chief of the nation's armed forces. A special electoral college, made up of members from the parliament and the provincial assemblies, elects the president for a maximum of two terms of five years each. The president retains certain constitutional powers, including the ability to dissolve the National Assembly in the event of governmental deadlock. The parliament can likewise call for the president's impeachment with a two-thirds vote.

The prime minister serves as the head of government and usually represents the majority party in the National Assembly. The prime minister advises parliament on matters of state and the agenda of the executive branch. He also appoints the ministers of the federal cabinet, who head the executive departments and advise the prime minister on policy issues. When the government was restructured in 1994, thirty-three executive departments were established.

The Council of Advisors, or parliament, consists of an upper house, the Senate, and a lower house, the National Assembly. Either house can originate and approve legislation, but all budget bills start in the National Assembly. The president can block legislation from either house unless both houses override the president with a majority vote.

The National Assembly consists of 342 members, of whom 272 are elected by direct vote from the four provinces. In addition, sixty seats are reserved for women and ten seats are reserved for representatives of religious minorities. The special seats are filled by a proportional representation system. Members serve for five-year terms unless the president dissolves the house before regularly scheduled elections.

The one hundred senators are elected directly by the provincial assemblies. Some Senate seats are reserved for women, representatives of religious minorities, and representatives of Pakistan's federally administered tribal areas. Senators are elected for six-years terms, with half of the membership reelected every three years. Unlike the National Assembly, the Senate cannot be dissolved by the president.

In the judicial branch, the Supreme Court justices are appointed by the president and may remain in office until the mandatory retirement age of sixty-five. The Federal Shariat Court, which specializes in Islamic law, is headed by a presidentially appointed chief justice and seven justices, three of whom must be Islamic scholars, known as *ulema*. The Shariat Court has both federal and provincial jurisdiction and is charged with determining whether any legislative proposal violates Islamic law.

The judicial branch also contains the office of *wafaqi mohtasib* (ombudsman), an official whose task is to ensure accountability of the federal government. The mohtasib can award damages to persons who suffer as a result of failed administration. The president appoints the mohtasib for a four-year term.

Political Parties and Factions

Pakistan has multiple political parties. Throughout the nation's history, some of the parties have joined military-led coalitions to control the central government.

The Pakistan Muslim League (PML-Q) is a pro-military party formed in 2000–2001. It supports President Pervez Musharraf (1943–), who won election 2002 after taking power by military coup. The PML-Q is a moderately conservative party focused on economic and administrative reform and the expansion of federal powers.

The Muttahida Majlis-e-Amal (MMA) is a coalition party composed of several of Pakistan's most powerful religious organizations, including Jamaat-e-Islami, Pakistan's oldest religious party. The MMA, which has majority support in the North West Frontier Province and Baluchistan, reorganized the provincial governments to conform to strict Islamic law. The MMA enjoys a high level of grassroots support across the country but has been criticized for its support of radical and militant Islamic factions.

The People's Party of Pakistan (PPP) was founded in 1967 as a democratic opposition to military control of the central government. The PPP advocated a more egalitarian democracy and a peaceful transition toward socialist governance. Its leader, Benazir Bhutto (1953–), became Pakistan's first female prime minister; she was forced into exile in Dubai following allegations of corruption. The PPP has since redefined itself as the People's Party of Pakistan Parliamentarians (PPPP).

The Grand National Alliance (GNA) is a coalition of major regional political parties. Organized in 2002, the GNA has gained significant influence in regional governments and has taken a sufficient number of seats in parliament to affect key votes. The GNA supports the PML-Q government and the military administration of Musharraf.

Since independence, the government has limited the activities of certain parties whose members oppose the existing formulation of Pakistan or its status as an Islamic state. For example, the Communist Party of Pakistan (CPP) and the National Democratic Party (NDP) have both been banned or restricted since the 1947 constitution.

Major Events

Pakistan has unresolved conflicts with India concerning national borders. At the time of the partition, the territories of Jammu and Kashmir, led by the Maharaja Hari Singh (1895–1961), opted to remain neutral territory. The Pakistani government believed that it should control Kashmir because a majority of the population was Muslim. In 1948 the Pakistani military invaded Kashmir, which led to a retaliatory troop deployment by India. The First Indo-Pakistani War ended with a cease-fire, and Kashmir was divided between the two countries (India gained control of about 54 percent of the territory).

In 1965 minor skirmishes erupted near the borders of Kashmir and escalated into full military engagement. Pakistan was unable to win additional territory in what is called the Second Indo-Pakistani War. The conflict ended after two months, with more than six thousand casualties reported for both sides. The United Nations mandated a cease-fire, and leaders from both nations met in the Soviet Union to negotiate a settlement.

Indian Muslims demonstrating in London in 1946 to support the partition of India and Pakistan.   © *Hulton-Deutsch Collection/Corbis*

The Third Indo-Pakistani War is also called the Bangladesh Independence War. When Pakistan was created in 1947, its territory was divided geographically by India. In 1971 the Pakistani military initiated martial law to combat a growing independence movement in the eastern portion of the country. India sent troops to support the independence movement, which led to further military escalation. The conflict lasted fourteen days and resulted in more than eleven thousand casualties on both sides. In the aftermath, the eastern portion of Pakistan successfully seceded and became the independent nation of Bangladesh. In this conflict, India had achieved a clear victory; it captured more than ninety thousand prisoners. Animosity and distrust did not end, however.

Pakistan began developing nuclear weapons in 1972 under the direction of energy minister Zulfiquar Ali Bhutto (1928–1979), who would later serve as president and prime minister. (He was the father of Benazir Bhutto.) Throughout the 1970s and 1980s the Pakistani government purchased supplies and materials through still-unknown channels and worked on developing a weapons program. In 1988 it announced that after successfully con-

ducting five nuclear tests, it was in possession of sufficient nuclear material to launch a military attack.

In 1999 India and Pakistan fought a three-month conflict in the Kargil region of Kashmir. The war began when Kashmiri guerrillas crossed the cease-fire line and occupied parts of India. The Indian government repelled the invasion force and might have pressed its advantage with a retaliatory invasion of Pakistan if the United Nations had not intervened. Pakistan later refused to accept any responsibility for the occupation, claiming the incident was entirely caused by Kashmiri freedom fighters.

The conflict between India and Pakistan has led to continued instability within the Pakistani government. Following the Kargil War, Prime Minister Nawaz Sharif (1949–) attempted to dismiss Musharraf, who was the army's chief of staff. Musharraf responded by staging a military coup, which led to a period of military rule. Musharraf declared a national state of emergency and suspended the constitution until it could be amended. He then declared himself chief executive of the country for the transition period.

In 2001 Musharraf declared himself president, though the Supreme Court directed him to hold elections by 2002. When elections were held in October 2002, he retained the presidency with the aid of the PML-Q's majority in parliament. Fierce political debates continued for the following year, as the administration and opposition leaders debated constitutional restructuring. Amendment 17 of the document they accepted formally legalized Musharraf's military coup and his subsequent leadership. It also allowed him to run for reelection. Musharraf originally agreed to step down as the army's chief of staff in exchange for parliamentary support, but in 2004 he announced that he would not relinquish his military post until the country had achieved greater stability.

Twenty-First Century

Though Pakistan has restored its constitution, the country still faces instability, largely arising from continued conflict between extremist political and religious factions. Diplomatic meetings with India have temporarily stabilized the dispute over Kashmir; however, militants on both sides continue to call for military action to decide ownership of disputed territories. Pakistan also faces high levels of poverty and rapid depletion of its natural resources.

Since 2001 Pakistan has supported the U.S. "war on terror," despite widespread dissent from some political and religious groups. At the same time, however, terrorists from Afghanistan have been crossing the border into parts of Pakistan and using its mountainous areas as hideouts. Some analysts believe the government will not be able to keep the terrorist groups out; others believe the Pakistanis are actively harboring terrorist cells.

Pakistan is one of three member countries of the United Nations that have not ratified the Nuclear Non-Proliferation Treaty—the other two are India and Israel. Pakistan maintains that it will use its nuclear arsenal against India if it is threatened by a significant invasion force. According to some estimates, the Pakistani nuclear program may have developed between twenty and fifty nuclear warheads.

BIBLIOGRAPHY

Talbot, Ian. *Pakistan: A Modern History.* Rev. ed. New York: Palgrave Macmillan, 2005.

Cloughley, Brian. *A History of the Pakistan Army: Wars and Insurrections.* 3rd. ed. Oxford: Oxford University Press, 2006.

Ahmed, Akbar S. *Resistance and Control in Pakistan.* Rev. ed. London: Routledge Press, 2004.

⊕ Myanmar

Type of Government

Myanmar has been under the control of a military junta since 1988. It functions as an authoritarian state while retaining the structure of a socialist democracy. The highest-ranking member of the junta, who serves as head of state, commander of the armed forces, and head of government, is assisted by a council of military leaders. Myanmar's constitution calls for a unicameral legislative and judicial body elected by popular vote; however, the constitution and all offices of the national and regional governments have been suspended. The military junta governs through a series of committees at the national and regional levels.

Background

Myanmar, formerly known as Burma, is an Asian nation bordering China, India, and Bangladesh on the northwest, Laos and Thailand on the east, and the Bay of Bengal on the southwest. Humans have lived there since Paleolithic times; centuries of immigration have made it is a culturally and ethnically diverse nation. Its history is usually divided into periods dominated by each of the seven major ethnic groups.

The Mon people migrated into the region between 3000 BC and 1500 BC and established numerous kingdoms. Frequent migration from India added characteristics that still influence modern Burmese culture. The Pyu ethnic group, which was more dominant in the northern regions, had early diplomatic contact with China.

In AD 1057 an immigrant society developed at Bagan (Pagan) and defeated the last of the Mon kingdoms and accomplished the first unified national government. Bagan society absorbed elements of Mon, Indian, and Chinese culture and developed Buddhism as a state religion. Art and architecture flourished, while the military continued to expand its control by subduing most of the nation's tribal cultures. The stability of Bagan society was threatened by the rise of Kublai Khan (1215–1294) and the Mongolian Empire, so in 1277 the Bagan king Narathihapate (1254–1287) declared war on the Mongols. His forces were defeated at the Battle of Ngasunggyan.

Infighting between the Burmese, the Shan, and the Mon groups followed, until King Tabinshwehti (1512–1550), using both aggressive military tactics and diplomacy, created a powerful Burmese military regime. Though Tabinshwehti was killed before unification of the country was achieved, his successor King Bayinnaung (?–1581) continued the campaign and by 1551 united Myanmar under the TaungNgoo Dynasty.

The TaungNgoo greatly expanded the local economy and trade, while continuing aggressive military campaigns against, among others, the Ayutthaya (Siamese) Kingdom. The Portuguese had poor relations with the TaungNgoo; as Myanmar became important to European trade, the Portuguese began lending assistance to the TaungNgoo's rivals. Though the TaungNgoo nearly collapsed under the military pressure, by 1613 they had reunified the country. A period of cultural enlightenment ensued, producing a wealth of art, theater, music and literature. The TaungNgoo began to lose control over indigenous groups during the eighteenth century, and in 1752, a rebellion by the Bago ethnic group, aided by European military forces, brought an end to the dynasty.

In 1753 the Burmese king Alaungpaya (1714–1760) defeated the Bago people in a series of battles and established the Konbaung Dynasty. Rangoon, in the northern part of the region, was its capital. However, the Konbaung suffered continual military strife with the Bago, Chinese, Siamese and European peoples. Between 1766 and 1769, China's Qing Dynasty attempted four invasions of Myanmar but was defeated by the Konbaung armies. After abandoning hopes of conquest, China signed a cooperation and trade pact with the Konbaung, thereby strengthening the regime's political and economic power. The Konbaung were not as successful in diplomatic relations with European powers, and in 1811 broke diplomatic relations with the British.

In 1824 the Konbaung captured the Assam region of northeastern India, angering the British government and leading to the first Anglo-Burmese War (1824–1826). The British, in alliance with Siam (now Thailand), invaded Myanmar. The Konbaung were defeated and surrendered their Siamese territories in the Treaty of Yandaboo (1826). During the Second Anglo-Burmese War (1852) the British captured additional territories and effectively destabilized the regime. Internal struggles persuaded the Konbaung to enter into a military alliance with the French, which incited the British government to seize power. In 1885, during the Third Anglo-Burmese War, the British defeated the remaining Konbaung forces and annexed Myanmar.

Under British control Burma was designated as a province of India with a local government in Rangoon. Burmese natives maintained a militant resistance until the 1890s, eventually persuading the British to allow Burmese to participate in government and to travel to England for higher education.

Led by a new educated elite, a peaceful Burmese independence movement surfaced around 1900 and by the 1920s its leaders had persuaded British authorities to allow additional native representation in the legislature. Despite British concessions, many still believed that the British were exploiting the local labor force and the country's natural resources while showing little regard for public welfare or the maintenance of native culture. In 1930 Saya San (1876–1931), a monk turned political leader, started a peasant rebellion that eventually mobilized the entire populace. After a nationwide labor strike in 1936, the British separated Myanmar from India and established a local assembly.

The British attempted to control the independence movement by arresting key leaders and forcibly preventing demonstrations. When the British attempted to arrest political leader Aung San (1915–1947), he fled the nation and formed an alliance with Japan. In 1941 Aung San's Burmese Independence Army helped Japanese forces occupy the country—a maneuver to get the British out. As the Japanese military faltered toward the end of World War II, Aung San turned on his Japanese allies to secure the country's independence.

Between 1945 and 1947 Aung San and British authorities negotiated a treaty. Internal conflicts erupted—some political factions believed that Aung San was making unnecessary concessions to the British. In July 1947 members of a rival communist faction assassinated Aung San and most of his cabinet. Despite Aung San's death, negotiations were completed successfully, and Myanmar was granted independence as a democratic republic on January 4, 1948.

Government Structure

Myanmar is divided into seven administrative divisions and seven states. The constitution, which was instituted in 1974 and suspended in 1997, called for a unitary socialist government with legislative, executive, and judicial powers vested in a single body, the Pyithu Hluttaw (People's Assembly). The assembly had 489 members, who were elected for four-year terms by popular vote. From that body were chosen the Council of State and the Council of Ministers, which served as the executive branch. The Council of State had twenty-nine members; they chose a chairman, who was the president of the country. The Council of Ministers, which had twenty-two members, was headed by the prime minister. Three other councils—the Council of People's Justices, which functioned as a supreme court; the Council of People's Attorneys, which advised the government on legal matters; and the Council of People's Inspectors, which functioned as the governmental auditing and budgetary office—were also chosen from the People's Assembly.

The 1974 constitution was created during a period of military control under socialist leader Bo Ne Win (1911–2002). His Burma Socialist Programme Party (BSPP) controlled the nation until 1988, when Ne Win was deposed by a military coup led by the State Law and Order Restoration Council (SLORC). The council was renamed the State Peace and Development Council (SPDC) in 1997. When it suspended the constitution pending reformulation, the SPDC abolished all existing governmental bodies.

Under martial law the chairman of the SPDC serves as the nation's head of state and the leader of the armed forces. The SPDC appoints a prime minister to lead a cabinet composed of military leaders. All legislation is proposed and amended within subcommittees of the junta. The state judicial system is administered according to military law and has no oversight over the executive branch.

Political Parties and Factions

The National Unity Party (NUP) was founded in 1988 as the political representative of the Burma Socialist Programme Party (BSPP). When elections were held in

Myanmar's junta leaders at an Armed Forces Day parade in 2007. © *Law Eh Soe/epa/Corbis*

1990, the NUP also represented the SPDC. The NUP is considered a pro-military, conservative party focused on preventing insurgency and restoring the economy. The NUP favors socialist economic policies based on a combination of Marxism and Buddhist philosophy.

The National League for Democracy (NLD) was founded in 1988 under the leadership of Aung San Suu Kyi (1945–), the daughter of Aung San. In the 1990 elections the NLD won majority control but was prevented from taking power by the SPDC, which placed Suu Kyi under house arrest. The NLD, which calls for a transition to full democracy through fair elections, is supported by many Western nations.

The Shan Nationalities League for Democracy (SNLD) was formed in 1988 as the political arm of the Shan people, one of Myanmar's largest ethnic groups. The Shan also occupy portions of China, Thailand, and Vietnam. The SNLD is closely allied with the NLD and, during the 1990 elections, won sufficient votes to become the second-rank party in Myanmar. The SNLD favors a democratic election system but, unlike the NLD, focuses on protecting the rights of the nation's ethnic groups.

Major Events

Since it gained independence in 1948, Myanmar has experienced frequent conflicts between ethnic, military, and political groups. By the late 1950s government stability was threatened by armed communist blocs, militant factions of the Karen ethnic group, and a parliament split along ideological lines. In 1962 General Bo Ne Win staged a military coup and placed the country under martial law. In the following months Ne Win's military police violently ended student protests, conducted mass arrests of political adversaries, suspended the constitution, and abolished all government offices. The regime then established a centrally controlled, single-party state headed by the BSPP. In 1974 Ne Win drafted a new constitution that legitimized the military takeover and created a government run by the People's Assembly. He relinquished his military role to serve as president.

The BSPP government was based on the "Burmese way to socialism," which combines Marxism with Buddhist philosophy. In addition to the state control of industry and economy, Ne Win's socialism called for the expulsion of all foreigners and social and economic isolation from all foreign nations. All citizens of the country were encouraged to adopt the state's version of Buddhism.

Because of economic difficulties, Ne Win eventually opened the country to foreign investment, but not in time to forestall a real crisis. In 1988 the military violently ended a series of student protests, which led to widespread demonstrations. Ne Win resigned in July 1988. The country lapsed into a period of mob rule until the military, under the command of Saw Maung (1928–1997), took control of the government and declared martial law.

Saw Maung and SLORC used communist infiltration and insurrection as justification for abolishing national and local governments and replacing them with military councils. Among the councils' duties were economic reform and preparation of a new constitution. In 1989 SLORC changed the name of the country from Burma to Myanmar.

In 1990 general elections were held under the supervision of the military. The NLD party, led by Aung San Suu Kyi, who had been under arrest since 1989, won a majority. However, the junta refused to accept the validity of the elections or to allow the newly elected government to convene. Suu Kyi was again placed under house arrest. Her peaceful resistance movement came to the attention of international human-rights organizations. In 1991 she was awarded the Nobel Peace Prize. Foreign governments began to pressure SLORC to convene the new government and restore the constitutional process.

Between 1993 and 2000 the military arrested numerous NLD supporters and shut down most of the party's offices. In 2005 the military leadership, by then called the SPDC, convened a new constitutional convention but prevented representatives from the NLD or any other pro-democracy party from participating. Suu Kyi was kept under house arrest, except for short periods in 2001 and 2002. NLD operations relocated outside the country.

Twenty-First Century

As a result of the continuing friction between prodemocracy groups and the socialist military regime, the United States and the European Union have levied trade sanctions against Myanmar. Neither the United States nor the EU recognizes the SPDC as a legitimate government, and both have agreed to suspend all foreign relations until the SPDC allows constitutional reform. The SPDC has limited support within Myanmar, and faces continued ethnic and political insurgencies.

Serious poverty affects life in rural areas of the country, which has limited access to foreign investment to spur economic development. However, a wealth of natural resources and a productive agricultural system have allowed it to avoid a severe economic crisis.

BIBLIOGRAPHY

Steinberg, David I. *Burma: The State of Myanmar.* Washington: Georgetown University Press, 2001.

Thant Myint-U. *The River of Lost Footsteps: Histories of Burma.* New York: Farrar, Straus and Giroux, 2006.

Tin Maung Maung Than. *State Dominance in Myanmar: The Political Economy of Industrialization.* Singapore: Institute of Southeast Asian Studies, 2006.

⊕ Sri Lanka

Type of Government

Sri Lanka is a democratic socialist republic with power divided between executive, legislative, and judicial branches. The executive branch consists of the president, the prime minister, and the cabinet. The legislative branch is a unicameral parliament. The Supreme Court and the Court of Appeals function independently of the executive and legislative branches.

Background

Sri Lanka is an island nation in the Indian Ocean near the southern coast of India. Though archaeologists believe that humans have occupied Sri Lanka since 500,000 BC, recorded history begins in approximately 540 BC, when immigrants from southern India established the Thammana Kingdom. In the following centuries Indo-Aryan immigrants intermarried with the island's tribal inhabitants to become the Sinhalese, the founders of the country's native dynasties.

In the fifth century BC Sinhalese King Pandukhabhaya built Anuradhapura, the nation's first major city. Buddhism, the official state religion, was an inspiration for its architecture and culture: Shrines and stupas—mound-shaped religious monuments—were prominent.

Anuradhapura endured through a succession of monarchs but was strategically vulnerable to coastal invasion. In AD 1017 armies from India's Chola region occupied Anuradhapura and captured King Mahinda V (982–1029). After taking control of the city, the Chola armies moved the capital to the northwestern city of Pollanaruwa.

Sinhalese King Vijayabahu I (1055–1110) defeated the Chola in 1070 and established the next major Sinhalese dynasty at Pollanaruwa. He left no successor to the throne, so civil war erupted after his death. The kingdom was eventually united under Parakramabahu I (1153–1186), who transformed Pollanaruwa into one of the most culturally advanced kingdoms in Asia. He is especially known for establishing irrigation and reservoir systems that revolutionized agricultural production.

The Pollanaruwa era ended in 1215 with the invasion of an army from eastern India, under the command of Kalinga Magha. During the following two centuries the nation was fragmented into a series of transient kingdoms until Sinhalese King Parakramabahu VI (1415–1476)

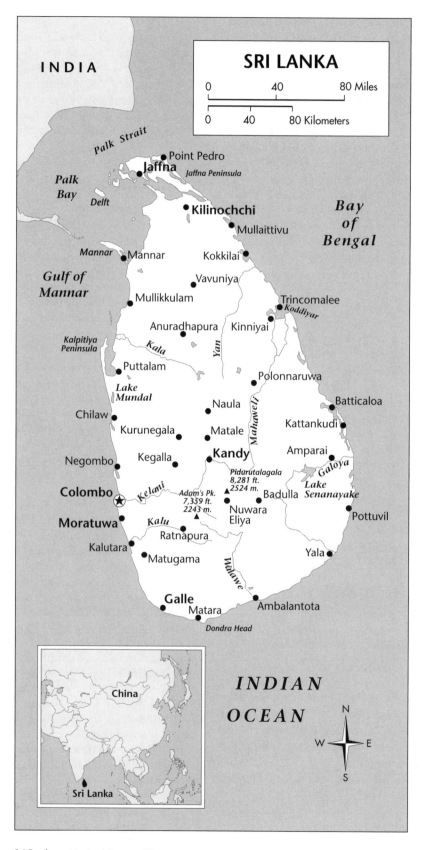

Sri Lanka. *Maryland Cartographics*

reunified the country and established a new capital in Kotte on the west coast. Portuguese traders arrived in Sri Lanka in the early sixteenth century and made commercial agreements with the Sinhalese rulers. By 1600 the Portuguese had assumed political control through economic dominance and the threat of military force.

While the Europeans ruled the west coast, a new dynasty, known as the Kandyan, developed in the central regions. The Portuguese attempted to expand their territory, but the Kandyans resisted militarily and, in 1617, formed an alliance with the Dutch government, one of Portugal's major rivals. With Dutch help the Kandyans captured the Portuguese city of Colombo and temporarily interrupted European control of the nation. Then in 1795 the British arrived in Sri Lanka. By 1815 they had defeated the native military and annexed Sri Lanka as a royal territory.

After establishing an administrative center in Colombo, the British transformed Sri Lanka into a key trading port while simultaneously developing the agricultural industry: Sri Lanka became a major producer of coffee, coconuts, and spices. The British also updated the nation's cities with improved transportation systems, established an industrial sector, and modernized the educational system, which was eventually opened to natives.

An independence movement developed soon after the British took control, but remained underground until the twentieth century. It surfaced in the 1930s, citing the denial of civil rights and labor exploitation. Between 1930 and 1940 the British reformed the constitution to allow native representation in the colonial government and to provide additional rights for citizens.

During World War II Sri Lanka was an important military base for allied operations against Japan; thousands of Sri Lankans provided labor. When the war ended in 1945 native representatives again resumed their petitions for independence. Through a series of negotiations a new constitution emerged, providing a timeline for independence while guaranteeing the British rights to military and economic operations in the region. On February 4, 1948, Sri Lanka (then called Ceylon) was granted full independence as a democratic republic.

Government Structure

The Sri Lankan constitution, adopted in 1978, provides universal suffrage for all persons eighteen years of age and older and specifies a proportional representation system for elections.

The executive branch of the government consists of the president, the prime minister, and the cabinet. The president, who functions as chief of state, head of government, and commander of the armed forces, is elected by popular vote for a maximum of two terms of six years each. Among the president's duties are appointing government officials and initiating legislative proposals. The

president also has the power to suspend or dissolve the parliament in the event of a government deadlock.

The prime minister, who serves as the president's chief deputy, is the leader of the majority party in parliament. Many of the prime minister's duties are executive in nature. For example, the prime minister nominates members of parliament to serve as cabinet ministers. The ministers, who are then appointed by the president, lead the nation's various agencies.

Sri Lanka has a unicameral parliament whose 225 members are elected for six-year terms. Voters in the twenty-five multimember electoral districts elect 196 legislators; the remaining 29 are allocated to the various parties according to their share of the national vote. Parliament is the sole lawmaking body and has oversight over most executive decisions, including the decision to declare war. The parliament can also impeach the president, dissolve the cabinet, and dismiss executive officers. The parliament functions through a system of committees that work with and advise the ministries.

The Supreme Court has jurisdiction over all lower courts and consists of eleven justices, including a chief justice, appointed by the president. They serve until retirement at age sixty-five. The Supreme Court is responsible for ensuring that laws do not violate the constitution. Sri Lankan law is based primarily on the British legal system but also incorporates elements of Roman, Dutch, Sinhalese, and Islamic law.

Political Parties and Factions

By the 1950s two major parties dominated national and regional elections, effectively making Sri Lanka a two-party state. Because of the prevalence of minor parties, however, neither major party has ever secured a majority without forming a coalition. In the twenty-first century, two major coalitions—the United Peoples Freedom Alliance (UFPA) and the United National Front (UNF)—became major contenders in national elections.

UFPA was founded by the Sri Lanka Freedom Party (SLFP), which has been one of Sri Lanka's largest political parties since its establishment in 1951. SLFP is a moderate socialist party that also represents Sinhalese nationalism. It is considered the more leftist or liberal of the major parties. The UFPA also includes the People's Liberation Front, the Communist Party of Sri Lanka, and the Muslim National Unity Alliance.

The UNF coalition was formed by the United National Party (UNP), Sri Lanka's oldest political party. UNP was the first party to head the Sri Lankan government and has held majorities during thirty-three of the country's fifty-seven years as an independent republic. Though UNP is a socialist democratic party, it is viewed as the more conservative party because of its focus on economic initiatives and military investment. The coalition also includes the Western People's Front and the

Ceylon Workers' Congress, both of which represent the nation's labor unions.

One of the major issues in Sri Lankan politics is the status of the country's Tamil ethnic group, which makes up 18 to 20 percent of the population. Ethnic divisions are now primarily political, though historically there has been a religious split between the predominantly Hindu and Muslim Tamil and the mostly Buddhist and Christian Sinhalese.

Militant factions, including the Liberation Tigers of Tamil Eelam (LTTE), have been waging a secessionist struggle against the Sri Lankan government since the 1970s. Though the government considers LTTE to be a terrorist organization and has banned it from participation in politics, the Tamil have developed a political coalition, the Tamil National Alliance (TNA), to lobby for legislation and for the establishment of an independent Tamil state. Some analysts believe LTTE or other militant factions covertly control the TNA. In any case, the coalition exacts some influence over legislative developments.

Major Events

In 1956 SLFP won the general election with a platform based on Sinhalese nationalism. Soon after it took control of the legislature, SLFP made Sinhalese the official language of Sri Lanka, despite the fact that 25 percent of the people spoke some form of the Tamil language. Tamil representatives protested, and the lobby for Tamil independence intensified. The subsequent debates led to increased factionalism and sparked incidents of racial violence.

In May 1958 mobs of Sinhalese nationalists attacked Tamil immigrants traveling through Pollonaruwa. The gangs then spread to the rural areas, where they attacked Tamil farm and plantation workers. As the mobs grew—they quickly numbered in the thousands—dozens of Tamil were killed, as were police who tried to intervene. Violence spread to Colombo, where Hindu temples were looted and burned and hundreds of Tamil were attacked in the streets. Sinhalese gangs committed acts of arson, rape, and murder. In the eastern province Tamil gangs began to commit revenge attacks, leading to the deaths of a number of Sinhalese.

The government declared a state of emergency and sent troops to Colombo. Thousands of Tamil were evacuated to Jaffna, the principal city in Sri Lanka's northern province. Although the violence ended within a few days, the divisions between ethnic groups had intensified. Militant Tamil factions developed, leading to a civil war in 1983. Government sources estimate that between 1983 and 2007 the civil war resulted in more than seventy thousand deaths. Thousands of others were left homeless or displaced.

LTTE is officially credited with starting the war by assassinating the mayor of Jaffna in 1975; however, LTTE's 1983 attack on the military near Colombo pre-cipitated the first major counteroffensive from the government. Faced with the government's superior military force, the Tamil began using assassinations and suicide bombings to disrupt military operations.

The Republic of India played a controversial role in the civil war by giving military and medical aid to Tamil rebels in the city of Jaffna. It parachuted tons of food into areas that were under siege by government forces. Some observers say the intervention was aimed at appeasing India's large Tamil population, which supported the independence movement in Sri Lanka. In 1987 Sri Lankan President J. R. Jayewardene (1906–1996) met with Indian Prime Minister Rajiv Gandhi (1944–1991) to negotiate a peace treaty. Among other minor concessions, the Sri Lankan government agreed to merge the northern and eastern provinces; to give additional governmental powers to the provinces; and to make Tamil an official language of the region.

By 1991 the disarmament agreement had failed, and racial violence erupted in Colombo, Jaffna, and surrounding areas. Military clashes led to thousands of deaths on both sides while gangs of militants roamed the country killing those believed to be enemy sympathizers. In 1993 a suicide bomber killed President Ranasinghe Premadasa (1924–1993).

Late in 2001 representatives from Norway mediated a cease-fire and arranged negotiations between the government and LTTE, which resulted in tentative agreements between combatants. When Sri Lanka was hit by the Indian Ocean tsunami in 2004, the government and Tamil representatives maintained the cease-fire to allow rescue and reconstruction operations.

Violence resumed in the northeast in 2005. In 2006 diplomatic intervention from the United States, Japan, and Norway led to a new cease-fire and plans for further negotiations. When peace talks came to a halt late in 2006, LTTE bombed a civilian bus, prompting the military to launch a series of air strikes. Fighting continued into 2007, as the military launched repeated naval and aerial assaults against Tamil strongholds. In April 2007 the Tamil revealed a newly formed aerial unit when they launched their first air strike against a government military installation.

Twenty-First Century

Sri Lanka's major challenge in the twenty-first century is the ongoing civil war. The military effort continues to drain the economy, prevents new investment, and contributes to unemployment and homelessness. The civil war has also weakened Sri Lanka's ability to conduct foreign relations because of the numerous human-rights violations committed by both the Tamil and the government.

Sri Lanka's economy and infrastructure were heavily damaged by the 2004 Indian Ocean tsunami, which left more than four hundred thousand people displaced. The economy showed signs of growth in 2005 and 2006,

Sri Lanka's Tamil Tigers rebel group parading in 2002.   © *Reuters/CORBIS*

spurred by the national reconstruction effort and the influx of foreign aid. The nation faces significant environmental issues, including rapid deforestation and the loss of native species because of population expansion and pollution.

BIBLIOGRAPHY

Clarance, William. *Ethnic Warfare in Sri Lanka and the UN Crisis.* London: Pluto Press, 2007.

De Silva, K. M. *A History of Sri Lanka.* Rev. ed. New Delhi: Penguin Books, 2005.

Hennayake, Nalani. *Culture, Politics, and Development in Postcolonial Sri Lanka.* Lanham, MD: Lexington Books, 2006.

⊕ State of Israel

Type of Government

The small Mediterranean nation of Israel is a parliamentary democracy with several distinctive features. A unicameral legislature, the Knesset, elects the president, who in turn oversees the formation of a coalition cabinet under a prime minister. Though more than 20 percent of the population of roughly six and a half million are Arab Muslims, Israel considers itself a Jewish state, and religious differences—both between Jews and Muslims and between secular and religious Jews—continue to play a key role in the formation and dissolution of the ruling coalitions.

Background

There has been a Jewish community in and around the city of Jerusalem, Israel's capital, for at least three thousand years. For most of that period, the region's residents, both Jews and non-Jews, were dominated by a succession of foreign powers. Some, like the Romans, were harsh masters; others, like the Ottoman Turks who ruled from 1517 to 1917, allowed significant local autonomy. With the growth of nationalism in the nineteenth century, however, came the Zionist movement of Theodore Herzl (1860–1904). Herzl and his followers believed that the fierce and unrelenting persecution of Jews throughout Russia and Eastern Europe meant that Jewish people would never be safe without a nation of their own.

There was much discussion about the site for such a state, with the British in 1903 offering part of their colony of Uganda. For the Zionists, however, the ancient Jewish homeland on the shores of the eastern Mediterranean was the only acceptable choice, and a small stream of Jewish immigrants began arriving in the area even before the region passed from Ottoman to British control toward the end of World War I. During the thirty years of British rule, however, Jewish immigration increased enormously for several reasons. One was the so-called Balfour Declaration in 1917, in which British Foreign Secretary Arthur James Balfour (1848–1930), expressed his support for a Jewish "national home" in the region then commonly known as Palestine. Many Jews who had seen Herzl's project as unrealistic became eager immigrants when Great Britain, rulers of Palestine and one of the most powerful nations in the world, endorsed it publicly.

The second major factor fuelling immigration to Palestine was the rise to power of anti-Semite Adolf Hitler (1889–1945) in Germany in 1933. Hitler and his followers deliberately created such a hostile atmosphere that German Jews had little choice but to abandon their homes and businesses and emigrate. Many chose Palestine. When World War II began in 1939, Hitler turned from a policy of forced emigration to deportation and murder, and Herzl's belief that Jews would never be safe in Europe gained a new and horrifying kind of credibility. The British, meanwhile, severely restricted Jewish immigration in an effort to avoid dangerous wartime conflicts with Palestine's Muslim population.

At the end of the war in 1945, thousands of Jews who had survived Hitler's death camps braved a British naval blockade to reach Palestine. Many of those who succeeded joined an armed independence movement. Given the rising tensions between the Arab and Jewish populations, however, the exhausted British needed little encouragement to withdraw. In 1948 the United Nations (UN) endorsed a plan to create two independent nations—one Jewish and one Arab—out of the territory Britain had controlled since 1917 (from 1917 until 1920 under a military administration, and thereafter under an international mandate approved by the UN's predecessor, the League of Nations). Under the UN plan, Jerusalem, a city holy to Jews, Muslims, and Christians alike, was to be under international administration, and the Jewish state was to have 55 percent of the land east of the Jordan River. A coalition of Arab states rejected the plan and invaded Jewish areas immediately after the British withdrawal in May 1948. The forces of the new nation of Israel, however, succeeded in driving the Arab armies out and stabilizing the frontiers.

Government Structure

Israel does not have a constitution in the conventional sense. Instead, a series of so-called Basic Laws define the structure and function of government. As of 2007, eleven Basic Laws were in force, with three more (Legislation, Rights in Trial, and Freedom of Expression and Association) in the drafting stage. Some provisions of the Basic Laws can be amended with the approval of an absolute Knesset majority (61 of the 120 members), others only with a special majority, which requires more votes.

The president, elected by the Knesset for a term of seven years, is head of state. The most important of a president's mostly ceremonial duties is the endorsement of a candidate for prime minister. For both practical and traditional reasons, the president usually chooses the leader of the largest party in the Knesset. A prime minister's first task is the construction of a coalition cabinet that will enjoy, at least for a time, majority support in the Knesset, and the leader of the largest party has the best chance to obtain that support. If the prime minister cannot construct a coalition, new elections are held, and the process begins again. Exceptions occurred in 1996, 1999, and 2001, when a short-lived change to the electoral laws mandated a direct, popular vote for prime minister. Widespread dissatisfaction with this arrangement soon caused the Knesset to revert to the previous system.

The prime minister and his cabinet form the core of the executive branch. Cabinet seats are allotted to political parties according to their importance to the coalition, so even a small party can win control of major ministries. The most powerful ministries are probably the Defense Ministry and the Interior Ministry. The size of the cabinet can vary, with some members serving "without portfolio"— that is, without attachment to a particular ministry. Opposition members can challenge a prime minister and his cabinet by demanding a vote of no confidence. If a majority in the Knesset sides with the prime minister, he or she remains in power. If the no-confidence vote is sustained, however, the government falls and new elections are scheduled. The old coalition remains in office until the election results are tabulated and a new coalition is formed.

Legislative powers are limited to the 120 members of the unicameral Knesset. Voters do not choose individual members, but they select the one party that best represents their interests. Seats are allocated to the parties in accordance with their share of the popular vote. The parties then choose individuals to fill their seats, usually on the basis of seniority. Bills may be introduced by individual members, blocs of members, the prime minister and his cabinet, or by individual cabinet ministers. Debate takes place in plenary sessions (attended by all members) and in committee meetings. Every bill must go through at least one reading in committee and three plenary readings; votes are taken on an item-by-item basis after the second plenary reading and on the bill as a whole after the third. Bills that fail in the second plenary reading may be returned to committee for redrafting. Bills that pass the third plenary reading are sent to the president, the prime minister, and the appropriate cabinet minister for signing into law.

Israeli law is based on English common law, a holdover from when Britain ruled the region. The influence of the Jewish, Muslim, and Christian traditions is frequently discernible in Israeli law, particularly in personal and family law, cases for which are often referred to special religious courts. At the head of the judicial branch is the Supreme Court, which is made up of twelve justices appointed by the Judicial Selection Committee. Cases are generally heard by panels of three or more justices. In addition to hearing appeals from lower courts, the Supreme Court acts as a High Court of Justice, with wide-ranging powers to investigate allegations of government misconduct, hear prisoners' petitions, and issue directives to ministries. Its power to review Knesset legislation, however, is limited.

Local affairs are handled by municipalities, local councils, or regional councils, depending on the size of the community. Municipalities exist in large towns and cities, local councils in small towns, and regional councils in rural areas. Local councils often join together in federations to save money or improve efficiency.

National elections are held at least every four years, and all citizens aged eighteen and over may vote.

Political Parties and Factions

No less than twelve different parties currently hold seats in the Knesset. The largest of these, with twenty-nine seats, is Kadima, a new center-right offshoot of Likud, traditionally the strongest of the conservative parties but much weakened in recent years. The founder of Kadima is Ariel Sharon (1928–), who was serving as prime minister when serious illness incapacitated him in January 2006. In his place, Ehud Olmert (1945–) was named acting prime minister; subsequent elections confirmed Olmert as prime minister in his own right.

Other major parties include Labor, the core of the moderate left wing, with nineteen seats; Shas, a conservative movement dominated by orthodox Jews, with twelve seats; Likud, with twelve seats; the conservative, religiously oriented National Union/National Religious Party, with nine seats; the far-right Yisrael Beiteinu, with eleven seats; and Gil, a single-issue party focused on the needs of pensioners and retirees, with seven seats. Arab citizens won four seats. As of October 2006, Olmert's coalition consisted of Kadima, Labor, Shas, Gil, and Yisrael Beiteinu.

Israeli pressure groups tend to focus on the conflict with the Palestinians. On one side are groups like Peace Now, which argues for a complete withdrawal from the Israeli-occupied Palestinian territories. Opposing them are a variety of organizations opposed to withdrawal on religious or nationalistic grounds. Many of these are dominated by Israelis who have built houses and settlements in the West Bank. Often, but not always, differences of opinion on the Palestinian question coincide with religious and cultural differences. Secular Jews tend to favor withdrawal, while the orthodox and ultra-orthodox communities generally oppose territorial concessions.

Major Events

Wars and uprisings have punctuated the history of modern Israel. The first major incident following the war in 1948 to gain independence was the Suez Crisis of 1956. When Egyptian President Gamal Abdel Nasser (1918–1970) announced his decision to nationalize the Suez Canal, a vital trade route between the Mediterranean Sea and the Red Sea, the Israelis took advantage of the turmoil and, with the tacit approval of the canal's French and British administrators, invaded Egypt's Sinai Peninsula and advanced easily toward the canal itself. International pressure eventually defused the situation, a UN peacekeeping force was established in the Sinai, and the Israelis withdrew. Tensions remained high, however. Though Nasser himself gained widespread respect throughout the Arab world for his defiance of Israel and its Western allies, the Egyptian army was clearly ill equipped to face Israeli forces.

In May 1967 Nasser successfully demanded the withdrawal of the UN force in the Sinai, closed the Gulf of Aqaba (south of the canal) to Israeli shipping, and sent Egyptian troops to join Iraqi forces gathering in Jordan. The Israelis, interpreting these actions as signs of an imminent attack, launched preemptive strikes by air and land. At the end of six days of fighting, the Arab armies had been routed, and Israel controlled five new territories, all with substantial Arab populations: east Jerusalem; the Golan Heights, along the northern border with Syria; the Gaza Strip, a narrow coastal region to the south; the West Bank of the Jordan River; and Egypt's Sinai Peninsula. The Camp David peace accords of 1979 returned the Sinai to Egypt, and a unilateral Israeli withdrawal from Gaza took place in 2005. The other territories remain under Israeli control and have seen substantial Israeli settlement. Nevertheless they are not part of Israel under international law.

The 1970s and 1980s in Israel were dominated by cycles of guerilla warfare, as the Israeli military reacted to bombings and shootings by Palestinian guerillas. The murder of eleven Israeli athletes during the 1972 Olympic Games in Munich, Germany, was an early example of the guerilla violence. A year later, in the last Arab attempt to overwhelm Israeli forces in pitched battle, was the so-called Yom Kippur War of 1973, when Egypt and Syria launched a surprise attack during the holiest period of the Jewish calendar. After several early setbacks, the Israelis, led by General (and future Prime Minister) Ariel Sharon, were victorious. Egyptian President Anwar as-Sadat (1918–1981) saw the defeat as a sign that his nation would never regain the Sinai without a comprehensive peace treaty. Negotiations soon began, and in 1979 Egypt officially recognized the state of Israel in exchange for the return of the Sinai. This deal, brokered by U.S. President Jimmy Carter (1924–) at Camp David, Maryland, is one of the rare diplomatic successes in the ongoing Arab-Israeli conflict.

Israeli soldiers removing a Jewish settler from the Gaza Strip in August 2005. © *Ariel Schalit/Pool/epa/Corbis*

In 1987 a popular uprising known as the *intifada*, Arabic for "shaking off," broke out throughout the West Bank and Gaza Strip. Riots, marches, and strikes paralyzed Palestinian neighborhoods, and photographs of angry young men throwing rocks and homemade bombs at Israeli soldiers were soon a familiar feature of newspapers around the world. Hundreds died. The first intifada came to an end in 1993 with the Oslo Accords, a series of agreements granting the Palestinians increasing autonomy in return for renouncing violence and recognizing Israel's right to exist. With widespread opposition among hardliners on both sides, however, most of the incremental steps outlined in the Accords were never implemented, and a second intifada broke out in September 2000.

Another problematic issue facing Israel is its relationship with its northern neighbor, Lebanon. In the 1970s Palestinian guerillas, many of them born in Lebanese refugee camps, used Lebanon, then in the grip of a brutal and chaotic civil war, as a base for operations against Israel. Israel responded in 1982 with an invasion and occupation of Lebanon. Most analysts agree that the operation was a disaster in terms of both casualties and public relations.

International protests were especially vehement after a group of Lebanese Christians allied with Israel killed hundreds of Palestinian refugees in two camps near the capital of Beirut. By 1985 Israeli forces had withdrawn to a security zone just north of the border, where they remained until 2000. The next few years were marked by the growing influence of Hezbollah, a militant group of Shiite Muslims that combine hostility toward Israel with an extensive array of social services. In July 2006 Hezbollah guerillas kidnapped two Israeli soldiers and killed three others. Israel responded with a massive but short-lived attack by air, sea, and land. A UN-brokered cease-fire was reached a month later, and Israeli troops eventually withdrew. The attack, which damaged but did not destroy Hezbollah, provoked widespread soul-searching among Israelis. The ramifications from the incident, which continued to unfold as of 2007, are likely to be significant, both inside Israel and beyond.

Twenty-First Century

Israel faces a number of serious social and political challenges. The largest of these is, of course, the conflict with the Palestinians, which colors every aspect of daily life and continues to prevent better relations with the nation's Muslim neighbors. Lasting peace treaties with Egypt and Jordan show that friendly relations are possible, but there is little evidence of new diplomatic initiatives on either side. Most worrisome to many Israelis is Iran. The UN's International Atomic Energy Agency estimated in 2007 that Iran is only three to eight years away from producing its own nuclear weapons, and Iran's president, Mahmoud Ahmadinejad (1956–), has called several times for Israel's destruction. Israel, for its part, is known to have had nuclear capabilities for several years. Intense diplomatic negotiations by Russia, the UN, and the European Union have so far failed to defuse the situation. Many diplomats feel regional peace and security are impossible without a comprehensive resolution of the Palestinian issue.

Israel also faces an impending identity crisis as the growth of the Jewish population, even when augmented by immigration, continues to be outstripped by the high birthrate of its Arab citizens. At current rates, Israel's Arabs will outnumber its Jews within a few decades. If and when that happens, Israelis may have to make a choice: continued democracy and the abandonment of the state's long-cherished Jewish identity, on the one hand; or a weakening of democracy and the maintenance of Jewish identity, on the other. Neither option is an appealing one for Israel.

BIBLIOGRAPHY

Cohen-Almagor, Raphael. *Israeli Democracy at the Crossroads.* London: Routledge, 2005.

State of Israel, Knesset. "Rules of Procedure." http://www.knesset.gov.il/rules/eng/contents.htm (accessed May 26, 2007).

State of Israel, Ministry of Foreign Affairs. "Israeli Democracy: How Does It Work?" http://www.mfa. gov.il/MFA/Government/Branches+of+ Government/Executive/Israeli+Democracy+ +How+ does+it+work.htm (accessed May 26, 2007).

⊕ Republic of Korea

Type of Government

The Republic of Korea, or South Korea, is a republic with powers divided between executive, legislative, and judicial branches. In the executive branch the president, who is elected directly by the population, serves as the head of state, head of government, and commander of the armed forces. The prime minister, who is appointed by the president, serves as his chief adviser and the head of the executive ministries. The legislative branch is unicameral and elected by a combination of direct and proportional representation. The judicial branch contains the Constitutional Court and the Supreme Court, with justices appointed by the president from a slate of nominees.

Background

Paleolithic societies in Korea and China were closely linked and shared important cultural roots, and in succeeding centuries Korea and China were often politically allied. At the start of the nineteenth century Korea adopted an isolationist policy and closed its ports to foreign trade, except for trade with China. In 1894 Japan, in its first war with China, defeated the Qing Dynasty's armies and forced them to relinquish control of Korea. Fearing an invasion by Japanese forces, Korea sought a protection pact with Russia. When Japan and Russia went to war in 1904, the Korean government attempted to remain neutral but Japanese forces occupied most of the peninsula. In 1910 Japan annexed the territory and established a colonial government.

The Japanese occupation lasted until 1945, during which time Japanese regents thoroughly modernized Korea's infrastructure but also attempted to obliterate all remnants of native culture—they forced natives to adopt Japanese names, for example, and to convert to the Shinto religion. An independence movement developed, but the Japanese repressed it with mass arrests and executions.

When the Japanese entered World War II in 1941, they conscripted thousands of Koreans into their army. In 1945 Japan surrendered to allied forces, and the Korean peninsula was split at the 38th parallel into two protectorates controlled by the United States in the South and the Soviet Union in the North. The major powers were unable to negotiate joint trusteeship and established two separate governments. In 1948 the southern portion of the peninsula became the Republic of Korea (ROK) and the northern portion became the Democratic People's Republic of Korea (DPRK).

Government Structure

Since the first constitution was approved in 1948, South Korea has enacted five constitutional reforms, each marked by the beginning of a new republic. The 1987 constitution provided universal suffrage for all persons twenty years of age and older. It maintained a parallel voting system, with a combination of direct election from single-seat constituencies and a proportional representation system by which special-interest groups and minority parties are guaranteed representation.

The executive branch, known as the State Council, consists of the president, the prime minister, and the cabinet ministers. The president, who is elected by direct vote to a single five-year term, has the power to propose legislation, submit budgetary initiatives, and declare war or emergency orders in times of crisis. The president also appoints the prime minister, cabinet ministers, and members of the judiciary. The president does not have the power to dissolve the legislature but may dismiss members of the executive branch.

The prime minister is first in line for presidential succession and serves as the president's chief adviser and liaison to the legislature. The prime minister assists the president with all administrative actions and recommends the appointment and/or dismissal of cabinet ministers who lead the country's eighteen ministries. The constitution requires the president to consult the prime minister before taking certain actions, such as proposing constitutional amendments, emergency orders, or budgetary resolutions.

South Korea's unicameral legislature, the Kukhoe (National Assembly), has 299 seats, 243 of which are filled by direct vote from single-member constituencies and 56 by proportional representation. Assembly members serve for four-year terms and are eligible for reelection. The assembly is organized into standing committees that loosely coincide and work with the executive ministries. It has the power to originate legislation, approve or amend most executive proposals, and impeach executive officers with a majority vote.

The judicial branch is independent of both the executive and legislative branches. Its highest body is the Constitutional Court, which was created in 1987 to handle cases involving constitutional law and impeachment. Its nine justices are appointed by the president—three directly, three chosen from recommendations made by the chief justice of the Supreme Court, and three from recommendations made by the National Assembly. They serve renewable six-year terms, but are required to retire at age sixty-five, except for the head of the court, who may serve to age seventy.

The Supreme Court is the final authority for all cases outside the mandate of the Constitutional Court. The nation's chief justice is appointed by the president for one six-year term with the consent of the assembly. The thirteen justices are appointed by the president on the recommendation of the chief justice and the consent of the assembly. They serve renewable six-year terms. One of the justices handles administrative matters and does not participate in judicial opinions. Below the Supreme Court are the state appellate courts, the provincial courts, and the regional courts.

South Korea has nine provinces and seven metropolitan areas, each of which maintains its own elected government.

Political Parties and Factions

The Uri Party was founded in 2003 to consolidate support for the campaign of President Roh Moo Hyun (1946–). It favors liberal policies, such as increased spending on social services and reduced emphasis on military and industrial growth. Party leaders also support conciliatory relations with North Korea and decreased military dependence on Japan and the United States. During the 2006 regional elections the Uri Party lost support in many parts of the country.

The Grand National Party (GNP), formed in 1997 through the consolidation of several conservative groups, is the largest minority party and the strongest opposition to the Uri Party. Its policies are conservative, emphasizing economic growth, lower taxes, strong military alliances, and a reduction in the size and authority of the central government. The 2004 election cycle was the first time since the party's inception that it failed to hold a majority in the National Assembly.

The Democratic Party (DP) was the largest liberal party in South Korea before the 2004 election cycle, when many of its key members left to form the Uri Party. When members of the DP joined with members of the GNP in calling for the impeachment of Roh in 2004—a decision overturned by the Constitutional Court—public opinion turned against the DP and greatly reduced its success in regional elections.

The Democratic Labor Party (DLP) was created in 2000 as the political arm of South Korea's trade unions and industrial organizations. It supports a more socialist form of democracy, with an emphasis on public involvement and activism. Major issues for the party include an increase in the minimum wage and restrictions on military activities. In March 2007 party leader Moon Sung Hyun (1952–) staged a month-long hunger strike at the presidential residence to oppose a trade agreement with the United States and to demonstrate the type of activism the DLP advocates.

Major Events

The nation's constitution has been reformulated five times since 1948, and the country has endured periods of military/autocratic rule punctuated by popular and military uprisings. The 1987 constitution marked the Sixth Republic of Korea.

The first republic was established on August 15, 1948, and held its first democratic election that same month, with Syngman Rhee (1875–1965) elected. The neighboring DPRK refused to accept the sovereignty of the ROK, believing that the peninsula should be unified under a single government.

On June 25, 1950, the DPRK, allied with the Chinese military, invaded the ROK. In July the U.S. military led a United Nations–backed force into South Korea to repel the invasion. During the early stages of what came to be known as the Korean War (1950–1953), the DPRK managed strategic gains but by 1951 had lost the advantage and retreated to the 38th parallel, which separated South from North. The war ended on July 27, 1953, with an armistice that established a demilitarized zone near the original demarcation line. It is estimated that more than three million civilians and combatants were killed during the three-year conflict, while both nations suffered severe economic and structural damage. The Korean War is considered part of the larger Cold War, in which communist and capitalist nations competed for alliances among developing nations in an effort to secure the future of their respective political ideologies.

In the decade following the war the administration was mired in internal conflicts and widely viewed as unresponsive to public sentiment. During the April Revolution of 1960 student and labor groups protested corruption in the government. Police fired into the crowds, killing several students, which led to an investigation by the National Assembly. On April 26, 1960, the president resigned, leaving the prime minister in control of the government.

In the following months the ROK adopted a parliamentary government, though it was unable to quell political unrest. On May 16, 1961, General Park Chung Hee (1917–1979) staged a military coup and assumed control. The coup, achieved without violence, was largely welcomed by the public and some members of the legislature.

In 1963, under pressure from the United States, Park agreed to hold general elections. He won by a narrow margin; the results were similar in 1967. Park also created the Korean Central Intelligence Agency, which functioned largely to protect his regime and control public disturbances.

During his first two terms Park made the highly unpopular decisions to begin normalization of relations with Japan and to support the United States during the Vietnam War. However, his foreign-relations initiatives vastly increased the country's resources, as both Japan and the United States began to provide economic aid and investment capital. By 1970 the industrial sector had grown to the point that the ROK was a competing force in international trade.

In 1971 Park and his legislative allies reformulated the constitution so he could run for a third term. He won the controversial election by a narrow margin, although

South Korean military parading through Seoul in 2003.   © *Kim Kyung-Hoon/Reuters/Corbis*

the opposition contested the legitimacy of his administration. In 1972 Park declared a state of emergency and instituted martial law.

With the government and constitution suspended, Park and his allies devised the Yushin Constitution, which granted Park unlimited presidential terms and the power to appoint large portions of the legislature so he could maintain a permanent majority. Park easily won the 1972 and 1978 elections, considered by many to be largely fraudulent.

In the 1970s Park began conducting secret negotiations with North Korea; however, when Park's wife was killed in an attempted assassination of him in 1974, Park shut down negotiations with the DPRK. Park spent the remaining years of his presidency somewhat removed from public scrutiny. In 1979 Kim Jae Gyu (1926–1980), the head of the intelligence agency, assassinated Park and several of his guards. Kim was later executed.

Park is often viewed as a dictator because of the excesses of his regime: persecuting political rivals, limiting the freedoms of the populace, and violating election laws to maintain power. However, Park's administration

was also largely responsible for helping South Korea to emerge from economic disaster to become one of the world's fastest growing economies and one of the strongest economic forces in Asia.

Twenty-First Century

Since the 1960s the economy has continued to grow, though like many Asian nations, South Korea suffered in the economic slump of the 1990s. After initiating a modest economic-recovery program, the ROK has returned to moderate growth. Today it boasts low unemployment rates and an export surplus.

Decades of rapid industrialization have led to a decline in the nation's natural resources. Air pollution and acid rain are among its most pressing environmental problems. Since 2000 the government has placed increased emphasis on developing renewable energy and reducing emissions from industrial sources.

Relations between the ROK and the DPRK have stabilized in recent decades, even though the DPRK is involved in major disputes with some of South Korea's allies, including Japan and the United States. Military alliances, investment, and relations with the DPRK continue to be major issues during each election period.

BIBLIOGRAPHY

Kyong Ju Kim. *The Development of Modern South Korea: State Formation, Capitalist Development and National Identity.* London: Routledge, 2006.

Oberdorfer, Dan. *The Two Koreas: A Contemporary History.* Rev. ed. New York: Basic Books, 2002.

Seungsook Moon. *Militarized Modernity and Gendered Citizenship in South Korea.* Durham: Duke University Press, 2005.

⊕ Democratic People's Republic of Korea

Type of Government

The Democratic People's Republic of Korea, or North Korea, defines itself as a democratic republic, but it functions as a single-party dictatorship under the leadership of the military. The commander of the military also serves as the general secretary of the leading political party. The party secretary oversees an executive cabinet consisting of a premier, a vice premier, and government ministers. North Korea has a unicameral legislature, which is constitutionally the nation's most important political body but is functionally subordinate to the leading political party. The judiciary is appointed by the legislature and serves mostly to maintain the authority of the ruling regime.

Background

After the Russo-Japanese War (1904–1905), Korea was annexed by Japan. Under a repressive colonial administration a strong independence movement arose, with an estimated two million people demonstrating against Japanese rule in rallies staged in 1919. The movement was strongly suppressed, with thousands killed by Japanese police and tens of thousands imprisoned. A government in exile was formed, and during World War II the Korean Liberation Army fought against Germany and Japan.

After World War II, the victorious Allied powers agreed that Japan would be stripped of its former colonies. Korea was split by the Allies into two parts, with the territory north of the 38th parallel administered by the Soviet Union and the territory south of that point administered by the United States. While the arrangement was intended to be a temporary trusteeship until the country could be united and granted its independence under a single, stable government, animosity between the communist Soviet Union and the ardently anti-communist United States led each side to promote leaders and a government structure sympathetic to its own goals. In 1948 this lead to the establishment of two different governments, the Democratic People's Republic of Korea (DPRK) in the north and the Republic of Korea (ROK) in the south, with each government claiming sovereignty over the entire Korean peninsula. War between the two factions broke out in 1950 and lasted until a peace treaty was signed in 1953.

Government Structure

North Korea's first constitution, adopted in 1948, was based on the communist ideology of German political philosopher Karl Marx (1818–1883) and Soviet leader Vladimir Ilich Lenin (1870–1924). The document, which was revised in 1972, 1992, and 1998, calls for representative government, with universal suffrage for all persons seventeen years of age and older. In reality, single-party control has led to a dictatorship in which most constitutional procedures are symbolic rather than functional.

The DPRK military, led by the National Defense Commission (NDC), is the country's largest employer and the center of the nation's economy. The chairman of the NDC is, according to decree, the head of government and the commander of the armed forces. Since the Korean War (1950–1953) the chairman of the NDC has concurrently served as general secretary of the Korean Workers Party (KWP). This close association between the NDC and the KWP means that a single person can assume control over the nation's government, military, and economy.

The executive branch consists of a cabinet headed by a premier and vice premier. The premier, who is appointed by the legislature, then chooses a foreign minister, a minister of the armed forces, a minister of public security, and a minister of state construction. Each has the authority to appoint deputy and assistant ministers. The executive branch has the constitutional authority to create legislation and to set the administrative agenda for the nation, but it does so under the supervision of the general secretary of the KWP.

North Korea has a unicameral legislature, the Supreme People's Assembly. Its 687 members are elected by popular vote, with elections held every five years. North Korea has three political parties; however, the majority party selects a list of candidates for the assembly who run in uncontested elections; some seats are reserved for representatives of minority parties. The assembly is constitutionally the highest political body in the country, with power to ratify, approve, and amend any legislation and/or administrative orders arising from the executive branch. However, as with the executive branch, the legislature is dominated by the leading political party and takes direction from the general secretary.

The judiciary consists of a Central Court, made up of a chief justice and two people's assessors, who are elected by the members of the assembly for five-year terms. The judicial system blends procedural rules from the Japanese, Russian, and German legal systems, with the courts serving largely to uphold the authority of the

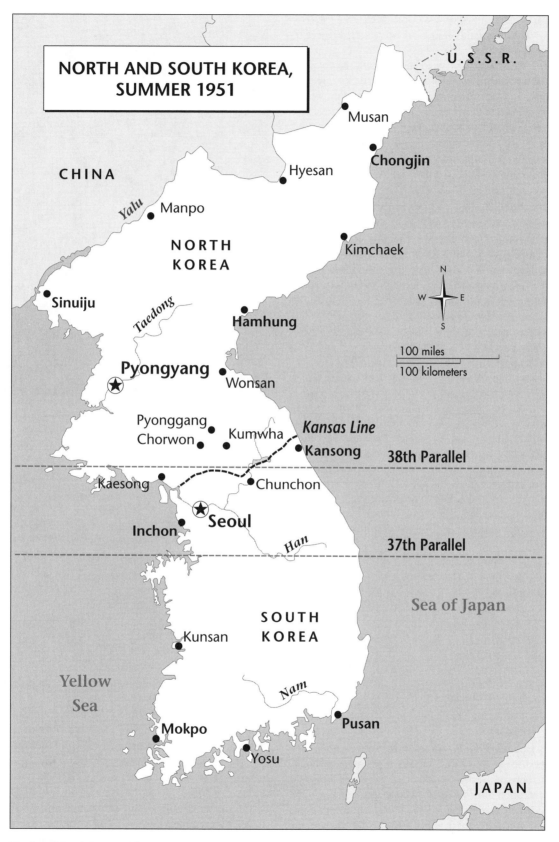

**NORTH AND SOUTH KOREA,
SUMMER 1951**

U.S.S.R.

CHINA

Musan

Chongjin

Hyesan

Yalu

Manpo

**NORTH
KOREA**

Kimchaek

N
W   E
S

Sinuiju

Taedong

Hamhung

100 miles
100 kilometers

Pyongyang ★

Wonsan

Pyonggang
Chorwon   Kumwha

Kansas Line

Kansong

38th Parallel

Kaesong

Chunchon

★ **Seoul**

Inchon

Han

37th Parallel

**SOUTH
KOREA**

Sea of Japan

Kunsan

**Yellow
Sea**

Nam

Mokpo

Pusan

Yosu

JAPAN

North and South Korea, 1951. © *Maryland Cartographics*

ruling party. The judiciary does not have oversight over executive decisions, and all judicial rulings are subject to executive approval.

The DPRK is divided into nine provinces and four municipalities, one of which is the capital city, Pyongyang. They are served by Provincial People's Assemblies, whose members are elected by popular vote for five-year terms. Provincial elections are also single-party, uncontested affairs and are subject to approval of the national assembly. Some seats in the provincial governments are reserved for minority parties.

Political Parties and Factions

The Korean Workers Party (KWP) was founded in 1945 by Kim Il Sung (1949–1994), the first leader of the DPRK. Since that time the KWP has been closely linked to the military and has controlled the nation as a single-party state. Minority parties are only allowed to function if they legally agree to accept the leadership and authority of the KWP. Originally the KWP was split into a number of ideologically distinct factions, but by 1960 Kim Il Sung's bloc had eliminated all competing groups and established itself as the leading political party. The KWP is a pro-military, communist party whose platform is based on the idea of *Juche* as explained by Kim Il Sung: "Man is the master of everything and decides everything."

The Korean Social Democratic Party (KSD) was formed in 1945 by a group of business leaders and political moderates who sought a more representative democracy. They took a pacifist stance toward foreign relations and advocated a peace agreement with the United States and its allies. Although the KSD represents the ideological opposition to the KWP, most political analysts believe it has little actual influence and serves mainly as a symbolic competitor.

The Chondoist Chongu Party was formed in 1946 as the political arm of the country's native Chondogyo religion, which is a blend of Confucianism, Taoism, and Buddhism. Early in the history of the DPRK the party was an active competitor to the KWP and secured sufficient representation to exert moderate legislative influence. After the Korean War the KWP effectively limited the Chondoist Party's political power but allowed it to function as a symbolic representative of one of the country's most influential religions.

Major Events

In 1945 Japanese colonial forces in Korea surrendered to the Soviet Army. In 1948, after failed attempts at reconciliation between Soviet–controlled North Korea and U.S.–controlled South Korea, two separate nations were created. When Soviet-trained General Kim Il Sung was elected premier, he proclaimed that the DPRK was the sole legitimate authority for the entire peninsula—he refused to acknowledge the political sovereignty of the ROK.

North Korean leader Kim Jong Il saluting a military parade in Pyongyang in 2005. © *Korea News Service/Reuters/Corbis*

The Korean War was devastating for both sides, with hundreds of thousands of combat deaths and civilian casualties in the millions. After the war, Kim Il Sung remained the nation's leader as the chairman of the National Defense Committee and the general secretary of the KWP. The alliance between the KWP and the military transformed the nation into a single-party regime, and in 1972 Kim Il Sung revised the constitution and named himself permanent president of the nation.

His government established control over all aspects of society, creating a "cult of personality" in which Kim's will translated directly into policy. The government functioned only as a subordinate bureaucracy. Kim used the perceived threat of capitalist invasion as justification for authoritarian rule and military control.

As Kim's rule continued, he developed the idea of Juche, making it the official state ideology in the 1972 version of the constitution. Juche is sometimes translated as "self-reliance" and is used in government literature to describe a state that is self-sustaining in economic and military terms. Its practical application was central planning: the government made massive investments in heavy industry and infrastructure. The concept of Juche also holds that it is the government's duty to mold the ideologies of the people and to mobilize the forces of communism.

Kim Il Sung is often referred to in political literature as the Great Leader, and since his death in 1994 he has been given the title of Eternal President. His son Kim Jong Il (1942–) succeeded him as chairman of the NDC and general secretary of the KWP. He has continued to lead the nation as an authoritarian regime.

Twenty-First Century

According to most outside observers, North Korea's economy is in a desperate state because of external debt, poor internal investment, and harsh climatic conditions. From 1995 to 2006 the country experienced severe flooding, which halted agricultural production and led to widespread food shortages. Since then the government instituted economic reforms, including redistribution of aid from China and South Korea and allowing limited decentralization of agricultural sales in an effort to boost production.

In 2002 North Korea withdrew from the Nuclear Non-Proliferation Treaty and announced its intention to develop a nuclear arsenal. In 2005—after negotiations involving the United States, Japan, South Korea, and Russia—North Korea agreed to abandon its nuclear program in exchange for international aid and protection agreements. However, the government conducted missile tests in July and October 2006, leading to military sanctions from China, Japan, South Korea, and the United States.

BIBLIOGRAPHY

Oh, Kongdan, and Ralph C. Hassig. *North Korea Through the Looking Glass*. Washington D.C.: Brookings Institution Press, 2000.

Oberdorfer, Dan. *The Two Koreas: A Contemporary History*. Rev. ed. New York: Basic Books, 2002.

Jeffries, Ian. *North Korea: A Guide to Economic and Political Developments*. Oxford: Routledge Press, 2006.

⊕ Bhutan

Type of Government

Bhutan is an absolute monarchy, although it has taken steps to become a constitutional monarchy with a parliamentary government. The executive branch consists of the king, who serves as chief of state, and an appointed prime minister, who serves as head of government assisted by an executive cabinet. Bhutan has a unicameral legislature. Some of its members are chosen by representative voting, and others are appointed by the monarch. The judicial branch consists of the Supreme Court and the High Court.

Background

Bhutan is located in the southeast portion of the Himalayas, between Tibet and India. Archaeological evidence suggests that the aboriginal Bhutanese migrated from Tibet before 2000 BC. Known locally as Druk Yul (Dragon Kingdom), Bhutan was divided into feudal kingdoms until the seventeenth century.

According to legend, the Tibetan monk Padmasambhava, also known as Guru Rinpoche, introduced Buddhism to the region in the eighth century AD. Bhutanese Buddhism is a branch of Mahayana Buddhism, which originated in Tibet. Buddhism played a major role in the development of Bhutanese culture, and the Drukpa sect remains the official state religion.

For centuries Bhutan was divided into numerous fiefdoms that battled for dominance. Each fiefdom developed its own linguistic, religious, and cultural characteristics; as the years passed those distinctions served to isolate each fiefdom from its neighbors.

In AD 1616 Tibetan Lama Ngawang Namgyal (1594–1651) arrived in Bhutan, fleeing the regime in Tibet. Namgyal, a former military leader, enlisted the aid of the wealthy fiefdoms to construct a series of *dzongs* (fortresses) in the valleys of western Bhutan to deter Tibetan raids. Namgyal established a new government, in which he served as the spiritual leader while governmental authority was vested in the *druk desi* (similar to a prime minister). Within a few decades most of the surrounding fiefdoms were absorbed into Namgyal's government.

Namgyal's armies stopped a Tibetan invasion in 1639, after which Namgyal was given the title *shabdrung*, an honorific indicating spiritual leadership in the Drukpa sect. The Mongolian armies attempted to invade Bhutan in 1644 and 1647 but were defeated by the Bhutanese. Namgyal's victories served to strengthen his authority and solidify the local government. After Namgyal's death in 1651, however, the druk desi system deteriorated as regional leaders began to separate from the central authority.

In the nineteenth century forces loyal to the druk desi decided to occupy the British-controlled territory of Assam in northeastern India. After several years of minor skirmishes in the *duars* (passages in the foothills) of Assam, Britain declared war. The Duar War (also known as the Anglo-Bhutanese War) lasted five months, from late 1864 into 1865. The scattered Bhutanese forces were unable to mount an effective resistance. In the 1865 Treaty of Sinchula, Bhutan surrendered Assam and Dewangiri, a portion of southeastern Bhutan, in exchange for an annual payment of fifty thousand rupees.

In 1903 British representatives traveled through Bhutan on a mission to Tibet. Ugyen Wangchuck (1861–1926), a local leader from the Tongsa region, guided the British on their journey and helped them to negotiate a treaty with Tibet. By acting as a mediator, Wangchuck won the respect of both the British and the Tibetans and enhanced his prestige among the Bhutanese. In 1907 the Bhutan monarchy was officially established with Wangchuck as the first king.

Though Bhutan behaved largely as a sovereign nation after the establishment of the monarchy, Britain treated Bhutan like a tributary. When the British relinquished authority over India in 1947, Bhutanese and Indian leaders negotiated the future relationship of their countries, resulting in the Indo-Bhutan treaty of 1949. Both countries agreed to remain independent in internal affairs, but India pledged to protect and represent Bhutan in foreign affairs and to continue annual payments for the use of the Dewangiri region.

Government Structure

As Bhutan's government makes the transition from an absolute monarchy to a constitutional monarchy, it has adopted elements of parliamentary government. Under the constitution adopted in 2005, the monarch serves as head of state while governmental power is jointly vested in the legislature and the executive branch, which consists of the prime minister and the cabinet. Bhutan is divided into eighteen administrative districts. In 2007 the Bhutanese government announced plans to convert to a democratic, multiparty system, with its first public elections in 2008. Each household would have a single vote.

The king (his official title is *druk gyalpo*, or Dragon King) functions as the chief of state and is responsible for addressing the nation, representing the country to foreign leaders, and nominating members to government posts. The king's chief advisers are the *je khenpo*, who represents the interests of the nation's Buddhist monks and the religious community, and the prime minister, who serves as the head of government.

The post of prime minister rotates annually between the five candidates who received the highest number of votes in the previous election cycle. The king nominates ten members of the legislature to serve on the cabinet of ministers; they are confirmed by the legislature. The prime minister and the cabinet handle all executive functions, including foreign policy, creation of budgets and legislative proposals, and administration of government policies.

The legislature, the unicameral Tshogdu (National Assembly), has one hundred fifty members, of whom thirty-five are appointed directly by the monarch, with the advice of the prime minister; ten are appointed to represent the state's religious communities; and the rest are elected by popular vote. All assembly members serve three-year terms. The legislature has the power to originate and amend legislation; has oversight over some executive decisions; and has the authority to remove the prime minister or the monarch with a two-thirds vote.

The judiciary consists of the Supreme Court and the High Courts, collectively referred to as the Royal Court of Justice. The National Judicial Commission, with the approval of the monarch, appoints justices for national and regional courts. Commission members are appointed by the legislature with approval of the executive branch. The Bhutanese legal system is based on Buddhist law; the penal code was revised in 2004.

Political Parties and Factions

Under the existing constitution, it is illegal to participate in the formation of political parties. However, in 2005 the king, Jigme Singye Wangchuck (1955–), by royal edict encouraged the formation of political parties in preparation for the country's 2008 shift to a democratic system.

Despite being illegal, political factions have played a major role in Bhutanese politics. Separatist organizations have arisen in some of the nation's territories while pro-democracy organizations have been petitioning for reforms since the 1950s. Most of Bhutan's political groups operate in exile in India or Nepal and are largely focused on representing the rights of the nation's ethnic groups. For example, the Bhutan State Congress (BSC), formed in 1952, was the nation's first political party and supported democratization and increased representation for the country's Nepalese population.

The Bhutan Peoples Party (BPP), a socialist democratic party formed in 1990, has operated in Nepal for several years. The BPP is Bhutan's largest political party and represents Bhutan's Nepalese population. The Bhutanese government has called the BPP a terrorist organization because it was involved in riots and instances of ethnic violence in 1991 and 1992. The BPP, in turn, has accused the Bhutanese government of arresting and deporting thousands of democracy supporters during the 1990s. In 2001 the BPP's founding president, R. K. Budathoki, was assassinated in Nepal.

The Bhutan National Democratic Party (BHDP) and the Druk National Congress (DNC) are pro-democracy groups, operating from exile in India. The BHDP is noted for its promotion of capitalist market reforms and liberal social policies while the DNC, formed in 1994, supports socialist democracy and increased representation for the Sarchops ethnic group.

Bhutan has a number of small communist parties operating in exile, some of which have instigated armed assaults on the government. The Bhutan Communist Party (BCP), located in Nepal, announced in 2003 that it intended to participate in the 2008 government in the hopes of encouraging a transition to communism. The BCP's political interests include repatriating exiled citizens and establishing free education and an employment-training system for all citizens.

Major Events

After assuming the throne in 1952, the third druk gyalpo, Jigme Dorji Wangchuck, initiated a series of political reforms that reduced the powers of the monarch. In 1953 Wangchuck formed the National Assembly, the nation's first legislative body, and established the post of prime minister.

Wangchuck also initiated programs to improve Bhutan's infrastructure and preserve the country's culture, establishing a national museum, a national library, and an official archive. After China invaded Tibet in

The Bhutan's parliament, a *dzong* known as the Fortress of the Golden Religion. © *Alison Wright/CORBIS*

1951 and 1959, Wangchuck strengthened Bhutan's relationship with India, hoping to discourage China from attempting to annex Bhutan.

In 1962 Prime Minister Jigme Palden Dorji initiated additional reforms that reduced the political influence of the Bhutanese Royal Army (BRA) and the state's religious lobby. In 1964 an army corporal assassinated Dorji. An investigation revealed a plot that included military leaders and the king's uncle (he was executed in 1964 for his part in the assassination). The assassination also revealed a growing split between loyalists and modernists within the central government. In 1965 the king's guards stopped an attempt to assassinate the monarch, after which a number of government officials were removed from their posts and exiled.

In 1968, in an attempt to consolidate support, Wangchuck issued an edict that changed the balance of power in the government: He granted the National Assembly the power to remove executive officers or the king by a two-thirds no-confidence vote. Though a formal constitution would not be written until the twenty-first century, the third druk gyalpo is often credited with taking the first steps toward democratization.

In the late 1980s and early 1990s, the fourth druk gyalpo, Jigme Singye Wangchuck, issued a series of edicts designed to "preserve native culture." The monarchy's focus on Buddhism and Bhutanese culture isolated the country's largely Hindu Nepali population. When the Nepalese within Bhutan began to gather into political groups and pressure the government for social reforms, the government responded with force, and violence erupted. During the following decade Bhutan evicted thousands of Nepalese from the southern territories into Nepal. The Nepalese government refused to allow the refugees to enter, so they were sent to UN refugee camps near the Bhutan border. Bhutan and Nepal have yet to create a mutually satisfactory plan for the repatriation of the refugees.

Beginning in 2000 Assamese separatists set up makeshift military bases in southern Bhutan and used them to launch attacks against Indian targets in Assam. The United Liberation Front of Asom (ULFA) and the National Democratic Front of Bodoland (NDFB) are the leading parties in the Assamese separatist movement.

Bhutanese representatives joined with Indian officials to negotiate with the ULFA in the spring of 2003. When the negotiations failed, the government issued an edict calling for members of the BRA, a volunteer military force, to begin training for military operations against the separatist bases. On December 15, 2003, the BRA and the

Indian military coordinated a set of attacks against the separatist strongholds, eventually routing the rebels from Bhutan. Dozens of Assamese were arrested or killed during the attack; a number of BRA members were killed as well. The 2003 operation was the first time the BRA had taken such action in more than a century.

Twenty-First Century

Bhutan's government is in a state of flux as the country prepares for the 2008 national elections. The first draft of the new constitution was produced in 2005. The fourth druk gyalpo, Jigme Singye Wangchuck, abdicated the throne to his son and successor, Jigme Khesar Namgyel Wangchuck (1980–) on December 15, 2006. The fifth druk gyalpo will lead the country during the 2008 governmental restructuring.

As that date approaches, the Bhutanese government is taking steps to solidify its relationships with other countries. For example, in 2007 Bhutan and India signed a new treaty, in which Bhutan no longer promised to be guided by India in foreign affairs, but agreed to maintain a close relationship of cooperation. The new treaty formally ended continued questions about the sovereignty of Bhutan. In addition, the government responded to criticism from human-rights organizations concerning the treatment of Nepalese refugees. It announced its intention to settle the refugee crisis before the 2008 elections.

BIBLIOGRAPHY

Hutt, Michael. *Unbecoming Citizens: Culture, Nationhood and the Flight of Refugees from Bhutan.* New Delhi: Oxford University Press, 2003.

Aris, Michael. *The Raven Crown: The Origins of Buddhist Monarchy in Bhutan.* Chicago: Serindia Publications, 2005.

Mathew, Joseph C. *Ethnic Conflict in Bhutan.* Jaipur: Nirala Publications, 1999.

⊕ People's Republic of China

Type of Government

The People's Republic of China is a communist state, jointly led by the Communist Party of China (CPC), the Central People's Government (CPG), and the People's Liberation Army (PLA). The CPC, which has direct control over most of the central government, operates through a series of committees containing party leaders, government officials and representatives of special-interest groups.

The central government is divided into executive, judicial, and legislative branches. The executive branch is led by the president, who serves as head of state, and the premier, who serves as head of government, assisted by vice premiers and an executive cabinet. The unicameral legislature has nearly three thousand members who are chosen from slates prepared by the Communist Party. The judicial branch contains a Supreme People's Court,

regional and local courts, and military courts. Within the army, most of the power resides in the Central Military Commission.

Background

Archaeological evidence indicates that China was occupied early in human history. The Xia Dynasty, the first recorded culture in China, existed from the twenty-first to the sixteenth century BC. It began as hunter-gatherer tribes and developed into agricultural communities.

During the Shang Dynasty (1700–1027 BC) and the Chou Dynasty (1027–220 BC), small bands of warlords grouped together and developed centralized bureaucratic structures. The Shang and Chou were threatened by raiding nomads from the west and north—during the following centuries such invasions would play major roles in the rise and fall of Chinese governments.

During the Spring and Autumn period (722–481 BC), the central authority disintegrated into regional kingdoms. Their rivalry was mirrored by competition among myriad philosophies, creating what was known as the Hundred Schools of Thought, which included Confucianism, Taoism, and Legalism. While the humanist political theories of the philosopher known as Confucius (551–479 BC) and his student Meng-tzu (c. 371–c. 289 BC) infiltrated the structure of local bureaucracies, Taoism—a search for harmony, usually through nature—spread throughout the rural communities.

By the end of the fifth century BC, seven kingdoms remained. The most powerful was the Kingdom of Qin, led by Ch'in Shi Huang Ti (259–210 BC). Because of their superior armed forces, the Qin conquered the other six kingdoms by 221 BC and achieved the first unification of China. Ch'in focused on developing an administrative structure that would enable a relatively small central government to administer to a large population. He also fostered the concept of Legalism, which argued that laws were to be obeyed out of fear, not respect.

During the Qin years the various military walls built during previous dynasties were joined into a three-thousand-mile-long wall, a precursor of the Great Wall of China completed centuries later. Soon after the death of Shi Huang-Tih, the dynasty collapsed under pressure from rebel groups.

The Han Dynasty emerged in 206 BC and instituted massive governmental and cultural reforms, bringing about China's first dynastic renaissance. For example, it instituted a Confucian civil service that recruited from the populace and became a fixture of Chinese bureaucracy, lasting until the twentieth century. Agriculture and commerce flourished as well, leading to foreign trade. The Han captured large portions of western China to establish the Silk Road—the trade route that carried Chinese silk to Rome. The Han Dynasty is considered one of the greatest in Chinese history. Today the nation's largest

China. *Maryland Cartographics*

ethnic group calls itself the Han out of reverence for that period.

As would become a pattern during centuries of imperial rule, the Han bureaucracy became dysfunctional through corruption, ineffective leaders who obtained rank through favoritism and family ties, and increasing dissatisfaction among the populace. In AD 220, after more than four hundred years of unified rule, China fragmented into civil war that lasted until the rise of the militaristic Sui Dynasty in 581. It played a transitional role similar to that of the Qin, for the Sui subdued rival powers but also became mired in internal conflict. The Sui fell to the Tang Dynasty, which would establish the second renaissance of imperial China.

The Tang invested heavily in culture, leading to the growth of a new elite. The artistic community flourished, producing lasting works of art, literature, and philosophy that continue to influence Chinese intellectuals. In addition, the Tang initiated massive programs to strengthen the nation's infrastructure. After three hundred years, however, central authority deteriorated, and dissatisfaction among the populace led to uprisings. The nation again lapsed into a period of upheaval, which is often called the Five Dynasties and Ten Kingdoms Period: Between 907 and 960 five distinct dynasties developed in the North, and at least ten kingdoms rose in the South.

When the Sung Dynasty came into power, it did not follow the example of earlier dynasties, which had vested significant administrative power in regional governors. Instead, the Sung strengthened central power through palace appointments. The next three hundred years were a time of cultural advancement and growth—the population is believed to have doubled to more than 100 million. The government had poor relations with foreign states, however, and faced continual pressure from nomadic groups in the northern and western regions. In 1279 Mongolian forces invaded and established the Yuan Dynasty. It lasted less than a hundred years, but was more open to foreign interaction than the Sung had been. Increased contact with Europe, Korea, and Central Asia led to cultural exchange, making the Yuan Dynasty an important time for the development of Chinese art and science.

The overextended Mongolian empire eventually became ineffective, leading to peasant revolts and economic strain. Zhu Yuanzhang (1328–1398), a former Buddhist monk turned military leader, conquered the last Mongolian emperor and founded the Ming Dynasty in 1368.

The Ming controlled China for more than three hundred years, a relatively prosperous time for the populace. They greatly expanded the educational and civil-service systems, and philosophy and art flourished—it was an era when earlier traditions in the arts were restored and perfected. Like previous dynasties, the Ming faced repeated Mongolian incursions as well as conflict with Japan over the Korean peninsula. Both economically and militarily taxed, they were unable to mount effective resistance to the Manchurian armies that established the Qing Dynasty in 1644.

Through military campaigns into Mongolia and Tibet, the Qing managed to pacify China's greatest threats, gaining complete control of the region; however, a strong resistance movement based on Han nationalism surfaced during the Qing, and the government faced continual threats of popular rebellion.

Chinese culture changed significantly with the arrival of western traders in the eighteenth and nineteenth centuries. Britain's main export to China was opium from India, and the drug had a devastating effect on society. When the Qing government tried to restrict opium sales in 1839, the British sent in troops, initiating the first Opium War, a three-year conflict in which the British dominated the Qing and, in the 1844 Treaty of Nanjing, gained control of the Hong Kong territory and unfettered rights to the opium trade.

Political leader Sun Yat-sen (1866–1925) formed the Tongmeng Hui, a revolutionary, republican organization built on three complementary goals: overthrowing the Qing dynasty; installing a parliamentary democratic system; and using socialism to end class struggles and promote popular welfare. The revolution began in October 1911 in Wuchang and spread throughout the country, gathering followers in each province. The Qing abdicated

the throne in 1912, and the Kuomintang (National People's Party) government took control. They renamed the country the Republic of China (ROC).

The ROC government suffered from internal struggles—some politicians wanted to establish a more authoritarian regime while others were pushing for democratic reform. KMT leaders Sun Yat-sen and Chiang Kai-shek (1887–1975) joined forces with the newly formed Communist Party of China (CPC) to take control of Beijing.

The KMT and the CPC eventually diverged in their plans for China, however. Mao Tse-tung (1893–1976) became the de facto head of the CPC, traveling the country and gathering a peasant militia to his cause. By 1928 the CPC army numbered more than ten thousand. Tensions between the KMT and the CPC turned into civil war. The KMT had the initial advantage. In 1934 the communists and their families, who numbered more than one hundred thousand, were forced to retreat some eight thousand miles from the south to avoid the pursuing KMT forces. The Long March, as it came to be called, lasted more than a year and significantly enhanced Mao's reputation among the populace. It also turned public opinion against the KMT.

During World War II the KMT developed strong ties with the U.S. government. Although the United States gave financial aid to the nationalist government, it was unwilling to commit to another military conflict. The KMT tried to regain popular favor through a series of reforms, but the tide of the civil war was turning: The KMT lost repeated engagements with the People's Liberation Army.

The communists captured Beijing in 1949 without significant resistance, and the remaining KMT forces fled to Taiwan, where Chiang Kai-shek declared the establishment of the new ROC government. The People's Republic of China was officially established in Beijing under control of the Communist Party of China.

Government Structure

The People's Republic of China (PRC) is divided into twenty-three provinces, five autonomous regions, and four municipalities. Voters in local districts elect the members of the local People's Congresses, choosing from nominees selected by the Communist Party. The local People's Congresses then elect members to serve in the provincial People's Congresses, who then elect the members of the National People's Congress (NPC).

The unicameral NPC is the highest political body in the government, containing 2,979 members who are elected for five-year terms. Approximately 70 percent to 75 percent of its members represent the Communist Party of China; the remaining seats are distributed among ethnic minorities, special-interest groups, the military, and minority parties. The tiered system of elections makes it unlikely that anyone would become a member of the NPC without the Communist Party's approval.

The NPC has the power to amend the constitution, enact laws, and elect the president and chairman of the Central Military Commission. Members of the NPC select one hundred fifty members to serve on its Standing Committee, which has the authority to enact or modify legislation between annual sessions of the NPC.

The head of the executive branch is the president, who is elected by the NPC for a maximum of two terms of five years and serves as chief of state and commander of the People's Liberation Army. The president makes government appointments, attends to foreign affairs, and addresses the public on behalf of the government. The president's chief deputy is the vice president, who is first in line for presidential succession.

The premier, who is generally a high-ranking member of the CPC, is the head of government and the State Council, which also contains four vice premiers and a number of state counselors and government ministers who oversee the executive departments. Members of the State Council are elected by the NPC for a maximum of two terms of five years. The State Council executes the daily functions of government.

The judicial branch consists of the Supreme People's Court, which has original and appellate jurisdiction over all of the lower courts. The court's two hundred judges are appointed by the NPC, with approval and consultation of the president, and may also be removed by NPC mandate. The courts are not independent of partisan politics and generally follow the directives of the Communist Party.

The Central Committee of the CPC appoints the Politburo, a council of some nineteen to twenty-five members, as its leadership. The Politburo then selects nine members to serve on the Politburo Standing Committee, which is considered the most powerful group in the PRC. The highest-ranking member of the Standing Committee is the general secretary, who is usually the president of the nation as well. The Politburo and its Standing Committee are responsible for translating the party agenda into legislation and executive action.

The People's Liberation Army reports directly to the Central Military Commission, a group of military leaders responsible for determining military policy. The commission exerts considerable influence over governmental policy but is subordinate to the Politburo and the National People's Congress.

Political Parties and Factions

The Communist Party of China dominates politics in the country, effectively making it a single-party state; however, the government allows opposition parties to remain active and to receive a controlled proportion of representation in the National People's Congress. The platform of the CPC, which was formed in 1921, is based on "socialism with Chinese characteristics," as developed by Premier Teng Hsiao-p'ing (1904–1997). It mixes private and state management of the economy.

The Revolutionary Committee of the Chinese Kuomintang (RCCK), founded in 1948 by members who defected from the nationalist-led KMT, and the Chinese Democratic League (CDL), formed in 1941, are minority parties that cooperate closely with the CPC-led government. The RCCK, which took part in setting up the first PRC government after separation from the ROC, is the largest minority party. The CDL is a special-interest party that represents the education industry and promotes free-market reforms.

The Chinese Democracy Party (CDP) is an illegal political organization formed in 1989 by pro-democracy supporters. When it was outlawed by the CPC, many of the party's leaders fled to the United States. The PRC is reportedly holding some members of the CDP on charges of attempting to overthrow the government. The CDP advocates a peaceful transition to a multiparty democracy and the release of all prisoners who were jailed for advocating democratic reform.

Major Events

After the establishment of the PRC in 1949, a rift developed between government and party leadership concerning the transition to socialism. While some believed in gradual reform through a series of modest advancement plans, Mao and other revolutionary leaders wanted to accelerate the nation's development with more aggressive social and economic policies.

In 1958 Mao initiated the Great Leap Forward, an ambitious series of educational and economic reforms intended to achieve ten years of cultural evolution in a five-year span. The intention was to develop agriculture and industry at the same time. However, so much labor was siphoned from agriculture to steel making and construction that food shortages became widespread. Thousands starved. The failure of the Great Leap deepened the rift between political factions. The central government began to assume more power while Mao and the revolutionary arm of the CPC were increasingly isolated.

In 1966 Mao launched the Great Proletariat Cultural Revolution, in which his newly formed student army, the Red Guards, detained, arrested, and executed thousands of opposition political figures, social activists, and others believed to oppose the revolutionary platform. The Cultural Revolution was intended to purge capitalist and antisocialist sentiment from the country but led to near anarchy as minor political cliques competed for power.

Mao accompanied his paramilitary operations with reeducation programs—aimed at ridding the country of old habits and old ideas—to create new literature, theater, academic materials, and art to support revolutionary ideals and the fundamentals of socialism. He even instituted a dress code. By 1969 the militant phase of the

Chinese Communist Party Chairman Mao Tse-tung. © *Bettmann/ CORBIS*

revolution had ended, and Mao had regained control of the party and the PRC government.

As the nation recovered from the revolution, a new political leadership guided by Premier Chou En-lai (1898–1976) began to steer the country toward a more conservative, socialist agenda. Along with Vice Premier Teng, Chou and his faction helped to end most of the programs initiated during the Cultural Revolution and to free many of the prisoners and exiles captured by the Red Guards.

Chou and Mao both died in 1976, after which members of Mao's radical faction attempted to regain control of the government. Teng's clique succeeded in winning popular and governmental support and was able to disarm the revolutionary faction. As part of Teng's conciliatory political strategy, the administration celebrated Mao as a national hero whose policies were corrupted by power-hungry advisers. Blame for the Cultural Revolution was therefore shifted onto Mao's closest allies, known as the Gang of Four, which included Mao's fourth wife, Jiang Qing (1914–1991). The Gang of Four were arrested and sentenced to death. Jiang's sentence was eventually commuted, but she remained in prison until she committed suicide in 1991.

Twenty-First Century

Market-oriented economic reforms in the 1980s and 1990s helped to strengthen China's economy and to make China a major competitor in international markets. China's greatest challenges in this century will include coping with overpopulation and loss of natural resources. China suffers from severe pollution, coupled with rapid deforestation.

China faces numerous issues in foreign affairs, including the continuing disagreement over the sovereignty of Taiwan. While the government considers Taiwan to be a part of the PRC, the Taiwanese government functions largely as an independent nation. The PRC has threatened to use military force against the island nation if Taiwanese leaders officially declare independence.

China's relationships with some members of the United Nations are strained because of unresolved human-rights issues. Human-rights organizations believe that China regularly holds hundreds of political prisoners and engages in human-rights abuses to control the populace.

BIBLIOGRAPHY

Fairbank, John King, and Merle Goldman. *China: A New History.* 2nd ed. Cambridge: Belknap Press, 2006.

Meisner, Maurice. *Mao's China and After: A History of the People's Republic.* 3rd ed. New York: The Free Press, 1999.

Yang Zhong. *Local Government and Politics in China: Challenges from Below.* Armonk: M. E. Sharpe, 2003.

⊕ Taiwan

Type of Government

Taiwan is a group of islands in the western Pacific, just off the coast of mainland China, that are governed as the Republic of China (ROC), a multiparty democracy. Taiwan's sovereignty has been debated since 1949, when its first leaders fled mainland China after a civil war. The government on the mainland, the People's Republic of China, considers Taiwan to be part of its territory. Some residents of Taiwan also see the islands as a province of China; other Taiwanese see the islands as a separate nation and want to declare independence.

The ROC government's powers are divided between executive, legislative, and judicial branches. The executive branch is made up of the president, who serves as chief of state, and the premier, who is the head of government, assisted by the vice premier and the executive cabinet. The unicameral legislature is elected through a combination of direct popular vote and proportional representation. The independent judiciary consists of a hierarchy of courts, with members of the Council of Grand Justices appointed by the president and lower-court justices hired through civil-service examinations.

Background

Taiwan is made up of one large island and smaller, outlying islands, less than one hundred miles off the southeastern coast of the Chinese mainland. It is surrounded by the Taiwan Strait, the East China Sea, the Philippine Sea, and the South China Sea.

Archaeologists believe that humans first occupied the islands at least thirty thousand years ago. Little is known about the original inhabitants, but around six thousand years ago Austronesian speakers arrived from the Malay Archipelago. Today, nine ethnic groups are recognized as descendents of the aboriginal culture. It is believed that Chinese began living in the islands during the sixth century AD, often intermarrying with aboriginals.

Dutch explorers began to visit Taiwan in the sixteenth century and, with the cooperation of the Ming Dynasty, had established a trading community on the eastern coast of the main island by 1624. The Spanish arrived during the same period and established a competing trading center. In 1642 the Dutch allied with aboriginal tribes to drive the Spanish from the island.

After defeating the Spanish the Dutch established the first centralized bureaucracy, brought in missionaries to convert the local population to Christianity, and established schools for both colonists' children and natives. The colonial economy was based on exports of agricultural products and livestock and supplemented by trade of other goods brought into Taiwan.

In 1644 the Manchurian Qing Dynasty defeated the Ming Dynasty on the mainland. A number of Han Chinese—the main ethnic group in China—migrated to Taiwan to escape the Qing. Under the leadership of Zheng Chenggong (1624–1662), they had captured the Dutch fort, Zeelandia, by 1661. The Kingdom of Zheng fought repeated engagements with Qing forces, culminating in a crucial defeat in 1683, which left Taiwan under Qing control. Although the Qing tried to limit immigration in hopes of preventing uprisings, by 1800 more than two million Han Chinese lived in Taiwan.

In the late 1800s the Japanese became interested in the islands and tried to claim them as their territory. The Qing defeated a Japanese invasion in 1871, but by 1890 were rapidly losing ground to Japanese forces. In 1894 full-scale war broke out between the two countries; Japan was the victor. Under the Treaty of Shimonoseki signed in 1895, China ceded Taiwan to Japanese control.

As was their typical colonization strategy, the Japanese attempted a complete cultural conversion, forcing the local population to learn the Japanese language, adopt Japanese names, and convert to the Shinto religion. They stopped armed uprisings with mass arrests and executions.

The independence movement was forced underground and divided into two factions, one favoring independence for Taiwan and the other favoring reunification with the mainland. As Japan entered its second war with the Chinese government in 1937, it tried to preempt further rebellion in the islands by allowing Taiwanese representation in the Japanese parliament.

While already engaged in war with China, the Japanese entered World War II. The United States supported the Kuomintang, or Nationalist, faction (KMT) in China and aided them in defeating the Japanese. When Japan surrendered in 1945, KMT got control of Taiwan. At the time, however, the KMT was losing ground in an ongoing civil war with the Communist Party of China. In 1949, under the command of Chiang Kai-shek (1887–1975), KMT leaders fled to Taiwan and established a military capital in Taipei. In October 1949 the communists declared the foundation of the People's Republic of China; they did not acknowledge the sovereignty of the ROC.

Government Structure

Taiwan is divided into eighteen counties, two municipalities, and two special municipalities, each maintaining a regional government. The constitution guarantees universal suffrage for citizens twenty years of age and older.

The central government is divided into five bodies, called "yuan": the Executive Yuan, the Control Yuan, the Examination Yuan, the Legislative Yuan, and the Judicial Yuan. The president of the republic, who serves as chief of state and commander of the armed forces, has authority over the executive, control, and examination yuan. The president's duties include appointing officials, declaring emergencies, and addressing the public on the government's behalf. The vice president serves as the president's chief deputy and handles administrative duties. The president and vice president are elected by popular vote for a maximum of two terms of four years.

The leader of the Executive Yuan is the premier, who is appointed by the president for a maximum of two terms of four years. The president and the premier collaborate on choosing a vice premier and eight cabinet ministers to manage the executive departments. As the head of government, the premier advises the legislature about the executive agenda and cooperates in developing legislation.

The Control Yuan, which functions as the central auditing agency, is also responsible for monitoring the conduct of government officials. It has twenty-four members selected by the president with the approval of the legislature. They serve six-year terms. Members of the Control Yuan are not permitted to have any political party affiliation or to hold any concurrent office in the government. The Control Yuan has the authority to recommend impeachment and censure as well as audit budgetary initiatives.

The Examination Yuan, which administers the nation's civil-service system, is the official employment department for the government. Its nineteen members are selected by the president for six-year terms.

Taiwan. *Maryland Cartographic*

The Legislative Yuan, the highest lawmaking body in the government, has 255 members, with 168 elected by direct popular vote from multimember constituencies. Forty-one of the remaining seats are filled by minority-party representatives through a proportional representation system, while eight other seats are divided between representatives of the People's Republic of China and the aboriginal population. The legislature has oversight over the executive offices and can call for the impeachment of any executive officer, including the president and the premier. The legislature initiates laws and constitutional amendments and approves all appointments.

The Judicial Yuan is the nation's highest judicial body. The fifteen-member Council of Grand Justices interprets and removes inconsistencies in the constitution and settles disputes between the national and local governments. Each member of the council is appointed by the president for one eight-year term. Other parts of the judicial system are the Supreme Court, the high courts, the district courts, and the courts for special administrative issues. The Supreme Court has original and appellate jurisdiction over all the lower courts but must follow the interpretations of the Council of Grand Justices. Justices at the lower levels are chosen by civil-service examinations and serve for life, although they can be removed for disciplinary reasons.

Political Parties and Factions

Taiwan is a multiparty democracy. Prior to constitutional reform in 1991, the country was controlled by one party, the Kuomintang (often called the Nationalist Party), which behaved as an authoritarian regime. During the elections of 2000 the KMT lost majority control to the Democratic Progressive Party (DPP), the first shift of power since the ROC was established on Taiwan.

The DPP leads the Pan Green Coalition, which is considered the more liberal or leftist coalition. The DPP, formed in 1986 by opponents of the KMT-run single-party state, was illegal until a constitutional amendment in 1991 legitimized multiparty competition. The DPP is often seen as an independence party, favoring complete political separation from the mainland; however, since it gained the majority it has taken incremental steps in support of independence without isolating or alienating voters who favor reunification.

In addition to the DPP, the Pan Green Coalition includes the Taiwan Solidarity Union (TSU) and the Taiwan Independence Party (TAIP). The TSU is an aggressively pro-independence party and has supported proposals to change the national flag, the national anthem, and the names of government buildings, roads, and offices to be more in keeping with native culture. The TAIP was formed in 1996 as a pro-independence offshoot of the DPP but failed to win popular support. Since 2001 it has been largely supplanted by the TSU.

The Pan Blue Coalition is made up of the Kuomintang (KMT), the People First Party (PFP), and the New Party (NP). Pan Blue is seen as the more conservative coalition and historically has favored reunification with the mainland or continuing the existing arrangement without seeking sovereignty. However, since the 2000 elections it has said less about reunification and more about maintaining the status quo. It also supports strong economic reforms, a stand that has allowed it to remain popular with the country's aboriginal population and labor groups.

The New Party (NP), formed in 1993 as an offshoot of the KMT, strongly favors reunification with the mainland and has maintained some influence in the legislature. The People First Party (PFP), formed in 2000, is a reunification-oriented party that focuses on economic cooperation with the PRC and greater international involvement.

Of the parties not in the major coalitions, only one—the Non-Partisan Solidarity Union (NPSU)—captured a significant number of seats in the Legislative Yuan. The NPSU takes no definite position on independence and bases its platform on government reform. Because neither the Pan Blue nor the Pan Green had a decisive legislative majority following the 2004 elections, the NPSU represents a tiebreaking vote on key issues.

Major Events

In 1947, after Taiwan was liberated from Japanese control, the KMT refused to acknowledge the independence movement and instituted martial law. On February 28, 1947, an elderly cigarette vendor was beaten while resisting arrest, which precipitated a conflict between police and pro-independence crowds. Protesters throughout Taiwan marched on government and police buildings. During the following three days rebel groups controlled large portions of several major cities. The KMT agreed to negotiate—while it built a military force. A week later KMT militia entered the cities and attacked rebel groups. By the end of March between ten thousand and twenty thousand civilians had been killed in what was later called the "2/28 Incident."

After Chiang Kai-shek established the ROC government in Taiwan, he maintained martial law in expectation of an imminent PRC attack. He controlled the media, the educational system, and the police. He also began to develop the military in hopes of regaining control over all of China.

In the 1950s the United States supported Taiwan as a way of gaining influence in the region and preventing the spread of communism. Between 1951 and 1960, the United States gave the ROC more than $1.5 billion. Chiang made vast infrastructure improvements and invested heavily in the military. Despite being controlled by a martial regime, Taiwan achieved economic prosperity.

During the Cold War the United States and the United Nations recognized the ROC as the legitimate government of China and refused to recognize the communist-controlled PRC. In 1971, however, the United States opened negotiations with the PRC in hopes of controlling the influence of the Soviet Union, which had been a close ally of the PRC. Later that year the United States adopted a "two Chinas" policy and agreed to recognize the PRC as a legitimate government.

Chiang Kai-shek's son, Chiang Ching-kuo (1910–1988), took control in 1978 and began to liberalize state policy. In 1987 he formally ended martial law, and in 1991 the multiparty political system was put into place.

Twenty-First Century

The major political issue in Taiwan is the relationship between the ROC and the mainland. The PRC has continually threatened military measures if Taiwan declares independence; to prove the point, in the mid-1990s the PRC conducted missile tests off the coast. The DPP, which leads the Pan Green coalition, has adopted a political model in which Taiwan is an independent nation, but it has taken no further measures to legitimize the separation from the PRC. Radical and nationalist groups oppose the status-quo policy and favor legitimizing independence through legislation.

Taiwan was hit hard by the Asian financial crisis in the late 1990s. However, its industrial sector has since rebounded, and unemployment and inflation are low. Taiwan continues to be one of the world's leading manufacturers of high-tech goods.

BIBLIOGRAPHY

Rubinstein, Murray A., ed. *Taiwan: A New History*. Rev. ed. Armonk: M. E. Sharpe, 2006.

Manthorpe, Jonathan. *Forbidden Nation: A History of Taiwan*. New York: Palgrave Macmillan, 2005.

Tucker, Nancy Bernkopf. *Dangerous Strait: the U.S.-Taiwan-China Crisis*. New York: Columbia University Press, 2005.

⊕ Oman

Type of Government

An arid nation at the southeastern end of the Arabian Peninsula, Oman—also known as the Sultanate of Oman—is a longstanding hereditary monarchy. Rapid economic and social changes since 1970 have been accompanied by a slower but equally persistent trend toward greater political participation. Highlights of this second trend include a 1996 royal decree, known as the Basic Law of the State, that created a bicameral, partially elected advisory body; in addition, voting rights were extended in 2003 to all citizens over the age of twenty-one. The king, or sultan, retains supreme legislative, judicial, and executive powers.

Background

The possession of ports along three major marine shipping channels (the Persian—or Arabian—Gulf, the Gulf of Oman, and the Arabian Sea) has had a major influence on the history of the region of Oman. A center of the lucrative frankincense trade for centuries, the area attracted traders from Africa, Asia, and the Mediterranean. Following the arrival of Islam in the seventh century, the region of Oman managed to avoid the unwanted attentions of foreign powers until the arrival of the Portuguese around 1500. After roughly a century and a half of Portuguese rule, Britain, France, and Persia began to compete for influence. Shortly after Ahmad bin Said was elected *imam*, or leader, of Oman in 1744, the Persians were expelled. Ahmad bin Said's dynasty persisted: The leader as of 2007, Qabus bin Said (1940–), is his direct descendant.

One of the major factors shaping Oman's history has been the tension between the cities of the coast, notably the capital of Muscat, and the impoverished, sparsely populated interior. Muscat, a major port, has traditionally been the focus of foreign interest and investment, while the interior has been the domain of conservative tribal and religious leaders. By the second half of the nineteenth century, the imam's authority was largely limited to the interior, while a separate institution, the sultanate of Muscat, controlled the capital. In 1920, under an agreement known as the Treaty of Seeb, the imam acknowledged the sovereignty of the sultan in return for the latter's acceptance of the imam's autonomy in matters limited to the interior. This arrangement lasted until 1954, when the reigning imam's death sparked a violent power struggle between his successor and the reigning sultan (and father of the current sultan), Said bin Taymur (1910–1972). With the assistance of British troops, the sultan expelled his rival and abolished the office of imam.

Great Britain had been the dominant foreign power in the region since the late eighteenth century. For the most part, however, British administrators in the area preferred informal, indirect control to direct rule. It was, therefore, a protectorate rather than a colony. The ambiguity inherent in this relationship persisted even after the British explicitly acknowledged Omani independence in a 1951 treaty, with many Arab nations charging that continued British control of Omani resources, notably oil, rendered the treaty meaningless. These issues were not fully resolved until the country's dramatic economic and social transformation under the current sultan.

In many ways, Oman's modern history did not begin until 1970, when Sultan Qabus bin Said deposed his father and vowed to bring an end to the country's severe isolation and poverty. When Qabus bin Said took power, the nation lacked electricity, telephone service, and running water, and there were only three schools. By diverting oil revenues from defense to social services, including universal access to education and health care, the sultan has overseen a remarkable social and economic transformation. Changes in the political system, however, have been slower to develop.

Government Structure

The current structure of government in Oman is a unique mix of traditional autocracy and progressive democracy. According to the most plausible explanation for this contradiction, Oman is still working to complete the transformation that began in 1970. While parts of the government have been updated, others have proved more resistant to change.

The sultan stands at the head of the executive, legislative, and judicial branches, and it is illegal to criticize him. The Council of Ministers, the sultan's cabinet of handpicked administrators, provides him with direct access to the agencies that handle the government's daily operations. Somewhat unusual is the presence of several regional administrators in addition to the heads of finance, education, health care, and other areas.

Laws are promulgated by royal decree. There is no elected body with the power to issue laws—the role of the bicameral Council of Oman is advisory only. Nevertheless, the Council has quickly become the most important outlet for the expression of public opinion. Its current bicameral structure dates from 1996, when the sultan established a new Council of State (known as Majlis al-Dawla) composed, as of 2006, of fifty-nine members appointed for renewable four-year terms. It now serves as the upper house. The lower house, known as the Consultative Council (or Majlis al-Shura), replaced an earlier body, the State Consultative Council (SCC), in 1991. Members of the SCC were appointed, but the Consultative Council has always been an elected body, and the gradual expansion of its electorate is the most prominent sign of the sultan's stated desire to increase political participation.

At first the government restricted voting rights to 50,000 citizens of its own choosing; this number soon rose to 175,000. In 2002, however, the sultan granted the vote to all citizens, male and female, over the age of twenty-one, with the significant exception of police and military personnel. The council's composition has changed as well, with the fifty-nine original members (one for each geographic district) now joined by twenty-four from the more populated districts. The chair of the council is an appointee of the sultan, who also reserves the right to invalidate election results. There are committees on a wide range of topics, and, as in the upper house, members are elected for renewable four-year terms.

Though both houses are advisory, they differ in their focus. The upper house investigates specific issues at the sultan's request, studies and reports on larger issues like education, and writes preliminary drafts of laws for the sultan's consideration. The lower house questions government employees on issues of mismanagement or corruption and drafts preliminary budget plans.

The participation of women in Omani politics stands in sharp contrast to the situation in neighboring states. For the 2003–2007 term, there were nine women in the upper house and two in the lower. Oman was the first Arab state in the region to allow women to run for office.

The nation's legal system is a mixture of tribal law, Islamic law, European law, and royal decree. A Supreme Judicial Council handles judicial appointments, oversees criminal prosecutions, and advises the sultan on legal issues. There are no jury trials, and the sultan remains the court of last appeal.

Oman is divided for administrative purposes into five regions and three governorates; these are divided in turn into a total of fifty-nine districts. At the head of each district is a *wali*, an official appointed by the interior minister. Chief among a wali's duties are public safety and tax collection. Governors appointed by the sultan and granted the rank of cabinet minister oversee the district leaders in the three governorates, which include many of the most densely populated districts.

Political Parties and Factions

There are no legal political parties in Oman. Omani society is more diverse than many outsiders assume, however, with several languages, ethnicities, and religions represented. Well over half a million foreign workers live in Oman, many from the Indian Subcontinent; as noncitizens, though, their political influence is quite limited. More influential are the several hundred distinct tribal groups, many of whose leaders, particularly among the nomadic peoples of the nation's rural interior, continue to adjudicate disputes and criminal offenses.

Despite the predominance of Islam, small Christian and Hindu groups do exist. The royal decree of 1996 specifically allows freedom of worship unless it interferes with maintaining civil order. More significant politically are the many Muslims whose religious views differ from those of the sultan. The sultan's family belongs, as do many Omanis, to the Ibadi sect, a traditional, highly conservative group. There are many Sunnis as well, however, particularly in the northern desert regions; prominent among these are the members of the Wahhabi (or Salafi) sect, the predominant branch in neighboring Saudi Arabia. Most of the radical militants seeking to impose their brand of fundamental Islam across the region have been Wahhabis. While their influence in Oman has been relatively modest to date—and their numbers are quite small in proportion both to other Wahhabis and to Omanis generally—the organization and cohesiveness of the militants make them the most formidable of the sultan's internal opponents.

Major Events

Oman's densely populated coastal region of Dhofar, near the border with Yemen, was the center of a tribal rebellion between 1964 and 1975. Originally organized as the Dhofar Liberation Front, the rebels later joined an umbrella group known as the Popular Front for the Liberation of Oman and the Arab Gulf. With considerable foreign aid, the sultan's troops managed to quell the rebellion by the end of 1975.

Twenty-First Century

Omanis will face a number of challenges in the years ahead. The oil revenue that has sustained an ambitious program of social services will soon disappear as the nation's remaining oil reserves are depleted. The government is eager to develop new industries to replace oil, but results to date have been mixed. Meanwhile, an ever-increasing demand for clean water is rapidly exhausting groundwater supplies, while many scientists believe global warming is worsening the oppressive heat waves for which Oman has long been notorious.

Radical Islamic fundamentalism poses a considerable threat to Oman's peace and security. The nation's close ties to the United States, highlighted by the U.S. military's use of Oman as a base for U.S. operations in Iraq, have made Oman a prominent target for radical groups seeking to destabilize regimes they consider insufficiently Islamic. Though there is little indication to date that such groups enjoy widespread support in Oman, the arrest and conviction of dozens of Omani citizens in 2005 for anti-government activity suggests that the problem is growing. Many observers worry, in particular, that the threat of Islamic fundamentalism may obstruct or even reverse the progress toward democracy that has distinguished the sultan's rule for nearly forty years.

BIBLIOGRAPHY

Ghubash, Hussein. *Oman: The Islamic Democratic Tradition.* London: Routledge, 2006.
Kechichian, Joseph A. *Political Participation and Stability in the Sultanate of Oman.* 2nd ed. Dubai, United Arab Emirates: Gulf Research Center, 2006.
Sultanate of Oman, Ministry of Information. "Government." *http://www.omanet.om/english/government/overview.asp?cat=gov* (accessed May 8, 2007).

⊕ Great Socialist People's Libyan Arab Jamahiriya

Type of Government

Libya considers itself a socialist country founded on Islamic law; however, in practice, Libya is a military dictatorship run by Muammar al-Qadhafi (1942–). The country is divided into hundreds of local congresses and committees, the participants of which elect the members of the General People's Congress (GPC), the legislative branch of the central government. The GPC elects a Secretary General, who is the head of state, and a General People's Committee, which functions as the executive branch of the government. The judicial arm includes a Supreme Court at the highest level and a Supreme Council for Judicial Authority that administers the judiciary.

Background

Libya is on the Mediterranean Sea in North Africa between Algeria and Egypt. Beginning about 6000 BC people farmed the coastal region while hunters and herdsman occupied the southern region, which had more water then but is now the Sahara Desert. Around 2000 BC Berbers settled the area, later to be controlled at various times from Egypt and Carthage until the Roman Republic conquered the region beginning in the third and second centuries BC.

In the fifth century AD, Germanic Vandals took the region from Rome, but the Byzantine Empire captured it from the Vandals in the sixth century. Arab invaders occupied the region beginning in the seventh century. Over the following centuries the Arabs' Muslim culture mixed with that of the native Berbers, and Arabic became the region's predominant language. The region was controlled by the Ottoman Empire from 1511 to 1711, by the Qaramanli dynasty until 1835, and again by the Ottoman Empire until 1911.

Italy invaded Libya in 1911 and formally established control by 1912. However, Italy continued to face armed resistance from Libyans until the country's complete conquest under Italian dictator Benito Mussolini (1883–1945) in 1932. Libya was a battleground during World War II from 1940 until 1943. Under the Treaty of 1947, Italy officially relinquished control of Libya to the Allied forces. The Allies could not agree what to do with Libya, so they decided to put the question to the United Nations. On November 21, 1949, the UN General Assembly voted to make Libya an independent state.

Libya declared independence under pro-British King Idris I (1889–1983) on December 24, 1951. It established a constitutional, hereditary monarchy, with separate parliaments for the provinces of Tripolitania and Cyrenaica. Political parties were prohibited. Libya became a member of the United Nations in December 1955.

Major oil reserves were discovered in Libya in 1959, turning the country from poor to rich as a nation. Ten years later, on September 1, 1969, military rebels led by twenty-eight-year-old Colonel Qadhafi deposed King Idris I, who was exiled to Egypt. Under the Constitutional Proclamation of December 1969, Qadhafi governed initially through the Revolutionary Command Council (RCC), abolished the monarchy, and called the country the Libyan Arab Republic. In 1977 Qadhafi replaced the RCC with the General People's Congress (GPC) and changed the name of the country to Great Socialist People's Libyan Arab Jamahiriya. The word "Jamahiriya" is an Arabic word Qadhafi created to mean "state of the masses."

Government Structure

While Libya calls itself a socialist country run by the people, Western sources consider it a military dictatorship run by Qadhafi. Its structure of government comes from two primary sources. In March 1977 the Declaration of the Establishment of the Authority of the People amended Libya's Constitutional Proclamation of 1969. In addition, a "Green Book" based on a speech Qadhafi delivered in 1975 contains much of the philosophical foundation for Libya's government. It contains a so-called third way, an alternative form of government that is supposed to lie somewhere between Western capitalism and the socialism of the former Soviet Union.

Viewed as a socialist state, the foundation for government in Libya is a collection of hundreds of municipalities called Basic People's Congresses. Each Basic People's Congress has a Basic People's Committee that administers local government. The members of the Basic People's Committees are elected by Libyan citizens over age eighteen. In turn, the Basic People's Committees elect members to regional People's Committees for regional People's Congresses. The regional committees elect the members of the General People's Congress, which comprises both the legislative and executive arm of Libya's national government.

The GPC has 760 members elected to three-year terms. Members must be at least eighteen years old and must hold leadership positions in the local congresses and committees. The GPC meets for only two weeks annually and has power to make laws for Libya. The GPC chooses a Secretary General, who serves as the head of state for Libya. The Secretary General serves as head of the five-member General Secretariat, also elected by the GPC. The General Secretariat handles affairs for the GPC in between its biennial assemblies. In addition to the Secretary General, the General Secretariat has secretaries for Women's Affairs, for Affairs of the People's Congresses, for Affairs of the Trade Unions, Syndicates and Professional Associations, and for Foreign Affairs.

The GPC also elects a General People's Committee, which effectively acts as the cabinet or executive arm of the government. The Committee is headed by its own Secretary General, who serves like a prime minister. Each of the other secretaries on the Committee leads one of the ministries, or departments, of the national government.

The judicial arm of the government contains a Supreme Court of Libya and various lower courts. The Supreme Court has five separate chambers, one each for civil and commercial, criminal, administrative, constitutional, and Islamic law cases. The GPC elects the judges of the Supreme Court. Appellate courts below the Supreme Court include three Courts of Appeal covering different regions, plus a Court of Appeals for cases under Islamic law. Below the appellate courts are Courts of First Instance, which handle trials in most cases, plus summary courts, which handle minor matters. According to the U.S. State Department, there are revolutionary and political courts that work outside the regular judiciary to try political crimes and offenses against the state. The laws of Libya are a combination of Islamic legal principles and the Civil Law tradition from Europe.

Qadhafi served as Secretary General of the GPC from its inception until 1979. Since then he has not had an official position, but Libyan government announcements refer to him as the brotherly leader and guide of the revolution. Western sources claim that despite his unofficial status, Qadhafi ultimately controls the military and government of Libya through the use of revolutionary committees with authority to review and control all government conduct.

Political Parties and Factions

Political parties have been illegal in Libya since its independence. A 1972 law defines illegal political activity as any activity based on a political ideology contrary to the principles of the revolution of 1969. The Arab Socialist Union is a state-authorized organization that mobilizes people for political involvement. As such, it effectively serves as the country's only lawful political party.

Political groups that operate in violation of state law can be exiled. During the 1980s Qadhafi targeted enforcement efforts at Islamic fundamentalist organizations, which represented a threat to his regime. When the Libyan military became a threat during the 1990s, including a failed coup attempt in 1993, Qadhafi replaced military rivals with supporters. In March 1997 the GPC adopted a law called the Charter of Honor to impose punishment on Libyans convicted of crimes of disorder. Some interpreted the law as an assault on opponents of Qadhafi's regime.

Major Events

After the revolution of 1969, Qadhafi took steps to rid Libya of foreign military bases, including those of Great Britain and the United States. Qadhafi worked at times to create a unified Africa and to create a united nation of Arabic states, but to no avail. During the 1970s and 1980s Libya battled with Chad over a region in that country known as the Aozou Strip, rich in mineral deposits. Libya finally withdrew in 1994 after the International Court of Justice ruled in Chad's favor in the dispute.

In 1979 the United States designated Libya as a state sponsor of terrorism, and already strained relations between the two countries deteriorated. In 1986 the United States bombed Libya in response to the bombing of a nightclub patronized by American military personnel in West Berlin, Germany. Two years later, terrorists with suspected connections to Libya bombed Pan Am

Libyan leader Muammar al-Qadhafi in 2005. © *AP/Wide World Photos*

Flight 103 over Lockerbie, Scotland, killing everyone aboard and eleven people on the ground. The attack led to economic and other sanctions against Libya by the United Nations, the United States, and others.

In September 1995 Libya began to deport thousands of Arab workers, primarily Palestinian, Sudanese, and Egyptian. Qadhafi claimed the action was necessary to open jobs for Libyans. Some interpreted the move as a protest against peace negotiations between Israel and the Palestine Liberation Organization.

In 1999 Libya complied with one of the UN's post-Lockerbie demands by turning over two Libyan intelligence officials for trial in Scotland. One, Abdel Basset al-Megrahi (1952–), was eventually convicted in the Pan Am bombing, while the other was acquitted.

Twenty-First Century

In the opening years of the twenty-first century, Libya took steps to mend its relations with Western nations. In August 2003 Libya agreed to take responsibility for its officials' actions in the Lockerbie bombing by paying compensation to the victims' families. That same month in a letter to the UN Security Council, Libya renounced terrorism. In December 2003 Libya announced plans to

eliminate its weapons of mass destruction. These actions led the United Nations and United States to lift sanctions against the country. In June 2006, just one month after both countries fully restored their mutual embassies, the United States lifted its designation of Libya as a state sponsor of terrorism.

BIBLIOGRAPHY

Simons, Geoffrey L. *Libya: the Struggle for Survival.* New York: St. Martin's Press, 1993.

United Nations Development Programme-Programme on Governance in the Arab Region. "Democratic Governance, Arab Countries Profiles, Libya." http://www.undp-pogar.org/countries/country.asp?cid=10 (accessed August 21, 2007).

Vandewalle, Dirk J. *A History of Modern Libya.* Cambridge: Cambridge University Press, 2006.

⊕ Cambodia

Type of Government

The Kingdom of Cambodia is a constitutional monarchy with a parliamentary government. Power is divided between executive, legislative, and judicial branches, with the president serving as the chief of state. Cambodia has a bicameral parliament that shares legislative responsibility with the executive branch. The judicial branch consists of the Supreme Council of the Magistracy, the Supreme Court, and lower courts.

Background

Cambodia borders Vietnam, Laos, and Thailand with a large coastal region along the Gulf of Thailand. Little is known about the prehistoric cultures of Cambodia, but archaeological evidence indicates that the country was occupied by bands of tribal residents before 4000 BC. The Funan Kingdom was established around 100 BC. By analyzing artistic and architectural remains, archaeologists have determined that the kingdom was closely related to early monarchies in India. It developed a complex naval economy and was involved in trade with China. Though the Funan never achieved full unification of Cambodia—military infighting was frequent—they remained in power until the sixth century AD.

By 802 Cambodia had become part of the Khmer civilization, a succession of dynasties throughout Southeast Asia. Jayavarman II (770–850) was the founder of the Kambuja Kingdom, from which the name Cambodia is derived. The Kambuja kings established their capital in an area known as Angkor.

Yasodharapura, built at the Angkor site between 889 and AD 910, was one of the largest cities in the world. It had a complex system of irrigation canals and reservoirs. Because Kambuja society was centered around religion, Buddhist and Hindu temples and monuments influenced its architecture.

From the eleventh through the thirteenth centuries the Kambuja kings struggled against periodic incursions by groups from Siam (today's Thailand), Vietnam, and Bagan (part of what is now Myanmar), who were interested in the productive potential of the Mekong Delta. The Thai kingdom of Ayutthaya sent periodic invasion forces that were repeatedly repelled.. However, the society at Angkor was eventually weakened by the economic and military strain, and in 1431 the Ayutthaya conquered the city, forcing the last of the Kambuja to flee west. Though portions of the Khmer civilization remained intact, a century of civil wars and defeat at the hands of foreign armies left it scattered.

In the sixteenth century the Khmer regained some of their previous economic and political control through the city of Lovek, where they traded with the Portuguese, the Indonesians, and the Ming Dynasty of China. However, the Thai finally forced the Khmer to submit in 1594 when they captured Lovek and installed a colonial government.

In 1863 the French arrived in Cambodia, hoping to win territory in Southeast Asia as part of their ongoing struggle against Britain. The French defeated the Vietnamese in the Mekong region and established trade routes in the area. Khmer King Norodom signed a treaty with the French in 1864, officially making Cambodia a French protectorate.

The French kept the Khmer monarchy in place as symbolic leadership but maintained careful control over all political developments to prevent uprisings. They made only minor adjustments to the infrastructure of Cambodia, building roads and a railroad line from their administrative center in Phnom Penh. They did little to improve the general prosperity of the populace. During the twentieth century the French granted the Cambodians greater access to education and involvement in government.

A Khmer independence movement surfaced during the 1920s, fueled by the emergence of an educated urban population. In the 1930s they appealed to the monarch for political and social reforms, but the monarchy had little power under French control. In 1941 the Japanese occupied the French portions of Vietnam and Cambodia. At first they allowed the colonial government to remain in place, but eventually they dissolved the government and encouraged the Cambodians to declare independence in hopes they would aid the Japanese war effort. Under King Norodom Sihanouk (1922–) Cambodia declared its independence in 1945.

The French attempted to regain control of Cambodia after Japan's surrender at the end of World War II and offered the Cambodian monarch a degree of self-governanceunder the French system, which Sihanouk accepted. The French supervised Cambodian elections, which were won by the newly formed Democratic Party. Although a constitution was drafted in 1947, it gave France significant influence over the military, police, and judiciary. In 1952 Sihanouk dissolved the legislature, suspended the constitution, and traveled to France for emergency negotiations. He convinced the French that Cambodia needed immediate, full independence to avoid political takeover from radical factions. On November 9, 1953, Cambodia was granted full independence.

Government Structure

Cambodia is divided into twenty provinces and four municipalities. While the provinces have their own administrative structure headed by a governor, the municipalities are administered directly by the central government. Since 1993 the constitution has granted universal suffrage to people eighteen years of age and older and established a system of direct popular election coupled with proportional representation.

The monarch is the symbolic head of state but has no direct power under the constitution. Succession of the monarchy is accomplished through the Royal Council of the Throne, which consists of the prime minister, the president, and select members of the legislature. The king meets with foreign dignitaries, addresses the public, and appoints officials on the recommendation of the legislature and the executive branch.

The prime minister, who serves as head of government and commander of the nation's armed forces, represents the ruling party and is appointed by the president after being recommended and approved by the legislature. After taking office, the prime minister directly appoints members of the Council of Ministers, who head the executive departments.

Cambodia's legislature is bicameral. The upper house, the Sénat (Senate), has sixty-one members who serve five-year terms. Two are appointed directly by the monarch, two are selected by the lower house of parliament, and the remaining members are elected by popular vote.

The lower house, the Radhsphea ney Preah Recheanachakr Kampuchea (National Assembly), has 123 members elected by popular vote for five-year terms. Its members select a president and vice president to preside over meetings and to represent the assembly to the executive.

The Senate and National Assembly cooperate in originating and passing legislation. They also have approval over executive actions. The monarch does not have veto power over legislation but often functions as an adviser to the public concerning legal changes. The legislature has the power to remove members from the executive branch, including the prime minister, with a two-thirds no-confidence vote.

The judicial branch includes the Supreme Council of the Magistracy, the nation's highest court, which has the responsibility of interpreting constitutional law. The Supreme Court has original and appellate jurisdiction over all lower courts but is subordinate to the Supreme Council in matters involving constitutional interpretation. Beneath the Supreme Court are the high courts, district courts, and local courts. Justices are appointed by the executive branch and approved by the legislature.

Political Parties and Factions

The Cambodian People's Party (CPP), which developed in 1991 as an offshoot of the Kampuchean People's Revolutionary Party (KPRP), gained control of parliament in 2003. Although the KPRP was a communist, pro-Vietnam party, the CPP has adopted a more moderate position and advocates free-market economic policies. Prime Minister Hun Sen (1951–) is the vice president of the CPP and a former member of the KPRP. After the 2003 elections the CPP did not hold a clear majority in the parliament, so it developed an alliance with the Funcinpec Party.

The Funcinpec Party, formed in 1991, is a royalist party. It was active in the resistance to the Vietnamese-installed government during the 1980s and gained significant political power in parliament in the 1990s. The Funcinpec was traditionally the CPP's strongest political adversary, but since the 2003 alliance it has attempted to support CPP policy.

The Sam Rainsy Party (SRP), a liberal democratic organization, was founded in 1998 by Sam Rainsy (1949–). It is the opposition to the CPP-Funcinpec alliance. In 2004 Rainsy publicly accused the CPP and Funcinpec of corruption, after which charges of criminal defamation were brought against him. He fled the country to avoid arrest. Rainsy was tried in absentia and found guilty but was later pardoned by the monarch. He returned to Cambodia in 2006.

Major Events

In 1963 King Norodom Sihanouk (1922–) amended the constitution of Cambodia, effectively naming himself head of government. A power struggle developed between Sihanouk and Prime Minister Lon Nol (1913–1985). During the Vietnam conflict, the Cambodian government declared itself neutral and allowed communist forces from Vietnam to occupy portions of its territory. In 1968 a domestic communist movement, the Khmer Rouge, launched an insurgency against the Cambodian government from bases in Vietnam. The United States responded by attacking Khmer targets in Vietnam, leading to additional instability.

In 1970 Nol ousted Sihanouk after it was revealed that Sihanouk was meeting with leaders of communist

King Norodom Sihanouk at a 1969 celebration commemorating Cambodia's independence. © *Bettmann/CORBIS*

countries and possibly negotiating a communist takeover of Cambodia. Nol ordered all Vietnamese forces to leave Cambodia. The Vietnamese, in alliance with the Khmer Rouge, attacked Cambodia directly while Sihanouk was in China. The Khmer Rouge captured Phnom Penh in 1975, deposing Nol's regime.

After taking power the Khmer Rouge changed the name of the country to Democratic Kampuchea. Its leader, Pol Pot (1925–1998), initiated an aggressive "purification" campaign—he intended to remove all members of elite Cambodian society to pave the way for a new communist system. Estimates vary, but Pol Pot is said to have ordered the execution of between 1.5 million and 7 million Cambodians who were seen as ideological, social, or governmental opponents of communism and the Khmer Rouge agenda.

The Khmer Rouge caused its own downfall by killing hundreds of Vietnamese in Cambodia and making military incursions into Vietnam. In 1979 Vietnamese forces entered Cambodia, marking the beginning of a decadelong struggle. A peace agreement was negotiated by 1991, but the damage caused by the Khmer Rouge dominated the political environment for the next decade.

Twenty-First Century

As Cambodia has recovered from civil war, human-rights organizations have charged the government with numerous violations, including unlawful detainment, torture, and murder of government opponents. In addition, the government is perceived to be corrupt, significantly reducing the foreign investment and aid available. One of the nation's greatest challenges in this century will be to reform its democratic procedures.

Unlike some neighboring nations whose economies experienced rapid expansion after 2000, the Cambodian economy is growing at a slow pace. Increases in tourism have the potential to stimulate economic growth, provided the government can control crime and stimulate growth in the recreation industry.

BIBLIOGRAPHY

Chandler, David P. *A History of Cambodia*. 3rd ed. Boulder: Westview Press, 2000.

Gottesman, Evan. *Cambodia After the Khmer Rouge: Inside the Politics of Nation Building*. New Haven: Yale University Press, 2004.

Lizée, Pierre P. *Peace, Power, and Resistance in Cambodia: Global Governance and the Failure of International Conflict Resolution*. London: Macmillan, 2000.

⊕ Republic of the Sudan

Type of Government

The government of the East African nation of the Sudan is in a transitional phase after decades of unrest and civil war. In 2005 a Comprehensive Peace Agreement (CPA)

between the government and southern rebels mandated a period of power-sharing and local autonomy before new general elections were to be held in 2008–2009. Despite these changes, the central government continues to be an authoritarian, militantly Islamic regime with a strong pro-northern orientation.

Background

Only slightly smaller than Alaska, Texas, and Montana combined, the vast Sudan is bordered by Egypt to the north; Libya, Chad, and the Central African Republic to the west; the Democratic Republic of the Congo, Uganda, and Kenya to the south; Eritrea and Ethiopia to the east; and the Red Sea to the northeast. For the most part, colonial administrators drew these borders with little regard for the region's ethnic, religious, and cultural diversity. As a result, the independent Sudan has never been a unified nation. On the contrary, it contains an enormous variety of distinct, cohesive groups, often with widely divergent interests. Thus nomads and farmers routinely fight over water and grazing rights; neighboring tribes pursue longstanding feuds; fundamentalist Muslims contend with secular Muslims, Christians, and the followers of native African faiths; and light-skinned Arabs and dark-skinned southerners view each other with distrust and antipathy. Each one of these conflicts is dangerous in itself. When they compound and complicate each other, however, as they did for decades in southern Sudan and as they continue to do in the western region of Darfur, the result has been turmoil and bitter civil war.

In ancient times the area of the Sudan was settled by various kingdoms and tribes from the north and the south, each bringing different religions, including Christian and Islamic faiths, to the region. From 1899 to 1956, the year of its independence, the Sudan was a joint colony, or condominium, of the British and Egyptians. For most of this period, the northern and southern regions were separately administered. Provisional constitutions in 1954 and 1956 envisioned the new nation as an Islamic republic, though Christianity and native faiths, not Islam, prevailed in the south.

Government Structure

An Interim National Constitution of 2005, closely based on the peace agreement of the same year, sets out a series of complex arrangements for power-sharing and regional autonomy. Chief of state and head of government in the new Government of National Unity (GNU) is President Omar Hassan Ahmed al-Bashir (1944–), who first came to power in a military coup in June 1989. According to the 2005 arrangement, the office of first vice president must be filled by the leader of the primary rebel movement, the Sudan People's Liberation Army/Movement (SPLA/SPLM). The leader of the SPLM at the time was John Garang (1945–2005), who held this office for only a few weeks before he died in a helicopter crash on

August 1, 2005. His successor in the SPLM, Salva Kiir (1951–), then became first vice president. Despite fears that the sudden death of the charismatic Garang might derail the new government, Kiir's succession went relatively smoothly. The cabinet, known as the Council of Ministers, continues to consist of presidential appointees, most of whom, unsurprisingly, belong to al-Bashir's National Congress Party (NCP).

Legislative powers are vested in a new bicameral body composed of a National Assembly and a Council of States. The old unicameral National Assembly was abolished. Until the elections scheduled for 2008–2009, 450 presidential appointees hold the seats of the new National Assembly. Unlike cabinet ministers, however, assembly appointments are not merely the expression of al-Bashir's personal preferences. On the contrary, the president must follow a precise distribution formula: 234 seats (52 percent) to his own NCP, 126 (28 percent) to the SPLM, 63 (14 percent) to other northern groups, and 27 (6 percent) to other southern groups. The Council of States, meanwhile, consists of 50 members, two from each of the country's 25 states. Apart from the five-year terms specified for both houses, details of the legislative and electoral processes are not yet finalized.

The structure and function of the judicial branch continues to be the subject of fierce debate. Powerful northern elements are still pushing for a nationwide system of sharia courts, which administer traditional Islamic law. The terms of the CPA, however, specifically exempt the southern states from sharia. In the north, however, sharia courts are to have jurisdiction over all individuals, regardless of religion. The capital of Khartoum presents special difficulties in this regard, for many southern refugees and other non-Muslims reside there. A special arrangement for the capital is therefore under discussion. In general, the legal system is a confused patchwork of sharia, English common law, and local tradition, with jurisdictional disputes a common complication in even the most routine cases. The upper courts, however, are relatively well defined, with Appeals Courts, a Supreme Court, and a special nine-member court empowered to review the constitutionality of legislation, government structure, and public policy.

Local affairs are generally handled through the twenty-five regional administrations with direction from the central government. As always, however, the south is an exception, with full autonomy for six years and its own constitution. In 2011, at the end of the autonomous period established in 2005 by the CPA, a referendum on independence is to be held. Oil revenues are split equally with the central government.

Political Parties and Factions

In addition to the NCP and SPLM, the transitional government includes members of the National Democratic Alliance (NDA), a coalition of small, mostly northern groups. Other groups, often based on regional or ethnic ties, exist outside the government, and often in violent conflict with it. One of the most troubling of these is a Uganda-based group, the Lord's Resistance Army (LRA), notorious throughout the region for kidnapping children and forcing them to take up arms. The most prominent of the opposition groups, however, are probably those fighting for greater autonomy in the enormous eastern region of Darfur. Roughly the size of France, Darfur supports a number of distinct rebel organizations, including the Justice and Equality Movement (JEM) and the Sudan Liberation Army/Movement (SLA/SLM). Opposing the rebels are loosely knit, government-backed militias known as the Janjaweed. The situation in Darfur is complex, with alliances shifting almost daily. In general, however, the conflict reflects longstanding animosity between darker-skinned farming peoples, represented by the rebels, and lighter-skinned nomadic peoples, represented by the militias. The extent to which the militias are acting merely as proxies for the government is a matter of debate. Al-Bashir's administration has repeatedly said it has no control over the militias, while the rebels cite reports of fighter planes and helicopter gunships as clear evidence of government involvement. Meanwhile an estimated two hundred thousand people have died since fighting began in 2003, and there is no end in sight.

Major Events

Immediately after gaining independence in 1956, with the new nation formed as an Islamic republic but with Christianity and other religions dominating the south, fighting between north and south broke out almost immediately. The first fifteen years of Sudan's independence were a time of constant turmoil, military rule, and periodic coups. The fighting came briefly to a halt in 1972, with the signing of a peace treaty in Addis Ababa, Ethiopia, between the government and the southern rebel movement known as Anya-Nya. A new constitution was drafted the following year, and a transition to peaceful civilian rule seemed imminent. The subsequent discovery of oil in the south, however, disrupted the fragile balance of power there, with the central government of General Gaafar Nimeiri (1930–) soon deploying troops in oil-rich areas in violation of the 1972 accords. By 1983 Nimeiri's stance had hardened further, as he did away with the treaty entirely and imposed sharia on the whole country. The south responded with a full-scale rebellion under SPLM leader John Garang. Despite several leadership changes—usually by coup—within the central government, the war dragged on for more than twenty years. By the time it ended with the CPA of 2005, the country was in shambles, and more than two million people, mostly civilians, were dead.

Sudan. *Maryland Cartographics*

The Sudan's region of Darfur constitutes another major problem for the nation. In September 2004 Colin Powell (1937–), then U.S. Secretary of State, announced that the Janjaweed's activities in Darfur constituted genocide (the state-sponsored extermination of a racial, ethnic or cultural group). Powell's comments provoked an angry and energetic denial from the Sudanese government, which nonetheless found itself facing increasing international pressure. The United Nations (UN), the European Union, the United States, the African Union (AU), aid organizations, and private citizens around the world demanded that President al-Bashir restrain and disarm the militias. There is some indication that al-Bashir was taken aback by the vehemence of the international outcry. He allowed the deployment of seven thousand peacekeepers from the AU and made some tentative movements toward a negotiated settlement in the area. He continues to reject proposals to replace the beleaguered and ill-equipped AU troops with a larger UN force, however, and the reputation of his government continues to slide.

Sudanese Prime Minister Ismail al-Azhari (center in white) formally proclaiming Sudan's independence on January 6, 1956, in Khartoum. © *Bettmann/CORBIS*

Twenty-First Century

The array of structural and economic problems now facing the Sudan would challenge even the most peaceful of nations. As it is, however, Sudan's conflicts make all other problems many times worse. Years of drought and environmental mismanagement, for example, have made millions of East Africans, including the people of Darfur, dependent on international food aid. Large-scale food delivery is never easy, even when the recipients are living in their own homes and villages. In Darfur, however, relatively few villages still exist. Hundreds have been burnt to the ground, their inhabitants—as many as two million people—driven into a barren, roadless countryside. War, in short, has turned a bad drought into a logistical and humanitarian nightmare.

Few observers are satisfied with the Sudanese government's response to this crisis. Even the most ardent admirer of President al-Bashir must admit that the situation in Darfur has destroyed the considerable store of international good will created by the successful peace treaty of 2005. Whether the reforms envisioned by that treaty will be enough to prod al-Bashir to make further changes is a question of fundamental importance for the nation's future.

BIBLIOGRAPHY

Beswick, Stephanie. *Sudan's Blood Memory: The Legacy of War, Ethnicity and Slavery in South Sudan.* Rochester, NY: University of Rochester Press, 2006.

Iyob, Ruth, and Gilbert M. Khadiagala. *Sudan: The Elusive Quest for Peace.* Boulder, CO: Lynne Rienner Publishers, Inc., 2006.

West, Deborah L., the Belfer Center for Science and International Affairs, and the Program on Intrastate Conflict and Conflict Resolution. *The Sudan: Saving Lives, Sustaining Peace.* Cambridge, MA: Harvard University, 2006.

⊕ Morocco

Type of Government

The North African nation of Morocco is a constitutional, hereditary monarchy. Since independence in 1956, there has been a gradual increase in political participation, a trend reflected in the establishment of a bicameral legislature in 1996. The king nevertheless retains significant power, notably the ability to appoint and remove the prime minister.

Background

Roughly the size of California, Morocco shares a border with Algeria to the east and the disputed territory of the Western Sahara to the south. To the north is the Mediterranean Sea and to the west, the Atlantic Ocean. Only the narrow Strait of Gibraltar separates Morocco from Spain to the north. These geographical features have shaped both Moroccan history and its current political and socioeconomic situations. Fishing and sea-based trade, for example, continue to be important economically, as they have been for centuries. But it is Morocco's proximity to western Europe—the Strait of Gibraltar is only eight miles wide at its narrowest point—that has probably been the single most important factor in the nation's history.

In the early Middle Ages Moroccans played a key role in the Muslim conquest of Spain, while the nineteenth and early twentieth centuries saw increasing European involvement in Moroccan affairs. Spain invaded northern Morocco in 1860; half a century later, in 1912, the French established a protectorate over most of the region (a smaller Spanish protectorate controlled the remainder, apart from a small international zone), maintaining it with increasing difficulty as support for independence grew. In 1956 Morocco signed accords with both France and Spain and became an independent state.

Mohammed V (1910–1961)—who had ruled as sultan of Morocco since 1927 and was the titular leader under the French protectorate—became king of the newly independent Morocco. As the twentieth leader of the Alaoui dynasty, Mohammed V claimed an ancestry stretching back to the Prophet Muḥammad, the founder of Islam. This lineage, expressed in the formal title Commander of the Faithful, is an important source of legitimacy. When Mohammed V died in 1961, his son took the throne as Hassan II (1929–1999). In 1999 Hassan II's son became king, ruling as Mohammed VI (1963–). Among

Mohammed VI's concerns as ruler are relations with neighboring Europe, which are defined by issues like fishing rights, boundary disputes (Spain maintains several tiny enclaves on the Moroccan coast despite strong local opposition), and illegal immigration. Despite the tensions such issues often provoke, the modern kingdom of Morocco is notable for its relatively close ties to the West, including a recent free trade agreement with the United States. These links have brought the monarchy into conflict with anti-Western Muslim fundamentalists, and it is this conflict that dominates Moroccan politics and much of Moroccan life in the twenty-first century.

Government Structure

In Morocco the monarch's extensive executive powers dominate the other branches of government. The king is head of state and commander in chief of the military. He appoints the prime minister and the other members of the cabinet, and he chairs the Supreme Council of the Judiciary, which recommends judges for appointment to the Supreme Court. He determines the course of foreign policy, negotiates treaties, and retains the power to dissolve the legislature and rule by decree. Both successions of kings since Morocco's independence have been smooth. Mohammed VI received extensive training in government and public policy while still crown prince.

The judicial branch uses a mixture of French, Spanish, and Islamic law. In addition to the Supreme Court, a special Constitutional Court reviews the constitutionality of laws and proposed amendments to the constitution itself. In 1962 voters approved Morocco's first constitution, which was based on a royal charter published in 1958. After declaring a state of emergency (an act the constitution specifically allowed him) in response to riots in 1965, Hassan II dissolved the legislature and ruled by decree for several years. A second, short-lived constitution in 1970 brought an end to the state of emergency, only to be replaced by a third in 1972. As of 2007, the 1972 version remained in force, though it was revised in 1992 and amended in 1996 to reflect changes in the legislative structure.

As currently constituted, the legislature is bicameral, with an upper house called the Chamber of Counselors and a lower house called the Chamber of Representatives. The 270 members of the upper house are elected for nine-year terms by municipal councils, trade unions, and other civic organizations. One third of the house faces election every three years. The lower house has 325 seats, which are filled by direct vote for five-year terms. A distinctive feature of the lower house is the reservation of thirty seats for women; for these seats, voters choose from specially prepared lists of female candidates. The king, government agencies, and members of the legislature can all introduce legislation, but the king must sign any bill before it becomes law.

For administrative purposes, Morocco is divided into about fifteen regions, with the precise number depending on a formal resolution of the situation within the disputed territory of the Western Sahara. Directly elected municipal councils handle most local matters.

Political Parties and Factions

Most Moroccan parties belong to one of three informal groupings: the National Entente, a conservative, pro-monarchy faction; a centrist group called the Center Union; and a moderately left-wing group, the Democratic Bloc. A separate bloc consists of several moderate Islamist parties—notably the Constitutional and Democratic Popular Movement—that seek greater adherence to Islamic law and tradition. These moderate parties were allowed to participate in parliamentary elections for the first time in 1997 as part of Hassan II's efforts to draw support away from the banned Islamic extremist wing. The results of this strategy as of 2007 seemed mixed at best, with a single banned group, Justice and Charity, enjoying the support of an estimated 250,000 Moroccans. In May 2006 international newspapers reported that Moroccan authorities had raided several Justice and Charity offices and detained more than three hundred members. The United Nations (UN) and other organizations have repeatedly criticized the monarchy's willingness to use such severe tactics to control political opponents; the government argues in response that radical fundamentalist groups like Justice and Charity are aiming at nothing less than the violent overthrow of the state.

Two other groups deserve mention as disadvantaged but potentially powerful forces in Morocco: women and the unemployed. In some rural areas of Morocco, more than 30 percent of the workforce is unemployed. Many of these are young people with few marketable skills or prospects; as a series of riots in the late 1990s demonstrated, the frustration of the unemployed can erupt into violence at any time. A person or group able to harness and direct this anger would present a formidable challenge to the monarchy. The situation of women has improved markedly in recent years, with their mandated presence in the lower house only the most visible of a wide range of government programs to enhance their skills and strengthen their voice. Women continue to lag behind men socially and economically, however, with an estimated literacy rate of only 40 percent (the rate for men is about 64 percent). Conservative groups have protested a series of legal reforms benefiting women as a violation of Islamic law, and domestic violence remains a serious problem.

All citizens over the age of eighteen are allowed to vote, and the wide range of parties encourages an atmosphere of vigorous debate. The public expression of extremist opinions, however, is not tolerated, and it is illegal to criticize the king, the monarchy, Islam, or the government's handling of the conflict over territory in

King Hassan II of Morocco, 1972. © *Christian Simonpietri/Sygma/ Corbis*

the Western Sahara. In January 2007 a Moroccan court convicted two journalists for publishing jokes judged offensive to the king, Islam, and public morals. They received suspended three-year sentences.

Major Events

In 1975, in what became known as the Green March, an estimated 350,000 Moroccans walked across the border to Western (or Spanish) Sahara, a vast region south of Morocco ruled by Spain, to assert their claim to the territory. The region is barren and sparsely populated but contains rich deposits of phosphates, minerals crucial to fertilizer production and other industrial applications. Spain conceded the territory and in 1976 withdrew and split its former colony in two, giving part to neighboring Mauritania and part to Morocco. A rebel organization known as the Polisario rejected the Spanish partition, easily driving out the Mauritanians and asserting independence. The Moroccans, however, proved more difficult for the Polisario to dislodge.

After roughly fifteen years of sporadic, sometimes intense fighting, Morocco won de facto control over the whole region, and a UN-sponsored cease-fire was achieved in 1991. As of 2007 there was still no permanent solution, however, and violence continued. Morocco considers the area an integral part of its territory and administers it as such. Meanwhile the Polisario has established the Sahrawi Arab Democratic Republic and demands a referendum on the question of independence. Morocco has responded with a plan for local autonomy but rejects the possibility of independence. A diplomatic end to the stalemate is necessary if both parties are to reach their full economic and sociopolitical potential, but several UN missions have failed to reach one, and there are few new diplomatic initiatives on the horizon.

Twenty-First Century

Even more pressing in modern Morocco than the Western Sahara, perhaps, is the problem of Muslim extremism. In the worst of several recent incidents, a total of forty-five people died in a coordinated series of suicide bombings in Casablanca on May 16, 2003. Since that time, suicide attacks have become increasingly common in Morocco, with at least three separate bombings in the first months of 2007. The most powerful of the extremist groups known to be operating in the kingdom is the Algeria-based Salafist Group for Preaching and Combat, recently renamed al Qaeda of the Islamic Maghreb (*Maghreb* is an Arabic term for the desert regions of North Africa). The name change reflects growing consolidation and transnational cooperation in what had been a highly fragmented movement. A number of local Moroccan organizations are affiliated with the Maghreb group, including the Moroccan Islamic Combatant Group, also known by its French acronym of GICM. Authorities believe that GICM members were involved in both the 2003 Casablanca bombing and an attack the following year in Madrid, Spain, that killed 191 people.

Morocco is particularly vulnerable to Muslim extremism because tourists from North America and western Europe are critical to the success of the economy, especially around the Moroccan cities of Marrakech and Casablanca. In the eyes of the extremists, attacking tourists is doubly attractive: It damages a so-called "insufficiently Islamic" state by driving away the tourists needed for that nation's economic growth, and it provides an opportunity to strike directly at the Western powers that the extremists consider implacable enemies of Islam. Moroccan officials are understandably worried, therefore, that their nation may become a magnet for Islamist extremists from all over North Africa and the Middle East. How the monarchy reacts to this threat will largely determine Morocco's course in the future. If increasing security costs divert money from education and economic development, for example, it may prove more difficult to reduce poverty, creating more problems for Morocco in years to come.

BIBLIOGRAPHY

Cohen, Shana, and Larabi Jaïdi. *Morocco: Globalization and its Consequences.* New York: Routledge, 2006.

Howe, Marvine. *Morocco: The Islamist Awakening and Other Challenges.* New York: Oxford University Press, 2005.

Kingdom of Morocco, Ministry of Foreign Affairs and Cooperation. "The Kingdom of Morocco." http://www.maec.gov.ma/en/default.html (accessed May 24, 2007).

⊕ Tunisia

Type of Government

The North African nation of Tunisia is a secular constitutional republic dominated in practice by the president and his political party, the Democratic Constitutional Rally (known by its French acronym, RCD); the latter dominates both halves of the bicameral legislature. The rule of Tunisia's current president, Zine El Abidine Ben Ali (1936–), has been marked by a mixture of progressive initiatives, including legally mandated equality for women, and autocratic policies, notably the harassment and detention of prominent dissidents.

Background

Slightly larger than the state of Iowa, Tunisia shares a border with Algeria to the west and southwest, and Libya to the southeast. Most of its roughly eleven million citizens live within a short distance of the northern or eastern coastlines. Home in antiquity to the powerful state of Carthage, the region fell to Muslim invaders in the seventh century AD. Several centuries of local autonomy followed under the ʾAbbāsids, based in modern Iraq, and other Muslim empires. The last of these was the Ottoman Empire, based in modern Turkey. The Ottomans arrived in 1574 and stayed until 1881, when a French force drove them out and established a protectorate. Local leaders remained in office, but it was the French who determined policy. Supporters of independence began to organize in the early 1900s, finally achieving success in 1956. A single man, Habib Bourguiba (1903–2000), ruled Tunisia as a one-party state for the next thirty years. He won four presidential elections in all, the first in 1959 and the last in 1974, when a constitutional change made him president for life. Amid increasing unrest, Bourguiba's interior minister, Zine El Abidine Ben Ali, seized control in a palace coup. He remained in power as of 2007.

Government Structure

Tunisia's 1959 constitution has been revised several times. Under its terms as of 2007, the president is head of state. He or she is elected by popular vote and serves a renewable term of five years. The president's powers are more extensive than in many other republics. His appointment of

Tunisian leader Habib Bourguiba arriving in Tunis Stadium, on the eve of Tunisia's first parliamentary elections after independence from France in 1956. © *Bettmann/CORBIS*

judges and regional administrators, for example, is rarely subject to judicial scrutiny or legislative approval. A similarly appointed cabinet under the leadership of the prime minister is available to assist the president in his executive functions, but the latter is solely responsible for setting policy. The legislature can override a presidential veto with a two-thirds majority, but the president's ability to rule by decree in an emergency or during a legislative recess limits the effectiveness of the override as a check on the power of the executive branch. Local affairs are in the hands of twenty-four regional governors (again presidential appointees), mayors, elected municipal councils, and a distinctive system of Governmental Councils made up of individuals appointed by the Interior Ministry on the governor's recommendation.

The legislative branch has been bicameral since 2002, when voters approved Ben Ali's plan to create an upper house called the Chamber of Advisors (or Councillors). The president dominates the new chamber, with 41 of its 126 seats occupied by presidential appointees. The remaining 85 seats are elected by various civic and municipal groups, including mayoral associations and trade unions. With the exception of the unions, these organizations are dominated by the RCD. The unions are allotted 14 seats,

but they have chosen not to fill them in protest of the RCD's advantages. Members serve for six years.

The lower house, known as the Chamber of Deputies, has existed since independence, but recent amendments to the constitution have altered its structure. There are currently 189 seats, a number of which are reserved for opposition parties. The remainder are filled by popular vote every five years. As in the presidential elections, all citizens aged twenty and over are eligible to vote, with the exception of military personnel on active duty. The lower house can introduce legislation, but bills introduced by the president have priority.

While Tunisia's constitution calls for an independent judiciary, there have been many plausible charges of governmental interference. In 2001 a judge named Mokhtar Yahyaoui lost his position after publicly protesting what he saw as the judiciary's subordination to the executive branch. Tunisia's highest court, known as the Court of Cassation, hears appeals from parties dissatisfied with decisions reached in the three regional appeals courts. Judges at all levels are chosen by the president after the Supreme Council of the Magistracy has submitted its recommendations. The Supreme Council, in turn, consists of selected appeals- and cassation-level judges and professionals from the Justice Ministry. There are also special courts for military and administrative matters; the latter is empowered to investigate government mismanagement and corruption. In general, Tunisian courts base their decisions on French civil law rather than traditional Islamic law, or sharia. A separate system of sharia courts was closed at the time of independence. The relative weakness of traditional law under the Tunisian system has facilitated the growing prominence of women in the nation's political and economic affairs, with gender equality now legally mandated in most situations. After the 2004 elections, more than 20 percent of the deputies in the lower house were women.

Political Parties and Factions

President Ben Ali's RCD is a descendant of the Neo-Destours ("New Constitutional") Party founded by Habib Bourguiba in 1934, more than two decades before independence. Though Bourguiba, then president for life, introduced a multiparty system in 1981, his party, renamed the Destourian Socialist Party, was so entrenched in public life and the bureaucracy that opposition groups had little chance. In the elections of that year, the National Front, an alliance of Bourguiba's party and a powerful trade union (the General Union of Tunisian Workers, or UGTT) won more than 94 percent of the popular vote. Following his seizure of power in 1987, President Ben Ali announced an amnesty for political prisoners and constitutional reforms to assist the opposition parties. In the first post-coup elections in 1989, however, Ben Ali ran unopposed after his two opponents were arrested, and his RCD won every assembly seat. In the next elections, in 1994, a new law guaranteed a number of seats (originally nineteen, later thirty-four) to opposition parties, with the number allotted to each party to be determined by its percentage of the national vote. Among the most important of the legal opposition parties are the Social Democratic Movement (MDS), the Popular Unity Party (PUP), and the Union of Democratic Unionists (UDU). Another popular group, the Progressive Democratic Party, boycotted the 2004 elections. Most analysts agree, however, that the major Islamist (radical Muslim) party, al-Nahda, would far outdraw the other opposition groups were it not banned under a constitutional provision prohibiting political organizations based on religion, race, region, or language.

Major Events

On April 11, 2002, a truck bomb outside a historic synagogue on the island of Djerba off the coast of Tunisia killed twenty-one people, most of them German tourists. The attack was widely attributed to Khalid Sheikh Mohammed, a leader of the al Qaeda terror network. Spanish police eventually arrested five people in connection with the blast, which badly damaged the tourism industry, a mainstay of the economy and a vital source of foreign earnings. After the bombing, many of the nation's nearly three hundred

thousand tourism workers lost their jobs. Many have since been rehired, but recovery has been slow.

Twenty-First Century

Like many Muslim nations, Tunisia is feeling increasing pressure from radical fundamentalists intent on the overthrow of secular (nonreligious) government. Many Tunisians worry, in particular, that fighters and weapons may be crossing the long, mostly unguarded border with Algeria, where violent clashes between government troops and rebels occur almost daily. Recent events seem to confirm those fears. In January 2007, for example, Tunisia's Interior Ministry reported that its forces had killed twelve rebels and arrested fifteen more in a gun battle south of Tunis, the capital. Several of the rebels had apparently entered the country from Algeria, and credible reports tied the Tunisian fighters to an Algerian organization called the Salafist Group for Preaching and Combat (recently renamed al Qaeda of the Islamic Maghreb), which is fighting for a single Islamic state encompassing all of North Africa (the Maghreb).

The rebels pose two major risks for Tunisia. The first and most obvious is the violence and destabilization that would occur if the insurgency spreads. A second and equally troubling problem, however, involves the government's reaction to the rebellion. Many Tunisians worry that Ben Ali's government may be willing to trade civil rights for security. Recent events seem to confirm this fear as well, with domestic and international human rights organizations reporting the harassment, detention, and torture of several prominent government opponents. Journalists work under heavy restrictions, with at least one man, Kamel El Tayef, convicted in 2002 for, among other charges, "disclosure of illegal facts by way of press." The president has repeatedly declared his determination to improve the nation's human rights record, but there have been few signs of lasting progress.

BIBLIOGRAPHY

Central Intelligence Agency. "Tunisia." *The World Factbook*. https://www.cia.gov/library/publications/the-world-factbook/geos/ts.html (accessed May 15, 2007).

King, Stephen J. *Liberalization against Democracy: The Local Politics of Economic Reform in Tunisia*. Bloomington, IN: Indiana University Press, 2003.

Perkins, Kenneth J. *A History of Modern Tunisia*. New York: Cambridge University Press, 2004.

⊕ Ghana

Type of Government

The West African nation of Ghana is a constitutional republic. The president serves as both chief of state and head of government. A new constitution in 1992 restored multiparty politics after a long period of authoritarian rule, and four different parties currently occupy seats in Parliament.

Background

Slightly smaller than the state of Wyoming, Ghana is bordered by the Ivory Coast to the west, Togo to the east, Burkina Faso to the north, and the Atlantic Ocean to the south. Its population of roughly twenty-three million is a diverse mix of tribes, religions, and at least ten distinct linguistic groups; English is the official language of the government. Ghana contains a variety of valuable natural resources, including gold, hydroelectric power, cocoa plantations, and timber, though the last of these is increasingly threatened by deforestation (tree clearing) and desertification (increasing desert land).

Gold and slaves were the primary attractions for European colonizers, beginning with the Portuguese in the late fifteenth century. By the end of the sixteenth century, the Dutch were firmly entrenched in the area. They lost interest in the region by the end of the nineteenth century, and the British established themselves as solely in control of the area with colonies named the Gold Coast and Togoland. The inhabitants of these colonies, after long struggles with British rule, eventually gained full independence in 1957, and the nation of Ghana was formed. Ghana was the first sovereign, postcolonial nation in sub-Saharan Africa.

Government Structure

The current constitution is notable for its straightforward simplicity. Executive powers are concentrated in the president, vice president, and cabinet. The president and vice president are elected on the same ticket for a maximum of two four-year terms. Parliament must approve all cabinet choices, half of whom must be Parliament members themselves.

The Parliament is a unicameral body of 230 members (increased from 200 in 2004), one from each constituency. Like the president, members are chosen by direct, popular vote for four-year terms by a universal electorate of citizens aged eighteen and over. In time of war, terms may be extended for a maximum of twelve months. All legislation approved by Parliament must be signed into law by the president, who can veto bills in most circumstances.

Judicial powers are vested in the Supreme Court of Ghana, which acts as the court of last appeal. It is also empowered to review the constitutionality of any law or government directive. Ghanaian law is based on British common law; the influence of local tradition is also evident. Though the court system has jurisdiction over all criminal and civil matters, tribal chieftains continue to wield significant, if informal, authority. An example of the government's failure to assert control over tribal matters took place in March 2002, when dozens of people died in a feud between tribal clans in the rural north, with little intervention by police or military personnel.

For purposes of local government, Ghana is divided into ten regional districts and more than one hundred subdistricts.

Political Parties and Factions

As of the 2004 elections, the largest bloc in Parliament was the New Patriotic Party (NPP) of Ghana's President John Agyekum Kufuor (1938–), with 128 seats and a moderately liberal platform. The next largest bloc, with 94 seats, was the National Democratic Congress (NDC), a populist group associated with former President Jerry J. Rawlings (1947–). The socialist People's National Convention (PNC) won four seats, while the Convention People's Party (CPP) founded by former President Kwame Nkrumah (1909–1972) took three. An independent candidate occupied the final seat.

With the exception of traditional tribal groups, there are relatively few factions within Ghanaian society, and religious tensions are notably absent. Though predominately Christian, Ghana has a sizeable Muslim minority (roughly 16 percent of the population), but there have been few Muslim-Christian battles of the sort that has plagued nearby Nigeria. While religious differences are relatively insignificant in Ghana, a larger gulf exists between economic classes. Though the average personal income in Ghana is roughly twice the average in its poorest neighbors, nearly a third of the population lives below the poverty line, and the poorest tenth accounts for only two percent of the nation's income. The result is an ever-widening gap between rich and poor. Many nations face similar situations, but the fragility of Ghana's new democracy formed after a series of coups (see below) makes it particularly vulnerable to the turmoil that often arises out of widespread socioeconomic resentment.

Major Events

The joy Ghanaians felt at gaining independence in 1957 was of short duration, for the administration of Prime Minister (later President) Kwame Nkrumah was soon marked by corruption, increasing economic malaise, and, despite the existence of a constitution, the widespread abuse and detention of dissidents. The notorious Preventive Detention Act of 1958 allowed security forces to detain critics of the regime for five (later ten) years without trial. With the exception of Nkrumah's CPP, political groups were banned. Opposition grew nonetheless, and in 1966 a group of army officers and police personnel staged a successful coup, ousting Nkrumah, dissolving Parliament, and suspending the constitution. Though a new constitution and multiparty politics returned briefly in 1969, another coup brought the army back into power in 1972. This cycle repeated itself in 1979, when the drafting of a new constitution and an anticipated return to multiparty democracy provoked a third, more violent coup. The leader of the coup, Jerry Rawlings, surprised many observers by accepting the new constitution, holding elections, and handing power over to the new government. Two years later, however, Rawlings staged another coup. This time he suspended the constitution and banned opposition parties; the Provisional National Defense Council (PNDC), a seven-member board chaired by Rawlings, exercised all legislative and executive power.

In 1992 increasing domestic and international pressures induced the PNDC to allow the drafting of yet another constitution. This one, the fourth (or fifth, if a transitional constitution in effect at independence is included), remained in force as of 2007. Rawlings won two four-year terms (1992 and 1996) as president under the new multiparty system; despite his authoritarian style, his populist policies had won him many supporters. By law, Rawlings was ineligible for a third term in 2000. John Kufuor took his place after a well-managed and widely admired election, and he won reelection in 2004.

Under Kufuor's rule, Ghana has been a major beneficiary of the recent international movement to reduce the burden of public debt in the developing world. In February 2002 two major lenders, the World Bank and the International Monetary Fund (IMF), offered Ghana a debt relief package worth more than three billion dollars. Three years later those institutions joined another major lender, the African Development Fund, in agreeing to forgive 100 percent of the money owed by Ghana and seventeen other nations. In theory, the money that would have gone overseas to service the debt will now be available for education, health care, environmental protection, economic development, and other pressing needs. The danger, in Ghana and elsewhere, is that those funds will disappear through corruption, mismanagement, and unchecked military spending. The lenders attempted to reduce that risk by making the relief contingent upon continued improvements in governance. To date, Ghana seems to be making satisfactory progress, with a recent survey by the Ghana Statistical Service showing significant reductions in poverty. The nation's poorest regions, however, showed little improvement.

Twenty-First Century

President Kufuor's government enjoys a remarkable reserve of international goodwill. The combination of moderate economic growth and revived democracy is often cited by the international press as an African success story. Ambitious, widely praised plans call for a 50 percent reduction in poverty by 2015, and World Bank predictions suggest that Ghana may soon become the first state in West Africa to reach the tier of middle-income nations. Past wounds are being addressed as well, with President Kufuor's establishment of a Reconciliation Commission to investigate human rights abuses under previous regimes.

Amid these signs of progress, serious problems remain. Rapid population growth and an unceasing migra-tion from rural areas have overwhelmed Ghana's cities, resulting in pollution, crime, and substandard housing. Meanwhile, unemployment, severe deforestation, and toxic mining waste plague the countryside. But Ghana's greatest challenge may be to prevent the chaos and violence that has engulfed many of its neighbors, including Sierra Leone, Liberia, the Ivory Coast, and Togo. The example of the Ivory Coast is particularly foreboding, for it, too, was once considered a success story. Older Ghanaians, of course, need not look abroad to appreciate the danger that political turmoil, coups, and authoritarianism pose to economic and social progress. The universally acknowledged fairness of the last two elections (2000 and 2004), however, is cause for hope.

BIBLIOGRAPHY

Amoah, Michael. *Reconstructing the Nation in Africa: The Politics of Nationalism in Ghana.* London: Tauris Academic Studies, 2007.

Boafo-Arthur, Kwame. *Ghana: One Decade of the Liberal State.* London: Zed Books, 2007.

Hasty, Jennifer. *The Press and Political Culture in Ghana.* Bloomington, IN: Indiana University Press, 2005.

Malaysia

Type of Government

Malaysia is a constitutional monarchy. Every five years the country's Council of Rulers elects a new king for Malaysia from among the heads of the country's ruling families. The king serves as a largely ceremonial head of state, while the prime minister, chosen by parliament from among members of its ruling party, serves as the head of government. Malaysia's bicameral, or two-chambered, parliament consists of a directly elected House of Representatives and an appointed Senate. The judicial branch of government is headed by the Federal Court, the High Court of Borneo, and the High Court of Malaya.

Background

Located in Southeast Asia, Malaysia consists of thirteen states divided by ocean into two distinct regions. West Malaysia is situated on the Malay Peninsula, a landmass jutting out from the southernmost reaches of Thailand. Across 330 miles of the South China Sea is situated East Malaysia, consisting of two states stretched across the northern reaches of the world's third-largest island, Borneo. All thirteen states of Malaysia have access to the sea, which has played a pivotal role in the country's history, especially the development of its ethnic and religious composition.

The ancestors of Malaysia's oldest residents, the Malays, are thought to have migrated from South China and settled the Malay Peninsula sometime around 2000 BC. In the seventh century AD early regional empires established their authority along the peninsular coastline and demanded tribute from ships traversing Malayan coastal waters. As early as the fourteenth century the Strait of Malacca, located off the southwestern coast of the Malay Peninsula, was a strategic stopping point and trading post for ships and cargo traveling the waters between China and India. Early traders, reluctant to complete the long and arduous journey between India and China, are thought to have met and bartered goods in sheltered coves along the coastline. Faint traces of Hinduism from India and Buddhism from China arrived in this manner, and these religions were absorbed early into Malaysian customs and traditions. By the early fifteenth century Muslim traders from India settled in the region and brought with them the religion that continues to be practiced by the majority of Malaysia's people.

Historically, the Malay Peninsula had never been unified politically but rather divided into small kingdoms defined by river valleys and other natural boundaries. Sultans (territorial kings) ruled these kingdoms. The island of Borneo was similarly organized, but even more fragmented. Today's thirteen Malaysian states include nine that were previously ruled as sultanate kingdoms.

Around AD 1400 an exiled Sumatran prince founded the kingdom of Malacca along the straits where the present-day state of Melaka is situated. Traders from India had already introduced the Muslim religion to the area, and the prince converted, afterwards making Malacca a center of the Islamic faith. Malacca prospered with trade and expanded its religious and political influence into the rest of the Malay Archipelago (the many islands that make up the region).

The Portuguese were the first Europeans to lay claim to the shoreline along the Strait of Malacca. Their arrival incited trading rivalries and violent attacks on foreign vessels, causing larger ships to avoid the area in favor of safer waters elsewhere. The Dutch captured the straits and kingdom of Malacca in 1641, but the importance of the area declined. In 1786 the British established their first foothold in Malaysia, when the sultan of the kingdom of Kedah leased the island of Penang to London's East India Company. Sir Thomas Stamford Raffles (1781–1826), a company administrator, went on to found the island city-state of Singapore off the Malay Peninsula's southern tip in 1819. British influence solidified when the Anglo-Dutch Treaty of 1824 gave Britain control of the Malacca Strait. The British collected Singapore, Penang, and Malacca into a political entity called the Straits Settlements in 1826. British oversight resulted in numerous and profound changes to Malayan economic and political life, including the systematic establishment of rubber plantations and tin mines on the Malay Peninsula and the importation of laborers from India and coastal China to work them.

Numerous territorial disputes ensued among the Malayan sultans still exercising local rule over much of the peninsula. British officials took advantage of the unrest in the 1870s and convinced the sultans to let them intervene and establish "advisory" positions among the various royal courts. Eventually the British ruled the peninsular Malay States in all matters except local customs and religion. In 1905 the British persuaded the states of Perak, Pahang, Selangor, and Negeri Sembilan to unite in the Federated Malay States. Later, the Unfederated Malay States of Johor, Perlis, Kelantan, Terenggand, and Kedah emerged, under less direct British control but all under the protection of the British Crown. The additional territories of Singapore, Penang, and Melaka were for all practical purposes British colonies.

Across the South China Sea, the present-day Malaysian states on the island of Borneo—Sarawak and Sabah—remained under the control of the powerful Muslim state of Brunei until the nineteenth century. In 1841 the sultan of Brunei gave the British adventurer Sir James Brooke (1803–1868) land in return for favors and awarded him the title Raja of Sarawak. Brooke and his successors expanded the territory given them. Other sultans to the east also granted land to Europeans. In 1882 the British purchased the other European-held lands and British North Borneo (the modern-day Malaysian state of Sabah) and Sarawak became British protectorates in 1888. Both states were prime producers of rubber and logs.

The Malay Peninsula, Sarawak, and North Borneo were seized and occupied by the Japanese armed forces during World War II. In 1946, when the British returned following the war, they established the Malayan Union. The Union drew together the former Federated and Unfederated States with Penang and Malacca to form a single British Crown colony. All residents of the Malay Peninsula, regardless of ethnicity, were granted Malayan citizenship; English became the colony's official language; and ruling sultans relinquished their sovereignty.

A Malayan independence movement began to emerge after World War II but was complicated by ethnic rivalries. The Malay, Chinese, and Indian communities were deeply divided along religious, linguistic, and ethnic lines. Malays remained concerned that, with independence, the more economically powerful ethnic Chinese and the Indian community, who together made up nearly 50 percent of the total Malayan population, would grow too politically powerful. The Malayan Union collapsed in 1948, largely due to opposition to the sultans' loss of sovereignty and the granting of citizenship to non-Malay residents. The Malayan Union was succeeded by the Federation of Malaya, which contained the same territories but passed some powers back to the individual states and their sultans and revoked many of the rights newly granted to non-Malay residents.

In response to the emerging independence movement, Britain continued to prepare for Malayan independence, and in 1955 the country's first free elections were held. The results brought to power the Alliance, a coalition of three political parties representing the three main Malayan ethnic groups. The British government and the victorious Alliance worked out plans for a Malayan constitution, which provided for a federal state; a parliament of one elected and one appointed chamber; citizenship for non-Malay residents; and preference for Malays in acquiring civil service jobs, scholarships, and licenses. The Federation of Malaya finally obtained independence from Britain in 1957. The eventual Federation of Malaysia, formally established in 1963, included the states of the Malay Peninsula, the island of Singapore, and the states of Sarawak and Sabah on the island of Borneo. After political and economic discord arose, Singapore left the federation in 1965 to establish its own independent republic.

Malaysia is a multilingual country. Its official language is Bahusa Malaysia, a standardized form of the Malay language that has many different local variants and is spoken across the Malay Archipelago. Ethnic Chinese residents of Malaysia speak a variety of dialects of Chinese, including Cantonese and Mandarin. A variety of Indian languages, including Urdu and Hindi, are spoken by the country's ethnic Indian population.

Government Structure

Malaysia's head of state is its king, or Yang di-Pertuan Agong, meaning "paramount ruler." He is elected by the Council of Rulers, a body consisting of the heads of the nine hereditary royal families of Malaysia. To avoid rivalry among Malaysia's royal families, and to spread power among them, the constitution calls for a different king to be elected by the Council of Rulers from among Malaysia's ruling families every five years. The king's role is largely ceremonial, but as in many other constitutional monarchies, his signature is required for all new laws to take affect, and he remains commander in chief of the armed forces.

Like other former British colonies in Southeast Asia, Malaysia's constitution preserves elements of the British style of parliamentary government. Malaysia's parliament is bicameral, totaling 157 members. Members of its House of Representatives are elected by voters aged twenty-one and older. Members of Malaysia's Senate are appointed by the king or elected by members of their respective state legislatures. Parliament introduces legislation, debates and approves new laws, and amends old ones. The majority party in parliament is responsible for choosing Malaysia's prime minister, who is officially appointed by the king. The prime minister chooses cabinet ministers from among the majority party in parliament.

The highest court in the Malaysian judiciary is the Federal Court, which reviews cases on appeal from the High Court of Malaya, in West Malaysia, and the High Court of Borneo, in East Malaysia. Judges are appointed to these highest courts by the king, who acts on the advice of the prime minister. The Malaysian judiciary functions independently, without any governmental or political interference. In some Malaysian states religious courts may decide matters of Islamic law and custom.

Each of the thirteen member states of Malaysia has its own legislature and may decide issues of local importance, such as agricultural and land policy, for itself.

Political Parties and Factions

The Alliance, Malaysia's most influential political organization, emerged out of the independence movement of the post–World War II era. It acquired multiethnic leadership but ensured separate representation of Malaysia's three main ethnic groups by establishing three component parties: the United Malays National Organization (UMNO); the Malayan Chinese Association (MCA); and the Malayan Indian Congress (MIC). The three-party alliance won an overwhelming victory in the Federation of Malaya's first nationwide elections in 1955, just prior to independence. Now known as the National Front (or Barisan Nasional), the Alliance's member parties, particularly UMNO, continue to dominate Malaysian politics. More than twenty other political parties are registered in Malaysia.

Major Events

In 1948, shortly after the end of World War II, the Malayan Union was faced with a pro-Communist rebellion consisting mostly of poor ethnic Chinese determined to replace colonial rule with a Communist government. The twelve-year armed rebellion, which resulted in some eleven thousand deaths, came to be known as the Emergency. The tide of rebellion finally began to turn against the Communists in 1954, but they continued their armed struggle even after the nation's independence in 1957. Violence and Malaya's state of emergency finally came to an end in 1960, but the region's Communists did not formally lay down their arms until 1989.

In 1967 Malaysia joined with Singapore, Indonesia, the Philippines, and Thailand to form the Association of Southeast Asian Nations (ASEAN). Joined by Brunei in 1984 and by Vietnam, Laos, Cambodia, and Myanmar in the 1990s, ASEAN seeks to reduce tensions and increase collaboration among its member nations. Accelerating the region's economic growth, cultural development, and social progress are among its aims. In 1999 ASEAN's member nations agreed to pursue development of a free trade zone in Southeast Asia by eventually eliminating duties on most goods traded in the region. Estimated to take effect in the year 2010 or later, the proposed zone will be the world's largest free trade zone, encompassing some 1.7 billion people and trade valued at $1.2 trillion. In May 2002 ASEAN's ten member countries pledged to form a united front against terrorism in response to the September 11, 2001, terrorist attacks in the United States. They

Tunku Abdul Rahman, the ruler of Malaya, signing the independence agreement in Kuala Lumpur, 1957. © *Hulton-Deutsch Collection/CORBIS*

linguistic differences from damaging their ability to govern. Malaysia's multiethnic society consists of 60 percent ethnic Malays and 26 percent ethnic Chinese, while Indian and indigenous peoples constitute the remainder of the population.

International organizations have criticized Malaysia's human rights record, particularly certain internal security laws that allow the detention of suspects without charge or trial. National security concerns are also sometimes cited as a reason for additional restrictions on the media, which, according to international news organizations, already work under some of the toughest censorship laws in the world. Newspapers must renew publication licenses annually, and these may be suspended or revoked by Malaysia's home secretary.

In 2006 the government unveiled the Vision for 2020, a multibillion-dollar plan to tackle the country's rural poverty, promote economic growth, and help Malaysia join the community of developed nations by the year 2020.

BIBLIOGRAPHY

Andaya, Barbara Watson, and Leonard Y. Andaya. *A History of Malaysia*. New York: Palgrave Macmillan, 2001.
Hooker, Virginia Matheson. *A Short History of Malaysia: Linking East and West*. New South Wales: Allen & Unwin, 2003.
Osborne, Milton. *Southeast Asia: An Illustrated Introductory History*, 5th ed. New South Wales: Allen & Unwin, 1990.

⊕ Guinea

Type of Government

The West African nation of Guinea is nominally a constitutional republic. In practice, however, it is an increasingly authoritarian presidential regime with stringent limits on opposition parties and the press.

Background

Not to be confused with the nearby nations of Equatorial Guinea and Guinea-Bissau, Guinea is roughly the size of Wyoming, with a rapidly growing population of roughly just under ten million as of 2007. No less than three of its immediate neighbors—Liberia and Sierra Leone to the south, and the Ivory Coast to the southeast—have been plagued in recent years by violent unrest and civil war. Conditions in Liberia and the Ivory Coast seem to have stabilized, but large areas of Sierra Leone remain lawless. Guinea also shares borders with Guinea-Bissau and Senegal to the northwest, and Mali to the northeast. To the west is the Atlantic Ocean.

Guinea falls within a broad region called francophone (French speaking) West Africa, and French is the official language. Three events mark the period of French

established a regional security framework, including joint training programs, exchange of intelligence information, and the introduction of national laws governing arrest, investigation, and extradition of suspects.

Southeast Asian financial markets took a sudden, precipitous decline in 1997 when investors lost confidence in a number of Asian currencies and securities. While impact on Malaysia was less significant than on other Asian countries, the economic decline forced the government to scale back or postpone several prominent infrastructure projects.

Twenty-First Century

Computer disk drives, palm oil, rubber, and timber are among the products and exports for which Malaysia is well known. The government's future economic plans call for increased manufacturing of high-value products and an expansion of the services industry. Preservation of Malaysia's valuable tropical forests, particularly on the island of Borneo, is a continuing environmental concern.

In February 2007 Malaysia, along with neighboring Brunei and Indonesia, signed a "Rainforest Declaration" and agreed to conserve forest and other areas that are home to rare species of animals.

Malaysian governments are challenged by their need to keep substantial and divisive religious, ethnic, and colonization. In 1891, after roughly a century as a vaguely defined French protectorate, Guinea was reorganized as a distinct colony. Then, in 1946, the French tried to dissipate growing demands for independence by allowing Guinea's educated elite to send elected representatives to the National Assembly in Paris. The unintended result was the creation of a small framework of experienced, politically savvy leaders determined to break all ties with France. The most prominent of these was a union leader named Sékou Touré (1922–1984), whose Democratic Party of Guinea urged voters in a 1958 referendum to reject continued ties with France. They did so overwhelmingly, and on October 2 of that year, Guinea became the first independent nation in francophone West Africa, with Touré as president. The French, for their part, immediately withdrew their resources and personnel, in many cases destroying files and other needed materials. The chronic mismanagement evident throughout the current government is still traceable in part to the chaotic, often angry atmosphere of 1958.

Government Structure

The Fundamental Law of 1990 serves as Guinea's constitution and provides for the separation of legislative, judicial, and executive powers. The president, who serves as head of state and commander in chief of the military, is elected by direct, popular vote for a seven-year term. If no candidate wins a majority, a new election is scheduled. Both the prime minister, who serves as head of government, and the other members of the cabinet are presidential appointees.

The original version of the Fundamental Law mandated a two-term limit for the president. In 2001, however, President Lansana Conté (1934–) demanded a referendum on a proposed amendment that would remove this limit, thereby enabling him to remain in office. In protest, opposition groups boycotted the referendum, and voter turnout was extremely low as a result. Of the votes that were cast, however, ninety-eight percent approved the change.

Legislative powers are vested in a unicameral body known as the People's National Assembly. Its 114 members are directly elected for five-year terms, with one third representing single-seat constituencies and the remainder chosen from national lists drawn up by each party. As in presidential elections, voting in parliamentary elections is open to all citizens aged eighteen and over.

The judicial system consists of a three-tiered hierarchy. At the bottom are the Courts of First Instance, followed by the Courts of Appeal. At the top is the Supreme Court, with very limited powers to review legislation and government policy. Guinean law is a rapidly evolving mixture of French codes, tribal codes, local tradition, and presidential decree. In 1997, for example, the government announced the establishment of a State

Security Court to oversee the trials of nearly one hundred soldiers involved in a mutiny the previous year. Opposition groups argued in vain that the Fundamental Law made no provisions for such a court.

Political Parties and Factions

Deep tribal divisions split the nation, though Guinea has not yet seen the level of violence such rifts have caused elsewhere in West Africa. There are three major tribal groups, each with its own language: the Puehl (the largest), the Malinke, and the Soussou. Former President Touré systematically favored his own group, the Malinke; current President Conté quickly reversed the situation when he seized power, initiating discriminatory policies against the Malinke while favoring his own tribe, the Soussou. Though many Malinke are prominent members of the opposition, there are as yet few political parties formed exclusively along tribal lines. The largest of the opposition parties in the Assembly is the Union for Progress and Renewal (UPR), which won twenty seats in the 2002 elections. President Conté's Party for Unity and Progress (PUP), meanwhile, holds eighty-five seats. As in other recent elections, however, two of the most popular opposition groups, the Rally for the Guinean People (known by its French acronym of RPG) and the Union for Republican Power (UFR) declined to participate.

Major Events

The time of Guinea's independence in 1958 was fraught with chaos. In retrospect, Touré's refusal to incur any obligation to France or its allies was a serious mistake, because it deprived the new nation of desperately needed funds and expertise. Grandiose, ill-advised development schemes and widespread corruption soon aroused deep resentment, but Touré's authoritarian tactics prevented organized opposition and he remained in sole control for more than twenty-five years. When he died in 1984, a military coup to oust his associates enjoyed broad support. Among the coup's leaders was Conté, who soon eliminated potential rivals by turning ruthlessly against his fellow conspirators. International pressure eventually forced Conté to allow popular, multiparty elections, and he remains in power as of 2007 not as a military strongman but as a thrice-elected president. Many domestic and international observers have questioned the legitimacy of his victories, however, as all three (in 1993, 1998, and 2003) came after elections compromised by systematic fraud. In addition, the 2003 elections took place without the participation of several major opposition parties, who urged their supporters to boycott the vote as a sham. Conté reportedly received 95 percent of the votes cast, but low voter turnout suggests that the opposition's boycott, not the president's popularity, was primarily responsible.

The Guinea government was accused of more wrongdoings when in October 2002 the international press reported the discovery of several mass graves, each containing hundreds of bodies, near the Guinea town of Kindia. The victims are believed to have died on a single night in October 1971 at the hands of forces loyal to Touré, who was then moving ruthlessly against dissidents and critics. Guineans today often allude to Touré's campaigns of repression with a reference to Boiro Camp, a National Guard installation where many of the worst incidents took place. After the Kindia graves were discovered, a group called the Children of the Victims of Boiro Camp announced their intention to bring a suit for wrongful death before the International Court of Justice (ICJ) in the Dutch city of The Hague. Guinea has accepted ICJ jurisdiction "with reservations," so such a suit is theoretically possible. Given the group's announced desire to subpoena President Conté, however, there is little chance of securing the current administration's cooperation.

Civil unrest has been a constant feature of Guinean life since independence. In some respects, however, the situation has worsened over the last decade. The fighting that began to engulf Sierra Leone, the Ivory Coast, and Liberia in the late 1990s, for example, drove hundreds of thousands of refugees into Guinea; some estimates put the number as high as half a million. Many—perhaps most—have since returned home, but a chaotic atmosphere still prevails in many areas, particularly near the Liberian border. Rebel forces from Liberia almost certainly entered Guinea with the refugees, and most of the considerable violence reported on Guinea's side of the border is probably attributable to those rebels. The actual situation remains unclear, however, in part because of the Guinean government's restrictions on journalists. Particularly unclear is the extent, or even the existence, of a purely Guinean rebel movement.

Twenty-First Century

Guinea faces a number of severe problems. Less than 36 percent of adults can read, and the life expectancy for both men and women is only about fifty year of age. The crumbling infrastructure is already inadequate, but the population continues to grow at one of the fastest rates in the world. Environmental degradation, particularly deforestation, is severe, and recent inflation has put a variety of basic necessities out of the reach of most families. Such challenges would test even the most open, compassionate, and farsighted leader. President Conté, unfortunately, has not often displayed those qualities. His response to a series of nationwide strikes in February 2007, for example, was to declare martial law, thereby granting his security forces the ability to detain anyone indefinitely. Similarly, he has reacted to the publication of unfavorable news by ordering the arrests of the journalists involved. This kind of repression may restore order temporarily, but it will likely not strengthen his position. Widespread, well-documented human rights abuses have brought international condemnation and the imposition of severe economic penalties; in 2003, for example, the

International Monetary Fund (IMF) canceled a comprehensive debt-relief package that has helped other poor nations dramatically improve living conditions. Guinea, meanwhile, continues to slip backwards.

BIBLIOGRAPHY

Fung, Karen, and Stanford University Libraries. "Africa South of the Sahara: Guinea." http://www-sul. stanford.edu/africa/guinea.html (accessed June 1, 2007).

International Crisis Group. "Stopping Guinea's Slide." http://www.crisisgroup.org/home/index.cfm? id=3509&l=1 (accessed June 1, 2007).

Norwegian Council for Africa. "The Index on Africa: Guinea." http://afrika.no/index/Countries/ Guinea/index.html (accessed June 1, 2007).

⊕ Republic of Cuba

Type of Government

The Republic of Cuba has been, since the adoption of its constitution in 1976 a socialist republic, governed by the National Assembly People's Power, a legislative body that selects a Council of State as the nation's executive branch. The President of the Council of State is the head of state and head of government of Cuba. Since 1976 the president has been Fidel Castro, who has been Cuba's ruler in name or fact since the Revolution of 1958–59.

Background

The island nation of Cuba is located at the northern rim of the Caribbean Sea, less than 100 miles south of Florida, immediately north of Jamaica and west of the island of Hispaniola. The island has, by far, the largest land mass in the Caribbean, accounting for about half the land in the West Indies. Cuba was one of the islands explored by Christopher Columbus (1451–1506) on his first trip to the New World, in 1492. At that time the island's native inhabitants were the Ciboney and Taíno Native American tribes.

The first European settlement in Cuba came in 1511, when the Spanish conquistador Diego Velázquez de Cuéllar (1465–1524) established a colony on the eastern end of the island. The Spaniards soon forced the natives into service; as in other areas of the Caribbean and South and Central America, the native population soon dwindled due to the new settlers' abuse, as well as the exotic diseases the Spaniards brought with them from Europe. By approximately 1523, the colonists began importing slaves from Africa to maintain the island's labor pool for the hard work of growing coffee and sugar cane.

Cuba's proximity to Florida and the Gulf of Mexico made it an ideal hub for Spain's activities in the region. Conquistadors such as Hernando de Soto (c. 1500–1542) and Hernán Cortés (1485–1547) embarked on their assaults on the mainland from Cuba, and when their expeditions were successful, the boats loaded with riches would stop in Cuba on their way back to Spain.

Spain's power began to ebb in the late eighteenth century, and throughout the nineteenth century its empire in the New World disintegrated. By 1819 the Spanish were forced out of Florida and had lost control of their colonies in Mexico and South America, but they maintained control over Cuba.

In October 1868 the Ten Years' War, a guerilla conflict between Spanish loyalists and Cuban nationalists, began. This revolutionary movement was ultimately stifled, but not before it motivated a young Cuban intellectual living in exile, the poet and journalist José Martí (1853–1895), to begin planning his own independence movement. Establishing a base of operations in New York, Martí spent more than a decade marshalling his forces and building up the Cuban Revolutionary Party (PRC) in preparation for a new war against Spain.

In February 1895, Martí issued his call to arms, and his force of expatriate rebels landed in Cuba. Less than three months into the war, however, Martí was killed in a battle with Spanish forces at Dos Rios. The rebels continued the war without him, making little headway in three years of fighting.

Martí's war led indirectly to Cuba's independence from Spain. In February 1898 the U.S. battleship *Maine*—docked in Havana harbor to protect American citizens who might get caught in the fighting—was rocked by a mysterious explosion, leading the United States to declare war on Spain in what became known as the Spanish-American War. Unlike the Cuban revolutionary efforts, the conflict between the United States and Spain was resolved rather quickly, leaving the United States in control of Spain's colonies: Puerto Rico, Guam, the Philippines and Cuba.

Liberation by the United States was not the independence from Spain that Martí's nationalists had had in mind. The American occupiers set up a provisional Cuban government almost immediately, and they also made many improvements to the island's sanitation and infrastructure. By 1901 Cuba had a new constitution establishing a republican government; however, independence from the United States came with strings attached. The new constitution gave the United States the right to establish a naval base on the island and permission to intervene in Cuba's affairs as it saw necessary. These provisions, along with a noteworthy increase in American business interests on the island, fostered resentment among Cubans toward their liberators.

In the two decades after independence, the United States staged military interventions to suppress rebellions and protect U.S. business interests in 1906–09, 1912, and 1920. After this period of instability, the nation came under the rule of the dictator Gerardo Machado y Morales (1871–1939) from 1925 to 1933, and then under the control of Colonel Fulgencio Batista (1901–1973), the soldier who led the coup against Machado's administration. Batista controlled Cuba through a string of puppet presidents until he ran for president himself in 1940. Batista was ousted in the 1944 elections by a former political ally, only to restore himself to power eight years later in a military coup.

Batista's 1952 coup prompted a young attorney and fledgling politician, Fidel Castro Ruz (1927–), to form his own revolutionary movement. On July 26, 1953, a small force led by Castro attacked an army barracks near Santiago de Cuba. The attack was a total fiasco—about half of Castro's guerillas were killed, the other half captured—but Castro made such a spectacle of his subsequent trial that it earned him international fame. Freed from jail through a general amnesty in 1955, Castro was exiled to Mexico, where he gathered supporters for another attempt to depose Batista. This group—which included Castro's brother, Raúl (1931–), and Argentine revolutionary Ernesto "Che" Guevara (1928–1967)—established itself in the Sierra Maestro Mountains in December 1956. The rebels' presence drove the Batista administration to increasingly oppressive measures, which eventually eroded the regime's international support. Even the United States, with whom Batista had enjoyed good relations, began to turn away from him. On New Year's Eve 1958 Batista abdicated his office, leaving Castro's rebels in control of the government.

Government Structure

In the immediate aftermath of the revolution, Castro's coalition of opponents to the Batista regime ruled by decree. During this period, surviving Batista loyalists were summarily executed and private property was expropriated, with Castro acting as the interim state's premier—essentially, an autocratic head of government.

Cuba did not become a Marxist state, however, until 1961, when Cuba's deteriorating relationship with the United States spurred Castro to seek the sponsorship of the Soviet Union, which was the leading proponent and exemplar of communism, an ideology developed by the German political philosopher Karl Marx (1818–1883). Castro's declaration of Marxism did not change the Cuban government's ways of doing business, except to the extent that industries which had merely been controlled by the Castro regime were now officially nationalized.

A more formal structure for the Castro government was created by the constitution of 1976. Under that constitution, Cuba's legislative power is vested in the National Assembly of People's Power. Since 1993, the members of the Assembly have been directly elected to five-year terms in national elections with universal suffrage for all Cubans over the age of 16—as long as they have never applied to emigrate from Cuba. However, elections occur within a single-party system—in the

2003 elections, all of the candidates approved by the PCC won seats in the Assembly.

The Assembly, in turn selects a thirty-one member Council of State, which can exercise legislative power between sessions of the Assembly. The Council of State's president is both head of state and the head of government in Cuba. Six of the remaining members of the Council of State are selected to serve as vice presidents to the president, who has, since the institution's inception, been Castro. In addition to being members of the Council of State, the president and vice presidents also head Cuba's Council of Ministers, which is in charge of the executive branch of the government.

The judicial branch of the Cuban government is headed by the People's Supreme Court. Although the judiciary is technically an independent branch of government, all judges are selected by the National Assembly. Trials in Cuba are not heard by juries, but rather by mixed panels of judges composed of certified professional judges and lay judges.

Political Parties and Factions

The only legally sanctioned political party in Cuba is the Cuban Communist Party (PCC). The PCC effectively controls the government through the National Assembly. On a local level, the party exercises control over the people of Cuba through Committees for the Defense of the Revolution (CDR). These committees function on a neighborhood level, reporting "counterrevolutionary" activity, and often take it on themselves to harass or intimidate any citizens suspected of disloyalty to the regime.

A substantial, and very politically active, Cuban expatriate community exists in the United States, particularly in the state of Florida. This community is extremely active in U.S. politics, influencing America's policies toward Cuba and supporting economic sanctions and trade embargoes against the Castro regime. The expatriates also influence events within Cuba, providing financial support to family members left behind on the island and giving aid to the many illegal dissident organizations operating within Cuba.

Major Events

Castro's Cuba soon ran afoul of the island nation's most powerful neighbor, the United States. The United States initially granted the Castro regime diplomatic recognition, but throughout 1959 and 1960 diplomatic relations deteriorated as the Cuban government increasingly confiscated property owned by American citizens and corporations, while the U.S. government retaliated by cutting sugar imports from Cuba, until, by October 1960, Cuba had nationalized all American property on the island and the United States had imposed a trade embargo against Cuba. Cuba increasingly came to depend upon assistance from the Soviet Union, first as a trade partner, and later as an ally against the United States.

Cuban President Fidel Castro addressing new schoolteachers on the opening of the school year in 2003. © *Claudia Daut/Reuters/Corbis*

In January 1961 the U.S. government cut off diplomatic relations with Cuba, and in April, a U.S.-supported group of Cuban expatriates invaded the island. The invasion was planned by the U.S. Central Intelligence Agency during the administration of Dwight Eisenhower (1890–1969), but put into action shortly after the inauguration of his successor, John F. Kennedy (1917–1963). Kennedy's administration was more concerned than his predecessor's about negative publicity should their involvement in the invasion become public. When the force of 1,500 expatriates landed at the Bay of Pigs, they did so without promised American air support to protect them from the Cuban air force. In a matter of days the invasion was repelled and the expatriates were captured.

The failed invasion deepened the relationship between Cuba and the Soviet Union. Within eighteen months of the invasion, the Soviets had built nuclear missile installations on Cuba, precipitating the international incident known as the Cuban Missile Crisis. For two weeks in October 1962 the United States and Soviet Union threatened each other with nuclear war while Cuba was "quarantined" by the U.S. Navy. Disaster was averted when the Soviets agreed to withdraw their weapons in return for the dismantling of similar American missile installations in Turkey, along with a commitment that the United States would not invade Cuba.

Even after the crisis was averted, Cuba continued to be an important strategic asset to the Soviet Union, and the Soviets subsidized the Cuban economy by purchasing Cuban sugar at above-market rates. In return, Cuban soldiers fought in Soviet-sponsored wars around the globe during the 1970s and 1980s. For example, Cuban military assistance was key to the victory of the communist Popular Movement for the Liberation of Angola (MPLA) in 1976.

In the early 1990s, however, the disintegration of the Soviet Union meant an end to Cuba's subsidies and led to the collapse of the Cuban economy. Relations with the United States did not improve, and the U.S. embargo continued, as did the Castro regime's repression of dissent within Cuba.

Twenty-First Century

The Cuban economy has never recovered from the loss of Soviet sponsorship, thanks in large part to the U.S. trade embargo. There is severe rationing of food for most of the population, and after a brief period of openness in the 1990s, the government has spurned foreign investment.

Going forward, the biggest questions surrounding Cuba have to do with its leader since 1959, Fidel Castro. As Castro approaches his 80s, many wonder whether the Cuban government will be sustainable after he dies. Castro's participation in Cuba's day-to-day governance has been greatly curtailed since he underwent intestinal surgery in August 2006; nonetheless, he continues to be Cuba's leader, and the party leadership continues to insist that he will stand for reelection despite his infirmities. Castro has concentrated so much of the regime's power upon himself, and stifled internal opposition so effectively, that his eventual death may leave a vacuum that no one in his government will be able to fill.

BIBLIOGRAPHY

Hudson, Rex A., editor. *Cuba: A Country Study.* Washington, D.C.: Federal Research Division, Library of Congress, 2002.

Zanetti, Oscar, and Frank Wright. *Sugar and Railroads: A Cuban History, 1837–1959.* Chapel Hill, NC: University of North Carolina Press, 1998.

The Web Site of the Government of the Republic of Cuba, http://www.cubagob.cu/ingles/default.htm (accessed August 6, 2007).

⊕ Antarctic Treaty Summary

Type of Government

Nearly ten times the size of Alaska, the continent of Antarctica is a vast expanse of ice sheets, glaciers, and floating ice shelves. Apart from scattered scientific research stations and transient tourists, it is uninhabited. A reliable system of governance is nonetheless necessary, because its unique climatic and geographic features make it critically impor-

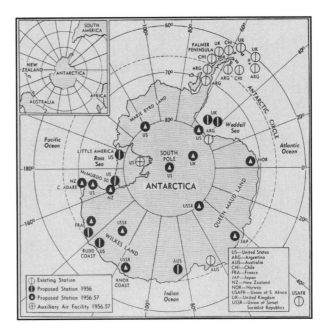

Map of international research stations in Antarctica, 1956. © *Bettmann/CORBIS*

tant to a wide variety of scientific disciplines, including climatology, geology, biology, and oceanography. To ensure that scientists of all nations are able to conduct their research in an atmosphere free of political intrigue and commercial exploitation, twelve nations signed the Antarctic Treaty in 1959, creating a form of governance called the Antarctic Treaty Summary. Several other nations have since joined the agreement, and a separate protocol mandating measures for the preservation of the continent's ecology was added in 1991.

Background

The first humans to glimpse Antarctica are thought to have been a group of seal hunters in 1820. Despite heavy use of the shipping channel around Cape Horn, roughly six hundred miles away at the southern tip of South America, few sea captains were rash enough to venture farther south; even in the summer months, the risk of collision with floating ice was enormous. A few tentative explorations took place over the next hundred years, but large-scale expeditions did not become feasible until the technological advances that happened during World War I. It was, above all, the development of long-range aircraft that opened the continent to scientific study and to territorial claims by a variety of nations, including France and Great Britain. Other countries, notably the United States and the Soviet Union, conducted expeditions but generally refrained from asserting territorial claims. The most notorious claim was made in 1939, when a German aerial expedition claimed an extensive territory for Adolf Hitler (1889–1945) and the German Reich.

The British Antarctic Survey research station at Halley. Antarctica is populated primarily by researchers sponsored by countries that have signed the Antarctic Treaty. *© Robert Weight; Ecoscene/CORBIS*

World War II had relatively little impact on Antarctica. By the 1950s, however, cold war rivalries and a growing awareness of the continent's scientific importance had brought new claims by Chile, Argentina, Australia, and others, as well as a wave of building activity. The culmination of this period of energy and enthusiasm was the declaration of 1957–1958 as an International Geophysical Year (IGY), an ambitious, multinational research program with a strong emphasis on Antarctica. The IGY proved a model of international cooperation in the sciences, and its success prompted widespread awareness of the need to preserve the continent for scientific purposes. In 1958 U.S. President Dwight D. Eisenhower (1890–1969) invited eleven other nations with major interests in the region to begin work on a comprehensive treaty. Negotiations began in June of that year, and the treaty was signed on December 1, 1959. Following ratification by all twelve parties (the United States, the United Kingdom, the Soviet Union, South Africa, Argentina, Chile, New Zealand, Australia, Belgium, France, Japan, and Norway), the treaty became binding in June 1961. A number of other nations have since joined the agreement, including India, Poland, and Brazil.

Government Structure

Terms of the treaty are valid for fifty years and cover all areas south of sixty degrees latitude with the exclusion of the high seas. The first provisions call for only peaceful, nonmilitary uses of the area and for cooperation in research, including the exchange of data, personnel, and equipment. The parties also agree not to obstruct or interfere with another's research, though each has the right to inspect the facilities of the others. Disputes are to be settled through negotiation, arbitration, or, in the last resort, by appeal to the International Court of Justice. The testing of nuclear weapons and the dumping of nuclear waste are banned. There are also provisions for the review and modification of the original agreement, notably a review to be held after thirty years if one of the parties requests it.

Finally, there is the matter of territorial claims. For these the treaty essentially preserves the status quo, prohibiting new claims but leaving earlier ones in place. Because these claims fall within a gray, unadjudicated area of international law, the treaty's drafters wisely made no attempt to resolve them, instead deferring the issue to the jurists of a later generation.

Political Parties and Factions

Though political parties do not exist, differences of opinion do arise with some regularity. The most significant of these occurred in 1988, when thirty-three nations signed a Convention on the Regulation of Antarctic Mineral Resource Activities, or CRAMRA. Mining and other types of resource extraction fell outside the scope of the 1959 treaty, but technological advances in the interim had reduced the obstacles Antarctica's forbidding environment posed to these activities. CRAMRA imposed restrictions on mining but did not prohibit it. Reaction was swift and vehement, with widespread feeling that any mining was a violation in spirit (though not in letter) of the original treaty. As a result, CRAMRA was rescinded. Superseding it in 1991 was a new protocol on environmental protection, Article VII of which bans any mineral activities unrelated to scientific research.

Major Events

Global climate change poses a major challenge to the treaty nations, because it threatens the unique environment the treaty seeks to preserve. Antarctica's landscape has always been in flux, as icebergs break off into the sea and ice shelves melt and reform. Recently, however, scientists have noted a dramatic increase in melting activity. In 2005, for example, satellite photos revealed that surface snow had melted over an area the size of California. May 2007 marked the beginning of an International Polar Year (IPY), an event similar to the IGY of 1957–1958. The focus of the IPY, however, is squarely on climate change.

Twenty-First Century

Over the past fifty years, scientists have noted a rise of two and a half degrees Celsius in the average temperature of the Antarctic Peninsula, the continent's most accessible region. Scientists note that this warming trend, moreover, seems to be increasing in speed and intensity. If Antarctica's ice—roughly ninety percent of the world's total—continues to melt into the ocean, the implications for the continent, and for plant and animal life around the globe, are ominous.

BIBLIOGRAPHY

Antarctic Treaty Secretariat. "Antarctic Treaty Secretariat." http://www.ats.aq/ (accessed May 26, 2007).

Intergovernmental Panel on Climate Change. "Intergovernmental Panel on Climate Change." http://www.ipcc.ch/ (accessed May 26, 2007).

International Polar Year. "IPY 2007–2008." http://www.ipy.org/ (accessed May 26, 2007).

Introduction to The End of Colonialism (1960–1988)

Two world wars and a crippling economic depression within thirty years left European society exhausted and its military forces depleted. Western Europe recovered economically but could no longer maintain the colonial structures through which it had exerted global power. After World War II nationalist movements for self-determination won victories worldwide, and the world's political map rapidly transformed as former colonies and protectorates became independent states. The United Nations, co-founded by 51 countries in 1945, grew to 144 member states by 1975.

Some countries, such as the island nations of the Pacific Ocean and the Caribbean Sea, achieved a peaceful transition to self-government. In much of Africa, however, freedom arrived through armed struggle. Algeria gained independence after eight bitter years of war with France. Many African nationalist leaders, such as Jomo Kenyatta (c. 1894–1978) of Kenya and Patrice Lumumba (1925–1961) of the Congo, were jailed for their activities. The tide was turning toward independence, however, and between 1955 and 1965, most of the African continent escaped colonialism's chains.

Political liberation, sadly, was only the first hurdle in Africa's recovery from centuries of foreign interference. The new nations faced daunting problems: revenue shortages, external debt, disputes over borders drawn by the colonial powers, inexperience with governing, ethnic conflicts, civil wars, and famine. A number of leaders turned dictatorial and assassinated their opponents. Some corrupt authorities amassed personal fortunes while neglecting their responsibilities. Political stability and economic development continued to elude much of sub-Saharan Africa into the twenty-first century, while the AIDS pandemic ravaged the continent.

As colonialism collapsed in these decades, the Cold War between the United States and the Soviet Union shaped the evolving world picture. Many newly independent states embraced the free markets and democratic institutions promoted by the United States. Others adopted the communist worldview of the Soviet Union or the People's Republic of China, emulating their model of one-party rule with a state-directed economy. In Vietnam Communist forces led by Ho Chi Minh (1890–1969) defeated the French, then the Americans, in a thirty-year war costing three million lives. In neighboring Cambodia, the Maoist Khmer Rouge rebels, led by the infamous Pol Pot (1928–1998), took power in 1975. More than one million Cambodians went to their deaths before a Vietnamese invasion ousted the oppressive Khmer Rouge in 1979.

Conflict continued to brew in the Middle East, due to the displacement of Palestinians by the formation of Israel. Israel defeated Egypt, Syria, Jordan, and Iraq in the Six-Day War of 1967, seizing and occupying territories that remained under dispute into the twenty-first century. Egypt and Syria started the next Arab-Israeli war in 1973, on the Jewish holiday of Yom Kippur. This time, the oil-producing Arab states imposed an embargo on the United States and Israel's other supporters. The "oil shock" drove up the price of petroleum on world markets, revealing to the industrial West the dangers of dependence on foreign energy sources.

An Islamic revolution in Iran drove the country's autocratic, Western-backed leadership from power in 1979. Iran's new leader, the Ayatollah Ruhollah Khomeini (1900?–1989), symbolized the face of Islamic confrontation with the West. Iran's revolution also fractured its relations with the secular government of Iraq, led by Saddam Hussein (1937–2006), and the two Persian Gulf nations warred from 1980 to 1988. The United States quietly armed both sides of the conflict, then backed Hussein more openly. The support would be short-lived.

The End of Colonialism (1960–1988)

⊕ Republic of Cameroon

Type of Government

By constitution Cameroon is a multiparty republic. In reality, however, it operates as a presidential regime, in which the executive branch is dominant. The president and members of the unicameral legislature are chosen by direct, popular vote. The judicial branch is constitutionally independent but is functionally subordinate to presidential influence.

Background

Archaeological evidence suggests that humans have been living in what is now Cameroon continuously for at least fifty thousand years. The first known inhabitants of the region were members of the Bantu ethno-linguistic group and Baku Pygmies. In subsequent centuries a succession of migratory groups lived in the region. Then, in the fifth century AD, the Sao Kingdom, which originated near the Nile River, conquered the native tribes and established the first major empire. It lasted until the fifteenth century, when it was overtaken by the Kotoko Kingdom.

Portuguese explorers visited Cameroon during the reign of the Kotoko, forming economic relationships with the kings but no lasting presence in the region. The Bornu Empire conquered the Kotoko in the 1800s and transformed Cameroon into a predominantly Muslim nation. The Islamic rulers established a thriving slave trade with Portugal and other European nations.

By the mid nineteenth century, British, Portuguese, and French missionaries had established permanent settlements in Cameroon. In 1884 German Chancellor Otto von Bismarck (1815–1898), who had overseen the unification of Germany, decided to expand his country's colonial territories to Africa. He negotiated with Britain, Denmark, France, and Spain to divide up Africa for colonization, obtaining the "rights" to the Cameroon coast. He then dispatched explorer and statesman Gustav Nachtigal (1834–1885) to negotiate with the Bornu and to establish the first German colony.

The Germans expanded inland, setting up military installations and agricultural communities. Some of the native tribes resisted the occupation but were overwhelmed by the superior German military; by 1890 Germany had eliminated the last pockets of resistance. In 1914, at the start of World War I, Britain and France united against Germany and forced the Germans to vacate their colonies in Africa. By 1916 the allied powers had gained control of Cameroon.

Britain and France divided Cameroon into two parts, with Britain retaining what is now Nigeria and a small strip of Cameroon between the Sea of Chad and the coast, while France controlled the remaining territory. In the 1919 Treaty of Versailles, which ended World War I, Germany officially relinquished its African colonies. The British and the French met with the League of Nations to legitimize their territorial agreements and formally divided Cameroon into two administrative territories.

Though both Britain and France experienced economic gains from territorial Africa, neither nation was able to maintain control over the native populace. The independence movement grew quickly in French Cameroon, which was the larger and more economically prosperous of the two. Though the French altered their territorial government to allow greater native participation, many Cameroonians believed that the French were exploiting local labor and resources. By the 1940s work boycotts, protest gatherings, and political lobbies were being organized. The Union des Populations du Cameroun (Union of the Peoples of Cameroon), or UPC, became the most radical pro-independence group during the 1950s.

The French refused petitions for independence, prompting more radical action and eventually armed rebellion. When the independence war began in 1955, the French officially designated the UPC as an illegal terrorist organization. As they tried to destroy the UPC, other independence organizations began to rise, and it soon became clear to the French that independence was inevitable.

In 1958 Amadou Ahidjo (1924–1989), who had served within the colonial government as an emissary to France, helped found the Union Camerounaise (Cameroonian Union), or UC, a moderate independence organization that favored maintaining strong economic and social ties to France. Ahidjo established the first Republic of Cameroon in 1956, though the French had not formally relinquished control. Independence was "granted" by France in 1960, after which Ahidjo remained the leader of the new government.

Although the independence movement in British Cameroon never turned violent, by late 1960 the British government had decided to relinquish its control. Hoping to avoid a civil war, Britain sponsored a plebiscite in 1961 that allowed the British Cameroonians to determine their political allegiance—they could either join the newly established Republic of Cameroon (former French Cameroon) or become part of Nigeria. The vote was split, with the northern portions of the territory joining Nigeria and the southern region becoming part of the Republic of Cameroon.

Government Structure

Cameroon is divided into ten provinces, each headed by a provincial governor. All local leaders are appointed and funded by the central government. A revised constitution, adopted in 1996, provides for multiparty elections and a stronger legislative system, but it still grants most of the power to the executive branch.

According to that constitution, the president serves as head of state and commander of the armed forces while the prime minister serves as head of government. In practice, the prime minister is subordinate to the president and functions as the president's chief deputy. The president, who is elected by direct, popular vote to serve up to two terms of seven years, has the power to appoint and dismiss members of the judiciary, provincial governors, military leaders, sixty-four cabinet ministers, and executive officers of approximately one hundred corporations that are wholly or partly owned by the state. The president is not bound to confer with the legislature before restructuring the government and has the freedom to utilize emergency powers and presidential degree without oversight. The 1996 constitution abolished censorship, but the president still maintains control over television, radio, and print media and has the authority to shut down media organizations.

The unicameral National Assembly has one hundred eighty members, who are elected by direct, popular vote for five-year terms. They can run for re-election. The president has the authority to extend or dissolve legislative terms. Legislation originates in both the executive and legislative branches and is passed by a simple majority vote in the legislature. The president has the power to veto legislation. When the National Assembly approved constitutional reforms in 1966, it called for the establishment of a one-hundred-member Senate and a new system of state councils. As of 2007 the government had not yet fulfilled those constitutional requirements.

The Ministry of Justice, which is part of the cabinet, is in charge of the judicial branch. Justices of the Supreme Court are appointed directly by the president with the consultation of the minister of justice. The Supreme Court functions as a council of presidential advisers and has little power to defend constitutional law without presidential approval. Below the Supreme Court are the high courts, with justices appointed by the National Assembly. They supervise the nation's regional and district courts.

In addition to the central and provincial governments, Cameroon maintains an informal system of local leadership based on tribal and ethnic affiliation. The federal government sometimes provides stipends as a way of keeping local leadership responsive to central authority.

Political Parties and Factions

The Rassemblement Démocratique du Peuple Camerounaise (Cameroon People's Democratic Movement), or RDPC, is Cameroon's dominant political party and represents the French-speaking majority in Cameroon. The RDPC evolved from the Cameroonian Union. President Paul Biya (1933–), Prime Minister Ephraïm Inoni (1946–), a majority of the National Assembly, and 44 percent of the executive ministers are members of the RDPC.

The Front Social-Démocratique (Social Democratic Front), or SDF, is the leading opposition party. Formed by politician and business leader Ni John Fru Ndi (1941–), it receives support from the nation's English-speaking minority and special-interest groups. The SDF opposed the RDPC during the 1992, 1996, and 2004 elections. Fru Ndi has repeatedly accused the RDPC and Biya of corrupting election procedures; some believe that Fru Ndi was the official winner of the 1992 presidential election. In the 2004 elections Fru Ndi received 17.4 percent of the popular vote.

In 1991 Amadou Ndam Njoya (1942–) founded the Union Démocratique du Cameroun (Democratic Union of Cameroon), or UDC. It focuses on the rights of the nation's ethnic minorities and draws support, like the closely related SDF, from the English-speaking minority. During the legislative elections of 2002, five members of the UDC won seats in the National Assembly. Unlike the SDF, Ndam Njoya and the UDC work closely with the RDPC.

Major Events

The republic's first president, Amadou Ahidjo, faced substantial resistance from the Union of the Peoples of Cameroon and used its threat to justify authoritarian policies. For example, he censored the media and prohibited opposing political parties. By 1970 Ahidjo's military had defeated the UPC but was facing potential rebellion. The president's attempts to expand the industrial sector were unsuccessful, and poverty remained rampant.

At first Ahidjo did little to integrate the French and British territories, allowing both to remain under the control of local administrations. In 1972 a new

Cameroon's prime minister, Ahmadou Ahidjo, at independence ceremonies in 1960. *© Bettmann/CORBIS*

constitution effectively ended the autonomy of former British Cameroon, leading to protests in the English-speaking community. The government maintained control through the police and militia but the threat of rebellion intensified.

Ahidjo abdicated the presidency in 1982, claiming health concerns, and left the office to his successor, Biya. Ahidjo hoped to remain in control by retaining leadership of the CU, but Biya responded by replacing Ahidjo's cabinet members with his own supporters and enacting legislation that reduced the influence of the CU. Ahidjo and Biya became political opponents. In 1984 Ahidjo's supporters attempted a presidential coup, but failed, leading to Ahidjo's exile.

Biya's restructured political organization, the RDPC, maintained most of the former administration's policies, including the prohibition of opposition parties and restriction of civil liberties. As dissent became widespread and the economy floundered, however, Biya allowed moderate democratic reforms. Changes to the constitution, proposed and adopted between 1990 and 1992, intended to establish a multiparty democratic system. The legislative and presidential elections of 1992 were controversial, as many felt that Fru Ndi had defeated Biya. The election results, as announced by the government,

indicated that Biya had won 39 percent of the popular vote and Fru Ndi had won 37 percent. After Fru Ndi and other opponents complained of election fraud, they were placed under house arrest.

The constitution was amended in 1996, allowing for further democratic reforms and calling for an upper chamber in the parliament and a system of state councils to provide greater regional representation for the populace. The presidential elections of 1997 were boycotted by most of the opposition parties, who did not believe that Biya's administration would allow a fair election. That move allowed Biya to win re-election with more than 90 percent of the popular vote.

Twenty-First Century

In 2000 the legislature voted to create the National Elections Observatory (NEO), an independent organization to monitor elections for fraud and other irregularities. The local and legislative elections of 2002 were considered the most democratically legitimate in the nation's history, though questions of misconduct remained. For the 2004 presidential elections, the NEO was joined by several international human-rights organizations to monitor election procedures. The NEO certified that the results were reliable, despite some irregularities. Biya won re-election in 2004 with more than 70 percent of the popular vote. His term expires in 2011.

The Cameroonian economy has shown signs of improvement since the 1990s, but poverty is still widespread. The government has worked with international aid organizations, including the World Bank and the International Monetary Fund, to reduce the nation's debt and to improve the infrastructure. A better human-rights record and more political stability could potentially encourage additional foreign investment.

BIBLIOGRAPHY

Ardener, Edwin. *Kingdom on Mount Cameroon: Studies in the History of the Cameroon Coast, 1500–1960.* Rev. ed. Edited and with an introduction by Shirley Ardener. New York: Berghahn Books, 2003.

Gros, Jean-Germain, ed. *Cameroon: Politics and Society in Critical Perspectives.* Lanham: University Press of America, 2003.

Mukum Mbaku, John, and Joseph Takougang. eds. *The Leadership Challenge in Africa: Cameroon Under Paul Biya.* Trenton: Africa World Press, 2004.

⊕ Togo

Type of Government

Togo is a republic that is in transition to a multiparty democracy. The powerful executive branch is headed by a president who serves as head of state and a prime minister who serves as head of government. The unicameral legislature, the National Assembly, is elected by popular vote. The legal code is based on French law and African tribal law.

Background

Togo is located on the southern coast of West Africa. It is bordered on the north by Burkina Faso, to the west by Ghana, and to the east by Benin. The southern coast, along the Gulf of Guinea, is the seat of the nation's capital, Lomé.

With the advent of the West African slave trade in the sixteenth century, the southern coast of Togo became a major center for raiding and shipping of slaves. The cultivation of cassava, coconuts, corn, and other crops was introduced to provide food for slave ships and became the basis for the local economy. The French settled in several villages in the seventeenth century, and for a time in the eighteenth century the region was claimed by Denmark. In 1884 it became a German protectorate called Togoland. Borders were established through treaties with the British, who ruled the Gold Coast (modern-day Ghana) to the west, and the French, who controlled Dahomey (now Benin) to the east.

During World War I (1914–1918), Togoland was invaded by both the British and French and the country was thereafter split in two, administered by Britain and France under a mandate from the League of Nations. After World War II (1939–1945) the two regions became United Nations "trust territories" in preparation for independence and self-government. Questions of independence were complicated by the fact that the Ewe people, who made up a large percentage of the population and had been scattered between the Gold Coast, British Togo, and French Togo, demanded some form of reunification. The residents of British Togo voted to join the Gold Coast in 1957, becoming part of the newly independent Ghana. To the east, French Togo became an autonomous republic within the French union in 1955, retaining its UN trusteeship status. A 1956 constitution established an elected executive body headed by a prime minister responsible to the legislature, which was elected by universal adult suffrage.

In 1956 Nicolas Grunitzky (1913–1969) became prime minister. In 1958 Sylvanus Olympio (1902–1963) was elected to that position, and on April 27, 1960, Togo became a sovereign nation under Olympio's leadership. A new constitution, promulgated in 1961, provided for a powerful executive and a weak legislature. Olympio thereafter secured his position in an election from which Grunitzky's party was barred.

Government Structure

Togo's head of state is the president, who is elected every five years and can serve up to three terms. The head of government is the prime minister, who is appointed by the president. The cabinet, called the Council of Ministers, is appointed by both the president and prime minister.

The eighty-one members of the unicameral National Assembly are elected to five-year terms without term limits. The National Assembly is, by the terms of the constitution, responsible for legislation and can also vote no confidence in the government with a two-thirds majority. This then forces the ruling party to create a new government, and if a new government cannot be created, new elections are held. A Seniority Board, whose members are effectively under presidential control, determines the budget for the National Assembly. Thus the executive retains significant influence over the legislative branch.

The Togolese legal code is based on French law and on African tribal law. The judiciary is headed by a Supreme Court and is complemented by tribal leaders who rule on matters of traditional law. Defendants are presumed innocent and guaranteed a public trial.

Togo is divided in five administrative regions— Kara, Plateaux, Savanes, Centrale, and Maritime—which are further divided in thirty prefectures, all with local administrators. A policy of decentralization has granted increased powers to the local governments.

Political Parties and Factions

Numerous political parties in Togo were active before and just following independence in 1960. The strongest of these were the Committee of Togolese Unity (Comité de l'Unité Togolaise or CUT) led by Olympio, and the

Togo President Gnassingbé Eyadéma, 1985. © *James Andanson/ CORBIS SYGMA*

Togolese Party for Progress (Parti Togolais du Progrès or PTP), headed by Grunitzky. However, from 1969 until 1991, opposition parties were disallowed, and Togo was a one-party state, ruled by the Togolese People's Rally (RPT), led by Gnassingbé Eyadéma (1937–2005) and founded in 1969 as the official state party.

Since 1991 other parties have emerged, but they face many obstacles from the dominant RPT. Predominant among the opposition parties are the Union of the Forces for Change (UFC), led by Gilchrist Olympio (1936–), son of the former President Sylvanus Olympio. The Togolese Youth Movement (also known as Juvento) is one of the oldest opposition parties, having been banned from the 1961 elections. The Rally for Democracy and Development (RSDD) has also won seats in the National Assembly, as has the Union for Democracy and Social Progress (UDPS) and the Believers' Movement for Equality and Peace (MOCEP). In the 2005 presidential elections, the Union of Forces for Change allied itself with five other smaller opposition parties to win 39 percent of the vote against the RPT candidate, Faure Gnassingbé (1966–), son of President Gnassingbé Eyadéma, who died in 2005.

Major Events

Since independence in 1960, Togo has experienced bloody coups and one-party rule. President Olympio was killed in 1963 by a young military man, Gnassingbé Eyadéma. Thereafter, Grunitzky was brought out of his Paris exile to lead the nation as president, only to be deposed by Eyadéma in a bloodless coup. Eyadéma established himself as supreme ruler, establishing the RTP in 1969 and banning opposition parties. Eyadéma created a cult of personality around himself and strove to rid the country of its European cultural influences and return it to its African roots. Part of this effort included the changing of his first name from Étienne to Gnassingbé, his African second name, and nationalizing industries once controlled by the French and others.

In late 1979 Eyadéma declared a new republic and promised a transition to more civilian rule with a mixed civilian and military cabinet. He was re-elected as president in uncontested elections in 1980 and 1986. Also in 1986 an attempted coup against the Eyadéma government failed. Anti-government riots broke out in 1991, partly spurred by the momentous world events of 1989 and 1990, with autocratic regimes falling in the Soviet Union and Eastern Europe. Eyadéma legalized opposition parties, created a new constitution, and for a time was replaced by a prime minister. However, with the help of the army, Eyadéma regained control, and in the 1993 elections won 96 percent of the vote. Most observers declared these elections fraudulent.

At Eyadéma's death in 2005, he was the longest-serving ruler in Africa. The military immediately installed his son, Faure Gnassingbé, as president, despite constitutional guarantees for an orderly and democratic succession. Under strong international protest, Gnassingbé held elections in 2005, winning 60 percent of the popular vote. Under an agreement with opposition parties, he included the opposition leader as the prime minister in his new government in 2006.

Twenty-First Century

The largest challenge to government stability in Togo is the transition to a multiparty democratic system. After an extended period of military and single-party dominance, the country's transition toward a multiparty system has been tenuous and accusations of political manipulation and voter fraud have accompanied recent elections. The 2006 move to install the opposition leader and respected politician Yawovi Agboyibo (1943–) as the new prime minister was a step in the right direction, according to international observers.

BIBLIOGRAPHY

Curkeet, A. A. *Togo: Portrait of a West African Francophone Republic in the 1980s.* Jefferson, NC: McFarland and Co., 1993.

Decalo, Samuel. *Historical Dictionary of Togo.* 3rd ed. Lanham, MD: Scarecrow Press, 1996.

Web Site of the Government of the Republic of Togo. http://www.republicoftogo.com (accessed May 16, 2007).

⊕ Madagascar

Type of Government

The government of Madagascar is a representative democracy with powers divided between independent executive, legislative, and judicial branches. The executive branch is headed by the president, who is head of state, while the prime minister is head of government. The legislative branch is made up of a bicameral, or two-chamber, parliament consisting of a Senate and National Assembly. While the executive branch and National Assembly are decided by direct election, members of the Senate are selected by the president and local legislative bodies. Madagascar was a one-party state from the time of its independence in 1960 until 1992.

Background

Located off the coast of Mozambique in the Indian Ocean, Madagascar is the world's fourth-largest island. The capital is Antananarivo. Portuguese traders began visiting the island around AD 1500 and named the island in 1502. Early European efforts to colonize the island were defeated by the indigenous population, the Malagasy, and pirates using the island as an outpost. The Malagasy were divided into three separate kingdoms: the Merina (central Madagascar), the Sakalava (western), and the Betsimisaraka (eastern). Local leaders made deals with the European traders to try to give them an edge over rival kingdoms. By the end of the eighteenth century, the Merina kingdom, led by King Andrianampoinimerina (who ruled from 1787 until his death in 1810), had emerged as the dominant force.

Both Great Britain and France wanted Madagascar as a colony, and in 1840 Paris signed a treaty with the Sakalava kingdom. Britain tried to annul the treaty, leading to a war from 1883 to 1885. Great Britain ultimately agreed to the establishment of a French protectorate in Madagascar in exchange for British control over Zanzibar. France formally annexed Madagascar in 1896, sending the royal family into exile.

Following World War II, Madagascar became a French overseas territory, which meant its residents were French citizens, some received the right to vote, and the island was granted three seats in the French parliament and a territorial assembly for limited autonomy. However, most of the seats in the local assembly went to Europeans, not Malagasy, which angered the indigenous population.

In March 1947 French forces put down a nationalist uprising in Madagascar; some eleven thousand people died in the battle. When the French Overseas Reform Act was passed in 1956, most territories—including Madagascar—became autonomous entities within the broader so-called French Community. All citizens were to have equal rights, irrespective of ethnicity, and the Malagasy were able to participate more in local administration. In 1959 the republic gained a constitution that provided for a strong presidency, and Madagascar gained independence from France on June 26, 1960.

Government Structure

Under the 2007 constitution, Madagascar has an executive branch led by a president, prime minister, and cabinet. The president is popularly elected for a five-year term and may serve a maximum of two terms. The president selects the prime minister from a slate of candidates drawn up by the National Assembly. The prime minister nominates the council of ministers.

Legislative authority is vested in a bicameral legislature, consisting of a National Assembly and a Senate; however, the Senate did not meet between 1972 and May 2001. The National Assembly has 160 members; 116 are popularly elected, while the president appoints the other 44. All serve five-year terms. The ninety members of the Senate are selected by both the president (thirty seats) and local legislatures (sixty seats). Senators serve six-year terms. Parliament and the prime minister initiate legislation, and the National Assembly can force the prime minister's resignation through a vote of no confidence. The president can dissolve the National Assembly.

Judicial authority is exercised by a Supreme Court, a Court of Appeals, a High Court of Justice, and a High Constitutional Court. The legal code is based on French law, while traditional courts handle some civil and criminal cases. The High Constitutional Court ruled on the outcome of the 2002 presidential election, a ruling considered to be an indication of judicial independence.

The country was divided into six autonomous provinces until 2002, when the country was redivided into twenty-two regions to improve local representation. The 2007 constitution formally dissolved the autonomous provinces. The central government appoints chiefs for each region. All Madagascar citizens may vote at the age of eighteen.

Political Parties and Factions

Madagascar's political parties tend to be formed around individual political figures rather than ideologies. Five main parties won seats in the 2002 National Assembly elections. With 103 of the 160 seats, the I Love Madagascar party headed by Madagascar President Marc Ravalomanana (1953–) is by far the dominant force. The National Union for Development and Democracy headed by Albert Zafy (1927–) is second with twenty-two seats, followed by Rally for Social Democracy (five seats), Vanguard of the

Malagasy Revolution (three seats)—the successor to the National Front for the Defense of the Revolution headed by Didier Ratsiraka (1936–)—and the Economic Liberalism and Democratic Action for Reconstruction Party (two seats).

Major Events

While the first decade of Madagascar's independence was relatively calm, the second was marked by frequent, violent turnovers in the executive branch and increasing limitations on opposition groups. In addition to poverty, one of the leading issues facing the nation was foreign policy, specifically regarding whether Madagascar should continue its longtime relationship with France or focus on Africa.

Madagascar's first president, Philibert Tsiranana (1912–1978), was reelected unopposed in March 1972, but he resigned on May 18, 1972, in the face of widespread demonstrations and strikes against his semiauthoritarian government and preferential treatment of French interests. A coalition government of civilians and military officers, led by General Gabriel Ramanantsoa (1906–1978), tried to quell the unrest and ordered France to close its military base on the island, but Ramanantsa resigned on February 5, 1975. His successor, Lieutenant-Colonel Richard Ratsimandrava (1931–1975), ruled only six days before being assassinated. For the next four months a provisional military regime under Gilles Andriamahazo (1919–1989) controlled Madagascar, until Ratsiraka, then a naval officer and foreign minister, assumed executive power in June 1975. Ratsiraka ruled for the remainder of 1975 as chairman of the Supreme Revolutionary Council. He took the office of president in January 1976, after a December 21, 1975, constitutional referendum approved the appointment. When his seven-year term ended, Ratsiraka was reelected on November 7, 1982.

Ratsiraka ruled with a hybrid military-socialist regime that sought to "feed, house, clothe, teach, and transport the population." He also promoted the Malagasy language and culture over French influences. Ratsiraka led the National Front for the Defense of the Revolution, which technically was a coalition of political parties. However, no group could participate in elections if they were not a member of the Front, making Madagascar a de facto single-party state.

Ratsiraka nationalized banks and key industries, and the Supreme Revolutionary Council directed the economy in addition to national security. Ratsiraka also strengthened relations with the Soviet Union, China, and other members of the Communist bloc. Economic conditions worsened through the late 1970s and early 1980s due to a combination of drought and economic austerity measures demanded by the International Monetary Fund. As popular unrest increased, especially in urban areas, the government of Madagascar increasingly cracked down on dissent. When the demonstrations and

Madagascar President Philibert Tsiranana holding a press conference, 1962. *© Bettmann/CORBIS*

strikes only increased, President Ratsiraka finally began to make some economic concessions in the late 1980s and allowed limited political competition in 1990. His regime nearly collapsed in August 1991 when government troops fired on a crowd of four hundred thousand pro-democracy protestors, killing more than thirty people. At this point Ratsiraka agreed to relinquish many of his powers, and work began to reform the Malagasy government.

The Panorama Convention of October 31, 1991, outlined the framework of a transitional government and began an eighteen-month process of creating a new constitution and governing regime. The Malagasy Christian Council of Churches organized a National Forum to draft the new constitution, under guidance from the High Constitutional Court. As the forum worked, civic violence spread across the island. After seven weeks of violence, Ratsiraka agreed to dissolve the cabinet in July 1992 and released opposition leader Zafy from prison.

Presidential elections were held November 25, 1992. Despite calls for his exclusion from the political process, Ratsiraka ran for the presidency but lost to Zafy. Four years later, Zafy was impeached on charges of corruption, and Prime Minister Norbert Ratsirahonana (1938–) completed the presidential term until new elections were held in 1997. This time Ratsiraka won, and he began a process to write yet another constitution, one that would restore the extensive powers he had enjoyed as president in the 1970s and 1980s. The new constitution adopted in 1998 took powers away from parliament and assigned them to the president.

The first presidential election under the 1998 constitution took place in December 2001. Ratsiraka and Ravalomanana, then the mayor of Antananarivo, each claimed victory. Ratsiraka refused to vacate the office, and his supporters began closing roads and destroying bridges leading to Madagascar's major cities. Five of the six provinces threatened to secede rather than accept Ravalomanana. Dueling governments, violence, and strikes crippled the country for the next seven months until Ratsiraka fled the country. Ravalomanana's I Love Madagascar party swept the December 2002 parliamentary elections, and he launched a major program of economic development and anticorruption measures.

Madagascar amended the new constitution in April 2007 to expand presidential powers during emergencies, make English an official language, and remove the description of the country as a "secular state."

Twenty-First Century

Most of Madagascar's sixteen million residents live in extreme poverty. The World Bank estimates that some 70 percent of the population gets by on less than $1 per day, and food shortages are common. Most citizens are subsistence farmers, but because Madagascar is an island, there is little land available for expansion. Farmers typically burn their leftover crops at the end of winter, a practice that has claimed about 75 percent of the country's forests since 1994. The loss of forests, in turn, contributes to erosion, a critical problem for an island. The country also lacks clean drinking water and adequate sewage systems.

The government needs funds to develop other sectors of the economy, but the political turmoil of recent years has made international financial institutions wary of investing in Madagascar. While France has long been an investor, Madagascar is now courting Germany and the United States. The government is working to improve tourism infrastructure and received a considerable boost in tourism following the release of the 2005 animated movie *Madagascar*.

Madagascar's political turmoil has affected the country in other ways: The highly disputed 2001 presidential election damaged the political process among the citizens of Madagascar. The government has been promoting "national reconciliation," but slim voter turnout levels since 2001 reveal an increasing level of apathy among the population in the twenty-first century.

BIBLIOGRAPHY

Allen, Philip M. *Madagascar: Conflicts of Authority in the Great Island*. Boulder, Co: Westview Press, 1995.

Brown, Mervyn. *A History of Madagascar*. Princeton, NJ: Marcus Wiener Publishers, 2000.

Jolly, Alison. *Lords and Lemurs: Mad Scientists, Kings with Spears, and the Survival of Diversity in Madagascar*. New York: Houghton Mifflin, 2004.

Democratic Republic of the Congo

Type of Government

The Democratic Republic of the Congo (DRC) is a parliamentary republic, operating under a constitution adopted in 2006 after a prolonged period of authoritarian rule. The government is divided into executive, legislative, and judicial branches, with a majority of the power vested in the presidency. The bicameral legislature is constituted through direct, popular vote. The judicial branch includes a Constitutional Court, a Court of Cassation (the highest court of appeals), and a High Military Court.

Background

The region that makes up the DRC was inhabited during Paleolithic times by a succession of hunter-gatherer groups. Archaeologists believe that the Baku Pygmies were among the first to occupy the area, followed by members of the Bantu ethno-linguistic group. Little is known about the early states that transformed into complex societies between the first and fourteenth centuries AD.

The Kingdom of Kongo was one of the region's first major civilizations, originating in what is now Angola and spreading into the Congo in the fourteenth century. Between the fourteenth and the nineteenth centuries, a number of native African states entered the area, including the Luba Empire in the South and the Kuba Kingdom in the North.

The first European to visit the region, Diogo Cão, explored the Congo River for the Portuguese crown. Later Portuguese explorers opened a trading station on the coast of Angola and developed treaties with the Kingdom of Kongo. They met resistance from others.

By the middle of the nineteenth century, African and Arab traders from the Sahel region south of the Sahara Desert were raiding the Congo to capture resources and slaves. The Portuguese supported and participated in the slave trade, which increased resistance from native groups. The slave traders built powerful military installations during the 1860s, most of which were eventually conquered by the Belgians, who arrived in the 1870s.

For Belgian King Leopold II (1835–1909), annexing the Congo region was personal. He dispatched ships to the Congo Basin and had his men establish trading stations and forge diplomatic relations with the native kingdoms. When the major European nations met at the Berlin Conference of 1884—their intention was to divide up Africa for their own colonization—they accepted Leopold's claim to the territory and set its boundaries.

Leopold established the Belgian Free State in 1885 and spent the next decade removing slave traders and native groups that would not submit to his authority. Though the territory initially belonged to Leopold himself, Belgium annexed it in 1908 and funded efforts to develop the local economy and set up an administration.

Leopold's Belgian Free State became known for excessive exploitation of the natives, who were forced into labor by private companies that leased portions of the territory. When the Belgian legislature decided to annex the territory, it reduced the autonomy of private companies, which improved conditions for native workers, but it refused to allow native participation in the government. The Belgian government converted the region into a mining center; it was especially rich in diamonds and metals. Although the Belgians allowed some educational reforms in the late 1940s, the local independence movement became dissatisfied with the pace of change and launched a military rebellion.

Shortly after France allowed the native inhabitants of the neighboring Republic of Congo to decide whether they wanted to remain a part of France, militants staged protests and riots in Kinshasa, the capital of the DRC. Though the Belgian government originally proposed a thirty-year plan for independence, mounting pressure and threats of violence forced it to accelerate the process.

The Belgian government negotiated with nationalist representatives, including the popular leaders Patrice Lumumba (1925–1961) of the leftist Congolese National Movement and Joseph Kasavubu (c. 1913–1969) of the Alliance des Bakongo (ABAKO), a political party. Full independence was granted on June 30, 1960.

Government Structure

The DRC is divided into ten provinces, with one special district—the capital city, Kinshasa, is designated as both a city and a provincial region. A revised constitution, adopted in 2006, called for restructuring the government to create twenty-nine administrative districts by 2009. Provincial governors and legislatures and city mayors are chosen by direct, popular vote.

The DRC constitution guarantees shared executive power between the president, who serves as head of state and commander of the armed forces, and the prime minister, who serves as head of government. The president, who is elected by direct, popular vote for a maximum of two terms of five years each, appoints the prime minister from the leading party in the legislature. With the prime minister's approval, the president then appoints thirty-five ministers to serve in the executive cabinet. The president also has the power to appoint and dismiss federal justices and members of the military. Legislative approval is

required for the president to enact emergency orders or to declare war.

In the bicameral legislature, the National Assembly has five hundred members, who are chosen by a combination of direct, popular vote in single-member constituencies and proportional representation in multiple-member constituencies. They serve five-year terms. The upper chamber, the Senate, has 108 members elected by the provincial assemblies to serve four-year terms. Legislators in both houses can stand for re-election. They initiate all legislation and approve executive appointments. They do not have the power to remove the president; however, the legislature can be dissolved by presidential decree in cases of deadlock. The Senate was responsible for drafting the constitution adopted in 2006.

The judicial branch is nominally independent but, because the president has the power to nominate and dismiss justices of the nation's highest courts, remains highly responsive to presidential policy. In addition, the legislature, which has the power to approve presidential appointments, is usually dominated by the president's political party. The highest courts are the Constitutional Court, which has jurisdiction in all cases involving constitutional law, treaties, and international agreements, and the Court of Cassation, the highest appellate court. The High Council of the Judiciary is composed of senior members of the judiciary who discipline, promote, nominate, and remove justices from other courts. The president, the legislature, and the High Council of the Judiciary each appoint three members to the Constitutional Court to serve five-year terms.

Political Parties and Factions

Since the new constitution was adopted in 2006, the leading party has been the Parti du Peuple pour la Reconstruction et le Démocratie (People's Party for Reconstruction and Democracy), or PPRD, founded by President Joseph Kabila (1971–). During the 2006 presidential election, Kabila received more than 45 percent of the popular vote, prompting a second-round runoff election with Jean-Pierre Bemba (1962–). Kabila won more than 58 percent of the vote in the second round and, after judicial arbiters reviewed the election results, was declared the winner. In 2006 the PPRD won 111 seats in the National Assembly and secured a small majority in the Senate.

The Mouvement pour la Liberation du Congo (Movement for the Liberation of the Congo), or MLC, is the major opposition to the PPRD–led government. The MLC won sixty-four seats in the National Assembly in 2006, and its presidential candidate, Bemba, received the second highest percentage of the popular vote. Bemba and his party initially challenged the election results, prompting the judicial review. Bemba eventually withdrew his challenge and announced that his party would cooperate with the PPRD.

Children carry the new flag of the Democratic Republic of Congo on July 1st, 1960, when the country received its independence from Belgium. © *Bettmann/CORBIS*

The Parti Lumumbiste Unifié (Unified Lumumbist Party), or PALU, won thirty-four seats in the 2006 legislative elections. PALU's ideology is based on the political work of Patrice Lumumba and supports decentralization. Party leader Antoine Gizenga (1925–) was named prime minister by Kabila in December 2006.

Major Events

When the nation achieved independence, Kasavubu was elected president, and Lumumba became prime minister. Almost immediately a secessionist regime in the Katanga region rebelled against the newly elected government. The Belgian government sent in troops to aid the rebels. Lumumba appealed to the United Nations for military aid; after receiving no support, he turned to the Union of Soviet Socialist Republics. Alarmed by Lumumba's actions, Western powers turned against him and supported Kasavubu in an attempt to dismiss the prime minister. Lumumba refused to vacate his post and called for the resignation of Kasavubu. In September 1960, General Mobutu Sese Seko (1930–1997) seized power in a coup, dismissing Kasavubu and arresting Lumumba. In 1961 Lumumba was killed, presumably by Mobutu's forces.

The nation disintegrated after Mobutu's coup. While Katanga and other regions proclaimed independence under local leaders, Mobutu controlled the western portions of the territory. With the aid of the United Nations, however, Mobutu was able to consolidate power and, by 1966, had reestablished the central government. Although Mobutu abolished the parliamentary system and installed a presidential, single-party regime, he also helped to build the economy by improving foreign relations and increasing foreign investment. Throughout the 1970s the nation, then called Zaire, enjoyed relative political stability; however, a number of alternative political parties continued to lobby for democratization.

Mobutu's government began to crumble in the 1980s when an economic downturn led to public protests and eventually to riots. After several moderate liberalization measures failed, Mobutu allowed the formation of a coalition government with members of then illegal opposition parties. The coalition did not succeed, partly because the economy continued to deteriorate and rebel groups gained prominence. The arrival of thousands of Hutu and Tutsi refugees from ethnic conflict in neighboring Rwanda also exacerbated political and social instability.

In 1997, while Mobutu was in Europe undergoing treatment for cancer, rebel leader Laurent-Désiré Kabila (1939–2001) seized control of the government and established the Democratic Republic of Congo. Mobutu died in 1997. Kabila's government was an initial success, although a rebel faction arose in the eastern region with military aid from Uganda and Rwanda. Kabila met with Ugandan and Rwandan military representatives to resolve the conflict. Although Kabila promised to hold elections in 1999, the date was postponed, which led to additional hostilities between the administration and rebel groups. In 2001 Kabila was assassinated—the plot against him involved members of the military and the central government—and replaced by his son, Joseph Kabila.

Twenty-First Century

Joseph Kabila successfully installed a transitional government that operated from 2001 to 2006. He appointed four vice presidents from opposition parties, legalized multiparty elections, and forged peace agreements with Rwanda, Uganda, and South Africa. Though the political situation remained fairly unstable, the coalition government was able to advance many of its goals. Kabila's first-round victory in the 2006 election was questioned by his opponent, Bemba, and ignited a resurgence of violence. After a judicial review certified the results, Kabila won the second-round election. Both he and Bemba urged their followers to heed the result. Domestic and foreign observers reported that the elections were not significantly hampered by voting or procedural irregularities.

BIBLIOGRAPHY

Nest, Michael Wallace, François Grignon, and Emizet F. Kisangani. *The Democratic Republic of the Congo: Economic Dimensions of War and Peace.* Boulder, Co: Lynn Rienner Publishers, 2005.

Nzongola-Ntalaja, Georges. *The Congo From Leopold to Kabila: A People's History.* London: Zed Books, 2002.

Oppong, Joseph R., and Tanya Woodruff. *Democratic Republic of the Congo.* New York: Chelsea House Publications, 2007.

⊕ Somalia

Type of Government

Torn by civil war, the East African nation of Somalia has lacked an effective central government since 1991. A transitional government was established in 1994, but its authority is largely limited to the single town of Baydhabo. Though its institutions—notably a cabinet, president's office, and assembly—continue to function, internal disagreements have kept it too weak to confront the warring factions that dominate the country.

Background

Roughly half the size of Alaska, Somalia occupies the barren but strategically important Horn of Africa, the peninsula that separates the Indian Ocean from the Gulf of Aden and the Red Sea. Its neighbors are Djibouti, to the northwest; Ethiopia, with a population more than eight times as large as Somalia's (seventy-six million and nine million, respectively), to the west; and Kenya, to the southwest. In the late nineteenth century, France, Great Britain, and Italy each established colonies in the area: French Somaliland (modern Djibouti), British Somaliland, and Italian Somaliland. The last two of these merged upon independence in 1960 to become the Somali Republic.

Serious problems arose immediately. The notion of a single central authority was still new to the largely nomadic peoples of the region, and their brief experience of it under colonialism did little to relieve their skepticism. Clan loyalties, religious movements (notably fundamentalist Islam), regional interests, and ethnic aspirations all undermined the unity of the new state. Though often forgotten today in light of Somalia's relative homogeneity (eighty-five percent of the population is Somali, with Bantu and Arab communities comprising the remainder), ethnic issues were a major factor in the 1960s, as a small but vocal movement pressed for a new state that would incorporate Somali populations in neighboring Djibouti, Ethiopia, and Kenya. In 1969 the military officer Mohammed Siad Barre (1919–1995) took advantage of the republic's chronic instability to stage a coup and impose an authoritarian socialist regime. Siad Barre remained in power until 1991, when a varied collection of clan-based militias, disaffected soldiers, and ordinary citizens drove him into exile. Chaos and civil war followed.

Government Structure

Amid the ongoing violence, there have been several attempts to establish a transitional government as an initial step toward reconciliation and recovery. The first of these failed in 2003 when its three-year mandate expired without significant progress. The second was organized the following year as part of a joint peace initiative by Kenya and the Intergovernmental Authority on Development (IGAD), with a mandate for five years. Known officially as the Transitional Federal Government, or TFG, its headquarters are in the town of Baydhabo northwest of Mogadishu, the capital. Its component organizations include a unicameral National Assembly of two hundred and seventy-five members, a cabinet of ninety members, and the offices of president and prime minister. Despite the almost universal support of the international community, the TFG remains weak, torn by internal disputes and the conflicting agendas of its members. These disputes are particularly evident in the Assembly, the membership of which is entirely clan-based. Each of the nation's four major clans holds sixty-one seats, with the thirty-one remaining seats allocated to smaller clans and subclans. One of the Assembly's first acts was the election of Abdullahi Yusuf Ahmed (1934–) as president and Ali Mohammed Ghedi (1952–) as prime minister. Ghedi, in turn, appointed the members of the cabinet, subject to Assembly approval.

No organized legal system exists. There are local Islamic courts in some districts, and informal tribunals based on local legal tradition (called *xeer*) in others. For the most part, however, Somalis rely on their clan leaders to represent their interests and protect them from crime. By the same token, local government exists only as an optional extension of the dominant clan leader's personal authority.

Political Parties and Factions

There are no political groups in the conventional sense. Instead, there are clans and subclans, the leaders of which are generally known as warlords. Occasionally, several clans will unite, usually for a limited, ad hoc purpose. When that purpose is the overthrow of authority, as it was in 1991, these alliances function as armed rebel groups. Unlike rebel movements elsewhere, however, many of which rely on a shared ideology like Marxism or fundamentalist Islam to maintain unity, clan alliances in Somalia tend to dissolve on the smallest of pretexts. Given that tendency, many analysts are worried for the future of the Transitional Federal Government, which is essentially a collection of clans fused together by a one-time application of international pressure. Among the more prominent members of the TFG are the Somali National Alliance (SNA), dominated by the Hawiye, one of the nation's four largest clans (the others are the Rahanwayn, Isaaq, and Darod); the Somali Salvation Alliance (SSA), dominated by members of the Abgal subclan within the Hawiye; and the Rahanwayn Resistance Army (RRA).

Of the groups opposed to the TFG, the most powerful remains the Council of Islamic Courts of Somalia (CSIC), also known as the Islamic Courts Union. One of the few groups in Somalia not based on clan membership, the CSIC is a coalition of Mogadishu business leaders, conservative Islamic clerics, and armed Islamic militias. CSIC's first goals were the restoration of order to the capital through the observance of sharia, or strict Islamic law, and the expulsion of clan-based militias. While it achieved these in June 2006, its victory was short-lived, for a coalition of Ethiopian troops and TFG forces had driven it from the capital by the end of the year. The CSIC nevertheless remains a formidable opponent, in part because of the discipline and unity its Islamist ideology confers. It still controls large districts in southern Somalia, and its ultimate goal remains the destruction of the TFG and the establishment of a sharia-based Islamic state.

Major Events

In 1991 Siad Barre found himself facing two major clan-based rebellions: the Somali National Movement, or SNM, in the northwest and the United Somali Congress, or USC, in the south. The SNM, which had been engaged in fierce but intermittent fighting for a decade, took advantage of Siad Barre's preoccupation with the new southern threat to proclaim the establishment of an independent republic to be called Somaliland, with borders roughly corresponding to the old frontiers of British Somaliland. In effect, the SNM's actions amounted to a unilateral abrogation of the 1960 merger. Though Somaliland has not won international recognition, its administration is widely viewed as more stable and more viable than the transitional government to the south. Somaliland's governmental framework includes a bicameral parliament, an elected president and vice president, and a cabinet of ministers. While successful multiparty elections have apparently been held (local elections in 2002 and presidential elections the following year), the general absence of foreign embassies, international nongovernmental organizations, and independent news outlets makes it difficult to verify the government's electoral claims. Sharia was introduced in 1998.

Somaliland is not the only region to withdraw from the rest of the country. Several leading clans in the area east of Somaliland declared the autonomy of their region in 1998. Though the new state, called Puntland, has designated a president and a constitutional commission, as of June 2007 it had not yet formally declared independence. There is widespread speculation that Puntland's leaders may have decided that unrestricted local autonomy under the purely nominal rule of the transitional government is preferable to the additional burdens and expenses formal independence would impose. If the central government is ever in a position to restrict that autonomy, a declaration of independence might well follow. In the meantime, Puntland's clans seem content with the status quo, and the region is one of the quietest in Somalia.

In 1992 U.S. troops were deployed to Somalia with two related tasks: to facilitate the delivery of humanitarian supplies to civilians and to restrain several warlords, notably General Mohammed Farrah Aidid (1934–1996) of the USC. A UN peacekeeping force followed. When gunmen loyal to Aidid killed twenty-three Pakistani peacekeepers in June 1993, U.S. troops returned in force. A series of policy missteps and intelligence failures prevented stabilization of the situation, however, and on October 3 and 4, 1993, two U.S. helicopters were shot down in Mogadishu, killing eighteen troops. Under heavy pressure from the American public, U.S. President Bill Clinton (1946–) withdrew his forces, leaving a vacuum Aidid and other warlords quickly filled.

Twenty-First Century

Somalia's continued existence as a nation is in considerable doubt. Even if the civil war were suddenly to end, the nation would still face a staggering array of problems, including persistent drought, rapid desertification, and endemic malnutrition. Somalia has one of the highest

A Somali standing defiantly in front of the wreckage of an American armored personnel carrier, part of a mission to rescue the crew of a U.S. Army helicopter shot down in Mogadishu, 1993. *© TORONTO STAR/CORBIS SYGMA*

population growth rates in the world and one of the lowest literacy rates. The civil war has pushed these problems to the background, but they pose nearly as great a challenge to the nation's existence as the war does. Sustained assistance from the international community is critical, but it will not arrive in sufficient quantities until some domestic organization or alliance is able to stabilize the situation. Given the casualties sustained by U.S. and UN forces, further foreign intervention is unlikely. Only one nation, Ethiopia, has intervened recently, and its motives are not above suspicion. Both Somalia and Ethiopia have a history of involvement in the other's civil conflicts. It is clear that predominately Christian Ethiopia does not want a fundamentalist Islamic state on its doorstep, particularly given the restive ambitions of its own sizeable Islamic community. The two nations have been rivals for decades, and it is reasonable to assume that Ethiopia's recent intervention is intended in part to lay the groundwork for its eventual emergence as a regional superpower.

BIBLIOGRAPHY

Abdi Kusow, ed. *Putting the Cart before the Horse: Contested Nationalism and the Crisis of the Nation-State in Somalia.* Lawrenceville, NJ: Red Sea, 2004.

Menkhaus, Kenneth John. *Somalia: State Collapse and the Threat of Terrorism.* London: Routledge, 2004.

Mohamoud, Abdullah A. *State Collapse and Post-Conflict Development in Africa: The Case of Somalia (1960–2001).* West Lafayette, IN: Purdue University Press, 2006.

⊕ Benin

Type of Government

Benin is a republic, with government power distributed among independent executive, legislative, and judicial branches. The executive branch is led by the president, who serves as both chief of state and head of government. The president is elected by popular vote to a five-year term. The legislative branch consists of a single chamber, the National Assembly, or Assemblee Nationale. Assembly members are elected by direct popular vote to four-year terms. The judicial branch includes the Constitutional Court, which reviews the constitutionality of legislation and decides disputes between the president and the National Assembly; the Supreme Court, which is the nation's highest court for nonconstitutional judicial review; and the High Court of Justice, which hears cases involving crimes against the nation committed by government officials.

Background

The Republic of Benin is located on the northern coast of the Gulf of Guinea in West Africa, on a bay called the Bight of Benin, and occupies about as much land as Tennessee. It is bordered on the west by Togo and the east by Nigeria. Other neighboring countries are Burkina Faso to the northwest, and Niger across the River Niger to the northeast. Benin occupies the part of Africa that was once Dahomey, an important West African kingdom that rose to prominence in the seventeenth century. Dahomey's origins can be traced to a group of Aja people from the coastal kingdom of Allada. These Aja moved northward into territory controlled by the Fon people, eventually achieving dominance over them and establishing a stable kingdom.

The first Europeans in Dahomey were the Portuguese, who set up a trading post at Porto-Novo on the coast of what is now Benin. As the slave trade continued to expand, the Portuguese were followed by traders from England, Holland, Spain, and France. During the early eighteenth century, the English, French, and Portuguese all built forts in the region. Dahomey's kings amassed great wealth through slave trade, and they used guns obtained from their European trade partners to conquer neighboring kingdoms.

Benin's modern geographical boundaries are the result of rivalries between English and French colonists during the partition of Africa that took place in the late nineteenth century. After jockeying with the English for dominant position in Porto-Novo and surrounding territories, the French finally subdued Dahomey and established a colony there in 1894.

Dahomey remained under French control through the first half of the twentieth century, becoming a component colony of the federation of French West Africa in 1904. In 1958 Dahomey became an autonomous republic within the French Community. A new constitution was adopted and a legislative assembly elected the following year. In 1960 the republic declared its complete independence from France.

Government Structure

After assuming power in a 1972 military coup, Major Mathieu Kérékou (1933–) essentially ruled by decree. The National Council of the Revolution, with Kérékou as its leader, became the nation's ruling authority in 1973. Two years later, Dahomey was renamed Benin. As required by law, the National Council dissolved itself in 1979 and was replaced by the 336-member National Revolutionary Assembly (NRA). The NRA elected Kérékou president in 1980 and 1984.

A new constitution adopted in 1990 established a multiparty system and established that the president be elected by popular vote to a five-year term, with a two-term maximum. The constitution also created a directly elected National Assembly, composed of eighty-three seats. There is universal suffrage for persons at least eighteen years old.

Benin is divided into twelve provinces, each of which contains several districts. Councils are elected at the village, town, commune, district, and provincial levels. While the process of devolving authority to increasingly local levels has been taking place since 1990, progress has been slow, as the central government has resisted handing over control of budgets and other key decisions to local officials.

Benin's legal system was originally based on French and customary law. Kérékou changed that in 1981, when he introduced a system of people's courts, with a Central People's Court presiding over all judicial activities. The overhaul of Benin's government in 1990 brought the creation of a new Constitutional Court, with responsibility for judicial review of all constitutional matters beginning in 1993. The 1990 constitution also created a High Court of Justice, which decides issues involving abuses by government officials, and a Supreme Court, the nation's highest court for reviewing nonconstitutional matters.

Benin's constitution contains a wide range of protections for citizens. Human and civil rights are safeguarded, and citizens accused of crimes enjoy the presumption of innocence and the rights to counsel, to a fair public trial, to confront witnesses, and to examine government evidence. The constitution also protects the privacy of citizens, and outlaws unwarranted police searches of private property.

Political Parties and Factions

There are many political parties in Benin, with smaller ones banding together in short- or long-term coalitions as they seek influence in the National Assembly. The Force Cowrie for an Emerging Benin (Forces Cauris pour un Benin Emergent; FCBE), a party aligned with newly elected President Thomas Yayi Boni, gained prominence by winning a plurality of seats in the Assembly in March 2007. One of the biggest coalitions in recent years has been the Union for the Future of Benin (Union pour le Bénin du Futur; UBF), formed in 2002 as more than fifty parties and factions supporting Kérékou joined forces for that year's elections. UBF is led by Bruno Amoussou, president of the Social Democratic Party. Another key component party of UBF is the Action Front for Renewal and Development (Front d'Action pour le Renouveau et le Developpement; FARD), founded in 1994 by five deputies aligned against then–Prime Minister Nicephore Soglo (1934–). Another major party is the African Movement for Democracy and Progress (Mouvement Africain pour le Democratie et le Progres; MADEP), led by Idji Kolawole, a former Minister of Foreign Affairs and president of the National Assembly. Prior to the March 2003 elections, these and several other parties made up the Presidential Movement, a broad alliance that controlled the National Assembly in support of Kérékou. Among opposition parties during the Kérékou era, Benin Revival (Le Renaissance du Bénin; RB), formed by Rosine Soglo, the former prime minister's wife, has been influential, as has the Democratic Renewal Party, led by Adrien Houngbedji (1942–).

Major Events

A period of extreme political instability followed independence. Military coups took place in 1963, 1965 (two of them), 1967, 1969, and 1972. Kérékou, brought to power in the 1972 coup, established a Marxist-Leninist communist state called the People's Republic of Benin, with a single ruling party, the People's Revolutionary Party of Benin (PRB), in charge. A National Revolutionary Assembly was elected—from a slate composed entirely of candidates from the People's Revolutionary Party—in 1979, and the following year this Assembly elected Kérékou to a new term as president. Later in 1980, Kérékou visited Libya, where he forged a friendly relationship with Libyan leader Muammar al-Gaddafi and converted to Islam.

With worldwide communism on the decline, and with Benin in social and economic turmoil, a national conference was convened in 1990 to discuss the future of the nation. The National Conference—the first such gathering anywhere in Africa—turned into a public gripe session about the Kérékou era. On December 2, 1990, a new constitution was adopted through a public referendum, and a transitional government was named to replace Kérékou. National elections for the presidency and legislature were held in March 1991, with Nicephore Soglo emerging victorious in the race for prime minister. This sequence of events—the first successful transfer of power in Africa from a dictator to a freely and democratically elected leader—has been referred to as a "civilian coup," and it foreshadowed similar developments in a number of African countries.

During the early stages of the new republic, there was a fair amount of tension between the executive and legislative branches, and following a wave of protest and continuing economic strife, a second National Convention was held. A new round of Assembly elections was held on March 28, 1995. A presidential election was held the following year, and remarkably, Kérékou defeated Soglo in a runoff to regain the presidency. Kérékou defeated Soglo again in a 2001 rematch. The following year, Benin undertook a program of decentralization, which brought the first municipal elections since the end of one-party rule in 1990. Some three million voters elected mayors and other local officials, posts that had previously been appointed by the national government.

Twenty-First Century

As the 2006 elections approached, the 72-year-old Kérékou announced that he would not seek to have the constitutional provision placing an age limit of 70 on presidential candidates changed, in effect meaning that he was stepping down as leader of Benin. The 70-year-old Soglo was likewise ineligible to run. With these two power-

houses out of the picture, Thomas Yayi Boni, a political outsider and former director of the West African Development Bank, was elected president of Benin. In National Assembly elections held in March 2007, the FCBE, a party associated with Yayi, won a plurality of seats, giving the new president substantial leverage in the legislature.

International observers hailed Benin's most recent elections as free and generally clean, and while corruption still exists, its government is one of the more open democracies in the region. Nevertheless, the nation continues to be mired in extreme poverty. Its economy is dependent on subsistence farming and cotton production. The main challenge of the twenty-first century is to preserve the stability of its government while fostering economic development of a more diverse nature, including development of new agricultural sectors and Western tourism.

BIBLIOGRAPHY

Ben-Amos, Paula. *Art, Innovation, and Politics in Eighteenth-Century Benin.* Bloomington: Indiana University Press, 1999.

Caulfield, Annie. *Show Me the Magic: Travels Round Benin by Taxi.* London: Penguin, 2003.

Houngnikpo, Mathurin C. *Determinants of Democratization in Africa: A Comparative Study of Benin and Togo.* Lanham, MD: University Press of America, 2001.

⊕ Niger

Type of Government

Niger is a republic, with a semi-presidential government based on the 1999 constitution that brought about the country's Fifth Republic. The president, who serves as head of state, may serve for two five-year terms. The prime minister, who functions as head of government, is appointed by the president, who chooses one of three candidates proposed by the majority in the legislature. The president also appoints all cabinet ministers and high-ranking military and civilian officers. The legislative branch consists of a 113-member National Assembly. The judicial system, based mostly on French civil law with modifications based on customary law, is headed by a Supreme Court as well as a seven-member Constitutional Court, which has jurisdiction over electoral and constitutional matters.

Background

The Republic of Niger covers an area close to twice the size of Texas. A landlocked nation, Niger is bordered on the north by Algeria, on the east by Chad, and on the south by Nigeria. Its other neighbors are Libya to the northeast, Benin and Burkina Faso to the southwest, and Mali to the west. About four-fifths of Niger is desert, and it is one of the hottest countries in the world.

Archaeological evidence suggests that humans have been in Niger for more than 600,000 years, and that a vibrant economy based on agriculture and cattle herding was being conducted by a mixed population of Libyan, Berber, and Negroid peoples in the Sahara as many as 6,000 years ago. The written history of the region begins in the tenth century with Arab texts chronicling events of that era. Several city-states had been founded along the southern border of what is now Niger by the fourteenth century. The Songhai Empire took control of the area in the early sixteenth century, but by the end of that century Moroccan invaders had seized the region. By the beginning of the nineteenth century, several groups competed for political control of the region, including the Hausa, Tuareg, Bornu, and Fulani peoples. European explorers also began arriving in the area around this time.

By 1900 the French had made military inroads into the region, and in 1901 the military district of Niger was established as part of a larger entity called Haut-Senegal et Niger. Rebellions against the French persisted all the way through World War I, and the region did not become peaceful until 1922, the year France officially made Niger a colony. During its colonial period, Niger had a governor, but was mainly ruled via a governor-general in Dakar, Senegal, who took orders from Paris. From 1932 to 1947, Niger and Upper Volta—now called Burkina Faso—were administered jointly by the French. After World War II, the French granted citizenship to the inhabitants of all of its African colonies, including Niger, and gradually began devolving power to local government officials. Niger became an autonomous state within the French Community in 1958, and two years later it became fully independent, with Hamani Diori as its first president.

Government Structure

During Niger's first several years of independence, Diori maintained friendly relations with France, and consequently received substantial financial, military, and technical support from the French, enabling him to retain firm control of the government. However, in the aftermath of the devastating drought that affected the entire region in the late 1960s and early 1970s, Diori was deposed in a 1974 military coup orchestrated by his former chief of staff, Lieutenant Colonel Seyni Kountché (1931–1987).

Following the coup, Kountché assumed the presidency, adopting a foreign policy that was largely pro-Western. He fought off a coup attempt in 1983. In November 1987 Kountché died and was succeeded as president by army chief of staff Ali Seybou.

Soon after taking office, Seybou sought to establish a one-party system in Niger, forming the National Movement for Developing Society (MNSD) in 1989. Around this time, however, democracy movements were sweeping the region, and the public clamored for the participation of multiple parties in the country's legislative system. In Niger, this movement was led by trade unions, which held a two-day general strike to protest

Seybou's actions. In 1991 a National Conference was held to hammer out the parameters for a new constitution. The conference yielded an interim government led by Amadou Cheiffou, which was to work in tandem with the incumbent government to plan for multiparty elections. Elections were postponed due to rebellion in the north, but a new constitution was adopted by national referendum in December of 1992.

In February 1993, Niger held its first multiparty elections. In a close vote, Mahamane Ousmane (1950–) emerged as winner of the March runoff election for president. MNSD won 29 seats in the National Assembly, more than any other party, but the Alliance of Forces of Change (AFC), a coalition of nine opposition parties led by Prime Minister Mahamadou Issoufou, gained control of the legislature by taking 50 of 83 assembly seats. The new government's first order of business was to contend with a growing, mostly Tuareg insurgency in the north. A truce was reached with the biggest Tuareg group, the Liberation Front of Air and Azaouak, but with several different Tuareg factions in the picture, fighting continued across the region.

The AFC coalition showed signs of stress over the next few years, and in the legislative elections of 1995, the MNSD, in alliance with another party, the Democratic and Social Convention, seized control of the National Assembly. A year later control of the assembly became moot, as Colonel Ibrahim Baré Mainassara (1950–1999) led a coup that ousted Ousmane. Baré and his military regime dissolved the National Assembly and held sway until another military coup in 1999.

Niger's current government is based on the 1999 constitution that brought the nation's Fifth Republic. This constitution created four new government entities: the Constitutional Court, which frequently overrules presidential decrees and rejects candidates for local office; the Superior National Defense Council; the Council of the Republic, a conflict resolution body; and the Economic, Social, and Cultural Council.

At the local level, Niger is divided into eight regions or departments, which are in turn composed of thirty-six districts and a capital district. As democracy has improved in recent years, more power has been devolved to these local units.

Political Parties and Factions

The MNSD, originally the sole legal political party in Niger, has remained a powerful force. Mamadou Tandja (1938–) was elected president in 1999 and 2004 as the MNSD candidate. In the 2004 legislative elections, the MNSD, in coalition with a handful of smaller parties collectively called the Alliance for the Forces of Democracy, captured 37 percent of the votes cast and won forty-seven of the Assembly's 113 seats.

Niger's primary opposition party is the left-wing Nigerien Party for Democracy and Socialism (PNDS), led by Issoufou, the former prime minister, who came in second in the 2004 presidential election. PNDS won seventeen seats in the 2004 legislative elections, but in alliance with a few other parties on the left it controls a total of twenty-five seats, making it the second most powerful bloc in the National Assembly.

The Democratic and Social Convention, led by former president Ousmane, is another potent political force, controlling twenty-two seats in the National Assembly.

Major Events

Niger's economy prospered during the 1970s under Kountché, largely thanks to a uranium boom. In the early 1980s, tensions arose with Libya. Disturbed by Libya's military adventures in Chad, Kountché broke off diplomatic relations with Libya in 1981. While relations improved and diplomatic ties were restored the following year, Niger remained wary of Libya's potential to meddle in its affairs, particularly with regard to rebellious Tuaregs in northern Niger.

Upon seizing control of Niger's government in a 1996 coup, Baré dissolved the National Assembly, suspended the constitution and all political parties, and arrested the president, prime minister, and legislative leaders. He promised a swift return to civilian rule, but the international community was not convinced. Donor nations withdrew much of their desperately needed financial assistance. A new constitution that increased the power of the executive branch was drafted, and multiparty elections were scheduled for May 1996. Baré proclaimed himself the winner and his party captured the majority of Assembly seats in elections universally condemned as being tainted by massive fraud. While running a multiparty democracy in name, Baré beat down the opposition with wholesale civil rights violations and harassment of the media.

In April 1999, Baré was assassinated and his government toppled in a military coup led by Maj. Daouda Mallam Wanké (1954–2004). As with the previous coups in Niger, Wanké pledged a rapid return to civilian democratic government. He formed a National Reconciliation Council to oversee the transition back to constitutional rule. Niger's voters approved a new constitution in July 1999, and legislative and presidential elections were held that fall. In an election called free and fair by international observers, Tandja was elected president with nearly 60 percent of the vote. His MNSD party also did well in the National Assembly elections, capturing thirty-eight of eighty-three seats. One of the new Assembly's first actions was to declare amnesty for those who had taken part in the 1996 and 1999 coups. Successful elections in 2004 resulted in Tandja's reelection and continuing domination of the Assembly by MNSD.

Twenty-First Century

With the exception of a 2002 rebellion by a small group of soldiers dissatisfied with their salaries and working conditions, relative calm has prevailed in Niger's political arena since the establishment of its Fifth Republic in 1999. Nevertheless, the ruling MNSD coalition faces monumental challenges. Food shortages arise frequently, including a serious one in the second half of 2005 that brought much criticism of the government. The opposition party PNDS accused the Tandja regime of diverting aid, and blamed it for reacting slowly to the crisis. A difficult climate and persistent poverty will continue to challenge Niger in the coming years.

BIBLIOGRAPHY

Lund, Christian. *Law, Power and Politics in Niger: Land Struggles and the Rural Code*. London: Lit Verlag, 1998.

Miles, William F. S. *Hausaland Divided: Colonialism and Independence in Nigeria and Niger*. Ithaca, NY: Cornell University Press, 1994.

Niger, Background Paper. Washington, DC: International Monetary Fund, 1996.

⊕ Burkina Faso

Type of Government

Burkina Faso is a republic with a president who serves as chief of state and chairs a council of ministers, from among which he or she appoints a prime minister. The president serves for a term of five years; this was reduced from seven years by an amendment to the constitution in 2000. The legislative branch consists of a single house, the 111-member National Assembly. Members of the assembly are elected by popular vote to a five-year term. At the head of the judicial system is the Supreme Court. Courts of appeals in Ouagadougou and Bobo-Diolasso are at the next level below.

Background

Burkina Faso, formerly known as Upper Volta, is a landlocked nation located in the "hump" of West Africa. With an area of about 106,000 square miles, its footprint is a little bigger than that of the state of Colorado.

The pre-colonial history of the land that is now Burkina Faso is to a large extent the story of the Mossi people. Oral history suggests that the Mossi arrived in the region during the eleventh through thirteenth centuries as warriors from Central or East Africa. Once there, they seized control of the area from weaker aboriginal people, including the Ninigi tribes. The Mossi established five separate kingdoms in the region—Tenkodogo, Yatenga, Gourma, Zandoma, and Ouagadougou—each ruled by its own king, with Ouagadougou the most powerful of the states. Over the next few centuries, the Mossi battled frequently against their powerful neighbor empires, Mali and Songhai.

Europeans did not arrive in the region until the 1870s, by which time the Mossi kings' power and reach had declined substantially. The French, after first gaining a strong foothold in surrounding countries, entered the Mossi-controlled territory in 1896, and within the year, they had succeeded in taking Ouagadougou. For the Mossi, subjugation by the French was not entirely unwelcome; at least it provided a measure of protection against the neighbors with whom they had a long history of hostility. Upper Volta, as the region was called, was designated a military zone by the French in 1899, and from 1904 to 1919 it was part of the broader French colony of Upper Volta-Senegal-Niger. Upper Volta became a separate colony in 1919.

In 1932 the French dissolved Upper Volta and divided its territory among Niger, French Sudan (now Mali), and the Ivory Coast. The traditional ruling structures of the Mossi remained intact, however, and the king of Ouagadougou maintained an intermediary role between the French and their Mossi subjects. It remained the goal of traditional Mossi leaders to eventually restore Upper Volta as a territorial entity, and following World War II it once again became a French colony. In 1958 the people of Upper Volta overwhelmingly voted to make their country an autonomous republic within the French Community. Upper Volta became a fully independent nation two years later. The new nation's constitution, ratified in November 1960, strengthened the presidency, established a single-chamber legislature, and created the groundwork for a multi-party system.

Government Structure

Under its first president, Maurice Yaméogo, leader of the Volta Democratic Union, the government of Upper Volta quickly moved toward authoritarianism, and Yaméogo banned all opposition parties. A one-party slate of candidates was put up for election in 1965, and the opposition, along with a broad range of civil servants, trade union members, students, and others, was outraged. A general strike was called in 1966, and with the support of trade unionists, a military coup ensued. Yaméogo was replaced as president by Sangoulé Lamizana (1916–2005), a high-ranking military leader and former army chief of staff. Lamizana organized a government with himself as its leader, and announced that civilian rule would be restored after four years of government by the military.

Upper Volta's "Second Republic" was born with the adoption of a new constitution in 1970. Lamizana was to carry on as president for an additional four years, with the power to appoint a prime minister, whom the National Assembly was authorized to expel. In legislative elections in December of that year, the African Democratic Rally (Rassemblement Democratique Africain; RDA) party took control of the Assembly, and RDA leader Gérard Kango Ouedraogo was named prime minister. When chaos erupted in the legislature in 1974, Lamizana again intervened and reestablished military rule. This led to the ratification of yet another new constitution in 1977,

establishing Upper Volta's "Third Republic." Lamizana prevailed in the presidential election held the following spring, and the RDA won a plurality of seats in the legislature. The fragile new government was shaken further by labor strikes in the fall of 1980. In November of that year, Colonel Saye Zerbo led a military coup. Zerbo and his allies suspended the constitution, banned political parties, and established a ruling body called the Military Recovery Committee for National Progress. Zerbo's regime did not last long. In November 1982 he was overthrown by an alliance of radical and conservative military factions.

The government was headed by the newly created Council for the People's Salvation (CSP), with Surgeon-Major Jean-Baptiste Ouédraogo as president and Capt. Thomas Sankara (1949–1987), one of the radical military leaders who orchestrated the coup, as prime minister. Sankara soon made moves to switch the country's allegiances from the United States and the West toward friendlier relationships with anti-Western states such as Libya, Cuba, and North Korea. He renamed the nation Burkina Faso, which translates approximately as "Land of Upright Men." During the months that followed, Sankara was toppled by conservatives, then restored to power via yet another coup. He became head of state and formed an anti-imperialist, Marxist-Leninist government headed by a ruling body called the National Revolutionary Council. Revolutionary councils were formed at every level of society to replace existing civil structures.

Disillusioned by Sankara's increasingly totalitarian ways, an old ally of his, Captain Blaise Compaoré (1950–), led a 1987 coup in which Sankara was killed. Compaoré took over as president. His Popular Front government adopted a friendlier attitude toward free enterprise and the West, and within a few years renounced communism. A new constitution was drafted in 1991, calling for a multiparty National Assembly and a directly elected president, who would serve a seven-year term. Compaoré ran for president unopposed, and his party, the Popular Democratic Organization-Worker's Movement (ODP-MT) gained control of the Assembly. Compaoré has been reelected twice, most recently in 2005.

Political Parties and Factions

The Congress for Democracy and Progress (CDP) was formed in 1996 through the merger of ODP-MT with about ten other parties that supported Compaoré. The CDP proceeded to dominate the 1997 legislative elections, winning 101 of 111 seats in the National Assembly. The party took 57 seats in the 2002 elections.

The RDA is a descendant of the national movement born after World War II to spark independence in the various French colonies of West Africa. The party was revived in Burkina Faso in 1991, and came in third place in Assembly elections the following year. In 2002 RDA partnered with another party, the Alliance for Democracy and Federation, to win seventeen seats. ADF was founded in 1990 by the son of former president Maurice Yaméogo.

Another major party in Burkina Faso is the Party for African Independence (PAI), which was active in the 1970s as a pro-Soviet Marxist party, and later banned by Sankara. PAI reemerged in the 1990s and has won a handful of seats in subsequent Assembly elections.

Major Events

Burkina Faso has been plagued by political instability throughout its history as an independent nation. To some degree, this was the result of France's obliteration of most of the country's pre-colonial structures of authority. During its first twenty years of independence, Burkina Faso cycled through a series of alternating civilian and military governments, ratifying—and subsequently suspending—three constitutions along the way. The 1980s marked Burkina Faso's flirtation with communism under Sankara. He had served as prime minister under the moderate president Jean-Baptiste Ouédraogo, before being forced out in a 1983 purge. Sankara seized power just a few months later by orchestrating the third overthrow in as many years in Upper Volta.

In 1985 Burkina Faso went to war against Mali over a narrow stretch of land that had been contested by the two countries for more than a decade. The skirmish was finally settled in December 1986, when the International Court of Justice ruled that the territory should be divided in roughly equal portions. Both countries accepted the decision.

Many of the revolutions that have taken place in Burkina Faso have been presaged by labor unrest on the part of trade unionists, who have managed to retain their independence and influence through most of the nation's history. Sankara's presidency was marked by frequent tussles with labor leaders. Compaoré's overthrow of Sankara in 1987 was generally cheered by trade unions and civil servants. Upon his ouster, Sankara was immediately shot, along with twelve of his aides.

Twenty-First Century

As one of the poorest countries in the world, Burkina Faso's challenges in the twenty-first century are immense. Four-fifths of the population is involved in subsistence farming, and the country suffers from inadequate infrastructure and a low literacy rate. Many people migrate to neighboring countries to find employment; the money that comes into Burkina Faso in this way is second only to cotton exports as a source of revenue. Steadier trade with other countries in the region, and extended peace in those countries, are keys to political stability and improving economic conditions in Burkina Faso.

BIBLIOGRAPHY

Engberg-Pedersen, Lars. *Endangering Development: Politics, Projects, and Environment in Burkina Faso.* Westport, CT: Praeger, 2003.

Englebert, Pierre. *Burkina Faso: Unsteady Statehood in West Africa.* Boulder, CO: Westview Press, 1996.

Mack-Williams, Kibibi. *Mossi.* New York: Rosen Publishing Group, 1996.

⊕ Republic of Côte d'Ivoire

Type of Government

Côte d'Ivoire is a republic whose executive branch is led by a president popularly elected to a five-year term. The president serves as both head of state and chief executive. The legislative branch consists of a National Assembly, whose 225 members are also elected to terms of five years. Côte d'Ivoire's judicial system is modeled on the French system, but also contains fragments of traditional law. The highest levels of the nation's judicial system are the Supreme Court, the High Court of Justice, and the State Security Court. The Supreme Court is divided into four chambers—constitutional, judiciary, administrative, and auditing.

Background

Côte d'Ivoire, or the Ivory Coast, rests on the southern coast of Africa's western bulge, sandwiched between Ghana to the east and Liberia to the west. Other neighboring countries include Guinea to the northwest, and Burkina Faso and Mali to the north. Roughly rectangular in shape, Côte d'Ivoire covers about the same area as the state of New Mexico.

The early history of the area now occupied by Côte d'Ivoire is murky. While civilizations have clearly thrived there for many centuries, most of the peoples currently living there are relatively recent arrivals. French missionaries first arrived in what is now Côte d'Ivoire in the mid-seventeenth century, initially landing at the coastal town of Assinie. In 1843 Admiral Louis-Edouard Bouet-Willaumez set up French outposts at Assinie and Grand Bassam, and signed treaties with the local kings of those regions.

After withdrawing to coastal areas briefly after the Franco-Prussian War of 1870, the French expanded further into the region toward the end of the nineteenth century. Given the name Côte d'Ivoire, the area became an official French colony in 1893 with well-defined borders with the Gold Coast (now Ghana) and Liberia. The northern borders would not become clear for another half-century.

In 1904 France consolidated its holdings in the region into the Federation of French West Africa, and Côte d'Ivoire became one of the federation's component territories. Between World War I and World War II, Côte d'Ivoire became a fairly large-scale producer of such tropical products as cocoa, coffee, and mahogany. A long-smoldering independence movement gained steam during the 1940s, when a group of plantation owners led by Félix Houphouët-Boigny (1905–1993) formed the African Agricultural Union (Syndicat Agricole Africain; SAA), which began pressuring French colonial authorities about the conditions under which they were forced to operate.

Following World War II, Côte d'Ivoire was given the status of an overseas territory of France, with representation in the French parliament and an elected territorial assembly. Houphouët-Boigny morphed the SAA into a full-blown political party called the Democratic Party of Côte d'Ivoire (Parti Démocratique de la Côte d'Ivoire; PDCI), which was aligned with the African Democratic Rally (Rassemblement Democratique Africain; RDA), a regional nationalist organization operating across French colonial West Africa. Côte d'Ivoire became an autonomous state within the newly established French Community in 1958. Two years later, the Republic of Côte d'Ivoire declared itself fully independent of France, with Houphouët-Boigny as the nation's first president. A new constitution was adopted in October 1960.

Government Structure

The 1960 constitution called for creation of a unicameral National Assembly, which the PDCI has dominated throughout the nation's history. In fact, between 1960 and 1990 it was the only party allowed by law. The constitution located most political power in the hands of the president, with a legislature acting more or less as a rubber stamp for the president's policies. The constitution contained provisions for judicial review of actions by the executive branch, but since the president controlled judicial appointments, this review authority was rarely exercised. Two plots to overthrow Houphouët-Boigny's government failed in 1963, and in the aftermath of those attempts the president consolidated his control over the PDCI and seized most of the nation's key ministerial posts.

Côte d'Ivoire underwent a period of democratic reform in 1990, following several months of agitation and labor unrest. For the first time in decades, opposition parties were legal. In elections that fall, Houphouët-Boigny was reelected by an overwhelming majority of voters. The PDCI still dominated the National Assembly, winning 161 of 175 seats, with the Ivoirian Popular Front (Front Populaire Ivoirien; FPI) picking up nine seats. The position of prime minister was also created that year. The National Assembly was expanded to 225 seats with the adoption of a new constitution in 2000. Since 2002, Côte d'Ivoire has been torn apart by an uprising that has essentially split the Muslim north from the government-controlled south, with additional forces vying for power from the west as well. International efforts since then have focused on reunifying the nation under a new power-sharing agreement that would include all parties involved in the scuffle.

Political Parties and Factions

The PDCI was founded in 1946 by Houphouët-Boigny, who represented Côte d'Ivoire in the French National Assembly from 1946 to 1959 before leading the nation's drive toward independence. Houphouët-Boigny became Côte d'Ivoire's first president in 1960 and served until his death in 1993, by which time he had become Africa's longest-serving head of state. Forty years of PDCI domination came to an end with the 1999 coup led by Gen. Robert Guei.

The FPI was founded in 1982 by Laurent Gbagbo (1945–), a history professor then in exile in France. Initially an illegal party, the FPI gained legal status in 1990, and quickly became the leading opposition party in Côte d'Ivoire. When elections were called for in 2000 following the military coup the previous year, Gbagbo was the obvious choice to be the FPI's presidential candidate, and he won the election. The FPI's base of power resides in the nation's trade union movement.

The Rally of Republicans (Rassemblement des Republicains, RDR) was formally created in 1994 by a breakaway group from the ruling PDCI, and has been a major party ever since. RDR is best known as the party of Alassane Ouattara (1942–), the former prime minister forced out after losing the power struggle over who would succeed Houphouët-Boigny. RDR is strongest in the Muslim northern part of Côte d'Ivoire. RDR has frequently boycotted national elections since the mid-1990s to protest restrictions placed on the party by the PDCI.

Major Events

During the late 1960s and early 1970s, Côte d'Ivoire experienced several outbreaks of political unrest. In 1969 widespread rioting resulted in the arrests of about 1,500 unemployed youths, and the following year there were uprisings in several cities. A failed coup followed in 1973, after which seven army officers were sentenced to death and many others given stiff prison sentences. Many of these individuals were pardoned or had their sentences reduced a few years later, as Houphouët-Boigny sought to bolster his popularity nationwide. He and his PDCI party retained their firm hold on the government throughout the rest of the 1970s and the 1980s. Côte d'Ivoire enjoyed a period of strong economic growth, emerging as one of the wealthiest nations in black Africa.

Following the reforms of 1990, discontent among the populace continued to grow. A number of opposition leaders were jailed after mass demonstrations broke out in 1992. After Houphouët-Boigny died in 1993, a close ally, Assembly Speaker Henri Konan Bédié (1934–), became acting president, as per the constitution. A rivalry emerged between Bédié and Prime Minister Ouattara.

In 1994, a faction of the PDCI broke away to form the RDR, planning to run Ouattara as its presidential candidate in 1995. Bédié countered by passing a law requiring that all future presidential candidates not only be Ivoirian by birth, but also have been born to Ivoirian-born parents. They must also have lived in the country for at least ten years, and for five years continuously immediately prior to the election. This new law effectively disqualified Ouattara from the upcoming presidential election. Most opposition parties, including the RDR and the FPI, boycotted the 1995 elections, resulting in lopsided wins for Bédié and the PDCI.

Bédié's policies revolved around a concept called *Ivoirité*, which was essentially an attempt to favor "true" ethnic Ivoirians. Naturally, such policies alienated Côte d'Ivoire's large immigrant and Muslim populations; corruption within his administration alienated many others. This growing discontent eventually culminated in the overthrow of Bédié in 1999 by Gen. Guei, his former minister for employment. While Guei's seizure of power had broad support among many portions of the population, including the support of both the FPI and Ouattara, he was not able to sustain that support. A surge of backing for Gbagbo carried him to victory over Guei in the 2000 presidential election. Legislative elections that year resulted in a fairly evenly divided Assembly, with the FPI taking 96 seats and the PDCI 94, and the other 35 seats divided among minor parties and independent candidates.

Major fighting erupted in Côte d'Ivoire in the fall of 2002, as a military coup, in which Guei was probably involved, blossomed into a broader uprising by rebels in the Muslim north against Gbagbo's southern-heavy government. Guei was killed during the fighting. The coup failed, but the country was effectively broken in half, with the northern section under the control of the rebel group, which called itself the Patriotic Movement of Côte d'Ivoire (Mouvement Patriotique de Côte d'Ivoire; MPCI). In November 2002, a new front in the war emerged in the western part of the country with the rise of two more rebel groups. These rebel factions, along with the MPCI, collectively became known as the New Forces.

Peacekeeping troops from France and a handful of African nations intervened, and a cease-fire was declared in early 2003. A French-brokered agreement called the Linas-Marcoussis Accord was reached in late January 2003, calling for a new reconciliation government, with Gbagbo in charge, that included representatives of the New Forces. United Nations peacekeepers remained on hand to help stabilize the fragile situation. Violence continued to flare up over the next two years, including the bombing of a French military installation that killed nine French soldiers and an American civilian.

The fall 2005 elections were postponed amid the turmoil, and the peace process outlined by the Linas-

General Robert Guei holding a press conference in Abidjan after overthrowing the government of Ivorian President Henri Konan Bedie, in 1999. *Jean-Philippe Ksiazek/AFP/Getty Images*

Marcoussis Accord was extended for another year. A new prime minister, Charles Konan Banny, was appointed by African mediators and given broad powers to implement reunification measures. Negotiations and maneuvering toward reunification continued through 2006. After weeks of private negotiations led by Gbagbo, New Forces leader Guillaume Soro, and Burkina Faso President Blaise Compaoré (1950–), a new reunification plan, called the Ougadougou Accord, was put into place in March 2007. It called for elections within ten months, and the gradual return of government officials to the northern part of the country as of the middle of 2007. Soro became prime minister in April.

Twenty-First Century

Côte d'Ivoire was on track for an economic recovery prior to the rebellion of 2002. Since then, the country's economy has been locked into a stagnant state, as efforts to stabilize the government and reunite warring factions have overshadowed any efforts to bolster the economy and address the staggering poverty under which many

Ivoirians live. Côte d'Ivoire's future will hinge on its success or failure in reunifying the nation in a way that meets the very different political and economic needs of the country's various regions and ethnic populations.

BIBLIOGRAPHY

Clark, John F., and Gardinier, David E. *Political Reform in Francophone Africa*. Boulder, CO: Westview Press, 1997.

Rapley, John. *Ivoirien Capitalism: African Entrepreneurs in Cote d'Ivoire*. Boulder, CO: L. Rienner Publishers, 1993.

⊕ Chad

Type of Government

Chad is a parliamentary republic. By constitution, power is divided among executive, legislative, and judicial branches; in practice, much of the authority lies with the executive. The president serves as head of state and commander of the armed forces, while the prime minister serves as head of government. The unicameral parliament is constituted by direct, popular vote. The judicial branch includes a Supreme Court and a Constitutional Council, as well as district and regional courts.

Background

Based on archaeological evidence, historians assert that Chad has been continuously occupied by African tribes since the Prehistoric Period. The first major civilizations to occupy the region were the Berber and Arab ethnic groups that migrated to Chad between the eighth and ninth centuries AD. Through intermarriage and military conquest, immigrant and native populations coalesced into a number of kingdoms that competed for control of the region's natural resources.

From the ninth century three major kingdoms—the Kanem-Bornu, the Bagirmi, and the Wadai—dominated the political and social landscape. The Kanem-Bornu and the Bagirmi were composed largely of Arabic descendants and played a role in bringing Islam to Chad and surrounding regions, while the Wadai was a non–Islamic African kingdom that remained a political force in the region, to varying degrees, into the twentieth century.

From the seventh to the nineteenth centuries, Muslim traders frequently led incursions into the territory to capture slaves. The dominant African kingdoms, such as the Wadai, were better able to resist the slave trade, while smaller kingdoms and transient tribal unions were often obliterated by it. In the eighteenth and nineteenth centuries, European slave traders expanded their operations in Africa, both cooperating and competing with Muslim slave traders, thereby putting additional pressure on native states.

By 1893 Sudanese warlord Rabih al-Zubayr (1842–1900), a slave trader, controlled most of Chad, as well as portions of what are now Sudan and the Central African Republic. His forces eliminated many of the native kingdoms. While his forces were moving into Chad and Sudan, France was also expanding its territorial empire. French forces encountered Rabih's military in the late 1890s and were repelled after a short engagement. The French initially attempted diplomacy, but when Rabih attacked and killed a French detachment in 1899, the French ordered a large contingent of troops from Gabon to confront Rabih's army. In the 1900 Battle of Kousseri in Cameroon, the French defeated Rabih's forces and claimed ownership of all of the warlord's territories.

In 1910 the French territories of Chad, the Central African Republic, the Congo, and Gabon were joined into a single administrative unit, Afrique Équatoriale Française (French Equatorial Africa), or AEF. As Chad was the most remote part of the AEF, it was allowed a certain degree of autonomy. France's main interest in Africa was to exploit its agricultural lands—the most substantial crop was cotton—and mineral deposits for export. Toward that end, the government allowed corporations to assume control of vast portions of the territory.

In 1940–1941 Chad joined the Free France Movement, which was established by French General Charles de Gaulle (1890–1970) to resist the Vichy regime that controlled France after it surrendered to the Nazis. As a result of Chad's involvement, the Free French parties invested heavily in Chad and made its governor, Félix Eboué (1885–1944), the governor-general of the AEF. Eboué, who was of mixed African and French descent, advanced the cause of decentralization and lobbied for local representation in the territorial assemblies. The constitution was amended to allow native participation in 1945, the year after Eboué died.

During the next decade Chadians attempted to implement changes in the political structure, though French officials still dominated the local government and placed restrictions on local assembly. The independence movement was vibrant but not violent. As its colonial era drew to a close, France gradually allowed greater autonomy for its territories. In 1958 Chad became an autonomous region of France; two years later it was granted full independence.

Government Structure

Chad is divided into eighteen administrative districts, each run by a presidentially appointed governor and regional assembly. The capital city, N'Djamena, is under central authority and headed by an appointed mayor. The administrative structure of the republic is in transition, however; the constitution was amended in 2005 to allow regional leaders to be elected by popular vote.

The president, who serves as chief of state and commander of the armed forces, appoints the prime minister, military leaders, the judiciary, and heads of state-owned industries. Elected by direct, popular vote, the president can

François Tombalbaye, president of Chad, in Paris, 1963. © *Bettmann/ CORBIS*

serve an unlimited number of five-year terms; in the constitutional referendum of 2005, some 65 percent of the voters agreed to remove the presidential term limit, although the vote was boycotted by many political parties. The president, who must have the approval of the legislature for budgetary and military proposals, can dissolve the legislature in cases of persistent deadlock.

The unicameral National Assembly has 155 members, who are elected by direct, popular vote for four-year terms. They can run for re-election. The primary duty of the assembly is to produce and review legislation and to approve executive policy. The constitution adopted in 1996 called for the formation of a second chamber, the Senate, but the plan was not initiated. The 2005 constitutional referendum replaced the proposed Senate with an Economic, Social, and Cultural Council, which has yet to be formed.

The judicial branch is constitutionally designated as independent of the executive, but in practice, presidential appointments keep the judiciary responsive to executive policy. The nation's highest court is the Supreme

Court, which consists of a chief justice and fifteen justices, all appointed by the president with approval of the legislature. They serve nine-year terms. The Supreme Court has final appellate jurisdiction over all lower courts. The Constitutional Council, consisting of nine justices, presides over cases involving constitutional law, treaties, and international agreements. The president of the republic and the president of the legislature appoint justices to the Constitutional Council, with the approval of the legislature.

Political Parties and Factions

The Mouvement Patriotique de Salut (Patriotic Salvation Movement), or MPS, organized in the 1990s as an antigovernment rebel group near the country's border with Sudan, has been the majority party since the presidential elections of 1996 and parliamentary election of 1997. The MPS is a centrist political party, focused on ending civil war and advancing economic reforms. MPS presidential candidate Idriss Déby (1952–) won 64 percent of the popular vote in 2006. The party won 110 seats in the last legislative elections, held in 2002.

The Rassemblement pour la Démocratie et le Progrès (Rally for Democracy and Progress), or RDP, was founded in 1992. It represents the interests of Chadian Muslims and the Kanembu ethnic group, who are descendants of the Kanem-Bornu Empire. The RDP ran candidates for the legislature and presidency in 1996 and supported the MPS party during the 2002 elections, winning twelve seats in the National Assembly. The RDP boycotted the 2005 constitutional referendum on removing the presidential term limit.

The Rassemblement National pour le Développement et le Progrès (National Rally for Development and Progress), or RNDP, was founded by Delwa Koumakoye (1949–). Koumakoye ran for president in 1996 and received approximately 2 percent of the popular vote. The party was active in the 1997 legislative elections but did not win any seats in the assembly. By the 2002 legislative elections, the visibility of the RNDP party had grown; it won five seats in the assembly. Koumakoye received the second-highest number of votes in the 2006 presidential election; his party was one of the few that did not take part in a boycott. Koumakoye was appointed prime minister in 2007.

In addition to the major political parties, Chad has a number of radical and rebel groups that, while not competitive in national elections, exert influence over legislative development. For example, the Forces Unies pour le Changement (United Front for Democratic Change), the nation's largest and most powerful rebel group, began as an alliance of several smaller groups opposed to the Déby administration. It initiated armed attacks against government forces in 2005 and 2006 but was repelled by the Chadian army and French peacekeeping troops. Déby's administration agreed to negotiate, but the organization has remained a threat to government security.

Major Events

Chad's first president, François "N'Garta" Tombalbaye (1918–1975), was hampered by problems inherited from French administration. The nation was divided into distant economic markets with little communication and integration and was rife with interethnic and tribal conflict. As a result Tombalbaye's policies became progressively authoritarian. In 1962 the administration banned all political parties except the ruling Parti Progressiste Tchadien (Chad Progressive Party), and the following year dissolved the legislature. Political groups rose in opposition to Tombalbaye's regime and staged frequent protests; the police often responded with force. When rioting occurred in 1963, Tombalbaye established a new criminal court to prosecute and imprison political opponents.

By the late 1960s Tombalbaye's policies had deepened ethnic, religious, economic, and social divisions. He was seen as a representative of the southern, foreign-educated portions of society, while many in the western and northern parts of the country believed their interests were not being represented. In addition, Tombalbaye's policies weakened the government's standing with the Islamic population, increasing religious tensions. Anti–Tombalbaye factions in the North eventually gathered behind the Front de Libération Nationale du Tchad (National Liberation Front of Chad), or FROLINAT, a rebel group that attempted to overthrow the government militarily.

Under pressure from France and domestic groups, Tombalbaye agreed to widespread reforms and the release of political prisoners. He allowed Islamic and northern leaders to play a larger role in local governments and increased government aid for ethnic groups living at the periphery of the nation. The reforms temporarily reduced civil disturbances; however, they were insufficient to stop many of his opponents. In 1975 Tombalbaye was assassinated in a coup led by members of the military.

Former military leader Félix Malloum (1932–) became president after Tombalbaye's death. Malloum's administration attempted to end civil strife by appointing northern leader Hissène Habré (1942–) as prime minister in 1978. The union between Malloum and Habré did not last, however. Malloum eventually fled the country when civil war broke out between forces loyal to Habré and those loyal to FROLINAT leader Goukouni Oueddei (1944–).

The civil war involved dozens of militant groups and political factions. Oueddei's faction gained the aid of the Libyan military because of a political deal: Upon victory, Oueddei said, Chad would cede to Libya the Aouzou Strip, an area along its northern border. Libya had long claimed ancestral ownership of the territory and was enticed by its uranium deposits. In response the United States and France lent military support to Habré's south-

ern faction. The civil war resulted in stalemate, with neither side winning much new territory.

In 1990 Habré's regime was overthrown in a military coup, and Déby was installed as president. He persuaded the Libyan government to allow the International Court of Justice to determine the disposition of the Aouzou Strip; in 1994 the court said the strip was the property of Chad, effectively ending Libyan involvement in the civil war.

Although Oueddei never officially relinquished control of the northern territories, between 1994 and 1996 more than a dozen rebel groups signed peace agreements to end hostilities in the region. Déby reinstated the parliamentary government. Déby won 69 percent of the popular vote in the presidential election of 1996.

Twenty-First Century

Déby was reelected in 2001, although many opponents claimed the government corrupted the vote-tabulation system. After a referendum in 2005 eliminated the presidential term limit, he competed in the 2006 election and was reelected to a third term, winning more than 60 percent of the popular vote; many parties boycotted the election in protest of the abolishment of the term limit, however. International observers contended that the election was fraught with irregularities, but they also commended the Déby administration for its efforts to end the civil war.

BIBLIOGRAPHY

Azevedo, Mario J. *Roots of Violence: A History of War in Chad*. Oxford: Routledge, 1998.

Meredith, Martin. *The Fate of Africa: From the Hopes of Freedom to the Heart of Despair*. New York: PublicAffairs, 2005.

Nugent, Paul. *Africa Since Independence: A Comparative History*. New York: Palgrave Macmillan, 2004.

⊕ Central African Republic

Type of Government

By constitution the Central African Republic (CAR) is a parliamentary democracy with executive, legislative, and judiciary branches. In practice, however, it operates as a presidential regime with close ties to the military. The president, who is elected by popular vote, serves as head of state and commander of the armed forces. The prime minister, who serves as head of government, is chosen by the unicameral legislature, which is constituted through direct, popular vote. The judicial branch is constitutionally independent, although, like the rest of the government, it is subordinate to presidential policy. The nation is divided into prefectures and subprefectures, whose leaders are appointed by the president.

Background

Archaeological evidence indicates that the Central African Republic has been occupied continually since Paleolithic times. In the seventh century AD the nation was occupied by a succession of imperial dynasties. With the rise of the Islamic slave trade in neighboring nations, the Central African Republic became the site of numerous slave camps, and the native tribes were threatened with capture and exportation. By the nineteenth century the Banda, the Baya, and the Ngbandi were the primary ethnic groups.

At the same time the French were sending expeditions into the area from their outposts in the Congo. They negotiated trade agreements with local leaders and, by 1897, were claiming the CAR as French territory. As they explored the interior, they confronted Sudanese slave trader Rabih al-Zabayr (1842–1900), who had established a formidable empire in neighboring Chad. In 1899 they dispatched Ferdinand de Béhagle (1857–1899) to negotiate with Rabih, but he imprisoned De Béhagle and his party. The French retaliated with a military detachment, which was defeated in its first encounter with Rabih's forces. The French then sent additional troops from Gabon and ended Rabih's empire, claiming possession of all of the warlord's territories.

In 1905 the French organized the CAR, Chad, the Congo, and Gabon into a single administrative unit known as Afrique Équatoriale Française (French Equatorial Africa), or AEF, and in the next several decades developed its agricultural production, focusing on such plantation crops as coffee, cotton, and rubber, and mining operations—the region was rich in gold and diamonds. They allowed private companies to lease and operate portions of the territory without any governmental oversight. Forced labor was common, and the natives were allowed few rights.

An underground independence movement led several failed rebellions. After the Kongo-Wara uprising of 1928–1931, led by workers groups in the South, the French forced large portions of the population into prisons and work camps. When a second rebellion erupted in 1935, France committed additional troops to the region at significant expense to its ailing economy.

During World War II CAR natives joined the Free French Movement, which was founded to resist the Vichy government that controlled France after it surrendered to the Nazis. Following the war the independence movement gained greater support among the French populace. A final rebellion in 1946 persuaded the government to allow moderate democratic reforms: It granted French citizenship to all CAR natives and allowed the formation of local assemblies.

In 1946 Roman Catholic priest Barthélemy Boganda (1910–1959) became the first African elected to the French National Assembly; from there he led the legislative effort for emancipation, working to enact a new voting system and eventually to dissolve the AEF. When the nation became an autonomous French territory in 1958, Boganda served as its first prime minister.

Boganda died in a plane crash in March 1959, shortly before the country gained its full independence. His relative and political ally David Dacko (1930–2003) took over as the nation's second prime minister and presided over the official independence ceremonies in August 1960. After independence Dacko became the nation's first president.

Government Structure

The Central African Republic is divided into fourteen prefectures, each of which is divided into subprefectures. The leader of each prefecture is appointed by the president of the republic. The capital region, Bangui, is considered an autonomous *commune*, or township, and is administered by the central government. According to the revised constitution, which was adopted in 2004, the central government operates as a parliamentary democracy, with officials chosen in two-round runoff elections: Several candidates stand for office in the first round; the two candidates who get the most votes then compete in a second round to determine a winner by simple majority.

The executive branch is the most powerful in the government. The president, who is elected by direct, popular vote for a maximum of two terms of five years, serves as head of state and commander of the armed forces. The president appoints military leaders, the judiciary, prefects, subprefects, mayors, council members, and leaders of the state-controlled industries, which include mining and some agricultural enterprises. In times of emergency the president may rule by decree, temporarily suspending the government and granting himself authority to dismiss any governmental official.

According to the constitution, the leading political party in the legislature appoints the prime minister, who serves as head of government. The prime minister then appoints the cabinet, whose members run the various executive departments. In actuality the president has significant influence over all ministerial appointments. The executive branch shares legislative responsibility with the parliament.

The unicameral National Assembly has 105 members, who serve five-year terms and can stand for re-election. The assembly has the power to originate legislation and, according to the constitution, is required to approve executive actions, treaties, and emergency orders. The executive exerts considerable control over the legislature's efforts.

The highest court in the CAR is the Constitutional Court, which handles all cases involving constitutional law. Its justices are appointed: three by the president of the republic, three by the president of the National Assembly, and three by a committee of justices from

Jean-Bédel Bokassa, who seized power in the Central African Republic in a military coup, declared himself Emperor Bokassa I in 1977. © *Richard Melloul/Sygma/CORBIS*

lower courts. Below the constitutional court are the Court of Cassation, which is the final appeals court; the Court of Appeals; and the district courts. Courts in most regions of the CAR are poorly funded and operate infrequently, so most criminal cases are referred to courts in the capital region. Observers have noted that the president exerts considerable influence over the operation of the judiciary.

Political Parties and Factions

Convergence Nationale "Kwa Na Kwa" (National Convergence Party), the dominant political organization in the 2005 election, was founded to support President François Bozizé (1946–), who ran for office as an independent candidate. The party's platform is based on ending the rebel insurgency and initiating democratic and economic reforms.

The Mouvement pour la Libération du Peuple Centrafricain (Movement for the Liberation of the Central African People), or MLPC, was founded in 1979 by Ange-Félix Patassé (1937–), who was president of the

republic from 1993 to 2003. The MLPC opposed the government of David Dacko and supported a platform of increased participation in a streamlined government. In the 2005 elections the MLPC was the primary opposition party to Bozizé and the National Convergence, winning eleven seats in the legislature.

The Rassemblement Démocratique Centraficaine (Central African Democratic Union), or RDC, was founded by former military leader André-Dieudonne Kolingba (1935–). The party was in power until Kolingba was replaced by Patassé in the 1993 elections. Like the other major parties, the RDC is democratic and centrist in basic policies. During the 2005 elections the RDC won eight seats in the legislature, placing third in terms of popular support.

The CAR has a number of minor ethnic and special-interest parties, and during the Bozizé administration, which has focused on democratization, numerous new lobbyist groups have emerged. The defining characteristics of many of them remain unclear.

Major Events

After gaining independence, the CAR kept close economic and political ties to France, which helped to maintain the nation's agricultural export revenues. In 1962 Dacko named the Mouvement d'Évolution Sociale de l'Afrique Noire (Movement for the Social Evolution of Black Africa), or MESAN, as the nation's sole legal political party. Other signs that he was developing an authoritarian regime led to widespread public dissatisfaction. In December 1965 Dacko was overthrown in a military coup led by Jean-Bédel Bokassa (1921–1996).

Although Bokassa initially had public support, he quickly lost that support when it became clear he intended to establish a more authoritarian regime than his predecessor's. Bokassa abrogated the constitution and appointed a cabinet of military leaders to help him rule. In 1976 he crowned himself emperor—the ceremony cost some $200 million—and renamed the nation the Central African Empire. The regime violently stopped any attempts to form opposition groups.

For four years the French government continued its financial support of the Bokassa government in hopes of maintaining its supply of diamonds and raw materials for industry. In September 1979, however, it removed the dictator from power, largely because he was mismanaging the state's mining industry and reducing French profits. The French government reinstated Dacko as president in 1980. Dacko's administration was faced with the imminent threat of public uprising and was forced to rely on the French military to stay in power. In 1981 André Kolingba (1935–), at the time a general, staged a military coup that removed Dacko from power, after which Kolingba formed a provisional military government.

Kolingba's government was led by the Comité Militaire de Redressement National (Military Committee for National Recovery), or CRMN, which functioned as an authoritarian regime but allowed some local participation in the government. Kolingba dissolved the CRMN in 1985—he remained as president—and allowed the formation of a National Assembly with limited public representation. Kolingba and the assembly drafted a new constitution that included provisions for elections. Patassé defeated Kolingba in the 1993 presidential elections, becoming the first democratically elected president since the nation gained its independence.

Patasse's government was faced with frequent turmoil as rival leaders, many representing the military, attempted to organize rebellion. With the help of the French military Patassé avoided three attempted coups in 1996. Shortly thereafter France removed its military from the nation. Patassé was reelected in 1999; further unrest followed.

Twenty-First Century

In 2001 and 2002 two coup attempts were foiled with the assistance of the Libyan military, which intervened in defense of trade agreements between the two nations. In 2003, however, a bloodless coup by Bozizé (1946–) successfully overthrew Patassé. After suspending the constitution and abolishing the government, Bozizé immediately began a campaign to forge peace agreements with rebel leaders. He also promulgated a new constitution, which was adopted in 2004. In the elections held in 2005, Bozizé won the presidential vote, and his party held a slight majority in the newly formed legislature.

In 2006 and 2007 the government fought repeated skirmishes with insurgent groups. The administration continued to negotiate with their leaders, however, and in 2007 signed a peace agreement with the Union of Democratic Forces for Unity (UFDR), a powerful rebel organization.

The CAR is one of the most economically impoverished nations in the world. Though the region is rich in natural resources, centuries of European exploitation followed by decades of political turmoil have prevented the nation from achieving economic growth and stability. More than half of the nation's agricultural production goes to subsistence. The CAR's diamond mining and refinement industry accounts for more than half of the nation's export revenue, but is underdeveloped.

BIBLIOGRAPHY

O'Toole, Thomas E. *The Central African Republic: The Continent's Hidden Heart*. Boulder, Co: Westview Press, 1986.

Titley, Brian. *Dark Age: The Political Odyssey of Emperor Bokassa*. Montreal: McGill-Queen's University Press, 2002.

Villalón, Leonardo A., and Peter VonDoepp, eds. *The Fate of Africa's Democratic Experiments: Elites and Institutions* Bloomington: Indiana University Press, 2005.

⊕ Republic of the Congo

Type of Government

The Republic of the Congo, long known as Congo-Brazzaville, is a presidential republic. The president, who serves as head of state, head of government, and commander of the armed forces, is assisted by an appointed cabinet of ministers. Members of the bicameral legislature are chosen in multiparty elections. The judicial branch is headed by a Constitutional Court and a Supreme Court.

Background

The nation was first inhabited more than forty thousand years ago by hunter-gatherer tribes. The Baku pygmies were among the first to settle in its dense forests and savannahs. They were followed by the Bantu ethnolinguistic group, which established hundreds of kingdoms, the largest of which were the Kongo, the Luango, and the Tio, that survived for many centuries.

In 1482–83 Portuguese explorer Diogo Cão became the first European to visit the region. Subsequent expeditions from Portugal established trade agreements with some of the larger kingdoms. Initially, most African states welcomed Portuguese trade; in fact, the Kingdom of Kongo sent emissaries to Europe to meet with Portuguese leaders. However, as the European and Muslim slave trade grew, relations between native and European kingdoms deteriorated. By the nineteenth century most of the native kingdoms had been compromised by the slave trade and European encroachment.

At the end of the nineteenth century the British, the French, the Belgians, and the Portuguese all claimed portions of the Congo River basin. In 1880 French explorer Pierre Savorgnan de Brazza (1852–1905) obtained a treaty with the Kingdom of Tio that gave France the strongest claim to the Congo. The French then expanded their export communities along the Congo River and, after defeating slave-trading sultanates and native kingdoms, controlled what are now the Republic of Congo, Chad, Gabon, and the Central African Republic. Beginning in 1905 they administered the territories as a single administrative division, Afrique Équatoriale Française (French Equatorial Africa), or AEF, with Brazzaville as the capital.

The French leased large portions of the AEF to export companies and gave them fairly free rein. Millions of native Africans were forced into labor by mining and agricultural corporations. The most famous of France's construction projects was the Congo-Ocean Railway, built between 1924 and 1934. It is estimated that more than fifteen thousand Africans died during the construction of the rail system; thousands more lived in extreme poverty in work camps along the construction line.

During the 1940s Congo-Brazzaville became the African headquarters of the Free France Movement, established by French General Charles De Gaulle (1890–1970) to resist the Vichy government that controlled France after it surrendered to the Nazis. Félix Eboué (1884–1944), who had been governor of Chad, led the movement in Africa. He was also the first native African to serve as governor-general of the AEF. Under Eboué's leadership, the AEF liberalized its policies and allowed more native representation. Forced labor was abolished, and the Congolese were granted French citizenship. Congo-Brazzaville was designated as a French territory in 1946, after which the Congo was permitted to elect representatives to the French National Assembly.

The French government eventually decided to dissolve the AEF and allowed each territory to vote whether it wanted to seek full independence. The Congo voted to become an autonomous republic within the French community, renamed the Republic of the Congo, and began forming political parties and working toward elected leadership. The Republic of Congo gained its formal independence in August 1960.

Government Structure

The Republic of the Congo promulgated a new constitution in 2002, adopting a multiparty democratic system. It is divided into ten regional units, each led by a regional governor. The capital, Brazzaville, is designated as a *commune* and is administered by the central government.

The president, who serves as head of state, head of government, and commander of the armed forces, is elected by popular vote for up to two terms of seven years. Although the constitution provides for a prime minister—Isidore Mvouba (1954–) was appointed in 2005—the role of the prime minister has not been defined. Mvouba has served as the president's chief deputy. The members of the Council of Ministers, who are appointed by the president, direct the nation's executive departments. The president also has the power to appoint members of the judiciary and leaders of the military. The executive branch cooperates with the legislature in creating and amending laws.

The 2002 constitution established a bicameral legislature. The upper chamber, the Senate, has sixty-six members, who are elected for six-year terms by local, district, and regional councils. The National Assembly has 137 members, who are elected by popular vote for five-year terms. Members of both houses can run for re-election. The executive and legislative branches are independent, with neither branch having the power to dissolve or dismiss the other.

The Constitutional Court is designated as the nation's leading judicial organization and has authority over constitutional law, treaties, and international agreements. Below the Constitutional Court is the Supreme Court, which has final appellate jurisdiction over all lower courts. Justices are nominated and approved by the legislature and then appointed by the president for lifetime terms. Neither the president nor the legislature has the power to remove justices from the Supreme Court. Though the constitution calls for an independent judiciary, observers have noted that the executive branch exerts significant control over the courts.

Political Parties and Factions

The Parti Congolais du Travail (Congolese Labor Party), or PCT, established in 1997, is the nation's dominant political party; it controls the executive branch and holds legislative majorities. The PCT is a socialist-democratic party that supports a strong central government. Denis Sassou-Nguesso (1943–), who has been president since 1997, led the development and adoption, by referendum, of the 2002 constitution. During the 2002 legislative elections, the PCT secured fifty-three seats in the National Assembly.

The PCT is allied with the Forces Démocratiques Unies (United Democratic Forces), or FDU, which also nominated Sassou-Nguesso as its presidential candidate in 2002. The FDU, whose policies are similar to those of the PCT, won thirty seats in the National Assembly, the second highest total, which increased Sassou-Nguesso's support in the legislature.

Many of the nation's larger parties, including the Union Panafricaine pour la Démocratie Sociale (Pan African Union for Social Democracy), boycotted the 2002 elections because they believed Sassou-Nguesso's supporters would use intimidation and fraud to control the election results. The only significant party to challenge the PCT and FDU in 2002 was the Union pour la Démocratie et la République–Mwinda (Union for Democracy and Republic), or UDR, under the leadership of André Milongo (1935–). It won six seats in the National Assembly. More than a thousand independent and politically aligned candidates registered to compete in the 2007 legislative elections.

Major Events

After gaining independence in 1960, Congo-Brazzaville maintained close relations with France, which provided military and economic aid. The efforts of the nation's first president, Fulbert Youlou (1917–1972), were compromised by ethnic and political turmoil, and within three years he was removed from power in a military coup. He was replaced by Alphonse Massamba-Débat (1921–1977), a leader of the nation's socialist party. He attempted to transform the nation into a communist regime, forming economic and military alliances with the People's Republic of China and the Union of Soviet Socialist Republics (USSR). In 1966 Massamba-Débat established a single-party presidential system and, two

Fulbert Youlou, president of the Republic of the Congo, with U.S. President John F. Kennedy in 1961. *© Bettmann/CORBIS*

years later, dissolved the parliament. In 1968 a group of military and radical political leaders staged another coup, removing Massamba-Débat from power and establishing an interim government.

In 1969 a new communist regime was established under the leadership of Marien Ngouabi (1938–1977), whose new Marxist party renamed the nation the People's Republic of Congo. It also established a socialized system that limited popular assembly and political opposition. Ngouabi's administration prevented seven coups before he was assassinated in 1977 by a group of military leaders, who were said to have had ties to Massamba-Débat. Ngouabi's Marxist regime remained in power, however, appointing Joachim Yohimbe-Opango (1939–) to serve as president. Massamba-Débat and several of his political allies were executed for their part in the assassination of Ngouabi. Two years later, amid accusations of corruption and deviation from party policy, Yohimbe-Opango was forced to resign and sent into exile. Sassou-Nguesso was installed as the nation's next president.

During the 1980s, with the USSR as the nation's chief military and economic ally, the People's Republic of Congo was transformed into a moderate socialist state with liberalized economic policies. Sassou-Nguesso improved relations with France during that period, after

he allowed moderate democratic reforms. Still, the economy suffered from poor internal and foreign investment and the burden of governmental debt. After the collapse of the Soviet Union, Sassou-Nguesso was forced to surrender to the economic crisis and agreed to allow multiparty elections. Congo-Brazzaville underwent political reconstruction and was renamed the Republic of the Congo.

In 1992 the nation held its first democratic elections since independence, and socialist party candidate Pascal Lissouba (1931–) won a runoff election against Sassou-Nguesso, receiving more than 60 percent of the vote. Opposition parties disputed the election results, however; they accused the government of using invalid counting methods and other forms of voter fraud. The political situation quickly deteriorated. Sassou-Nguesso's allies, led by former military leaders, launched an armed rebellion against the government, taking control of parts of Brazzaville. Lissouba attempted to control the uprising but was unsuccessful. In 1997 he and his allies fled to London to avoid capture, and Sassou-Nguesso reclaimed the presidency.

Sassou-Nguesso established a transitional government that lasted until 1999. The nation was then under martial law while the regime faced continuous insurgency—most notably from an ethnic group in the southern Pool region who call themselves Ninjas, after the caped Japanese warriors. In 2003 Sassou-Nguesso held a series of meetings with opposition leaders and succeeded in securing peace agreements.

Twenty-First Century

Since the 2003 peace accords, the Republic of the Congo has enjoyed a reprieve from civil war and seen signs of economic improvement. The administration has worked with other governments, the World Bank, and the International Monetary Fund to encourage foreign investment, which became possible when relative political stability was achieved. Despite those efforts, thousands of Congolese live in severe poverty.

BIBLIOGRAPHY

Clark, John F., ed. *The African Stakes of the Congo War.* New York: Palgrave MacMillan, 2002.

Edgerton, Robert. *The Troubled Heart of Africa: A History of the Congo.* New York: St. Martin's Press, 2002.

Jan Van Eyck Acadamie. *Brakin: Brazzaville-Kinshasa; Visualizing the Visible.* Baden, Switzerland: Lars Müller Publishers, 2006.

⊕ Gabonese Republic

Type of Government

The Gabonese Republic has a multiparty government, with powers divided between executive, legislative, and judicial branches. The executive branch consists of the president, prime minister, and an appointed cabinet of ministers. The president utilizes dismissal and appointment powers to dominate the legislature and the judiciary. The bicameral legislature is constituted through direct, popular vote. The judicial branch is constitutionally independent but functionally subordinate to executive policy. The president appoints the governors of the nation's nine administrative divisions.

Background

Archaeologists have found artifacts in Gabon, a small country on the western coast of Africa, that indicate the presence of numerous hunter-gatherer tribes as early as 7000 BC. By AD 1100 the Bantu were the dominant ethnic group, which was divided into a number of kingdoms—the Fang and the Loango were the largest and controlled most of the interior of the region. The Portuguese first visited Gabon in the 1470s, but efforts to establish settlements were hindered by disease.

In the fifteenth century the native Gabonese were under pressure from Islamic slave traders, who intermittently raided villages near the coast to acquire slaves. British, French, and Dutch traders also conducted expeditions to Gabon, hoping to establish rubber plantations

and harvest the region's elephants for ivory. The French won the competition for Gabon in 1839, when French explorer Louis Bouët-Willaumez (1808–1871) met with King Antchouwé Kowe Rapontchombo—he was known as King Denis—of the Asigas branch of the Mpongwe Kingdom. They signed treaties that established Gabon as a protectorate of France.

In 1875 Pierre Savorgnan de Brazza (1852–1905) was dispatched to explore and evaluate the economic potential of the Gabonese interior. De Brazza met and negotiated with several tribes along the Ogooué River, obtaining treaties that permitted the establishment of settlements. However, disagreements over the development of those settlements into colonies led to turmoil in the French Assembly, so the French were unable to commit further resources to Gabon. Tensions eased after the 1885 Berlin Conference, at which the major European powers divided up Africa for their own colonization. They also established rules for trade and river navigation and abolished the commerce in slaves.

In 1886 France established colonial headquarters in Gabon and brought in military detachments to defend it against resistance from native tribes. During the next decade the French engaged in repeated conflicts with the powerful Fang kingdom, which was eventually forced to submit to the colonial government. The French integrated the Fang into their colonial efforts by using them as guides and enforcers. They also converted them to Roman Catholicism; the converted Fang then became missionaries to spread the religion throughout Gabon. The French continued to encounter some resistance into the twentieth century, and thousands of Gabonese were placed in prison and labor camps.

After World War I the strain on the French economy prevented the government from effectively preventing the rise of an anticolonial lobby among the Gabonese. To avoid popular rebellion the French gradually instituted democratic reforms and allowed some native representation in local assemblies. Following World War II the Gabonese independence movement became more powerful, lobbying for greater participation in the government.

By the 1950s the French government was making plans to relinquish its colonial commitments. As French Equatorial Africa was dissolved, each nation was given a choice to remain a French territory or to seek full independence. In a 1958 public referendum the Gabonese voted to become an autonomous republic within the French community. In the following two years the French worked with local leaders to prepare a constitution and organize elections. The Gabonese Republic was formed in October 1960. Fang ethnic leader León Mba (1902–1967) became the first president of the republic.

Government Structure

The Gabonese Republic is divided into nine provincial regions, each of which is divided into thirty-six prefectures and eight subprefectures. The president appoints governors, prefects, and subprefects to head the provisional governments, while members of the provincial and prefectural assemblies are elected by popular vote.

The president, who holds the most powerful office in the central government, is elected by direct, popular vote for seven-year terms (term limits for the president were abolished in a 2003 referendum). The president has the power to name a prime minister, who serves as the head of government and consults with the president concerning all appointments to the executive cabinet. The president can also dissolve the legislature, suspend pending legislation, and introduce legislation through referendum. In addition, the president has the power to appoint and dismiss members of the military and the judiciary without the approval of the legislature.

Under constitutional reforms approved in 2007, the legislative branch is bicameral, consisting of the National Assembly, with 120 members elected by direct, popular vote for five-year terms, and the Senate, with ninety-one members elected by the municipal assemblies to six-year terms. The National Assembly and the Senate cooperate in initiating and approving legislation. Though constitutional revisions in 1991 granted the legislature approval power over some presidential decisions, in practice the legislature is subordinate to presidential decree. The legislature does not have the power to remove the president or prime minister from office.

The judicial system is based on French law, with some elements of tribal law. The lowest level of the judiciary consists of the trial courts, which are located within the prefectures and subprefectures. A system of appellate courts has jurisdiction over the trial courts, and the appellate courts are subject to review by the Supreme Court, which is divided into three chambers: judicial, administrative, and accounts. Gabon's constitution also calls for the establishment of a Constitutional Court, which has jurisdiction over constitutional law, treaties, and international agreements. The Gabonese judicial branch is constitutionally designated as independent of both the legislature and the executive branch, but it actually functions as a kind of advisory group for the president.

Political Parties and Factions

The Parti Démocratique Gabonais (Democratic Party of Gabon), or PDG, was formed in 1968 as the political vehicle of president Albert-Bernard "Omar" Bongo (1935–). Bongo invited leaders from opposition and allied parties to join the PDG in forming a coalition government. Those who declined to join with the PDG were not permitted to take part in the government until reforms in 1991 legalized multiparty elections.

The PDG focuses on economic development and infrastructural investment. During the presidential elections of 2005, Bongo received 79 percent of the popular

Omar Bongo, President of the Gabonese Republic, in 1968. *© Bettmann/CORBIS*

vote, running against four opposition candidates. The PDG also fared well in the legislative elections of 2006, winning eighty-two seats in the National Assembly and fifty-five seats in the Senate. During the legislative elections, the PDG formed a coalition government with a number of closely aligned parties. The coalition controls ninety-nine of the 120 seats in the National Assembly.

The Union de Peuple Gabonaise (Gabonese People's Union), or UPG, is the primary opposition party. The UPG was founded in 1991 by Pierre Momboundou (1945–), who was the party's presidential candidate in 1998 and 2005. The UPG supports greater popular involvement in the government and opposed the 2003 referendum to remove term limits on the presidency. In the 2005 presidential election, Momboundou received approximately 13 percent of the popular vote, coming in a distant second to Bongo. In the 2006 legislative elections, the UPG party won eight seats in the National Assembly.

The Union Gabonaise pour la Démocratie et le Développement (Gabonese Union for Democracy and Development), or UGDD, was founded in 2005 to oppose the PDG coalition government. The UGDD's leader, Zacharie Myboto (1938–), a former secretary of state, broke away from the PDG in protest of Bongo's policies. Myboto ran as an independent presidential candidate in 2005—the government had not yet officially recognized the UGDD—and won 6.6 percent of the popular vote, or third place. In 2006 the UGDD won four seats in the National Assembly.

Major Events

When Gabon achieved independence, neither of the two primary political parties of the time—the Bloc Démocratique Gabonais (BDG) and the Union Démocratique et Sociale Gabonaise (UDSG)—had enough members to command a majority in the executive branch or the legislature. Mba, the leader of the BDG, and Jean-Hilaire Aubame (1912–1989) of the UDSG agreed to form a coalition government, with Mba serving as president.

In 1963 Mba forced the UDSG members of the cabinet to resign and ordered an election to reconstitute the legislature. Accusing Mba of authoritarianism, the Gabonese military and UDSG supporters staged a coup, removing Mba from power for one day until the French military intervened and reinstated his administration. Aubame was arrested and sentenced to ten years in prison for his role in the coup.

In the 1964 elections the BDG won a majority in the legislature and Mba was reelected president, with Bongo serving as vice president. Mba died in office in 1967, and Bongo became president. In the following months Bongo abandoned the BDG and announced the establishment of a single-party government under his newly formed PDG.

Bongo's party immediately initiated legislation to increase the scope of presidential power. He was reelected in 1975, in 1979, and in 1986, while the nation enjoyed relative stability—his administration succeeded in mediating rivalries between ethnic groups and developed the nation's export industries. Economic prosperity prevented armed uprising, despite high levels of poverty in Gabon's poorest regions.

Economic depression hit Gabon in the 1980s and led to an increase in antigovernment sentiment. Protests and workers' strikes eventually persuaded Bongo to allow moderate democratic reforms. In 1990 he met with seventy-four rival and ally political organizations in a conference to decide the future of the nation. The conference resulted in constitutional amendments that ended the single-party system and allowed multiparty legislative and presidential elections. Other amendments established a Senate and an independent judiciary and provided for a basic bill of rights with greater protection for civil liberties, including freedom of the press.

Bongo voluntarily resigned from office and allowed the creation of a transitional government under Prime Minister Casimir Oyé-Mba (1942–). Bongo's reforms satisfied many in the population, but some militant groups continued to protest and to call for immediate regime change. The president's security forces prevented two coup attempts prior to the elections in 1990. After the votes had been counted, the PDG retained its control by forming a coalition with several allied parties. Bongo won re-election in a controversial 1993 election, which was boycotted by many of the opposition parties—they accused Bongo and his allies of rigging the procedures.

Political disturbances continued as opposition leaders refused to accept the results of the presidential election. Hoping to protect their economic interests in the region, the French government sent negotiators to Gabon to bring an end to governmental deadlock. Eventually a deal was struck: The major political parties formed a coalition government and agreed to a power-sharing arrangement. Political divisions among the nation's minor parties prevented them from organizing support behind a single candidate for the 1998 elections, allowing Bongo to win re-election amidst allegations of fraud and intimidation.

Twenty-First Century

Bongo was reelected in 2005 by a wide margin, as the opposition was again unable to unite behind a single candidate. The PDG has also maintained its legislative and municipal majorities, although representation for opposition parties has been growing at the local level. Political opponents continue to accuse Bongo and the PDG of election fraud, but international and domestic monitoring agencies have reported that elections since 2000 have been largely representative of public opinion as gauged through polling. Bongo held a controversial referendum in 2003, which removed term limits from the presidential office (term limits had been removed in 1967 and reinstated in the constitution of 1991).

Economically, the Gabonese are heavily dependent upon petroleum exports and trade with France. The government retains ownership of many of the nation's largest corporations, but has made moves toward privatization. It has also invested heavily in the nation's eco-tourism industry. Gabon is rich in natural resources and has become an important site for ecological and biological research.

BIBLIOGRAPHY

Gray, Christopher. *Colonial Rule and Crisis in Equatorial Africa: Southern Gabon, 1850–1940.* Rochester: University of Rochester Press, 2002.

Nugent, Paul. *Africa Since Independence: A Comparative History.* New York: Palgrave Macmillan, 2004.

Yates, Douglass A. *The Rentier State in Africa: Oil Rent Dependency and Neocolonialism in the Republic of Gabon.* Trenton: Africa World Press, 1996.

⊕ Cyprus

Type of Government

Cyprus (Kypros in Greek and Kibris in Turkish) is a divided country with two separate ruling bodies. In the south is the Republic of Cyprus, the internationally recognized government, which has a representative democracy with a division of powers between executive, legislative, and judicial branches. The executive branch is headed by a president who serves as both head of government and head of state. The legislature comprises one body, the Vouli Antiproson (House of Representatives), whose members are chosen by popular vote. The judiciary is headed by the Supreme Court, with three judges appointed by the president. In the north is the Turkish Republic of Northern Cyprus (TRNC), recognized only by Turkey. It has a president and a prime minister, and the members of its legislature, the Cumhuriyet Meclisi (Assembly of the Republic), are elected directly by voters in the north.

Background

The third-largest island in the Mediterranean Sea, Cyprus is 44 miles from the southern shore of Turkey and 500 miles east of the Greek mainland. The island's ethnic mix is about 75 percent Greek and 20 percent Turkish. Most of the Greek population follows the Greek Orthodox faith, and most of the Turkish population is Muslim.

Kypros means "copper," and it was the island's copper that first attracted settlers in the Stone Age. By about 2200 BC the island was renowned throughout the Mediterranean for its bronze-making industry and for the population's devotion to the cult of Aphrodite, the Greek goddess of love. By 1400 BC, the island was colonized by settlers from Greece but soon fell under the control of the Phoenicians and in the sixth century BC, was captured again by the Egyptian navy. Persia wrested the island from Egyptian control, but Alexander the Great (356–323 BC) returned it to Greek control in 333 BC. Rule passed to Rome in 58 BC, and about four hundred years later to the Byzantine Empire. Byzantine rule lasted until 1191, when the island was conquered by Richard I of England (1157–1199), also known as Richard the Lionhearted, as he was returning home from the Third Crusade. Richard in turn sold the island to the order of the Knights Templar, who gave Cyprus to the ruler of Jerusalem, Guy de Lusignan (1129–1194), in fulfillment of debts. Lusignan's descendants ruled Cyprus for the next three hundred years until the island was annexed briefly by Venice and then came under the rule of the Turkish Ottoman Empire, beginning in 1571.

During the following three hundred years of Turkish rule, the seeds of discontent were sown between Greek and Turkish Cypriots. In 1878 the United Kingdom was entrusted with the protection of the island at the Congress of Berlin, which limited Russian power following the Russo-Turkish War of 1877–88. The British intended to use the island as a bulwark against Russian expansion in the Middle East. In 1915, after Turkey entered World War I on the side of Germany and Austria-Hungary, Britain annexed Cyprus, eventually administrating the island as a Crown colony.

However, the Greek population had long desired *enosis* (union) with Greece, and after World War II, the enosis movement was carried forward by the Ethniki Organosis Kipriakou Agonos (National Organization of Cypriot Struggle; EOKA). Founded by a retired army officer, Lieutenant Colonel Georgios Grivas (1898–1974), and supported by Cypriot Archbishop Makarios III (1913–1977), EOKA launched a rebellion to rid the island of its British occupiers. To that end, British police, military, and government offices and personnel were targeted by EOKA, and the capital, Nicosia, as well as other large cities on the island, such as Limassol and Larnaca, fell into a state of siege. Greek Cypriots quit the police force and were replaced by Turkish Cypriots. When the British deported Makarios in 1956, the insurgency escalated, with more than two thousand casualties reported.

The Turkish Cypriots, fearing union with Greece, began demanding partition of the island, a position supported by Turkey. Turkish Cypriots formed their own militia, the Türk Mukavemet Teşkilat (TMT), to fight EOKA. Negotiations between Britain, Greece, and Turkey, begun in 1955, broke down repeatedly, but finally a settlement was reached in 1959 under which the island was granted its independence and Greek Cypriots gave up their demands for unification with Greece, while Turkish Cypriots agreed to cease their call for partition.. Independence was declared on August 16, 1960, and Archbishop Makarios was elected the first president.

Acknowledging the country's contentious ethnic mix, Cyprus's 1960 constitution instituted a number of checks and balances and power-sharing measures. Most critically, the constitution prohibited both the union of Cyprus with Greece and the partition of the country into separate Greek and Turkish enclaves. However, the complexities of the constitution were difficult to implement, and fighting broke out repeatedly between Greek and Turkish Cypriots. In 1974, after Greek military officers attempted to overthrow Makarios—believing that he had come to terms with an independent Cyprus and abandoned the struggle for enosis—the Turkish military invaded, taking control of approximately one-third of the island. In 1983 the northern region was declared the Turkish Republic of Northern Cyprus (TRNC), which is recognized only by Turkey. The TRNC includes the administrative districts of Kyrenia, small parts of Nicosia, and most of Famagusta.

Government Structure

The government in the Republic of Cyprus functions according to the 1960 constitution, but without Turkish participation since the TRNC's withdrawal from the government. The constitution provided for a strong executive branch with a president who would be a Greek

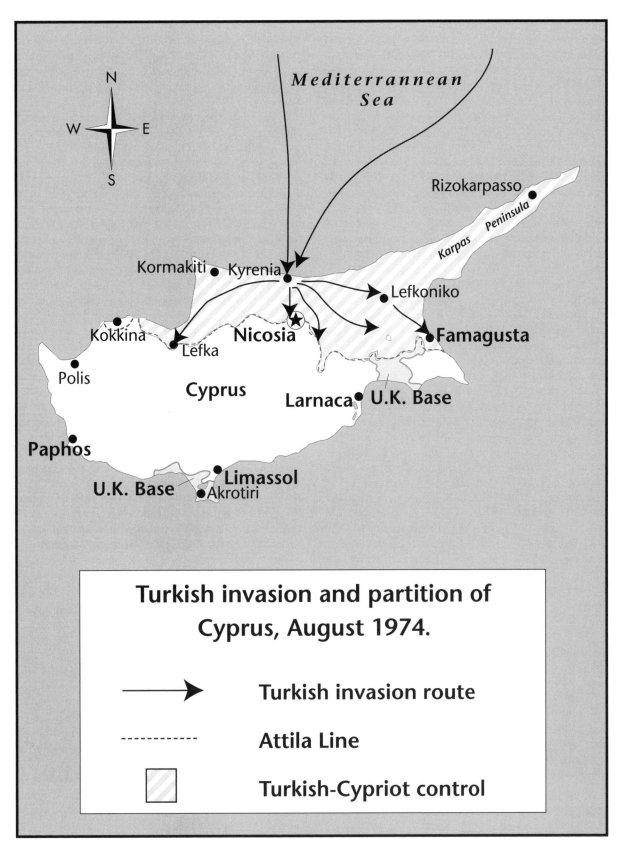

Turkish invasion and partition of Cyprus, 1974. *Map by Eastword Publications Development. Gale, a part of Cengage Learning*

Cypriot and a vice president who would be of Turkish descent. Both were to serve for a term of five years and be elected by popular vote of their respective communities. (Suffrage in Cyprus is universal and begins at age eighteen.) Each was also granted the power of veto over legislation and over decisions of the Council of Ministers, which was to be made up of seven Greek Cypriots and three Turkish Cypriots chosen jointly by the president and vice president. The constitution stated that the Ministry of Finance, the Ministry of Defense, and the Ministry of Foreign Affairs must each be headed by ministers of Turkish background. The Council of Ministers was to advise the president and vice president on policy decisions. As head of state in addition to being head of government, either or both executives were entitled to represent their country abroad, and both served as commanders-in-chief of the armed forces.

The members of the House of Representatives were to be elected by the two ethnic communities, with 35 positions reserved for Greeks and 15 for Turks. In 1985 the number of representatives was increased to 80, but only the 56 seats reserved for Greek Cypriots are filled. These members are elected by proportional representation to five-year terms. Decisions in the House of Representatives are made by simple majority rule, and the members share, along with the appointed members of the Council of Ministers, the right to propose new legislation.

Similarly, the Supreme Court was set up for an equitable distribution of power. Appointed by the president and vice president jointly, one of the judges was to be Greek, one Turkish, and the third, the president of the court, of neither ethnic background, and therefore considered neutral. This court was to rule on matters referred to it by the president or vice president that were considered prejudicial to either ethnic community. Below the Supreme Court is a High Court, which was to be made up of two members each from the Greek and Turkish communities appointed jointly by the executive branch, and beneath that there are other subordinate courts. The Cypriot legal system borrowed from British law the concept of the presumption of innocence, the right of appeal, the protections of due process, and the right to a fair and public trial.

A separate government was established in the TRNC, with a president elected by popular vote and prime minister appointed by the president. The Assembly is a unicameral body with fifty members elected for five-year terms by proportional representation. The judiciary is headed by a Supreme Court, which is made up of a president and seven judges.

Political Parties and Factions

The three major parties in the Republic of Cyprus are the center-right Democratic Party (DIKO), the center-right Democratic Rally (DISY), and the communist Progressive Party of Working People (AKEL).

The Democratic Party was established in 1978 by Spyros Kyprianou (1932–2002), and was led by Tassos Papadopoulos (1934–) until he became president in 2003. As of 2006, the Democratic Party was the third-largest party with eleven of the 56 seats in the House of Representatives.

DISY is the second-strongest party, with nineteen of the fifty-six members of the House of Representatives. It was founded in 1976 by Glafcos Clerides (1919–), who served as president of Cyprus from 1993 to 2003.

The strongest and oldest political party in the Republic of Cyprus is AKEL, founded in 1926 as the Communist Party of Cyprus (KKK). During the partition conflict, AKEL was the political leader of the independence movement and lobbied against enosis and partition. Renamed AKEL in 1943, the party was first led by Ploutis Servas (1907–2001) until 1989 and then by Dimitris Christofias (1946–), who is currently the president in the House of Representatives. Since the 1940s, AKEL no longer opposes enosis but instead has argued for a gradual process of unification with Greece. In the 2006 elections, AKEL won 31.1 percent of the vote, and the party has worked in coalition with DIKO and other smaller parties, including the Movement for Social Democracy (EDEK), founded in 1970.

In the Turkish, northern zone of Cyprus, the National Unity Party (UBP), founded in 1975 by Rauf Denktaş (1924–), is conservative in outlook and remained in power from its inception until the 2005 elections. At that time, Mehmet Ali Talat (1952–), of the Republican Turkish Party (CTP), came into office, and the CTP took twenty-five of the fifty seats in the Turkish National Assembly. Other minor parties in the north include the Democratic Party (DP), with five seats in the National Assembly, and the Peace and Democratic Movement.

Major Events

After the de facto partition of the country in 1974, the island was relatively free of violence until confrontations in 1996 in which two people were killed and fifty injured, escalating domestic and international tensions. In 1998 the Republic of Cyprus announced its intent to deploy missiles that were capable of reaching the Turkish coast, which brought complaints from Turkey and threatened to undermine the delicate balance of power on Cyprus. The missiles were subsequently deployed on Crete instead.

Potential European Union (EU) membership, contingent upon settlement of the long-time dispute, brought both sides back to the bargaining table under the UN-sponsored "Annan Plan" for reunification. However, with the failure of these talks, EU membership was granted only to the Republic of Cyprus in 2004.

Twenty-First Century

Cyprus continues to grapple with the effects of the island's partition. There are more than 200,000 displaced

Archbishop Makarios, the first president of Cyprus, addressing a demonstration against NATO intervention to prevent civil war, 1964. © *Bettmann/CORBIS*

persons from both north and south who still hope to be able to return to their homes. In 2003 President Denktaş of the TRNC eased travel restrictions between the north and south, and since that time more than twelve million border crossings have taken place.

In 2006 Cypriot President Tassos Papadopoulos met with Turkish Cypriot leader Mehmet Ali Talat for the first time in two years, leading to further talks between the two leaders. As an act of good will, in 2007 the Greek Cypriot government destroyed part of the Green Line, a barrier in the capital of Nicosia dividing the Turks and Greeks, a gesture applauded by Turkish Cypriots.

BIBLIOGRAPHY

Borowiec, Andrew. *Cyprus: A Troubled Island*. Westport, CT: Praeger Publications, 2000.

Cyprus, a Country Study. 4th ed. Edited by Eric Solsten. Washington, DC: Government Printing Office, 1993.

Republic of Cyprus. "Government Web Portal." http://www.cyprus.gov.cy/portal/portal.nsf/ dmlcitizen_en/dmlcitizen_en?OpenDocument (accessed March 30, 2007).

⊕ Senegal

Type of Government

Senegal is a democratic republic with separate executive, legislative, and judicial branches. The powerful executive branch includes a president elected by popular vote every five years and an appointed prime minister. The legislature is the unicameral 120-member National Assembly. The legal code is based on French civil law.

Background

Dakar, the westernmost point in Africa, is the capital of Senegal. The country is located on the Atlantic Ocean, with Mauritania bordering it to the north, Mali to the east, and Guinea and Guinea-Bissau to the south. Senegal also surrounds The Gambia on three sides. Inhabited since prehistoric times, this region was ruled by the Empire of Ghana from the eighth to the eleventh centuries AD, a period during which much of the population was converted to Islam. That religion is still the predominant faith in Senegal.

The thirteenth century saw the rise of the Jolof Kingdom (also called Djolof), a confederation of six states of the Wolof people who still populate the country and give it one of its two main languages (French is the second). By the fifteenth century, when the region first came into contact with Europeans, the Jolof Kingdom was at its peak of power.

In the fifteenth century, the Portuguese, under Prince Henry the Navigator (1394–1460), explored the West Africa coastline and established some small settlements along the Senegal River. The French later established more permanent settlements, such as that at Saint-Louis Island, which was founded in 1659. With the onset of the slave trade from West Africa, both Saint-Louis and Gorée Island became strategic launching sites for slave ships and were contested by several European powers. The British took control of some parts of Senegal for a time, but by 1840 the entire region had come under French control. In 1895 the region was designated part of French West Africa, an administrative federation of eight French colonies. The cultivation of peanuts, which continues to be one of the country's main crops, was established in the mid nineteenth century.

After World War II, a new generation of young leaders arose in Senegal, including the poet Léopold Sédar Senghor (1906–2001) and the socialist leader Lamine Guéye (1891–1968), both of whom campaigned for the abolition of forced labor, improvement in standards of living, and the granting of French citizenship to the colony's subjects. Senghor founded the Senegalese Democratic Bloc (BDS) in 1948, and Guéye led the Senegalese Party of Socialist Action (PSAS); both parties were formed by splitting from the French Socialist Party (SFIO). Elected to the French National Assembly, these two men were instrumental in leading the country to independence, which was achieved in June 1960.

Senegal joined the French Sudan in the short-lived Mali Federation, but by August both of these entities had declared independence from one another. French Sudan was renamed the Republic of Mali, and Senegal held its first presidential elections the following month with Senghor winning the position. He would remain in power for the next two decades as head of an authoritarian regime that did not permit opposition parties.

Government Structure

Though more than 90 percent Muslim in population, Senegal is governed as a secular republic. By the terms of its constitution (amended by referendum in 2001), the country is governed by three separate branches.

The strong executive branch includes a president who is head of state and is elected for a maximum of two five-year terms. The president in turn appoints a prime minister from the majority party or coalition in the legislature. The prime minister functions as head of government and appoints a cabinet, called the Council of Ministers.

Legislative power rests with the unicameral National Assembly. Comprising 120 members elected every five years by universal adult suffrage, the National Assembly is the sole body with the power to write laws. Though the president does not have absolute veto power, he or she may ask the National Assembly to reconsider a bill, in which case the bill must be passed again by a three-fifths majority.

The constitution declares the independence of the judiciary from the executive branch, the legislature, and the armed forces. However, the judges of the country's highest courts are appointed by the president after nomination by the minister of justice. The legal system is based on French civil law. Criminal defendants are presumed innocent until proven guilty and are afforded public trials and the right to legal counsel.

Local government is carried out through eleven administrative regions, each headed by an appointed governor and an elected local assembly. These regions are further divided into twenty-eight departments, which are in turn sub-divided into ninety-nine districts. Since 1996 a policy of decentralization has given authority for taxation and other local matters to local governments.

Political Parties and Factions

Senegal has a multi-party democracy with more than sixty-five functioning parties. The most important parties are the Socialist Party of Senegal (Parti Socialiste du Sénégal, or PS) and the Senegalese Democratic Party (Parti Démocratique Sénégalais, or PDS). These work alone and in concert with minor parties to form the main governing and opposition parties in the country.

The PS was Senegal's ruling political party from the year of independence in 1960 to 2000. Led by Léopold-Sédar Senghor until his retirement in 1980, the PS was for many years the only political party allowed in Senegal. With Senghor's resignation, his deputy, Abdou Diouf (1935–) became president, a position he held until 2001. Diouf is credited with opening up the political process in Senegal by allowing the establishment of other parties.

One such party to come into being as a result of new regulations was the liberal PDS, founded in 1974 and led by Abdoulaye Wade (1926–), who became the main opposition leader to the PS. Wade ran for president several times before finally defeating Diouf in 2000 with

Senegalese President Abdulaye Wade (right) and separatist leader Diamacoune Senghore (left), 2001. *Seyllou Diallo/AFP/Getty Images*

a coalition of forty other parties under the umbrella of the Sopi ("Change") Coalition. Wade was again elected president in the 2007 elections, winning about 56 percent of the vote.

Other smaller parties that function independently or in coalition with either the PS or PDS include the African Party for Democracy and Socialism or And-Jef (also known as PADS/AJ); the African Party of Independence; the Democratic and Patriotic Convention (also known as Garab-Gi); the Democratic League-Labor Party Movement (LD-MPT); the Gainde Centrist Bloc (BGC); the Independence and Labor Party (PIT); the National Democratic Rally (RND); and the Union for Democratic Renewal (URD).

Major Events

The first crisis facing Senegal after independence was the conflict between President Senghor and his more radi-

cally socialist prime minister, Mamadou Dia (1910–). Accused of plotting a coup against the Senghor government, Dia was arrested and thereafter the post of prime minister was abolished. The president thus became both head of state and head of government, a situation that did not change until the position of prime minister was reinstated in 1970, with Abdou Diouf taking that position. Diouf later succeeded Senghor as president. Diouf, however, again abolished the position of prime minister in 1983, and it was not reinstated until 1991.

In 1982 Senegal and The Gambia formed the Confederation of Senegambia with Diouf as president. The two countries agreed to join their armed and security forces, form an economic and monetary union, and coordinate foreign policy and communications. However, this confederation was dissolved seven years later.

Strained relations with Mauritania resulted from the killing of hundreds of Senegalese in a border dispute in

1989. Senegalese rioters in turn took to the streets of Dakar, killing Mauritanians. Further rioting led to most Mauritanians resident in Senegal being expelled from the country and to border clashes between the two countries. Diplomatic relations between the two countries were not renewed until 1992.

Conflict has also erupted within Senegal. Since 1983, in the southernmost province of Casamance near Guinea-Bissau, a separatist group called the Movement of Democratic Forces of the Casamance (MFDC) has challenged the armed forces and central government in what has become a guerrilla war. The conflict has also spilled beyond the borders of Senegal, leading to the Senegalese bombing of suspected rebel camps in Guinea-Bissau. Ceasefires have come and gone, but the conflict has yet to be resolved.

Abdoylaye Wade became Senegal's third president in 2000. The handover of government was largely peaceful, and Wade was suddenly elevated from leader of the opposition—a position he had maintained for a quarter of a century—to leader of the country. Although Wade made social overtures by initiating the construction of new schools around the country, dissatisfaction with his government was still exhibited by strikes by many in the public sector, such as teachers and postal workers. Nevertheless, Wade was reelected in 2007.

Twenty-First Century

Senegal has proved to be among the most steady democracies on the African continent and has never suffered a coup. It has also continued to maintain close relations with France. However, it faces a real threat to its political stability with the ongoing conflict with the MFDC and its demands for the secession of Casamance. Although a peace agreement was signed in December 2004, the peace process has not gone forward due to internal dissent among the leaders of MFDC. In 2006 thousands of villagers in the region were uprooted by fierce fighting between government troops and the MFDC and fled into The Gambia. Thousands have been killed in the conflict and many more thousands made homeless. The violence also threatens Senegal's relations with The Gambia and Guinea-Bissau.

BIBLIOGRAPHY

Clark, Andrew Francis. *Historical Dictionary of Senegal.* 2nd ed. Metuchen, NJ: Scarecrow Press, 1994.

Gellar, Sheldon. *Senegal: An African Nation between Islam and the West.* 2nd ed. Boulder, CO: Westview Press, 1995.

Government of Senegal Web Site. http://www.gouv.sn (accessed May 15, 2007).

Gritzner, Janet H. *Senegal.* Philadelphia: Chelsea House, 2005.

⊕ Mali

Type of Government

Mali is a multiparty democracy, with sixteen different political parties represented in its National Assembly in 2007. Several other parties play important roles in local government. The legislative branch of government consists of the 147-seat National Assembly. The executive branch is led by a president, who serves as both head of state and commander-in-chief of the armed forces. The president appoints a prime minister, who in turn selects a cabinet. At the head of Mali's judicial branch is the Supreme Court, which holds both judicial and administrative powers. The Supreme Court has nineteen members, each appointed for five years.

Background

Mali is a landlocked West African country with an area of about 479,000 square miles, or roughly twice the size of Texas. Its neighbors include Algeria to the north and northeast, Mauritania to the northwest, Niger on the east, Senegal to the west, Guinea to the southwest, and Burkina Faso and Côte d'Ivoire to the south.

The area now occupied by Mali has a history stretching back to the empire of Ghana, dating to about the fourth century AD. During its peak years, the Ghana Empire covered eastern Senegal, southwest Mali, and southern Mauritania. This empire engaged in steady and profitable trade with Arab peoples across the Sahara Desert. By the thirteenth century, the Ghana Empire had collapsed, and the Mali Empire had risen to take its place as the dominant force in the region.

Under the fourteenth-century king Mansa Musa (c. 1280–1337), the Mali Empire became an important center of Muslim scholarship, and Tombouctou, or Timbuktu, became key in trans-Sahara trade. Over the next few hundred years, however, the Mali Empire collapsed, disappearing entirely by the seventeenth century. While Mali was disintegrating, the Songhai Empire was rising to prominence just to the east. Songhai captured Tombouctou in 1468. The region came under Moroccan control in the late sixteenth century, but within a hundred years it had become fragmented into a number of smaller states.

The French began their advance into the area now called Mali around 1880. Between 1882 and 1898, the French met with opposition led by the Mandingo leader Samory Touré (1830–1900). Touré was eventually captured and exiled, and the French conquest of Mali was completed in 1898. Under French rule, the territory was called French Sudan, and was part of the federation known as French West Africa. After World War II, the people of French Sudan were granted French citizenship and representation in the French parliament. In 1958 French Sudan was renamed the Sudanese Republic, and along with the other territories of French West Africa, it became an autonomous republic within the French Community.

In January 1959, representatives from a handful of the region's emerging nations—the Sudanese Republic, Senegal, Dahomey (now Benin), and Upper Volta (now Burkina Faso)—came together in Dakar, Senegal, to draft a constitution for a new entity to be called the Federation of Mali, named after the old African empire. However, only the Sudanese Republic and Senegal ended up ratifying the constitution; they became the federation. The federation, which became a fully independent state in June 1960, did not last long. After months of bickering over domestic and foreign policy, the federation was dissolved in August 1960, and the former Sudanese Republic declared itself an independent nation under the name Republic of Mali, with Modibo Keita (1915–1977), a cofounder of the African Democratic Assembly, as its initial leader.

Government Structure

Under Keita, Mali was a one-party socialist dictatorship built on the model of the People's Republic of China. Over the next few years, public discontent grew as the economy struggled and poverty deepened. In November 1968, Moussa Traoré (1936–), a lieutenant (and later a general) in the military, overthrew Keita in a bloodless coup. Mali's constitution of 1960 was thrown out, and the fourteen-member Military Committee for National Liberation took control of the government. The new regime opened Mali up to economic investment from nonsocialist countries.

Traoré became president of Mali in 1969. His regime worked to turn the nation's economy around, but its efforts were thwarted by an extended drought that plagued the entire region for several years, beginning in 1968 and peaking in 1972–73. The severity of the drought left about one-third of the population desperately impoverished. A new constitution designed to move Mali toward civilian rule was approved in 1974. It established a one-party state, but left the existing military leaders in power for the time being. A new political party, the Democratic Union of the Malian People (UDPM), was formed in 1976. One-party elections were held in 1979, with Traoré receiving 99 percent of the votes cast. Discontent with his single-party rule grew stronger over the next year, and in 1980 his stranglehold on the government was challenged by massive student-led demonstrations. Traoré put down the demonstrations in brutal fashion. Three attempted coups were likewise crushed.

After a failed coup attempt by a group of disgruntled army and police officers in 1978, a new constitution was drafted. The new constitution reaffirmed Mali's one-party system, and Traoré was elected president once again. The political landscape in Mali remained relatively calm during the early 1980s, and Traoré was reelected in 1985.

Modibo Keita, the first president of the Republic of Mali, in 1961. *AFP/Getty Images*

By 1990 large segments of the population were growing dissatisfied with their country's one-party system, and calls for a more democratic government grew louder. In March 1991, amid growing dissatisfaction and intensifying rioting, Traoré's government was ousted in a coup orchestrated by Lieutenant Colonel Amadou Toumani Touré (1948–). Touré and his allies arrested Traoré, suspended the constitution, and set up a predominantly civilian transitional government led by a 25-member ruling committee. The Transitional Committee for the Salvation of the People (CTSP) quickly appointed a civilian-led government, and in August 1991 a new constitution was drafted. The new constitution, officially adopted in January 1992, allowed for the formation of multiple political parties and outlined new election procedures. Between January and April of that year, elections were held for president, National Assembly, and municipal offices, and on June 8 Alpha Oumar Konaré of the Alliance for Democracy in Mali (ADEMA) party assumed the presidency. ADEMA also won 76 seats in the National Assembly, out of 116 total at the time.

Political Parties and Factions

In 2007 sixteen political parties participated in Mali's National Assembly, with no party or coalition controlling a majority of seats. The largest number, sixty-six seats, belonged to a coalition called Espoir 2002 (Hope 2002), an alliance led by Rally for Mali (Rassemblement pour le Mali; RPM), whose leader, Ibrahim Boubacar Keita, came in second to Touré in the 2007 presidential election.

ADEMA is close behind Espoir in power, with fifty-five seats in the National Assembly. A third coalition, Convergence for Alternance and Change (Convergence pour l'Alternance et Changement), controls ten seats. Six seats are controlled by African Solidarity for Democracy and Independence (Solidarité Africaine pour la Démocratie et l'Indépendance; SADI), a party headed by a former student leader in the movement that instigated protests that contributed to the 1991 downfall of the Traoré.

The Union for Republic and Democracy (URD) party is an emerging force in Mali. Formed in 2003, primarily by former ADEMA members, URD received the second highest vote total nationwide in the 2004 communal and municipal elections.

Major Events

The devastating drought of the late 1960s and early 1970s led to tumultuous internal political struggles in Mali. Another severe drought that lasted from 1982 to 1985 did not have as much of a destabilizing effect on Mali's fragile political and economic situation. In late 1985, violence erupted between Mali and Burkina Faso over control of a narrow strip of land along the border between the two nations. An agreement forged by the International Court of Justice settled the matter a year later.

In 1990 massive popular upheaval brought down Traoré's single-party government. After his ouster, Traoré was tried and convicted for his role in the massacre of protesters. Before the transitional government led by Amadou Toumani Touré handed over power to Konaré's newly elected civilian government in 1992, it made an important accomplishment: the negotiation of a peace treaty with Tuareg rebels in the northern part of the country. The Tuaregs are a people of Berber descent who live in an area that includes parts of Mali, Libya, Algeria, Burkina Faso, and Niger. The truce allowed thousands of Tuareg refugees to return home to Mali from the neighboring countries to which they had fled.

Konaré was reelected as president in 1997, in an election marked by violence and boycotts by several opposition parties. Multiparty legislative elections were held a few months later, and ADEMA won an overwhelming majority of seats in the National Assembly. Amid allegations of "serious irregularities," the Constitutional Court voided the results of the elections, but ADEMA also dominated when new elections were held. Having served his constitutionally permitted two terms, Konaré did not run again in 2002; as a result, all the parties that had boycotted the 1997 election participated

this time. Running as an independent candidate, Touré was elected president in 2002. In National Assembly elections that year, no party emerged with a majority of seats. RPM gained a small plurality, with sixty-six seats, over a coalition of parties led by ADEMA.

The election of Touré in 2002 marked the first successful transfer of power from one democratically elected government to another in Mali's history as an independent nation. Over the next few years, under a government appointed by Touré to represent all key constituents, Mali was one of the most stable democracies in Africa. Touré was reelected in April of 2007, receiving 71 percent of the votes in a field containing seven other candidates.

Twenty-First Century

As of 2007 Mali remained a relatively stable democracy. Much of the population still relies on fishing and small-scale agriculture for survival, but the country holds substantial reserves of gold and other in-demand minerals. Mali's greatest challenge will be maintaining the delicate peace between leaders in the capital, Bamako, and the Tuaregs and other Muslim groups in the north, who sometimes feel marginalized by the southern-based government.

BIBLIOGRAPHY

Conrad, David, C. *Empires of Medieval West Africa: Ghana, Mali, and Songhay.* New York: Facts on File, 2005.

Davies, Susanna. *Adaptable Livelihoods: Coping with Food Insecurity in the Malian Sahel.* New York: St. Martins, 1996.

Mann, Kenny. *Ghana, Mali, Songhay: The Western Sudan.* Parsippany, NJ: Dillon Press, 1996.

⊕ Federal Republic of Nigeria

Type of Government

Nigeria is a federal republic with a popularly elected president—who serves as head of state, commander of the armed forces, and head of government—assisted by a vice president and an executive cabinet. The legislature's two independent chambers, whose members represent constituencies in the nation's thirty-six states and the federal capital, cooperate to develop laws and approve budgets. The judicial branch is led by the Supreme Court, with justices appointed by the president upon approval of the legislators.

Background

Archaeological surveys of Nigeria indicate that tribal societies occupied the region from at least 2000 BC. By the ninth century BC many of the native tribes had coalesced into agricultural societies on the Jos Plateau. Through immigration and military conquest, they gradually came under the control of a series of powerful kingdoms.

In the sixteenth century the Kanem-Bornu Kingdom, which originated around Lake Chad in the ninth century, controlled what is now eastern Nigeria. The Kanem-Bornu adopted Islam in the thirteenth century and, by the fifteenth century, were trading slaves and other commodities along the trans–Saharan trade routes. The Benin Kingdom, which controlled the central forests and the southern coast, was the first of the Nigerian kingdoms to be visited by Portuguese explorers, who arrived in the fifteenth century. Benin society, which had highly developed artistic and sculptural traditions, was dominated by spiritual rituals. Stories of those rituals, including tales of human sacrifice, spread throughout Europe and fueled the perception that African societies were "uncivilized."

In the sixteenth century Portuguese, British, French, and Dutch traders began purchasing slaves from merchants operating on the coast. In the following centuries millions of native Nigerians were captured and shipped to the colonies of the European powers.

In 1804 Usuman dan Fodio (1754–1817), a Muslim reformer from the Fulani tribal group, began a holy war to unite the tribes in northern Nigeria. He and his followers had eclipsed the Kanem-Bornu by 1809 and became the leaders of the Islamic slave trade from their capital city, Sokoto. By the mid nineteenth century the Fulani and the Benin were the most powerful states in the country.

After the British abolished slavery in 1807, they engaged in diplomatic and military efforts to disrupt the slave trade. For example, in the 1840s British negotiators met with leaders in the coastal city of Lagos, which had become the most active port in the Nigerian slave market. When negotiations proved unsuccessful, the British invaded and captured the city in 1851. Within forty years Britain controlled the coast and had begun to negotiate with the Benin, who controlled the central region. Britain's aim was to "civilize" the Benin by persuading them to prohibit slavery and human sacrifice. When the Benin captured and killed a diplomatic detachment from Britain, the British army invaded Benin territory and toppled the monarchy.

In Lagos and Benin the British concentrated on developing an export industry while simultaneously conducting military expeditions into the northern parts of the region. The British army captured Sokoto in 1903, thereby subduing the last major kingdom in Nigeria. During the next decade the British established a colonial administration that maintained tribal and ethnic leaders under the supervision of appointed governors.

The British slowly improved—and urbanized—the infrastructure of Nigeria and developed the agricultural industry. Though Nigerian nationalists occasionally surfaced and engaged in protests, the British were able to restrain the population through economic incentives and a carefully metered system of reforms. In the 1920s the British allowed limited native representation in local governments and promoted foreign education for natives. In 1951 the British promulgated a new constitution that provided a timeline for full independence. Constitutional revisions in 1954 and 1956 divided the territory into three semiautonomous regions, each led by a territorial parliament.

Between 1951 and 1959 the British supervised the development of the nation's first political parties, divided along regional and ethnic lines. Three major parties emerged: the National Council of Nigerian Citizens (NCNC), the Action Congress (AC), and the Northern People's Congress (NPC). When elections were held in 1959, none of the major parties won a controlling majority, so the NCNC and NPC formed a coalition government. Nigeria officially gained its independence in 1960 and became a representative republic.

Government Structure

In 1999, after decades of intermittent military control, Nigeria adopted constitutional reforms that reinstated a civilian government. It operates as a federal republic, with governmental powers divided between executive, legislative, and judicial branches.

Nigeria is divided into thirty-six states and one federally administered capital region. Within each state, residents elect a chief executive, or governor, who serves a four-year term and can stand for re-election. In addition, each state has a single legislative chamber, known as the State Assembly. The states are further divided into a total of 774 local government areas, or LGAs, each of which has a council headed by an elected chairman.

At the federal level, the president is popularly elected for a maximum of two terms of four years and serves as head of state, head of government, and leader of the armed forces. The president is assisted and advised by a vice president, who is also a leading member of the legislature, and a Federal Executive Council, or cabinet. Its ministers are appointed by the president from a list of candidates submitted by the legislature. The president has the power to create legislative and budget proposals, declare emergency and military actions, and to call for the dissolution of the legislature in cases of governmental deadlock.

Nigeria's legislature, known as the National Assembly, is bicameral. The lower chamber, the House of Representatives, has 306 members elected by popular vote. The Senate, or upper chamber, has 109 members, with three elected from each state and one elected from the capital region. Members of both houses serve four-year terms and can stand for re-election.

Legislation may originate in either chamber, but cannot become law until it receives majority votes in both chambers and the consent of the president. The assembly also has the authority to approve presidential appointments, emergency orders, and budgetary proposals.

The Nigerian legal system is based on English law, but twelve states have adopted Islamic law. The state assemblies appoint justices, either secular or Islamic, to serve on state courts. The Supreme Court, the highest body in the federal judiciary, has final authority over all criminal and civil disputes. It consists of a chief justice and not more than twenty-one justices, who are appointed by the president and approved by the legislature.

Below the Supreme Court are the Court of Appeal and the Federal High Court. Members of the Court of Appeal are appointed by the legislature upon the advice of a special judicial advisory committee. The constitution stipulates that three members of the Court of Appeal must have knowledge of Islamic law. The Federal High Court has jurisdiction in all cases involving federal spending and taxation.

Though the 1999 constitution established a balanced governmental system with an independent judiciary, in practice the president exerts significant influence over the operation of the legislature and the courts. From 1999 to 2007 democratic reforms increased multiparty and civilian participation in the government; however, critics repeatedly accused the president of wielding authoritarian power.

Political Parties and Factions

The People's Democratic Party (PDP) is the leading party in Nigeria. Former military leader Olusegun Obasanjo (1937–) became the first PDP president in 1999 and won a second term in 2003, though monitoring agencies noted numerous irregularities in the elections. Umaru Yar'Adua (1951–), the PDP presidential candidate in 2007, reportedly won more than 60 percent of the popular vote, although those elections were also marred by controversy. The PDP is viewed as a socially conservative party, but it also supports moderately liberal economic policies.

The All-Nigeria People's Party (ANPP) is the second-largest political party and the main opponent of the PDP. In 2003 the ANPP controlled ninety-six seats in the House and twenty-seven seats in the Senate, representing the largest percentage of any minority party. Its candidate, Muhammadu Buhari (1942–), got the second highest number of votes in the 2007 presidential election, approximately 18 percent. The ANPP is known as a radical, conservative party and generally represents the interests of northern Nigerian ethnic groups.

The Action Congress (AC) was formed in 2006 when several minority parties merged. Atiku Abubakar (1946–), the former vice president, was the AC's presidential candidate in 2007 but was disqualified following allegations of corruption. Abubakar and his supporters accused the PDP party of engineering the disqualification. Unlike other minority parties, the AC refused to join in a coalition with the PDP government after the 2007 elections. The AC party is viewed as the more

socially liberal party and focuses primarily on democratic reforms and increasing civilian representation in the government.

Major Events

In 1966 members of the Ibo ethnic group, in eastern Nigeria, rebelled against the ruling government coalition, accusing it of favoring northern Nigeria over the other provinces. The Ibo assault resulted in the deaths of the leaders of all three regional territories; military reprisals led to the death of many Ibo. In 1967 Ibo military leader Chukwuemeka O. Ojukwu (1933–) led the eastern province in seceding from the nation to found the Republic of Biafra.

The federal government refused to acknowledge Ojukwu's government and threatened to invade. The United States and Britain gave military and financial aid to Nigeria in hopes of preventing disunion. When France agreed to aid Biafra's independence movement, the conflict quickly escalated into civil war. Between 1967 and 1970 thousands were killed in military engagements, and the situation in Biafra deteriorated as the Nigerian military cut off crucial imports of food and medical supplies. Ojukwu surrendered in 1970 and fled to the Côte d'Ivoire.

Following the civil war Nigeria was led by a military regime under Colonel Yakubu Gowon (1934–), who adopted a policy colloquially known as "No Victor, No Vanquished," which included measures to reintegrate the Ibo into Nigerian society. At the same time the discovery of oil reserves spurred economic growth and led to an explosion in industrial employment. Gowon slowly adopted democratic reforms but failed to consolidate power over the military, and his regime was overthrown in a bloodless coup led by Murtala Muhammad (1938–1976) in 1975.

Muhammad instituted a four-year plan to restore democracy, but the oil market plummeted, causing a financial crisis that made the population turn against the government. Muhammad was assassinated in 1976 and replaced by Obasanjo. Throughout the 1980s and 1990s the Nigerian government was in a state of flux. While the government alternated between civilian and military leadership, legislation and economic initiatives were insufficient to address poverty levels. In the mid 1980s, the government became more authoritarian, restricting all popular demonstrations and arresting thousands of political dissidents.

In the late 1990s, when the government was suspected of assassinating several popular civilian political leaders, protests and demonstrations became more frequent. As the nation appeared close to popular revolt, the military government adopted constitutional reforms and, in 1999, held general elections. Obasanjo, who had relinquished his military title and returned as a civilian

Nigerian President Olusegun Obasanjo receives the government seals from his predecessor, Abdulsalami Abubakar, in 1999.   *Jean-Philippe Ksiazek/AFP/Getty Images*

candidate, won the 1999 elections to become the twelfth president of Nigeria.

Twenty-First Century

Beginning shortly after the election of Obasanjo in 1999, several northern states declared their adherence to Islamic law, partly in response to Obasanjo's devout Christianity. Hundreds died in intermittent conflicts between Muslims and Christians; the government was forced to intervene and declare military law. Peace agreements allowed some states to maintain Islamic law, so long as it did not conflict with the federal legal system.

Obasanjo won re-election in 2003, though many believed that the government had corrupted election procedures. In 2006 Obasanjo proposed a constitutional amendment to remove term limits on the presidency. Vice President Abubakar opposed the amendment. When he was chosen as the 2007 presidential candidate for a coalition of opposition parties, Obasanjo attempted to have him removed from the government, citing corruption. Abubakar made counterallegations. Obasanjo's regime succeeded in barring Abubakar from running in

the election, and Yar'Adua, the candidate of Obasanjo's party, won. International observers, noting irregularities in voting and tabulation, said the elections should be considered invalid.

BIBLIOGRAPHY

Smith, Daniel Jordan. *A Culture of Corruption: Everyday Deception and Popular Discontent in Nigeria.* Princeton: Princeton University Press, 2006.

Tijani, Hakeem Ibikunkle. *Nigeria's Urban History: Past and Present.* Lanham: University Press of America, 2006.

Udogu, Emmanuelle Ike. *Nigeria in the Twenty-First Century: Strategies for Political Stability and Peaceful Coexistence.* Trenton: Africa World Press, 2005.

⊕ Islamic Republic of Mauritania

Type of Government

Mauritania is a multiparty republic. Its executive branch is led by a president, who serves as chief of state and is elected for a renewable term of six years. The president appoints a prime minister and a Council of Ministers. The legislative branch consists of a two-chamber parliament, made up of an eighty-one-member lower house called the National Assembly, and a fifty-six-member upper house, or Senate, both selected directly by municipal officials. Mauritania's judicial system is based on a mixed set of principles. Social and family matters are based on Islamic law, known as sharia, while commercial cases are subject to a Western-style legal code.

Background

Mauritania is a West African nation located on the continent's Atlantic coast. Slightly larger than Texas and New Mexico combined, Mauritania's coastal neighbors are Western Sahara to the north and Senegal to the south. Its other neighbors are Algeria to the northeast, and Mali to the east and south.

The land that is now Mauritania has a long, rich history. In the eleventh century, a Mauritania-based group of Muslim Berbers known as the Almoravids conquered most of northwest Africa and a large portion of Spain. The Almoravids had an alternatingly hostile and friendly relationship with neighboring black African empires, particularly Ghana. In the twelfth century, the Almoravid empire was conquered by the Mali Empire, which had succeeded Ghana in influence in the area. The region was subsequently controlled by the Songhai Empire, which in turn fell to Moroccan invaders in the late sixteenth century. Meanwhile, Arab tribes from the east gradually overtook the Berbers to dominate Mauritania. The Mauritanian Thirty Year War, which took place from 1644 to 1674, represented the Berbers' unsuccessful final stand against the encroaching Arabs, though Berbers remained an important cultural influence.

The Portuguese were the first European traders to arrive in Mauritania, first appearing in the fifteenth century, and they were eventually followed by the French, Dutch, and English. France took the lead in exploring the inland regions, and signed numerous treaties with local leaders. After decades of French control, Mauritania was officially established as a French colony in 1920, becoming one of the eight territories that made up the federation called French West Africa. During the colonial period, black Africans from various neighboring territories trickled into Mauritania, creating the conditions for ongoing political tensions between those who like to see Mauritania primarily as part of the Arab world and those who would prefer to align the country with sub-Saharan Africa. Like the other territories in the federation, Mauritania's status changed following World War II. In 1946 the colony gained a greater degree of control over internal matters, and a Mauritanian Territorial Assembly was formed. Political power gradually shifted into the hands of local leaders over the next decade. In 1958 Mauritania became a self-governing republic within the French Community. The Islamic Republic of Mauritania gained complete independence from France two years later.

Government Structure

Moktar Ould Daddah (1924–) served as Mauritania's president from its inception as an independent republic until July 1978, when he was ousted in a military coup. The coup came at a time when Daddah's government was weakened by a military dispute with Morocco over the resource-rich territory called Western Sahara, which was formerly controlled by Spain. Following the coup, the constitution was suspended and the National Assembly was dissolved, as was its dominant political party, the Mauritanian People's Party (PPM). In 1980 Lieutenant Colonel Khouna Ould Haydalla emerged as chief of state and chair of the newly created Military Committee for National Salvation. Haydalla fought off a coup attempt in each of the next two years. His regime was finally toppled in December 1984 in a coup led by Col. Maaouya Ould Sid'Ahmed Taya (1943–), who became the new chief of state. He and his Democratic and Social Republican Party (PRDS) dominated Mauritanian politics for more than two decades.

Taya instituted a multiparty system during his reign, but elections were far from free and democratic. Leaders of opposition parties were routinely harassed and arrested. One politician, Cheikh Sadibou Camara of the Union for Democracy and Progress (UDP), was arrested twice during the 1990s for stating publicly that slavery was still happening in Mauritania. Journalists who reported on stories reflecting the government in an unfavorable light were similarly silenced. The United States revoked Mauritania's trade privileges in 1993 due to its poor human rights record.

Taya was ousted in a 2005 military coup. Colonel Ely Ould Mohamed Vall was named head of the transitional Military Council for Justice and Democracy. Vall promised a return to civilian rule within two years, and his government made good on that vow with elections in 2007. Politics in Mauritania were opened considerably, as parties long suppressed by the Taya regime were allowed to participate fully.

Political Parties and Factions

Parliamentary elections in 2007 were dominated by Al-Mithaq, a coalition of moderate Islamist independents.

The Republican Party for Democracy and Renewal (PRDR) is the new incarnation of the PRDS. Following the 2005 coup that ousted Taya, the PRDR renounced its predecessor's pro-Israel positions. The PRDR is now a minority party in the Mauritanian legislature, but still controls a significant handful of seats in each house.

The Rally of Democratic Forces is led by Ahmed Ould Daddah, the half-brother of Mauritania's first president. This party, in coalition with another party called the Union of the Forces for Progress, is the second most potent political force in the Mauritanian legislature.

Other key parties include the Rally for Democracy and Unity, which captured nearly 10 percent of the popular vote in the most recent national elections; and a coalition composed of the People's Progressive Alliance and the Mauritanian Party of Unity and Change.

Major Events

Tensions between the black minority, mostly located in the country's south, and its Arab majority have been central to Mauritania's political dynamics since the nation achieved independence. Flagrant human and civil rights abuses have repeatedly led to protests among blacks. Slavery was not officially banned in Mauritania until 1981, and there were no criminal penalties for slavery until August 2007. International antislavery organizations contend that slavery continues in Mauritania today.

Throughout its history as an independent nation, Mauritania's ties to the Arab world have grown closer. In 1973 Mauritania joined the Arab League and withdrew from the franc zone (countries using French currency). Mauritania has nevertheless retained strong relations with Western Europe and the United States, and received substantial aid from those countries (as well as from the Arab states) during the massive drought that plagued the Sahel region—the border zone between the Sahara Desert to the north and the more fertile Sudan region (not to be confused with the country Sudan)—during the late 1960s and early 1970s.

Mauritania's military skirmish over Western Sahara in the mid-1970s set the stage for the political instability that followed over the next several years. In November 1975, Mauritania, Morocco, and Spain reached a settlement under which Spain was to withdraw from the area. Mauritania and Morocco agreed on borders. Mauritania was granted control of a small portion of the region, but the nation's weak military was unable to defend it successfully against nationalist guerillas known as the Polisario.

In the wake of the 1984 coup that brought Taya to power, Mauritania became a society starkly divided along racial/ethnic/class lines. The main division was between the Maurs (or Moors)—the privileged class that has dominated the Mauritanian government—and black Africans, many of whom are the descendants of slaves, or in some cases have even remained slaves themselves. Members of the black population, which is mainly concentrated along the Senegal River, which marks the nation's southern border, formed an underground movement called the Front for the Liberation of Africans in Mauritania (FLAM).

Hostilities between the different ethnicities came to a head in 1989 when race riots in the capital city of Nouakchott erupted in the midst of a border dispute with Senegal. Hundreds of Senegalese were killed in the city. In Senegal outraged blacks retaliated by attacking members of the Moorish trading community. Refugees poured over the border in both directions, and Mauritania deported thousands of longtime residents who were of Senegalese origin. In late 1990 and early 1991, a violent purge took place in which about five hundred Mauritanian soldiers, most of them black, were killed. All of this was seen as part of a broad "Arabization" process being undertaken by Taya's regime.

In 1991 Taya granted opposition parties legal status, and the following January he was elected president in Mauritania's first-ever multiparty presidential election, receiving nearly two-thirds of the vote. The election was widely regarded as being horribly tainted by fraud, however, resulting in a boycott of the March legislative elections by six of the fourteen opposition parties. Consequently, Taya's PRDS captured sixty-seven of seventy-nine seats in the National Assembly. The 1997 presidential election yielded an even more lopsided result: Taya won with 90 percent of the vote, amid opposition leaders' cries of widespread fraud and irregularities.

PRDS continued to dominate Mauritanian politics into the twenty-first century despite mounting protests by opposition parties. Much of this opposition was based on Taya's pro-Western/pro-U.S. foreign policy and, perhaps more significantly, his establishment of full diplomatic ties with Israel, a risky political move in a predominantly Muslim country. Mauritania was one of only three members of the Arab League with such ties. Outside observers assessed Mauritania's 2001 Assembly elections as being relatively free and fair. In 2003 the government successfully repelled a coup attempt orchestrated by Sala Ould Henena, an army officer who had been fired because of his opposition to the government's connections with Israel. Two days of fighting in Nouakchott left six people dead and forty injured. Taya was reelected to the presidency that year, receiving more than 60 percent of the vote.

Taya's support deteriorated over the next two years, and there was little public outcry when he was deposed in 2005. In elections held in 2007, Sidi Ould Cheikh Abdallahi was elected president.

Twenty-First Century

The military coup of 2005 ushered in a new period of hope for Mauritania. The newly elected civilian government, voted into power in 2007 in elections generally regarded as free and fair by international observers, faces significant challenges. The first will be to remain a stable force in a nation frequently shaken by violence, mired in extreme poverty, and pulled in opposite directions by the influence of radical Islam and the prospect of useful financial relationships with the West. The new government's ability to maintain productive ties with both its fellow Muslim nations and with economic powers like the United States will be the determining factor in its success.

BIBLIOGRAPHY

Claderini, Simonetta. *Mauritania*. Santa Barbara, CA: Clio Press, 1992.

Handloff, Robert E. *Mauritania: A Country Study*. 2nd ed. Washington, DC: Library of Congress, 1990.

Stewart, Charles C. "North-South Dialectic in Mauritania: An Update." *Maghreb Review 11*, no. 1 (1986): 40–45.

⊕ Sierra Leone

Type of Government

Sierra Leone is a constitutional democracy with an executive branch headed by a president who serves as both head of government and head of state. The legislative branch consists of the unicameral House of Representatives, which has 124 members. The judicial branch includes a Supreme Court, a Court of Appeal, and a High Court of Justice, with judges appointed by the president.

Background

Located on the Atlantic Ocean in West Africa, Sierra Leone is bordered by Guinea to the north and east and Liberia to the south. Portuguese explorers visited the coast in the fifteenth century and named the region Sierra Leone, or "lion mountains."

The slave trade plagued the region from the sixteenth to the nineteenth centuries. The first colony on Sierra Leone was founded in the late eighteenth century by British philanthropists as a home for runaway slaves and for blacks discharged from the British army and navy. It was initially administered by the Sierra Leone Company, headed by the British abolitionist Granville Sharp (1735–1813). However, the initiative was unsuccessful, and in 1808 the coastal zone was turned over to the British government. In 1896 a British protectorate was declared for the inland regions as well.

The returned slaves, called Krios (Creoles), had originally come from all parts of Africa. Rather than assimilating the customs of the local black population, they took on some of the manners and lifestyle of the British overlords, establishing themselves as a strong merchant class along the coast. The Creoles, along with the British, became the target of animosity from local tribes, as indigenous groups staged repeated rebellions against the British and Creole authorities. Meanwhile, Freetown became an administrative center for British holdings in West Africa.

A constitution was promulgated in 1924, and the country held its first elections for a legislative council. The next step in independence was the 1951 constitution, which allowed for majority rule and thereby allowed native Africans to gain control of the government. The House of Representatives was established in 1957, and the following year Milton Margai (1895–1964) became the country's first prime minister. Sierra Leone gained independence from England on April 27, 1961, and became a commonwealth of the British government. Since independence the country has been wracked by military coups and civil war.

Government Structure

Sierra Leone's executive branch is headed by the president, who is elected every five years by universal suffrage. The president in turn appoints a cabinet, which is approved by the legislative branch. The president and cabinet together function as both head of state and head of government.

The legislative branch is represented by the House of Representatives. Of its 124 members, 112 are elected by popular vote every five years. Twelve seats in the House of Representatives are filled by paramount chiefs—the highest level traditional or tribal chief in a region—who are chosen in separate elections.

The country's legal code is based on British common law with some aspects of African traditional law. Magistrate courts are held in the capital of Freetown and in various regions. Appeals from these lower courts first go to the High Court. Appeals from High Court decisions may be made to the Court of Appeal and finally to the Supreme Court, which consists of a chief justice and three other justices, all appointed by the president in consultation with the Judicial and Legal Service Commission.

The three provinces of Sierra Leone—Eastern, Southern, and Northern—are administered by a resident minister. (There is also one administrative area, Western.) These provinces are further subdivided into twelve districts, each administered by a paramount chief and council elders. There is also an elected council and mayor in the cities of Freetown, Bo, Kenema, and Makeni.

Political Parties and Factions

The diversity of political parties has suffered through the more than four decades of Sierra Leone's independence. Ruled for a time by a one-party system, the country also experienced a period in the 1990s when all political parties were banned. However, since the re-establishment of democratic government in 2002, the country has divided politically into three main parties: the Sierra Leone People's Party (SLPP), the All People's Congress (APC), and the Peace and Liberation Party (PLP). These parties often are differentiated by regional and tribal affiliations rather than by stated political goals.

Established in 1951, the SLPP was the nation's leading political party until the elections of 1967, deriving its support predominantly from southern constituencies and the Mende tribal group. Milton Margai was an early leader of the party and became the first prime minister after independence. However, from 1967 to 1996, the party was either out of power or banned. After the SLPP candidate Ahmad Tejan Kabbah (1932–) won the popular vote in the 1996 elections to become president, his government was overthrown in a military coup in May 1997, which lasted about ten months before Kabbah was restored to power. With free elections in 2002, Kabbah won again, this time with about 70 percent of the vote, and his party took 83 of the 112 seats in the House of Representatives.

The APC has been traditionally linked with the northern regions of Sierra Leone and the Temne and Limba tribes. Founded in the late 1950s by Siaka Stevens (1905–1988), who was also a co-founder of the SLPP, the APC became the main opposition party following the 1962 elections. The APC came to power with the 1967 elections, with Stevens at the head, and was later led by President Joseph Saidu Momoh (1937–2003). The party became the sole legal party in the nation in 1978, a situation that lasted until 1992. In the 2002 elections, the APC won twenty-two seats in the House of Representatives.

The third major party in Sierra Leone is the PLP, formed by followers of Johnny Paul Koroma (1960–2003?), who led a military coup in 1997. It won two seats in the 2002 elections. Another party involved in the violence of the 1990s is the Revolutionary United Front (RUF). Originally a rebel army, the RUF became a political party in 2002 with the cessation of hostilities.

Major Events

The decades since the 1961 independence of Sierra Leone have been turbulent, though the first years did see orderly changes of government. With the death of Milton Margai in 1964, power was passed to his half-brother, Albert Margai (1910–1980), who held power until 1967. With the electoral victory of the APC, Siaka Stevens became the new prime minister. However, a military coup quickly ended civilian government. Coup followed coup, until Stevens was returned to power in 1968. He remained in power until 1985, increasingly centralizing power. Another coup attempt in 1971 induced Stevens to ask for help from neighboring Guinea. In 1978 Stevens turned Sierra Leone into a one-party state, with the APC the only legal political party. Prime Minister Stevens ruled until 1985, when he appointed the former military officer Joseph Saidu Momoh to be his successor. Momoh was elected president in the 1985 elections; there were no challengers.

Under Momoh there were increasing abuses of power. By 1991 he was pressured into overhauling the constitution, once again allowing a multiparty system. However, by this time there was already a violent insurgency underway in eastern Sierra Leone near the Liberian border. Led by Foday Sankoh (1937–2003) and his Revolutionary United Front (RUF) troops, this insurgency soon spread into a violent and bloody civil war. RUF troops began with the stated aims of returning the

A diamond mine in Sierra Leone, 1996. © *Patrick Robert/Sygma/Corbis*

power and wealth of Sierra Leone to the common people. But once they controlled the lucrative diamond mining in the country, the RUF was able to fuel a full-scale rebellion that resulted in tens of thousands of deaths and the displacement of more than two million people, or about one-third of the population. The RUF was noted for its brutality, including mass killings, maiming, rape, and the use of child soldiers.

Meanwhile Momoh was overthrown in another military coup, but the new military government also proved ineffective at stopping the RUF. Multiparty elections were held in 1996, with Kabbah taking power, only to be overthrown in a further coup led by Lieutenant Colonel Johnny Paul Koroma, who took the title of Head of the Armed Forces Revolutionary Council (AFRC). A joint junta was set up between RUF and AFRC to control the country. A Nigerian-led peacekeeping force, ECOMOG, reinstated Kabbah in 1998, but AFRC and RUF continued to fight. The Lomé Peace Agreement was signed in 1999, bringing the RUF's Sankoh into power as vice president and establishing the United Nations Mission in Sierra Leone (UNAM-SIL) to keep the peace. After violence erupted again in 2000, Sankoh and the RUF were stripped of power. A new ceasefire was established and disarmament and reintegration of the rebels began to take place. By 2002 more than seventy thousand had been disarmed, and President Kabbah, re-elected in free elections that same year, declared the decade of civil war to be over.

A Truth and Reconciliation Commission was established as well as a UN-sponsored Special Court for Sierra Leone to try those responsible for crimes against humanity. However, these have had limited success, and the 2005 report by the Truth and Reconciliation Commission was not fully accepted by the Sierra Leone government. Also in 2005 the UNAMSIL peacekeeping mission in Sierra Leone formally ended.

Twenty-First Century

The greatest single challenge to security in Sierra Leone continues to be the potential for political instability. The country's troubled history has bred numerous factions, and the Special Court for Sierra Leone has faced difficulties in bringing some defendants to trial. Many of these prosecutions have proved to be politically unpopular, and there are fears that order cannot be maintained in such proceedings. Attempts to bring the country together through the Truth and Reconciliation Commission likewise proved less than successful, with even President Kabbah, in his testimony before the commission, appearing to be partisan and defensive, rather than statesmanlike.

The transition from war to peace is also threatened by the poor conditions in the country as a whole. Sierra Leone consistently appears on the United Nations list of "least livable" countries, with life expectancy of just forty years and one of the highest infant mortality rates in the world. Much of the country's public infrastructure, shelter, and education and health facilities have been compromised or destroyed during the extended conflict, and thousands still await relocation from refugee camps. In August 2007 there were high hopes for the presidential election, the first since the end of the civil war.

BIBLIOGRAPHY

Alie, Joe A. D. *A New History of Sierra Leone*. New York: St. Martin's, 1990.

Binns, Margaret. *Sierra Leone*. Santa Barbara, CA: Clio Press, 1992.

Gberie, Lansana. *A Dirty War in West Africa: The RUF and the Destruction of Sierra Leone*. Bloomington, IN: Indiana University Press, 2006.

Thompson, Bankole. *The Constitutional History and Law of Sierra Leone (1961–1995)*. Lanham, MD: University Press of America, 1997.

⊕ Kuwait

Type of Government

Kuwait is governed by a constitutional monarchy with a hereditary emir as the head of state and a prime minister, appointed by the emir, as the head of the government. In addition, the Kuwaiti government includes a unicameral legislature, the Majlis al-'Umma, or National Assembly, consisting of fifty members who are elected by popular vote to four-year terms. Kuwait operates under a constitution ratified in 1962 that declares Islam the state religion and justice, equality, and liberty the pillars of society.

Background

Kuwait is a flat, barren country that is located on the northwest coast of the Persian Gulf. Its only major natural resource is oil. On its landward sides, Kuwait is bounded by Iraq to the west and north and by Saudi Arabia to the south. It comprises a land area of 6,880 square miles, which is about the size of New Jersey. Its livable, developed area, however, is much smaller, leading nearly all of the population to live in or near Kuwait City, the capital. Citizens of Kuwait are significantly outnumbered by immigrant laborers. Of the roughly three million people who live in Kuwait, approximately two-thirds are noncitizens who are working in Kuwait, including 22 percent Arabs from other countries and 39 percent Asian non-Arabs. The remainder comprises Bedouns (Arabs who have no formal citizenship) and Bedouins (traditional nomads).

Kuwait's modern history dates to the early seventeenth century, when several tribes migrated to the coast from the Arabian Desert. Kuwait's ruling family, the al-Sabahs, trace their lineage to the reign of Sheikh Sabah ibn Jaber I (d. 1762) starting in 1756. In 1899, seeking to guard against advances in the area by the Ottoman Turks (and to secure funding for the royal family), Kuwait's leader, Sheikh Mubarak al-Sabah (1837–1915), signed a treaty that assured British protection of the tiny nation in return for Kuwaiti help in promoting British interests in the region. The arrangement was formalized again in 1914, when Kuwait was officially recognized by Britain as an independent nation under its protection. On June 19, 1961, the agreement with the United Kingdom was terminated by mutual consent, and Kuwait became a fully sovereign and independent nation.

Prior to the discovery of oil in 1938 and its exploitation starting in the 1940s, Kuwait was poor, with an economy dependent upon pearl diving, fishing, and ship building. Kuwait controls about 10 percent of the world's oil reserves. Only Saudi Arabia and Iraq have larger proven reserves. As oil is essentially Kuwait's only natural resource, other than fish from the Persian Gulf, nearly all food products and agriculture must be imported into Kuwait.

Government Structure

Emir Sabah al-Ahmad al-Jabir al-Sabah (1929–) has been the head of the state of Kuwait since January 2006. As such, he appoints the prime minister, who serves as the head of the government. A cabinet-level Council of Ministers is appointed by the prime minister and approved by the monarch. Kuwait's unicameral legislature, the National Assembly, consists of fifty members elected by popular vote to four-year terms. In addition, all cabinet ministers serve as members of the National Assembly by virtue of their cabinet positions.

Kuwait's first National Assembly was elected in 1963, but from 1976 to 1981 the National Assembly was suspended by the emir, who holds the right to dissolve parliament when an impasse is reached. Elections occurred in 1981 and again in 1985, but the National Assembly was again dissolved. When the Kuwaiti government fled to Saudi Arabia during the 1990 occupation of its country by Iraq, the emir promised that political reforms would take place once he could return to Kuwait. The Iraqis were ousted in 1991, and new elections for the Kuwaiti National Assembly occurred in 1992. In 2006 the emir dissolved the National Assembly after its members determined they could not reach an agreement on redistricting the country's electoral constituencies. Members of parliament were advocating consolidating districts in an effort to reduce corruption and eliminate opportunities for election tampering. Elections to replace parliament were conducted in June 2006, and the new government quickly approved a plan that designated five constituencies, which would each elect ten representatives to the National Assembly.

The Kuwaiti legal code is a mix of civil law and Islamic sharia law, with the latter used for all disputes related to family and personal matters. At the local level lay courts deal with both civil and criminal cases. Courts of Appeal, however, are separated into those that hear personal and civil cases and those that hear criminal and commercial cases. Respective Sunni and Shia courts decide family law matters for Muslims, and a separate domestic court functions for non-Muslims. Kuwait's constitution guarantees an independent judiciary, but the executive branch (the emir) appoints the judges and retains control over its budget.

Another arm of the government, created specifically for the independent oversight of the government's finances, is the Kuwait Audit Bureau. It monitors the expenditure of public funds. Using its oil and investment revenues, the Kuwaiti government provides many public services to its citizens. Public education, including undergraduate studies at college, is free for students, and health care is provided for all citizens without charge. Kuwaitis are provided with retirement income, marriage bonuses, and employment.

The right to vote in Kuwait is restricted to individuals who are twenty-one years old and have been Kuwaiti citizens for at least twenty years. However, members of the police or military are not allowed to vote. Women were granted voting rights in May 2005 and participated as voters and candidates in parliamentary elections for the first time in June 2006.

Political Parties and Factions

Political parties and organizations are not legally sanctioned in Kuwait. However, a number of political groups act as de facto parties, and like-minded members of the National Assembly (such as Shia activists, secular liberals, tribal groups) do act as voting blocs. Sunni Muslims outnumber Shia and other Muslims by a ratio of two to one.

Although trade unions are permitted, less than 5 percent of the labor force are union members, and the only legal trade union is the Kuwait Trade Union Federation, which is supervised and financially subsidized by the government.

Major Events

From the time of its declaration of independence in June 1961, Kuwait has had an uneasy relationship with its neighbor Iraq, which claimed Kuwait's land as its own, based on territory once held by the Turkish Ottoman Empire. Kuwait's oil fields and ports were highly sought after by landlocked Iraq. Although the United Nations upheld Kuwaiti sovereignty, and in 1963 Iraq formally recognized Kuwait's independence, tensions between the two nations, and between the Sunni and Shia Muslim groups, continued to grow over many years. In the 1980s Kuwait supported Iraq in the Iran-Iraq war, an act that angered Kuwait's Shia minority, which launched terrorist acts in protest. The American embassy was bombed and a Kuwait Airways plane was hijacked. Explosions killed civilians in bombings at waterfront cafes.

In 1987, at the request of the Kuwaiti government during the Iran-Iraq War, U.S. military forces were used to protect Kuwaiti oil vessels in the Persian Gulf. Because the U.S. Navy is prohibited by law from escorting vessels operating under foreign ownership, the oil tankers were given U.S. registry and flew American flags for the duration of the operation.

In 1990 Iraqi president Saddam Hussein (1927–2006) accused Kuwait of waging economic warfare against Iraq by, among other charges, overproducing oil to drive down prices and illegally drilling oil from the shared Rumaila oil field. That summer, on August 2, Iraqi forces invaded Kuwait, asserting that Iraq was reclaiming its rightful territory. Kuwait's royal family and much of its population fled to Saudi Arabia. When Iraq did not withdraw from Kuwait as ordered by the United Nations, an offensive was orchestrated by an international coalition of military forces with the United States in the lead. Iraqi forces retreated on February 26,

Kuwaiti oil fields left burning by the Iraqi army after they were driven out of Kuwait by U.S.-led forces in 1991.   © *Peter Turnley/CORBIS*

1991 (setting fire to many oil fields along the way). Kuwait spent more than $5 billion to repair the infrastructure damage caused by the invasion, and vast tracts of land polluted by the oil fires remained unusable into the twenty-first century. In 1994 Iraq formally recognized the independence and borders of Kuwait, although it continued to perform threatening military maneuvers near the Kuwait-Iraq border. As a result, the United States, the United Nations, and others continued to keep military and peace-keeping operations in Kuwait.

Twenty-First Century

In 2003 Kuwait allowed the U.S. military to use its country for staging the American invasion of Iraq that successfully ousted the regime of Hussein. With the threat of its aggressive neighbor removed, Kuwait turned its attention to domestic issues. The most significant development in Kuwaiti government since 2000 has been the entrance of women into national politics. After more than forty years of debate, women were granted the right to vote and to hold office in May 2005. Shortly afterward Massouma Mubarak (1951–) was named a cabinet minister, and she became the first woman to hold a government post in the history of

Kuwait. However, in June 2006, in the first election in which women were able to participate as both candidates and electors, none of the twenty-eight female candidates won a seat in the assembly. Instead, Islamic reformists strengthened their numbers in the parliament. In June 2007 the assembly passed legislation that barred women from working between 8 P.M. and 7 A.M. and codified the types of businesses in which women would be allowed to work. While many observers quickly criticized the discriminatory nature of the law, religious conservatives applauded the decision as a step toward preserving Islamic tradition with respect to women's role in society.

BIBLIOGRAPHY

Casey, Michael S. *The History of Kuwait.* Westport, CT: Greenwood Press, 2007.

Cordesman, Anthony J. *Kuwait: Recovery and Security after the Gulf War.* Boulder, CO: Westview Press, 1997.

U.S. Central Intelligence Agency, *The World Factbook,* "Kuwait." https://www.cia.gov/library/ publications/the-world-factbook/geos/ku.html (accessed August 15, 2007).

⊕ Samoa

Type of Government

Samoa is a constitutional monarchy with a prime minister who serves as head of government. The Samoan government combines elements of the traditional *matai* (chief) system of governance and the European parliament. The unicameral Fono Aoao Faitulafono (National Legislative Assembly) is the main decision-making body.

Background

Samoa, which is located in the southern Pacific Ocean among the island nations of Polynesia, comprises four inhabited islands—Upolu, Savai'i, Manono, and Apolima—and five uninhabited islands. The nation must be distinguished from American Samoa, an unincorporated territory of the United States that occupies the eastern part of the Samoan archipelago. Samoa's capital is Apia, on the northern coast of Upolu Island. Until 1997 the nation was known as Western Samoa.

The Samoan archipelago was settled as early as 1000 BC, when migrants arrived from other Polynesian islands (most likely Tonga). Early Samoan society was based on kinship ties and focused on agricultural and maritime activities. Before European contact, each Samoan village was governed by a council of matai.

European involvement in Samoa began during the nineteenth century, when the English missionary John Williams (1796–1839) succeeded in converting Samoa's most powerful matai, Malietoa Vainu'upo, to Christianity; most of his subjects followed suit. The United States, Britain, and Germany all had settlements on the islands by the second half of the century, and the three nations struggled for control of the archipelago. In 1889 they reached an agreement (known as the Berlin Act) to ensure Samoa's neutrality. A decade later, however, the United States annexed the eastern islands, and Germany took the western islands (first called German Samoa, then Western Samoa).

In German-controlled Samoa, the colonial occupiers immediately attempted to centralize political power by restricting the authority of the matai. The act fueled sentiments for independence and spurred the formation of a nonviolent movement known as O le Mau a Pule, or Mau ("strongly held view"), which challenged the authority of the German governor.

After World War I New Zealand occupied Western Samoa, expelling the Germans and administering the islands first as a League of Nations–mandated territory and later as a trust set up by the United Nations. The independence movement intensified as the Mau became a more organized political force.

Following World War II a council of state and a legislative assembly were established for Samoa, and in 1954 a constitutional convention was held. Western Samoa became an independent nation in 1962, the first of the Pacific microstates to achieve that status. Samoa remains a full member of the Commonwealth of Nations (also called the British Commonwealth), a voluntary association of more than fifty independent nations that are former colonies or territories of the British Empire.

Government Structure

The structure and functions of government are outlined in the nation's constitution, which was adopted upon independence in 1962. The constitution initially provided for a monarchy headed by two co-chiefs of state (O le Ao le Malo) serving lifetime appointments; it specified that if one chief died, the other would serve as the sole monarch until his death. When the constitution was promulgated in 1962, Samoa's two highest-ranking matai were appointed as monarchs. Upon the death of co-ruler Tupua Tamasese Mea'ole (1905–1963), Malietoa Tanumafili II (1913–2007) served as sole chief of state. When he died in 2007, a three-person Council of Deputies acted as interim chief of state until a successor could be appointed. As spelled out in the constitution, the Samoan legislature appointed a new chief of state to a five-year term, with no term limits: Tupua Tamasese Tufuga Efi (1938–) took office on June 17, 2007. The position is largely ceremonial, with duties performed on the recommendation of the prime minister.

The head of government in Samoa is the prime minister, who is chosen by the majority party in the legislature and forms a government at the invitation of the chief of state. The prime minister is advised by a cabinet of twelve members, who are appointed by the chief of state. Cabinet members remain in their positions as long as they have the confidence of the legislature.

The unicameral National Legislative Assembly is made up of forty-nine members who serve five-year terms: Forty-seven members represent village-based electoral districts, while two seats are reserved for non–Samoan nationals who are separately elected. Only matai are eligible to run for election to the village-based seats.

Samoa's legal system is based on British common law but incorporates elements of Samoan customary law. The Supreme Court is the ultimate judicial authority. The chief justice is recommended by the prime minister and appointed by the chief of state. Supreme Court justices also preside over the Court of Appeal, which consists of three justices; this court may only hear cases referred by the Supreme Court. Lower courts include the Magistrate's Court, which handles criminal matters, and the Land and Titles Court, which hears civil cases. Some criminal and civil cases are heard by village *fonos* (traditional courts), which follow different procedures from those of the official courts.

At the local level Samoa is divided into eleven administrative districts. Within each district are thousands of *aiga* (extended families), each of which selects a chief as its leader. The chiefs, in turn, form village councils that attend to local concerns.

Tofilau Eti Alesana, Samoan political leader who served as prime minister from 1982 to 1985 and again from 1988 to 1998, shown here in 1985. © *Nik Wheeler/CORBIS*

Political Parties and Factions

During the first decade after independence, Samoa had no formal political parties. Members of the legislature followed the traditional "consensus" practice of deferring to the highest-ranking chief, a holdover from the indigenous *fa'amatai* system of governance. From 1962 to 1975 Fiame Faumuina Mataafa (1921–1975), the highest-ranking matai after the dual chiefs of state, served as prime minister, running for election virtually unopposed.

Political parties emerged in the 1970s as members of the legislature began to express differences of opinion. Since 1982 the Human Rights Protection Party has dominated Samoan politics. The main opposition party is the Samoan Democratic United Party. Minor political parties include the Samoa Party, the Samoa Progressive Party, and the Christian Party.

Major Events

From 1908 to 1962 the native Samoans resisted foreign rule, first by Germany and later by New Zealand. The primary organization behind their resistance was the

nonviolent O le Mau a Pule, or Mau, movement, which arose in the early twentieth century in response to German efforts to restrict the authority of local matai and centralize political power. In 1908 demonstrators led by Lauaki Namulau'ulu (1838–1915), a high-ranking orator chief, challenged the authority of the German governor. The uprising was quickly put down, however, when the governor called in German warships. Lauaki and his supporters were exiled to the Mariana Islands.

In the 1920s the Mau, led by Olaf Frederick Nelson (1883–1944), whose mother was Samoan, emerged as a more organized alliance agitating for Samoan independence. In 1929 New Zealand outlawed the organization and sent Nelson into exile. Later that year government troops fired on unarmed Mau demonstrators, killing many. The Mau was recognized as a legal political entity in 1935 and continued to work toward independence until 1962, when that goal was achieved.

Twenty-First Century

Samoa faces significant economic challenges. For most of its history, the nation's economy has depended heavily on agricultural production, particularly cash crops such as coconuts, bananas, and taro. A series of cyclones in the 1990s devastated coconut and banana crops, and a taro leaf blight in 1994 decimated the taro crop, the nation's largest export. These setbacks were exacerbated by the Asian financial crisis of the late 1990s. The Samoan government has responded to these challenges by attempting to diversify its economy, especially through development of its tourism industry.

BIBLIOGRAPHY

Fischer, Steven Roger. *A History of the Pacific Islands.* New York: Palgrave Macmillan, 2002.

Lawson, Stephanie. *Tradition Versus Democracy in the South Pacific: Fiji, Tonga, and Western Samoa.* Cambridge: Cambridge University Press, 1996.

⊕ Rwanda

Type of Government

The central African nation of Rwanda is a rapidly evolving constitutional republic. Many recent changes, including a new system for allocating legislative seats, were mandated by a new constitution ratified in 2003. Others, including a growing reliance on traditional village tribunals, represent ad hoc responses to crisis.

Background

Roughly twice the size of Connecticut, Rwanda is a densely populated, landlocked nation of ten million. Sharing its borders are Burundi, to the south; Tanzania, to the east; Uganda, to the north; and the Democratic Republic of the Congo (formerly Zaire), to the west. There are two primary ethnic groups: the majority Hutu, also known as Bahutu, and the minority Tutsi, or Batutsi. The deeply troubled relations between these two groups have shaped Rwandan history. Though the Hutu seem to have been the first to establish themselves in the region, the Tutsi had arrived, probably from the east, by the end of the fifteenth century. For more than four hundred years, they ruled the Hutu in a feudal system of nobles and peasants.

European colonists reached Rwanda relatively late. The first were the Germans, and for a short period (1899–1915) the region was administered as part of German East Africa. In the midst of World War I, however, troops from the Belgian Congo seized the colony as enemy territory. When the war was over, the League of Nations, forerunner of today's United Nations, declared the area comprising present-day Rwanda and Burundi a "trust territory"—a preparatory step toward self-government—under Belgian administration. Known as Ruanda-Urundi, the territory's legal status changed again at the end of World War II, when the UN assumed formal responsibility from Belgium, though Belgian administrators remained in their positions. Ethnic resentments grew in the late 1950s, and a Hutu insurrection toppled the Tutsi monarchy that the Belgians had left in place to mediate their relations with the mostly Hutu population. Thousands of people, mostly Tutsis, died, and at least one hundred and fifty thousand Tutsis fled across the borders. By 1962 the UN had dissolved the trust, the Belgians had withdrawn, and the Hutu rebels, organized as the Party of the Hutu Emancipation Movement, or PARMEHUTU, took charge of the new nation of Rwanda. Independence became official on July 1, 1962.

Grégoire Kayibanda (1924–1976), PARMEHUTU's leader, won the first presidential elections. He remained in office until 1973, when a military coup by Major General Juvénal Habyarimana (1937–1994) overthrew his administration. Habyarimana, in turn, ruled for more than twenty years with a fluctuating but always substantial degree of authoritarianism. He soon banned all parties except his own National Revolutionary Movement for Development (MRND), and the military quickly permeated both government institutions and civil society. The ratification of a new constitution in 1978 did little to change the situation, and Rwanda remained a charade of democracy; though three presidential elections were held (1978, 1983, and 1988), for example, Habyarimana was the only candidate on the ballot each time. In 1990 increasing domestic and international pressures finally forced him to announce plans for a new, multiparty system, but severe economic problems and rising ethnic tensions soon dashed hopes for reform. The largest single problem was an armed rebellion launched by a Uganda-based Tutsi group, the Rwandan Patriotic Front (RPF). Many of the RPF's fighters were the children of Tutsis who had fled the Hutu insurgency of the 1950s, and a significant propor-

tion received formal military training in the Ugandan army. This training, combined with Ugandan support and, above all, the desire to avenge their parents' exile, made the troops of the RPF formidable opponents. After two years of war, Habyarimana, a Hutu, and the rebels signed a ceasefire and agreed in principle to share power. With the arrival of a UN peacekeeping force the following year, there was renewed hope for political, social, and economic progress.

In 1994, however, both Habyarimana and the president of Burundi died in a plane crash. While the cause of the crash remains unknown, there are strong indications that the plane was shot down, presumably by Tutsi rebels or Hutu extremists angered by the ceasefire settlement. Whatever the cause, Habyarimana's death provoked one of the century's worst episodes of ethnic violence as Hutu extremists murdered more than eight hundred thousand Tutsis and moderate Hutus. It was in the aftermath of this genocide, and in response to it, that the current structure of Rwandan government was established.

Government Structure

Under the terms of the 2003 constitution, the executive branch consists of a president, a prime minister, and a cabinet, called the Council of Ministers. Both the prime minister and the other members of the cabinet are presidential appointees. The president is elected by direct, popular vote for a seven-year term, and there are no limits to the length of his or her tenure.

The structure of the legislative branch is far more distinctive. The upper house, called the Senate, has twenty-six seats, twelve of which are filled indirectly by vote of the nation's elected local councils. Eight seats are allocated to presidential appointees, two to representatives of Rwandan universities, and the last four to representatives of the Political Organizations Forum, an assembly of all recognized political parties. Senate members serve eight-year terms. The lower house, called the Chamber of Deputies, has eighty seats, fifty-seven of which are filled by direct, popular vote. The remaining twenty-seven are filled indirectly, with twenty-four allocated to women chosen by local organizations and three to representatives selected by youth groups and associations of the disabled. Deputies serve five-year terms.

Ongoing efforts to try more than one hundred and thirty thousand individuals suspected of involvement in genocide have complicated the structure of the judicial branch. The basic system consists of a Supreme Court, appellate courts called High Courts of the Republic, provincial courts, and local courts. These apply a legal code based on German, Belgian, and tribal law. Alongside the traditional court system, however, are several venues established in an effort to bring at least a significant fraction of genocide perpetrators to justice. The most prominent of these is the International Criminal

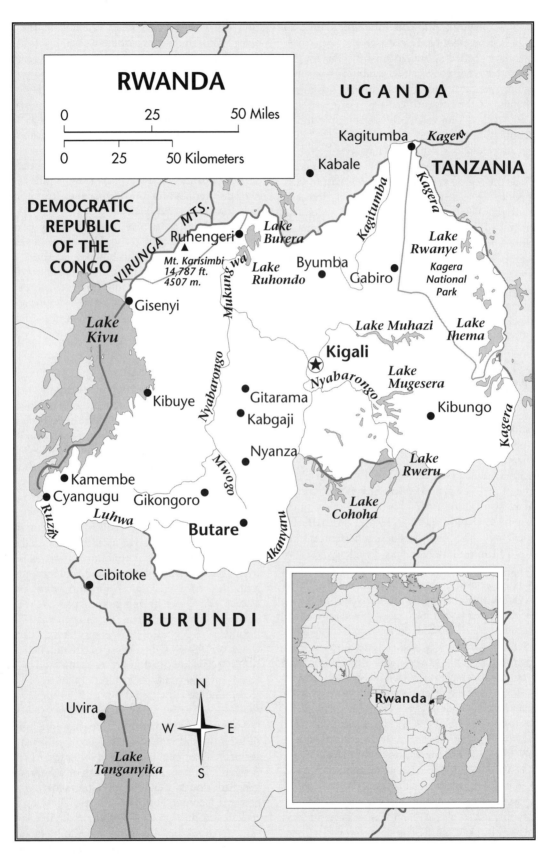

Rwanda. *Maryland Cartographics*

Rwandan Tutsis massacred in the 1994 genocide. © *Baci/CORBIS*

Tribunal for Rwanda (ICTR), established under UN auspices just over the border in Arusha, Tanzania. The ICTR focuses on authority figures suspected of instigating or participating in genocide. Despite several dozen convictions, its success has been limited for several reasons, notably its high cost, slow pace, and tense relationship with Rwandan authorities, who remain responsible for the trials of low-level participants. Despite significant foreign aid and enormous effort, the Rwandan court system remains woefully unequipped for a task that would overwhelm many better-funded systems. Authorities have therefore turned to public village tribunals. The *gacaca*, as these informal courts are known, are not a perfect solution; impartiality, for example, is difficult to obtain in a setting in which every judge, witness, and observer is likely to know the defendant. This intimacy, however, has also proved useful at times, for many witnesses unable or unwilling to testify before a professional judge are willing to do so before their peers and neighbors. While it is too early to assess the effectiveness of the gacaca system, it represents the kind of innovative, locally based reform many observers are now urging governments across Africa to develop.

Political Parties and Factions

On July 4, 1994, RPF forces seized the capital of Kigali in a victory that marked the end of the genocide. Nearly thirty percent of the nation's population had already fled, including many Hutu extremists fearful of Tutsi revenge. Running water, electricity, and telephone service no longer existed. Under these circumstances, the formation of a transitional government by the end of the month was a remarkable achievement. Though the president of the so-called Government of National Unity was a Hutu, Pasteur Bizimungu (1950–), the most powerful individual in the country was the Tutsi rebel Paul Kagame (1957–), who served simultaneously as vice president, minister of defense, and leader of the RPF. When internal disagreements toppled the transitional government in 2000, Kagame took over the office of president. Three years later, he won the first elections since the genocide with more than ninety-five percent of votes cast. In light of Kagame's authoritarian tendencies, however, many observers questioned the authenticity of the results. In the subsequent legislative elections, Kagame's RPF secured forty of the fifty-seven available seats in the Chamber of Deputies. The Social Democratic Party (PSD) took ten, and the Liberal Party (LP) won the remaining seven. Several parties are banned as extremist, notably Bizimungu's Party for Democratic Renewal (PDR). Supporters of the prohibited groups claim Kagame is simply using the extremist label to stifle dissent.

Major Events

In 2004 the International Criminal Tribunal sentenced Sylvestre Gacumbitsi (c. 1947–) for his role in the single worst incident of the genocide: the murder in April 1994 of more than twenty thousand unarmed civilians in and around the parish church of Nyarabuye, near the border with Tanzania. Gacumbitsi was acting in his capacity as mayor of the district, witnesses recounted, when he told Tutsi civilians that the church was a safe haven. Thousands believed him. It was then, prosecutors charged, that he told the extremist Hutu militias (known as "Interahamwe") to search the church grounds. Gacumbitsi's crimes illustrate one of the most tragic features of the genocide: the victims' misplaced trust in institutions that either failed to protect them, as the Nyarabuye church and other religious organizations failed, or delivered them to their killers, as Gacumbitsi's local administration did. Belated though it was, the conviction of the former mayor proved an event of profound emotional and symbolic significance throughout the country.

Twenty-First Century

Rwanda faces a number of significant challenges. Some of these, such as the increasingly serious environmental issues of deforestation and desertification, are shared by nations across Africa and around the world. Others, such as the need for continued Hutu-Tutsi dialogue and reconciliation, are Rwanda's alone. But the single most pressing problem may be a regional one. Decades after the upheavals associated with the end of colonialism, violence and instability continue to plague the nations of central Africa, particularly the Democratic Republic of the Congo. Though the Congolese Civil War, one of the longest and most brutal conflicts in recent memory, officially came to an end in 2002, the eastern Congo—the region closest to Rwanda—remains a vast, essentially lawless region of armed rebels, criminal gangs, and refugees. Both the Rwandan and Ugandan governments have endorsed repeated military incursions into Congolese territory in pursuit of rebels they claim present a critical threat to their administrations. Many analysts, however, are more concerned about the destabilizing effects these cross-border raids may be having on the Congo. Given the support Rwanda currently enjoys in the international community and its remarkably quick recovery from the physical damage of the 1994 crisis, the chance that scattered and disorganized Hutu rebels will be able to launch a successful invasion from the Congo seems relatively remote. The effects of the Rwandan army's incursions, however, are all too clear: civilian casualties, ruined crops, and refugees. If President Kagame is sincere in his frequently expressed determination to build a peaceful and prosperous nation, he will have to help stabilize the regional situation. The first step in the creation of a new Rwanda may lie just beyond its frontiers.

BIBLIOGRAPHY

Dallaire, Roméo, and Brent Beardsley. *Shake Hands with the Devil: The Failure of Humanity in Rwanda.* New York: Carroll & Graf, 2004.

Mamdani, Mahmood. *When Victims Become Killers: Colonialism, Nativism, and the Genocide in Rwanda.* Princeton, NJ: Princeton University Press, 2001.

Waugh, Colin M. *Paul Kagame and Rwanda: Power, Genocide and the Rwandan Patriotic Front.* Jefferson, NC: McFarland & Co., 2004.

⊕ Burundi

Type of Government

Burundi is a parliamentary republic with the executive branch led by the president, who is both chief of state and head of the government. The legislative branch is made up of a bicameral parliament comprising the National Assembly and the Senate. The judicial branch is headed by the Supreme Court.

Background

Burundi is a small, landlocked country in Central Africa. It shares borders with Rwanda, Tanzania, and the Democratic Republic of the Congo (DRC). The original inhabitants of Burundi were a people called the Twa. Ethnic Hutus arrived in the area in the fourteenth century and established themselves as the dominant culture. In the fifteenth century the Tutsi people began to settle the region and take control. Over time, Burundi became a monarchy presided over by Tutsi kings. That dynasty ruled for several centuries.

Except for a few short visits, European explorers and missionaries paid little attention to Burundi until the late nineteenth century. European influence finally began in 1899, when the country was incorporated into German East Africa. Belgian troops occupied the area in 1916, and after World War I Belgium received a mandate from the League of Nations to administer Ruanda-Urundi (what is now Burundi and Rwanda). The monarchy remained intact, however, as Belgium employed it in a system of indirect rule. In July 1962 Burundi gained its independence and a constitutional monarchy was established. The monarchy was overthrown in 1966, and a series of harsh, Tutsi-run military regimes followed.

Although the minority Tutsis had long held control over Burundi's majority Hutu population, the polarization and open hostility between the two did not erupt until after independence—especially with the advent of

Burundian refugees waiting to return home from Tanzania are directed by a United Nations refugee agency. © *Reuters/CORBIS*

the military governments. Those governments were particularly brutal, marked by violence, human rights violations, and oppression. Civil unrest and ethnic bloodshed were common: thousands of civilians were killed, thousands more were displaced, and the country entered a downward spiral.

In 1987 Major Pierre Buyoya (1949–) took over the Burundi government by means of a bloodless coup. Ethnic violence broke out the following year, killing thousands of Hutus and prompting Buyoya to institute a transition to democracy. A new constitution providing for a multi-party system was adopted in 1992, and Melchior Ndadaye (1953–1993), the country's first Hutu chief of state, ended military rule by becoming Burundi's first democratically elected president in June 1993. These developments toward stability were, however, abruptly terminated by Ndadaye's assassination by Tutsi soldiers. The result was immediate and protracted civil war.

The Hutu-Tutsi battle raged for nearly a dozen years, costing at least two hundred thousand lives. Peace negotiations were begun in 1998, and a transitional, power-sharing government was established in 2001. Violence continued to disrupt the process, but most rebel factions agreed to a ceasefire in time to allow voters to ratify a new constitution and elect a new parliament in

2005. Parliament elected a president (under extraordinary rules for the first post-transitional government only) that same year, and a ceasefire agreement with the last active rebel group was signed in 2006.

Government Structure

Burundi was established as a parliamentary republic with powers divided among executive, legislative, and judicial branches. Its constitution also contains provisions to ensure specific ethnic and gender representation. The executive arm is led by the president, who is both chief of state and head of the government. As per the constitution, in 2005 the first post-transition president was elected by a two-thirds majority of the parliament. After that the president is to be elected by popular vote to a five-year term and is eligible for a second term. There are two vice presidents: a first vice president, in charge of political and administrative affairs, and a second vice president, who oversees social and economic affairs. Both vice presidents are nominated by the president and endorsed by parliament. The executive branch also includes a twenty-member council of ministers, all of whom are appointed by the president.

The legislative branch is made up of a bicameral parliament comprising the National Assembly and the

Senate. The National Assembly consists of at least one hundred members who are directly elected to five-year terms. The constitution requires that the composition of the Assembly be 60 percent Hutu, 40 percent Tutsi, 30 percent female, and three Twa members. If the popular election does not return such a proportion, a National Independent Electoral Commission appoints additional members to ensure the obligatory representation is met. Thirty-four of the Senate's fifty-four members—one Hutu and one Tutsi from each of the sixteen provinces and Bujumbura (the capital)—are indirectly elected by an electoral college. Three seats are reserved for former heads of state and three for ethnic Twa. The remaining fourteen spots are appointed by the president, and women must comprise 30 percent of the overall body. Burundi has universal suffrage at age eighteen.

The judiciary is headed by a Supreme Court. Other courts include the Constitutional Court, three Courts of Appeals, and the Tribunals of the First Instance (17 at the provincial level and 123 local). The judiciary is still in its infancy, however, and struggles with problems of inefficiency and bias.

Political Parties and Factions

There are more than twenty registered political parties in Burundi, including two loose coalitions of Hutu and Tutsi majority parties—G-7 and G-8, respectively. The most prominent of the national mainstream parties are the Burundi Democratic Front (FRODEBU), National Council for the Defense of Democracy/Forces for the Defense of Democracy (CNDD-FDD), and Unity for National Progress (UPRONA).

FRODEBU was founded in 1992 as a Hutu-dominated party, although it boasted some Tutsi membership as well. In Burundi's first democratic elections, held in 1993, the party swept the parliamentary elections by winning sixty-five of eighty-one contested seats. The presidential elections were also a triumph, as they installed party leader Ndadaye as the country's first democratically elected president and first Hutu head of state. The euphoria over such momentous events was, unfortunately, cut short by Ndadaye's assassination only one hundred days into his presidency. The party continued to be active in government, however, contributing several key leaders, including three more presidents by 2003. Its leadership was also involved in the peace process that resulted in a new government and constitution in 2005. In those elections, FRODEBU demonstrated that it was still a force by securing 22 percent of the vote and twenty-five seats in the National Assembly.

The CNDD-FDD is a merger of two former Hutu rebel militia factions. The dominant FDD faction is especially notable in that its leadership was assumed by Pierre Nkurunziza (1963–) in 2001, six years after he had joined the Hutu rebellion. The CNDD-FDD finally signed a peace agreement with the transitional govern-

ment in 2003, and it went on to become a prominent organization within the new republic. The party came in first in the July 2005 parliamentary elections, garnering 59 percent of the vote and fifty-nine seats in the National Assembly. Nkurunziza was elected president of Burundi on August 26, 2005.

The predominately-Tutsi UPRONA is the oldest Burundian political party, with roots in the country's former monarchy. As such, it has necessarily undergone many adjustments and changes to suit the often-volatile times. Founded in 1959 by Prince Louis Rwagasore (1932–1961), UPRONA's original mandate was to oppose Belgian rule. That goal was attained in 1962, although the prince had been assassinated before seeing his dream come to fruition. The party then underwent an almost ironic transition in 1966, when it was proclaimed sole ruling party by leaders of the very military coup that had just overthrown the monarchy. The UPRONA proved equally resilient as it was variously embraced by subsequent military regimes and later, increasingly pluralistic governments. The path was often contentious, as the UPRONA and the FRODEBU became especially at odds during the civil war, but the party was on hand to sign the 2001 peace agreement and take its place alongside its rival party in the transitional government. It had lost much of its traditional prestige by the 2005 elections, but still managed to win 7 percent of the vote and ten seats on the National Assembly.

Political parties in Burundi are likely to continue to undergo transformation as the republic strives for stability. Integration of Hutu and Tutsi into the same parties has begun, but long-held resentments and acrimonies make the process slow and difficult.

Major Events

It is hard to overstate the significance of Burundi's civil war. Tens of thousands of people, including many civilians, were killed during the conflict. Hundreds of thousands more were either internally displaced or forced to become refugees in neighboring countries. The war's effects were compounded by a comparable conflict in neighboring Rwanda, which sent thousands of Rwandan refugees into Burundi. In addition, beyond the toll in human suffering, the devastation of war shattered the already precarious economy of one of the poorest nations in the world.

Twenty-First Century

The government of Burundi faces formidable economic and social challenges. Approximately 68 percent of the populace lives on less than a dollar per day. The literacy rate is less than 60 percent, and only about half the nation's children attend school. HIV/AIDS is an immense problem, as an estimated one in fifteen adults is affected by the disease. Food and medicine are widely unavailable, although the end of the war and resulting increased stability in the government has improved the flow of international assistance. In addition, the government is largely made up of former rebel leaders that have little experience in democratic leadership or building a solid infrastructure. For all these reasons, and others, Burundi remains heavily dependent on foreign aid. However, the perseverance required to come to a peace agreement among rebel factions, despite years of internal conflict and setbacks, indicates a commitment to change in Burundi. Whether that commitment can be translated into the creation of a lasting national unity will be the country's greatest challenge in the twenty-first century.

BIBLIOGRAPHY

Lemarchand, Rene. *Burundi: Ethnic Conflict and Genocide.* New York: Cambridge University Press, 1997.

Scherrer, Christian P. *Genocide and Crisis in Central Africa: Conflict Roots, Mass Violence, and Regional War.* Westport, CT: Praeger, 2002.

Sommers, Marc. *Fear in Bongoland: Burundi Refugees in Urban Tanzania.* Oxford, New York: Berghahn Books, 2001.

⊕ Democratic and Popular Republic of Algeria

Type of Government

Algeria is a multiparty republic. The president, who serves as head of state, is popularly elected to a five-year term. The president appoints a prime minister, who serves as head of government and presides over the cabinet, called the Council of Ministers. The legislature is a bicameral parliament consisting of the National People's Assembly and the National Council. The three-tiered judiciary includes lower courts that resolve civil disputes and some criminal cases, provincial courts that conduct more serious criminal trials and hear appeals, and a Supreme Court.

Background

On the southern coast of the Mediterranean Sea between Morocco and Libya, Algeria reaches southward into Africa's Sahara Desert. When French forces conquered the country in the nineteenth century, they called it Algérie, based on the Arabic name al-Jazair.

The native people of northern Africa who inhabited the region were called Berbers by the ancient Greeks. From the fifth century BC, the Berbers endured waves of invasion by the Phoenicians, Romans, Vandals, and Byzantines. Arabs invaded between the eighth and eleventh centuries, bringing Islam, Muslim culture, and the Arabic language. The Ottoman Empire controlled the region from the sixteenth century into the nineteenth century.

After a brief period of independence following Ottoman rule, Algeria was invaded by France in 1830. Algerians resisted conquest in a series of wars that ended in the mid 1870s, and the Algerian population fell by nearly one-third during this time. Under colonial rule, Algerians had fewer rights than the French, who occupied the country to take advantage of its natural resources.

On November 1, 1954, Algerian nationalists who had organized as the National Liberation Front (FLN) launched a revolution. The war, characterized by attacks on civilians that killed more than 30,000 French and perhaps 1.5 million Algerians, lasted until a cease-fire agreement in March 1962, when France agreed to hold a referendum on independence. On July 1, 1962, Algerian voters chose independence, and France declared the country independent two days later. Algeria became a member of the United Nations on October 8, 1962.

In a process controlled by the FLN, Algerians approved a constitution in 1963, and Ahmed Ben Bella (1918–) became the country's first president. The constitution initially created a socialist government, but the country later became a republic. The constitution was amended five times between 1976 and 1996, and constitutional government has been suspended during times of violent civil conflict.

Government Structure

Algeria's head of state is a president elected for up to two five-year terms. The president leads the armed forces, supervises foreign affairs, negotiates and ratifies treaties, and presides over the prime minister and cabinet. The president appoints many officials, including the prime minister and cabinet, civil and military officials, and the governors of Algeria's forty-eight provinces, or *wilayas.* The president also appoints one-third of the members of parliament's upper chamber, the National Council. The president has power to make law in special circumstances, but parliament must approve such decrees. In presidential elections, if no candidate receives a simple majority in the first round of voting, a run-off election is held between the top two candidates.

Along with the president, the prime minister and cabinet function as the executive branch of the government to administer the country's laws and policies. The prime minister nominates cabinet members subject to the president's approval. The prime minister has power to introduce legislation and, with the cabinet, executes the laws and programs adopted by the parliament. Parliament holds the power to investigate the actions of the prime minister and cabinet members. Its lower chamber, the National People's Assembly, can call for a vote to censure the prime minister and cabinet. If two-thirds of the Assembly votes for censure, the prime minister and cabinet must resign.

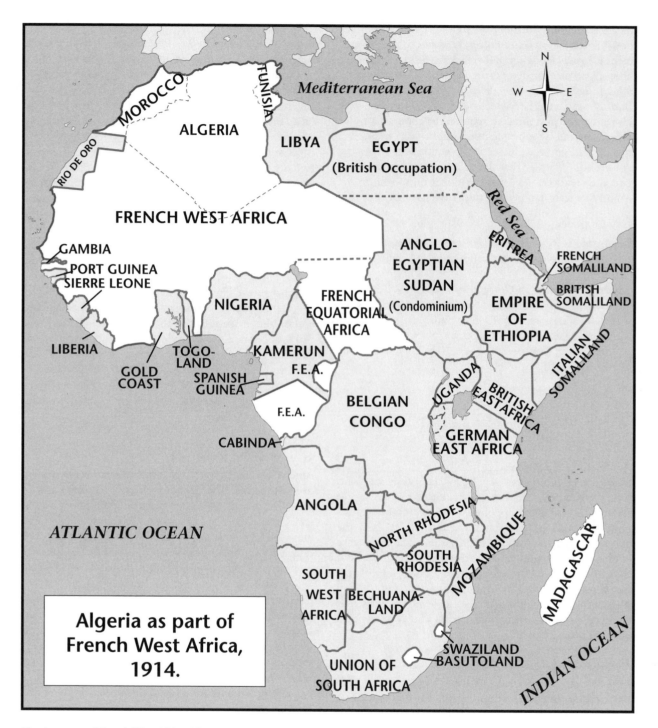

Algeria as part of French West Africa, 1914. *Map by Eastword Publications Development. Gale, a part of Cengage Learning*

Algeria's legislature is a bicameral parliament. It meets in two ordinary sessions annually, each lasting at least four months, and may meet for extraordinary sessions under certain conditions. The lower chamber is the National People's Assembly. It contains 389 members elected by the people for five-year terms, with eight seats reserved for Algerians living abroad. The Assembly is the only chamber with power to introduce legislation. Laws pass the chamber with a simple majority vote. If, however, the president requests a second reading, a law must receive a two-thirds vote to pass. After consulting the leaders in parliament and the prime minister, the president has power to dissolve the Assembly, in which case the country holds elections within three months.

The upper chamber of parliament is the National Council. It has 144 members who serve six-year terms. The president appoints one-third of the members, and council members from Algeria's provincial and other local governments elect the other two-thirds. The Council does not have power to introduce legislation, but it must approve laws by a three-fourths vote for them to take effect.

Algeria has a judicial system that is independent in theory under the constitution, although all judges are appointed by the executive branch without legislative approval and can be removed at will. The Supreme Court of Algeria sits atop the system. It has separate chambers for civil and commercial, social, criminal, and administrative cases. The Supreme Court hears appeals from provincial appellate courts that sit in each of Algeria's forty-eight provinces. The provincial courts handle various cases and hear appeals from tribunal courts, which sit at the lowest level of the hierarchy to decide civil, commercial, and some criminal cases. Algeria's laws are a combination of Islamic law and the civil code tradition inherited from France.

The judiciary has various bodies that operate outside the Supreme Court's hierarchical system. The Constitutional Council is the final authority on electoral matters and on deciding whether laws violate the constitution. The Council of State has power to hear certain administrative matters. The Tribunal of Conflicts adjudicates disputes over whether a case belongs before the Council of State or the Supreme Court. Finally, the Supreme Judicial Council, headed by the president, administers the judiciary.

Algeria is divided into forty-eight provinces, each of which has a governor appointed by the president and a council elected by the people. The provinces are divided further into municipalities with their own mayors and assemblies. The power of local governments is restricted mostly to implementing programs mandated by national law. Algerians who are at least eighteen years old have the right to vote.

Political Parties and Factions

For more than two decades after independence in 1962, the National Liberation Front (FLN), which launched the revolution of 1954, was Algeria's only legal political party. When they revised their constitution in 1989, Algerians ended FLN's monopoly. To operate lawfully, however, a party must be approved by the Ministry of Interior, which also has the power to dissolve parties. The Organic Law Governing Political Parties forbids parties from organizing based on race, religion, gender, language, or region.

Algeria's parliamentary system is designed to allow political participation by many parties. Twenty-four parties competed in legislative elections for the National People's Assembly in 2007, with just one party failing to win any

seats. With the momentum of history and its former monopoly, the FLN has usually been the most powerful political party during Algeria's modern independence. It won the most seats, though less than a majority, in Assembly elections in 2007. The next two most successful parties were the National Democratic Rally and the Movement of Society for Peace, both of which were allies of FLN in a coalition called the Presidential Alliance. Other influential parties included the Movement for National Reform, Workers' Party, Algerian National Front, Islamic Renaissance Movement, Party of Algerian Renewal, and the Movement of National Understanding.

Major Events

Algeria's history since independence in 1962 is characterized by its movement from socialism toward republican democracy with periods of violent civil strife and authoritarianism. In June 1965 a nonviolent coup led by Houari Boumédienne (1927–1978) and the Council of the Revolution exiled Algeria's first president, Ben Bella. Boumédienne ruled as head of state until 1976 and then as elected president until his death in 1978.

The FLN, then Algeria's sole lawful political party, nominated Chadli Bendjedid (1929–) to replace Boumédienne. Bendjedid was elected in 1979, 1984, and 1989. His administration brought a loosening of socialism and the growth of capitalism, all of which fueled the rise of government opposition by Islamic fundamentalist groups.

In 1989 Algerians amended their constitution to allow multiple political parties. The militant Islamic Salvation Front (FIS) thrived in municipal elections in 1990 and in a round of parliamentary elections in 1991. Faced with potential control of the National People's Assembly by FIS, Bendjedid dissolved the party on January 4, 1992, and then resigned a week later. A High Council of State assumed control of the presidency and canceled parliamentary elections, triggering violence. On January 16, independence hero Muhammad Boudiaf (1919–1992) returned from exile to be president, only to be assassinated in June as the government continued to suppress the FIS. Algeria entered a decade of state violence and Islamic terrorism that killed approximately 100,000 people. The primary terrorist organization was the Armed Islamic Group.

Liamine Zeroual (1941–) served as head of state from 1994 to 1999. In April 1999 Algerians went to the polls to elect a new president. While seven people sought the position, all but FLN candidate Abdelaziz Bouteflika (1937–) withdrew at the last minute under the belief that the results were rigged. Bouteflika was declared the winner with 70 percent of the votes cast.

Twenty-First Century

Following his inauguration, Bouteflika proposed a Civil Concord policy to grant amnesty to everyone who

French paratroopers controlling a crowd of pro-independence demonstrators in Algiers, 1961. © *Bettmann/CORBIS*

fought against the government in the 1990s except those guilty of "blood crimes" such as murder and rape. Algerians approved the policy in a referendum election in September 2000. Algerians reelected Bouteflika in 2004. The election was tarnished by accusations of preferential press coverage for Bouteflika by the state media and by governmental action taken against the FLN when it nominated a candidate other than Bouteflika. After reelection, Bouteflika proposed to build on the Civil Concord of 2000 with a Charter for Peace and National Reconciliation. The charter would grant amnesty to individuals who laid down arms against the government, pardon certain people convicted of armed violence, absolve government security forces for responsibility for their violence, and yet compensate victims of terrorism and families of people who had disappeared during the fighting.

Algerians approved the charter in a referendum in September 2005, but implementation proceeded slowly. Violence in the country continued, perpetrated by groups such as the Salafist Group for Preaching and Combat (GSPC), which pledged allegiance to the terrorist organization al Qaeda. In 2007 GSPC changed its name to al Qaeda in the Islamic Maghreb.

BIBLIOGRAPHY

Ageron, Charles. *Modern Algeria: A History from 1830 to the Present*. Translated and edited by Michael Brett. Trenton, NJ: Africa World Press, 1991.

Ruedy, John. *Modern Algeria: The Origins and Development of a Nation*. Bloomington: Indiana University Press, 2005.

Stora, Benjamin. *Algeria, 1830–2000: A Short History*. Ithaca: Cornell University Press, 2001.

⊕ Jamaica

Type of Government

Jamaica is a constitutional parliamentary democracy within the British Commonwealth. Its head of state is the British monarch, Queen Elizabeth II (1926–), who is represented locally by a governor general. Internally, power is shared between the executive branch, whose prime minister (the leader of the majority party or coalition) is head of government; a bicameral legislative branch, made up of an appointed Senate and an elected House of Representatives; and a judicial branch, led by a Supreme Court, whose judges are appointed by the governor general on the advice of the prime minister.

Background

The island nation of Jamaica lies in the West Indies, south of Cuba and west of the island of Hispaniola. The name of the island comes from Spanish sailors' corruption of the native Arawak name for the island, Xaymaca, "land of wood and water." Sighted in 1494 by Christopher Columbus (1451–1506), the island was settled by the Spanish in 1509; subsequently the Arawak inhabitants were enslaved and virtually annihilated by disease. To replace their work force, the Spanish planters then turned to African slaves, who were first imported to the island after 1517.

The island remained under Spanish control until it was captured by the British naval commander Sir William Penn (1621–1670) in 1655. After several years of small-scale warfare against Spanish holdouts on the island, the British established control, and the island was officially ceded to England in 1670. British rule was consolidated by co-opting local pirates and buccaneers, such as Sir Henry Morgan (1635–1688), who raided foreign vessels and added to the wealth of the island. Morgan was made lieutenant governor of Jamaica in 1674. Port Royal became the capital; however, it was destroyed by an earthquake in 1692. The island population grew quickly under British rule: there were 4,205 people in Jamaica in 1662; 17,272 in 1672; and 47,365 in 1696. The vast majority of these were African slaves.

The British established the plantation system on the island, using their imported slave labor to grow sugar cane, and the island became a leading supplier of sugar. Several uprisings took place in the eighteenth century, with Maroons—slaves who had escaped their owners and fled to the interior—leading revolts against the planters. At first the Maroons were able to win a degree of autonomy from the British, but by the end of the eighteenth century, most of them had been rounded up and shipped off to other countries. The island's population swelled to more than two hundred thousand, 90 percent of whom were slaves from Africa. In 1808, when the British Parliament finally ended the slave trade, the African population on the island was over three hundred thousand. Slavery was abolished in 1833, and by 1838 all the slaves on the island had been emancipated.

However, with the freeing of the slaves, sugar production plummeted, and without an effective economic base, the island soon sank into a severe depression. In 1865 impoverished former slaves rioted in Morant Bay, killing nineteen people. The British suppressed the uprising, effectively ending any question of Jamaican independence. In the late nineteenth century, the widespread establishment of banana plantations replaced the island's former reliance on sugar cane. Still, many freed slaves left Jamaica to find employment and better economic opportunities on neighboring islands, and, after the U.S. Civil War, in the United States. Native Americans from South America were imported to do much of the labor, and agricultural production was further diversified. In 1884 a new constitution gave the island a renewed measure of autonomy.

Through the first half of the twentieth century, nationalist sentiments grew among the majority black population. With the advent of the worldwide depression of the 1930s, which resulted in rising unemployment in Kingston and other Jamaican cities, riots broke out to protest lack of work and British racial policies. These riots spurred the British to accelerate the move toward autonomy: universal adult suffrage was introduced in 1944, and a new constitution was approved that provided for a house of representatives chosen by popular vote, although ultimate authority continued to reside with the Colonial Office in London and the appointed governor of Jamaica.

Jamaica was granted internal autonomy in 1953, and five years later the nation became a member of the West Indies Federation, a group of ten territories sponsored by the British. However, the nationalist leader of the Jamaica Labour Party and a leader of the resistance to colonial power, Sir Alexander Bustamante (1884–1977), campaigned against the federation, maintaining that Jamaica did not have sufficient decision-making power within the group. This led to a 1961 referendum in which Jamaica chose to withdraw from the federation. On August 6, 1962, Jamaica became an independent member of the Commonwealth, with Bustamante the first prime minister.

Government Structure

Jamaica's current constitution was adopted in 1962, establishing a parliamentary system after the British model. The hereditary monarch of the United Kingdom, who is the head of state, appoints a governor general whose role is largely ceremonial. The prime minister and the cabinet form the real executive power in Jamaica. The prime minister is the leader of the ruling party in the House of Representatives, or the chosen leader of a coalition government. The prime minister advises on the choice of a fifteen-member cabinet, which is then submitted by the governor general. No fewer than two and no more than four of the members of the cabinet are selected from the members of the Senate.

The legislative branch is made up of two houses: the Senate and the House of Representatives. The twenty-one members of the Senate are appointed, thirteen by the prime minister and eight by the leader of the opposition. The sixty members of the House of Representatives are elected by popular vote (Jamaica enjoys universal suffrage from age eighteen) and serve five-year terms. New elections must be called within five years of a new government taking office; the prime minister, however, can ask for elections to take place before that time. The Senate may initiate bills and also review legislation submitted by the House of Representatives, but it is not allowed to delay budgetary bills by more than a month or other legislation for more than seven months. A two-thirds majority is needed from both houses for constitutional amendments.

Jamaica's judicial system is based on British law. The judges of the Supreme Court, which handles matters of constitutional law, are appointed by the governor general on the advice of the prime minister. The Court of Appeals is the highest appellate court in Jamaica; in some circumstances, cases may be appealed to the Privy Council of the United Kingdom.

Jamaica is divided into fourteen parishes. Each has an elected council that exercises limited powers of local government.

Political Parties and Factions

Jamaica is basically a two-party system, with the People's National Party (PNP) and the Jamaica Labour Party (JLP) competing for control of the presidency and the legislature. Both of the primary parties have strong connections to labor unions.

Founded in 1938 by Norman Manley (1893–1969), the PNP is the older of the two main parties in Jamaica and is generally considered the more liberal and leftist of the major parties. With strong ties to the National Workers Union (NWU) and membership in the Socialist International, the PNP advocates populist causes, including social justice and free education. The party held power under the leadership of the founder's son, Michael Manley (1924–1997), from 1972 to 1980 and again from 1989 to Manley's retirement in 1992. Manley was replaced by Percival James Patterson (1935–), who was elected a record number of three times, and when he retired in 2006, he was replaced by Jamaica's first female prime minister, Portia Simpson-Miller (1945–).

The JLP was founded in 1943 by Alexander Bustamante, becoming the political arm of the Bustamante Industrial Trade Union. The JLP ruled Jamaica in the first decade of independence, first with Bustamante as prime minister from 1962 to his retirement in 1964, and then under Sir Donald Sangster (1911–1967) and Hugh Shearer (1923–2004). The party was led by Edward Seaga (1930–) from 1974 to 2005 and has been headed by Bruce Golding (1947–) since that time.

Additionally, the center-right National Democratic Movement (NDM) was founded in 1995, and the more populist United Peoples Party (UPP) was established in 2001. These parties have thus far been marginal in terms of membership numbers, and neither has links with any particular trade union.

Sir Alexander Bustamante, Jamaican nationalist leader and first prime minister, c. 1960. © *Grey Villet/Time Life Pictures/Getty Images*

Major Events

While Jamaica's political system has been relatively stable, severe economic problems have created correspondingly severe social problems. With unemployment at around 15 percent, high interest rates, and growing international debt, the country has had to face difficult choices in its legislative policies. Violent crime, particularly in the capital of Kingston, has further exacerbated the economic situation, reducing revenues from tourism. Many criminal gangs are known to have connections to members of the JLP or PNP. Gangs have also become involved in the international drug trade, making Jamaica a transshipment point.

Violence also plagues the political arena, with dozens killed each election cycle as a result of partisan passions. The most violent political year in the country's history was 1980, in which more than eight hundred people were reportedly murdered, most as a result of political violence. Another milestone in the island's violent history took place on July 7, 2001, when more than twenty people were killed when Jamaican security forces entered a community in the West Kingston area to contain violence between rival political gangs.

Twenty-First Century

Jamaica continues to make great efforts to increase its tourist trade and has become a major destination for Caribbean cruises: in 2003 Jamaica attracted more than a million cruise visitors. The government has also invested in developing hotels and recreational accommodations at all the major coastal facilities in an effort to attract additional visitors. However, tourism has suffered from natural disasters, including hurricanes, which accounted for over $90 million in damages in 2004.

The government and political parties are also increasingly addressing the issue of violence in Jamaican society. In 2002 party leaders agreed to a political code of honor and to discourage their followers from violence. Nonetheless, sixty persons were killed due to political violence in the 2002 elections. In 2005 both major political parties also required their members to renounce any ties to criminal gangs. Under Prime Minister Portia Simpson-Miller, the Justice System Reform Programme was initiated in an attempt to review and overhaul the Jamaican justice system, and crime-fighting units were increased in western Jamaica.

BIBLIOGRAPHY

Black, Clinton V. *A History of Jamaica*. Harlow: Longman, 1988.

Government of Jamaica. "Jamaica Information Service." http://www.jis.gov.jm/default.asp (accessed March 31, 2007).

Jamaica in Slavery and Freedom: History, Heritage and Culture, edited by Kathleen E. A. Monteith and Glen Richards. Barbados: University of the West Indies Press, 2002.

Mordecai, Martin, and Pamela Mordecai. *Culture and Customs of Jamaica*. Westport, CT: Greenwood Press, 2001.

⊕ Trinidad and Tobago

Type of Government

The Republic of Trinidad and Tobago is a parliamentary democracy with power shared between executive, legislative, and judicial branches. The executive branch is led by the prime minister—normally the leader of the majority party in the House of Representatives—who is head of government, and a president—chosen by an electoral college of the members of the Senate and House of Representatives—who is head of state. The legislature is bicameral, with an appointed Senate and an elected House of Representatives. The judiciary is based on English common law; the Supreme Court reviews legislative acts. Its justices are appointed by the president.

Background

Trinidad and Tobago is located in the southern Caribbean and consists of two main islands, Trinidad and Tobago, as well as twenty-one smaller islands. Originally settled by tribes from South America, including the Arawak and Carib, the islands were sighted by Christopher Columbus (1451–1506) in 1498. Spanish settlers established the first permanent settlements on the island in the sixteenth century. As the indigenous population was hostile toward European immigrants, the Spanish government invited missionaries from across Europe to settle on the islands in hopes of converting more of the native population to Catholicism. Throughout the eighteenth century, Britain contested the Spanish claim to the islands resulting in numerous skirmishes between Spanish and British naval groups. In the nineteenth century, under the threat of full invasion, Spain agreed to cede the islands to British control.

The early economy of Trinidad and Tobago, like those of many other Caribbean islands, relied heavily on sugar cane plantations, which were replaced by cacao in the late nineteenth century. After slavery was abolished in 1834, the British imported thousands of contract workers from India, adding to the racial mix. In 1899 the two islands were combined into a single colony.

By 1910 oil had become a key export, of particular importance after the cacao trade was badly hurt by disease and the Great Depression in the 1930s. By 1925 partial self-government had been granted to the island, and following World War II the islands were briefly part of the West Indies Federation, a step toward decolonization. Trinidad and Tobago gained independence on August 31, 1962, as a member of the British Commonwealth of Nations, and in 1976 the nation adopted a republican constitution.

Government Structure

For the first fourteen years of its independence, Trinidad and Tobago acknowledged the British monarch as the chief of state, with the governor-general acting as the local representative of the Queen. With the new constitution in 1976, however, ties to the British monarchy were severed and the country became one of the first republics within the Commonwealth. The office of president was created to take over the duties of head of state and commander in chief of the military. The prime minister and cabinet head the government and are responsible to the legislative branch.

The legislature, or parliament, is made up of the upper chamber, the Senate, with thirty-one members. Sixteen of these members are appointed by the president, in consultation with the prime minister; six are appointed by the president in consultation with the leader of the opposition; and nine are appointed solely by the president. The lower chamber, the House of Representatives, consists of forty-one members elected by universal adult

Instrumental in the independence of Trinidad and Tobago, Eric Eustace Williams served as prime minister from 1961 until his death in 1981. © *Bettmann/CORBIS*

suffrage for five-year terms. Elections may be called before the full term is concluded by the president at the request of the prime minister, or after a vote of no confidence in the House of Representatives.

The Supreme Court of Judicature of Trinidad and Tobago is made up of the High Court of Justice and the Court of Appeals. The chief justice must be a judge of the High Court, and other judges are appointed by the president in consultation with the prime minister and the leader of the opposition. The Supreme Court of Judicature has jurisdiction in civil and criminal cases. The Caribbean Court of Justice—based in Trinidad and Tobago—was inaugurated in 2005 and is the highest court of appeal.

Administratively, the nation is divided into nine regional corporations, two city corporations, three borough corporations, and one ward, Tobago. That island was granted limited autonomy in 1977 and full internal self-government in 1987. The nation's capital is Port-of-Spain.

Political Parties and Factions

Though there are numerous political parties in Trinidad and Tobago, in practice the country has a two-party system, with the major parties being the People's National Movement (PNM) and the United National Congress (UNC).

Founded in 1955 by the "Father of the Nation," Eric Williams (1911–1981), the PNM is the major conservative party. Williams became the first prime minister in 1956, serving in that capacity until his death in 1981. It is largely supported by citizens with African ancestry.

The UNC was formed in 1988 as a result of a split in the multiracial National Alliance for Reconstruction (NAR), which held power from 1986 to 1991. The UNC won a majority of seats in 1995 and held the majority until 2001, when the PNM once again took power. The UNC is supported largely by citizens of East Indian descent.

Major Events

Oil revenues have supplied Trinidad and Tobago with the highest standard of living in the Caribbean. However, racial tensions between East Indian and black residents have been a major threat to government stability. A state emergency was declared in 1970 when rioting broke out against the East Indians; in 1990 black militants attempted a coup against the multiracial government headed by the NAR.

Twenty-First Century

Sugar, long the country's chief crop, received its final blow in 2003 when the 9,000-member workforce of the government-owned sugar producer, Caroni Ltd., was laid off. Since 2003 the island's sugar industry has produced only enough sugar for local demand while the petroleum industry became the nation's chief source of export revenues, accounting for more than 20 percent of the Gross Domestic Product (GDP).

Aside from such economic issues, blending the disparate elements of the country's multiracial community continues to be the most difficult challenge for Trinidad and Tobago's political leaders.

BIBLIOGRAPHY

Besson, Gérard, and Bridget Brereton. *The Book of Trinidad*. 3rd ed. Port of Spain, Trinidad and Tobago: Paria Publishing, 1992.

Government of the Republic of Trinidad and Tobago. "Trinidad and Tobago Government Portal." http://www.ttconnect.gov.tt/Egov/Portal/Default.aspx (accessed April 2, 2007).

Winer, Lise. *Trinidad and Tobago*. Philadelphia, PA: J. Benjamins, 1993.

⊕ Uganda

Type of Government

The central African nation of Uganda is a constitutional republic that has recently made a transition to unrestricted multiparty politics after decades of one-party rule. The executive branch, headed by a president who is both head of state and head of government, continues to dominate over the legislative and judicial branches.

Background

Slightly smaller than the state of Wyoming, Uganda is a fertile, densely populated, and landlocked nation of thirty million. Its immediate neighbors are Sudan, to the north; Kenya, to the east; Tanzania, to the south; Rwanda, to the southwest, and the Democratic Republic of the Congo (DRC), to the west. These boundaries correspond closely to those demarcated by the British when they established the Protectorate of Uganda with a series of treaties around 1900, bringing a number of independent and often hostile tribes together under a single administration. The result was increased ethnic tension as individual tribes competed for British favor, and these rivalries persisted after independence and remain an important factor in Ugandan politics. Of the nation's ten major ethnic groups, the largest is the Baganda, who nevertheless comprise only seventeen percent of the population. The Baganda were a privileged group under the British, and their king, known as the *kabaka*, was an important mediator between the colonial administration and the various tribes.

The transition from protectorate to independent nation was relatively peaceful, gradually proceeding through stages of increasing autonomy. Full independence came on October 9, 1962, with Milton Obote (1924–2005) of the Uganda People's Congress serving as the new nation's first prime minister. Obote quickly met resistance in his efforts to centralize and consolidate power, particularly from the Baganda, who remembered the power they themselves had enjoyed before independence. When Obote, a member of the Lango tribe, suspended the constitution in February 1966 and dismissed the kabaka from his mostly ceremonial post as head of state, the stage was set for ethnic rebellion and civil war.

Though increasingly repressive methods kept Obote in power for another five years, opposition was building, and in January 1971 the commander of Uganda's military, Idi Amin (c. 1925–2003), staged a successful coup. Within a week, he had dismissed parliament, amended the constitution, and declared himself president. Amin and his followers persecuted ethnic minorities, expropriated businesses and private property, and massacred civilians, killing hundreds of thousands of Ugandans during his corrupt and brutal eight-year reign. In 1979 a coalition of Tanzanian troops and Ugandan rebels finally ousted Amin. A series of ineffectual transitional governments then ruled briefly before elections in 1980 returned Obote to power, this time as president. Again Obote tried to centralize power, and again he met stiff resistance. In 1985 a group of army officers overthrew Obote, only to be overthrown themselves the following year by the National Resistance Army, a rebel group under Yoweri Museveni (1944–). Museveni became president, an office he still held in 2007. In his long tenure, he has overseen a remarkable if uneven economic recovery, a new constitution, and the recent transition to multiparty politics.

For many years, Museveni was strongly opposed to a multiparty system, which he contended would merely institutionalize the ethnic rivalries and factional disputes that had devastated the country. Instead, he insisted that all Ugandans join his National Resistance Movement (originally the political wing of his rebel army), which he characterized not as a party but as a universal movement for Ugandan progress. Opposition parties were tolerated, but prohibited from fielding candidates in elections. Despite Museveni's assertions to the contrary, most analysts described Uganda in this period as a one-party state. In March 2003, however, the government's own National Executive Committee recommended removal of the restrictions on opposition parties, subject to a national referendum. When the referendum passed in July 2005, Museveni had little choice but to acquiesce, and a constitutional amendment formally established the multiparty system now in use.

Government Structure

Despite these changes, President Museveni retains enormous power. Under the current constitution, promulgated in 1995 and amended a decade later, the president is both head of government and head of state, and is solely responsible for appointing the prime minister and the other members of the cabinet. His or her choices, however, are limited to current members of the National Assembly. The issue of term limits remains controversial. The original version of the 1995 constitution limited presidents to a maximum of two five-year terms, a restriction that would have barred Museveni from seeking another term in light of his elections in 1996 and 2001. In a remarkable display of executive power, however, the president pushed a constitutional amendment removing the two-term limit through the National Assembly. Freed to stand for a third term in 2006, he easily won the popular vote, and thus the election.

Legislative powers are vested in the unicameral National Assembly. Of its three hundred and thirty-two seats, two hundred and fifteen are chosen by direct, popular vote; thirteen are held by ex-officio members; seventy-nine are selected by women's groups; ten by the army; and five each by labor groups, associations of the disabled, and youth groups. Members serve five-year terms.

The nation's legal code is a mixture of British common law and tribal tradition. At the top of the court system is the Court of Appeal, judges for which are appointed by the president and approved by the National Assembly. Between the local courts and the Court of Appeal is the High Court, similar in jurisdiction and authority to a U.S. federal court. High Court judges are chosen by the president without Assembly involvement.

Uganda's system of local and regional government is extensive, largely because President Museveni reversed

Field Marshall and President Idi Amin Dada ruled Uganda from 1971 until 1979. © *AP/Wide World Photos*

the centralization policies of Milton Obote and Idi Amin soon after taking office. A hierarchical system of elected nine-member councils has broad authority at the village, parish, subcounty, county, and district levels. In 2007 there were seventy-nine districts, but that number may change as restructuring efforts continue.

Political Parties and Factions

President Museveni's NRM continues to dominate the Assembly, controlling one hundred and ninety-one of three hundred and thirty-two seats as of elections in February 2006. The major opposition party, with thirty-seven seats, is the Forum for Democratic Change (FDC), led by Kizza Besigye (1956–). Though Besigye was once a close ally of the president, he has become one of Museveni's harshest critics, characterizing the administration as a "dictatorship." Museveni, for his part, had Besigye arrested on rape and treason charges in November 2005, only weeks before the two were scheduled to face each other in the presidential election. The charges were later dropped on a technicality, however, and Besigye remains Museveni's most powerful domestic opponent. None of the other parties represented in the National Assembly has more than nine seats. These are held by the Ugandan People's Congress, former president Obote's party. Obote's wife Miria now leads the organization.

Despite Uganda's relative stability under the current administration, a number of rebel groups continue to harass soldiers and civilians in outlying districts. By far the most notorious of these is the so-called Lord's Resistance Army (LRA), the creation of a reclusive, self-styled holy man named Joseph Kony (c. 1962–). In October 2005, the International Criminal Court charged Kony and four of his top lieutenants with a range of crimes including rape, murder, kidnapping, and the enslavement of children, many of whom he has reportedly used in combat. As of June 2007, however, Kony was still at large, probably in the jungles of the DRC or southern Sudan, and sporadic but violent attacks by his forces have continued throughout northern Uganda. While the LRA is probably too weak to mount a serious challenge to Museveni's government, it has a proven capacity to sow panic and disrupt civilian life. There have been several preliminary attempts at negotiation, but in light of the two parties' failure to agree even on the location for further talks, few Ugandans are confident of a peaceful settlement.

Major Events

The precise number of Idi Amin's victims will probably never be known. Conservative estimates put the number at three hundred thousand. While all tribes and segments of society were at risk, Amin preyed particularly on the small Lango and Acholi tribes, probably because these were disproportionately represented in Obote's administration. By the end, almost everyone in the country had seen a friend, village acquaintance, or family member disappear into one of Amin's prison camps. Any pretext sufficed for arrest, but the true motive was usually ethnic hatred, greed, or, most commonly, a combination of the two. In 1972, for example, he expelled en masse all citizens of Asian extraction, primarily immigrants from the Indian subcontinent who had arrived during the protectorate. He then seized all businesses owned by these citizens and distributed them as gifts to his associates, many of whom simply plundered what they could and abandoned the ruined remains. The economic damage inflicted by Amin, though still evident throughout the country, can be repaired; the social and psychological damage has proved much harder to heal. Amin himself, meanwhile, died peacefully in his bed in a Saudi Arabian hospital in 2003.

Twenty-First Century

Uganda has made significant progress under Museveni's administration. Most areas of the country are secure, the economy is growing at a respectable pace, and public criticism of the government is generally tolerated. Local government is thriving, and the country's response to the AIDS crisis has been one of the most energetic and effective in Africa. Deep structural problems remain, however. Annual population growth of nearly 4 percent is not sustainable in a country that is already one of the most densely populated on the continent. Adding to the growing burden on resources and infrastructure is the largest number of refugees in Africa, including well over two hundred thousand from Sudan, almost thirty thousand from the DRC, and twenty thousand from Rwanda.

The refugee problem is a reflection of the regional instability that is probably the nation's single biggest challenge. The so-called Great Lakes region straddling the Congolese and Rwandan borders is one of the most lawless areas in the world. Inhabiting its rough terrain is a diverse collection of rebel groups, army deserters, criminal gangs, and frightened civilians. The Rwandan and Ugandan armies have repeatedly sent troops into the DRC in pursuit of rebels. In 2005 the Congolese government formally protested the most protracted of these incursions, the Ugandan invasion of 1998–2003, before the International Court of Justice (ICJ) in The Hague, Netherlands. That invasion helped spark what has become known as the Second Congolese War, a conflict that eventually killed millions. In December 2005, the ICJ ruled in the DRC's favor, ordering Uganda to pay damages for the organized plundering of resources (notably illegal logging) in areas held by its troops. It is unclear if or how Uganda will pay the settlement. What is clear, however, is the need for the nations of central Africa to put aside their conflicting interests long enough to stabilize the region. Uganda's recent progress makes it the best candidate to lead such an initiative.

BIBLIOGRAPHY

Kutesa, Pecos. *Uganda's Revolution, 1979–1986: How I Saw It.* Kampala, Uganda: Fountain Publishers, 2006.

Rubongoya, Joshua B. *Regime Hegemony in Museveni's Uganda: Pax Musevenica.* New York: Palgrave Macmillan, 2007.

Uganda Riding the Political Tiger: Security and the Wars in the Greater Lakes Region, edited by Aaron K. Kabweru Mukwaya. Kampala, Uganda: Makerere University, 2004.

⊕ Kenya

Type of Government

Kenya is a constitutional republic struggling to overcome a legacy of one-party politics, ethnic tension, and widespread corruption. Reform efforts faltered when the legislature failed to approve a new constitution in November 2005.

Background

Kenya, which lies in East Africa along the Indian Ocean, has been inhabited for hundreds of thousands of years. Some of the oldest human ancestors have been found in the Rift Valley, a significant feature of the country's geography. In the intervening centuries a variety of ethnic groups developed agrarian communities and kingdoms. Today Kenya's population of 37 million includes descendants of the Kikuyu, who represent about 22 percent of the people; the Luhya, 14 percent; the Luo, 13 percent; and the Kalenjin, 12 percent.

Arab and Persian traders arrived in the first century AD; they had developed settlements along the coast by the eighth century. Around 1500 the Portuguese made their own attempts at establishing a colony, which led to conflict, initially with the Arabs and Persians but later with representatives of the British and Dutch monarchies. The most intense colonization began under the Germans, who in the 1880s took control of thousands of square miles from the ocean to the mountain highlands of what are now Rwanda and Burundi. When they were defeated in World War I, however, the Germans lost their overseas territories. The League of Nations, the predecessor of today's United Nations, divided the colonies among the nations that won the war, and Britain was granted control of Kenya.

After several decades of administering the region as the East Africa Protectorate, the British formally announced the creation of Kenya Colony in 1920. Anticolonial sentiment among native Kenyans spread quickly in the following decade, particularly among the Kikuyu, many of whom worked for white settlers and resented the poor pay and treatment they generally received. The Young Kikuyu Association, founded in 1921 (after 1925 it was known as the Kikuyu Central Association), provided a forum for the airing of grievances and demands. Until the end of World War II, those demands did not generally include independence; instead, Kikuyu activists aimed for stronger representation of native interests within the framework of the colonial administration.

The Kikuyu continued to play a prominent role when the struggle for independence began in earnest in the early 1950s. Jomo Kenyatta (1889–1978), the first president and universally recognized father of independent Kenya, was a Kikuyu, as were the Mau Mau, a group of violent anti–British rebels. Kenya achieved full independence on December 12, 1963.

Government Structure

The government operates under the constitution of December 1963, which has been substantially amended nine times. There is widespread recognition of the need for a new constitution to protect the rights of individuals and to reduce the power of the president, but legislators refused to accept a draft version in 2005. There has been little progress since.

The executive office continues to dominate the legislative and judicial branches, though not as completely as it did under Kenyatta and his successor, Daniel arap Moi (1924–). Elected by direct vote for a maximum of two terms of five years, the president serves as both chief of

President Jomo Kenyatta, the first president of the Republic of Kenya, in 1964. © *Bettmann/CORBIS*

state and head of government; there is no prime minister. The president appoints the vice president and the cabinet, as well as the chief justice of the Court of Appeal, the nation's highest judicial venue. An unusual constitutional amendment orchestrated by Moi in 1994 requires the victor in a presidential race to win both the popular vote overall and at least 25 percent of the vote in five of the nation's eight regions or face a run-off with the second-place candidate. The amendment was widely interpreted as an ethically questionable attempt by Moi to thwart his opponents, many of whom had regional bases of power.

Legislative authority is vested in the unicameral National Assembly, also known as the Bunge. Of its 224 members, 210 are elected by direct, popular vote for five-year terms; two are ex officio; and twelve are allocated to the various parties in proportion to their overall vote. The president formally appoints those twelve, but they are selected by the parties.

The Kenyan legal system is a mixture of British common law, tribal tradition, and a smaller element of Islamic law, or sharia. In addition to presiding over the Court of Appeal, the chief justice chairs the High Court, which rules on constitutional issues and other civil and criminal matters of its choosing. As many as eleven associate justices may sit on the Court of Appeal, but ordinarily only three hear a given case. The High Court, in contrast, may have as many as fifty associates. Local and district courts handle the bulk of the nation's judicial business.

For purposes of local administration, the country is divided into seven provinces and one urban equivalent, the capital of Nairobi. Certain districts, notably in the Western and Rift Valley Provinces, have experienced significant ethnic turmoil in recent years.

Political Parties and Factions

Two political parties existed at independence: the Kenya African National Union (KANU), the party of Jomo Kenyatta, and the Kenya African Democratic Union (KADU), which was primarily an organization of smaller

Two guerillas renouncing their ties to the Mau Mau revolutionary group in Kenya by licking the sacrificial blood of a goat off sticks, 1952. © *CORBIS*

ethnic groups concerned about the dominance of the Kikuyu and Luo peoples. KADU favored a more decentralized system than the one KANU proposed. The two rivals formed a coalition briefly in 1962, but elections held in May 1963 gave KANU sole control of the transitional government. After independence most KADU members joined KANU, and for several years thereafter Kenya had no real opposition parties.

In 1966 Kenyatta's vice president, Oginga Odinga (1911–1994), a Luo leader, resigned to form a new party, the Kenyan People's Union (KPU). Odinga's primary motivation was his belief that Kenyatta's economic policies were too capitalistic. Many of his supporters, however, were also disappointed by Kenyatta's continued reliance on the Kikuyu at the expense of the Luo and other groups. When the popular Luo politician Tom Mboya (1930–1969) was assassinated in 1969, ethnic unrest mounted, and the KPU was banned. Kenya then entered a long period of de facto one-party rule under KANU. In 1982 a constitutional amendment formally established Kenya as a one-party state. Under foreign and domestic pressure, the assembly repealed that amendment in 1991, and new opposition groups flourished.

As of the 2002 elections, KANU remained a major force in the assembly, holding sixty-four seats, although it was no longer the most powerful group. That distinction went to the National Rainbow Coalition (NARC) of President Mwai Kibaki (1931–), which won 125 seats. NARC's power has declined significantly since the elections, however. In a dispute over the drafting and review of the new constitution, NARC split in 2005. Those members who remained loyal to Kibaki renamed themselves NARC-Kenya, or NARC-K, while the dissidents joined KANU to form a new coalition, the Orange Democratic Movement-Kenya, or ODM-K. ODM-K's considerable influence in the assembly was revealed in November 2005, when it orchestrated the defeat of the Kibaki administration's proposed constitution.

Only one other party has more than a handful of seats in the assembly: the Foundation for the Restoration of Democracy-People (FORD-P), which holds fourteen. FORD-P was formed when the original FORD split in two; the other faction is known as FORD-Kenya (FORD-K); it is not a major power in the assembly. Outside the assembly a number of powerful pressure groups operate, urging political and economic reform. The most prominent is probably the National Convention Executive

Council (NCEC), a coalition of nongovernmental organizations and religious groups. Labor groups, a variety of Christian denominations, and the Supreme Council of Kenya Muslims are also active.

Major Events

The vast majority of the Kenyans agitating for independence in the 1950s did so peacefully. A few groups, however, were willing to use violence, especially the Mau Mau, a well-organized secret society within the dominant Kikuyu tribe. The Mau Mau launched an armed campaign in 1952 against civic institutions, police stations, and white settlers. In response, colonial authorities declared a state of emergency. As the insurrection spread, more than twenty thousand Kikuyu were detained without trial in guarded camps, where they were pressured to renounce any anticolonial feelings they may have had. Aside from its fundamental cruelty, the detention program was a catastrophic failure; faced with a clear example of colonial injustice, most detainees, even those who had previously shunned politics, returned from the camps avid and energetic nationalists.

While Kenya has remained relatively free of armed conflict since independence, violent incidents do occur with some regularity. In 1998 the U.S. embassy in Nairobi was bombed (another bomb exploded simultaneously outside the U.S. embassy in neighboring Tanzania). More than two hundred people in Nairobi died, most of them Kenyan bystanders, and nearly four thousand were injured. The bombers were Islamic extremists with close ties to al Qaeda, the Muslim jihadist group; the connection is a continuing concern for Kenyan officials. Several factors, notably the nation's porous borders with Somalia and Sudan—both are extremist strongholds—and its attractiveness to foreign tourists, have increased Kenya's vulnerability to terrorism and to the economic dislocations that often follow it. In the aftermath of the embassy bombing, for example, the tourism industry, one of the nation's leading employers and a major source of foreign exchange earnings, fell into a deep recession. Though it soon recovered, the industry declined again in November 2002, after Islamic extremists attacked an Israeli-owned hotel in Mombasa, a port city on the Indian Ocean. Thirteen people were killed.

Twenty-First Century

Despite moderate economic growth in 2006, Kenya's overall unemployment rate remains at 40 percent; it is even higher in isolated rural areas. At least half the population lives below the poverty line. While foreign aid constitutes a major portion of the budget, several major donors, including the International Monetary Fund and the World Bank, have said they will suspend aid completely if the administration continues to ignore the problem of corruption. Though certain kinds of graft—giving gifts to public officials, for example—have

traditionally been tolerated in Kenya, the situation turned considerably worse in this century, partly because the already inadequate salaries paid civil servants have failed to keep pace with inflation. In 2005 Kenyan media reported that corruption during Kibaki's first two years in office had cost consumers and taxpayers close to a billion dollars—a staggering sum in a country where the government's annual revenue is about $4.5 billion.

BIBLIOGRAPHY

Bujra, Abdalla, ed. *Democratic Transition in Kenya: The Struggle From Liberal to Social Democracy.* Nairobi: African Centre for Economic Growth, 2005.

Kihoro, Wanyiri. *The Price of Freedom: The Story of Political Resistance in Kenya.* Nairobi: MvuleAfrica Publishers, 2005.

Murunga, Godwin R., and Shadrack W. Nasong'o, eds. *Kenya: The Struggle for Democracy.* London: Zed Books, 2007.

⊕ United Republic of Tanzania

Type of Government

Tanzania, a constitutional, multiparty republic on Africa's eastern coast, was founded in 1964 when two newly independent nations united: Tanganyika, an enormous region on the mainland, and Zanzibar, a collection of small islands just offshore. The terms of the union guarantee Zanzibar considerable autonomy, with an entirely separate executive and legislative structure.

Background

Arab traders had been paying regular visits to Zanzibar and the mainland coast for at least seven hundred years by the time a Portuguese expedition arrived in 1498. Portuguese rule was never firmly established, however, and other, more profitable colonies soon diverted administrators and resources from the region. So Arab traders from Oman, on the southeastern coast of the Arabian peninsula, met little resistance as they gradually increased their political authority in the region; their commercial dominance, which the Portuguese had never seriously challenged, increased as they encouraged trade with Persians (whose descendants in Tanzania are known as Shirazis) and the Indian subcontinent. By the middle of the nineteenth century the Omani sultan, Seyyid Said (1791–1856), had established a wealthy and influential court at Zanzibar, where he received foreign dignitaries and oversaw much of the world's spice market.

European interest in the region had revived by the 1880s, however, and within a decade the German government had deprived the Zanzibar sultanate of its mainland properties. The Germans incorporated the territory into a new colony called German East Africa, which soon extended from the coast to the mountain highlands of what are now Rwanda and Burundi, hundreds of miles away. In return for British acquiescence during this expansion, the Germans agreed to recognize Zanzibar's status as a British protectorate; the sultan was allowed to remain in office to mediate relations between the islanders and the new mainland administration.

German East Africa, meanwhile, proved short-lived, as Germany lost all of its overseas possessions following its defeat in World War I. The League of Nations, the predecessor of today's United Nations, divided the colony and distributed the pieces to the victors as trust territories. The British won Tanganyika and retained control of Zanzibar.

The geopolitical shifts that followed World War II encouraged the development of nationalist, pro-independence movements in colonies across Africa, including Tanganyika and Zanzibar. The leader of Tanganyika's movement was Julius K. Nyerere (1922–1999), who founded the Tanganyika African National Union (TANU) in 1954. The movement in Zanzibar was more diffuse, with two ethnically based parties, the Afro-Shirazi Party (ASP) and the Arab-dominated Zanzibar Nationalist Party (ZNP), competing for the leadership role. In both colonies incremental increases in autonomy led relatively quickly to full independence. Tanganyika became an independent nation on December 9, 1961, and a constitutional republic under Nyerere the following year. Zanzibar achieved independence in 1963, when the sultanate was transformed into a constitutional monarchy.

As the new nations struggled to establish themselves, the advantages of a union became immediately apparent: Tanganyika had available land and an eager workforce, but lacked a well-developed economic infrastructure; Zanzibar had extensive port facilities and most other necessities for economic growth, but was too small for regional influence. The prospect of a union was especially attractive to the islands' African majority, who resented the Arabist overtones of the new administration and longed to be part of greater Africa. Less than a month after independence, ASP led a successful revolt against the new king. ASP's leader, Abeid Karume (1905–1972), took office as president and quickly moved to unite the islands with the mainland. On April 26, 1964, the United Republic of Tanganyika and Zanzibar was established; several months later, its name was shortened to the United Republic of Tanzania.

Tanzania today is an ethnically and religiously diverse nation of 40 million. Sharing the mainland are the members of at least one hundred and thirty tribes, dozens of linguistic groups, and three major religious traditions (Islam, Christianity, and native belief). There is some correspondence between these affiliations; certain tribes, for example, are predominately Muslim, others predominately Christian. The social and cultural situation on the mainland is so complicated, however, that few such generalizations are possible. The addition of Zanzibar only adds to the complexity, for it offers a marked contrast to the mainland in a number of ways. While Tanganyika's major faiths were roughly equal in popularity, for example, Zanzibar was almost entirely Muslim. Its ethnic divisions, moreover, were not based on tribal affiliation but on cultural affinities and skin tone, with most islanders classifying themselves as Arab, mixed Arab-African, Shirazi, Indian, or African. Despite these differences, the union of Tanganyika and Zanzibar has remained intact for more than forty years, largely because of an unusual administrative framework.

Government Structure

The basic structure of Tanzanian government is set out in the 1964 union agreement and the 1977 constitution (which was amended in 1984 and 1992). Executive powers are vested in the president and vice president, who are elected together by direct, popular vote for a maximum of two terms of five years. The president is both chief of state and head of government. A prime minister and cabinet assist in setting policy and overseeing its implementation. The president is solely responsible for cabinet appointments, including the position of prime minister, but his choices are limited to current members of the National Assembly. That unicameral body, also known as the Bunge, is the nation's primary legislature. It has 274 seats. Two hundred and thirty-two are elected by direct, popular vote for five-year terms; thirty-seven are women nominated by the president; and five are chosen by another legislative assembly, Zanzibar's House of Representatives. The relationship between the two legislatures is complex. In general, the National Assembly makes two kinds of laws: some that apply to the nation as a whole and some only to what was Tanganyika. The Zanzibar House is a much smaller body, with fifty members elected by direct, popular vote for five-year terms; its laws apply only to the islands and are implemented by Zanzibar's president, whose authority does not extend to the mainland. Zanzibar's president serves a five-year term.

Judicial powers are vested in a hierarchy of courts. At the top is the Court of Appeal, with five judges appointed by the president. One of the five serves as chief justice. Lower in the hierarchy are the High Court, whose justices are presidential appointees; and the district and primary courts, whose judges are appointed by the chief justice. The nation's legal code is a mixture of British common law, local and tribal tradition, and Islamic law, or sharia. While special Islamic courts are available throughout the country for cases involving inheritance, divorce, and other aspects of family law, the influence of sharia is especially strong in Zanzibar, which has its own High Court, district courts, and primary courts. The jurisdiction of the national Court of Appeal, however, covers Zanzibar as well as the mainland.

Local government is organized on the basis of twenty-six regional districts. A variety of district councils—city, municipal, town, and rural—have broad authority under a longstanding decentralization initiative.

Political Parties and Factions

Nyerere's TANU dominated the country for more than a decade following independence, particularly after the constitution of 1965 formally established Tanzania as a one-party state. That formulation was slightly misleading, however, as the union agreement that remained in force guaranteed Zanzibar a party of its own, ASP. The result was the curious coexistence of two legal parties in an avowedly one-party state. In 1977 Nyerere used the occasion of the new constitution to merge TANU and ASP into a new organization, Chama Cha Mapinduzi (the Revolutionary Party of Tanzania), or CCM. The one-party limitation remained until 1992, when the constitution was amended to allow opposition parties.

In the 2005 National Assembly elections, two major opposition groups won seats: Chama Cha Demokrasia na Maendeleo (Party of Democracy and Development), or CHADEMA, took five seats and the Civic United Front (CUF) won nineteen. In a clear indication of its continuing dominance, the CCM controlled 206 seats; fringe parties won the last two. Results in the Zanzibar House of Representatives were more balanced, with the CCM taking thirty of the fifty seats and the CUF nineteen. One seat remained vacant pending a new vote, after the returns from that constituency were voided amid allegations of electoral irregularities and fraud.

Major Events

Increasing resentment toward German rule led in 1905 to one of the first anticolonial rebellions in Africa. Now largely forgotten outside Tanzania, the Maji Maji uprising continued until German troops overwhelmed the last bands of rebels in 1907. Though brutality existed on both sides, the Germans were clearly responsible for most of the atrocities. While the death toll directly attributable to the conflict remains controversial, a minimum number of one hundred thousand is widely accepted. Nearly all of the casualties were Africans. Fifty years later, lingering memories of the rebellion encouraged the growth of Nyerere's independence movement.

On August 7, 1998, car bombs exploded simultaneously outside the U.S. embassies in Dar es Salaam, Tanzania, and in Nairobi, Kenya. While the Tanzanian blast, which killed about a dozen people, was not as lethal as the one in Kenya, which killed more than two hundred, both nations lost the sense of security they had previously enjoyed. When investigations revealed the bombings to be the work of foreign nationals with ties to the Islamic extremist group al Qaeda, many Tanzanians, mindful of their nation's deep religious divisions, worried that the incident would spark sectarian violence.

Tanzania's first president, Julius Nyerere, celebrating his country's independence in 1961.   © *Bettmann/CORBIS*

While those fears proved mostly groundless in the immediate aftermath of the bombing, tensions between the Muslim and Christian communities have increased in the years since, and analysts fear the growing influence of fundamentalist preachers in both camps may signal the rise of local extremist movements.

Twenty-First Century

Tanzania continues to make impressive economic gains at the national level, including nearly 6 percent annual growth in its gross domestic product. Concern is widespread, however, that these gains are not improving the living standards of most citizens. Nearly 40 percent of the population continues to live below the poverty line, and 80 percent remain dependent upon subsistence agriculture for their livelihoods. Diseases such as AIDS and malaria, meanwhile, have overwhelmed an aging and ill-equipped health-care system. While substantial foreign aid has arrived, a cultural reluctance to discuss private matters of health and sexuality continues to obstruct the public health initiatives that aid is intended to fund. Because relatively few Tanzanians are willing to be tested for the AIDS virus, for example, it is difficult to know how and where to allocate antiretroviral drugs and other limited resources. While these problems are not limited to Tanzania, they have been exacerbated by the administration's failure to adopt a more open and transparent style.

Unfortunate legacies of the one-party state are evident throughout the administration, notably its sensitivity to criticism, its reluctance to publicize unpleasant or unfavorable news, and its use of strong-arm tactics. One of the most shocking events in this century occurred in January 2001, when police killed twenty-two civilians during an antigovernment protest on the island of Pemba (part of Zanzibar). Such incidents impede the administration's ability to move the nation forward politically, socially, and economically.

BIBLIOGRAPHY

Mbogoni, Lawrence E. Y. *The Cross vs. the Crescent: Religion and Politics in Tanzania From the 1890s to the 1990s.* Dar es Salaam, Tanzania: Mkuki na Nyota Publishers, 2005.

Shayo, Rose. *Parties and Political Development in Tanzania.* Johannesburg: Electoral Institute of Southern Africa, 2005.

United Republic of Tanzania. Official Web site. http://www.tanzania.go.tz [accessed July 8, 2007].

⊕ Malawi

Type of Government

The African nation of Malawi is a constitutional republic. Its 1995 constitution—modeled in part on the constitution of the United States—curtailed the unchecked executive power that characterized the thirty-year administration of the nation's first president, Dr. Hastings Banda (c. 1897–1997), who ruled from 1964 to 1994.

Background

Roughly the size of Ohio, Malawi shares borders with Mozambique, to the south and east; Tanzania, to the north and northeast; and Zambia, to the west. Though landlocked, it shares control of Lake Nyasa (also known as Lake Malawi), one of Africa's largest bodies of fresh water, with its eastern neighbors.

Malawi's thirteen and a half million people, one of the fastest-growing populations in the world, represent a wide variety of ethnic and tribal groups, the largest of which are the Chichewa and Chinyanja peoples. This diversity is in part a legacy of colonialism, for the British administrators who established the Nyasaland Districts Protectorate in the area in 1891 largely ignored tribal boundaries when demarcating the territory. It is not surprising, therefore, that a sense of national unity and purpose took several decades to develop. By the middle of the twentieth century, however, a near universal desire for independence had begun to overcome traditional tribal divisions. By all accounts, the return of the long-time expatriate Banda in 1958 greatly accelerated this

process. As head of the Malawi Congress Party (MCP), the principal pro-independence group, Banda endured a brief period of imprisonment before persuading the British to accept a series of incremental steps toward independence. By 1963, the British had ceded authority in most areas of government, and on July 6, 1964, Nyasaland became the independent nation of Malawi. Two years later, a permanent constitution replaced the last of several transitional versions, with President Banda serving as both chief of state and head of government.

Despite the relatively peaceful and orderly transition to independence, the shortcomings of the new government quickly became apparent. Banda refused to yield any significant power to the National Assembly or the other constitutionally mandated institutions of democratic government. Systematic purges of potential rivals within the MCP began within months of independence, and the arrest and detention of suspected dissidents likewise became routine. In 1970 Banda formally suspended the constitution, orchestrated his own appointment as president for life, and required all citizens to join the MCP. Less than six years after independence, Malawi had become a full-fledged dictatorship.

Through intimidation and bribery, Banda would remain in power for another twenty-four years. In 1992, however, protests by the nation's Roman Catholic bishops sparked a nationwide reform movement. International non-governmental organizations, aid donors, and underground opposition groups together forced Banda to allow free, multiparty elections for both the National Assembly and the presidency. In the elections of May 1994, the MCP remained a significant force in the Assembly, taking fifty-five of one hundred and ninety-three seats. The previously underground United Democratic Front (UDF), however, won eighty-four seats. President Banda, meanwhile, was voted out of office. Elections were held again in 1999 and 2004, with mixed results. While the multiparty system has survived, there have been widespread incidents of electoral fraud, voter intimidation, and political violence. There have been positive signs as well, however, notably the development of an independent press.

Government Structure

Even in the post-Banda era, the influence of the president extended well beyond the executive branch. Under the terms of the 1995 constitution, the president is elected by direct, popular vote for a five-year term. The cabinet consists of forty-six members, all presidential appointees. The president also chooses a chief justice to preside over the nation's six-member High Court, the other five members of which are appointed on the recommendation of the Judicial Service Commission. A Supreme Court of Appeal, composed of the chief justice and an even number of other presidential appointees, handles appeals from the High Court and reviews the

Dr. Hastings Banda, the first prime minister and later first president of Malawi who ruled from 1961 to 1994. *AP/Wide World Photos*

constitutionality of legislation passed by the National Assembly. Local Magistrates' Courts handle the bulk of the nation's judicial business in accordance with English common law and local tradition.

Legislative powers are vested in a unicameral National Assembly of one hundred and ninety-three seats. Members are elected by direct, popular vote for five-year terms in elections concurrent with the presidential vote. The president, however, retains the power to postpone legislative elections or to dissolve the Assembly before the end of its five-year term.

The elected officials of the nation's twenty-seven administrative districts handle most local matters.

Political Parties and Factions

In the 2004 elections, no party was able to obtain a legislative majority. The largest single party, the UDF, won seventy-four seats, or thirty-eight percent of the total. The UDF's influence, however, was sharply curtailed in 2005, when the newly elected president, Bingu wa Mutharika (1934–), renounced his membership in the party and established his own group, the Democratic Progressive Party (DPP). Though the DPP is not represented in the current Assembly, its power is significant.

In addition to the UDF, there are two other major parties in the Assembly. One of these is the MCP, long associated with former president Banda; it holds sixty seats, or thirty-one percent of the total. The other, with sixteen seats (eight percent), is the Republican Party (RP). Like the UDF, the RP has been weakened by internal dissent. Independent legislators hold twenty-four seats (twelve percent), minor parties hold eighteen (nine percent), and there is one vacancy. Opposition groups tend to be strongest in the remote northern region.

Major Events

One of the first achievements of the multiparty state was the disbanding of the Malawi Young Pioneers, the Banda regime's primary paramilitary force and a notorious violator of human rights. Despite the apparent success of the anti-Pioneer campaign, few Malawians believed it would bring a significant reduction in political violence. There were soon indications, in fact, that some Pioneers had escaped to Mozambique to regroup and rearm. These reports proved difficult to confirm, and the situation in many remote border areas remains unclear. In any event, the disappearance of the Pioneers did not mean an end to political violence, as many of the new parties quickly organized paramilitary forces of their own. The most visible of these has been the UDF's Young Democrats.

Succeeding Banda as president in 1994 was Bakili Muluzi (1943–), secretary general of the UDF; five years later, he won reelection in a vote widely condemned as fraudulent. Though the 1995 constitution prohibits presidents from serving more than two terms, Muluzi's supporters began to agitate for an amendment that would allow him to run again in 2004. Amid a looming constitutional crisis, gangs of Young Democrats began to harass journalists and other prominent opponents of the proposed amendment. Their campaign of intimidation soon backfired, however, with several national newspapers denouncing the perpetrators. When the international press took note of the situation, Muluzi was forced to step down. The episode thus illustrates one of the paradoxes of Malawian democracy: the nation's press has become a powerful force for change even, or perhaps especially, under the most repressive and intimidating administrations.

Twenty-First Century

One of the poorest nations in the world, Malawi faces a staggering array of problems. Recurrent drought over the past decade has largely destroyed the agricultural sector that employs ninety percent of the population. Health and educational services are nearly nonexistent in many areas, and one in every four Malawians carries the HIV virus. Malnutrition, malaria, cholera, and other preventable conditions are endemic in many areas. As a result, life expectancy for both men and women is only forty-three, or roughly half the figure for the most developed nations.

All of these problems are worsened by rampant corruption, in part because international donors are reluctant to send aid if it is likely to be diverted for private profit. Though bribery and embezzlement were particularly widespread under Banda's regime, they have tainted more recent administrations as well. In one of the most widely publicized cases, Muluzi, while still in office, reportedly spent tens of thousands of dollars in state funds on his own wedding.

BIBLIOGRAPHY

A Democracy of Chameleons: Politics and Culture in the New Malawi, edited by Harri Englund. Somerset, NJ: Transaction Publishers, 2002.

Lwanda, John Lloyd. *Politics, Culture and Medicine in Malawi: Historical Continuities and Ruptures with Special Reference to HIV/AIDS*. Zomba, Malawi: University of Malawi, 2005.

Sindima, Harvey J. *Malawi's First Republic: An Economic and Political Analysis*. Lanham, MD: University Press of America, 2002.

⊕ Malta

Type of Government

Malta is an independent parliamentary democracy within the British Commonwealth. Its chief of state is a president elected for a five-year term by the House of Representatives. The government is headed by a prime minister, who is the leader of the ruling party in the House of Representatives, and a cabinet, chosen by the president and prime minister. The legislative branch is unicameral, and the sixty-five members of the House of Representatives are elected for five-year terms. The highest levels of the judicial branch include the Constitutional Court and Court of Appeal. Judges for both courts are appointed by the president on the advice of the prime minister.

Background

Located in the Mediterranean Sea about sixty miles south of Sicily, the nation of Malta is made up of the inhabited islands of Malta, Gozo, and Comino, and the uninhabited islands of Comminotto, and Filfla. Its strategic location in the shipping lanes of southern Europe has long made it an attractive prize for various countries. Malta had a rich civilization more than six thousand years ago, evidenced by the number of prehistoric temples such as those at the World Heritage site of Mnajdra.

By 700 BC, the Phoenicians had colonized the islands, using the islands as a naval post in their explorations of Europe. The African kingdom of Carthage took control of the islands in about 400 BC, followed by the Romans in 218 BC. After the dissolution of the Roman Empire, Malta was under the control of the Byzantine Empire and then in the ninth century was conquered by Arab armies. During the period of Arab rule, the Maltese language, which borrows heavily from both Arabic and Italian, began to develop.

Sicilian Normans followed the Arabs in the eleventh century, and in 1523, Holy Roman Emperor Charles V (1500–1558) ceded the islands to the Knights of St. John of Jerusalem. For the next three centuries these wealthy and powerful "Knights of Malta" administered Malta, building palaces, churches, gardens, and fortifications. They fended off a Turkish siege shortly after taking control of the island and maintained control until they were unseated by the French in 1798. Napoleon (1769–1821) used the islands as a garrison for his expedition against Egypt.

The French, unpopular conquerors, were in turn dislodged by the British, who incorporated the islands into the British Empire in 1814. The British established Malta as fleet headquarters and a way station for India, via the Suez Canal. For the next 150 years, the islands remained part of the Empire, playing a vital role in disrupting Axis shipping during World War II, for which the Maltese people earned the George Cross from a grateful King George VI (1895–1952).

Malta's Prime Minister Lawrence Gonzi, 2005.   © *Darren Zammit Lupi/Reuters/Corbis*

Following the war, Malta was granted self-rule, but the Malta Labour Party (MLP) favored integration with the United Kingdom, which would allow the Maltese Parliament to retain responsibility over all affairs except defense, foreign policy, and taxation, while the citizens of Malta would in effect become British citizens with their own representation in the British House of Commons. This proposal was passed by referendum in 1956, though the voting was boycotted by the other major Maltese political group, the Nationalist Party (PN), and by the Roman Catholic Church. Malta was granted independence on September 21, 1964, and a constitution was promulgated, which initially kept Queen Elizabeth II (1926–) as chief of state, with an appointed governor general who took responsibility for executive decisions. The nation became a republic on December 13, 1974, with the establishment of a new constitution providing for a president as head of state.

Government Structure

By the terms of the 1974 constitution, a parliamentary system similar to the United Kingdom's Westminster system was established. The Il-Kamra tad-Deputati (House of Representatives) consists of between 65 and 69 members elected by direct universal suffrage for

terms of five years. These members are elected according to a proportional representation formula known as the "single transferable vote" system, which has been in place in Malta since 1947. Under this system, the voter ranks the candidates in order of preference. An individual's vote is then given to his or her most preferred candidate, but if that candidate has already met a vote quota sufficient to be elected, or if the candidate is eliminated, then the vote transfers to the voter's next preferred candidate. The House may be dissolved for elections before the end of the five-year period on the advice of the prime minister and may also express no-confidence votes against any government that does not enjoy majority support in the parliament, thereby removing that government. The House of Representatives is responsible for legislation; the president may not veto such legislation.

The president, who serves as head of state in a largely ceremonial position, is elected by the House of Representatives. The president in turn appoints as prime minister the leader of the majority party in the House, and also a cabinet on the recommendation of the prime minister. In the case that a party wins the majority of the popular vote yet still fails to garner a majority of seats in the House of Representatives, that party is supplied with extra seats to give it a voting majority. Thus the number of representatives can fluctuate according to need. The prime minister is the head of government and appoints a cabinet from among the members of the House of Representatives to help him or her govern.

The judicial branch consists of a Constitutional Court, the Court of Appeal, the Court of Criminal Appeal, the Civil Court, the Criminal Court, the Courts of Magistrates, the Gozo Courts, the Small Claims Tribunal, the Juvenile Court, and Commissioners of Justice. The Constitutional Court hears appeals in cases involving violations of human rights, interpretation of the constitution, and validity of laws. It also deals with corrupt electoral practices. Its chief justice and all other judges are appointed by the president in consultation with the prime minister.

The Local Councils Act of 1993 subdivided Malta into 54 local councils and 14 on the small island of Gozo. Councils are elected every three years.

Political Parties and Factions

The two major Maltese political parties are the Partit Nazzjonalista (Nationalist Party; PN), and the Partit Laburista (Malta Labour Party; MLP).

Founded in 1880 as the Anti-Reform Party by Fortunato Mizzi (1844–1905), the PN party's platform was originally based on the independence movement and opposed British taxation and interference with the local economy and education system. By 1926 it had assumed the Nationalist Party name and was anti-colonial in outlook. Connections with Italy damaged the party during World War II, but following the war the PN regained its popularity with the electorate as it became the leading party to oppose merging with the United Kingdom. The PN has been the majority party for most of the time since independence and has produced three prime ministers during that same time: Giorgio Borg Olivier (1911–1980), from 1962 to 1971; Eddie Fenech Adami (1934–), from 1987 to 1996 and 1998 to 2004; and Lawrence Gonzi (1953–), who became prime minister in 2004.

The MLP, a social democratic party, was founded in 1949 by the prime minister at the time, Paul Boffa (1890–1962). Traditionally a workers' party, it favored integration with Britain following World War II. It has been the main opposition party in Maltese politics since independence, and has supplied three prime ministers in that same time: Dominic Mintoff (1916–), from 1971 to 1984; Carmelo Mifsud Bonnici (1933–), from 1984 to 1987; and Alfred Sant (1948–), from 1996 to 1998.

Major Events

British military forces were finally withdrawn from Malta in 1979 after the expiration of a defense agreement between the two nations. Thereafter, despite its membership in the Commonwealth, Malta pursued a neutral course in international relations, joining for a time the Movement for Non-Aligned Countries.

In April 2003, in a referendum, Malta's voters expressed their willingness to join the European Union (EU). Official membership came about on May 1, 2004. EU membership, however, proved a divisive issue in Maltese politics, with the MLP strongly opposing it as an endangerment to the country's neutrality, and the PN supporting such membership. Malta sends five members to the European Parliament, three from the MLP and two from the NP.

Twenty-First Century

The strongest challenge to the government of Malta is continuing illegal immigration from North Africa, specifically Libya. In 2005, Malta took part in talks between European countries and African countries to resolve the immigration problem, but in 2006, the illegal immigrant situation reached critical levels, with conditions deteriorating in detention centers. EU border patrols, including troops from Malta, were in place by late 2006 throughout the southern Mediterranean.

BIBLIOGRAPHY

Berg, Warren G. *Historical Dictionary of Malta.* Lanham, MD: Scarecrow Press, 1995.

Goodwin, Stefan. *Malta: Mediterranean Bridge.* Westport, CT: Bergin & Garvey, 2002.

Government of Malta. "Government of Malta Information & Services Online," http://www.gov.mt (accessed April 4, 2007).

⊕ Zambia

Type of Government

The African nation of Zambia has been a constitutional republic, at least in name, since independence in 1964. In practice, however, Zambian democracy has been repeatedly compromised by authoritarian regimes, notably the so-called "one-party participatory democracy" of president Kenneth Kaunda (1924–), who ruled from 1964 to 1991. A new constitution, adopted in 1991 and amended five years later, remains in force. Among its most distinctive provisions are those granting the president extensive powers over all three branches of government (executive, legislative, and judicial).

Background

Roughly the size of Texas, Zambia shares borders with seven nations: Angola, to the west; Namibia, to the southwest; Zimbabwe, to the southeast; Mozambique and Malawi, to the east; Tanzania, to the northeast; and the Democratic Republic of the Congo, to the

October 24, 1964, independence ceremony for Northern Rhodesia, thereafter known as Zambia. © *Bettmann/CORBIS*

northwest. Its eleven and a half million citizens speak more than seventy-five native languages in addition to English, the primary language of business and government. This linguistic variety reflects the nation's enormous ethnic and tribal diversity. Among the major tribal groups are the Bemba, Lunda, and Tonga peoples.

Zambia's landlocked position protected it from the encroachments of European colonizers until the last decades of the nineteenth century. In 1891 a private British corporation, the British South Africa Company, began administering the region in return for a monopoly over its rich deposits of copper and other minerals. The British government assumed control in 1924, reorganizing the territory, then known as Northern Rhodesia, as a protectorate. In 1953 Northern Rhodesia was attached to two other British possessions, Nyasaland (now Malawi) and Southern Rhodesia (now Zimbabwe), to form the so-called Federation of Rhodesia and Nyasaland. This organization provoked widespread resentment and was dissolved shortly before Zambia's independence.

Though sporadic demands for independence were heard as early as the 1930s, traditional tribal rivalries delayed the development of an organized independence movement. In this respect, Northern Rhodesia resembled colonies across Africa. The prominence of the mining industry, however, gave local activists a rare advantage.

While the decentralized, agricultural basis of most colonial economies made labor organization difficult, the copper mines of Northern Rhodesia were concentrated in a single region (Zambia's Copperbelt Province, near the Congolese border) and utterly dependent on the skills of native workers. These conditions facilitated the establishment of the African Mineworkers' Union, which provided crucial training and management experience to many of the independence movement's most effective leaders. By the end of the 1950s, two rival organizations had emerged to challenge the legitimacy of British rule: the African National Congress (ANC; not to be confused with the South African anti-apartheid group of the same name) and the more radical United National Independence Party (UNIP). A tense alliance between the two groups forced the British to yield, and on October 24, 1964, the protectorate of Northern Rhodesia became the independent nation of Zambia. UNIP held a majority of seats in the first National Assembly, and its leader, Kenneth Kaunda, took office as Zambia's first president. He would remain in power for the next twenty-seven years.

Government Structure

The president, elected by popular vote for a five-year term, enjoys extensive powers under the 1991 constitution. As chief of state, head of government, and commander of the armed forces, the president's ability to appoint (and fire) subordinates extends across all three branches of government and does not require legislative approval. The vice president, members of the cabinet, and Supreme Court justices are all presidential appointees. The only significant limitation on the president's power to make these selections is a requirement restricting cabinet posts to members of the National Assembly.

Legislative powers are vested in a unicameral National Assembly with two distinctive features. One is a provision requiring a two-thirds majority (rather than a simple majority, as in most republics) for a bill to pass. The other involves the Assembly's membership. All but eight of the one hundred and fifty-eight members are chosen by direct, popular vote for five-year terms in elections concurrent with the presidential race. The other eight members are presidential appointees; five of these can serve in the cabinet as well.

The structure of the Zambian legal system is based on the British model, while the law code is a mixture of English common law and local tradition. A Supreme Court is the court of final appeal. The constitution mandates the appointment of at least nine justices, but the number hearing a particular case varies, and may be as low as three. Below the Supreme Court are the High Court, which hears particularly serious or complex cases, local Magistrates' Courts, and a variety of specialized tribunals.

All citizens eighteen and over are eligible to vote. Nine provincial governors, appointed by the president, oversee government operations at the local and regional levels.

Political Parties and Factions

The 2006 elections gave Assembly seats to three major parties and several minor ones. The largest bloc is the Movement for Multiparty Democracy (MMD), which controls roughly half of the one hundred and fifty-eight seats. The next party, with forty-four seats, is the Patriotic Front (PF), best known for its strident opposition to "interference" by the International Monetary Fund (IMF) and the World Bank. Though these organizations have provided significant aid in the past, the conditions they impose on recipients, often involving painful cuts in government spending, have angered many Zambians. The PF's platform is therefore popular but problematic, for the party's leaders have not yet explained how they would manage without the assistance previous administrations have considered a crucial part of the nation's budget.

The third major bloc in the Assembly is the United Democratic Alliance (UDA), a coalition of UNIP, the United Party for National Development (UPND), and the Forum for Democracy and Development (FDD). The primary purpose of the UDA, which holds twenty-seven seats, is to offer a viable alternative to voters disenchanted with both the ruling MMD and the PF.

Major Events

Shortly after Zambia declared its independence, the strength of Kaunda's authoritarian tendencies gradually became apparent. In 1973, amid growing unrest, he replaced multiparty rule with an unusual, even eccentric, system called "one-party participatory democracy." Though all parties with the exception of UNIP were banned, elections continued to take place, with several candidates—all UNIP members—vying for each seat in the National Assembly. In presidential elections, however, Kaunda was the only candidate. To maintain power, the president increasingly relied on patronage and bribery, which together swallowed an enormous portion of the budget. The 1980s were a period of ballooning public debt, rising inflation, and a growing dependence on foreign aid. Widespread unrest and growing international pressure finally forced Kaunda in 1990 to allow opposition parties and to schedule multiparty elections for the following year. A new party, the Movement for Multiparty Democracy (MMD), won these decisively, taking one hundred and twenty-five of the one hundred and fifty available Assembly seats; UNIP took the remaining twenty-five. In the presidential race, the MMD's candidate, the trade union leader Frederick Chiluba (1943–), ousted Kaunda with no less than 81 percent of the popular vote. After dominating Zambian politics for nearly three decades, UNIP was out of power.

Hopes for positive change were soon dashed, however, as corruption scandals and internal conflict increasingly compromised Chiluba's administration. Nationwide unrest prompted the president to arrest dissidents, censor the press, and twice declare a state of emergency. To prevent Kaunda, a native of Malawi, from entering the 1996 presidential race, Chiluba pushed through a constitutional amendment restricting the office to Zambian natives. UNIP boycotted the elections in protest, and MMD won one hundred and thirty-one Assembly seats in a vote widely condemned as rigged. Chiluba remained in office for a second term. The cycle of protests and government crackdowns continued, reaching a climax when Chiluba announced plans to eliminate the constitutional provision limiting presidents to two terms. In 2001, several months before the next round of elections, the United States, the United Kingdom, and other major donors threatened to cut off aid unless the president abandoned his plans for a third term. He did so, and the MMD's new candidate, Levy Mwanawasa (1948–), narrowly won the election. He was reelected in 2006.

Twenty-First Century

There are some signs of progress. Despite constant harassment, the nation's journalists and religious leaders continue to expose abuses and press for reform. Zambia's mineral deposits, still its chief source of foreign earnings, are vast, and its literacy rate of 80 percent is higher than the rates in five of its seven immediate neighbors (only Namibia, at 85 percent, and Zimbabwe, at 91 percent, surpass it). Zambia has also managed to avoid the civil wars that have engulfed much of the continent since the end of the colonial era. Decades of fighting in the Democratic Republic of the Congo, for example, have claimed more than two million lives, with no end in sight. To the civilians fleeing these conflicts, Zambia appears a peaceful haven. Tens of thousands of refugees, most from Angola and the Congo, crowd Zambia's cities, further straining an already overburdened infrastructure.

The problems facing Zambia at the turn of the twenty-first century would challenge even the most stable and prosperous of nations. Roughly seventeen percent of the population is infected with the virus that causes AIDS, a disease that had already killed eighty-nine thousand Zambians by 2003. Life expectancy is only thirty-eight years, one of the lowest figures in the world. Severe air and water pollution, much of it from mining and smelting operations, has devastated the landscape and threatens prospects for the so-called "eco-tourism" that is driving economic growth elsewhere in Africa, notably in nearby Botswana. The most basic problem, however, remains poverty. The vast majority of Zambians are subsistence farmers earning less than a dollar a day. Alleviating poverty of that magnitude will require substantial and sustained aid from abroad. That aid is unlikely to arrive in the necessary quantities, however, until the ruling party—whether MMD, UNIP, PF, or another group—stops using the machinery of government to build private fortunes and harass opponents.

BIBLIOGRAPHY

Phiri, Bizeck. *A Political History of Zambia: From Colonial Rule to the Third Republic, 1890–2001.* Trenton, NJ: Africa World Press, 2006.

Promoting and Sustaining Economic Reform in Zambia, edited by Catharine Hill and Malcolm F. McPherson. Cambridge, MA: Harvard University Press, 2004.

Rakner, Lise. *Political and Economic Liberalisation in Zambia, 1991–2001.* Uppsala, Sweden: Nordic Africa Institute, 2003.

⊕ Republic of the Gambia

Type of Government

After a military coup in 1994, a new Gambian constitution provided for separate legislative, judicial, and executive branches of government and a guarantee of human rights. In practice, however, the country has been ruled since that time by an autocratic executive, Yahya Jammeh (1965–), whose grip on the country has only tightened since failed coup attempts in 2000 and 2006.

Background

The Republic of the Gambia, or The Gambia for short, is located on the western coast of Africa. The smallest country in Africa, it is a narrow slice of land following the Gambia River for two hundred miles to its mouth in the Atlantic and is surrounded on three sides by Senegal. The first records of Gambia are derived from the records of Muslim traders who crossed Africa to establish posts for the slave and mineral trade. Islam gained numerous converts in the region, and 92 percent of the population is Muslim today. The area was settled by Wolof, Malinke, and Fulani people in the thirteenth century and became part of the Mali Empire in the fourteenth century.

The Portuguese took over the slave trade in the fifteenth century and then sold off trading rights along the Gambia River to the British. During the seventeenth century the English and French vied for control of the slave trade in the region until the Treaty of Versailles (1783) gave England uncontested possession of The Gambia. Though the British government officially abolished the slave trade in 1807, illegal trading persisted for decades. Over the course of the slave trade era, more than three million slaves were taken from the region.

The present capital of Banjul was established as a military post in 1816; from 1821 to 1888, The Gambia was administered by the British government of Sierra Leone. In 1889 it achieved separate status again, with Banjul becoming a Crown colony and the rest of the area a British protectorate. Executive and legislative councils were established in 1901, and the area began a long journey toward independence.

During World War II (1939–1945), Gambian soldiers assisted in Allied operations in Burma, and the nation became an important port for naval and aerial operations. Following the war, the independence movement accelerated. Universal adult suffrage was introduced in 1960 and a thirty-four-member House of Representatives was established. The office of prime minister was created in 1962, and in the general elections of that same year Dawda Kairaba Jawara (1924–), the leader of the People's Progressive Party (PPP), became the first prime minister supervising a year-long transition toward self-governance. In 1965 the country became a constitutional monarchy (recognizing the British monarch) and an independent nation within the British Commonwealth.

Government Structure

The Gambia's executive branch is led by a president, elected to five-year terms, who acts as both head of state and head of government. The president appoints a vice president and cabinet to assist in running the government and governing the country. There are no term limits on the presidency, and the chief executive wields extensive authority.

The legislature is unicameral, with the fifty-three-member National Assembly responsible for enacting legislation. Forty-eight of its members are elected by universal suffrage every five years; five of the members are appointed by the president.

The country's legal system is a mixture of English common law; the law of the Koran (the Muslim holy book), which is called sharia; and African traditional law. For example, magistrate and divisional courts determine most civil cases, but Muslim courts may apply sharia law in some cases involving Muslim citizens, while in traditional matters, chiefs rule on customary law and local affairs. The Supreme Court is the highest court of appeal in The Gambia.

The country is divided into five administrative divisions—Lower River, Central River, North Bank, Upper River, and Western—and one city, Banjul. These are further subdivided into 35 districts, each administered by a chief who in turn is assisted by councilors and village mayors.

Political Parties and Factions

Though several political parties exist, The Gambia is essentially a one-party state, with the authoritarian Alliance for Patriotic Reorientation and Construction (APRC) wielding power. The party came into being in 1996 to support Yahya Jammeh in his bid to become elected president. Jammeh, who led a coup deposing then president Jawara in 1994, won the 1996, the 2001, and the 2006 presidential elections, and his party took 42 seats in the National Assembly in 2006.

Five smaller parties coalesced in 2005 into the National Alliance for Democracy and Development (NADD). Their goal was to end the rule of Jammeh and return power to the people. The parties forming this coalition were the People's Democratic Organization for Independence and Socialism (PDOIS), the National Democratic Action Movement (NDAM), the National Reconciliation Party (NRP), the People's Progressive Party (PPP), and the United Democratic Party (UDP). Of these, the PPP was the oldest, formed in 1958. Under the leadership of Dawda Kairaba Jawara, it held power from 1970 to 1994 when Jammeh seized power, suspended the constitution, and banned opposing political parties. The ban on some opposition parties (but not the PPP) was lifted for the 1996 elections. It was not until 2001 that the ban was lifted on all political parties.

Major Events

On April 24, 1970, The Gambia became a republic following a majority-approved referendum, and Jawara was the first president. Jawara stayed in power for a quarter of a century, being reelected in 1982, 1987, and 1992. He survived a left-wing coup attempt in 1981, and in the following year led his country to join with Senegal in the Confederation of Senegambia. This confederation sought to combine the armed forces of the two nations and to unify their economies and currencies. However, The Gambia withdrew from the confederation in 1989.

During his long years in office, Jawara supported democratic institutions, but critics also complained of corruption in his administration and of a general decline in the quality of governance at all levels. He was deposed from office in 1994 when the Armed Forces Provisional Ruling Council, or AFPRC, seized power in a bloodless military coup. Jammeh was chairman of the AFPRC and became head of state. While the junta suspended the constitution and banned political activity, Jawara took refuge in an American warship on call in The Gambia at the time. A failed counter-coup was staged the next year in an attempt to return the country to civilian rule. Jammeh, however, consolidated his power. Facing censure and criticism from the West, he turned to other nations, such as Iran, Cuba, and Taiwan, for support.

To secure legitimacy for his regime, Jammeh scheduled presidential elections for 1996; however, leading opposition parties such as the PPP were banned from participation. Not surprisingly, Jammeh won more than 55 percent of the vote. Established as president, he called for legislative elections in early 1997. Again, with major opposition parties excluded from participation in this election, Jammeh's APRC took 32 of the 45 contested seats.

Despite the nominal return to civilian government, Jammeh's administration continued to wield extraordinary powers. The government cited a coup attempt in 2000 as grounds for increasing its control over the media; many foreign observers, however, felt the government was only using the alleged coup as a pretext for a government clampdown on political action. Government clashes with student protesters resulted in the deaths of fourteen. Jammeh's government postponed local elections, kept up its campaign against the freedom of assembly for political parties, and relied increasingly on the death penalty. On social issues, Jammeh was strongly opposed to women's rights and supported the practice of female genital mutilation.

In the 2001 elections, all political parties were allowed to participate. However, with Jammeh's control of the media, other candidates did not receive the same public exposure as the president. Opposition parties including the UDP, the PPP, and the Gambia People's Party (GPP) formed a coalition but were unable to defeat the incumbent. Jammeh only took 53 percent of the vote amid charges of voter fraud. Some observers complained that thousands of voters of the Diola people, which is Jammeh's own ethnic group, were transported illegally across the border from Senegal to vote. In legislative elections, the ruling APRC took 45 of the 48 contested seats.

Following the election, Jammeh granted amnesty to the former president Jawara, who had been living in exile, on condition that he not participate in politics. In 2002 the government continued to tighten its control on the media when the National Assembly passed a "gag" rule to limit supposedly sensationalist reporting. In 2004 a new law was passed providing for journalists found guilty of libel or sedition to be jailed. This was followed by the murder of a well-known newspaper editor who was a strong critic of the government.

In 2006 a planned military coup attempt against Jammeh was uncovered, and its leaders were arrested or fled the country. In the 2006 presidential elections, Jammeh took two-thirds of the popular vote in a contest that pitted his APRC against the five-party coalition NADD.

Twenty-First Century

The Gambia faces several important political issues in the twenty-first century, including the continuing effort to maintain the democratic system and prevent the outbreak of violence between political factions. In addition, there are ongoing questions over the role that Islamic law should play in the country's legal system. President Jammeh has said that he wants to bring Koranic law formally into the legal system on an equal footing with the civil code. Such an action poses the threat of a strong president using Islamic law as a tool for political repression.

On the international level, the Gambian government has been forced to address the arrival of thousands of refugees from Senegal's Casamance region, largely in 2006. Though The Gambia and Senegal signed a friendship and cooperation treaty in 1991, tensions between the two countries have persisted as the recent refugee crisis has led to an increase in arms dealing, smuggling, and crime along the nation's borders.

BIBLIOGRAPHY

Hughes, Arnold, and Harry A. Gailey. *Historical Dictionary of the Gambia.* 3rd ed. Metuchen, NJ: Scarecrow Press, 1999.

Hughes, Arnold, and David Perfect. *A Political History of the Gambia, 1816–1994.* Rochester, NY: University of Rochester Press, 2006.

Koslow, Philip. *Senegambia: Land of the Lion.* Philadelphia, PA: Chelsea House, 1997.

⊕ Maldives

Type of Government

The government of the Maldives is a presidential republic with near absolute power vested in the executive. The president is head of state, head of government, and even the supreme religious leader. The political system is highly centralized, and power is held mainly by a small group related to the president. The executive branch is headed by the president, who selects the cabinet, part of the parliament, and all judges.

Background

Maldives is a chain of 1,191 coral islands, grouped into what are known as atolls, in the Indian Ocean, south of India and west of Sri Lanka. Only about two hundred of the islands are inhabited. Maldives was gradually populated beginning in the twelfth century AD as sailors, traders, and settlers migrated southward from Sri Lanka and India. The population converted from Buddhism to Islam in 1153, and Sunni Islam is the official religion today.

Due to its isolation, Maldives has been able to survive as a self-governing, independent country for centuries. The country was a sovereign Islamic sultanate for almost the entire period between 1153 and 1968. Portugal claimed ownership of the islands from 1558 until they were defeated by Sultan Muhammad Thakurufaanu Al-Azam in 1573. The Dutch government, controlling nearby Ceylon, reached an agreement whereby the sultanate paid tribute to the rulers of Ceylon in return for protection. When Great Britain took control of Ceylon in 1815, it also assumed responsibility for Maldives. Colonial Ceylon became independent Sri Lanka in 1948, and Great Britain and Maldives negotiated a new agreement that eliminated tribute payments.

A 1952 referendum abolished the sultanate in favor of a republic, but the royal family, the Didis, continued to dominate the government. Amir Didi, already Sultan Amin Didi's designated heir, became president on January 1, 1953. Many Maldivians resented Didi's progressive reforms, such as emancipation of women, and he was removed from office in September 1953. Two of his cousins temporarily served as copresidents. Parliament voted to restore the sultanate in 1954, to be led by Muhammad Fareed Didi and Prime Minister Ibrahim Ali Didi.

Maldives became independent in 1965, and a November 11, 1968, referendum replaced the sultanate with a second presidential republic. Ibrahim Nasir (1926–), a member of the royal family who had been prime minister since 1965, became president, a post he occupied until 1978.

Government Structure

Under the constitution of 1968, Maldives has an executive branch headed by the president, who is head of state, head of government, and commander-in-chief. The president is nominated by parliament and approved by national referendum. Presidents may serve an unlimited number of five-year terms. Maumoon Abdul Gayoom (1937–) was elected president in 1978 and re-elected five times (1983, 1988, 1993, 1998, and 2003). His brothers occupy key advisory roles within the government, including speaker of parliament, minister of trade, and minister of atoll administration. President Gayoom is also minister of defense and national security, minister of finance, and governor of the national monetary authority. There is no prime minister, although the president is assisted by an eleven-member cabinet, most of whom are relatives.

The Maldivian legislative branch consists of a unicameral (one-chamber) parliament, the Majlis, with fifty members. Each administrative district sends two representatives to parliament, while the president appoints an additional eight. The representatives typically have other state responsibilities in local governments or as heads of state-owned firms. All parliament representatives serve five-year terms.

Judicial authority in Maldives is exercised by a High Court, as well as a civil court, criminal court, family and juvenile court, and 204 general courts. The legal code draws from Islamic law, and customary punishments such as banishment are common. The president appoints all judges; he may fire judges or overturn High Court decisions at will. There are no jury trials for criminal cases.

Local governance is complicated by the diffuse structure of Maldives. The numerous islands are grouped into twenty districts, while the capital city, Male, is the twenty-first district. Each district is ruled by an atoll chief, appointed by the president. All citizens of Maldives are permitted to vote at the age of twenty-one.

A man surveying the devastation on Kolhufushi Island, in the Maldives, after the December 2004 tsunami. © *Anuruddha Lokuhapuarachchi/ Reuters/Corbis*

Political Parties and Factions

Political parties were banned in Maldives prior to June 2005. Before then, candidates for parliament ran as independents. Four parties have registered—Adalath (Justice), Dhivehi Raiyyethunge, Islamic Democratic Party, and Maldivian Democratic Party—and members of parliament have begun to announce their affiliations.

Major Events

Maldives has enjoyed relative calm since independence and the 1968 constitution, a calm some analysts attribute to the common Islamic beliefs shared among most of the population. Critics, however, blame the government for maintaining peace by restricting opposition activities. Demands for representative government are increasing, with the number of protests growing since the last presidential referendum in 2003.

By 1978 President Nasir's popularity had plummeted, even among the ruling elite. He was criticized for his autocratic political style, and poor economic policies had left a hungry population protesting over rising prices for food. Consequently, Nasir announced he would resign in 1978. The Majlis appointed diplomat Gayoom as the next president.

Gayoom has survived three coup attempts. In 1980 Nasir loyalists hired British mercenaries to try to overthrow Gayoom, but their plot was discovered before they could act. A local businessman, Reeko Ibrahim Maniku, unsuccessfully tried to buy the 1983 presidential nomination for himself by bribing judges and members of parliament. Tamil mercenaries from Sri Lanka attempted to overthrow the Maldivian government on November 8, 1988, shortly after Gayoom was inaugurated for a third term. They wanted to use Male as a gunrunning outpost and raise funds through the Maldivian tourist sector. President Gayoom appealed to New Delhi for assistance, and Indian troops put down the invasion within twenty-four hours.

The most serious challenge to Gayoom's rule occurred in the summer of 2004. In June he convened a special session of parliament to consider constitutional amendments, including limiting presidents to two five-year terms, increasing judicial independence, ending the president's right to appoint eight members of parliament, and legalizing political parties. Parliament was scheduled to take up the reform package on August 16.

But on August 12 a group of protestors assembled outside the police headquarters in Male, demanding the release of four political activists. The number of protestors grew overnight to around five thousand people, and they began calling for the dismissal of several hard-line members of the government. Gayoom declared a state of emergency on August 13, invoking a constitutional provision that the president could suppress peaceful, democratic protests. As part of the crackdown, at least two hundred opposition leaders and several members of parliament were arrested, and Gayoom briefly cut Maldivian access to the Internet.

Twenty-First Century

Maldives faces three challenges in the years ahead: accommodating demands for democracy, rebuilding the tourist sector, and stemming environmental damage.

The December 26, 2004, Asian tsunami struck Maldives and severely damaged the country's lucrative tourist and fishing industries. About 10 percent of the population lost their homes. The estimated price tag for reconstruction was set at $1 billion—double the country's annual gross domestic product.

Parliamentary elections had been scheduled for December 31, 2004, but were successfully held three weeks later, on January 22, 2005. However, four of Gayoom's main critics were arrested on corruption charges ahead of the vote, complicating their campaign efforts. Pro-Gayoom candidates won twenty-eight of the forty-eight elected seats, giving Gayoom another compliant parliament. His reforms have been shelved, but popular protests for democracy continue.

The islands of Maldives rise only a few feet above sea level, making them prone to erosion and flooding. Global warming could lead to rising sea levels that eventually could submerge the country. The government launched a land reclamation project in 1997 to alleviate housing shortages, but any progress was literally washed away by the 2004 tsunami. Furthermore, the islands are rapidly losing their freshwater supply, and the country's poor sanitation systems threaten the environment.

BIBLIOGRAPHY

Ellis, Royston. *A Man for All Islands: A Biography of Maumoon Abdul Gayoom.* New York: Times Editions, 1998.

Hockly, T. W. *The Two Thousands Islands: A Short Account of the People, History and Customs of the Maldive Archipelago.* New Delhi: Asian Educational Services, 2003.

⊕ Singapore

Type of Government

A parliamentary republic, Singapore elects a president as its head of state. The Council of Presidential Advisers advises the president on proposed budgets and appointments to important government posts, including the selection of the country's prime minister. The prime minister serves as the head of government and is chosen by the president from among the members of parliament's majority party. Singapore's parliament is unicameral, or one-chambered, and designed to accurately reflect the country's ethnic diversity. Singapore's judicial system is headed by the Supreme Court, which is divided into a High Court and separate courts of appeal for civil and criminal cases.

Background

An island city-state off the southern tip of the Malayan Peninsula in Southeast Asia, Singapore declared its independence from its northern neighbor, Malaysia, in 1965; it shares much of Malaysia's history and political development but remains economically and ethnically distinct. Composed of one main island and fifty smaller surrounding islands, Singapore is known for both its high standard of living and strict social controls. A causeway and bridge link the main island to the southern tip of Malaysia.

Settlement on the island of Singapore, or Singapura ("Lion City"), goes back at least to the thirteenth century when it became a flourishing trading center known as the Port of Temasek. Regional rivalries are thought to have destroyed Temasek in the fifteenth century, and it was left largely uninhabited until 1819, when Sir Thomas Stamford Raffles (1781–1826), an official with the British East India Company, established a new trading station there to provide a secure base for the company's trade with China. Located between China and India, Singapore commanded three convenient sea channels leading from the Strait of Malacca to the South China Sea. In 1824 the sultan, or ruler, of the southern Malayan kingdom of Johore ceded the offshore island to the East India Company, which governed the island with assistance from the British Crown government in India.

Singapore became home to a substantial population and rapidly became a major transit point for shipping, especially for merchant ships traveling the stretches of ocean between India and China. Southeast Asian–produced materials shipping through the area were spices, gold, resins, rare gums, and other produce from the region's rain forests, mines, and plantations. When Raffles founded Singapore he intended it to remain a free port and imposed no import or export duties, wharf fees, marine or port dues, or other charges on shipping. Movement of goods and people in and out of the port was not regulated. With some minor concessions, Singapore remained a free port until the latter half of the twentieth century. Its lucrative activity attracted settlers from the Malay Peninsula, India, and eventually large numbers of merchants, craftsmen, and planters from

China. Over the next century, Singapore's population would grow to be largely Chinese. By the beginning of the 1900s, greater numbers of women had joined Singapore's Chinese society, and the region became more settled as families and schools were established.

After World War I ended in 1918, Britain declared the island of Singapore its main Eastern Asian naval base and began extensive military construction there, which was completed in 1938. Singapore's excellent harbor continued to attract maritime trade until the city became the leading seaport of Southeast Asia. Among other commerce, the tin and rubber exported from Malayan mines and plantations flowed through Singapore.

In 1826 the British Crown combined Singapore, Malacca, and Penang into a Crown colony known as the Straits Settlements. Singapore was not included in the Malayan Union (organized by Britain after World War II) or the Federation of Malaya (organized in 1948). Singapore remained a colony of the British Crown, however, until 1959, when it was granted local self-government. In 1963 it gained formal independence from Britain and became part of the newly established Federation of Malaysia. Political and ethnic tensions with the Malay-dominated central government of Malaysia, many due to Singapore's predominantly urban Chinese population and highly commercial economy, eventually led to Singapore's withdrawal from the federation in August 1965. It established itself as a completely independent sovereign state within the British Commonwealth and proclaimed itself a republic in December 1965.

Government Structure

Voting in Singapore is compulsory for all citizens twenty-one years of age and older. Singapore's constitution provides for a unicameral parliament, which as of 2007 consisted of eighty-four elected members and six members appointed by Singapore's president. To ensure representation of ethnic minorities in parliament, some constituencies are designated as Group Representation Constituencies (GRCs). These constituencies are represented not by a single candidate but rather by teams of three to six candidates, one of whom must be a Malay, Indian, or a person belonging to another minority community. In the interest of engaging opposition parties in government, Singapore's president may appoint to parliament up to six opposition candidates who fail to win election. These Nominated Members of Parliament (NMPs) are given limited voting rights. The maximum term for parliament is five years, but elections may be called within that time. If parliament is dissolved, a general election must be held within three months.

Singapore's original constitution of 1965 called for its president to be elected by parliament every four years. Since a 1991 amendment to the constitution, Singapore's president has been directly elected by the people for a term of six years. In addition to serving as the country's head of

Lee Kuan Yew, Singapore's first prime minister. He served as prime minister from 1959 to 1990, and in 2007 he still maintained the title of "Mentor Minister" in the Singaporean government. © *Library of Congress*

state, the president has the right to veto appointments to public office or government budgets proposed by parliament. The president also has authority to examine the government's investigations into cases of corruption, as well as the government's use of powers granted it under the Internal Security Act and the so-called "religious harmony" laws.

The 1991 constitutional amendment also provided for the establishment of a Council of Presidential Advisers. Singapore's president is obliged to consult the council before vetoing proposed government budgets or appointments to key government posts. The Council of Presidential Advisers is composed of six members, two of whom are appointed by the president, two by the prime minister, one by the chief justice of Singapore's Supreme Court, and one by the chair of the public service commission. Members of the council serve an initial term of six years, followed by eligibility for reappointments of four years each. The chair of the council steps in to assume the duties of the president when the president is unavailable.

Singapore's prime minister is appointed by the president from among the members of the majority party in parliament, which since 1959 has been the People's Action Party (PAP). The prime minister heads Singapore's government and appoints a cabinet consisting of a senior minister, two deputy prime ministers, and eleven others. In addition to law, foreign affairs, health, and other ministries, Singapore's government includes the Ministry of Environment and Water Resources; Ministry of Information, Communication, and the Arts; and Ministry of Community Development, Youth, and Sports.

Singapore's judiciary includes the national Supreme Court as well as subordinate magistrate, district, and lower courts. Singapore's Supreme Court is headed by a chief justice and is divided into the High Court, the Court of Appeal for civil cases, and the Court of Criminal Appeal for criminal cases. Judges of the Supreme Court are recommended by the prime minister and appointed by the president after consultation with the chief justice of the court. Singapore's constitution provides for an independent judiciary.

Political Parties and Factions

PAP has remained Singapore's dominant political party since its founding in 1954 and has won every general election since 1959. Led initially by Lee Kuan Yew (1923–), a London-trained lawyer who emerged victorious in the struggle for power in newly independent Singapore, PAP dominated Singapore politics until Yew's resignation in 1990. Popular support for PAP, which continues to dominate Singapore's government, likely results from policies that stress law and order, economic growth, and improved standards of living. Singapore remains a multiparty nation, but critics of PAP's long hold on power cite strict media controls—including recently imposed restrictions on the use of the Internet for political campaigning, a ban on publication of opinion polls during elections, and a 1998 ban on television appearances by political parties—as PAP-imposed regulations that make it difficult for opposition parties to campaign and win votes. Virtual monopoly ownership of print and broadcast media, as well as a history of successful defamation lawsuits by PAP politicians against opposition politicians, are seen as additional elements stifling political debate.

Singapore's strongest opposition party is the Workers Party, which has been critical of what it sees as undemocratic practices within the PAP government. Along with the other major opposition party, the Singapore Democratic Party, the Workers Party is tolerated but subject to what critics of the government characterize as almost continual harassment.

Major Events

In 1967 Singapore joined with Malaysia, Indonesia, the Philippines, and Thailand to form the Association of Southeast Asian Nations (ASEAN). Joined by Brunei in 1984 and by Vietnam, Laos, Cambodia, and Myanmar in the 1990s, ASEAN seeks to reduce tensions and increase collaboration among its member nations. It works to accelerate the region's economic growth, cultural development, and social progress. In 1999 ASEAN's member nations agreed to pursue development of a free trade zone in Southeast Asia by eventually eliminating duties on most goods traded in the region. Estimated to take effect in the year 2010 or later, the proposed zone will be the world's largest free trade zone, encompassing some 1.7 billion people and trade valued at $1.2 trillion. In May 2002 ASEAN's ten member countries pledged to form a united front against terrorism in response to the September 11, 2001, terrorist attacks in the United States. They established a regional security framework, including joint training programs, exchange of intelligence information, and the introduction of national laws governing arrest, investigation, and extradition of suspects.

Southeast Asian financial markets took a sudden, precipitous decline in 1997 when investors lost confidence in a number of Asian currencies and securities. In 1998 the Singapore economy slipped into its first recession in thirteen years, but in 2000 the government announced positive economic growth after two years of budgetary uncertainty, indicating the economy had weathered the crisis.

An outbreak of severe acute respiratory syndrome (SARS) in 2003 shook Singapore medically and financially. Stringent precautions to halt the spread of the potentially fatal disease, which is known to have killed thirty-three people in Singapore, included closing markets, screening air passengers with thermal imaging, and establishing quarantines. Tourists stayed away and local people stayed home, creating a sharp economic downturn for the island.

From 1998 to 2005 an outbreak of international piracy plagued the waters of the Strait of Malacca and Strait of Singapore, disrupting shipping. Small ships that ferried goods to port from large container vessels proved particularly vulnerable. Narrow shipping channels and numerous shallow reefs slowed the speed of oceangoing vessels, and thousands of islands along the straits offered potential shelter to pirates. While sea piracy had been a recurring problem in the area for centuries, Singapore successfully reduced piracy during this latest outbreak by instituting joint naval and air patrols with neighboring Malaysia and Indonesia.

Twenty-First Century

Like neighboring Malaysia, Singapore is sometimes referred to as one of Asia's economic "tigers." Its prosperous economy is centered on electronics manufacturing, financial services, and a growing tourism industry. Its port—the original source of its wealth and renown—continues to thrive.

While ethnic Chinese make up the majority of Singapore's residents, the city-state remains multilingual and religiously, as well as ethnically, diverse. Singapore has four major languages: English, Malay, Mandarin Chinese, and Tamil. Its population practices any of four major religions: Taoism, Buddhism, Islam, and Christianity. Singapore's thriving economy and cultural diversity stand as the country's strong points, but its limited land area and population density create environmental challenges in a number of areas. Waste disposal, air pollution from transportation vehicles, and pollution from the country's petroleum industry are ongoing concerns. Singapore's success as a financial hub makes its institutions vulnerable to money laundering attempts, despite strict laws and enforcement.

BIBLIOGRAPHY

Osborne, Milton. *Southeast Asia: An Illustrated Introductory History.* New South Wales: Allen & Unwin, 1990.

Singapore Government. *SINGOV: Government Information.* http://www.gov.sg (accessed June 20, 2007).

Turnbull, C. M. *A History of Singapore: 1819–1975.* Singapore: Oxford University Press, 1985.

⊕ Guyana

Type of Government

Guyana is a republic with a mixed presidential and parliamentary system. The president holds the power in the executive branch, appointing a prime minister and cabinet. The president is not directly elected, but rather is the leader of the party that receives the most votes in elections for the unicameral legislature, the National Assembly. A judiciary with appointed judges includes the Court of Appeal and the High Court.

Background

The English-speaking country of Guyana is located on the northeastern coast of South America, bordered by Venezuela to the west, Suriname to the east, and Brazil to the south. The tropical nation takes its name from an Indian word that means "land of many waters," and the country is indeed crisscrossed by numerous rivers through the verdant rain forest that covers 80 percent of the country.

Though first sighted by Spanish explorers in 1499 and a century later by English explorers under Sir Walter Raleigh (1554–1618), the region that became known as Guyana was not settled by Europeans until the arrival of the Dutch in 1616 under the auspices of the Dutch West India Company. The Carib, Warrou, and Arawak tribes that inhabited the region were soon devastated by diseases brought by the Europeans, to which they had no immunity. The Dutch established three separate colonies

in the region: Berbice, Demerara, and Essequibo. These colonies flourished in the eighteenth centuries as a result of sugar cane, coffee, and cotton plantations worked by slave labor imported from Africa. A major slave revolt in Berbice protesting harsh treatment by the Dutch occurred in 1763, led by the national hero of Guyana, Cuffy. The slaves held many plantations in Berbice for months before the Dutch could put down the rebellion.

Meanwhile, the British had also made attempts to colonize the region and finally took control in the late eighteenth century. The Dutch formally ceded the area to Britain in 1815, following the Napoleonic Wars; in 1831 the three former Dutch colonies officially became the British colony of British Guiana, remaining under British control until independence in 1966. Another major slave revolt took place in 1823, with between ten and twelve thousand slaves rebelling in Demerara. After the revolt was put down, more than thirty of the slave leaders were executed.

After 1834, when slavery was outlawed in the British Empire, a new labor source had to be found for the sugar plantations. This new workforce came in the form of indentured or contract laborers, mostly from India, who were allowed to emigrate if they worked on the plantations for five years. Other nations—China, Scotland, Ireland, Germany, Malta, and Madeira—also contributed workers, but the overwhelming majority was East Indian. The practice of importing labor was halted in 1917; however, its legacy is apparent in modern Guyana, in which about half of the population is of East Indian descent and a little more than a third of African descent. In general, the Afro-Guyanese became the core of the urban population, while those of East Indian descent made up the rural population. Racial tensions between these two groups has proved to be a continuing problem in Guyana.

Politics in the country have likewise had a long tradition of turbulence. In 1928 British Guiana became a Crown colony and a constitution was adopted, giving women the right to vote. The first modern political party, the People's Progressive Party (PPP), was founded in 1950 by Forbes Burnham (1923–1985) and Cheddi Jagan (1918–1997). The PPP's mission was to achieve independence for Guyana. Its leadership reflected an attempt at multiracial cooperation, as Burnham was of African descent and Jagan of East Indian. With the first popular elections in 1953, Jagan was elected the chief minister of the newly instituted House of Assembly. However, Jagan's Marxist views alarmed London, and the new government and its constitution were suspended within months.

Subsequently, Burnham broke with the PPP and founded his own party, the People's National Congress (PNC). Political divisions soon developed along racial and ethnic lines. With the advent of self-rule in 1961, Jagan became the country's first premier, though the British governor still retained veto power over the locally elected legislature. Jagan's leftist views continued to concern England and the United States, where Jagan had been educated. Those two countries collaborated in an attempt to destabilize the democratically elected government by fomenting strikes and racial violence. A constitutional conference was called in London in 1963, and Guyana was guaranteed independence under the condition that it adopt proportional representation in its elections, a move intended to counter the PPP strength. With the 1964 elections, the PPP was unable to gain a majority, and Burnham became prime minister, working in coalition with another smaller party.

On May 26, 1966, Guyana achieved full independence and British troops left the country that same year. Four years later the country became the Cooperative Republic of Guyana, replacing the British monarch with a president as ceremonial head of government. Burnham continued to rule the country until his death in 1985. His rule was marked by a turn toward autocracy, suppression of personal liberties, the nationalization of industry, and fraudulent elections. Burnham was also accused of having opponents assassinated, including the leader of the opposition Working People's Alliance party, Walter Rodney (1942–1980), who was killed by a car bomb. In 1980 Burnham pushed through a new constitution establishing an executive presidency with broad powers. The years of his leadership were marked by continued racial tension and economic depression.

Government Structure

By the terms of the 1980 constitution, the president is, in effect, both head of state and head of government. As such he or she exercises executive power and appoints as well as supervises the prime minister and cabinet ministers. The president is not elected by popular vote; rather, he or she is the leader of the majority party in the National Assembly. The presidency can thus be changed by a shift in the majority in the National Assembly.

Legislative power resides in the sixty-five members of the National Assembly; forty of these are chosen on the basis of proportional representation and twenty-five are elected by regional administrative districts. The president may dissolve the assembly and call new elections at any time before the usual five-year electoral period.

The judicial branch consists of the Court of Appeal, headed by a chancellor appointed by the president, and the High Court, led by a chief justice who is also appointed by the president.

Guyana is divided into ten administrative regions, each headed by a chairman who presides over a regional democratic council. Local communities are administered by village or city councils. The capital, Georgetown, is administered directly by the central government.

Political Parties and Factions

The two main political parties in Guyana are the PPP and the PNC. The country functions as a two-party

Forbes Burnham, prime minister of Guyana from 1966 to 1980 and president from 1980 to 1985. *Photographs and Prints Division, Schomburg Center for Research in Black Culture, The New York Public Library, Astor, Lenox, and Tilden Foundations*

democracy, and these major parties have controlled political life since independence.

The PPP is the oldest Guyanan party, founded in 1950 by Burnham and Jagan. At its founding it was anticolonial and focused on establishing multiracial political alliances and instituting leftist economic policies. Since then the PPP has become primarily the party of the rural East Indian Guyanans. The party came to power in 1992 under the leadership of Cheddi Jagan, who was succeeded upon his death in 1997 by his American-born wife, Janet Jagan (1920–), and then in 1999 by Bharrat Jagdeo (1964–). Jagdeo and the PPP also won the 2001 and 2006 elections.

The PNC was founded in 1955 by Burnham after his split with the PPP. Primarily the party of black Guyanese voters, the PNC remained in power from independence until 1992. With the death of Burnham in 1985, party leadership and the presidency were taken over by Hugh Desmond Hoyte (1929–2002). Hoyte attempted to reform both the party and Guyanese politics, renouncing socialist ideology in 1987. Under pressure from the international community, Hoyte ensured that the 1992 elections were fair and open. The party lost the elections in 1992, 1997, 2001, and 2006, and renamed itself the People's National Congress Reform-One Guyana (PNCR-1G) in the 2006 elections.

Several other smaller political parties, such as the Working People's Alliance, work in coalition with the PPP and PNC. One of the stronger new parties is the Alliance for Change, which took 8.1 percent of the vote in the 2006 election and won five seats in the National Assembly. In general, ethnic and racial divisions are more important than ideological concerns in determining party affiliation, as most parties in Guyana favor a socialist or mixed economic system.

Major Events

Guyana came into the international spotlight in 1978 with the mass suicide of members of a religious cult, the People's Temple, which had moved to the country from San Francisco four years earlier and established a settlement known as Jonestown.

With the death of President Burnham in 1985, his successor, Hoyte, began to move away from socialist policies and the virtual one-party rule Burnham had established, moving the country toward a market economy. This trend continued under the presidency of Cheddi Jagan, who came to power in 1992, ending long years of PNC monopoly power. With Jagan's death in 1997, his widow, Janet Jagan, was elected president, becoming the country's first female head of government. In 1999 ill health forced her to turn over power to Jagdeo, who won free and open elections in 2001 and 2006.

Border disputes broke out in 2000, disrupting Guyana's economic re-emergence. Venezuela revived claims it had made in 1889 that more than half of Guyana's territory belongs to Venezuela. Meanwhile, Suriname to the east disputed the border in a coastal region that is rich in oil deposits. Both disputes were outstanding as of 2007.

Twenty-First Century

Guyana is one of the poorest countries in the world, and its economy has been constrained by heavy levels of foreign debt. In the early years of the twenty-first century, the World Bank, International Monetary Fund, and Inter-American Development Bank provided Guyana with debt relief totaling more than $700 million.

The biggest challenge to Guyana's rather fragile democracy is the tensions resulting from racial and ethnic divisions. Following the 2001 election of Jagdeo, who is of East Indian descent, members of the Afro-Guyanese population held protests and riots, claiming election fraud even though international monitoring agencies declared that the elections appeared legitimate. However, the 2006 elections, which were again won by Jagdeo and the PPP, were without significant incident, and the results were approved by international monitoring agencies. The People's National Congress Reform party, which had been one of the PPP's strongest critics

among the nation's minority parties, accepted the results of the election.

Another threat to democracy in Guyana is an increase in violent crime associated with the international drug trade, which is developing armed groups in the country to protect its interests.

BIBLIOGRAPHY

Guyana News and Information. http://www.guyana.org (accessed April 5, 2007).

Guyana and Belize: Country Studies, 2nd ed., edited by Tim Merrill. Washington, DC: Library of Congress, 1993.

Williams, Brackette F. *Stains on My Name, War in My Veins: Guyana and the Politics of Cultural Struggle.* Durham, NC: Duke University Press, 1991.

⊕ Botswana

Type of Government

Botswana, officially known as the Republic of Botswana, is a parliamentary democracy. The executive branch is headed by the president, who is both head of state and head of government. The legislative branch is made up of a bicameral (two-chamber) parliament consisting of a House of Chiefs and a National Assembly. The parliament elects the president, who in turn appoints the vice president.

Background

Botswana is a landlocked country in southern Africa, bordering Zimbabwe, Zambia, South Africa, and Namibia. Almost two-thirds of the land is part of the Kalihari Desert. The area now known as Botswana is the historic homeland of the Batswana tribe, which dates to the fourteenth century. Throughout the centuries the region was regularly attacked by the Matabele, a Zulu tribe located in modern-day Zimbabwe, until Khama III (1837–1923), chief of the Bamangwato branch of the Batswana, successfully defeated the Matabele in the early 1880s. However, the Boers of South Africa then became a threat to the Bamangwato. Rather than fight the Boers alone, Khama appealed to the United Kingdom for protection. Britain created a protectorate, Bechuanaland, in 1885 and divided it into two halves: British Bechuanaland, south of the Molopo River, and Bechuanaland Protectorate, north of the Molopo. British Bechuanaland was assigned to South Africa in 1895, and Britain assumed that the Bechuanaland Protectorate would also eventually be incorporated into South Africa. However, when South Africa withdrew from the British Commonwealth in 1961, Batswana leaders lobbied to become an independent state.

To prepare for the handover, executive and legislative councils were created in 1961, followed by a constitution in 1965. Bechuanaland elected a provisional parliament, with Seretse Khama (1921–1980; grandson of Khama III) as prime minister. Botswana became an independent country on September 30, 1966, and Khama became the first president of the independent state. He died in 1980, shortly after winning a fourth term as president in October 1979.

Government Structure

The president is the country's chief executive, chief of state, and commander in chief of the armed forces. The National Assembly elects the president by simple majority, and the president then selects a vice president and cabinet of ministers from members of parliament. The president has the power to declare war, dissolve parliament, and veto legislation.

Legislative power is vested in the National Assembly and the House of Chiefs. Originally the National Assembly had thirty-two elected seats, but with adjustments based on the national census this number has increased to sixty-three. Fifty-seven seats are chosen by popular election, and four are selected by the majority party. The president and attorney general are nonvoting members of the Assembly. The House of Chiefs is an advisory body with fifteen members, including the chiefs of the eight main tribes and four chiefs representing minority districts. These twelve House members elect the last three members. Both chambers have five-year terms, although the eight tribal chiefs have permanent seats.

Legislation originates in the National Assembly and goes to the president for approval. If the president vetoes a bill that is later passed again by the National Assembly, he must sign the bill or dissolve parliament. Similarly, the parliament must be dissolved in case of a no-confidence vote. Legislation related to tribal matters has to clear the House of Chiefs before it goes to the Assembly.

Botswana's judicial system is based on a combination of Roman-Dutch and local customary law. The 1965 constitution outlines a court system consisting of a High Court, a Court of Appeals, and magistrates' courts in each district. The Judicial Services Commission, chaired by a chief justice appointed by the president, advises the president on judicial appointments. Customary courts handle marital and property matters according to tribal law. Botswana introduced a court of appeals for customary law in 1986.

Botswana is divided into nine districts and five towns, each of which is governed by a commissioner and council. The central government appoints the commissioners, while district and town councils are composed of both appointees and locally elected representatives. Citizens can also express their views through *kgotla*, a traditional village council.

Botswana has universal suffrage; a constitutional amendment in 1995 reduced the minimum voting age from twenty-one to eighteen years of age. All ethnic and tribal groups are able to participate in the political process. The constitution guarantees freedom of religion and does not specify an official state religion.

Political Parties and Factions

The Botswana Democratic Party (BDP) has dominated politics since Botswana was established in 1966. Founded in 1961 by Seretse Khama and Quett Ketumile Masire (1925–), the BDP sought to achieve independence through peaceful, democratic means, and it dominated the 1965 elections. Despite internal tensions between urban technocrats and rural populists, the BDP still won 51.7 percent of the popular vote in the 2004 parliamentary election, followed by the Botswana National Front (26 percent) and the Botswana Congress Party (17 percent). The opposition parties tend to be concentrated in urban areas, but attempts to form an alliance against the BDP in 1994 collapsed even before election day.

Major Events

Following the death of President Khama in 1980, Vice President Masire became president, finishing out Khama's five-year term. Masire was elected president in his own right in 1984 and again in 1989. His presidency was marked by tensions within his Botswana Democracy Party over who would be his political heir, national political unrest over a corruption scandal within the cabinet, popular demands for electoral reform, and rioting. Masire resigned on April 1, 1998, and his vice president, Festus Mogae (1939–), became president. In October 1999 parliament later appointed Mogae president in his own right, and Mogae named Ian Khama (1953–; son of Seretse Khama) as his vice president.

In 1994 deteriorating economic conditions in Botswana led to significant changes in the political system. The size of the parliament was increased to forty-four seats, with all but four directly elected. Opposition members sought to establish procedures for absentee voting, because some 20 percent of the population seeks employment as migrant workers and therefore cannot vote in their home precincts. Constitutional amendments approved in 1995 lowered the voting age from twenty-one years to eighteen years and set a two-term limit (still of five years per term) on the presidency. The new restriction did not apply to the incumbent president, however, and would only come into force with his successor. The government did not agree to introduce absentee voting.

Botswana is heavily influenced by events in neighboring South Africa. It is a member of the South African Customs Union, which has been administered by South Africa since the union's creation in 1969, and used the South African currency until 1976.

The government of South Africa repeatedly sought a mutual security agreement with Botswana, partly due to fears that opponents of the South African regime could operate out of bases in Botswana. When the Botswana government refused such a security alliance, South African commandos raided Botswana several times during the 1980s. With the collapse of the apartheid (racial segregation) regime in Pretoria in the early 1990s, Botswana and South Africa established formal diplomatic relations in 1992.

Twenty-First Century

Botswana is widely regarded as a stable republic, with regular elections conducted in a free and fair manner. It has managed to maintain civilian leadership and has a reputation as the least corrupt country in Africa. However, opposition forces call for direct election of the president and proportional representation in the National Assembly.

The country's most pressing problem is the spiraling crisis of the human immunodeficiency virus (HIV) and acquired immunodeficiency syndrome (AIDS). World health officials estimate that nearly four of every ten people in Botswana are infected by HIV/AIDS. The life expectancy rate has dropped from 65 years of age in 1990 to 33.87 years of age in 2005. The health crisis has created a drain on the economy, which previously had one of the highest growth rates in the world thanks to the country's extensive diamond mines. The government has implemented a comprehensive program to address the HIV/AIDS crisis, pledging to provide medications to all infected citizens through the national health program.

BIBLIOGRAPHY

Leith, J. Clark. *Why Botswana Prospered*. Montreal: McGill University Press, 2006.

Peters, Pauline E. *Dividing the Commons: Politics, Policy, and Culture in Botswana*. Charlottesville: University of Virginia Press, 1994.

Tlou, Thomas, and Alec Campbell. *History of Botswana*. Gabarone, Botswana: MacMillan Botswana, 1997.

⊕ Lesotho

Type of Government

The government of Lesotho is a parliamentary constitutional monarchy. The executive branch is headed by a hereditary monarch who is the ceremonial head of state, while the prime minister is head of government. The legislative branch is made up of a bicameral, or two-chamber, parliament made up of an appointed Senate and an elected National Assembly. The king appoints all judges.

Background

Lesotho is a small kingdom of two million people, completely surrounded by South Africa. It is the homeland of the Basotho nation, founded in 1818 when chief Moshoeshoe I (1786–1870) gathered the survivors of Zulu and Matabele raids into a territory that would eventually be designated as Basutoland. When the African raids from the north began to abate, the Basotho encountered Boer challengers from the Orange Free State, who seized considerable amounts of Basotho land. Great Britain had already begun to colonize the region, and Moshoeshoe I appealed to Britain for protection. Basutoland became an autonomous Crown protectorate in 1868, but three years later it was incorporated into Britain's Cape Colony over Basotho objections. In 1879 Cape Colony administrators decided to reserve part of the Basotho lands for white settlers and ordered the Basotho to disarm. The Basotho refused and open conflict began. The Gun War lasted from 1880 to 1881, when Cape authorities agreed to a settlement with the surprisingly well-armed Basotho. After three more years of unrest, Great Britain detached Basutoland from the Cape Colony in 1884, making it an autonomous Crown colony.

Along with Botswana and Swaziland, Lesotho was a British protectorate at the turn of the twentieth century, and Great Britain had intended for all three to eventually be incorporated into South Africa. But when Pretoria increasingly embraced racial discrimination, Britain began to prepare the three colonies for independence. A Basutoland National Council and a constitutional commission were created in 1960. Two political parties emerged at this time: the conservative Basutoland National Party (BNP) and the left-wing Basutoland Congress Party (BCP). The BNP won the April 29, 1965, National Assembly elections, which also ratified the new constitution. BNP leader Joseph Leabua Jonathan (1914–1987) became prime minister, and he called for a vote on full independence in April 1966, which was achieved October 4, 1966. Moshoshoe II (1938–1996) was proclaimed king of Lesotho.

Government Structure

Despite the long history of the Basotho monarchy, the king has actually exercised little power in Lesotho's history. He has been dependent upon other institutions, such as the military, to retain his throne, and King Moshoeshoe II was exiled twice. Prior to 1993 the king appointed the prime minister and cabinet, but those powers were taken away by the 1993 constitution, leaving him as only a ceremonial head of state. The king is selected by a College of Custom, drawing upon traditional laws.

Executive authority is exercised by the prime minister, who is head of government and selects the cabinet. The head of the political party with the parliamentary majority automatically becomes prime minister.

Legislative sovereignty is invested in a bicameral parliament consisting of a National Assembly and a Senate. The National Assembly has 120 seats, eighty chosen directly and forty allocated via proportional

Lesotho's King Moshoeshoe II arriving in Maseru after months of solitary confinement in the United Kingdom, 1992. © *Reuters/CORBIS*

representation. Members serve five-year terms. The Senate has thirty-three members; twenty-two are local chiefs, while the ruling party selects the other eleven members.

Lesotho's judicial system draws upon English common law and Roman-Dutch law. There is a High Court, Court of Appeals, and local courts. The king chooses the chief justice based on recommendations from the prime minister and other judges based on recommendations from a Judicial Service Commission. Most justices are citizens of South Africa. Local governance is carried out via ten administrative districts, and the central government appoints each district administrator. All citizens of Lesotho are permitted to vote at the age of eighteen.

Political Parties and Factions

Three parties have dominated politics in independent Lesotho. The BNP, founded in 1959, stressed the need to maintain good relations, including formal diplomatic ties, with South Africa. BNP leader Joseph Leabua Jonathan became Lesotho's first prime minister, and the party controlled parliament until 1993.

The BCP is Pan-African (an effort to politically unite all African nations) and recommended keeping strong ties with all African states except South Africa. Founded in 1952 by Ntsu Mokhehle (1918–1999), the BCP was more aggressive in pursuing independence than the BNP. The BCP became the most popular party in Lesotho around 1970, but Prime Minister Jonathan manipulated the electoral system to prevent it from gaining control of parliament.

The two traditional parties of BNP and BCP have been eclipsed by the Lesotho Congress for Democracy (LCD), whose members broke from the BCP in 1997.

LCD won the 1998, 2002, and 2007 parliamentary elections, but by successively smaller margins. A new party, the All Basotho Convention, broke from the LCD in 2006 and has become the leading opposition party. It is led by former foreign minister Thomas Thabane (1939–).

Major Events

As voting was underway on January 27, 1970, Prime Minister Jonathan cancelled the election when initial returns suggested that the opposition BCP would dominate the new legislature at the expense of his own Basutoland National Party. To further his grip on power, Jonathan suspended the constitution and arrested the BCP's leaders and the king. Later the Netherlands granted the king asylum.

Jonathan ruled by decree for the next sixteen years, but not without challenges. In January 1974 BCP partisans attacked police posts. Jonathan accused them of attempting a coup and arrested, executed, or exiled many of them. The Lesotho Liberation Army, affiliated with BCP in exile, continued to attack or bomb targets for the remainder of Jonathan's tenure. Opposition parties refused to participate in the 1985 parliamentary elections, claiming fraud, causing Jonathan to cancel the balloting entirely. Disputes with South Africa about members of the African National Congress (South Africa's majority political party) allegedly hiding in Lesotho led Pretoria to stage raids into Lesotho and periodically close the border.

In 1986 the military overthrew Prime Minister Jonathan, established a Military Council to rule the state, and restored the king (Moshoeshoe II). As the head of the Military Council, Lieutenant General Justin Lekhanya (1938–) created a system in which the monarch formally had supreme executive and legislative authority, but the six-man Council dominated the king. When the king refused to fire senior officers as ordered in 1990, Lekhanya deposed Moshoeshoe II in favor of the king's son, Mohato Bereng Seeiso, who became King Letsie III (1963–). Moshoeshoe received asylum in Great Britain.

Lekhanya was overthrown by Major General Phisoane Ramaema in April 1991. Ramaema legalized political parties and led a return to a constitutional regime. When the BCP swept the 1993 parliamentary elections, Ramaema ceded power to BCP founder Mokhehle without incident. At this point Letsie III tried to abdicate in favor of his father, but his proposal was rejected.

In August 1994 Letsie III fired Prime Minister Mokhehle and created a new ruling council. The new regime was an international outcast, and over a two-year period a compromise was brokered between Letsie III and the BCP. The king agreed to reinstate the BCP government if it would reinstate his father as monarch, but during the negotiations Moshoeshoe II was killed in an automobile accident.

The BCP fired Mokhehle as party chief in 1997, maintaining that he was too old and no longer effective. However, a large faction followed Mokhehle into a new party, the LCD, which immediately formed a parliamentary majority. LCD won all but one seat in the 1998 parliamentary elections, and LCD leader Pakalitha Mosisili (1945–) automatically became prime minister. However, the BCP and BNP refused to accept the results. Rioting and a police mutiny ensued, and the government asked members of the South African Development Community for help. Troops from Botswana and South Africa subsequently entered the country and restored order.

An all-party interim government was established, which recommended changing the electoral system to proportional representation. The LCD won the 2002 election, taking 77 of the 120 seats in parliament. In 2006 the LCD split, with foreign minister Thabane and seventeen members of parliament forming a new party, the All Basotho Convention (ABC). As the LCD no longer controlled parliament, Mosisili dissolved the assembly and called elections for February 2007. The LCD took 82 of the 120 seats in that poll, but the new ABC party, which finished second, disputed the results and called a general strike.

Twenty-First Century

Most Basotho are subsistence farmers and do not produce enough to feed the country. The government has been making a tremendous push to improve agriculture yields, expand the economy, and create an industrial base. It is working to privatize industry in the hopes of attracting foreign investment and has participated in International Monetary Fund poverty-reduction programs. However, until the health of the workforce improves, such efforts will have a limited impact. Lesotho has the third-highest prevalence rates for the human immunodeficiency virus (HIV) and acquired immunodeficiency syndrome (AIDS) in the world, with 28.9 percent of the population infected.

BIBLIOGRAPHY

Ferguson, James. *Anti-Politics Machine: "Development," Depoliticization, and Bureaucratic Power in Lesotho.* Minneapolis: University of Minnesota Press, 1994.

Gill, Stephen J. *A Short History of Lesotho from the Late Stone Age Until the 1993 Elections.* Lesotho: Morija Museum and Archives, 1993.

Rule, Stephen, and Ntsoaki Mapetia, eds. *Lesotho 2000: Public Perceptions and Perspectives.* Pretoria, South Africa: Human Sciences Research Council, 2002.

⊕ Barbados

Type of Government

Barbados is a parliamentary democracy and an independent nation within the British Commonwealth. The British sovereign is head of state and is represented locally by a governor general. A prime minister, the leader of the majority party in the bicameral parliament, is the head of government, assisted by a cabinet. The parliament consists of a Senate and House of Assembly. The judiciary is independent and is based on English common law. It consists of magistrate courts and a Supreme Court.

Background

Barbados is an island nation located in the western Atlantic, just outside of the Caribbean Sea and about three hundred miles northeast of Venezuela. The island had been inhabited by Arawak Indians and then Carib Indians, but had been abandoned by the time the British first established a colony there in 1627. For the next 339 years, the island remained under British control; however, Barbados has a long history of local autonomy: its first House of Assembly was created in 1639.

The early colonists cultivated tobacco and cotton, and by the 1640s the main crop had become sugar cane. African slaves worked the sugar plantations of the island, turning sugar into a profitable industry for the British settlers. The African population grew until it constituted 90 percent of the island's inhabitants. Settlers from Ireland and Scotland were brought as indentured servants, and these Celtic people became a third class between the British masters and the African slaves, serving in the local militia. The Celtic settlers allied themselves with the slave populations several times throughout the history of Barbados and helped to foment slave rebellions.

Though the slave trade was halted in 1804, slavery continued in Barbados until it was abolished throughout the British Empire in 1834. In 1816 the island's largest slave revolt took place; thousands were killed and 144 slaves were later executed. Even with emancipation, the black population continued to be a disenfranchised underclass. High-income qualifications for voting kept them from the decision-making process, and lack of education guaranteed they would be fit for only unskilled work on the plantations. The economy remained heavily dependent on sugar, rum, and molasses production through most of the twentieth century.

However, by the 1930s, the descendants of former slaves began to agitate for more rights. This movement was spearheaded by Sir Grantley Adams (1898–1971), one of the founders of the Barbados Labour Party and the country's first premier. Adams advocated universal suffrage, educational rights for the black population, and workers' protection, while remaining loyal to the British government. The black population was further galvanized in 1937 by the deportation of the pioneering trade unionist Clement Payne (1904–1941). Four days of rioting ensued, which became a turning point in social justice on the island. Thereafter, many of the reforms that Payne had proposed, including the introduction of trade union legislation, were enacted. Further reforms followed: in 1942 income qualifications for voting were lowered, and by 1950 a universal suffrage system was instituted. In 1954 Adams became premier, and in 1958 Barbados became one of the ten members of the short-lived West Indies Federation, with Adams serving as the Federation's first and only prime minister.

Adams, however, continued to support the British monarchy, a position that put him at odds with younger leaders, such as Errol Walton Barrow (1920–1987), who was the founder of the Democratic Labour Party and is often called the "Father of Barbados Independence." Promoting a reform agenda, Barrow replaced Adams as premier in 1961 and instituted free public education, among other progressive legislation. The West Indies Federation was dissolved in 1962, and for four years Barbados was once again a self-governing colony of the British. Finally, on November 30, 1966, the country became an independent state and a member of the Commonwealth of Nations.

Government Structure

Like many former British colonies, Barbados adopted a parliamentary democratic monarchy as its government structure. According to the 1966 constitution, while the British monarch is the official head of state, and is represented locally by an appointed governor general, that is largely a ceremonial office. Real executive power is wielded by the prime minister and the members of his or her cabinet, who are chosen from the members of parliament. Both the prime minister and the cabinet are responsible to the parliament.

The bicameral legislature is made up of the House of Assembly and the Senate. The thirty members of the House are elected every five years. (Suffrage is universal

The Barbados parliament building in Bridgetown. *Altrendo/Getty Images*

in Barbados, and begins at the age of eighteen.) The leader of the party achieving a majority of sixteen seats becomes prime minister, while his or her counterpart in the minority party is leader of the opposition. Elections can be called at any time if a prime minister wishes a new mandate from parliament, or if parliament expresses a vote of no confidence in the government. The twenty-one members of the Senate, on the other hand, are appointed by the governor general—twelve in consultation with the prime minister, two in consultation with the leader of the opposition, and seven at the governor general's own discretion.

The judicial branch is divided into magistrate courts, which are authorized by statute, and the Supreme Court, which is provided for in the constitution of Barbados. The Supreme Court is also divided in two parts, consisting of the high court and the court of appeals. Each of these has four judges, appointed by the governor general in consultation with the prime minister and the leader of the opposition. The Chief Justice serves on both the high court and the court of appeals. In 2005 the Trinidad-based Caribbean Court of Justice was inaugurated, functioning as the highest court of appeal and replacing the Privy Council in the United Kingdom. Barbados joined this court in 2006.

Political Parties and Factions

The three most important political parties are the Barbados Labor Party (BLP), the Democratic Labor Party (DLP), and the National Democratic Party (NDP). The oldest of these is the BLP, which has been in power since 1994.

Founded in 1938 by Grantley Adams, the BLP is a member of the Socialist International. The BLP's platform advocates more inclusive social services, including improvements to the public housing, educational, and medical systems. Moderately left of center, the BLP is led by Owen Arthur (1949–), who became prime minister in 1994.

The DLP was founded in 1955 and was the majority party from 1961 to 1976, led by Errol Barrow. It was also in power from 1986 to 1994, under the leadership of Lloyd Erskine Sandiford (1937–). Its policies are similar to those of the BLP.

The third-largest party, the NDP, was formed in the late 1980s by former members of DLP and supports a moderate platform. In 2006, the leftist People's Empowerment Party was formed, with the goal of putting the means of production under public ownership.

Major Events

Under the stewardship of Grantley Adams and later his son, J. M. G. M. ("Tom") Adams (1931–1985), Barbados was considered one of the leaders among the island nations of the Caribbean, setting the tone in foreign relations and trade. Tom Adams, who served as prime minister from 1976 until his death in 1985, sent Barbadian troops to St. Vincent in 1979, to help the newly independent nation put down a separatist revolt on Union Island. Barbados also supported the U.S.-led invasion of Grenada in 1983.

Despite its actions in Grenada, Barbados has retained friendly relations with Cuba. After initially breaking off diplomatic contact with Cuba in anticipation of joining the Organization of American States in 1967, Barbados reestablished relations with Cuba in 1973. In recent years, Barbados has become an advocate against the United States' embargo against Cuba.

Twenty-First Century

Traditionally reliant on sugar cane as its economic mainstay, Barbados has transformed its economy to become one of the most prosperous countries in the developing world through the development of tourism, financial services, and light manufacturing. On the United Nations Human Development Index, which measures life expectancy, education, and per capita income, Barbados is ranked third in the Americas, behind only Canada and the United States.

Barbados is considering changing its status as a parliamentary monarchy within the Commonwealth. In 2000 the government commissioned a panel to explore the benefits of adopting a republican system, with an elected president serving as head of state. In 2005 the parliament approved a bill allowing for a referendum to decide the matter.

BIBLIOGRAPHY

Barbados: Thirty Years of Independence, edited by Trevor Carmichael. Kingston, Jamaica: Ian Randle, 1996.

Beckles, Hilary. *A History of Barbados: From Amerindian Settlement to Nation-State*. New York: Cambridge University Press, 2007.

Government of Barbados. "Barbados Government Information Service." http://www.barbados.gov.bb (accessed April 4, 2007).

⊕ Nauru

Type of Government

Nauru is governed as a parliamentary republic. Its government combines elements of the European system of parliamentary conventions and the American presidential model. Nauru's federal government comprises separate executive, legislative, and judicial branches. The president serves as both head of state and head of the government. The unicameral parliament carries out legislative functions.

Background

The Republic of Nauru is a small island nation located in the southwestern Pacific Ocean, approximately twenty-five miles south of the equator. With a population of just over thirteen thousand and an area of only eight square miles, it is the world's smallest independent republic. The nation has no official capital; rather, the seat of government is located in the Yaren administrative district on the island's southwestern coast. Nauru is one of three phosphate rock islands in the South Pacific (the others are Makatea in French Polynesia and Kiribati).

Until the end of the eighteenth century, Nauru was inhabited solely by people of Polynesian origin. They lived in relative isolation from outside cultural influences, which gave rise to a distinctive language. Traditional Nauruan society was divided into twelve matrilineal clans (groups of families sharing a common maternal ancestor).

The island was first sighted in 1798 by the British captain John Fearn (1768–1837), who named it Pleasant Island. Nauru began to attract serious attention in Europe during the 1830s, when it became a stopping point for whaling ships in search of fresh water and supplies. The Europeans brought with them weapons, disease, and liquor. The introduction of guns exacerbated conflict among the indigenous people, leading to decades of bloody warfare. Between 1843 and 1888 Nauru's population dropped from fourteen hundred to just nine hundred.

Nauru became a possession of Germany according to the terms of the Anglo-German Convention of 1886, and two years later, the island was incorporated into Germany's nearby Marshall Islands protectorate. The German colonial administration succeeded in putting an end to the clan warfare.

At the beginning of the twentieth century, the discovery of large deposits of phosphate—a key ingredient in the production of fertilizers—marked a turning point in Nauru's history, as nations struggled for control of the island and its natural resources. In 1906 Germany authorized the British-owned Pacific Phosphate Company to begin phosphate-mining operations on Nauru. During World War I, the island was occupied by Australian forces, who expelled most of the Germans. After the war Nauru became a mandated territory of the

Workers strip-mining for phosphate on Nauru, 1968. Phosphate is the island nation's major export, and its mining poses environmental hazards for the smallest independent republic in the world. © *Bettmann/CORBIS*

League of Nations, which assigned joint responsibility for the island and its resources to Great Britain, Australia, and New Zealand. These nations created the British Phosphate Commission to control Nauru's phosphate-mining operations.

Nauru was occupied by another imperial power during World War II. From 1942 to 1945, Japan controlled the island, forcing more than twelve hundred Nauruans into unpaid labor on the nearby atoll of Truk (modern Chuuk, part of the Federated States of Micronesia) and using the island as a military base. Australia reclaimed the island in 1945 and returned the enslaved Nauruans to their homes on January 31, 1946, a date that is now celebrated as Independence Day. The following year, the United Nations appointed the trio of Great Britain, Australia, and New Zealand to head Nauru's colonial government once again, although Australia handled the actual administration of the island.

Nauru continued under the administration of Australia until it was granted self-government in 1966. In

1968 the island became fully independent following a two-year constitutional convention. That year, Nauru adopted its own constitution and elected Hammer De Roburt (1923–1992) as the nation's first president.

In 2006 Nauru was designated a special member of the Commonwealth of Nations (also called the British Commonwealth), a voluntary association of more than fifty independent nations that are former colonies or territories of the British Empire. Its special status means that Nauru can participate in all Commonwealth activities and receive all benefits of membership but cannot attend meetings of the heads of government.

Government Structure

According to the 1968 constitution, the president of Nauru serves as both head of state and head of the government. The president is elected from among the members of the legislature to serve a three-year term. However, the legislature may end the president's term at any time by passing a motion of no confidence. Executive authority is vested in the cabinet, which consists of four to six members who are appointed by the president from among the members of the legislature. The cabinet is ultimately responsible to the legislature.

Nauru has a unicameral (single-chamber) legislature called the Parliament. This body is made up of eighteen members representing eight multi-seat constituencies; seats are apportioned to the constituencies based on population. Members are elected by popular vote to three-year terms. Voting is compulsory for all citizens over the age of twenty.

Nauru's highest judicial authority is the Supreme Court, headed by a chief justice; members of the court are appointed by the president. The Supreme Court has the authority to interpret the constitution. Appeals are handled by the Appellate Court, which consists of two members. In rare cases, appeals of Supreme Court decisions may be heard by the High Court of Australia. Parliament has no authority to overturn judicial decisions. Below the Appellate Court are the District Court and Family Court, each of which is headed by a resident magistrate. The constitution also provides for two quasi-courts, the Public Service Appeal Board and the Police Appeal Board; the chief justice of the Supreme Court presides over these bodies. Nauru makes extensive use of a traditional reconciliation process, thereby keeping many cases out of the formal judicial system.

At the local level, Nauru is divided into fourteen administrative districts. The Nauru Island Council advises the government on local matters, but it holds little formal political power.

Political Parties and Factions

Nauruan politics is best characterized as a loose multi-party system. Political parties in Nauru have little formal structure, as they are focused largely on the personality of the leader, and do not play a significant role in the island's politics. Three parties were formed during the late twentieth and early twenty-first centuries: the Democratic Party, the Nauru First Party (Naoero Amo), and the Centre Party. However, most candidates for political office run as independents. In the parliamentary elections of 2004, for example, fifteen of eighteen candidates were listed as independents.

For two decades after independence, Nauruan politics was dominated by DeRoburt, the nation's first president. Since the 1990s Nauru has experienced great political instability as one president after another has been unseated by incessant no-confidence votes.

Major Events

Phosphate mining has been at the center of Nauruan politics throughout its history. In 1967 Nauru purchased the British Phosphate Commission, which had controlled phosphate operations on the island since 1919. The company was nationalized in 1970, becoming the Nauru Phosphate Corporation. Phosphate operations made the tiny island nation one of the richest per capita in the world for nearly two decades. Most Nauruans lived comfortably on the earnings derived from the nation's phosphate industry—each citizen received a share of the profits—and thus many remained unemployed by choice. By 2000, however, Nauru's phosphate stores were nearly depleted, and the nation now faces considerable environmental damage.

Twenty-First Century

The depletion of Nauru's phosphate reserves, its sole source of wealth, has plunged the country into an economic crisis. Whereas Nauru once had the second-highest gross national product per capita, it now faces extreme poverty. The island is dependent on foreign aid, primarily from Australia. In return, Nauru operates a detention center for immigrants seeking asylum in Australia. (Many have been rescued after being stranded at sea while trying to reach Christmas Island, an Australian territory in the Indian Ocean.) Although the government had invested much of its phosphate revenues in a trust fund in anticipation of the inevitable transition away from mining, poor investments and corrupt management left the fund nearly bankrupt by the 1990s. In an attempt to generate income, the island has become an important center for offshore banking, making it an attractive location for money laundering schemes.

BIBLIOGRAPHY

McDaniel, Carl N., and John M. Gowdy. *Paradise for Sale: A Parable of Nature.* Berkeley: University of California Press, 2000.

"Paradise Well and Truly Lost—Greed, Phosphate and Gross Incompetence in a Tropical Setting: The History of Nauru Really Is Stranger Than Fiction." *The Economist,* December 22, 2001.

⊕ Republic of Mauritius

Type of Government

An isolated island in the Indian Ocean east of Madagascar, Mauritius is a constitutional republic with an unusual legislative structure and a vibrant multiparty system.

Background

Mauritius is a small country, roughly two-thirds the size of Rhode Island. Its stable, democratic government and steady economic growth have made it one of postcolonial Africa's greatest success stories. The country's history begins in 1598, when the Dutch founded a small and ultimately unsuccessful settlement on the previously uninhabited island they called Mauritius. By the time the French arrived in 1715, it was again uninhabited, as the last Dutch settlers had departed several years earlier. Renamed the Ile de France, Mauritius remained in French hands for a century, eventually passing to the British in 1814 under the Treaty of Paris. In 1835 British administrators abolished the slave trade that had brought tens of thousands of Africans to the island for work on French and British sugarcane plantations. Faced with an impending labor shortage, the British began to import indentured servants from Asia, particularly from the Indian subcontinent. Most were Hindus, who now form the largest ethnic group on the island. The next largest group is the Creoles, who trace their ancestry back in varying degrees to the slave population. There are also sizeable communities of Indian Muslims and Chinese, as well as a very small, mostly French-speaking elite. All of these groups are politically active today, and several political parties are based primarily on ethnic ties.

Mauritius's isolated location ensured a high degree of local autonomy under colonial rule, with a Legislative Assembly in existence as early as 1947. Full independence came in 1968. Sir Seewoosagur Ramgoolam (1900–1985), leader of the Mauritius Labor Party, served as the nation's first prime minister.

Government Structure

The 1968 constitution provides for a strong executive branch. Both the president, who serves as chief of state, and the vice president are elected by majority vote of the National Assembly for a maximum of two five-year terms. The president then appoints a prime minister to serve as the head of government. In theory, there are no restrictions on the president's choice; by tradition, however, the leader of the largest bloc in the Assembly is chosen. The other members of the cabinet, known as the Council of Ministers, are also presidential appointees, though the president's choices here are made only after consultations with the new prime minister.

Legislative powers are vested in a unicameral National Assembly of seventy members, sixty-two of whom are elected by direct, popular vote for five-year terms. The main island (also known as Mauritius) is divided into twenty regional constituencies, each of which sends three members to the Assembly. The outlying island of Rodrigues comprises the twenty-first constituency; it sends two members. The remaining eight seats are allocated to various underrepresented ethnic groups under a complex system administered by the Electoral Supervisory Commission. All bills passed by the legislature must be signed by the president to become law. If the president refuses, he or she must resign. Proposed amendments to the constitution require a special three-quarters majority.

Though the structure of the Mauritian legal system is based closely on the British model, its legal code draws heavily on the Napoleonic Code of nineteenth-century France. At the top of the legal structure is a Supreme Court of eleven judges, one of whom, the chief justice, is appointed by the president after consultation with the prime minister. Assisting the chief justice is the senior puisne (a French legal term meaning "junior") judge, whom the president appoints on the chief justice's recommendation. The other nine puisne judges are appointed by the president on the recommendation of the Judicial and Legal Service Commission. In contrast to the U.S. Supreme Court, where justices enjoy lifetime appointments, Supreme Court justices in Mauritius face mandatory retirement at the age of sixty-two.

The primary appeals courts, the Court of Criminal Appeal and the Court of Civil Appeal, are divisions of the Supreme Court. Other venues include an Intermediate Court, which handles serious civil and criminal matters, ten district courts, and several specialized tribunals. Ordinarily, the Supreme Court serves as the court of last appeal. In rare circumstances, however, decisions of the Supreme Court may be appealed to the Judicial Committee of the Privy Council, a London-based, three-member panel empowered to hear cases from a variety of former British colonies.

For administrative purposes, Mauritius is divided into nine administrative districts and three offshore dependencies. A variety of elected councils (city, town, village, or rural district) handle local affairs.

Political Parties and Factions

As of the 2005 elections, the single largest bloc in the National Assembly was the Social Alliance (SA), a coalition dominated by the Mauritian Labor Party (MLP) and the Mauritian Social Democrat Party (PMSD); it controlled forty-two of the seventy seats. The MLP's leader, Navinchandra Ramgoolam (1947–), the son of the first prime minister, was elected prime minister. The second largest bloc, with twenty-four seats, was a coalition of the Militant Socialist Movement (MSM) and the Mauritian Militant Movement (MMM). The MSM's leader, Pravind Jugnauth (1961–), is the son of the president, Anerood Jugnauth (1930–). The Jugnauth and Ramgoolam dynasties illustrate the extent to which

Courtyard of the Mauritius Government House in Port Louis.   © *Giraud Phi/CORBIS SYGMA*

a small group of mostly Hindu families continues to dominate the island's politics.

The four seats not controlled by the two major coalitions are held by the Organization of the People of Rodrigues (OPR), a regional, heavily Creole group based on the outlying island of Rodrigues. Of the parties that failed to win seats in the 2005 election, the most significant and controversial is the conservative Muslim group Hezbollah (Arabic for "Party of God"). Unrelated to the Lebanon-based organization of the same name, the Mauritian Hezbollah is strongest in poor Muslim neighborhoods victimized by drug traffickers. In keeping with the strictest interpretations of traditional Islamic law, or sharia, Hezbollah advocates the imposition of the death penalty for those convicted of selling or distributing illegal substances. There is strong evidence that Hezbollah has occasionally taken violent action against drug traffickers without the knowledge or approval of authorities. Though most Mauritians condemn such behavior as vigilantism, many supporters of Hezbollah argue, with some justification, that certain members of the government have close ties to the criminal networks that control drug trafficking. To rely on the government to protect the public from traffickers is in their view naive and counterproductive. Debate on this

point continues. What is clear, however, is the growing alienation of many in the Muslim community. Drug addicts and Hezbollah activists alike are convinced that the Hindu-dominated government cares little for Muslims and will never grant them their rightful share in the so-called "Mauritian miracle" of sustained economic and social development.

Major Events

Like the Muslims with whom they have close ties, the Creoles continue to struggle with poverty and unemployment. Though all communities have benefited to some extent from the island's sustained economic growth, the distribution of good jobs, adequate housing, and other dividends has been uneven. The reasons for this discrepancy are complex, but racism is certainly a factor. This was the context for the nation's worst incident of civil strife since independence. In February 1999, Kaya (born Joseph Reginald Topize, c. 1960), a popular singer of Creole ancestry, died in police custody following his arrest on a minor drug charge. The circumstances of his death were highly suspicious, and many Mauritians, Creoles and non-Creoles alike, believe police officers beat him to death. News of his death sparked three days of riots across the capital city of Port Louis.

Eleven people were killed, including another popular Creole singer, and dozens of businesses looted or destroyed. The city quickly recovered, but Creole frustrations remain, and there has been little sign of reform within the police department.

In the immediate aftermath of the terrorist attacks of September 11, 2001, the U.S. government charged that banks registered in Mauritius had laundered money for al Qaeda and other terrorist organizations. Like many island nations, Mauritius is a center of the largely unregulated offshore banking industry, the practices of which are often of questionable legality. As Mauritius has more than nine thousand of these enterprises, the U.S. charge was plausible, and the existence of the militant Hezbollah organization did little to allay fears. In the years since, however, the United States has found the Mauritian authorities to be energetic allies in the war on terror, particularly after the 2002 passage of a stringent antiterrorism bill, and a recent report by the U.S. Central Intelligence Agency downplays the role of Mauritian banks in the funding of terror networks.

Twenty-First Century

Mauritius has undergone a remarkable socioeconomic transformation since independence. In 1968 more than eighty percent of the island's economy depended on the highly variable prices of the international sugar market. While sugarcane is still a major export, the agricultural sector as a whole provides only about five percent of the nation's gross domestic product and less than fourteen percent of its jobs. The tourism, textile, technology, and banking industries, meanwhile, have enjoyed decades of almost uninterrupted growth. The tax revenues generated by these new industries have made possible an ambitious program of state-funded social services, particularly health care. The result has been a dramatic decrease in infant mortality and a corresponding increase in life expectancy. Mauritius now boasts one of the highest life expectancies in Africa (sixty-nine years for men, seventy-six for women). The literacy rate of roughly 84 percent is also one of the highest in the region.

Continued progress is not assured, however. Like sugarcane, tourism is an unstable industry. The growth of tourism in Mauritius has been interrupted several times, notably by international news reports of the 1999 riots. In each case, the industry quickly recovered. Every reported incident of civil unrest, however, has the potential to cause a prolonged slowdown. In addition, the increasingly rapid deterioration of the island's coral reefs threatens fishing and scuba diving, two of the island's major attractions for foreign tourists.

The largest problem, however, is economic inequality. Ironically, this is in part a result of Mauritius' success. If the economy were still dependent on labor-intensive sugarcane production, as it was in 1968, poverty would be much more widespread among all ethnic groups. As it

is, however, the highly visible success of individual entrepreneurs, most from the Hindu community, emphasizes the poverty that continues to afflict the Muslim and Creole populations. While the government's distinctive method of allocating Assembly seats has increased the political participation of these two historically underrepresented groups, integrating them into the new Mauritian economy may prove more difficult.

BIBLIOGRAPHY

Boswell, Rosabelle. *Le Malaise Créole: Ethnic Identity in Mauritius.* New York: Berghahn Books, 2006.

Republic of Mauritius. "Government Web Portal." http://www.gov.mu (accessed June 30, 2007).

Sacerdoti, Emilio. *Mauritius: Challenges of Sustained Growth.* Washington, DC: International Monetary Fund, 2005.

⊕ Swaziland

Type of Government

Swaziland is an independent monarchy within the British Commonwealth. The monarch holds supreme executive, legislative, and judicial power, which is exercised on his behalf by both formal and traditional institutions. Under the 2005 constitution, the hereditary monarch, King Mswati III (1968–) is head of state, while the prime minister is head of government. The legislative branch is made up of a bicameral, or two-chamber, parliament consisting of a Senate and a House of Assembly. The king appoints one-third of the members of both houses of parliament and all judges of the judicial branch. The government tightly controls the media and restricts freedom of speech—especially reports about the royal family—and freedom of assembly.

Background

Swaziland is a landlocked country in southern Africa. It is almost completely surrounded by the Republic of South Africa, with the exception of a small strip in the northeast that borders Mozambique. Its geographical position makes it highly reliant on the South African economy and vulnerable to security threats from South Africa. The British Crown owns nearly two-thirds of the land, with the remainder held by private, predominantly foreign owners. The center of government is the capital of Mbabane.

Swaziland's dominant ethnic group, the Swazi, emerged from the Bantu-speaking peoples around the beginning of the nineteenth century, but they faced continual threats from the larger Zulu tribes to the north. Europeans began to settle in modern-day Swaziland near the end of the nineteenth century. In the 1840s the Swazi ruler, Mswati II (1821–1868), had asked the British government, which already had colonies in southern Africa, for assistance in quelling the Zulu attacks, and Crown representatives successfully brokered a settlement. European settlers soon began to move to the region, interested in its land and potential wealth.

In the 1880s King Mbandzeni (1855–1889) began selling rights to Swaziland and resources to the Europeans, and Great Britain stepped in to establish a provisional government to represent the interests of the Swazi people. British representatives in the South African province of Transvaal administered Swaziland from 1894 until the outbreak of the Second Boer War in 1899, when Great Britain transferred the territory to the British high commissioner for Southern Africa.

Elections were held in 1921 for a new European Advisory Council that would represent the interests of Europeans in Swaziland. The growing racial discrimination in South Africa convinced Great Britain that its remaining protectorates should become independent states. Britain recognized the head of the Swazi nation, called *ngwenyama*, as the local authority in 1944. Discussions about creating an independent Swaziland began in 1963, and administrators drafted a constitution that provided for a new legislative council. Local leaders began to create political parties ahead of elections to the legislative council in 1964. In an effort to promote traditional Swazi values, King Sobhuza II (1899–1982) established the Imbokodvo National Movement (INM), which swept the elections, winning all twenty-four council seats. The council immediately sought independence, and Swaziland became an independent, constitutional monarchy within the British Commonwealth on September 6, 1968.

Government Structure

Supreme authority is vested in the king, a member of the Dlamini dynasty, who is assisted by both a traditional advisory council (Liqoqo, later known as the Supreme Council of State), parliament, and a cabinet. While the king is responsible for governing, his mother is the spiritual leader and serves as regent if the king is a minor. The 1963 constitution created a division of powers, but on April 12, 1973, King Sobhuza II unilaterally repealed the constitution, declared a state of emergency, and began to rule as an absolute monarch, with all powers vested in the Crown. His move came after the May 1972 parliamentary elections, in which his INM lost three seats to the Ngwane National Liberatory Congress. Sobhuza declared unity to be the traditional Swazi way of life, dissolved parliament, and outlawed political parties.

Swaziland's order of succession is loosely based on the male candidate's mother. When Sobhuza died in 1982, a power struggle erupted among his fifty wives, sixty-seven sons, and the Liqoqo. Initially Queen Regent Dzeliwe Shongwe, "senior wife," became head of state, but she was largely a figurehead, because real power was vested in the Liqoqo, which was in conflict with the prime minister and cabinet. Two years later the Liqoqo removed Dzeliwe when she refused to fire Prime Minister Mabandla Dlamini. The Liqoqo installed Queen Regent Ntombi in 1984. Simultaneously, Prince Makhosetive, then fifteen years old and Ntombi's son, was named his father's successor. For the next three years Makhosetive completed his education abroad, and the Regent ruled in his stead. After turning eighteen, Makhosetive was crowned King Mswati III on April 25, 1986, and he eliminated the Supreme Council of State.

Under the 2005 constitution, the king is still head of state and commander-in-chief of the military, but he can no longer rule by decree. He can veto legislation and dissolve parliament without cause. The king is advised by the Swazi National Council (SNC), a reorganized incarnation of the Liqoqo. The SCN helps select tribal chiefs and justices of traditional courts; its decisions can override those of the cabinet, if the king agrees. The king selects the prime minister—usually a member of the royal family—from the members of parliament. The prime minister makes recommendations about cabinet appointments to the king.

Legislative power resides with the king. Before becoming law, legislation must pass through parliament and be approved by the king. Under the 2005 constitution, the House of Assembly has sixty-five members, fifty-five chosen by popular election and ten appointed by the king. The royal appointments must include five women and five representatives of marginalized groups. As of 2007 the Senate was composed of thirty members: ten selected by the House of Assembly and twenty appointed by the king. Within these allotments the House must have five women, and the king must nominate eight women.

Swaziland is divided into four administrative districts that are supervised by royally appointed commissioners. There are also traditional courts, fifty-five subregional districts, known as *tinkhundla*, governed by tribal chiefs, and another 366 chiefdoms.

Although the judiciary is formally independent, judicial power effectively resides in the executive branch. There is a Supreme Court and a High (formerly Appeals) Court, both appointed by the king, as well as magistrate courts in each of the four administrative districts. Statutory courts are governed by a legal code based on South African Roman-Dutch law, while a parallel set of traditional courts based on unwritten customary law also operates. Judges in the High Court serve two-year terms and are generally citizens of South Africa. No court has jurisdiction over the royal family.

All Swaziland citizens eighteen years of age and older are permitted to vote. The 2005 constitution grants freedom of religion, which is largely observed, although religious groups must register with the government. Women did not have equal rights prior to the 2005 constitution, and they are still poorly protected, particularly in traditional courts. Children and property belong to the husband.

Delegates from Swaziland attending a 1963 meeting with British officials to discuss the nation's future. © *Hulton-Deutsch Collection/CORBIS*

Political Parties and Factions

Political parties were allowed under Swaziland's original 1963 constitution but banned by the 1973 state of emergency. Political parties are not formally banned under the 2005 constitution, but they are not allowed formal registration, a situation leaving them in limbo. Without a voice in their government, Swazis have used political associations to challenge the central government. These include the antimonarchist People's United Democratic Movement (Pudemo), the Ngwane National Liberatory Congress (NNLC), and the African United Democratic Party. Pudemo and NNLC are the largest of these groups, and they have occasionally joined forces with the Swaziland Federation of Trade Unions and the National Association of Civil Servants to stage protests.

Major Events

While Swaziland has not experienced invasions or external threats to its sovereignty, there have been internal challenges to the king's absolute rule, usually associated with parliamentary elections. In 1973 King Sobhuza II

unilaterally repealed the constitution after his political party lost three of the twenty-four seats in the May 1972 parliamentary elections. Sobhuza's death ten years later caused a four-year succession crisis, because he had no designated successor.

Under the 1978 constitution, the National Assembly consisted of fifty members: ten appointed by the king and forty chosen through an electoral college made up of representatives of each local tinkhundla. The king chose which candidates were presented to the electors. Throughout the 1980s opposition groups called for changing to direct election of members of parliament. Direct election was used in the 1993 and 1998 parliamentary elections and enshrined in the 2005 constitution.

With political parties banned, the Swaziland Federation of Trade Unions and the National Association of Civil Servants staged strikes in 1995, calling for political reforms. Mswati III responded by outlawing trade unions. Another round of strikes in 1996 led to the creation of a Constitutional Review Commission to survey the people about what type of government they prefer. But instead of heeding public demands for democratization, two of the king's brothers crafted a constitution that solidified the king's absolute control. The docile parliament approved the document in 2005.

The largest rebellion against King Mswati III came in November 2002. The national Court of Appeals had issued two rulings against the king: One rejected the legal basis of his frequent decrees, and the other ordered the end of the exile imposed on Chief Mliba Fakudze and some two hundred of his followers. The king refused to accept the rulings. In response, all six Court of Appeals judges resigned; no cases were heard in this venue for two years. Prime Minister Dlamini, aware of international criticism of the Swazi government, ultimately coaxed the judges into returning by promising to obey court decisions. The court reconvened in 2004.

Twenty-First Century

Swaziland faces three major challenges in the twenty-first century: the human immunodeficiency virus (HIV) and acquired immunodeficiency syndrome (AIDS); high-level corruption; and persistent demands for democratization. Nearly 40 percent of Swaziland's population is infected with HIV/AIDS, the highest prevalence rate in the world; some 20 percent of the population has been orphaned by the disease. Current life expectancy in Swaziland is 33.2 years old, the lowest in the world. Without extensive intervention efforts, the disease will decimate the Swazi people. In 2001 the king ordered teenaged girls to take a five-year vow of chastity, to stem the spread of the disease. The law is highly unpopular, and the king's practice of taking multiple wives, many of them selected as teenagers, has caused tremendous resentment.

The lavish lifestyle of the ever-expanding Swazi royal family has become public knowledge, and anger has been rising over the use of state monies to support excesses such as a $45-million royal jet, a $500,000 automobile, and palaces for the king's thirteen wives. Budget deficits are generally the result of overspending by the royal family on personal expenses. Furthermore, compounding these problems related to Swaziland's royalty, the population and international community are calling for King Mswati to share power with his people.

BIBLIOGRAPHY

Davies, Robert H., Dan O'Meara, and Sipho Dlamini. *The Kingdom of Swaziland: A Profile.* London: Zed Books, 1986.

Nugent, Paul. *Africa since Independence: A Comparative History.* New York: Palgrave Macmillan, 2004.

⊕ Equatorial Guinea

Type of Government

By constitution Equatorial Guinea is a multiparty republic. The president serves as head of state and commander of the armed forces while an appointed prime minister serves as head of government. A unicameral legislature is constituted by direct, popular vote. The nation's leading legal body is the Supreme Tribunal, with justices appointed by the president. In practice, however, the government is authoritarian, with power concentrated in the executive branch.

Background

Equatorial Guinea, one of the smallest countries in Africa, consists of a small territory on the continent's western coast, known as Rio Muni, and several nearby islands, the largest of which is Bioko. The first inhabitants of Rio Muni were hunter-gatherer tribes from nearby regions, including the Baku pygmies. Between the twelfth and thirteenth centuries AD, members of the Bantu ethno-linguistic group occupied the region and established a procession of transient states. In the following centuries the Fang tribe, the region's largest ethnic group, controlled the coastal area of the mainland, until it was driven into the interior in the seventeenth century by Muslim slave traders.

The Bubi tribe settled the island of Bioko in the thirteenth century and lived in isolation until the arrival of Europeans in the fifteenth century. Portuguese explorer Fernão do Pó was the first European to visit Bioko; for many years thereafter the island was named for him. The Portuguese established plantations on Bioko, utilizing imported slave labor, and eventually occupied Rio Muni as well. In 1798 Portugal and Spain negotiated a treaty that gave Spain control of Bioko and Rio Muni in exchange for territory in South America.

Though the Spanish hoped to use their African colonies for the slave trade, disease—especially yellow fever and malaria—hindered attempts to form lasting settlements. Unable to utilize the territories, the Spanish leased Rio Muni and Bioko to Britain. When the British abolished the slave trade in 1807, they began using Bioko and Rio Muni to monitor and disrupt that kind of commerce. In fact, Bioko became a haven for freed slaves who could not be repatriated. The integration of former slaves from a number of African and West Indian nations led to the development of a creole-linguistic population.

The Spanish eventually reclaimed Equatorial Guinea and established their own administration. By the mid nineteenth century, they were using Bioko as a penal colony and developing plantations for coffee and cotton production. Though an independence movement emerged toward the end of the nineteenth century, conflict between Spanish authorities and the native inhabitants was rare.

After the Spanish Civil War (1936–1939) the territorial administration began to disintegrate. In 1959 the government reclassified both Bioko and Rio Muni as autonomous provinces of Spain, granting Spanish citizenship to all residents. In 1963 the Spanish held a plebiscite, or common vote, asking the population to decide whether to maintain Spanish colonial status. The population voted for autonomy, resulting in a new administrative system in which Spain controlled the central government but native leaders had regional authority. The Spanish established health-care facilities and encouraged native participation in public education, which led to Equatorial Guinea's having one of the highest literacy rates in Africa.

After leaders of the independence movement petitioned Spain for further democratic reforms, the colonial government held a public referendum on a new constitution, which was approved. Legislative elections followed. In October 1968 Equatorial Guinea was granted full independence.

Government Structure

The republic is divided into seven administrative districts. Provincial governors are appointed directly by the president, and provincial assemblies are elected by popular vote. Each province is further divided into districts and municipalities.

The executive branch is organized according to a parliamentary model, with a president serving as head of state and commander of the armed forces and a prime minister serving as head of government. The president, who appoints ministers to serve in the executive cabinet, has the power to create law by decree and to negotiate and implement treaties and international agreements without legislative oversight. The president also has the power to dissolve the legislature and call for new elections. According to the constitution, the president is elected by direct, popular vote to serve a maximum of two terms of seven years.

The Chamber of Representatives is constituted by popular vote from the nation's seven administrative districts, which function as multimember electoral units. The one hundred representatives, who serve five-year terms, can stand for re-election. By constitution the Chamber has the responsibility to develop legislation, but in practice it is subordinate to the executive branch. It has no power to approve and ratify treaties negotiated by the president or to approve the president's use of emergency powers.

The judicial branch is headed by the Supreme Court, with sixteen justices appointed directly by the president to serve five-year terms. Though the constitution calls for an independent judicial branch, the Supreme Court rarely opposes presidential authority. Below the Supreme Court are the appellate courts, the district courts, and the local courts. The penal code combines elements of Spanish law and tribal customs.

Political Parties and Factions

The Partido Democrático de Guinea Ecuatorial (Democratic Party of Equatorial Guinea), or PDGE, was estab-

lished by President Teodoro Obiang Nguema Mbasogo (1942–) in 1987, at which time it was the nation's only legal political party. It has controlled the government ever since. In the 2002 presidential poll Obiang reportedly won more than 97 percent of the popular vote, though observers believe election procedures were seriously flawed. The PDGE rules in an alliance with minor political parties; in the 2004 legislative elections, they won ninety-eight of the one hundred seats in the Chamber of Representatives.

The Convergence for Social Democracy (CPS) is the only opposition party that was able to elect members to the legislature during the 2004 elections. The CPS nominated Celestino Bonifacio Bacale for president in 2002, but according to official figures, he won only 2 percent of the popular vote. Bacale and the CPS accused Obiang's party of fraud and intimidation during both elections. The CPS's platform focuses on democratizing political procedures and instituting socialist economic initiatives.

For many years several independence movements have existed on Bioko—they seek independence from the central government. The largest group is the Movimiento para la Auto-determinación de la Isla de Bioko (Movement for Self-Determination of Bioko), or MAIB. MAIB, like several similar organizations, is led by the Bubi ethnic group, which constitutes the majority on the island. During the administration of the nation's first president, Francisco Macías Nguema (1924–1979), the Bubi tribe and the independence movement were nearly eliminated by internal security forces. Since Obiang took office in 1987, MAIB has experienced a slight resurgence but is still considered illegal and operates in secret.

Major Events

The nation's first constitution, established in 1968, provided for a strong executive office. Nguema, who was a member of the Fang ethnic group, quickly utilized that authority to establish a dictatorial regime. Portions of the constitution were abrogated in the 1970s; for example, the multiparty system was replaced with a single party, the Partido Nacional de los Trabajadores (United National Workers Party), or PUNT.

Nguema, who named himself "president for life" in 1972, violently suppressed civil liberties and political opposition. More than 30 percent of the population was killed or fled the country between 1970 and 1976, which brought the nation close to economic collapse. Despite protests from foreign governments and human-rights organizations, Nguema continued to detain, arrest, and execute political adversaries. Meanwhile, the people who remained in the country lived in extreme poverty, and the nation's infrastructure deteriorated.

In 1979 Nguema's regime was overthrown in a military coup led by Obiang, his nephew. Nguema was eventually arrested, convicted of genocide, and executed.

Teodoro Obiang Nguema Mbasago, President of Equatorial Guinea, with French President Jacques Chirac in 2005.   © *LUC GNAGO/Reuters/Corbis*

Obiang established a transitional government under the leadership of a military council. Although he allowed some civilian participation in the government and, with the advice of the United Nations Commission on Human Rights, enacted a new constitution in 1982, his regime was essentially authoritarian.

After his party was accused of rigging the 1989 elections, Obiang announced his intentions to revise the political system and allow other parties to participate. While some revisions were made, Obiang won the 1996 election with more than 90 percent of the popular vote, according to government tallies. Numerous groups accused the government of voter intimidation and fraud. Under pressure from foreign governments and human-rights groups, he reconstituted his cabinet to include members of opposition groups and other political parties among his ministers, but his efforts were criticized as ineffective and largely symbolic.

Twenty-First Century

Though the nation has had significant export revenues—it is one of the world's leading suppliers of oil—most of the money has ended up in the hands of political leaders. Little has been done to reduce poverty and unemployment and repair the nation's infrastructure.

Obiang was re-elected in 2002; according to government sources, he won more than 97 percent of the popular vote. His political party also won majorities in the 2004 legislative and municipal elections. In both instances, domestic and international observers criticized the regime for utilizing intimidation to prevent legitimate outcomes.

In 2004 the government prevented a coup attempt, later called the "Wongo coup," which involved Zimbabwean and South African mercenaries working on behalf of exiled political leaders. Prominent British business leaders—including Mark Thatcher (1953–), the son of former prime minister Margaret Thatcher (1925–)—provided financial support. Some analysts believe the coup leaders intended to gain control over the nation's oil industry by installing a puppet government.

BIBLIOGRAPHY

Hyden, Goran. *African Politics in Comparative Perspective.* New York: Cambridge University Press, 2005.

Klitgaard, Robert E. *Tropical Gangsters: One Man's Experience with Development and Decadence in Deepest Africa.* New York: Basic Books, 1990.

Roberts, Adam. *The Wonga Coup: Guns, Thugs, and a Ruthless Determination to Create Mayhem in an Oil-Rich Corner of Africa.* New York: PublicAffairs Books, 2006.

⊕ Tonga

Type of Government

Tonga is governed as a constitutional monarchy headed by a king or queen. The nation's constitution puts considerable power in the hands of the royal family and a small group of hereditary nobles. The Tongan monarch serves as head of state, and the prime minister serves a lifetime appointment as head of the government. The unicameral Legislative Assembly, which is dominated by royal appointees and representatives of the nobility, has limited powers.

Background

The Kingdom of Tonga is located in the southwestern Pacific Ocean among the island nations of Polynesia. Tonga comprises 171 islands, 48 of which are inhabited, spread over an area of 290 square miles. The islands are divided into three groups: Vava'u in the north, Haapai in the center, and Tongatapu in the south. The nation's capital is Nuku'alofa, located on Tongatapu, the largest island. Tonga is the only surviving independent kingdom in the South Pacific.

Tonga was settled by migrants from Southeast Asia nearly three thousand years ago. During the tenth to twelfth centuries, a line of Tongan kings and queens (known as the Tu'i Tonga) was established, and Tongan chiefs gained power throughout the South Pacific. Some historians have argued that a Tongan empire existed between 1200 and 1500 AD.

Although Dutch explorers made contact with the Tongan Islands in 1616 and 1643, Europeans did not gain a foothold there until the late eighteenth century. English captain James Cook (1728–1779) visited the islands in the 1770s, naming them the Friendly Islands. European contact, particularly the introduction of firearms, disrupted native life, leading to a period of violence and disorder during the nineteenth century. Order was restored when the warrior and orator chief Taufa'ahau (d. 1893) united Tonga as a kingdom in 1845, taking the title King George Tupou I (in honor of England's King George III [1738–1820]) and establishing the dynasty that rules Tonga to this day. Under King George's leadership, Tonga became an independent nation with a constitution and a parliamentary system of government. Tonga signed agreements with Germany, Great Britain, and the United States recognizing its independence.

Fearing German territorial ambitions in the South Pacific—one of the few areas of the world left for European colonization—Tonga signed a treaty of friendship with Britain in 1900, making the islands a British protectorate. According to the terms of the treaty, the British consul took responsibility for Tonga's foreign affairs and military defense, but the Tongan monarch retained authority over local matters. Tonga achieved complete independence from Great Britain in 1970 under an agreement negotiated by Queen Salote Tupou III (1900–1965).

Tonga remains a full member of the Commonwealth of Nations (also called the British Commonwealth), a voluntary association of more than fifty independent nations that are former colonies or territories of the British Empire.

Government Structure

The Tongan monarch—King George Tupou V (1948–) in 2007—serves as head of state. The monarch's responsibilities are largely ceremonial: opening and closing sessions of the legislature, greeting foreign dignitaries, and serving as a symbol of national unity. The monarch's position is hereditary; since 1875, five monarchs of the Tupou line have ruled Tonga. The Privy Council, which is composed of the monarch and members of the cabinet, assists the king in carrying out his constitutional duties and acts as the highest executive authority in Tonga. When the legislature is not in session, the Privy Council has the power to make ordinances, which become law if approved by the Legislative Assembly.

The head of government is the prime minister, who is appointed to a lifetime term by the monarch. The prime minister is assisted by the deputy prime minister, who also serves for life. The cabinet is composed of the prime minister, deputy prime minister, ministers of the Crown (who head the major departments of government), and the governors of the Vava'u and Haapai island groups, all of whom serve lifetime appointments.

Queen Salote Tupou III of Tonga visiting with Lord John Waverly in London, 1953. © *Hulton-Deutsch Collection/CORBIS*

In 2005 the cabinet membership was expanded to include four elected members from the legislature (two each from the nobles' and the people's representatives) who serve three-year terms.

Tonga has a unicameral (single-chamber) legislature called the Fale Alea, or Legislative Assembly, which exercises limited powers. This body is made up of thirty members: Twelve seats are reserved for cabinet ministers; nine members are chosen by the nation's hereditary nobles from among themselves, referred to as "nobles' representatives"; and nine members are elected by popular vote to three-year terms, referred to as "people's representatives." The Legislative Assembly meets for four to five months of each year.

Tonga's judicial system comprises the Supreme Court, whose judges are appointed by the monarch; the Court of Appeals, whose members are chosen and approved by the Privy Council; the Magistrates' Court; and the Land Court.

At the local level, Tongans elect town officials who handle village administration and district officials who exercise control over groups of villages.

Political Parties and Factions

Tonga is a class-based society, with a sharp division between the nation's hereditary nobles and the majority commoners, who have little political power. The monarchy and the nobility together control most of the government: Most cabinet ministers and all judges are appointed by the monarch, as are twenty-one of thirty seats in the legislature.

In this environment, political parties exist chiefly as pressure groups. The nation's first organized political party, the People's Democratic Party, was formed in 2003. The Human Rights and Democracy Movement, an association of commoners who aim to bring greater democracy to Tonga, is also active in Tongan politics. In the elections of 2005, this group controlled seven of the nine popularly elected seats in the Legislative Assembly.

Major Events

In 2005 a nationwide strike of civil servants and widespread pro-democracy demonstrations prompted the Legislative Assembly to form a committee to consider political reform. The committee's report, published the following year, called for the direct election of a majority of seats in the legislature, though it recommended the monarch retain the authority to appoint the prime minister and cabinet ministers. The People's Committee for Political Reform, a pro-democracy group of public servants, businesspeople, and political activists, rejected the proposal and organized rallies to call for immediate and sweeping reform. In late 2006 rioting gripped the capital of Nuku'alofa; several demonstrators were killed and 80 percent of the city's central business district was destroyed. The Tongan government declared a state of emergency, which remained in effect as of September 2007.

Twenty-First Century

Democratic reform is Tonga's most important challenge in the twenty-first century. Leading human rights organizations, including Amnesty International and Freedom House, have rated Tonga as one of the least democratic nations in the world. The Tongan government has responded to calls for reform by jailing pro-democracy activists and imposing restrictions on local media. Significant pro-reform sentiment exists nevertheless within Tonga and is supported by international organizations and regional neighbors, including New Zealand. However, these efforts chiefly focus on increasing elected representation in government and not on an end to the monarchy.

BIBLIOGRAPHY

Fischer, Steven Roger. *A History of the Pacific Islands.* New York: Palgrave Macmillan, 2002.

Lawson, Stephanie. *Tradition versus Democracy in the South Pacific: Fiji, Tonga, and Western Samoa.* New York: Cambridge University Press, 1996.

⊕ Fiji

Type of Government

Fiji is governed as a parliamentary republic. Its government combines elements of the European model of parliamentary conventions and a traditional tribal system

Commodore Frank Bainimarama giving a press conference on December 6, 2006, in Suva, Fiji, after staging the country's fourth coup d'etat in twenty years. *Phil Walter/Getty Images*

of governance. The president serves as head of state, and the prime minister serves as head of government. Fiji has a bicameral (two-chamber) legislature made up of the House of Representatives and the Senate. In December 2006 Fiji's democratically elected government was overthrown in a military coup, triggering widespread international condemnation.

Background

The Republic of the Fiji Islands is located in the South Pacific Ocean, northeast of New Zealand. Fiji comprises some three hundred islands and five hundred islets spread over an expanse of more than a million square miles. Of this territory, about one hundred islands are inhabited. Most of Fiji's population resides on the two largest islands, Viti Levu ("Great Fiji") and Vanua Levu. The nation's capital is Suva, on the southern coast of Viti Levu.

The Fiji islands were settled in the first and second centuries BC by people of Melanesian origin. Early Fijian society was structured hierarchically, with people organized into clans based on kinship ties; these clans were led by chiefs and often formed confederacies with one another. Warfare among the clans was common.

Although Dutch explorers sighted the Fiji islands as early as 1643, the area did not attract much attention from Europeans until the nineteenth century. European settlement increased as the islands became a source of sought-after commodities, including sea cucumbers, which were considered a delicacy in Europe and Asia, and sandalwood. In addition, Europeans found a hospitable climate for plantation agriculture in Fiji. European contact, particularly the introduction of firearms, disrupted native life and exacerbated conflict among the clans, making it impossible for any single chief to exercise control over such a disparate area. In 1874 the Fijian chiefs ceded control of the islands to Great Britain, and Sir Arthur Hamilton Gordon (1829–1912) was appointed governor of the colony.

Under Gordon's stewardship, the British Crown ruled the Fiji islands indirectly, preserving the traditional political power of the chiefs and shielding the native Fijians from the exploitation that typically accompanied European colonization. The islands' sugar plantations were staffed with indentured workers imported from India. Many of these workers remained in Fiji after the conclusion of their servitude—at the request of the colonial government—but they had few political rights, no land, and little opportunity for advancement. Racial tensions developed as lower-status "Indo-Fijians" (as the Indian workers and their descendants became known) began to outnumber Europeans and native Fijians, who continued to dominate social and political life. This tension would become a hallmark of Fijian politics.

The move toward independence in Fiji was not the result of internal agitation, as it was in most Pacific Island nations, but of international pressure. The nation's constitution, developed during the 1960s, sought to strike a balance between the principles of parliamentary democracy and traditional tribal life and to bridge racial divisions within Fiji's population. The new political arrangement extended the vote to all adult citizens, but it retained the native Fijians' land rights and gave the chiefs the power to veto constitutional change—provisions that sowed the seeds of future conflict. In 1970 Fiji became a dominion within the Commonwealth of Nations (also called the British Commonwealth), a voluntary association of more than fifty independent nations that are former colonies or territories of the British Empire.

For nearly two decades after independence, Fiji's government was dominated by the Alliance Party, which was pledged to the principles of multiracial democracy. Since 1987, however, Fiji has experienced a series of coups d'état (violent overthrows of the government) and constitutional changes that has left its political infrastructure in jeopardy.

Government Structure

The structures and functions of Fiji's government are outlined in the nation's 1997 constitution. In December 2006 the democratically elected government was overthrown by a military coup; therefore, the role and functions of the nation's political institutions remain in flux.

According to Fiji's 1997 constitution, the nation has both a president who serves as head of state and a prime minister who is head of the government. The president is elected by the Great Council of Chiefs (Bose Levu Vakaturaga), a fifty-five-member body made up of the chiefs of Fiji's ethnic clans, and confirmed by the prime minister. The president serves a five-year term. Although the role is largely ceremonial, the president holds important "reserve" powers that officeholders have employed during Fiji's many political crises. Notably, the president serves as commander in chief of the military and symbolizes the unity of the nation.

The executive authority of government lies primarily in the hands of the prime minister and the cabinet. The prime minister is appointed by the president. Typically, the prime minister is the leader of the majority party (or coalition of parties) in the House of Representatives; if there is no clear leader, the president selects an individual who is acceptable to a majority. The cabinet is composed of ten to twenty-five members who are appointed by the president on the recommendation of the prime minister. By design, the cabinet should mirror the composition of the House of Representatives, with each party that has more than eight seats in the House represented proportionally in the cabinet.

Fiji has a bicameral legislature composed of the House of Representatives, referred to as the "lower house," and the Senate, called the "upper house." The House of Representatives is the more powerful of the two chambers: It determines the makeup of the government and initiates all legislation, whereas the Senate only has the power to review legislation and to amend or reject bills passed by the House.

The House of Representatives is made up of seventy-one members who serve five-year terms. Candidates are elected from single-member constituencies by a system of preferential voting (also known as alternate choice or instant run-off voting) in which voters rank candidates in order of preference; a candidate must achieve a majority in order to be elected. Fiji has two types of electoral districts: open and communal seats. The twenty-five open seats may be filled by candidates of any ethnic group, and all Fijians are eligible to vote in these contests. The remaining communal seats are apportioned to electoral districts representing particular ethnic groups: native Fijians (23), Indo-Fijians (19), Rotuman Islanders (1), and other minority groups (3).

The Senate is made up of thirty-two members who also serve five-year terms. Candidates are formally appointed by the president, but they are selected by different groups: the Great Council of Chiefs (14), the prime minister (9), the leader of the opposition party (8), and the Council of the Rotuman Islands (1).

Fiji's judiciary is independent of the executive and legislative branches of government. The highest judicial authority is the Supreme Court, whose five judges are appointed by the president. Four of the five judges also act as serving judges in Australia or New Zealand. Lower courts include the Court of Appeals, the High Court, and Magistrates' Courts.

At the local level, Fiji is divided into four administrative districts, each governed by a commissioner who is appointed by the national government. Districts are further divided into provinces, each administered by a provincial council. Native Fijians also maintain ethnic councils that handle matters pertaining to ethnic Fijians.

Political Parties and Factions

Modern politics in Fiji is marked by sharp ethnic divisions, and political parties are delineated along these lines. Two parties dominate the legislature: the Sogo-sogo Duavata ni Lewenivanua (United Fiji Party), which mainly represents native Fijians, and the Fiji Labor Party, which is supported by Indo-Fijians. The United Peoples Party, a minor party, represents the interests of Fiji's ethnic minorities, primarily Europeans and Chinese.

Major Events

Fiji has experienced four coups d'état over the span of two decades: two in 1987, one in 2000, and the most recent in 2006. These developments have transitioned Fiji from a Commonwealth dominion to a republic to a military regime.

In 1987 democratic elections resulted in an Indian-dominated electoral coalition in government, prompting widespread protests among native Fijians, who wished to maintain their traditional political dominance. The leaders of the new government were deposed in a coup led by Lieutenant Colonel Sitiveni Rabuka (1948–), who withdrew Fiji from the Commonwealth and declared the nation a republic. Rabuka led a second coup the same year after British authorities attempted to restore civilian rule. In 1990 a new constitution was implemented under Rabuka, ensuring the native Fijians' political dominance.

Fiji's Indian population declined after the 1987 coups, but those who remained agitated for a return to the 1970 constitution. Rabuka's government relented in 1997, and a Constitutional Review Commission promulgated a new constitution that granted Indo-Fijians a greater voice in government. Elections held under the new constitution in 1999 resulted in the first government headed by an Indian prime minister, Mahendra Chaudhry (1942–). However, the government was again deposed in 2000 following a coup led by civilian businessman George Speight (1956–). The military, which had opposed Speight's armed faction, took over and installed a government dominated by native Fijians and headed by Prime Minister Laisenia Qarase (1941–).

Lingering bitterness over the 2000 coup, largely centered on plans to grant amnesty to those involved, exacerbated tensions between Qarase's government and the military, led by Commodore Josaia Voreqe Bainimarama (known as Frank Bainimarama; 1954–). In December 2006 Bainimarama ousted Qarase's democratically elected administration and shut down the parliament in a military coup. In January 2007 Bainimarama was appointed interim prime minister.

Twenty-First Century

The military takeover in Fiji has been universally condemned by the international community. In December 2006 the Commonwealth of Nations suspended Fiji's military regime from its councils pending the restoration of democracy, and several nations (including the United States and New Zealand) imposed sanctions on the country. Prime Minister Bainimarama has promised to hold elections by 2010 and restore democracy. To this end, as of 2007 Fiji was conducting a population census in order to implement a redistricting plan and was searching overseas for an independent supervisor of elections.

BIBLIOGRAPHY

Fischer, Steven Roger. *A History of the Pacific Islands.* New York: Palgrave Macmillan, 2002.

Lawson, Stephanie. *Tradition versus Democracy in the South Pacific: Fiji, Tonga, and Western Samoa.* New York: Cambridge University Press, 1996.

⊕ Bahrain

Type of Government

The Kingdom of Bahrain became an independent nation in 1971 and has been led by a hereditary constitutional monarchy since 2002. The king is the head of state, and an appointed prime minister is the head of the government. Bahrain has a bicameral legislature, the Majlis al-Watani, or National Assembly. Its lower house is elected by the people, and its upper house is appointed by the king. Executive power is vested in the king together with his appointed council of ministers; legislative power rests with the king and the National Assembly.

Background

Bahrain encompasses an archipelago of three-dozen low-lying desert islands located in the Persian Gulf between the Qatar peninsula and the eastern coast of Saudi Arabia. The largest island is referred to as Bahrain or Manama, which is the name of the nation's densely populated capital. The main island also contains Mina Salman, the country's primary port. Bahrain's total land area is about 240 square miles, an area roughly four times that of Washington, D.C.

The Bahrain region has been settled since 3000 BC, but its current state was largely shaped by European intervention starting in the sixteenth century. From 1522 until 1602 Bahrain was controlled by the Portuguese, and then Arabs and Persians battled over the islands. In 1782–83, the al-Khalifa family, originally from Kuwait, captured Bahrain from the Persians for good. Afterward, to retain its hold on the region, particularly against intrusion by the Turkish Ottoman Empire, the ruling family sought the assistance of England, which made Bahrain a British protectorate in the nineteenth century. The first of several protective treaties between Bahrain and Britain was made in the 1820s.

Large supplies of oil were discovered in Bahrain in 1932. Bahrain was the first Arab Gulf state to discover and prosper from the extraction and sale of oil. The government-owned Bahrain Petroleum Company refinery was built in 1935, the same year the British stationed

Members of the Bahraini parliament arriving to that body's first session in 27 years, December 14, 2002. © *Reuters/CORBIS*

their regional naval headquarters in Bahrain. In 1968 the two nations agreed to end their long-standing arrangement, and Britain announced it would be pulling its military out of the area by 1971. Bahrain initially planned to join the eight other states in the region that were also losing British protection (Qatar and the seven sheikdoms currently part of the United Arab Emirates), but was unable to agree on terms. Bahrain became independent on August 15, 1971.

Of the nation's nearly 700,000 residents, 63 percent are ethnic Bahraini, with the remaining 37 percent being a mix of Asians (19 percent), Arabs (10 percent) and Iranians (8 percent), many of whom are in the country as laborers. Some 98 percent of Bahrain's residents are Muslim, the state religion, with about 70 percent of those being Shia and 30 percent identifying as Sunni. Although some two-thirds of the indigenous population is Shia Muslim, the ruling family and the majority of government, military, and business leaders are Sunni Muslims. It is legal to practice other religions, and the country is home to a small number of Christians.

Government Structure

King Hamad is the chief executive or head of the state. Khalifa bin Salman al-Khalifa (1935–) is the prime minister, the head of the government. The Council of Ministers (or Cabinet) is appointed by the king and is led by the prime minister, who is also appointed by the king. The Bahraini legislature, called the National Assembly, consists of the Shura Council, or Consultative Council (forty members appointed to four-year terms by the king), and the Council of Representatives or Chamber of Deputies (forty members directly elected by the public to serve four-year terms). In keeping with the traditional Islamic administrative system of *majlis*, people are allowed to petition the king directly—even if, in reality, this generally occurs only to exchange pleasantries.

In terms of more localized government, the kingdom also includes five governorates, each managed by an appointed governor, and twelve administrative subdivisions or municipalities. All citizens age eighteen and older have the right to vote. Women were granted the right to run for political office in 2002, but none succeeded in that election. The entrance of women into the Bahraini government began with the appointment of Nada Haffadh as Minister of Health in 2004 and Fatima Al-Balooshi as Minister of Social Development in 2005.

The constitution includes numerous provisions guaranteeing social programs that bolster family life. The government provides medical care at no or low cost and free education from primary school to a technical college level (about twelve years). Since the 1970s a public welfare system has funded unemployment, sick leave, maternity benefits, and a pension system.

Political Parties and Factions

The ruling family of Bahrain, the al-Khalifas, are related to the al-Sabah family of Kuwait and Saudi Arabia's ruling clan, the House of Sa'ud. Officially, political parties are banned in Bahrain. However, political societies, or blocs, have been tolerated since 2001 and were formally sanctioned in 2005. The political societies range from the communist left to the Islamist right. Various factions include branches of Hizbollah and other pro-Iranian militant Islamic groups.

Since the constitutional reforms were approved in 2001 and 2002, several public service, human rights–oriented nongovernmental and advocacy organizations have been founded, including the Bahrain Human Rights Society and the Supreme Council for Bahraini Women. Beginning with municipal elections in 2002, a variety of political groups fielded and campaigned for candidates. In the parliamentary and municipal elections of 2006, Al Wifaq, the largest Shia political society, won the largest number of seats in the publicly elected Council of Representatives. Trade unions, all of which belong to the General Federation of Workers Trade Unions in Bahrain, were allowed beginning in 2002.

Major Events

At the time of its independence, the country was led by Sheikh Isa bin Sulman al-Khalifa (1933–1999), the nation's monarch, who became both emir and prime minister of the newly formed independent state. Bahrain created a constitution and elected its first parliament in 1973. However, two years later, in August 1975, after the prime minister charged that the national assembly was hampering the effectiveness of the government, the emir disbanded the parliament. He then ruled by decree. When Sheikh Isa died in March 1999, his son Sheikh Hamad bin Isa al-Khalifa (1950–) ascended the throne.

During the 1990s Bahrain experienced violent protests, including hotel and restaurant bombings orchestrated by the marginalized Shia majority (with suspected Iranian involvement). More than 1,000 people were arrested and held without trial. They were released when political reforms took hold after 2001.

During the 1991 Gulf War, Bahraini pilots flew air strikes over Iraq, and the country was used as a base for military operations. Bahrain has since provided logistical and base support toward enforcing United Nations sanctions and preventing the illegal smuggling of oil from Iraq.

In November 2000, seeking to bring political reform to his country, Sheikh Hamad established a committee to transform Bahrain from a hereditary emirate to a constitutional monarchy. The National Action Charter, created by the committee, was overwhelmingly approved in a national referendum in February 2001. A year later, on February 14, 2002, Sheikh Hamad declared Bahrain to be a constitutional monarchy—instead of an emirate—and

his title changed from emir to king. Municipal elections occurred in May 2002, the first since 1957, and the bicameral parliament was restored. Public elections for the Chamber of Deputies, the lower house of parliament, were held in October. The other house is the Consultative Council, which has equal voting rights to the elected branch and is appointed by the king. The full assembly held its first legislative session from December 2002 to December 2006. Elections for the subsequent parliament occurred in the fall of 2006.

In addition to the reformed parliament, a new constitution was also effected in February 2002. It declares Islam the state religion and Islamic sharia law the basis of Bahraini law, but expressly protects freedom of religion. The constitution guarantees education, social welfare, rights of private ownership, and equality before the law. As part of his restructuring plan the king established an independent body to investigate government embezzlement. He pardoned all political prisoners and detainees, including those who had been imprisoned, exiled, or detained on security charges. He also abolished a system that permitted the government to detain individuals without trial for several years.

The Supreme Judicial Council was created in 2001 to establish a judiciary independent of the government. Bahraini law is based on both Sunni and Shia sharia religious laws, tribal law, and other civil codes and regulations.

Twenty-First Century

Revenues from oil and natural gas currently account for about 76 percent of Bahraini government income. However, Bahrain's oil reserves are considered relatively small, and as of 2006, its reserves were expected to last only another ten to fifteen years. In anticipation of its oil reserves shrinking, Bahrain is making a concerted effort to lessen its dependence on oil revenues. As such, the nation is also focusing its commerce on international banking, aluminum smelting, and petroleum processing. Efforts are also underway to make Bahrain a regional hub for higher education. In 2004 negotiations resulted in the U.S.-Bahraini Free Trade Agreement, which reduced or eliminated tariffs on trade between the two countries and provided substantial opportunities for U.S. corporate investment in Bahrain.

In 2001 the International Court of Justice settled a long-standing boundary dispute between Bahrain and Qatar. In resolving the case, the Court awarded the ancestral home of the al-Khalifa family—Zubara on the Qatar peninsula—to Qatar based on the fact that Qatar had held Zubara since the nineteenth century. The Hawar Islands, however, were awarded to Bahrain, in a decision based on a previous determination by Britain during its colonial administration. The 2001 decision also established a maritime boundary between the disputants and ended tensions over underwater rights and possession of reefs. The reefs, in particular, posed significant legal issues as they were submerged during high tide but at low tide could be occupied like islands.

BIBLIOGRAPHY

Al-Arayd, Jawad Salim. *A Line in the Sea: The Qatar v. Bahrain Border Dispute in the World Court.* Berkeley, CA: North Atlantic Books, 2003.

Kingdom of Bahrain, eGovernment. http://www.bahrain .gov.bh (accessed on August 15, 2007).

U.S. Department of State, Bureau of Near Eastern Affairs. *Background Note: Bahrain.* http://www.state.gov/ r/pa/ei/bgn/26414.htm (accessed on August 15, 2007).

⊕ Qatar

Type of Government

The State of Qatar is a hereditary monarchy derived from the al-Thani family and led by an emir. A former British protectorate, Qatar achieved independence in 1971. It functions under a constitution enacted in 2005, which states that Qatari society is based on the values of justice, benevolence, freedom, equality, and high morals. The constitution declares Islam the state religion and sharia the basis of its legal system. It guarantees the right of private ownership and freedom of expression, and declares all persons equal before the law. Executive power rests with the emir, who is advised by a council of ministers. Legislative power is vested in the Al-Shoura Council, a unicameral body comprising both elected and appointed members.

Background

Qatar is a peninsula nation that extends northward from Saudi Arabia into the Persian Gulf. The nation's total land mass is about 4,400 square miles, or roughly the size of Connecticut and Rhode Island combined. Qatar's capital, Doha, sits on the eastern coastline and is home to nearly half of Qatar's population of approximately 907,000 people. About half of Qatar's residents are noncitizens, including foreign workers and nomadic Arabs. About 40 percent of the population is Arab, with 18 percent Pakistani, 18 percent Indian, 10 percent Iranian, and the rest representing many nations.

Although Qatar is surrounded by water on three sides, its interior is a mostly flat, gravel desert. Its greatest resources are oil and natural gas, the revenues from which have given the country one of the highest per capita incomes in the world. The nation is home to the world's largest single gas reserve, known as the North Field, which comprises an entire half of the Qatar peninsula.

The Qatar peninsula was originally settled by fishermen and Arab tribes emigrating from the interior deserts of what is now Saudi Arabia. The al-Khalifa family of Bahrain controlled the Qatar peninsula until the mid-nineteenth century, when the British helped the Bahrainis negotiate a land agreement with the al-Thani family, which had moved into the Qatar peninsula earlier in the century. Later in the century, the Ottoman Turks took control of the Doha region and appointed Sheikh Muhammad bin Thani as the region's governor. In 1893 the sheikh overthrew the Turks and secured control of Qatar by the al-Thanis. In 1916 Qatar became a British protectorate, which meant that in exchange for Britain's military protection, Qatar relinquished its autonomy in foreign affairs and other areas, such as the power to cede territory.

Prior to the discovery of oil in 1939, and its exportation a decade later (the delay caused by World War II), Qatar was a poor desert nation. Its economy was dependent upon the Persian Gulf pearling industry, which struggled beginning in the 1920s and eventually disappeared due to competition from Japan and cultured pearl manufacturers. When oil prices increased greatly in the 1970s, the subsistence-level economy of Qatar rose to one of enormous wealth. While much of Qatar's population is now middle class or wealthy, a poor underclass exists of immigrants, uneducated men, and widowed or divorced women.

In 1968, when Britain announced its intention to end its protective relationships with the Gulf sheikdoms, Qatar entered into negotiations to join with the other eight states then under British protection—Bahrain and the seven sheikdoms that are now the United Arab Emirates. When terms with Qatar could not be reached, the sheikdom pulled out of the alliance. On September 3, 1971, Qatar declared itself as the independent State of Qatar.

The emir at the time of independence was Sheikh Ahmad bin 'Ali al-Thani (1917–1977), a man who so preferred the luxuries available outside his country that he formally announced Qatar's newfound independence from his Swiss villa instead of from his palace in Doha. In 1972 the Deputy Ruler and Prime Minister Sheikh Khalifa bin Hamad al-Thani (1932–), with the support of much of the al-Thani family, deposed his cousin, who at the time was vacationing in Iran.

Government Structure

Sheikh Hamad bin Khalifa al-Thani (1950–) is the emir of Qatar, the head of the state. The rule of Qatar is passed on within the al-Thani family. Members of the family serve throughout the government, which is run by the prime minister, who is appointed by the emir.

While the emir is the ultimate ruler, he serves according to sharia (Islamic law) and is expected to rule by consultation and consensus. Qatari citizens retain the right to appeal directly to him. The emir is advised by a cabinet-level Council of Ministers, the highest executive arm in the state, which he appoints. According to the constitution of 2005, the emir enacts laws upon the

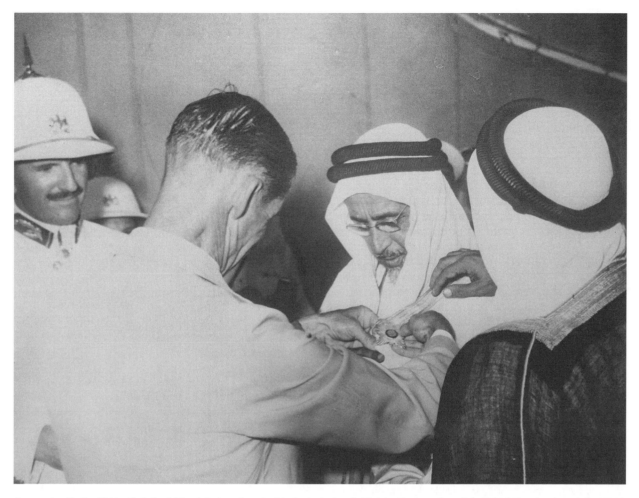

Qatar ruler Sheik 'Ali bin Abdulla al-Thani, being pinned with the insignia of a Knight Commander of the British Empire aboard the HMS *Newfoundland* in 1954.   © *Bettmann/CORBIS*

recommendation of the Council of Ministers and after consultation with the Advisory Council, a unicameral body consisting of thirty elected members and fifteen appointed by the emir. However, as of 2007 national elections still had not been held for the council representatives, and all serving members had been appointed.

The judiciary is appointed as well. The Qatari legal code is a mix of civil law and Islamic religious law, with all disputes related to family and personal matters being decided by Islamic sharia courts.

Qatari local government consists of ten municipalities, many with their own Municipal Councils. Since 1999, elections have been held for seats on these councils. All citizens age eighteen and older are allowed to vote.

Political Parties and Factions

Qatar has no political parties or organizations. However, since 2004 workers have been allowed to form unions and to take strike actions. As political dissidents are dealt with firmly, there are no organized opposition groups.

Any opposition to government and specific leaders has been among factions of the expansive al-Thani royal family, which is currently estimated to have 20,000 members.

Major Events

During his reign, Khalifa bin Hamad worked to preserve Qatar's traditional Islamic values. At the same time, he increased spending on social programs and reduced the financial allowances pocketed by the ruling family from the nation's oil and natural gas revenues. (It was believed that the former emir, Ahmad bin 'Ali al-Thani, was taking a quarter of the industry's revenues, and the family as a whole might have consumed up to half of the monies.) Khalifa bin Hamad is credited with building Qatar into a modern state.

By the late 1980s Hamad bin Khalifa al-Thani was running the daily operations of the country. In 1995 the son deposed and exiled his father, who had become an absentee leader and was believed to be mismanaging Qatar's oil revenues. Although Khalifa bin Hamad claimed to still be the emir of Qatar, setting up a government in exile in the United Arab Emirates, more than a dozen years later his son still remained in power. In 2004 the former emir was allowed to return to Qatar for the funeral of his wife.

As Qatar's emir, Hamad bin Khalifa has worked to diversify Qatar's economy and introduce democratic reforms under the constitution of 2005. Thus far, he has extended freedoms to the press, women, and local municipalities.

Twenty-First Century

In 2001 Qatar resolved its long-standing border disputes with both Bahrain and Saudi Arabia. In resolving the case against Bahrain, the International Court of Justice awarded the ancestral home of the Bahraini al-Khalifa family—Zubara—to Qatar based on the fact that Qatar had held Zubara since the nineteenth century. The Hawar Islands, however, were awarded to Bahrain, in keeping with a decision issued by Britain during its colonial administration. The ruling also established a maritime boundary, determined underwater rights, and awarded possession of reefs. The reefs, in particular, posed significant legal issues as they were submerged during high tide but at low tide were exposed and were proposed sites for development.

The Qatari government funds the Al-Jazeera satellite television network, the largest Arab-owned, worldwide cable news network. It became widely known outside the Arab region in 2001 when it was the only news service allowed to operate in Afghanistan and when it broadcast recorded statements by al Qaeda leader Osama bin Laden (1957–). Despite its government funding, Al-Jazeera is considered the most unrestricted news source in the Arab world. It launched an English-language companion channel in November 2006 that is available via satellite or cable systems in more than eighty million homes worldwide and ranks with the BBC and CNN among the most prominent international television news sources.

Qatar has been a leading supporter of U.S. military activities in the Middle East, contributing to the liberation of Kuwait during the Gulf War of 1991 and supporting the U.S.-led invasions of Afghanistan and Iraq. The U.S. Central Command maintains its forward command center at Camp As Sayliyah in Qatar, which also hosts thousands of U.S. military personnel on rest and recuperation breaks from combat. Qatar itself has been the site of terrorist incidents, including the assassination of former Chechen president Zelimkhan Yandarbiyev (1952–2004) in a car bomb attack in February 2004 in Doha and a bomb explosion in an English theater near a British school in 2005.

BIBLIOGRAPHY

Al-Arayd, Jawad Salim. *A Line in the Sea: The Qatar v. Bahrain Border Dispute in the World Court.* Berkeley, CA: North Atlantic Books, 2003.

Embassy of the State of Qatar in Washington D.C. "Political System." http://www.qatarembassy.net (accessed on August 15, 2007).

⊕ United Arab Emirates

Type of Government

The United Arab Emirates is a federation of seven emirates—Islamic states ruled by an emir—each having once been a sheikdom under British protection. The hereditary rulers of the individual emirates comprise the Federal Supreme Council (FSC), which oversees the budget and enacts policies. The UAE federal government has specified authority and responsibility, particularly for foreign affairs, with other powers reserved to its member states.

Background

In December 1971, upon gaining independence from Britain, six Arab states—Abu Dhabi, 'Ajmān, Al Fujayrah, Ash Shāriqah, Dubayy, and Umm al Qaywayn—merged to form the United Arab Emirates (UAE). The union was joined two months later by Ra's al Khaymah. Each emirate is named after its principal city. Abu Dhabi is the capital of the UAE and is its largest and wealthiest city, followed by Dubayy, which is transforming itself into a cosmopolitan city for business, high-end tourism, and luxury living. At about 52,000 square miles—most of it vast, rolling sand dunes—the UAE is slightly smaller than Maine.

The UAE is located on the southern shore of the Persian Gulf and the western coast of the Gulf of Oman; its land borders are with Saudi Arabia and Oman. The UAE's strategic location, along the southern coast of the Strait of Hormuz, makes it a vital transit point for world crude oil.

Although the lands currently occupied by the UAE and neighboring Oman have been settled since 3000 BC, its more recent history can be traced to the Middle Ages, when the area was part of the Persian Kingdom of Hormuz, which controlled the approaches to the Persian Gulf. By the sixteenth century the coastal region was a main trade route between Asia and Europe. Portugal was an occupying power for much of the sixteenth and seventeenth centuries, followed for a time by the Netherlands and then, during the nineteenth century, Britain. However, piracy was so rampant that the region came to be called the "Pirate Coast." Rivalries also raged between the Qawasim sheiks, who ruled the Ra's al Khaymah region (frequently challenging the British at sea) and the al-Nahyan, founders of Abu Dhabi and Dubayy. In 1820 the largest sheikdoms signed agreements whereby the sheiks would not challenge British interests in the region and the British would provide the sheikdoms with external protection and internal autonomy over their own lands and people. While under British rule in the nineteenth century these emirates were called the Trucial States. Over time the various sheikdoms, which included the seven UAE emirates as well as Bahrain and Qatar, came to be called the Federation of Arab Emirates. In 1968 Britain announced it would be removing its military forces from the area. When the British left in 1971, Bahrain and Qatar declared their independence. The remaining emirates came to organize themselves as the United Arab Emirates.

The UAE's first president was Abu Dhabi's leader, Sheikh Zayed bin Sultan al-Nahyan (1918–2004). He ruled until his death in 2004, when his son Sheikh Khalifa bin Zayed al-Nahyan (1948–) was chosen by the rulers of the seven emirates to take his place.

Government Structure

The UAE is a federation composed of seven autonomous city-states, each with a hereditary ruler. Those seven rulers, called the Federal Supreme Council (FSC), are responsible for creating and supervising UAE policies, laws, and the federation's budget. The seven members of the FSC elect from among themselves a president and a vice president, each of whom serves for five years. Since 2004, the UAE's president, its chief of state, has been Sheikh Khalifa ibn Zayid al-Nahyan of Abu Dhabi. The vice president and prime minister is Sheikh Muhammad bin Rashid al-Maktoum (1949–) of Dubayy.

Upon the formation of the UAE in 1971, an interim constitution was created. That constitution was reaffirmed every five years, over the next twenty-five years, until it was made permanent in 1996. Under the constitution, the seven rulers of the FSC also appoint a Council of Ministers, which has budgetary and legislative responsibilities. That council shares its work with the forty members of the Federal National Council (twenty members appointed by the FSC and twenty elected to two-year terms) as well as with the citizen-run National Consultative Council. However, the FNC and NCC do not possess authority to enact laws.

Although there are elective seats on the Federal National Council, in 2006 the UAE's electorate amounted to just 6,689 Emiratis (including 1,189 women) who are appointed by the rulers of the seven emirates. (That is roughly 1 percent of the UAE's Emirati citizenry.) In that year's elections, 456 candidates including 65 women ran for 20 contested FNC seats; one woman from Abu Dhabi won a seat.

Although the UAE is a federated nation, each emirate retains significant autonomy. The rulers of each emirate hold power based on their family history and, in keeping with tribal traditions, citizens in each emirate can communicate directly with their rulers. The evolution of the local governments in each emirate from a traditional to modern structure varies depending upon its local ruler. Under the constitution, each emirate reserves considerable powers, including control over mineral rights (oil) and revenues. Such local authority means that laws and practices can differ greatly between regions of the UAE.

A federal court system introduced in 1971 applies to all emirates except Dubayy and Ra's al Khaymah. The Federal Supreme Court is made up of a president and up to five judges, each appointed by the UAE's president with approval of the Federal Supreme Council. The judiciary is considered to be independent of the executive and legislative branches. All emirates have secular courts to adjudicate criminal charges, civil, and commercial disputes and Islamic courts to review family and religious matters. There are no jury trials.

Political Parties and Factions

As the leaders of the country are the hereditary rulers of each emirate, the United Arab Emirates has no national elections or official political parties or organizations.

The people of the United Arab Emirates are called Emirati(s) and the official language is Arabic, with English often being used as a second language. Islam is the state religion, with the population of Sunni Muslims (96 percent of the population) vastly exceeding that of Shia Muslims and other religions. Unlike in many other Muslim countries, where alcohol is prohibited, all but one of the emirates (Ash Sharjah) does allow alcohol consumption by non-Muslims. Although the UAE is very modern and in many aspects westernized, the emirates are religiously conservative about public behavior, especially between the sexes, and most locals still dress in traditional clothing.

In 2007 the population of the UAE was believed to be about 4,400,000, with less than a quarter of the population being native Emiratis, and as such UAE citizens. Due to an influx of labor for the country's many construction projects and the domestic needs of its many wealthy households, the vast majority of the UAE population consists of less wealthy Arabs—Palestinians, Egyptians, Jordanians, Yemenis, Omanis—as well as many Iranians, Pakistanis, Indians, Bangladeshis, Afghanis, Filipinos, and Eastern Europeans.

Major Events

Since the discovery of oil in the UAE in the late 1930s, and its commercialization after World War II, the UAE has been transformed from an impoverished region of small desert principalities into a modern nation with an extremely high standard of living. Prior to being an oil exporter, the UAE's economy was dependent on pearling, fishing, farming, and herding. Since the rise of oil prices in the 1970s, the petroleum industry has dominated the economy. The UAE has huge proven oil reserves and is estimated to be the sixth-largest oil exporter in the world.

Twenty-First Century

After the terrorist attacks against the United States on September 11, 2001, the U.S. government froze the

Immigrant workers lining up for work in Dubayy, 2005. The United Arab Emirates' economy is driven by foreign labor. © *CAREN FIROUZI/ Reuters/Corbis*

bank assets of nations and individuals believed to have assisted in the attacks or of funding terrorist activities. As a banking hub for the Middle East, many UAE financial institutions fell under international scrutiny. However, when the United States launched its assault against Iraq in 2003, the UAE permitted the U.S. military to station troops and operations within the emirates.

Even though the UAE has huge amounts of oil, the nation is diversifying its economy so as not to be entirely dependent on petrodollars. The UAE aspires to create a sophisticated service economy and become a leader in Islamic and international finance. Abu Dhabi and Dubayy are growing cities, each busy with construction projects of architecturally distinctive hotels, high-rise towers, and luxury waterfront communities geared toward wealthy residents and tourists. Abu Dhabi is working to transform itself into a destination for arts and culture in the Middle East, and its government has secured the rights to open branches of Paris's Louvre Museum and New York's Guggenheim Museum as part

of a development project called the Cultural District of Saadiyat Island ("Island of Happiness").

While many of the UAE's regional neighbors suffer from war, religious conflict, and extreme poverty, Emiratis shop in high-end, air-conditioned, western-style malls with designer boutiques. They can also ski at an indoor ski lodge (complete with manufactured snow) and cool off in a massive water amusement park. The UAE has been compared to Las Vegas, without the gambling.

In 2006 legislation was approved by the UAE's Cabinet to address the problem of human trafficking. In part due to its expansive growth, the United Arab Emirates is a destination country for adults and children trafficked from Asia, Eastern Europe, Africa, and poorer Middle Eastern nations for involuntary servitude and sexual exploitation. Many other underprivileged people who come for what they believe are legitimate jobs have been imprisoned by their employers or have had their passports confiscated. In a related measure, the practice of using children as camel jockeys was outlawed in 2005.

In its 2006–07 sessions, the National Consultative Council passed advisory recommendations relating to religious leadership, environmental protection, health and safety standards, and infrastructure improvements. The Cabinet ministers remained focused on six areas outlined in a government strategy developed in December 2005 that established goals and initiatives in such areas as social development, economic development, government sector development, justice and safety, infrastructure, and rural development.

BIBLIOGRAPHY

Davidson, Christopher M. *The United Arab Emirates: A Study in Survival.* Boulder, CO: Lynne Rienner Publishers, 2005.

Rugh, Andrea B. *The Political Culture of Leadership in the United Arab Emirates.* Basingstoke, England: Palgrave Macmillan, 2002.

UAE Ministry of Information and Culture. *United Arab Emirates Yearbook 2007.* http:www.uaeinteract.com (accessed August 15, 2007).

⊕ Bangladesh

Type of Government

The 1972 constitution of Bangladesh created a parliamentary democracy based in part on the British, or Westminster, model of parliament. As such, many British customs and procedures are incorporated into the structure of government and rules of the legislature. A president presides as head of state but plays a mostly ceremonial role. Ruling power resides with the prime minister, who is head of government with extensive administrative responsibilities. Although the Westminster model usually provides for two houses of parliament, the Bangladeshi parliament has only one house of elected representatives.

Background

Bangladesh is in South Asia, bordered by India and Myanmar. Slightly smaller than the state of Iowa (55,598 square miles), it has been known in other eras as East Bengal and East Pakistan. When the country gained independence from Pakistan in 1971, it embraced the name People's Republic of Bangladesh.

The area that is now Bangladesh has been home to various civilizations since at least the fourth century BC. It was part of the Hindu Maurya Empire that reached its height about 207 BC. Hinduism remained the dominant religion until around 1200 AD, when Muslim invaders established political control over the region. Islam took a firm hold with the presence of Turkish, Persian, and Afghan invaders during the thirteenth and fourteenth centuries. Eighty-eight percent of the populace now adheres to Islam.

French and British East India companies arrived in the region called Bengal in the early eighteenth century.

The British eventually established firm control and created the Bengal Presidency as part of their colonial empire in India. Hindus and Muslims began to resent both the British and each other in the late nineteenth century. To improve administration and placate the Muslims, the British decided to split the large Bengal Presidency in two in 1905. The Muslim areas of eastern Bengal and Assam became a separate province, but were reunited only six years later after increased violence plagued the region.

In 1936 the idea of a separate Muslim state again gained popularity. By 1947 the British split the region into religious provinces. Hindu India became flanked by the Muslim states of Pakistan to the west and Bengal, renamed East Pakistan, to the east. Although separated by a thousand miles of Indian territory, both Muslim states were to be overseen by the governing powers of Pakistan. From that moment in 1947 until 1971, when Bangladesh gained independence, the relationship between the two halves of Pakistan was challenged by political instability and economic differences. Linguistic, cultural, and ethnic differences also caused estrangement and resentment between them, especially among the people of East Pakistan being ruled from afar.

During a time of martial law in 1971, civil disobedience and violence with the army in East Pakistan led the Pakistani president to postpone the session of parliament. In response, civil war broke out, and Bengali nationalists declared their region to be the independent People's Republic of Bangladesh. By the end of 1971 India intervened, and the independent state of Bangladesh was born.

Bangladesh adopted a constitution that established a parliamentary democracy. Four principles guided its formation: nationalism, secularism, socialism, and democracy. Bangladesh is one of the few democracies in the Muslim world. An amendment in 1988 replaced the guiding principle of secularism with Islam as the state religion. Constitutional government has been suspended several times throughout much political turmoil since independence.

Government Structure

Bangladesh gained independence from Pakistan in 1971 and established a constitution by 1972. Since then the constitution has been modified by amendments in 1974, 1979, 1986, 1988, 1991, 1996, and 2004. The constitution provides a parliamentary democracy with three branches of government.

The executive branch of government has two leaders, a president and a prime minister. The president is elected by parliament every five years and can serve no more than two terms. The president's role is mostly ceremonial. A 1996 constitutional amendment, however, created a unique structure for the transfer of power at the end of a prime minister's term. At such time a

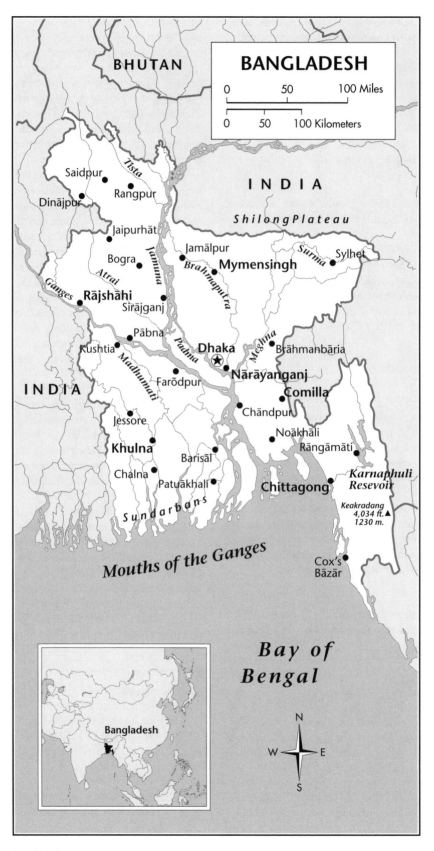

Bangladesh. *Maryland Cartographics*

caretaking government relieves the outgoing prime minister's government, oversees elections within ninety days, and assists in transferring power to the newly elected government. During the caretaking government, the president acquires expanded powers and plays an important role in the transition.

The prime minister is a member of parliament and is appointed by the president based on ability to command the confidence of other members of parliament. Often the leader of the political party with majority representation in parliament is selected to the post. The prime minister is the guiding force for policy in Bangladesh and wields the administrative powers of the government. The prime minister nominates the Cabinet of Ministers for appointment by the president. Ninety percent of the ministers must be members of parliament as well. The ministers serve as the heads of the executive departments of government.

The legislative branch of government is a unicameral parliament (Jatiya Sangsad). It has three hundred members who are elected by universal suffrage at least every five years. In 2004 a constitutional amendment created another forty-five seats to be reserved for women. At the next election these additional seats will be distributed among political parties in proportion to the number of seats they already hold in parliament.

The Bangladeshi Constitution provides an independent judicial system also modeled after the British system. A Low Court and a Supreme Court exist to hear civil and criminal cases. Civil laws include elements of both Hindu and Islamic religious principles relating to various social matters. The Low Court consists of magistrate courts. The Supreme Court has two divisions. The High Court hears original cases as well as reviews cases decided in the Low Court. The Appellate Court hears appeals from the High Court. Trials are public, and citizens have rights of counsel and appeal.

Local governance is provided through six regional divisions of the country, each of which are divided into *zila* (districts). Each zila is composed of *upazila* (subdistricts) or *thana* (police stations). In metropolitan areas, each thana contains divisions of wards and then *mahallas*. In other areas, upazilas and thanas contain unions consisting of multiple villages. Divisions, zilas, and upazilas are overseen by unelected government officials. Municipalities have chairpersons, and cities have mayors who are elected for terms of five years. Elections are held at the union or ward levels for each chairperson and several members of council. Parliamentary action in 1997 assured that in unions, three of every twelve council seats are reserved for women.

Political Parties and Factions

There are more than one hundred political parties in Bangladesh, but only thirty to forty have an active presence, with five wielding the most political power. The

party most in control of the government is the Bangladesh National Party (BNP). It represents conservative, right of center politics. Its main opponent is the Awami League (AL). The AL represents center and center-left politics. The Jatiya Party is another popular party with similarities to both the BNP and the AL. Extreme right views define the Jamaat-e-Islami Party and the Islami Oikyo Jote. Both call for an increased role for Islam in national politics. The extreme left is represented mostly by the Bangladesh Communist Party and by factions of the Jatiyo Samajtantrik Dal advocating revolutionary changes in the government.

There is much intolerance among Bangladeshis with opposing views. Violent demonstrations and enforced strikes pepper the country no matter which party is in power. Opposition parties often organize boycotts of parliamentary sessions or elections. Parties in power take advantage of state resources to suppress opposing voices. They portray opposition activity as anti-state or treasonable. Politically motivated arrests are common.

Major Events

Since Bangladesh acquired independence in 1971, the government has been suspended by coups, martial law, and states of emergency. The first incident occurred in 1975 with the assassination of the president and prime minister, Mujibur Rahman (1920–1975), by a group of military officers. A counter-coup happened three months later, and by 1979 General Ziaur Rahman (1936–1981) had restored a parliamentary government with himself as leader.

Ziaur Rahman was assassinated too, eventually to be replaced by General Hussain Mohammad Ershad (1930–), who declared martial law. Martial law remained until 1986. Elections that year were irregular, ensuring the general his position as president until 1990, when opposition forced his resignation and new elections.

The elections of 1991 provided new hope for the government. After what has been considered one of Bangladesh's fairest elections, the president appointed parliamentary member Begum Khaleda Zia-ur Rahman (known as Khaleda Zia; 1945–) as the country's first female prime minister. By 1994 the government again began to lose support. Opposition parties organized demonstrations, boycotted sessions of parliament, and refused to participate in the elections of 1996. Khaleda Zia resigned under pressure, and parliament was dissolved for elections.

After an interim government oversaw elections, Hasina Wajed (1947–) came to power as the country's second female prime minister. Strikes, protests, and violent demonstrations continued. Violence increased leading up to the 2001 elections. When Wajed handed power to the caretaker government for elections, she became the first prime minister in the country's history to complete the full five-year term.

Bangladeshi founding father Sheikh Mujibur Rahman waving to a crowd after his release from jail in West Pakistan in January 1972. © *David Kennerly/CORBIS*

Twenty-First Century

Khaleda Zia regained the seat of prime minister after the elections of 2001. Political violence continued, however, especially as calls grew for Islamic law to be expanded within public life. In January 2007 a state of emergency was declared, and elections were postponed until 2008.

As a result of political corruption and strikes, Bangladesh has been challenged in establishing a strong infrastructure for its economy. Transportation, communication, and power are poorly developed. Rapid population growth, urbanization, underemployment, and food shortages pose further complications. Bangladesh might find some solutions by developing the successful garment industry established in recent years and tapping into the country's natural gas reserves.

Bangladesh confronts the global issues surrounding terrorism. Sitting at the crossroads of South and Southeast Asia, it has potential for terrorist movement and activity within and through its borders. Concerns center particularly around both Indian insurgents and extreme Islamic forces that may use Bangladesh as a convenient gathering point.

BIBLIOGRAPHY

Ahmed, Nizam. *The Parliament of Bangladesh.* London: Ashgate, 2002.

Malhotra, Inder. *Dynasties of India and Beyond: Pakistan, Sri Lanka, Bangladesh.* New Delhi: HarperCollins Publishers India, 2003.

U.S. Department of State, Bureau of South and Central Asian Affairs. "Background Note: Bangladesh." http://www.state.gov/r/pa/ei/bgn/3452.htm (accessed August 23, 2007).

⊕ Commonwealth of the Bahamas

Type of Government

The Bahamas is a parliamentary democracy on the British model. The executive branch is headed by a prime minister who serves as the head of government and a governor general who is head of state. The bicameral parliament is made up of an elected House of Assembly and an appointed Senate, with major legislative functions performed by the former. The independent judiciary includes lower courts, a Supreme Court, and a Court of Appeal.

Background

The Commonwealth of the Bahamas consists of about 700 islands and a further 2,400 islets lying fifty miles off the east coast of Florida. Of these, only about thirty islands are inhabited, with New Providence (seat of the capital, Nassau), being the most important. Other major islands include San Salvador (also once known as Watling's Island), Grand Bahama, the Abacos, Cat Island, and Eleuthera.

Christopher Columbus (1451–1506) visited San Salvador in 1492, after which the Spanish made numerous visits to the island to capture the native Lucayan people for slave labor. The Lucayan population, which was estimated at approximately 40,000 in the early sixteenth century, was completely eliminated within a quarter century of the Spanish arrival on the island. The islands were uninhabited until 1647, when a group of religious exiles from Britain and Bermuda, known as the Eleutherian Adventurers, established a small settlement on the island. Further waves of European immigrants arrived throughout the seventeenth century, many of whom imported slave laborers to the islands.

The archipelago was also used as a base of operation for many privateers, including the notorious Edward Teach, otherwise known as Blackbeard (d. 1718), who preyed on shipping and coastal settlements of the West Indies. Indeed, the Bahamas has had a long history of smuggling, from the days during the U.S. Civil War when Confederate blockade runners operated there, to alcohol smugglers during Prohibition, and as a station in the shipping routes for drug trafficking into the United States. It took a former pirate, Woodes Rogers (c. 1679–

The Bahamian Parliament House in Nassau. © *Mark E. Gibson/CORBIS*

1732), to clear the islands of buccaneers once the British established a crown colony there in 1717.

After the American Revolution, about eight thousand inhabitants of North America (from Florida, the Carolinas, and New York) loyal to England moved with their families and slaves to the Bahamas. These settlers brought farming and shipbuilding skills to the islands. In addition, many fugitive slaves from the United States fled to the islands following the 1834 end of slavery in the British Empire.

The Bahamas remained a British crown colony for two and a half centuries. In the decades before independence, the United Bahamian Party (UBP), which was supported by the white population, dominated the government and economy of the Islands. Increasingly, however, there was a movement to empower the 85 percent of the population that was black, and in 1953 the opposition Progressive Liberal Party (PLP) was formed to give blacks a voice in government. In 1964 the United Kingdom granted the Bahamas self-government, which meant that the country was in control of its domestic politics, while its defense and foreign relations were left to England. The following year a significant event occurred in parliament when, in protest over what he saw as unfair UBP practices, PLP leader Lynden Pindling (1930–2000) threw the golden mace

(the symbol of the House Speaker's authority) out the window of the House of Assembly chamber. This action galvanized the black population, and the PLP won control of the government in 1967 and led the Bahamas to full independence in 1973. Pindling remained in power as prime minister until 1992.

Government Structure

By the terms of the 1973 constitution, the Bahamas is an independent parliamentary democracy in the British Commonwealth. Formally, the country is headed by the British monarch, represented by a governor general. However, actual executive power lies with the prime minister—the leader of the majority party in parliament—and the cabinet.

The bicameral parliament consists of an elected House of Assembly and an appointed Senate. The forty members of the House of Assembly stand for election every five years (or earlier if the prime minister calls for elections) by popular vote. The Bahamas has universal adult suffrage for those eighteen and older. The major work of legislation is done by the House of Assembly. The sixteen members of the Senate are appointed by the governor general—nine on the advice of the prime minister, four on the advice of the opposition leader, and three on the advice of both the prime minister and leader of the opposition.

To manage local government issues, there are twenty-one administrative districts. Each of these is headed by a commissioner who answers to the national minister of local government.

The legal system is based on British common law. There is a right to be brought before a magistrate within forty-eight hours, a right to bail, a presumption of innocence, and a right to appeal. Magistrates' courts form the lowest level of courts in the country. Above these are the Supreme Courts in Nassau and Freeport, composed of a chief justice, two senior justices, and six justices, and the Court of Appeal, with three judges. Appointments to the high courts are made by the governor general in consultation with the Judicial and Legal Services Commission. Though other Caribbean nations voted to join the Caribbean Court of Justice as the last court of appeal, the Bahamas still refers such cases to the Privy Council of the United Kingdom. Capital punishment is in effect in the Bahamas.

Political Parties and Factions

Though several major parties operate in the country, the Bahamas essentially functions as a two-party system. The populist and liberal Progressive Liberal Party (PLP) and the center-right Free National Movement Party (FNM) are the major parties. Other minor parties include the liberal populist Bahamas Democratic Movement (BDM) and the liberal Coalition for Democratic Reform (CDR).

Formed in 1953, the PLP was in the forefront of the independence movement. Under Lynden Pindling, the party held power from 1967 to 1992, and regained power in 2002. That year, under the leadership of Perry Christie (1943–), the PLP won 50.8 percent of the vote and 29 seats in the forty-member legislature.

The PLP's main rival, the FNM, was formed from two earlier parties. First was the white-dominated United Bahamian Party (UBP), which had controlled the country from 1958 to 1967. Second was a splinter group to the PLP, the Free Progressive Liberal Party, which was to the right of the PLP leadership on many issues. These two merged to form the FNM, a socially liberal but economically conservative party. In the 1992 elections, led by Hubert Ingraham (1947–), the FNM took the majority of seats in the House of Assembly and held power for the next ten years.

The BDM is a liberal, democratic party formed in 1998 whose primary constituency is the disenfranchised youth living on the islands, which comprised more than 60 percent of the population in the 1990s. Its leaders made news with high-profile protests: chaining themselves to the symbolic mace in the House of Assembly in 2001, and then barring the entry of Prime Minister Perry Christie to the House of Assembly in 2005.

Major Events

Tourism and foreign investment became the major economic sectors in the Bahamas following independence. True to its former smuggling and privateering history, the islands, by the early 1980s, had also become a major center for the drug trade, with an estimated 80 percent of the cocaine reaching the United States having passed through the archipelago. The government of the Bahamas took measures to curb this illegal trade, and by 2003 this number had dropped to 10 to 15 percent. With its financial sector growing, the Bahamas also came under increasing international scrutiny for money laundering in its offshore banking sector.

This reputation for drug trafficking, along with an increasing crime rate, did damage to the country's tourist industry. In September 1999, Hurricane Floyd did extensive damage in the Abacos and Eleuthera, causing a significant dip in tourism revenues.

With the transfer of power to the FNM in 1992, Prime Minister Hubert Ingraham promised to focus on job creation. He also began a strenuous effort at privatization of national industries. During Ingraham's administration, a stock exchange, Bahamas International Securities Exchange, officially opened in 1999.

Twenty-First Century

The major challenge to the Bahamas in the twenty-first century is economic diversification. Tourism provides 40 percent of the nation's total GDP, tourism-related jobs employ roughly 50 percent of the workforce in the country, and nearly 90 percent of tourists to the Bahamas come from the United States. As a result, a downturn in the U.S. economy can directly and immediately affect the Bahamas. In an attempt to diversify, the government has reached out to countries such as China, opening an embassy in Beijing in 2006.

The financial sector of the Bahamas accounts for 15 percent of the nation's GDP. Since 2000 the government has been taking more active measures against money laundering by reducing its banking secrecy laws, thereby allowing other jurisdictions to track funds obtained illegally.

Privatization of state industries has continued under the PLP since 2002, with the selling of the country's airline, Bahamasair, and half of the Bahamas Telecommunications Corporation.

BIBLIOGRAPHY

Craton, Michael, and Gail Saunders. *Islanders in the Stream: A History of the Bahamian People.* Athens, GA: University of Georgia Press, 1992.

Government of the Bahamas. http://www.bahamas.gov.bs/bahamasweb2/home.nsf (accessed April 30, 2007).

Johnson, Howard. *The Bahamas: From Slavery to Servitude, 1783–1933.* Gainesville, FL: University Press of Florida, 1996.

⊕ Grenada

Type of Government

Grenada is a parliamentary democracy with an executive branch consisting of a governor general who is head of state and a prime minister who is the head of government. The legislative branch is bicameral, consisting of an appointed Senate and a House of Representatives whose members are elected every five years. The third branch of government is an independent judiciary.

Background

First named Concepción by Christopher Columbus (1451–1506) when he sighted the island in 1498, by the eighteenth century the island had changed its name to Grenada. Carib Indians had killed the original Arawak inhabitants by Columbus's time; they continued to control the island until French settlers seized the island in 1672, using the safe harbor that eventually became St. George's. The French ruled the island until the late eighteenth century, when it was ceded to Great Britain. It became a Crown colony a century later.

During the nineteenth century, sugar cane provided the major export crop. African slaves were brought in to work the plantations. A major slave revolt erupted in 1795, and the slave trade was made illegal in 1834 throughout the British Empire. Sugar production fell off accordingly, but by this time the island was already diversifying its agriculture, becoming a major source for nutmeg and cocoa. This decreased the importance of the large sugar cane estates and created a new middle-class of prosperous farmers.

In the nineteenth century Grenada was incorporated into the British Windward Islands Administration, and was governed on this basis until independence. By the mid-twentieth century, a labor movement had come to prominence in Grenada that also began demanding independence from England. Eric Matthew Gairy (1922–1997) founded the Grenada United Labour Party (GULP) in 1950, and became one of the strongest voices on the island for independence. In 1967 Grenada received full internal autonomy as an associate state of Great Britain, while foreign policy remained directed by the British government in London. Grenada was granted full independence on February 7, 1974, whereupon Gairy became the country's first prime minister.

Gairy proved to be erratic as a leader, cracking down on labor unions and being widely accused of human rights abuses via a secret police force. While he was out of the country in 1979, he was overthrown in a coup led by Maurice Bishop (1944–1983), leader of the New Jewel Movement, a Marxist group with ties to the Cuban leader Fidel Castro (1926–). Bishop became prime minister of the People's Revolutionary Government and did not allow elections. He in turn was killed in a coup by more hard-line Marxists on October 19, 1983. This was followed by a U.S.-led invasion to restore order and rid the country of Cuban troops. In 1984 the country returned to its earlier constitution.

Government Structure

Grenada is an independent parliamentary democracy within the Commonwealth of Nations (also called the British Commonwealth), a voluntary association of more than fifty countries that are former colonies or territories of the British Empire. It recognizes the British monarch as its head of state, represented locally by a governor-general whose role is largely ceremonial. Real executive power is wielded by a prime minister and a cabinet chosen from the majority party in parliament (but technically appointed by the governor-general).

The parliament is bicameral, made up of the House of Representatives and the Senate. The fifteen members of the House are elected every five years by universal suffrage among those age eighteen and older. Called the lower house, the House of Representatives conducts the majority of legislative tasks. The thirteen members of the Senate are appointed: ten by the prime minister and three by the leader of the opposition. The Senate's role is more advisory.

For administrative purposes, the main island is divided into six parishes—Saint Andrew, Saint David, Saint George, Saint John, Saint Mark, and Saint Patrick. In addition, Grenada includes a dependency comprising the neighboring islands of Carriacou and Petite Martinique.

The independent judiciary is based on English common law and statutes passed by the House of Representatives. The law provides for the right to a fair public trial, to a presumption of innocence, to remain silent, and to seek the advice of an attorney. The judicial system consists of magistrates' courts and the Court of Magisterial Appeal. Higher appeals go to the Eastern Caribbean Supreme Court, also known as the Supreme Court of Grenada and the West Indies Associated States. The final court of appeal is to the Caribbean Court of Justice in Trinidad.

Political Parties and Factions

Operating within a multi-party framework, Grenada has two dominant parties: the conservative New National Party (NNP) and the liberal National Democratic Congress (NDC). Minor parties include the left-leaning Maurice Bishop Patriotic Movement (MBMP) and the right wing, populist Grenada United Labour Party, which was founded in 1950 by Gairy. Both of these latter parties garnered only a single-digit percentage of votes in the 2003 elections, and neither won seats in parliament.

U.S. Marines landing on Grenada as part of a military intervention in 1983. © *Shepard Sherbell/CORBIS SABA*

The National Democratic Congress came to power in the wake of the U.S.-led invasion, when its leader, Nicholas Brathwaite (1925–), was appointed prime minister. However, the NDC lost the 1984 elections; Brathwaite served again as prime minister from 1990 to 1995, after which he retired from office.

Founded in 1984, the New National Party was the result of a four-way merger of smaller parties. Led by Herbert Blaize (1918–1989), the NNP soundly won the 1984 elections, and Blaize stayed in power until his death. Keith Mitchell (1946–) thereafter took over the party leadership, and led his party to majorities in 1994, 1999, and 2003.

Major Events

Order was quickly restored in Grenada following the U.S. invasion in October 1983, with free elections once again held in 1984 and the 1974 constitution restored. Shortly thereafter, all foreign troops left the island. Since the mid-1990s Grenada has been led by the free-market-oriented NNP. Ten years after the U.S. invasion, tourist arrivals in Grenada had grown by more than 300 percent and an international airport, Point Salines, had opened. In 1998 Castro arrived in Grenada for his first state visit

since 1983. During his stay he signed an economic agreement with Prime Minister Mitchell's government.

Grenada has, in addition to tourism and the cultivation of nutmeg, developed its financial services industry. Its offshore banking services have led to its being listed, in 2001 and 2002, as a tax haven by the Organization for Economic Cooperation and Development. Also, the collapse of the country's largest offshore bank, First International, and the suspension of several other banks' licenses pending a probe into financial irregularities, have led to further problems in that industry. Only five of the thirty-six banks in operation in 2001 remained in operation in 2003.

The country attempted to put its bloody history to rest by the establishment, in 2000, of a Truth and Reconcilement Commission to investigate crimes from the end of Gairy's rule through the Bishop regime. In 2006 the commission recommended new trials for those convicted of Bishop's murder.

The country is also prone to the vicissitudes of weather. In September 2004 Hurricane Ivan struck Grenada, killing scores of people and leaving more than two-thirds of the population homeless. About 90 percent of all buildings on the island were damaged in some way. The following year Hurricane Emily struck, causing an estimated $175 million in damage and destroying 90 percent of the recently planted banana crop.

Twenty-First Century

Tourism on the island has been in decline in the twenty-first century. The combination of a downturn in international tourism following the terrorist attacks of September 11, 2001, and a rise in crime rates in Grenada has produced sizeable shortfalls in that once lucrative segment of the economy.

Grenada is therefore attempting to diversify its economy, one of the largest challenges to the country's ongoing stability in the twenty-first century. Since 2001 Grenada has been attempting to foster foreign investment in the tourism, technology, and communications industries. In addition, the government has been placing emphasis on developing such ocean tourism sectors as yachting, scuba diving, and other recreational activities.

BIBLIOGRAPHY

Government of Grenada. http://www.gov.gd (accessed August 31, 2007).

Schoenhals, Kai P. *Grenada*. Santa Barbara, CA: Clio, 1990.

Steele, Beverley A. *Grenada: A History of Its People*. Oxford, UK: Macmillan Caribbean, 2003.

⊕ Guinea-Bissau

Type of Government

Guinea-Bissau is a parliamentary republic with a president who acts as head of state and a prime minister who functions as head of government. The legislative branch is the unicameral Assembleia Nacional Popular (National People's Assembly), whose one hundred members are elected by popular vote. The judicial branch is headed by a Supreme Court made up of nine judges who are appointed by the president.

Background

Formerly known as Portuguese Guinea, Guinea-Bissau is located on the western coast of Africa, bordered by Senegal to the north and Guinea to the east and south. Once the kingdom of Gabú, which was a part of the Mali Empire, by the mid sixteenth century Gabú was an independent state and Portuguese traders had begun to make inroads. In 1630 the Portuguese government established a colonial administration to supervise the territory, then called Portuguese Guinea.

The Portuguese used Portuguese Guinea as a staging ground for the exportation of African slaves to the New World. The modern capital, Bissau, was founded in the eighteenth century as a military and slave-trading center. With the decline of the slave trade in the nineteenth century, Bissau became the economic capital of the colony and in 1941 was designated as the adminis-

trative capital. During that time the Portuguese began exploring the interior, extending the borders of their colony to the east. Some tribes in the interior resisted the Portuguese occupation; it was not until almost the onset of World War I (1914–1918) that resistance was quelled and the current borders were established. After World War II, the colony was designated as a province of Portugal.

Four years later armed rebellion against the Portuguese occupation broke out. The Partido Africano de Independência da Guiné e Cabo Verde (African Party for Independence of Guinea-Bissau and Cape Verde; PAIGC), a guerilla band seeking independence for both Portuguese Guinea and another Portuguese colony, the offshore archipelago of Cape Verde, began an insurgency supported by arms from Cuba, China, and the Soviet Union. Led by Amilcar Cabral (1921–1973), the PAIGC managed to control most of the countryside by 1973, and the Portuguese were largely confined to towns and barracks. Cabral was assassinated in 1973, and leadership of the Guinea-Bissau branch of the PAIGC fell to his half-brother, Luis Cabral (1931–). The PAIGC declared independence on September 24, 1973. Following a military coup in Portugal in 1974, Portuguese Guinea was granted its independence as the Republic of Guinea-Bissau, with the name of the capital added to prevent confusion with its neighbor, the Republic of Guinea. A constitution was promulgated and Luis Cabral became the country's first president.

Government Structure

Guinea-Bissau's constitution, which has been amended several times, provides for a multiparty republican democracy. The president, who is head of state, is elected by universal suffrage for a five-year term with no term limits. In consultation with party leaders in the legislature, the president appoints a prime minister who is head of government; the prime minister in turn appoints a council of ministers. The prime minister can be replaced by a no-confidence vote in the legislature.

The unicameral legislature is the National People's Assembly, whose 102 members are elected to five-year terms. Two Assembly seats, which have been reserved for Guinea-Bissau citizens living overseas, are chosen by nationals living in Africa and Europe, but these were not filled in the 2004 elections.

The judicial branch of government is based on French law but also accepts the jurisdiction of the International Court of Justice. The lowest level of court for minor civil cases and misdemeanors is the Sectoral Court; there are twenty-four of these throughout the country. More serious criminal cases and civil cases of more than one thousand dollars go to one of the nine Regional Courts. The final court of appeal for both civil and criminal cases is the Supreme Court.

Local government is administered through the country's nine regions: Bafatá, Biombo, Bissau, Bolama, Cacheu, Gabú, Oio, Quinara, and Tombali. Each is governed by a regional council.

Political Parties and Factions

Before 1991 PAIGC was the only legal political party in Guinea-Bissau. However, with constitutional amendments allowing for a multiparty system, many parties have taken root. The PAIGC continues to be one of the most important, but the Partido da Renovação Social (Party for Social Renewal; PRS), has become a major opposition party, as has the Partido Unido Social Democrático (United Social Democratic United Party; PUSD). The Resistência da Guiné-Bissau-Movimento Bafatá (Resistance of Guinea-Bissau-Bafatá Movement; RGB-MB) also proved to be a strong opposition party in the 1990s but did not field a presidential candidate in 2005.

As noted, the PAIGC was founded in 1956 as a resistance movement against Portuguese rule. Once armed struggle was at an end in 1974, the PAIGC turned to a political role. It was the ruling party in Guinea-Bissau from independence until 2000, first under Luis Cabral and then under João Bernardo Vieira (1939–). The PAIGC returned to majority status in the legislature in the 2004 elections, but lost the 2005 presidential election to former president Vieira, who ran as an independent candidate. However, internal disputes caused the PAIGC to lose its parliamentary majority in 2005 when several members of the National People's Assembly quit the PAIGC.

The PRS was founded in 1992 by Kumba Yala (1953–), formerly a member of the PAIGC. Yala ran in the 1994 presidential elections but lost to Vieira. His party took twelve seats in the National People's Assembly. In 1999, following a coup that unseated Vieira, Yala again ran for president, this time defeating the PAIGC candidate, Malam Bacai Sanhá (1947–), who had been acting president. The PRS and its ally, RGB-MB, dominated Yala's cabinet. Yala was also victim of a coup, in 2003, but ran again for president in 2005, losing to Vieira.

In 2007 the PAIGC and the PRS joined with the PUSD and several other smaller parties to form a new government by unseating the former prime minister with a vote of no-confidence. The PUSD, a moderate political party, gained two ministerial posts in the new government.

Major Events

With the first post-independence elections, held in 1977, an overwhelming majority of the population voted for the PAIGC list of candidates. Luis Cabral was reelected president of Guinea-Bissau, and João Bernardo Vieira was confirmed as the nation's vice president. Cabral ruled until 1980, when he was deposed in a

military coup headed by Vieira. He ruled for four years with a Revolutionary Council composed of nine military officers and four civilian advisers. Then, in 1984, Vieira restored the civilian government and re-established the National People's Assembly, but made the PAIGC the only legal political party. Vieira survived three coup attempts, in 1983, 1985, and 1993.

After ruling Guinea-Bissau as a one-party state for a decade, Vieira denounced such single-party rule as undemocratic and repressive. In April 1991 Guinea-Bissau formally allowed other political parties to form. Despite such party competition, the PAIGC and Vieira maintained control of the country until 1998, when a violent military uprising was staged to protest Vieira's firing of one of the top military commanders, Brigadier General Ansumane Mané. About 300,000 residents of the capital city, Bissau, were forced to flee from the conflict. A ceasefire was negotiated but did not hold. Vieira finally called in help from neighboring Senegal and Guinea, a highly unpopular move that led to him being ousted from power in 1999. The nineteen years of his rule have been criticized as a period of little or no economic or political advancement for Guinea-Bissau. During this period the country remained one of the poorest in the world. However, in 1997, the country did join the Union Economique et Monétaire Ouest-Africaine (Economic Union of West Africa; UEMOA).

Following the Vieira coup, Guinea-Bissau was ruled by the military for a brief time, and a peacekeeping force from the Economic Community of West African States Monitoring Group (ECOMOG), was established in the country. Free elections in 2000 brought Kumba Yala of the PRS to power. Yala faced immense difficulties coming to office. There were still thousands of displaced persons in the country as a result of the recent fighting; in addition, a former leader of the military insurgency that unseated Vieira, General Mané, declared the presidential election fraudulent, which led to a divide between the government and the military from the outset of Yala's presidency. Mané was killed in 2000 in a shootout with government forces. Following this crisis, the Yala government was again in difficulties over the dismissal of three Supreme Court judges, an act criticized by the domestic opposition and by international observers. The National People's Assembly cast a no-confidence vote on the president, and Yala reacted by threatening to close the legislative body. In 2002 parliament was dissolved and new elections were scheduled, but they were postponed several times. The situation was further exacerbated when Yala fired the defense minister in 2003, straining the already poor relations between him and the military.

In September 2003 Yala was deposed in a bloodless military coup. A transitional government was again established, but various military factions mutinied in 2004, adding to the country's instability. Finally, presidential elections were held in 2005. Seventeen candidates ran for office; Yala

Rebels standing in front of the burned-out remains of the presidential palace in Bissau after the 1999 coup that toppled João Bernardo Vieira. © *Tiago Petinga/epa/Corbis*

was again the PRS candidate, while former president Vieira returned from six years of exile in Portugal, ran as an independent, and won with 55 percent of the vote.

In the spring of 2006, Guinea-Bissau was dealing with the threat of rebel activities on the border with Senegal. Troops from Guinea-Bissau became engaged in fighting with hard-line factions of the Casamance Movement of Democratic Forces (MFDC), a secessionist movement in Senegal whose bases of operation have spilled over into Guinea-Bissau.

Twenty-First Century

Guinea-Bissau's government has seen three military coups since 1974, and the danger of military intervention in politics continues. With an economy primarily dependent on agriculture, Guinea-Bissau is listed by the United Nations as one of the ten poorest countries in the world. Political instability has contributed to the government's inability to enhance the nation's infrastructure and public services.

On the international level, thousands of Senegalese refugees from Senegal's Casamance region fled into Guinea-Bissau in 2006 to escape political turmoil and violence. The presence of Senegalese refugees has highlighted the inefficiencies of the government's aid programs and has led to an increase in crime and violence along the Senegal border. Relations between Guinea-Bissau and Senegal have suffered from disputes over the disposition of the refugee population.

BIBLIOGRAPHY

Forrest, Joshua. *Guinea-Bissau: Power, Conflict, and Renewal in a West African Nation.* Boulder, CO: Westview Press, 1992.

Galli, Rosemary. *Guinea-Bissau.* Santa Barbara, CA: Clio, 1990.

Lobban, Richard, and Peter Karibe Mendy. *Historical Dictionary of the Republic of Guinea-Bissau*, 3rd ed. Lanham, MD: Scarecrow Press, 1997.

⊕ Palestine

Type of Government

Palestine is the historical name for a disputed territory that roughly comprises the current state of Israel, which acquired much of the territory when it became a state in 1948. The term "Palestinian" refers to the Muslim and Christian Arabs who inhabited the region before 1948. There are two main governments associated with the Palestinian people, many of whom dispersed to other countries when Israel became a state. The Palestine Liberation Organization (PLO) is the body recognized internationally as the representative of all Palestinians, in and out of Israel. The Palestinian National Authority is a parliamentary democracy authorized by Israel to govern Palestinian communities living in Israel in parts of the West Bank and the Gaza Strip.

Background

Egypt ruled the Canaanites in the region that is now Palestine from the sixteenth century BC to the twelfth century BC. The end of Egyptian rule coincided with the permanent settlement of Israelites, Hebrews, Philistines, and others, who warred with each other. The kingdom of Israel triumphed for a time until it fell to the Assyrians in the eighth century BC, at which point Israel ceased to exist. For the next seven centuries the region was controlled by Assyrians, Babylonians, the Persian Empire, Macedonia, the Egyptian Ptolemaic dynasty, and then the Seleucid kingdom. In history's first diaspora of Jews from their homeland, the Babylonians forced the Jews to leave the region, called Judaea, in 586 BC.

When the Roman Republic conquered the Seleucid kingdom, Pompey the Great (106 BC–48 BC) organized the government for the region that is now Palestine in 67 BC. The Roman Republic and then the Roman Empire and Byzantine Empire ruled until about 636 AD. The life of Jesus Christ (c. 6 BC–c. 30 AD) gave the region great importance to Christians. In 136 AD, history's second Jewish diaspora occurred when the Roman Empire exiled Jews from Jerusalem.

Palestine fell to Muslim invaders between 636 and 640 AD. Except for an interim when Christian crusaders invaded during the twelfth century, the region was ruled by a series of Muslim dynasties and empires, ending with the Ottoman Empire from 1516 to 1918.

During World War I, British and Allied forces captured Palestine from the Ottomans. At a peace conference in 1920, the Allies awarded Palestine to Great Britain, which governed until 1948. The first half of the twentieth century brought a Jewish movement for reestablishment of an independent Israeli state in their ancient homeland, now Palestine. Jews worked hard to immigrate to Palestine while Palestinian Muslims sought to maintain their dominance through population and land ownership. The Nazi persecution of Jews in Europe quickened their immigration. This led to an Arab revolt in Palestine from 1936 to 1939.

Nazi genocide of Jews during World War II generated international support for creating a homeland for the Jewish people in Palestine. On August 31, 1947, the

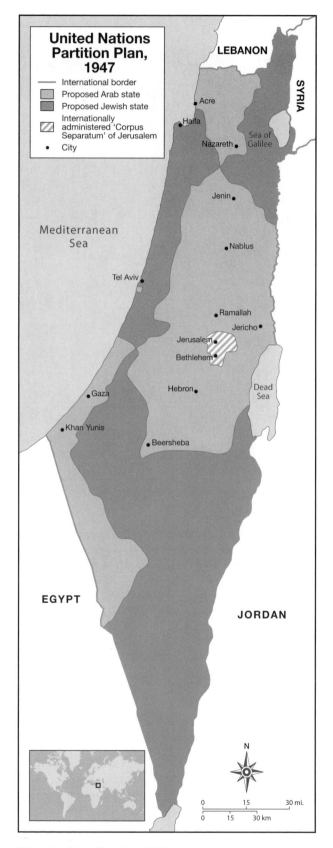

Palestinian Plan of Partition, 1947. *XNR Productions, Inc., Gale, a part of Cengage Learning*

United Nations Special Committee on Palestine recommended that Palestine be partitioned into an Arab state and a Jewish state. Palestinian Jews generally supported the proposal, but Palestinian Arabs generally opposed it, and fighting erupted in Palestine. Unwilling to enforce a disputed plan, Great Britain simply set May 15, 1948, as the date for the end of its control of the region. Israel became an independent state on May 14, 1948. The following day, armies from Egypt, Iraq, Syria, and Transjordan (now Jordan) attacked Israel, which won the war with a peace agreement by the summer of 1949. Transjordan retained the region of Palestine called the West Bank, and Egypt retained the Gaza Strip (though Israel would capture both regions in 1967).

Before Israel became a state, approximately 1.4 million Arabs lived in Palestine. About 150,000 remained in Israel after it became a state. The remainder lived in or fled to the West Bank, Gaza Strip, Lebanon, Jordan, Syria, and other Middle Eastern countries. Hundreds of thousands lived in refugee camps created by the United Nations. In time, dispersed Palestinians formed groups to fight for the destruction of Israel and the return of Palestine to the Arabs.

In 1945 seven states had formed the League of Arab States to coordinate their political and economic activity. At a meeting in Cairo, Egypt, in 1964 the Arab League decided to unite the various Palestinian groups into the Palestine Liberation Organization. The PLO's original charter declared its mission to destroy Israel and to support the rights of Palestinians to return to their homelands.

After decades of fighting, Israel and the PLO met secretly in Oslo, Norway, in January 1993. The Oslo Accords paved the way for them to sign a Declaration of Principles in Washington, D.C., in September 1993. By these agreements, Israel promised to transfer governmental responsibility in the West Bank and the Gaza Strip to the Palestinian National Authority over a period of five years. During that time Israel and the PLO were to negotiate the ultimate political status of those regions. As of 2007, however, they remained under Israeli control.

Government Structure

There are two main governments associated with the Palestinians. The first is the Palestine Liberation Organization. It is the internationally recognized representative of all Palestinians, in and out of Israel. The PLO's members are various Palestinian communities and organizations that formed after the creation of Israel in 1948. While the groups have different ideological foundations, their common goal and that of the PLO is the creation of an independent state of Palestine.

The PLO has a fifteen-member Executive Committee that manages the PLO's activities. The Executive Committee is headed by a chairman, who is the leader of the PLO. The Executive Committee and its chairman are elected by the Palestine National Council, the PLO's quasi-legislative body.

The Palestine National Council is composed of civilian representatives from the various Palestinian groups that are part of the PLO. The first Council had 422 representatives, but the number has increased over time. The Council normally meets once every two years, leaving daily operation of the PLO to the Executive Committee.

The second government associated with the Palestinians is the Palestinian National Authority, or Palestinian Authority. It is a parliamentary democracy that represents Palestinians living in the Israeli-controlled regions of the West Bank and the Gaza Strip. The Palestinian Authority was created in 1994 with Israel's approval. The Basic Law that contains its structure of government was approved by Palestinian President Yasser Arafat (1929–2004) in 2002.

The Basic Law creates a parliamentary democracy with executive, legislative, and judicial branches. The executive branch is led by a president, who is elected by Palestinians in Israel who are at least eighteen years old. The president appoints a prime minister, who in turn forms a cabinet for the executive branch. The president commands the armed forces and proposes and vetoes laws. He cannot be impeached.

The legislative branch of the Palestinian Authority is the Palestinian Legislative Council. It comprises 132 members elected from sixteen constituent Palestinian areas of Israel. Most council members are Muslim, but a small percentage of seats have been reserved for Christian and Samaritan Palestinians. Council members serve five-year terms.

The Basic Law creates a judiciary administered by a High Judicial Council. The judiciary has a Supreme Court and a system of lower courts. The Supreme Court has three components. The High Constitutional Court reviews legislation to ensure it is constitutional. The Court of Cassation decides civil and criminal matters. The High Court of Justice hears cases under administrative law.

Political Parties and Factions

After the creation of Israel in 1948, dozens of Palestinian organizations formed to work for the recovery of Palestine. The PLO gathered many under its leadership in 1964. The most influential has been the Palestinian National Liberation Movement, a center-left organization known as Fatah, which is a reverse acronym of its Arabic name. Fatah is a nationalist organization that embraces ideals of social democracy. The next two most powerful organizations have been the Popular Front for the Liberation of Palestine and the Democratic Front for the Liberation of Palestine, both communist organizations.

President of the Palestinian National Authority Yasser Arafat shaking hands with former U.S. President Jimmy Carter in 1996. © *Gilbert Liz/ CORBIS SYGMA*

The groups that have been most influential in the PLO have also been most prominent in the Palestinian Authority. Fatah, of which Arafat was a member, dominated the Palestinian Legislative Council until 2006. That year the Islamic Resistance Movement, called Hamas for its Arabic acronym, won a majority of seats on the Council.

Major Events

Israel and various Arab states have fought repeatedly since Israel became a state in 1948. During the Six-Day War in 1967, Israel captured the Gaza Strip from Egypt and the West Bank from Jordan. This placed large populations of Palestinians under Israeli control.

In autumn 1974 the UN General Assembly officially recognized the PLO as the representative body for Palestinians and gave it observer status in the United Nations. On November 13, PLO chairman Arafat spoke before the General Assembly to make the case for the rights of the Palestinians. Some countries, including the United States and Israel, continued to refuse to negotiate with the PLO while it supported the destruction of Israel. In March 1977, however, U.S. President Jimmy Carter (1924–) acknowledged the need for Palestinians to have a homeland and to participate in peace talks in the Middle East.

In 1987 a Palestinian uprising known as the *intifada* erupted in the West Bank and the Gaza Strip and continued for five years. In December 1988 Arafat announced that the PLO recognized Israel as a state and rejected terrorism. This enabled the U.S. government to negotiate with the PLO. Israel and the PLO officially recognized each other in letters between Arafat and Israeli prime minister Yitzhak Rabin (1922–1995) in 1993.

That year Israel and the PLO held secret meetings in Oslo, Norway, that led to creation of the Palestinian Authority in 1994. Israel agreed to transfer government of the West Bank and the Gaza Strip to the Palestinian Authority between 1994 and 1999, during which time the parties would negotiate the final status of those areas. Israel reserved the right to have military patrols in both regions during the transitional period. The transitional period did not go as planned. Terrorist groups on both sides took steps to derail the peace process, including the assassination of Rabin by an Israeli in 1995. Transfer of control to the Palestinian Authority and withdrawal of Israeli military forces went slower than agreed, and 1999 passed without final resolution.

Twenty-First Century

In July 2000 the United States hosted negotiations between Israel and the Palestinians, which failed. Soon another intifada erupted in the occupied territories, and in 2002 Israel resumed control there.

In 2005 Israel withdrew from parts of the West Bank and the Gaza Strip. In elections to the Palestinian Legislative Council in 2006, the group Hamas won a majority of seats. Fatah, which had controlled the Council previously, formed a coalition government with Hamas. Israel and other countries, however, rejected Hamas as a terrorist organization, and in 2007 fighting erupted between Hamas and Fatah forces in the West Bank and the Gaza Strip, leaving the region's future uncertain.

BIBLIOGRAPHY

Bickerton, Ian J., and Carla L. Klausner. *A History of the Arab-Israeli Conflict*, 5th ed. Upper Saddle River, NJ: Pearson Prentice Hall, 2007.

Sabbagh, Karl. *Palestine: A Personal History*. New York: Grove Press, 2007.

United Nations Development Programme-Programme on Governance in the Arab Region. "Democratic Governance, Arab Countries Profiles, Palestine." http://www.pogar.org/countries/country.asp?cid=14 (accessed August 22, 2007).

⊕ Mozambique

Type of Government

The east African nation of Mozambique is a constitutional republic struggling with the legacy of a prolonged civil war, which lasted from 1977 to 1992.

Background

Roughly the size of Texas and Louisiana combined, Mozambique dominates Africa's southeastern coast, with more than fifteen hundred miles of coastline. Six nations share its interior borders: South Africa and Swaziland, to the southwest; Zimbabwe, to the west; and Malawi, Zambia, and Tanzania, to the north. Despite significant fresh water resources, notably portions of the Zambezi River and Lake Nyasa (also known as Lake Malawi), irrigation is minimal, and a prolonged drought has devastated the subsistence agriculture that sustains the vast majority of the nation's twenty-one million citizens.

Though the Portuguese had established small trading posts there as early as 1498, the region was not formally declared a Portuguese possession until 1885. Independence movements in other colonies after World War II encouraged the development of Mozambican nationalism, and in 1962 a coalition of pro-independence groups formed the Mozambique Liberation Front, or FRE-LIMO, and began a guerilla campaign to force the withdrawal of the Portuguese. Brutal but intermittent fighting lasted more than a decade, with human rights abuses on both sides. Finally, in 1974, a coup in Portugal brought to power a new regime more sympathetic to the rebels' demands. The colonial administration abruptly withdrew, and on June 25, 1975, Portuguese East Africa became the independent nation of Mozambique. FRELIMO immediately took charge, instituting a socialist system and banning opposition groups. The party's authoritarian methods bred widespread resentment, and armed resistance to the new government began in 1977. The principal rebel group, the Mozambique National Resistance (RENAMO), was formed under the direction of the openly racist colonial regime in neighboring Southern Rhodesia (present-day Zimbabwe). Both Southern Rhodesia and, later, South Africa wanted to overthrow FRELIMO because of its strident Marxism and ongoing support of anti-colonial movements across Africa. While their ties to these two nations cast doubt on the motives and sincerity of RENAMO's leaders, the grievances that motivated most of the rank-and-file rebels were undoubtedly genuine.

By the time the General Peace Accord brought an end to the violence in 1992, the losses were staggering, with more than one hundred thousand dead and one million wounded. The displacement of two million farmers devastated food production, while the destruction of roads, railroads, and telephone lines brought communication and transportation nearly to a halt. The result was the further impoverishment of what was already one of the poorest nations in the world. Most Mozambicans now live on the equivalent of less than forty cents a day.

There are signs of progress nevertheless. In 1989 FRELIMO announced its abandonment of several Marxist strategies, notably collective farming, that had clearly failed to raise the standard of living. A new constitution, adopted the following year, mandated a shift to multiparty politics, and international observers certified several subsequent elections as free and fair, though they noted a number of local irregularities.

Government Structure

The 1990 constitution divides executive powers between the president, who serves as chief of state, and the prime minister, who serves as head of government. The president is elected by direct, popular vote for a maximum of two five-year terms. The prime minister is appointed by the president and assisted by the cabinet, known as the Council of Ministers. In addition to overseeing the government's day-to-day operations, the prime minister is responsible for presenting budget and policy proposals to the unicameral legislature, known as the Assembly of the Republic. The Assembly's two hundred and fifty members are chosen by direct, popular vote for five-year

Mozambique's first president, Samora Machel, died in office after a fatal plane crash in 1986.   © *Patrick Durand/CORBIS SYGMA*

terms, though the president may dismiss the current session and call for new elections at any time.

At the head of the judicial branch is the Supreme Court, which serves as the court of final appeal and reviews the constitutionality of legislation. Though the constitution provides for a separate court to adjudicate constitutional issues, such a court does not yet exist. Vacancies on the Supreme Court bench are filled either by presidential appointment or Assembly vote. Many of the nation's lower courts are specialized tribunals; the most important of these is probably the Administrative Court, which oversees the management of government programs and audits state spending. The legal code is a mixture of Portuguese law and local common law.

For administrative purposes, Mozambique is divided into ten provinces, each under an appointed governor. The capital city of Maputo has its own municipal administration. Elected town and district councils assist the provincial administrations in the handling of local affairs.

Political Parties and Factions

With the December 2004 elections, FRELIMO won one hundred and sixty seats in the Assembly, while a coalition dominated by RENAMO took the remaining ninety. A number of smaller parties participated in the vote but failed to win any seats. In the concurrent presidential vote, FRELIMO's Armando Guebuza (1943–) soundly defeated Afonso Dhlakama (1953–), the RENAMO coalition's candidate. The prime minister, FRELIMO's Luisa Diogo (1958–), is probably Africa's most prominent female politician.

In addition to the major political parties, a number of nongovernmental organizations wield considerable influence. Some of these, including the World Bank and the International Monetary Fund (IMF), are global in scope. Others, however, are domestic organizations with limited international contacts. These include the Mozambique League of Human Rights (LDH) and a similar group called Association for Human Rights and Development (HDH). It is noteworthy that the leaders of both are women. One of the few lasting benefits of FRELIMO's Marxist period was the group's willingness to allow women to serve in positions of authority, and the relative prominence of Mozambican women continues.

Major Events

Though many areas of Mozambique remain sparsely settled, there is an acute shortage of arable land. In part, this shortage is simply the result of geography, for much of the available land is too rocky or dry to produce a harvest with the basic tools available to subsistence farmers. Shortsighted decisions, however, have also played a role. One of these was the indiscriminate use of landmines by both government and rebel forces in the civil war. Despite intensive de-mining efforts by the United Nations and other international organizations, it will take decades to find and remove the estimated two million mines still hidden in the ground. In the meantime, farmers are understandably reluctant to cultivate new fields unless these have been professionally cleared. Only a small percentage of the nation's territory now meets that requirement.

The land issue grew more complex in the spring of 2000, when President Guebuza's predecessor, Joaquim Chissano (1939–), who served in that role from 1986 to 2005, made an unexpected announcement. In light of persistent efforts by the government of neighboring Zimbabwe to dispossess white farmers, Chissano said, the government of Mozambique was prepared to offer land grants to those evicted. The evictions were completed shortly thereafter, and at least a few farmers (the precise number is unclear) apparently accepted the offer. In July 2001 the Mozambique News Agency reported that "around" ten farmers from Zimbabwe had produced a harvest in the province of Manica, and that sixty-three more had applied for land. Most Mozambicans were deeply surprised that the proposal was made at all, given both the prominent role white Zimbabweans had played in fomenting Mozambique's civil war and the bleak circumstances of the country's own farmers. Chissano's supporters portrayed the offer as a practical, levelheaded effort to take advantage of foreign capital. Many of his critics, on the other hand, saw it as misguided and insensitive. There are probably elements of truth in each of these interpretations. Chissano is an able and respected politician, who moved easily from the presidency to a new role as the UN Secretary General's special envoy to Uganda. There is a growing consensus, however, that the quest for foreign investment has lured both the Chissano and Guebuza administrations into a number of ill-advised policies.

Twenty-First Century

In June 2007 the United States announced that it would provide $506.9 million in additional aid to Mozambique under a so-called Millennium Challenge Grant. The money is earmarked for clean-water projects, malaria eradication, and road construction. It is only the latest in a wave of donations and other international assistance that began with the establishment of the multiparty system. In 2005, for example, the leaders of the world's eight wealthiest nations (a group known as G-8) named Mozambique as one of eighteen countries to be granted immediate debt relief. The goal of the debt relief program, known as the HIPC (Highly Indebted Poor Countries) Initiative, is to allow poor but deserving nations to spend their tax revenues on health care and other social programs instead of loan repayment.

The aid now flowing to Mozambique is a testament to the nation's political progress since the end of the civil war, for the international community is generally reluctant to provide financial assistance (as opposed to food, medicine, and other humanitarian relief) to particularly brutal, corrupt, mismanaged, or authoritarian regimes. To be included in the HIPC Initiative, for example, beneficiaries must meet relatively stringent standards for good governance and show significant progress toward even higher standards. Enormous problems remain, however, and it is by no means certain that money will cure them. A sudden influx of money, in fact, may make a number of problems, particularly crime, much worse. If the aid donors succeed in their goal of raising living standards, it is likely that the incidence of so-called street crimes like robbery and burglary will indeed decrease. The incidence of embezzlement and other forms of corruption, however, may well increase, as both the opportunities for fraud and the potential profits of that fraud grow rapidly. It is not uncommon in developing nations for poorly paid government officials to "skim off" as much as a third of a grant's total value. While Mozambique has been making some progress in its struggle to discourage such practices, a recent case involving the son of former President Chissano suggests that corruption remains widespread. In May 2006 prosecutors in the capital of Maputo charged Nyimpine Chissano (1970–)—son of former President Chissano—with involvement in the 2000 murder of a journalist, Carlos Cardoso (1952–2000), who had been investigating corruption in the government's sale of the nation's largest bank.

If financial aid is not a cure-all, the question of how best to help the people of Mozambique again becomes an urgent one. There are no clear answers, but many economists are now recommending that donors consider funding thousands of small projects instead of the highly visible but expensive public works projects that have hitherto received most of the available money. The new approach is perhaps best illustrated by the "microcredit" model developed by Muhammad Yunus (1940–), founder of Bangladesh's Grameen Bank and winner of the 2006 Nobel Peace Prize. Microcredit involves lending small sums of money, often to rural women, to finance new businesses.

BIBLIOGRAPHY

Dinerman, Alice. *Revolution, Counter-Revolution and Revisionism in Post-Colonial Africa: The Case of Mozambique, 1975–1994.* London: Routledge, 2006.

Law and Justice in a Multicultural Society: The Case of Mozambique. Boaventura de Sousa Santos, João Carlos Trindade, and Maria Paula G. Meneses, editors. Dakar, Senegal: Council for the

Development of Social Science Research in Africa, 2006.

Nuvunga, Adriano. *Multiparty Democracy in Mozambique: Strengths, Weaknesses and Challenges.* Johannesburg: EISA, 2005.

⊕ Cape Verde

Type of Government

Cape Verde is a constitutional, multiparty democracy. The president is the head of state and is elected by popular vote for a five-year term. The prime minister—nominated by the legislature, or National Assembly, and approved by the president—is the head of government. The members of the unicameral National Assembly are elected by popular vote to five-year terms. The judicial branch is headed by the Supreme Court of Justice, which consists of nine justices.

Background

Cape Verde is an archipelago of ten islands located off the coast of West Africa. The northern group of six islands is called Barlavento, while the southern islands—which contain the largest island, São Tiago, and the capital, Praia—are called Sotavento.

The islands were uninhabited until the arrival of the Portuguese in 1462, and in 1495 they became part of the Portuguese Empire. Plantation agriculture was established on the islands with imported slave labor from Africa, and by the sixteenth century, Cape Verde was a major node in the slave trade. With the abolition of the slave trade in 1876, the prosperity of the islands declined. However, the deep harbor in the city of Mindelo on the northern island of São Vicente served to make Cape Verde an important shipping and commercial center.

In 1951 a growing nationalist movement forced Portugal to upgrade the status of Cape Verde from a colony to a province. In 1963 the Partido Africano de Independência da Guiné e Cabo Verde (African Party for Independence of Guinea-Bissau and Cape Verde, or PAIGC), a rebel group seeking independence for both Cape Verde and Portuguese Guinea, initiated a rebellion with military support from the Soviet Union, Cuba, and China. With the fall of the Portuguese government in 1974, the newly formed Portuguese government decided to relinquish control over the nation's colonial territories. Cape Verde gained its independence on July 5, 1975.

Government Structure

Cape Verde has had several constitutions since independence. The country is governed under a mixed presidential and parliamentary system. A strong president is the head of state and shares responsibility for foreign affairs and defense matters with the prime minister and cabinet. The president is elected by universal suffrage to a maximum of two five-year terms. The prime minister is nominated by the legislative body, the National Assembly, and is usually the leader of the majority party. The president officially appoints this nominee.

The seventy-two members of the National Assembly are elected by popular vote to five-year terms. The principal function of the National Assembly is to determine fundamental international policies and to pass domestic regulations and laws. The National Assembly can also vote no-confidence in the government, thus forcing a change of prime minister. However, day-to-day authority for government policy and implementation of such policy is the responsibility of the prime minister, in consultation with the cabinet and National Assembly.

The legal system of Cape Verde is based on the legal system of Portugal. Separate courts hear civil and criminal cases. The Supremo Tribunal de Justia (Supreme Court of Justice), is the final court of appeal. Its nine justices are appointed by the president, the Superior Board of the Magistrature; and the National Assembly to five-year terms. In general, the judicial system acts independently.

Local government is carried out via seventeen different *concelhos* (municipalities): Boa Vista, Brava, Maio, Mosteiros, Paul, Praia, Porto Novo, Ribeira Grande, Sal, Santa Catarina, Santa Cruz, São Domingos, São Filipe, São Miguel, São Nicolau, São Vicente, and Tarrafal.

The office of Provedor de Justiça (national ombudsman) was established in a 1999 amendment to the constitution. This independent organization protects citizens' rights.

Political Parties and Factions

Cape Verde was a one-party state until 1990. The PAIGC, established in 1956 as a guerilla organization, turned to politics in 1974 with a socialist platform. In 1975 the PAIGC became the sole party of the newly independent Cape Verde, and its leader, Aristides Pereira (1923–), the first president. PAICG changed its name to the African Party for the Independence of Cape Verde (PAICV) following a coup in Guinea-Bissau in 1980, and remained in power until 1991. It returned to power in 2001 and in the 2006 elections under Pedro Pires (1934–).

With the legalization of a multiparty system in 1990, several other parties were formed. Most important of these is Movimento para a Democracia (Movement for Democracy; MPD), which came into existence in 1990. In the 1991 elections it took a majority of seats in the National Assembly, and its presidential candidate, António Mascarenhas Monteiro (1944–), defeated the incumbent Pereira. In the 1996 elections, the MPD again controlled the National Assembly and returned to Monteiro to the presidency.

Divisions within the MPD in 1994 led to defections from the party by some key members and the creation of

Cape Verde President Pedro Verona Pires attending a 2006 summit of African heads of state. *Pius Utomi Ekpei/AFP/Getty Images*

another political party, the Party for Democratic Convergence (PCD), which won one seat in the 1995–96 elections.

The União Caboverdeano Independente e Democrática (Democratic and Independent Cape Verdean Union; UCID) is another opposition party in Cape Verde, as is the Party of Work and Solidarity (PTS). In the 2006 elections, a coalition of the UCID, PTS, and PCD, called the Democratic Alliance for Change (ADM), took two seats in the National Assembly.

Major Events

Following independence, Cape Verde and Guinea-Bissau were linked but independent republics. PAICG leader Aristides Pereira was elected president of Cape Verde and maintained that position until 1991. Cape Verde had close relations with Guinea-Bissau, working toward an eventual unification of the two countries, until a 1980 coup in Guinea-Bissau deposed its president, Luís Cabral (1931–), originally a Cape Verdean. The Cape Verde wing of the PAIGC thereafter left that party to found the African Party for the Independence of Cape Verde (PAICV), and diplomatic relations with Guinea-Bissau were interrupted until 1982. The PAICV went on to rule the country as the sole political party until 1990. The Pereira presidency was characterized by economic reforms to help the peasantry and a refusal to align with either the United States or the Soviet Union in the Cold War, though Pereira did, controversially, establish ties with both Libya and China.

Growing political pressure, however, forced the PAICV leadership to open up the political process. Opposition groups came together to form the Movimento para Democracia (Movement for Democracy; MPD) in Praia in April 1990, and in September of that year the one-party state was abolished. In presidential elections held in early 1991, the MPD candidate, António Mascarenhas Monteiro, defeated the incumbent PAICV candidate, Pereira, winning 72 percent of the vote. The MPD also took control of the National

Assembly in a political transfer of power that transpired smoothly and without violence. Monteiro also won the 1996 elections with 80 percent of the vote. However, in the 2001 and 2006 elections, the PAICV were again returned to power, under the leadership of Pedro Pires, who had served as prime minister under Pereira. The 2006 elections were very close, with Pires winning only 51 percent of the popular vote.

Twenty-First Century

Cape Verde is considered to be one of Africa's strongest democracies. However, the ruling PAICV does have its roots in the revolutionary movement that freed the country from Portuguese domination and ruled in one-party fashion for fifteen years. International observers still see a possible threat to democratic stability in that party's traditions. However, political transitions have been peaceful and orderly.

A further challenge to stability is the weakness of the economy. Throughout the country's history, and notably in the second half of the twentieth century, cycles of drought and accompanying economic hardship have led to heavy emigration. A large part of Cape Verde's economy depends on remittances, or money sent home, from this large expatriate population. Cape Verde has little in the form of natural resources, including fresh water, which must be imported to maintain supplies. Primarily a service economy, Cape Verde depends on transport and tourism for much of its income. Widespread poverty and unemployment are the norm; as of 2000, the unemployment rate had risen to over 21 percent, with more than 30 percent of the population living in poverty. Foreign financial aid is crucial to the well-being of Cape Verde's citizens, and the government has been attempting to forge stronger economic ties to the European Union to facilitate financial assistance programs.

BIBLIOGRAPHY

Lobban, Richard. *Cape Verde: Crioulo Colony to Independent Nation.* Boulder, CO: Westview Press, 1995.

Lobban, Richard, and Paul Khalil Saucier. *Historical Dictionary of the Republic of Cape Verde.* 4th ed. Lanham, MD: Scarecrow Press, 2007.

Shaw, Caroline S. *Cape Verde.* Santa Barbara, CA: Clio Press, 1991.

⊕ Union of Comoros

Type of Government

Comoros is governed as a federal republic with powers divided between independent executive, legislative, and judicial branches. After repeated coups and secessionist problems, a new constitution was adopted in 2001. Now each of the nation's three constituent islands elects its own president to administer local affairs, while a union president is responsible for issues affecting the entire country, such as defense, foreign policy, and finance. The union presidency rotates among the three islands.

Background

Comoros is a chain of three islands in the Indian Ocean—Grande Comore, Anjouan, and Mohéli—between Mozambique and Madagascar. A fourth island, Mayotte, opted to stay under French jurisdiction in 1975, but Comoros continues to claim it. With some 838 square miles in area, Comoros is about half the size of the state of Delaware and is home to about seven hundred thousand people. It is one of the poorest countries in Africa. The capital city, Moroni, is located on Grande Comore, the largest island.

The population is overwhelmingly (98 percent) Sunni Muslim and traces its origins to Africa, Indonesia, Europe, and the Middle East. The 2001 constitution makes Islam the state religion and does not provide for freedom of religion. President Ahmed Abdallah Mohamed Sambi (1958–) is an Islamic scholar, but he maintains that he does not plan to implement Islamic law.

Arab explorers brought Islam to the islands in the fifteenth century AD and created two sultanates to rule the islands. Portuguese explorers arrived in 1505, around the same time the Portuguese discovered Madagascar. Over the centuries, traders and sailors from Africa, the Persian Gulf, Indonesia, and Madagascar passed through the Comoros islands. French explorers landed in the islands in 1517 and often captured Comorans and sold them as slaves to work sugar plantations on other French territories. In 1843 the ruler of Mayotte transferred the island to France, and the leader of Mohéli signed a friendship treaty with France in 1865 but did not relinquish his island's independence. With control of Mayotte secured, France established a protectorate over Grande Comore, Anjouan, and Mohéli in 1886. By 1908 France had assigned administrative authority for the Comoros to the governor general of Madagascar.

On May 9, 1946, the islands became a French overseas territory with representation in the French National Assembly. Faced with demands for independence from the Comoro National Liberation Movement, based in Tanzania, France agreed to local rule in 1961, expanded local autonomy further on January 3, 1968, and agreed to transition toward total independence by 1978. Before the latter date, however, a referendum on independence was held on December 22, 1974. Three islands overwhelmingly voted for independence, but residents of Mayotte wanted to remain under French rule. While France insisted that the four islands hold separate votes on a draft constitution, the Comoran parliament unilaterally passed a declaration of independence on July 6, 1975, expelled French diplomats, and nationalized French property. The Comoran declaration of independence included Mayotte, but on February 7, 1976, resi-

dents there voted to remain a French territory. France welcomed Mayotte's association, but the United Nations has backed the Comoros claim to Mayotte.

Government Structure

The president is chief of state and appoints the Cabinet of Ministers. According to the 2001 constitution, every four years the union presidency rotates among the presidents of the three main islands, beginning with Grande Comore (2002), then Anjouan (2006) and Mohéli (2010). The entire population over the age of eighteen votes for the presidents, but only candidates from the designated island can run. Sambi of Anjouan was elected union president in May 2006, and the presidents of the other two islands serve as union vice presidents. The president has the power to appoint a prime minister, but the post has been vacant since the new constitution came into effect in 2002.

Legislative power is institutionalized in a unicameral (one-chamber) Assembly of the Union. The Assembly has thirty-three seats; fifteen members are selected by the individual islands and the remaining eighteen by universal voting. Members serve five-year terms.

The Comoran judicial system is based on a combination of Muslim and French law. At the top of the judicial system is the Supreme Court. The president appoints two members of the court, the Assembly of the Union selects another two members, the councils of the three islands each select one member, and the remaining members are former national presidents. The Constitutional Court oversees elections and has seven members: the union president, union vice presidents, the leader of parliament, and three members each appointed by the executive heads of the three islands.

Administratively, Comoros is organized as three islands (Grande Comore, Anjouan, and Mohéli) and four municipalities (Domoni, Fomboni, Moroni, and Moutsamoudou). Each island elects its own president and legislature.

Political Parties and Factions

Comoran political parties tend to be short-lived and be based around a particular issue, such as independence for an island, or a particular politician. President Ahmed Abdallah (1919–1989) led the Comoros Democratic Union from 1972 until 1982, when he outlawed all political parties and created the Comoran Union for Progress as the only legal party. The Comoran Union for Progress dominated politics throughout the 1980s, but in 1991 President Said Mohamed Djohar (1918–2006) abandoned it and multiparty elections began.

Leading parties as of 2007 included President Sambi's Islamic National Front for Justice, Convention for the Renewal of Comoros (CRC) headed by previous Comoros leader Azali Assoumani (1959–), and the Movement for the Comoros Party. The Camp of the Autonomous

Islands, which opposes the union president, holds the largest bloc of seats in the parliament.

Major Events

Since independence, the government of Comoros has endured coups, numerous coup attempts, and repeated secessionist strife. There were nineteen coups or attempted coups between 1975 and 2007, and in 1997 the islands of Anjouan and Mohéli declared their independence. For two decades, the real ruler of the country was a white French mercenary, Colonel Bob Denard (1929–), who formally headed the five-hundred-member presidential guard. Many observers believed Denard had the covert backing of France, which feared a Communist regime coming to power in the geographically strategic region.

Abdallah was president of the Comoran assembly when it declared independence, and he assumed control of the new executive branch on July 6, 1975. A coup led by Denard overthrew Abdallah on August 3, 1975, and Abdallah took refuge in France. Denard installed the former prime minister, Prince Said Mohammed Jaffar (1918–1993), as head of a new ruling Revolutionary Council. In January 1976 Ali Soilih (1937–1978) became president of the council. Soilih, in turn, was murdered by Denard's mercenaries on May 13, 1978, and Denard reinstalled Abdallah as head of the military council.

Abdallah issued a new constitution on October 1, 1978, that renamed the country the Federal Islamic Republic of the Comoros and increased individual island autonomy. Abdallah, the only candidate, subsequently won the October 22, 1978, election for president with 99.9 percent of the vote. He was reelected in September 1984 with 99.4 percent of the vote and moved to eliminate the post of prime minister. In 1989 Abdallah appealed to France and South Africa to eject Denard from the country, but on November 26, 1989, Abdallah was assassinated by Denard's Presidential Guard. As specified in the constitution, the head of the Supreme Court, at the time Said Mohamed Djohar, became acting president, and he succeeded in expelling Denard. Djohar subsequently won the 1990 presidential election and established a coalition government that survived three attempted coups.

Djohar's rule began to falter in 1992 when his son-in-law, then finance minister, was accused of corruption at a time when the economy was rapidly deteriorating. Djohar's allies won a slim plurality in the January 1992 parliamentary elections, but members could not agree on a cabinet and Djohar dissolved the parliament in June, calling for new elections in December. Parliament again objected to Djohar's cabinet appointments, and a wave of demonstrations and strikes spread across the islands. Denard resurfaced and seized this opportunity to invade, arrest Djohar, and install Colonel Ayouba Combo as head of a new Transitional Military Committee. France

In 1997, rebels on the island of Anjouan raised the French flag, hoping their island would be repatriated by France. © *RUET STEPHANE/CORBIS SYGMA*

responded by dispatching one thousand troops and arresting Denard. Opposition leaders Mohammed Taki and Said Ali Kemal ruled as co-interim presidents until Taki was elected president on March 16, 1996.

Soon after Taki took office, protests erupted in Anjouan and Mohéli, with residents demanding to secede from Comoros and rejoin France—even though France did not want them. In September 1997 Taki deployed the army to recapture the two islands, but it failed. Taki unexpectedly died in November 1998 under suspicious circumstances. Tadjiddine Ben Said Massounde (1933–2004) became acting president, only to be ousted in a coup on April 30, 1999.

The Organization for African Unity stepped in to broker an inter-island peace agreement, known as the Antananarivo agreement of April 2, 1999. However, the delegate representing Anjouan refused to sign the agreement, sparking attacks on Anjouans in Moroni. Azali Assoumani, then head of the Comoran armed forces, overthrew Massounde on April 30, 1999. On May 6 Assoumani took the titles of president, prime minister, and minister of defense.

He then suspended the constitution, dissolved all elected legislatures, and formed a twelve-member Committee of the State to run the country.

Assoumani sponsored a confederal power-sharing arrangement to resolve the secessionist crisis. Known as the Fomboni Accord of February 17, 2001, the agreement was based on the Antananarivo framework and was enshrined in a new constitution in 2001. The document requires incumbent leaders to step aside if they are to stand for reelection, so Assoumani resigned on January 16, 2002, before the April 14 presidential election. Assoumani then ran in the election and won the vote, but over the next few years his popularity began to fade. Two candidates boycotted the 2002 election, and Assoumani's CRC Party had a poor showing in the 2004 legislative elections. As his term of office neared an end and the presidency was due to rotate to a representative from Anjouan, Assoumani introduced a constitutional amendment that would allow him a second, consecutive term, but he soon abandoned the idea. Instead, he departed office on schedule, overseeing the first peaceful transition of power in the country's history.

Twenty-First Century

The Comoran government's main challenges are economic: securing additional investment and recouping funds lost due to corruption. With its turbulent political history, Comoros has had a difficult time raising foreign investment. Leaders must convince international lenders that the state is stable and their funds will be safe in the twenty-first century.

BIBLIOGRAPHY

Le Vine, Victor T. *Politics in Francophone Africa.* Boulder, CO: Lynne Rienner, 2004.

Weinberg, Samantha. *Last of the Pirates: The Search for Bob Denard.* New York: Pantheon, 1994.

⊕ São Tomé and Príncipe

Type of Government

The Democratic Republic of São Tomé and Príncipe has a multiparty government, based on a parliamentary model. The executive branch is jointly headed by a popularly elected president, who serves as head of state and commander of the armed forces, and an appointed prime minister, who serves as head of government. The unicameral legislature is constituted by popular vote. The judicial branch is independent of both the executive and the legislative branches and consists of a Supreme Court and lower courts.

Background

São Tomé and Príncipe are islands in the Gulf of Guinea, off the coast of western Africa. Archaeological evidence indicates that the islands were uninhabited before Por-

tuguese explorers arrived in the fifteenth century. In the following decades the Portuguese government allowed private citizens and corporations to occupy the islands and establish their own administrative systems without supervision from the central government in Lisbon. São Tomé was settled in 1483; communities first appeared on Príncipe in 1500.

The Portuguese companies brought African slaves to the islands to serve as laborers on sugar plantations. By the early sixteenth century the islands had become the most productive sugar producers in the Portuguese empire—which prompted the government to take control. It established a colonial administration on São Tomé in 1522 and on Príncipe in 1575.

Throughout the sixteenth and seventeenth centuries African laborers were shipped to the islands to maintain the plantation industry. When the sugar market declined, however, so did the prosperity of the islands. In the seventeenth century the local government on São Tomé deteriorated, and hundreds of slaves escaped into the mountains. They organized a resistance movement and staged frequent raids on the plantations. The Portuguese government lent the colonists financial aid and sent troops to the islands; a majority of the escaped slaves were eventually captured.

Following the lead of other European nations, Portugal abolished slavery in 1875, but it did not enact reforms to improve working conditions or wages for African plantation workers. In addition, the colonial government did not allow African laborers to gather into political groups or to seek representation in the local government. At the beginning of the twentieth century an independence movement developed on San Tomé, resulting in organized protests and demonstrations.

After World War I the Portuguese government paid little attention to the islands, once again allowing local plantation communities and export corporations to maintain their own authority. Most of the laborers were *forros* (freed slaves), who, by the 1950s, were refusing to work under the conditions and compensation offered by most plantation owners. Their actions caused severe labor shortages. In 1953 a major conflict erupted on São Tomé, when the plantation owners attempted to conscript forros into labor. During the resulting riots the Portuguese killed hundreds of forros in what became known as the Batepa Massacre.

Events on São Tomé strengthened the independence movement on both islands and led to the formation of the nation's first forro political groups. The Comité de Libertação de São Tomé e Príncipe, formed in 1960, became the Movimento de Libertação de São Tomé e Príncipe (Movement for the Liberation of São Tomé and Príncipe), or MLSTP, in 1972, led by economist and political leader Manuel Pinto da Costa (1937–). To avoid persecution by antiforro factions of the Portuguese administration, the MLSTP moved its headquarters to Gabon.

In 1974 Portuguese leader Marcello Caetano (1906–1980) was overthrown in the Carnation Revolution, and the new regime in Portugal wanted to divest responsibility of the nation's African territories. Portuguese leaders met with da Costa and other MLSTP leaders in Algiers, Algeria, and arranged a schedule for the transfer of sovereignty. In July 1975 São Tomé and Príncipe received their independence, with da Costa serving as the nation's first president.

Government Structure

The islands of São Tomé and Príncipe are divided into seven administrative districts, six on São Tomé and one on Príncipe. In 1995 the population of Príncipe voted to become an autonomous entity and is now governed by a five-member regional government. (While Príncipe is autonomous in domestic affairs, it is still officially joined with São Tomé for purposes of international representation and constitutional law.) Each of São Tomé's six regions is led by a five-member Regional Assembly, elected by popular vote for five-year terms. All citizens age eighteen and older have the right to vote.

In the executive branch the president serves as head of state and commander of the armed forces and the prime minister is head of government. Presidential elections are conducted according to a two-round runoff system; the winning candidate must achieve an overall majority in both rounds of voting. After election the president appoints a prime minister from nominees selected by the leading party of the legislature. The prime minister, in turn, appoints leaders of the nation's fourteen executive departments. Executive power is balanced by the legislative branch, which approves executive orders and appointments.

The unicameral National Assembly has fifty-five members, who are chosen through a system of proportional representation from multimember electoral districts. Legislators serve four-year terms; they can stand for re-election. The autonomous region of Príncipe is guaranteed representation within the National Assembly of São Tomé.

According to the constitution, the National Assembly is the most powerful body in the government. It creates and approves legislation and oversees constitutional amendments and international treaties. At its semiannual meetings it conducts legislative debates through a committee system. The members representing the majority party select the president of the assembly. When no party holds an absolute majority, coalition governments are formed.

The judicial branch is independent of both the executive and legislative branches and is responsible for executing the nation's penal code. The highest court in the nation is the Supreme Court, with justices appointed directly by the National Assembly, to serve lifetime terms. The Supreme Court has final appellate jurisdiction and is responsible for interpreting constitutional law. It also supervises the operation of the nation's regional and district courts.

Political Parties and Factions

The Movimento Democrático Força da Mundança–Partido da Convergência Democráica (Force for Change Democratic Movement–Democratic Convergence Party), or MDFM-PCD, which was created in 2001 to support President Fradique de Menezes (1942–), is the majority party in the legislature. In 2005 elections the MDFM-PCD received 36 percent of the popular vote and placed twenty-three candidates in the legislature. It formed a coalition with the Movement for the Liberation of São Tomé and Príncipe–Social Democratic Party. De Menezes was reelected in July 2006, receiving more than 60 percent of the popular vote.

The Movimento de Libertação de São Tomé e Prícipe–Partido Social Democrática (Movement for the Liberation of São Tomé and Príncipe–Social Democratic Party), or MLSTP-PSD, is an offshoot of the 1960s political party founded under the nation's first presidential administration. The party was initially a Marxist-communist organization but shifted its focus during the 1980s to a democratic platform. During the 2006 legislative elections, the MLSTP-PSD received the second highest percentage of the popular vote (29.5 percent) to place twenty candidates in the legislature. For the 2006 presidential elections, the MLSTP-PSD formed a coalition with the MDFM-PCD to nominate de Menezes for a second presidential term.

The Accão Democrática Independente (Independent Democratic Action Party), or ADI, was founded in 1992 to support Miguel Trovoado (1935–), the nation's first elected president after the democratic reforms of the 1990s. In 2001 the centrist ADI Party supported Fradique de Menezes in his first successful presidential campaign; de Menezes later left the party to join the MDFM-PCD. In the 2006 presidential elections, the ADI supported former foreign minister Patrice Trovoada (1962–), the son of the former president. He received 38 percent of the popular vote, or second place, in the second-round poll. In the legislative elections that year the ADI received 20 percent of the popular vote, winning eleven seats in the legislature.

Major Events

The government under the MLSTP and President da Costa was a socialist regime with economic and diplomatic ties to the Union of Soviet Socialist Republics, the German Democratic Republic (East Germany), Cuba, and the People's Republic of China. Between 1975 and 1980 da Costa arrested or exiled dozens of political leaders who opposed his policies. Miguel Trovoada, the nation's first prime minister, was dismissed in 1979 for opposing da Costa's domestic agenda. The following year da Costa had Trovoada arrested for treason and, after he had served a prison sentence, exiled to France.

The economies of São Tomé and Príncipe suffered in the 1980s, resulting in widespread public dissatisfaction. To avoid economic collapse da Costa began to sever ties with his former communist allies and to broaden foreign relations and trade with western nations. To prevent public unrest the administration also enacted a system of gradual democratic reforms. Da Costa pardoned political leaders who had been exiled or arrested for treason and allowed broader representation in the legislature. In 1987 the constitution was amended to allow independent and opposition party elections. The government also instituted a universal suffrage system for presidential elections, although the MLSTP was the only party permitted to nominate candidates for president. In 1988 da Costa reinstated the office of prime minister and appointed the former education minister, Celestino Rocha da Costa (1935–), who is his cousin.

Members of several opposition parties, who had been operating from exile in France, Gabon, and Cameroon, returned to São Tomé to compete in legislative elections. In 1988 Monso dos Santos and the Frente de Resistência Nacional de São Tomé–Renovada (National Resistance Front of São Tomé and Príncipe–Renewal), or FRNSTP-R, headquartered in Cameroon, launched a military expedition to overthrow the da Costa regime. Poorly armed, their coup attempt failed. Dos Santos and his supporters were arrested and imprisoned.

Da Costa's regime was under pressure from domestic and foreign agents promoting democratization and from the rise of radical and militant opposition groups. At the MLSTP conference of 1989 the party called for multiparty competition in presidential elections and the adoption of a two-term limit for the presidency. In addition, the new constitution abolished the death penalty, revised the nation's penal code, and constituted an independent judicial system. Dos Santos was pardoned by presidential decree and allowed to compete in the following elections.

In 1990 the MLSTP lost its legislative majority to a coalition of minority parties. The following year da Costa chose not to compete in the presidential elections, leading to a contest between minority-party candidates. Independent candidate and former prime minister Trovoada became the nation's first democratically elected president. Though some opposition groups objected to Trovoada's election, international observers regarded the elections as legitimate and relatively free from irregularities. In 1995 Trovoada was briefly displaced in a presidential coup, which was resolved within several months with the aid of international negotiators. Trovoada and the legislature had difficulty cooperating to enact economic reforms and infrastructural improvements. As a result, public sentiment turned against the

Brazilian President Luiz Inácio Lula da Silva with Fradique Menezes, president of the Republic of São Tomé and Príncipe, in 2003. © *Brazilian Presidency Handout/Reuters/Corbis*

government. Large-scale protests and demonstrations occurred in 1995 and 1996. Despite failing public support, Trovoada won re-election in 1996 with more than 52 percent of the popular vote.

Twenty-First Century

The democratic system organized in 1991 has remained relatively stable, despite contentious partisanship in the legislature. In 2001 Menezes was elected president. The military prevented two coups in 2003, after which Menezes invited opposition leaders to join in a new coalition government. During the 2006 legislative elections, Menezes's party won a significant majority in the legislature, allowing him to institute a greater portion of his governmental agenda.

São Tomé and Príncipe had long faced significant economic difficulties because it had a weak export economy. However, the discovery of oil beneath the shared waters between São Tomé and Nigeria offers the promise of new revenue; the government is cooperating with Nigeria to develop the oil industry. That investment, along with an increase in the price of cocoa, an export crop, have helped to foster moderate economic growth.

BIBLIOGRAPHY

Garfield, Robert. *A History of São Tomé Island, 1470–1655: The Key to Guinea.* Lewiston, NY: Mellen University Press, 1992.

Seibert, Gerhard. *Comrades, Clients and Cousins: Colonialism, Socialism, and Democratization in São Tomé and Príncipe.* Leiden and Boston: Brill Academic Publishers, 2006.

Torp, Jens Eric, L. M. Denny, and Donald I. Ray. *Mozambique, São Tomé and Príncipe: Economics, Politics and Society.* London: Pinter Publishers, 1990.

⊕ Papua New Guinea

Type of Government

Papua New Guinea is formally governed by a constitutional monarchy: the British monarch serves as head of state, and the governor-general acts as his or her local representative. In practice, however, the administration of the nation is carried out through a parliamentary democracy. The unicameral (single-chamber) National Parliament carries out legislative functions, and the prime minister is head of the government.

Background

The Independent State of Papua New Guinea is an island nation located in the southwestern Pacific Ocean. Papua New Guinea occupies the eastern half of the island of New Guinea (the Indonesian province of Irian Jaya makes up the western half) and encompasses some six hundred small islands, including the Bismarck archipelago (New Britain, New Ireland, New Hanover, and the Admiralty Islands) and Buka and Bougainville of the Solomon Islands. The nation's capital is Port Moresby, on the southwestern tip of New Guinea. The modern state of Papua New Guinea is home to more than seven hundred ethnic groups.

Before the arrival of Europeans on New Guinea, Malaysian and Chinese explorers had extensive contact with the island, coming to trade goods or find slave labor among the natives. Portuguese and Spanish mariners discovered the island during the sixteenth century, and Europeans explored its coastline for nearly three centuries before setting up any colonies there.

In 1828 the Dutch claimed the western half of the island (now a province of Indonesia) as part of the Dutch East Indies. In the 1870s Captain John Moresby (1830–1922) explored southeastern New Guinea; the British made this area a protectorate in 1884 and formally annexed it in 1888. By the turn of the century, Britain had shifted the responsibility for administering the territory to Australia. This arrangement was formalized in 1905 by the Papua Act, by which the colony was renamed the Territory of Papua. At the same time, the German New Guinea Company established dominion over the northeastern part of the island, declaring it a German protectorate, the Territory of New Guinea, in 1899. This region was administered directly by the German New Guinea Company until World War I, when it was occupied by Australia.

After the war, German New Guinea was governed by Australia as a mandated territory of the League of Nations. Following World War II, the Territories of Papua and New Guinea were placed under Australian control as a United Nations trust, with their joint capital at Port Moresby in the more remote Papuan region. The United Nations mandate provided the new territory with a legislature, judiciary, and local governments.

Calls for independence began to be heard during the 1960s, and in 1972 legislative elections gave a majority to Michael Somare (1936–), an advocate of self-governance for Papua New Guinea. Australia granted the territory self-governance in 1973, and Papua New Guinea achieved complete independence in 1975.

Papua New Guinea remains a member of the Commonwealth of Nations (also called the British Commonwealth), a voluntary association of more than fifty independent nations that are former colonies or territories of the British Empire.

Government Structure

Papua New Guinea's government is modeled on the British system of parliamentary conventions. The structure and functions of government are outlined in the nation's constitution, which was adopted upon independence in 1975.

The British monarch Queen Elizabeth II (1926–) is Papua New Guinea's head of state, although the role is purely symbolic. The monarch is represented in Papua New Guinea by a governor-general, who is elected by the legislature to a six-year term. Although the governor-general is invested with some executive authority—he or she formally appoints members of the cabinet, the chief justice of the Supreme Court, and other judges on the advice of a judicial commission—the position is largely ceremonial.

The head of government is the prime minister, who is elected from among the members of the legislature. Typically, the prime minister is the leader of the majority party (or coalition of parties) in the legislature; he or she forms a government at the invitation of the governor-general. Executive authority is vested in a cabinet called the National Executive Council, whose members are appointed by the governor-general on the prime minister's recommendation and lead the major departments of government.

Papua New Guinea has a unicameral (single-chamber) legislature called the National Parliament. This body is made up of 109 members who serve five-year terms. Eighty-nine members are elected from "open" electorates—single-member constituencies apportioned by population. The

Papua New Guinea Prime Minister Michael Somare addressing the United Nations General Assembly in September 2006. *Timothy A. Clary/AFP/Getty Images*

remaining twenty members are chosen by provincial electorates, so that there is one at-large member for each of Papua New Guinea's nineteen provinces and the National Capital District. Since independence, parliamentary elections have employed the simple majority system of voting; beginning in 2007, however, elections are conducted according to a "limited preferential vote" system in which voters rank candidates in order of preference.

The National Parliament has the authority to pass a motion of "no confidence" against the governing administration. In this case, a new government is formed, although no new elections are held, as in other parliamentary systems such as Great Britain or Canada. The no-confidence vote has been used frequently in modern Papua New Guinean politics, with the result that no government since independence has remained in power for a full five-year term. To bring some stability to the government, reforms were implemented in 2001 to disallow no-confidence votes within the first eighteen months of a new administration and during the twelve months preceding national elections (previously, no-confidence votes were allowed after six months).

Because Papua New Guinean politics operates as a multi-party system, seats in the National Parliament may be divided among many parties, giving no single party a clear majority (more than 50 percent). In this case, several parties may join together to form a coalition government, although such administrations are less sta-

ble than majority governments and typically have shorter life spans.

Papua New Guinea's legal system is based on English common law. The Supreme Court is the ultimate judicial authority and highest court of appeal. The court consists of six to eight members who are appointed by the Judicial and Legal Services Commission; the chief justice is appointed by the governor-general on the recommendation of the National Executive Council and the minister of justice. The Supreme Court has the power to interpret the constitution and hears appeals from the National Court, the nation's highest trial court. The Supreme Court and National Court share the same judges—the latter becomes the Supreme Court when the judges sit together as an appellate panel. The lower judiciary includes district, local, and village courts.

At the regional level, Papua New Guinea is divided into nineteen provinces and the National Capital District (the area in and around Port Moresby). As a result of reforms implemented in 1995, at-large members of the National Parliament now serve simultaneously as provincial governors. Although the provincial governments share some powers with the national government, Papua New Guinea is not a federal system; rather, the provinces are created by the national government and do not have "reserve" powers, as in federal governments such as the United States and Australia.

Political Parties and Factions

National politics in Papua New Guinea operates as a multi-party system—that is, many political parties compete for control of government. However, most political parties in Papua New Guinea are weak in structure. They are based largely on the personality of the leader rather than any cohesive ideology, and there is little of the party discipline seen in Western-style democracies. In practice, most members of the National Parliament function as independents, and it is common for candidates to switch parties to suit political ends. Legislation was passed in 1999 to prevent members of the National Parliament from switching parties while in office.

The large number of parties—more than forty in the 2002 parliamentary elections—combined with the traditional simple majority voting system, has ensured that no party can achieve a legislative majority. Electoral reforms have attempted to remedy this problem by changing to a preferential system of voting.

Of Papua New Guinea's many political parties, the major organizations are the National Alliance Party, the Papua and Niugini Union, the People's Democratic Movement, and the People's Progress Party.

Major Events

A secessionist movement in Papua New Guinea's Bougainville Province has been a source of conflict in the nation for nearly four decades. The province, which comprises Bougainville, Buka, and several other small islands, is geographically part of the Solomon Islands chain but belongs politically to Papua New Guinea. The province initially attempted to secede upon independence, citing concerns about the distribution of revenues from its lucrative copper-mining operation. An insurrection began in 1988, and rebels controlled the province until 1991, when national troops were sent in to restore order.

Secessionists continued to push forward, however, and during the decade-long rebellion that followed, control of the province shifted between rebel and government troops, claiming nearly 20,000 lives. A peace agreement was reached in 2001, according to which Bougainville formed an autonomous region within Papua New Guinea, implementing a separate constitution and electing its own president.

Twenty-First Century

Papua New Guinea's most important challenge in the twenty-first century is political stability. Years of repeated no-confidence votes, fluid party loyalties, and a voting system unsuited to its highly competitive political environment have left Papua New Guinea with little continuity in government. Electoral reforms implemented in the late 1990s and early 2000s are promising signs of progress toward stable government.

BIBLIOGRAPHY

Commonwealth Secretariat. "Papua New Guinea Country Profile." http://www.thecommonwealth.org/Year bookHomeInternal/138973/ (accessed August 25, 2007).

Waiko, John Dademo. *A Short History of Papua New Guinea*. Melbourne, Australia: Oxford University Press, 1993.

Zimmer-Tamakoshi, Laura. *Modern Papua New Guinea*. Kirksville, MO: Thomas Jefferson University Press, 1998.

⊕ Angola

Type of Government

Angola is a presidential regime, in power since 1992, that is making the transition to a multiparty, democratic republic. By constitution the central government is divided into three branches: the executive branch, which consists of the president, who is elected by popular vote, and the prime minister and the cabinet, who are appointed; the unicameral assembly, whose members are elected by popular vote; and the court system, which is overseen by the Supreme Court. The justices are appointed. In practice, the executive wields considerable influence over the other branches.

Background

The original inhabitants of Angola, members of the Khoisan linguistic group, were descendants of some of Africa's most ancient tribes. The region was sparsely populated by confederations of tribes until the sixth century AD, when the Bantu arrived. They established a series of nation states along Africa's western coast, known later as the Middle Atlantic Kingdoms.

The Kongo (Congo) Kingdom, which originated in the thirteenth century AD, was one of the most powerful. The *manikongo* (king of Kongo) ruled as an absolute monarch assisted by the *mani*, a group of aristocrats who functioned as regional governors. By the sixteenth century the Kongo Kingdom controlled six large provinces, stretching from Angola to what is now the Democratic Republic of Congo. The capital city, Mbanza Kongo, had a population of more than fifty thousand.

In 1482–83, Portuguese explorer Diogo Cão became the first European to visit the western coast of Africa. On behalf of the Portuguese crown, he and other explorers formed trade agreements with the Kongo kings, exchanging firearms for slaves, ivory, and minerals. The Portuguese also gave the manikongos privileges and property in Europe. King Nzinga a Nkuwu (?–1506) became the first manikongo to be baptized as a Christian; he took the name Joáo I. His son Nzinga Mbemba (c. 1460–c. 1545), who was baptized as Affonso I, became a well-known figure in Europe—he was known for exchanging correspondence with the pope and other Christian leaders.

In 1587 the Portuguese established two important trading posts, Luanda and Benguela (once called São Felipe de Benguela because it was built around São Felipe fortress), which became the largest ports in the region. The neighboring kingdom, Ndongo, formed an alliance with the Dutch and several other smaller kingdoms to resist Portuguese expansion. The Ndongo fought an extended series of engagements and, with the help of the Dutch, managed to capture Luanda. The Portuguese colony in Brazil, strengthened by years of imported slaves from Angola, launched an invasion force and recaptured Luanda in 1648.

The alliance between the Kongo and the Portuguese began to disintegrate, however, and in 1665 the Kongo attempted to seize Luanda. The Portuguese easily defeated the Kongo, and by 1671 the Ndongo had also submitted, leaving the Portuguese in control.

Angola was an important hub in the Atlantic slave trade until 1836, when Portugal, following the lead of Britain and France, abolished that form of commerce. By 1844 the Portuguese had transformed Angola into an agricultural center, exporting cotton and other crops, and an ivory export market. In 1850 Luanda was one of the continent's largest cities.

As Portugal moved from a monarchy to a parliamentary system in the early twentieth century, the government decided to make Angola a province of Portugal. Before provincial status was instated, however, the Portuguese strengthened their authority by removing tribal leaders who still controlled some of the more remote regions. That effort, completed by the 1920s, so angered and isolated the native population that a strong nationalist movement developed.

In the 1950s three militant factions battled each other and the Portuguese for control of the country. Movimento Popular de Libertação de Angola (Popular Movement for the Liberation of Angola), or MPLA, which had ties to the Portuguese Communist Party, was supported by the Union of Soviet Socialist Republics (USSR). Out of concern that communists would gain control of Central Africa, the United States agreed to aid the Frente Nacional de Libertação de Angola (National Front for the Liberation of Angola), or FNLA, which originated in 1960–61. The third group, the União Nacional para a Independência Total de Angola (National Union for the Total Independence of Angola), or UNITA, was formed in 1966 as an alliance of native tribal leaders. Although the independence armies rapidly overwhelmed the Portuguese military, their battle with each other intensified into civil war.

A 1974 presidential coup in Lisbon brought an end to Portugal's colonial empire. Angola was granted independence in November 1975. Each of Angola's leading factions also declared independence, however, establishing its own separate government. The outcome was a quarter century of escalating conflict.

Government Structure

In 1992 Angola made the transition from a single-party Marxist-Leninist republic to a multiparty democracy with powers divided between executive, legislative, and judicial branches. In practice, however, authority is concentrated in the executive branch. The president, who serves as head of state, commander of the armed forces, and head of government, appoints a prime minister, who functions as the president's chief deputy. The president also appoints as many as thirty members to the Council of Ministers, which oversees the executive functions of the government. The president is elected by direct popular vote to serve up to two consecutive or discontinuous five-year terms.

The unicameral National Assembly has 223 members, who are elected according to proportional representation: five assembly members serve each of the nation's eighteen provinces, and the remaining legislators are elected by the entire population as a single electoral unit. Legislators, who serve four-year terms, can stand for re-election. In cases of deadlock the president may, after consulting the cabinet, dissolve the National Assembly.

Angola's governmental procedures hinge on the Council of the Republic, a consultative body presided over by the president. Its members include the prime minister, the president of the National Assembly, the president of the Constitutional Court, the attorney general, the former president of the republic, the presidents of the political parties represented in the National Assembly, and ten citizens appointed by the president to represent special interests and industry. The Council of the Republic meets to deliberate on executive decisions and issues involving constitutional law.

The 1992 constitution designates an independent judicial branch; however, in practice the executive exercises a high degree of influence in judicial operations. The High Council of the Judicial Bench—which appoints, removes, and punishes court officials—is led by the president and includes three legal officials appointed by the president, five lawyers or judges appointed by the National Assembly, and ten judges elected from within the judicial system. The constitution calls for a Constitutional Court, with final authority in all matters involving constitutional law. As of 2007 the Constitutional Court had never been convened. The nation's highest functioning court is the Supreme Court, which is the final appellate authority and has oversight over all the nation's lower courts. The justices are appointed by the president.

Political Parties and Factions

The Popular Movement for the Liberation of Angola (MPLA), established in 1956, has been the nation's leading political party since the beginning of the civil war. Originally designated as a Marxist-Leninist political party, it controlled Angola as an authoritarian, communist state. After peace accords and the establishment of the 1992 constitution, the MPLA won the popular vote.

The National Union for the Total Independence of Angola (UNITA), established in 1966, is the second-largest political group. After independence and during most of the civil war, UNITA controlled a portion of the nation and established a democratic system. Though UNITA was originally a socialist party, its platform shifted during the 1980s in favor of a capitalist, democratic model. UNITA took part in the 1992 presidential poll and lost a close vote to the MPLA, leading to a brief relapse into civil war.

The National Front for the Liberation of Angola (FNLA), established in 1957, took a major role in the early independence movement and was originally supported by the United States and other pro-democracy foreign powers. The FNLA lost foreign support when its leadership broke away to form UNITA, leaving the remaining members of the FNLA without significant military backing. The FNLA took part in the 1992 elections, winning five seats in the National Assembly.

Frente para a Libertação do Enclave de Cabinda (Front for the Liberation of the Enclave of Cabinda), or FLEC, is a separatist political party located in the oil-rich Cabinda region. It repeatedly launched small-scale assaults on military convoys. In the 1990s the MPLA–led

UNITA forces parading under a portrait of their leader, Jonas Savimbi, in 1985, marking ten years of Angolan independence.   *© Reuters/ CORBIS*

government instituted reforms that addressed some of the separatists' complaints; however, many FLEC supporters have refused to take part in the central government.

The civil war led to the development of numerous other small, revolutionary parties. Only a few of them, including Partido Liberal Democrático (Liberal Democratic Party) and Partido Renovador Social (Social Renewal Party), held more than one seat in the assembly after the 1992 election.

Major Events

In the decade following independence the Angolan civil war became part of the "cold war" as the United States and the South African–supported UNITA faction attempted to drive the MPLA from Luanda. The United States and the USSR chose not to commit troops to the struggle, in fear of a major escalation, but Cuban and South African troops became directly involved, fighting several battles over disputed territory in neighboring Namibia. By 1980 the Cubans and South Africans had withdrawn from the conflict, but the Angolans continued their struggle.

During the 1980s the MPLA, under the leadership of José Eduardo dos Santos (1942–), and UNITA, under the leadership of Jonas Savimbi (1934–2002),

tried several times to develop a peace agreement. Prospects for a cease-fire improved when Santos and the MPLA moved away from their communist platform and began advocating the establishment of a democratic system. Peace talks sponsored by the United Nations in 1988 seemed promising, but then disintegrated, leading to another wave of violent attacks. Though the MPLA enjoyed greater support and had territorial advantages, Savimbi's UNITA controlled 80 percent of the nation's diamond industry, which provided the funding needed for an ongoing war.

Between 1975 and 1989 the civil war resulted in some six hundred thousand verified casualties (in reality, the death toll probably exceeded more than 1 million) and prevented any lasting infrastructural improvements. Eventually both sides realized that a peace agreement was becoming necessary for economic reasons. In 1991 the MPLA and UNITA reached agreement on a new constitution and made plans for general elections the following year. Dos Santos won the presidential election with 49.6 percent of the popular vote; Savimbi won 40.1 percent. UNITA refused to accept the result and launched an attack on Luanda. During the following two years more than 20 percent of the population was displaced and thousands more died in armed conflict.

The 1994 Lusaka Peace Accords produced only a transient peace because Savimbi refused to surrender profitable diamond-mining territories. Widespread suffering accompanied the final stages of the war—aid workers were unable to reach poor and displaced families in the nation's cities. In 2002 government troops killed Savimbi, which led to a cease-fire with UNITA leaders. Since 2002 the peace agreement has held, although separatist struggles have continued in some parts of Angola, including Cabinda province.

Twenty-First Century

After more than thirty years of civil war the populace faces extreme poverty. Access to food, medical care, and social services is insufficient. In addition, the government has a poor human-rights record, and accusations of corruption are common. Angola has potential, however, for it is rich in natural resources, including oil, diamonds, and other minerals.

Although the government operates within the framework of the 1992 constitution, dos Santos and the rest of the executive branch hold near-authoritarian power. However, the government announced plans to hold general elections in 2009, with a multiparty democratic system in place. Dos Santos said he would not run for re-election.

BIBLIOGRAPHY

Birmingham, David. *Empire in Africa: Angola and Its Neighbors.* Athens: Ohio University Press, 2006.

Chabal, Patrick, and Nuno Vidal, eds. *Angola: The Weight of History.* New York: Columbia University Press, 2007.

Guimarães, Fernando Andresen. *The Origins of the Angolan Civil War: Foreign Intervention and Domestic Political Conflict.* New York: Palgrave Macmillan, 2001.

⊕ Spain

Type of Government

The Spanish government is a parliamentary monarchy. The role of the monarch is largely ceremonial in Spain, and real power is wielded by the executive branch, which includes the President of the Government and a Council of Ministers. The legislature is the bicameral Cortes Generales (General Courts), which consists of the Congreso de los Diputados (Congress of Deputies) and Senado (Senate), both of whose members are elected every four years. The independent judiciary comprises various levels of regional and municipal courts, as well as a Supreme Court and a Constitutional Court.

Background

Spain is located on Europe's Iberian Peninsula. In addition to its continental landmass, Spain also includes the Balearic Islands in the Mediterranean Sea and the Canary Islands off the coast of western Africa.

The area was settled by Iberians, Celts, and Basques and by 206 BC had become part of the Roman Empire. Beginning in the early fifth century the Romans were partly supplanted by the Visigoths. Still, Roman garrisons remained on the southern coast until Muslim Berbers from North Africa conquered the peninsula between 711 and 718. Spanish Islam, or al-Andalus, became a stronghold of Muslim belief on the European continent for several hundred years. By the eleventh century, with immigration from Arab countries and conversion of Christians to Islam, it was estimated that Muslims outnumbered Christians in the region. Muslim cities such as Córdoba were among the richest and most advanced in Europe at the time.

From the eighth to the thirteenth centuries, Muslim and Christian armies competed for control of northern Spain. The struggle culminated in the Christian armies' conquest of Córdoba and Seville in the mid-thirteenth century, which effectively pushed the Spanish Muslims to the south. Christian campaigns continued into the fifteenth century, and with the capture of Granada in 1492 effectively drove the last of the Muslims from Spain. That year is also significant as the year the explorer Christopher Columbus (1451–1506) was commissioned by Queen Isabella I (1451–1504) and King Ferdinand II (1452–1516) to undertake a maritime expedition seeking a new trade route to Asia, thereby discovering the New World.

The unification of present-day Spain was begun by consolidation of the kingdoms of Castile and Aragon with the marriage of Isabella and Ferdinand in 1469. The union was completed by their grandson, the Holy Roman Emperor Charles V (also known as Charles I of Spain; 1500–1558), with the addition of León and Navarre to form the geographic basis of modern Spain. Charles ruled as king of Spain from 1516 to 1556, and together with his successor Philip II (1527–1598) created one of Europe's foremost powers of the time. In addition to the expeditions led by Columbus were those of Fernão de Magalhães (known in English as Ferdinand Magellan; c. 1480–1521). In 1519 Magalhães, a Portuguese in the service of Spain, began the first voyage to sail around the world. Although Magellan died before returning home to port, the Basque explorer Juan Sebastián Elcano (c. 1476–1526) assumed command of the expedition and completed the circumnavigation in 1522.

The sixteenth century is known as the golden age of Spain, with intellectual life developing rapidly and with the formidable Spanish Armada protecting and expanding the national boundaries. The Spanish Empire stretched across the globe, consisting of large tracts of South, Central, and North America, the Philippines, and parts of what are now Italy, Germany, Belgium, and the Netherlands. Great wealth grew from such overseas possessions. However, with the defeat of the Armada by England in 1588, Spain's power began to diminish. Subsequent wars on land with England, France, and the Netherlands further reduced its power and reach.

From the mid-nineteenth century, the political environment in Spain was divided between those who favored the continuation of the monarchy and those who sought a shift toward a representative, democratic system. The First Spanish Republic was declared in 1873, but lasted just under two years, ultimately put down by the military. Spain also lost most of its remaining colonies during this time; Cuba, Puerto Rico, and the Philippines were transferred to the United States after the Spanish-American War in 1898.

In 1923 General Miguel Primo de Rivera y Orbaneja (1870–1930) established a dictatorship. After his death, and in the wake of a strong anti-monarchist movement, the king left Spain, and the Second Spanish Republic was established. Under the new constitution, a workers' republic was declared. The government granted the vote to women, awarded autonomy to regions such as Basque Country and Catalonia, and emphasized the separation of church and state. It broke up large estates and established secular schools. Elections in 1936 put the leftist Popular Front party in power.

Right wing and monarchist groups rejected the new government, leading to civil war from 1936 to 1939. The two opposing parties were the Republicans, made up of democrats and left-wing groups, and the Nationalists, who favored the establishment of a right-wing dictatorship and were led by General Francisco Franco (1892–1975). International troops and military support served to make the war particularly brutal and bloody. Germany and Italy furnished soldiers and weapons to the Nationalists, while the Soviet Union and Mexico supported the Republicans. With the defeat of the Republican cause, Franco formed a new government, becoming both prime minister and *caudillo* (leader).

In 1947 the monarchy was re-established, but Franco remained in power as head of state until his death. The repressive nature of the Franco regime kept Spain apart from postwar Western European developments, although it was admitted to the United Nations in 1955. In 1969 Prince Juan Carlos Borbón (1938–) was designated to become the king of Spain after Franco's regime ended. Two days after the death of Franco in 1975, Juan Carlos I was sworn in as the King of Spain. Among his first acts was to replace Franco's prime minister with Adolfo Suárez González (1932–), under whom the legislature wrote a new constitution that established a parliamentary democracy. This constitution was approved by a national referendum in 1978.

Government Structure

Under the terms of the constitution, the king is the head of state. However, his powers are greatly limited and largely ceremonial. Although he proposes candidates to serve as head of government, these must still be approved by the congress. Executive authority rests with the President of the Government, who functions as a prime minister and who is approved by the democratically elected congress. The prime minister also designates a cabinet. The lower house of parliament, the Congress of Deputies, can force a government to resign by a vote of no confidence.

Legislative power is in the hands of the General Courts, which consists of two chambers: the Congress of Deputies with 350 members and the Senate with 259 members. All deputies and 208 senators are popularly elected to four-year terms under universal suffrage by adults age eighteen and older. The remaining fifty-one senators are chosen by the assemblies in the seventeen autonomous regions of the country. The Congress of Deputies elects the prime minister and shares authority to propose legislation with the Senate. While the Senate can amend or veto proposed legislation that comes to it from the Congress of Deputies, that veto can be overridden by a simple majority vote of the lower house.

By the terms of the 1978 constitution, Spain is divided into seventeen autonomous regions, *comunidades autonomas*, with locally elected governments responsible for such matters as schools and roads.

The judicial branch is made up of a variety of courts, both regional and national. The highest judicial body is the Tribunal Supremo (Supreme Court). Additionally, there is the Tribunal Constitucional (Constitutional Court), which judges the constitutionality of laws and decides disputes between the central government and the autonomous regions. Its twelve judges are elected for nine-year terms. On the regional level, the territorial high courts (*audiencias*) are the courts of last appeal in the seventeen regions of the country, while Provincial audiencias serve as appeals courts in civil matters and also hold the first hearings for criminal cases. The Audiencia Nacional (National High Court) has jurisdiction over criminal cases that cross regional boundaries and over civil cases involving the central state administration. A jury system was established in 1995, and a new penal code was enacted in 1996.

Political Parties and Factions

There are numerous political parties in Spain, ranging across the political spectrum and also advocating single issues, such as environmentalism. The two major parties operating in Spain are the Partido Socialista Obrero Español (Spanish Socialist Workers' Party; PSOE) and the Partido Popular (Popular Party; PP). There are also regional parties that function in Catalonia, Andalusia, Basque Country, and other areas.

One of the oldest parties in Spain, the PSOE was founded in 1879 by the labor leader Pablo Iglesias Posse (1850–1925) to protect the rights of workers, and was

Spanish general and future dictator Francisco Franco saluting troops in 1939. © *Bettmann/CORBIS*

and opening to the rest of the world. Spain joined the North Atlantic Treaty Organization (NATO) in 1982, and in 1986 became a member of the European Community, which later became the European Union (EU). In February 2005 Spain became the first nation to ratify the proposed European constitution in a national referendum.

Meanwhile, within Spain, recurring violence caused by Basque separatists proved to be a major problem for successive governments. Since the 1960s, political murders and kidnappings have terrorized not only the Basque region, but all of Spain. The Basque separatist organization Euskadi Ta Askatasuna (ETA) has claimed responsibility for such actions. In August 1995 terrorists attempted the assassination of King Juan Carlos, and over the years bombings have taken place in Madrid. More than a thousand people have been killed due to separatist violence. These include innocent bystanders in addition to the intended political, police, judicial, and military targets of ETA.

International terrorists have also chosen Spain as a target of violence. In 2004 members of the al Qaeda terrorist group bombed the Madrid railway, killing almost two hundred people and injuring another fourteen hundred. The bombings were allegedly in reprisal for the Spanish government's support of the U.S.-led invasion of Iraq the year before. About 90 percent of the Spanish population had been against such support, and in the 2004 elections, the Aznar government was badly defeated as a result.

inspired by the principles of Marxism. It was part of the Popular Front elected to power in 1936 and was thereafter banned by Franco. Today it is a social democratic party combining social reforms with a liberal capitalist economic policy. It won absolute majorities in both chambers of the General Courts in 1982, 1986, and 1989. It finished short of a parliamentary majority in 1993 and 1996. It was returned to power in 2004 under José Luis Rodríguez Zapatero (1960–).

The conservative, center-right PP is a coalition made up of the Alianza Popular, the Demócrata Popular, and the Partido Liberal. Formed in 1989, by the time of the 1996 elections the PP won a parliamentary majority with 156 seats, while their primary opponent, the PSOE, won 141 seats. Party leader José Maria Aznar (1953–) became prime minister and remained in office until the 2000 elections.

Of the numerous regional parties, the Basque Nationalist Party is one of the largest and strongest. Its main aim is to achieve independence for the Basque region.

Major Events

Following the establishment of a parliamentary monarchy in 1978, Spain entered a period of rebuilding

Twenty-First Century

The greatest single challenge to political stability in Spain continues to be the issue of regional separatism. After the events of September 11, 2001, and the Madrid bombings in 2004, the terrorist activities of ETA became less viable as a political tool. Thus, in 2006 ETA declared a state of permanent ceasefire. Despite that, however, in early 2007 a bombing at a Spanish airport left two dead. Peace talks between the government of Prime Minister Zapatero and ETA were terminated as a result. Catalonia also voted in a 2006 referendum for greater autonomy from Spain.

Illegal immigration, especially from Africa, has also become a major issue in Spain. In a 2006 poll, Spaniards named immigration (both legal and illegal) as the main problem facing the country.

BIBLIOGRAPHY

Barton, Simon. *A History of Spain*. Basingstoke, UK: Palgrave Macmillan, 2004.

Carr, Raymond. *Spain: A History*. New York: Oxford University Press, 2001.

Miller, Arthur. *Spain*. Philadelphia: Chelsea House, 1999.

⊕ Suriname

Type of Government

The small South American nation of Suriname is a constitutional republic marked by a distinctive electoral system and an enormous variety of political parties.

Background

Suriname is the smallest and youngest nation in South America. Less than five hundred thousand people live within a heavily forested territory slightly larger than the state of Iowa. By the end of the sixteenth century, its convenient location on the Caribbean coast (between the modern states of Guyana and French Guiana) had brought it to the attention of European explorers. Though Spain claimed the area in 1598, dense mangrove swamps along the coast discouraged intensive colonization. Consequently, when Dutch expeditions began settlement around 1616, the Spanish had little desire to stay and turned to other, more lucrative locations. Under the name of Dutch Guiana, Suriname would remain a Dutch possession from 1667, when it became an official colony, to the time of independence in 1975. Before independence, however, local autonomy had been steadily increasing for decades, with full autonomy in routine affairs established as early as 1954.

Issues of race and ethnicity were prominent throughout the colonial period, and they continue to play a major role in national politics. Modern Suriname has a diverse population, with substantial groups of African, Hindustani, and Javanese descent. The Africans, known locally as Maroons, are the descendants of slaves brought from West Africa in the seventeenth and eighteenth centuries. Some eventually intermarried with the Dutch and Native American populations; the offspring of these unions are known as Creoles and make up the largest single group in Suriname today (roughly 37 percent of the population). Other slaves, however, escaped into the jungles where they established no less than five distinct societies based closely on West African models. These are the Djuka, Quinti, Paramaccaner, Saramaccaner, and Matuwari groups, and together they make up about 10 percent of the population. The Hindustani (also known locally as East Indians), originally from northern India, and the Javanese, from the Indonesian island and former Dutch colony of Java, were brought to Suriname as menial laborers after the abolition of slavery in 1863. As of 2007 they represented roughly 31 and 15 percent of the population, respectively. The remaining 7 percent represent a variety of smaller groups, including isolated native villages in the interior and several Chinese communities.

Government Structure

Suriname's constitution of 1987 established a unicameral legislature, the National Assembly, with fifty-one seats. Members are elected by popular vote and hold their seats for five years. Terms are not staggered, as they are in the U.S. Senate; all seats are open in every election. In addition to drafting and passing legislation, the National Assembly elects the president and vice president. A two-thirds majority is required. If no candidate has received that majority after two votes, the election is transferred to a much larger body, the United People's Assembly (UPA). The UPA consists of 893 members, including the fifty-one members of the National Assembly. Every popularly elected municipal and regional official in the country takes one of the remaining 842 seats. In the UPA, a simple majority is enough to elect the president and vice president, both of whom can serve an unlimited number of five-year terms. The president is chief of state, head of government, and supreme commander of the armed forces. A Cabinet of Ministers, staffed by presidential appointees and chaired by the vice president, oversees the government's day-to-day operations. Finally, several ad-hoc councils are available to advise the president on policy. Chief among these is the National Security Council and the State Advisory Council. The latter, with the president acting as chair, has fifteen seats: Eleven are allocated to political parties on the basis of their strength in the National Assembly; two are allotted to labor unions; and the last two to business organizations.

The codes and structures of Dutch law, as amended by the Constitution and local tradition, form the basis of Suriname's legal system. At the top of the judiciary is the High Court of Justice, which serves as the court of last appeal. When vacancies occur on the High Court, the president fills them with lifetime appointments, usually on the basis of recommendations from the National Assembly, the National Order of Private Attorneys, and the State Advisory Council. Since the end of military rule, there has been a de facto moratorium on the use of the death penalty, and the Constitution guarantees the right to "personal liberty and safety."

Ten regional governors, appointed by the president, manage local affairs, chiefly through their oversight of the officials elected by each municipality and rural district. Traditional village leaders retain significant influence over both local matters and, through the Association of Indigenous Village Chiefs, national policy.

Political Parties and Factions

Despite its small size, Suriname supports a wide variety of political parties. Many of these—including the Javanese Indonesian Peasants Party (also known as the Party for National Unity and Solidarity of the Highest Order, or KTPI), the Creole National Party of Suriname (NPS), and the Hindustani Progressive Reform Party (also known as the United Reform Party, or VHP)—are rooted in ethnic identity. In practice, coalitions (alliances of parties) are necessary, even for the largest parties.

Runaldo Ronald Venetiaan (1936–), who by 2007 was serving his third term as president, owes his elections to the support of the New Front for Democracy and Development (NF), a large coalition of ethnic and labor-oriented parties. Though his own party, the NPS, is one of the country's largest, it is not strong enough to elect a president without recruiting smaller groups.

Of the fifty-one seats in the National Assembly, the ruling NF coalition won twenty-three in the 2005 election. The National Democratic Party (NDP), chaired by Désiré Bouterse (1945–), won fifteen seats, a reflection of the former military leader's enduring populist appeal. Another coalition, the People's Alliance for Progress (VVV), is dominated by the figure of Jules Albert Wijdenbosch (1941–), whose single term as president (1996–2000, between Venetiaan's first and second terms) was marked by severe economic difficulties, strikes, and widespread unrest; it won five seats. Two coalitions of minor parties took the remaining eight seats.

Major Events

Despite Suriname's careful preparations for its 1975 independence, including a constitution, the new nation soon faced a serious political crisis. In February 1980, sixteen low-ranking military officers staged a successful coup. Under the leadership of Bouterse, coup members suspended the constitution, dismissed the elected government, and instituted an authoritarian socialist regime. Economic and sociopolitical conditions steadily deteriorated, reaching a low point with the arrest and swift execution of fifteen leading dissidents in 1982. Under increasing international pressure, the Bouterse regime made a number of purely cosmetic changes to improve its image, notably the appointment of a nominally civilian cabinet. Bouterse remained firmly in control, however, and the subterfuge fooled almost no one. Continuing pressure from abroad, particularly the Dutch government's refusal to release critical financial aid, finally forced Bouterse to step down in 1987. Elections and a new constitution followed, but another, short-lived military coup in 1990 delayed the transition to civilian rule. New elections took place without incident the following year, however, and several more rounds, equally successful, have taken place since.

Additional upheaval has plagued Suriname. In the summer of 1986 a violent insurgency arose in the sparsely populated jungles of the interior. Former solider Ronnie Brunswijk led a group called the Jungle Commando in attacking government installations, utilities, plantations, and other targets. Bouterse, then in power, responded ferociously, burning homes and driving thousands of African Surinamese, the insurgents' primary ethnic group, over the border into French Guiana. The two sides eventually signed a peace treaty, but its articles were never fully implemented and many of the social and

Sargeant Ronnie Brunswijk led an unsuccessful guerrilla rebellion against Suriname's military leader in 1986. © *Patrick Chauvel/Sygma/ Corbis*

economic frustrations that fed the insurgency remain. As of 2007, rebel leader Brunswijk lead a small, nonviolent group called the General Interior Development Party, or ABOP.

Twenty-First Century

Despite the successful return to civilian rule, a number of serious problems remain in Suriname. Environmental degradation, including rapid deforestation and the pollution of inland waterways with mine waste, has limited opportunities for forms of sustainable development. The result is a vicious cycle, as limited alternatives increase the dependence on mining and logging, which in turn inflict more environmental damage. A fundamental transformation of the economy is therefore an urgent priority if the nation is to escape endemic poverty. Seven out of ten Surinamese live below the poverty line, and the percentage is even higher in rural areas. The recent discovery of oil off the coast will provide the government with a new source of needed revenue, but it is not clear how much of that money will reach those who need it most. Low wages for civil servants and the growing influence of organized crime have increased corruption and limited government effectiveness in one of the world's youngest and most vulnerable democracies.

BIBLIOGRAPHY

Forte, Maximilian Christian. *Indigenous Resurgence in the Contemporary Caribbean: Amerindian Survival and Revival.* New York: Peter Lang, 2006.

Hoefte, Rosemarijn, and Peter Meel. *Twentieth-Century Suriname: Continuities and Discontinuities in a New World Society.* Kingston, Jamaica: Ian Randle, 2001.

Thoden van Velzen, H. U. E., Wilhelmina van Wetering, and Dirk Van der Elst. *In the Shadow of the Oracle: Religion as Politics in a Suriname Maroon Society.* Long Grove, IL: Waveland Press, 2004.

⊕ Lao People's Democratic Republic

Type of Government

A multiethnic Communist state in Southeast Asia, the Lao People's Democratic Republic (Sathalanalat Paxathipatai Paxaxon Lao) was founded as a modern nation state in 1945 but possessed a monarchy dating back six centuries. Communist governmental authority rests with members of a unicameral (one-chambered) National Assembly elected by popular vote and an elected president, who serves as chief executive. A prime minister, leader of the majority party in the National Assembly, serves as head of government and is assisted by a Council of Ministers appointed by the president. The country's highest judicial authority is the People's Supreme Court in the capital city of Vientiane.

Background

Among the least developed and poorest of Asian nations, Laos found itself caught in the middle of decades of conflict in Southeast Asia during the twentieth century. A landlocked country, its historical, political, and cultural development have been heavily influenced by its neighbors. Laos is bordered on the east by Vietnam, on the south by Cambodia, and on the northwest by China and Myanmar; the vitally important Mekong River forms much of its western boundary with Thailand.

Laos is home to four distinct ethnic groups among the Lao, who make up the majority of Laos's inhabitants. The Lao Lum, or valley Lao, live in the country's lowlands and cities along the Mekong River. They account for two-thirds of the country's population. The Lao-Tai, or tribal Lao, live throughout the country, especially in the isolated higher mountain elevations. They are divided into the Black Tai and Red Tai, demonstrated by the color of tribal dresses worn by women. The Lao-Theung live throughout

Laos and into neighboring countries. They are thought to be descendants of original inhabitants whose presence in Laos dates back to prehistoric times. Also called the Mon-Khmer, their predominant religion is animism. The Lao-Soung, including the Hmong and Yao groups, probably migrated from southern China as recently as the late eighteenth century. Substantial groups of ethnic Chinese and Vietnamese live in Laotian cities. Urban life is limited to the former royal capital at Louangphrabang and the present-day capital of Vientiane, along with four of five other major towns. The rest of the country is primarily rural and agricultural with isolated valley communities near rivers and roads to provide access to markets and trading. Significant numbers of the rural tribal Lao subsist on hunting, gathering, and shifting agricultural cultivation.

Buddhism is practiced by 65 percent of the population and is sanctioned by the Communist government as the state religion. Confucianism is practiced by some urban ethnic Chinese and Vietnamese minorities. Animists, most living in isolated rural areas, constitute nearly 33 percent of the population. Christians constitute slightly over 1 percent. Lao is the country's official language; English, French, and Vietnamese are spoken by the elite in urban areas.

The Lao are a branch of the Tai people believed to have migrated from southern China sometime in the first millennium of the common era. The earliest known government entities in the central Mekong River basin—the center of Laotian economic life—were concentrations of political, economic, and military power known today as *mandalas*, to differentiate them from the modern notion of a nation-state. More powerful mandalas extracted tribute from other, smaller centers of power. In the fourteenth century a royal Tai leader, Fa Ngum (1316–1373), united many of these principalities into the Kingdom of Lan Xang, to which Laotian people trace their cultural and political ancestry.

In 1707 internal strife brought about the division of the Kingdom of Lan Xang into the three separate kingdoms of Vien Chan, Champassak, and Luang Prabang. Declining in power and regional authority, all three kingdoms came under the control of Siam (present-day Thailand) and became tribute-paying vassals of that state. In the late nineteenth century France gained control of all Siamese territory east of the Mekong River, part of the region that became known as French Indochina. Laos became a French protectorate in the early twentieth century.

Japan occupied Laos during World War II. In March 1945 the Japanese proclaimed the end of French colonial rule in Laos, compelling King Sisavang Vong (1885–1959) to issue a declaration of independence. A nationalist movement dethroned the king temporarily. French forces reoccupied Laos in 1946, and on August 27 France reestablished control over the country and reinstituted the monarchy. In May 1947 King Sisavang

Laotian King Savang Vatthana, who was forced to abdicate in 1975. © *Bettmann/CORBIS*

Vong promulgated a constitution providing for democratic government under a constitutional monarchy. The parliamentary democracy that emerged granted nominal executive authority to the king, who was assisted by a prime minister and Council of Ministers. The legislative branch of government was an elected fifty-nine-member National Assembly to whom the prime minister and cabinet were responsible.

In 1949 Laos gained limited autonomy when it became an independent sovereign state within the French Union. Communist-inspired Laotian Pathet Lao, or "land of the Lao," forces joined with the Vietnamese Viet Minh to fight against France in the First Indochina War in the early 1950s. By the end of the war the Pathet Lao controlled two Laotian provinces, while the remainder of the country remained a constitutional monarchy.

In 1954 the first Geneva Conference established a unified and fully independent Laos as a buffer state between Communist-aligned North Vietnam and Western-aligned Thailand. The Geneva Conference of 1962 created a coalition government for Laos, which included the Pathet Lao. The remainder of the 1960s was dominated by increased Laotian civil war and increased involvement in armed regional conflicts, particularly the Vietnam War. In 1973 a ceasefire was declared,

and 1974 saw the creation of the Laotian Provisional Government of National Unity, which included both Pathet Lao and rightist elements. Its collapse in 1975 was followed by the king's abdication, and the Vietnamese-backed Pathet Lao movement seized complete power in Laos and established the Lao People's Democratic Republic (LPDR), a Marxist-Leninist Communist government closely aligned with and modeled on Vietnam. It adhered to strict Communist economic strictures, including collectivization of agriculture, and ideologically orthodox social constraints. Government attempts to "reeducate" the country's elite and non-Communist-aligned leadership included forced labor camps and long periods of imprisonment. Human rights organizations estimate that approximately three hundred thousand Laotians "disappeared" within the borders of the country between 1975 and 2001. Even as of 2007, the ruling government of the LPDR did not tolerate dissent.

The mid-1980s brought a less centralized economy and a gradual increase in private enterprise. Farming returned to being a largely individual and family-based enterprise. The International Monetary Fund and other international sources continue to provide essential financial aid without which the economy would collapse. Once powerful, Vietnamese political and economic influence in

Laos began to diminish in the 1990s. The Laotian government today practices a kind of economic pragmatism that reconciles Communist ideology with marketplace realities. The government retains strict control of all communication media, including French and English language newspapers in urban areas.

Government Structure

Sixteen years after the establishment of the LPDR, the national legislature—the Supreme People's Assembly—completed the task of drafting a constitution and promulgated it in August 1991. It calls for a National Assembly: a unicameral, or one-chambered, legislature, which as of the 2006 elections consisted of 115 members elected by popular vote for terms of five years. The constitution also calls for executive power to be vested in a president and a Council of Ministers, headed by a prime minister, who serves as head of the National Assembly's majority party. Laos currently has only one legal political party, the Lao People's Revolutionary Party (LPRP).

The legal system in Laos is based on traditional regional custom and French legal norms and procedures, as well as socialist practice. Various provincial and appellate courts hear cases across Laos. The country's highest court is the People's Supreme Court, whose judges are appointed by a special committee of the National Assembly.

Political Parties and Factions

Since 1975, the LPRP has been Laos's only legal political party. Founded in 1955 by Prince Souphanouvong (1909–1995) and prominent politician Kaysone Phomvihan (1920–1992), both of whom were influenced by the regional Indochinese Communist Party, the party remained secret until the establishment of Communist government in Laos in 1975. The party's internal structure includes a politburo, responsible for decision-making at the highest level.

Major Events

More than 10 percent of Laotians, including most members of the political opposition, fled the country in the aftermath of the Communist takeover in 1975. Many settled in Thailand, while others landed in the United States, France, Australia, and Canada.

In 1997 Laos joined the Association of Southeast Asian Nations (ASEAN), which had first been established by Malaysia, Singapore, Indonesia, the Philippines, and Thailand in 1967. Brunei joined in 1984, followed by Vietnam, Cambodia, and Myanmar in the 1990s. ASEAN seeks to reduce tensions and increase collaboration among its member nations. It works to accelerate the region's economic growth, cultural development, and social progress. In 1999 ASEAN's member nations agreed to pursue development of a free trade zone in Southeast Asia by eventually eliminating duties on most goods traded in the region. Estimated to take effect in the year 2010 or later, the proposed zone will be the world's largest free trade zone, encompassing some 1.7 billion people and trade valued at $1.2 trillion. In May 2002 ASEAN's ten member countries pledged to form a united front against terrorism in response to the September 11, 2001, terrorist attacks in the United States. They established a regional security framework, including joint training programs, exchange of intelligence information, and the introduction of national laws governing arrest, investigation, and extradition of suspects.

Southeast Asian financial markets took a sudden, precipitous decline in 1997 when investors lost confidence in a number of Asian currencies and securities. In Laos the decline interrupted economic growth rates noticeable since partial privatization of the economy in the 1980s. The crisis inflicted particularly harsh damage on the value of the kip, Laos's national currency.

In 2003, closure of Laotian refugee camps in Thailand forced tens of thousands of Laotian exiles to return home, where they initially expected harsh reprisals. The government instead encouraged their peaceful settlement among politically moderate lowland populations.

Twenty-First Century

Laos is a mountainous country with thick subtropical forests covering much of the land. It lacks modern infrastructure in the way of roads, railways, and telecommunications. Electricity is available in only a few urban areas. Government plans in the twenty-first century call for major road improvements, including some scheduled to be done with Japanese financial support.

Subsistence agriculture provides 80 percent of total employment and accounts for half of the country's gross domestic product (GDP), which ranks among the lowest in Asia. Important crops are rice, sweet potatoes, corn, coffee, sugarcane, tobacco, cotton, tea, and peanuts. What light manufacturing exists depends on the processing of raw materials and natural resources. Key exports are garments, wood products, coffee, electricity, and tin. Proposed hydropower and road building projects are expected to increase demand for construction labor and create some additional revenue. The rivers of Laos hold enormous potential for the development of water storage and hydroelectric power. One major hydroelectric project is already operational, with another scheduled for completion in 2013. Opposition to hydroelectric development comes chiefly from international concerns regarding potential environmental and social costs.

The limited Laotian economy does not permit maintenance of a properly funded military, and there is little political will in the country to allocate sparse funding to the Lao People's Army and the country's air force, which have become degraded over time. Some international security situations are likely to remain unaddressed in the twenty-first century, drug trafficking among them. Northern Laos is part of Asia's infamous opium-producing

"Golden Triangle" region, which periodically produces problems with armed smugglers and trafficking along the Laos-Myanmar border.

Other illicit issues plague Laos, which shares with Cambodia and Thailand an active and recognized sex industry, largely centered in urban areas. It is also a transit and destination country for trafficking of human beings, usually economic migrants (immigrants seeking to improve their quality of life), who are used in prostitution. Laos does not yet fully comply with internationally agreed-upon minimum standards for elimination of human trafficking and has yet to make significant efforts to do so.

In the twenty-first century the citizens of Laos face serious health issues. Life expectancy in the country remains relatively low at fifty-four years for men and fifty-eight years for women. Malaria, influenza, dysentery, and pneumonia remain leading causes of death and are prominent public health concerns. Eighty percent of Laos's people live in rural areas, where medical care and public health services remain inadequate. Improvement of services is a high government priority.

BIBLIOGRAPHY

Evans, Grant. *The Land in Between: A Short History of Laos.* New South Wales: Allen & Unwin, 2002.

Savada, Andrea Matles, ed. *Laos: A Country Study.* U.S. Government Printing Office, 1995.

Stuart-Fox, Martin. *A History of Laos.* New York and London: Cambridge University Press, 1997.

⊕ Seychelles

Type of Government

The government of Seychelles is a multiparty republic with powers divided between independent executive, legislative, and judicial branches. The executive branch is headed by a president, who is head of state and head of the government. The legislative branch is made up of a popularly elected unicameral parliament. The president appoints top members of the judicial branch.

Background

Seychelles is an archipelago of 115 islands in the Indian Ocean, east of Kenya and northeast of Madagascar. The islands are divided into two distinct geographical categories: the forty-two granite islands have central hills surrounded by narrow coastlines, while the other islands are essentially large coral reefs. The coral islands have little freshwater and few are inhabited. Almost 90 percent of the population is concentrated on Mahé, the largest island and the site of Victoria, the national capital.

Portuguese explorer Vasco da Gama (c. 1460–1524) discovered the Seychelles in 1505, but the islands remained uninhabited for another 150 years. France staked a claim to the archipelago in 1742, when the governor of the African island nation of Mauritius sent an expedition. A second expedition followed in 1756 and named the islands for the French minister of finance under Louis XV (1710–1774). French colonists soon began coming to the area, often bringing African slaves to work on plantations. The result is a culture drawn from French, Asian, and African traditions, with Creole as the predominant language. France administered Seychelles as a dependency of Mauritius, with the governor general of Mauritius overseeing both territories.

Following the Napoleonic wars, Great Britain was awarded both Mauritius and Seychelles in the 1814 Treaty of Paris. Like France, Britain subordinated Seychelles to the governor general of Mauritius, but by 1888 Seychelles had grown prominent enough to warrant its own executive and legislative councils. Great Britain continued to upgrade the archipelago's status, until Seychelles became a Crown colony on August 31, 1903.

By 1964 Seychelles had two active political parties, the Seychelles Democratic Party (SDP) and the Seychelles People's Unity Party (SPUP). A constitutional convention in March 1970 led to the promulgation of a constitution and elections for a new parliament in November. The SDP won ten of the fifteen seats in the new parliament (SPUP took the other five), giving its leader, James Mancham (1939–), the post of chief minister.

In the 1974 parliamentary election, both parties campaigned for independence from Great Britain. London agreed and began a two-year transition process. A coalition government of both the SDP and the SPUP formed in June 1975 and asked Britain to constitute an advisory committee to help determine the electoral and constitutional parameters of an independent Seychelles. They agreed to add ten seats to the legislature, with each party responsible for selecting five members, and formed a new Cabinet of Ministers. Given the SDP's win in the 1974 election, it was allocated eight cabinet posts, while the SPUP received four. Mancham would become president, while the SPUP leader, Albert René (1935–), would be the new prime minister. Seychelles became an independent, sovereign state on June 29, 1976. Great Britain also reassigned the island of Desroches's two island groups, Aldabra and Farquhar, to the Seychelles government. They had been administered as part of the British Indian Ocean Territory since 1965 but had historical ties to Seychelles.

Government Structure

Executive authority in Seychelles is exercised by a president, who is simultaneously head of state and head of government. The president appoints the Cabinet of Ministers to advise him in his work. The president is popularly elected for a maximum of two five-year terms. James Michel (1944–) won his first term as president in July 2006.

The legislative branch of the Seychellois government is a thirty-four-member unicameral (single-chamber) parliament called the National Assembly. Twenty-five members of parliament are directly elected, while the other nine are chosen via proportional representation (PR). Parties must win at least 10 percent of the vote to be eligible for one of the PR seats. Members serve five-year terms.

Judicial authority is vested in a Supreme Court and an Appeals Court, and the legal code is based on English common law, French civil law, and customary law. The president appoints members of both courts. The chief justice must be a citizen of Seychelles, either through birth or naturalization, while the other members are hired from other British Commonwealth countries on seven-year contracts.

There are twenty-three district councils, and the dominant Seychelles People's Progressive Front (SPPF) appoints all members of the councils. All citizens of Seychelles are permitted to vote beginning at the age of eighteen.

Political Parties and Factions

Seychelles has three leading political parties. Founded in 1979, the socialist SPPF was the sole official party until 1992. It has been in power for thirty years, and it is often difficult to differentiate between party and state. The Seychelles National Party (SNP), led by Wavel Ramkalawan (1961–), is heir to the pre-independence Seychelles Democratic Party and currently is the primary opposition party in parliament. The Democratic Party (DP), led by former president Mancham, formed an alliance with the SNP for the 2007 parliamentary election, after failing to win any seats in 1998 and 2002.

Major Events

On June 5, 1977, while President Mancham was out of the country, supporters of Prime Minister René took control of the government and proclaimed him president. René then suspended the constitution and dissolved parliament. In response, some ten thousand citizens fled abroad. He ruled by decree until a new constitution was approved in a referendum in March 1979, but René refused to accept a multiparty political system. Instead, the socialist SPPF—a new incarnation of the Seychelles People's United Party—became the sole legal political party.

In November 1981 René survived a coup attempt by mercenaries hired to reinstate Mancham. Their plot was discovered, and the hired guns hijacked a flight and fled to South Africa. In August 1982 the Tanzanian military helped suppress an army mutiny.

René announced he would allow the registration of political parties on December 4, 1991. Many exiles, including Mancham, took this opportunity to return home and reestablish themselves in the Seychellois polit-

Albert René ruled the Seychelles from 1977 until his retirement in 2004. © *Zen Icknow/Corbis*

ical scene. By April 1992 eight political parties had applied to participate in elections for a constitutional commission to convene July 23–26. The commission, consisting of fourteen SPPF members and eight DP members, settled on a text for national reconciliation and a democratic constitution, which was approved in a national referendum in June 1993.

From July 23 to July 26, 1993, Seychellois voted for a new president and legislature. René was returned as president, and the SPPF won a parliamentary majority. The same pattern was repeated in 1998, 2001, and 2006. However, over time both René and the SPPF won their elections by narrower and narrower margins, suggesting the party was losing its dominant position. In 2001 René received 54 percent of the vote, while challenger Wavel Ramkalawan took 45 percent.

President René resigned in 2004 and appointed Vice President James Michel of the SPPF to be his successor. With presidential elections scheduled for 2006, René hoped two years would be enough for Michel to build popular support. The plan appeared to work, as Michel was declared winner of the July 2006 presidential election, taking 53.7 percent of the vote to the 45.7 percent officially recorded for his challenger, SNP leader Ramkalawan. When the National Assembly voted to prevent political parties from owning radio stations or newspapers, SNP members of parliament refused to attend Assembly sessions for the next six months. Ultimately, Michel dissolved parliament on March 20, 2007, and called early elections for May 10–12. The SPPF took twenty-three seats, while an alliance between the SNP and the DP took the remaining eleven.

Twenty-First Century

Seychelles has impressive levels of education, health care, and social security, thanks to the heavy government spending by René's socialist regime. However, those gains have left the country deeply indebted. In the twenty-first century the government needs to find ways to generate funds other than deficit spending. Plans are underway to increase the fishing and tourism sectors, attract foreign direct investment, and encourage import substitution industrialization (replacing imports with locally produced products). The government launched a privatization program in 1990 that has attracted some foreign investors.

BIBLIOGRAPHY

Hoare, Mike. *The Seychelles Affair*. London: Bantam Press, 1986.

McAteer, William. *Hard Times in Paradise: The History of the Seychelles, 1827–1919*. Mahé, Seychelles: Pristine Books, 2000.

Scarr, Deryck. *Seychelles Since 1770: History of a Slave and Post-Slave Society*. Trenton, NJ: Africa World Press, 1999.

⊕ Socialist Republic of Vietnam

Type of Government

A Communist state, Vietnam invests legislative authority in its elected National Assembly. From among its membership, the assembly selects a president to act as the nation's chief executive for a term of five years. The president chooses a prime minister from among other National Assembly members. The prime minister leads a cabinet of government ministers appointed by the president and approved by a vote of the National Assembly. Judicial authority in Vietnam rests with the national Supreme People's Court.

Background

Located in Southeast Asia, Vietnam is bordered on the north by China, on the west by Laos and Cambodia, and on the south and east by the South China Sea. Its twentieth-century history included decades of warfare and political disruption, including struggles for independence and years of immersion in an internationally

observed and controversial war between the nation's north and south that involved the United States. Around the globe, Vietnam remains identified with its war-torn past, but its youthful and enterprising population is cultivating greater commercial and technological involvement in the world, despite living in a closely guarded society.

Ancestors of the modern-day Vietnamese settled in the vicinity of the Red River Delta in northern Vietnam sometime during the first millennium BC. By the third century BC they had established the Kingdom of Van Lang, which was conquered by a Chinese military adventurer who incorporated the Red River Delta area into his own southern Chinese kingdom. A century later the expanding Chinese empire itself reached Vietnam and incorporated the Red River Delta. China ruled Vietnam for a thousand years, bringing significant change to Vietnamese society and introducing Chinese social and political institutions. Chinese architecture, art, and literature, as well as its written language, followed. In AD 939 Vietnamese rebels seized the opportunity presented by a period of imperial weakness and restored independence to Vietnam.

During several hundred years of independent rule, the Vietnamese Empire, known as Dai Viet, or "Great Viet," expanded to the south while developing its own social and political institutions. Two great dynasties, the Ly (1009–1225) and the Tran (1225–1400), fended off repeated Chinese attempts to reincorporate Vietnam. Subsequent dynasties and further territorial expansion eventually brought the entire Mekong River Delta under Vietnamese rule during the seventeenth century. Vietnam's first north-south division occurred when expansion inadvertently brought on civil war between two royal clans, the Trinh in the north of the country and the Nguyen in the south. The country eventually reunified under a third dynasty.

European colonial conquest reached Vietnam in the mid-nineteenth century. France succeeded in establishing a protectorate over central and northern Vietnam between 1858 and 1884. In 1895 Vietnam was included with the protectorates of Laos and Cambodia in the union of French Indochina.

Western-style nationalist movements opposed to French colonial rule began to appear after the end of World War I. They gained momentum when nationalist leader Ho Chi Minh (1890–1969) formed the Indochinese Communist Party in 1930. Following the collapse of the French government during World War II, Japan forced the French to accept a Japanese military occupation of Indochina. During this time the Japanese installed a puppet Vietnamese government with Bao Dai (1913–1997), the figurehead emperor of Vietnam, as head of state. After World War II, and the return of French rule, Ho Chi Minh's Viet Minh movement waged a successful eight-year war, known as the First Indochina War, for

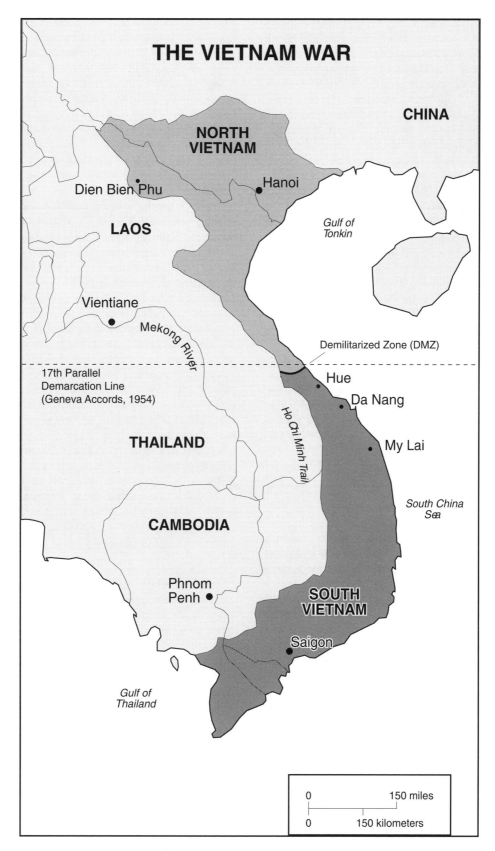

THE VIETNAM WAR

CHINA

NORTH VIETNAM

Dien Bien Phu

Hanoi

LAOS

Gulf of Tonkin

Vientiane

Mekong River

Demilitarized Zone (DMZ)

17th Parallel
Demarcation Line
(Geneva Accords, 1954)

Hue

Da Nang

Ho Chi Minh Trail

My Lai

THAILAND

South China Sea

CAMBODIA

Phnom Penh

SOUTH VIETNAM

Saigon

Gulf of Thailand

| 0 | | 150 miles |
| 0 | | 150 kilometers |

Important locations during the Vietnam War, 1964–1975. *Gale, a part of Cengage Learning*

Vietnamese independence from France. The French withdrew from the country in 1954 after sustained guerilla warfare and a decisive defeat at Dien Bien Phu. That same year, the Geneva Conference of world leaders divided Vietnam at the seventeenth parallel of latitude into separate northern and southern states. Vietnamese Communists held the north (the Democratic Republic of Vietnam), while non-Communist and pro-French elements took the south (becoming the Republic of Vietnam). In 1957 future conflict became imminent when a Communist insurgency began in South Vietnam.

Fearful that a so-called "domino effect" might take hold in Southeast Asia, if more countries established Communist governments, the United States began pouring economic and military aid into sustaining the South Vietnamese government. Beginning in 1964, American bombing raids and troop deployments increased until planes averaged one hundred sorties per day and troops engaged on the ground numbered five hundred thousand. At the height of conflict, 1.25 million American and South Vietnamese troops were deployed in the war effort.

As American politicians lost the political will to continue the conflict, troops were gradually withdrawn and negotiated settlements were sought. The final withdrawal of U.S. troops in 1975 allowed North Vietnamese forces to overrun South Vietnam and take the capital city of Saigon, renaming it Ho Chi Minh City. In July 1976 the Socialist Republic of Vietnam was officially proclaimed, and the country united under one government.

Government Structure

Elections for a new National Assembly were held just after reunification. Preoccupied with nationalization of industry and other economic and social changes, the National Assembly finally approved a new constitution for the country in December 1980. It declared Vietnam to be led by the Communist Party. The highest state authority was the unicameral, or one-chambered, National Assembly, whose members were elected to five-year terms by voters aged eighteen and older. The National Assembly appointed a cabinet of thirty-three ministers—the Council of Ministers—whose chairman acted as the country's premier. The Council of State, made up of twelve members, acted as the country's collective presidency. Its members were chosen from among the membership of the National Assembly and remained accountable to it.

In 1992 the Vietnamese National Assembly adopted the country's present constitution. It reaffirmed the authority of the Communist Party but held that the party must be subject to the law. It expressed support for a free market economy and replaced the Council of State with a single president to be elected by the National Assembly from among its membership for a term of five years. The president could appoint a prime minister, also from

among the National Assembly and subject to its approval. Legislative authority remained with the assembly, and its membership was calculated on the basis of one deputy for every ten thousand voters in urban areas and for every thirty thousand in rural areas. In theory, the National Assembly is Vietnam's sovereign power. In reality, it functions as a rubber stamp to ratify decisions already reached by the Vietnamese Communist Party leadership and the executive branch of the government. In recent years, however, greater numbers of candidates have run for election to the Assembly, including some nonparty candidates approved by the party. Deputies take an increasingly greater role in decision making and selection of key government officials. The number of women deputies in the National Assembly is increasing.

Vietnam's legal system is based on Communist legal theory and French civil law. Local courts are found throughout the country's administrative districts. Military courts, and special courts created by the National Assembly, initially handle certain cases. Vietnam's highest court is the Supreme People's Court, whose judges are appointed for five-year terms by the National Assembly according to the recommendation of the president. Although the constitution of 1992 provides for an independent judiciary, the Vietnamese Communist Party exercises close control of the entire government, and the judicial selection process favors candidates supportive of the party.

Vietnam's struggle with reunification included initial adherence to strict Communist economic strictures, including collectivization of agriculture. Elements of free enterprise and a market system began appearing in the 1980s, and a stock exchange opened in 2000. As of 2007, Vietnam's largest trading partner was the United States.

Political Parties and Factions

Ho Chi Minh founded the Indochinese Communist Party in 1930. It was formally dissolved in 1945 but operated secretly until 1951, when it emerged as the Vietnamese Workers Party. It assumed its current identity as the Vietnamese Communist Party upon the country's political reunification as the Socialist Republic of Vietnam in 1976. A party central committee guides affairs and elects the politburo, the party's highest policy-making body. The Vietnamese Communist Party remains the country's only legal political party. Nonaligned, or "independent," candidates may run for office but only with the party's approval.

Viet Minh, also known as the League for the Independence of Vietnam, was a front organization set up by the Indochinese Communist Party at the suggestion of Ho Chi Minh. It was designed to win popular support for independence and social and economic reform. Active at the province, district, and village level, it also organized women, writers, peasants, students, workers, artists, and religious organizations into national-level associations. When forces aligned with the Indochinese Communist Party seized power in Vietnam in 1945 and proclaimed the Democratic Republic of Vietnam, they used the Viet Minh and its associated organizations to achieve broader support in their struggle for independence from the French. The Viet Minh was instrumental in the fight against the French and their allies in the First Indochina War, which is sometimes called the Franco–Viet Minh War.

The Fatherland Front, a successor to the Viet Minh, was formed in North Vietnam in 1955, also as a vehicle for mobilizing popular support. A similar organization was established among South Vietnamese Communists in 1960 and named the National Liberation Front. At the fall of the Republic of Vietnam (South Vietnam) in 1975, the two organizations merged into one, still known as the Fatherland Front.

Major Events

Enactment of economic renovation policies in 1986, known as *doi moi* policies, has committed Vietnamese authorities to increased economic liberalization and the reform and modernization of the economy to allow for development of more competitive, export-driven industries. Chief Vietnamese exports include crude oil, marine products, rice, coffee, rubber, tea, garments, and shoes. While the doi moi policies remain controversial for some members of Vietnam's older Communist elite, the country is home to one of the fastest-growing economies in Southeast Asia.

In 1995 Vietnam joined the Association of Southeast Asian Nations (ASEAN), which had first been established by Thailand, Singapore, Indonesia, the Philippines, and Malaysia in 1967. Brunei joined in 1984, and during the 1990s Laos, Cambodia, and Myanmar became members. ASEAN seeks to reduce tensions and increase collaboration among its member nations. Accelerating the region's economic growth, cultural development, and social progress are among its aims. In 1999 ASEAN's member nations agreed to pursue development of a free trade zone in Southeast Asia by eventually eliminating duties on most goods traded in the region. Estimated to take effect in the year 2010 or later, the proposed zone will be the world's largest free trade zone, encompassing some 1.7 billion people and trade valued at $1.2 trillion. In May 2002 ASEAN's ten member countries pledged to form a united front against terrorism in response to the September 11, 2001, terrorist attacks in the United States. They established a regional security framework, including joint training programs, exchange of intelligence information, and the introduction of national laws governing arrest, investigation, and extradition of suspects.

Southeast Asian financial markets took a sudden, precipitous decline in 1997 when investors lost confidence in a number of Asian currencies and securities.

North Vietnamese leader Ho Chi Minh, 1950. *© Bettmann/CORBIS*

The crisis highlighted problems in Vietnam's economy and temporarily allowed opponents of economic reform to slow the process of liberalization and modernization. As the economic crisis subsided, however, reform continued, and Vietnam continued to improve its image among nations. In 2000 U.S. President Bill Clinton paid a three-day official visit to Vietnam, signaling the beginning of a new stage in the relationship between the two countries.

Twenty-First Century

Increasing crime rates in Vietnamese cities, plus endemic corruption and drug smuggling, are expected to continue challenging the resources of law enforcement agencies and the criminal justice system. Despite long-standing efforts to crack down on illicit drug use, the government continues to face the problem of opium, heroin, and methamphetamine addiction among its people.

Vietnam has set the year 2020 as a goal for becoming a developed nation. Significant disparities in wealth between urban and rural Vietnamese remain and are a cause of concern for Communist Party leadership.

Human rights groups have spoken out against Vietnam's suppression of political dissent and religious practice, which continues in the twenty-first century. The Ministry of Culture and Information controls the nation's press and broadcast media. Internet cafés are popular but are required to register the personal details of customers. Several publications have been shut down for violating narrow limits on reporting. Hundreds of magazines and newspapers are available, but television is the dominant medium. In addition to the government station in Hanoi, which broadcasts nationwide, there are numerous provincial stations. Some foreign channels are available by cable. The state-run radio features programs in English, French, and Russian, as well as Vietnamese.

BIBLIOGRAPHY

Ashwill, Mark, and Thai Ngoc Diep. *Vietnam Today: A Guide to a Nation at a Crossroads.* Boston: Intercultural Press, 2004.

Chapuis, Oscar. *A History of Vietnam: From Hong Bang to Tu Duc* (Contributions in Asian Studies). Westport, CT: Greenwood Press, 1995.

Duiker, William J. *Vietnam since the Fall of Saigon* (Monographs in International Studies). Athens: Ohio University Press, 1989.

⊕ Djibouti

Type of Government

Djibouti is a small but strategically important republic on the coast of northeastern Africa. A constitution passed in 1992 mandates a multiparty system with an elected president, an appointed prime minister, and a unicameral assembly.

Background

Djibouti's location overlooking one of the narrowest portions of the crucial Red Sea shipping lanes gives it far greater economic and military significance than its small size, inhospitable climate, and barren landscape would otherwise suggest. A major trade depot for centuries, Djibouti remains a primary conduit for goods entering and leaving East Africa. But persistent drought and instability in all three of its immediate neighbors (Eritrea, to the north; Ethiopia, to the west and south; and Somalia, to the southeast) have hindered efforts to reduce widespread poverty and an unemployment rate of fifty percent.

Djibouti's population is difficult to estimate for a variety of reasons, including a high but inconstant growth rate, underreported infant mortality, and significant numbers of nomads, illegal aliens, and refugees. Most 2007 estimates range between seven hundred and eight hundred thousand. The great majority of these are members of the Issa or Afar tribal groups. The Issas, who constitute sixty percent of the population, are a Somali people; the Afars, who constitute thirty-five percent, are not. Though relations between the two groups have never been warm, the establishment of the French colony of Somaliland in the nineteenth century thrust them into closer contact, deepening longstanding rivalries and fueling mutual resentments. In 1967 administrators changed the colony's name from French Somaliland to the French Territory of the Afars and Issas in a belated attempt to reduce tribal tensions. Despite significant autonomy under French rule, demands for full independence grew, in part because each tribe felt the French favored the other. On June 27, 1977, the French formally withdrew, and the new nation of Djibouti was born. A one-party system under President Hassan Gouled Aptidon (1916–2006) was established, and authoritarianism remained the rule until domestic and international pressures forced Aptidon to allow opposition parties and a new constitution. This document, accepted in a national referendum in September 1992, remains the basis of government.

Government Structure

Executive powers are split between the president, elected by direct, popular vote for a maximum of two six-year terms, and the prime minister he or she appoints. Assisting the prime minister in setting policy and overseeing government operations are the members of the cabinet, known as the Council of Ministers; these are also presidential appointees.

Legislative powers are vested in a unicameral, sixty-five seat assembly called the Chamber of Deputies. Members are elected by direct, popular vote for five-year terms. The party with the most votes in a particular constituency wins all the seats allocated to that constituency. It is possible, therefore, for a party to win as much as forty-nine percent of the popular vote without gaining a seat.

The legal system is a mixture of French law, local custom, and traditional Islamic law (known as sharia), though the last of these is limited to family and civil matters. The legal structure consists of lower courts, appeals courts, and a Supreme Court, which serves as the court of final appeal. Magistrates at all levels are appointed for life. Despite the separation of government powers mandated in the constitution, the executive branch has repeatedly intervened in judicial matters. Defendants sometimes lack legal representation, and there have been frequent reports of abuse by guards in the nation's jails and prisons. The death penalty was officially abolished for all crimes in 1995.

For administrative purposes, the nation is divided into six regions. At least two-thirds of the population lives in the capital (also called Djibouti).

Political Parties and Factions

Between 1981 and 1992, the sole legal party was President Aptidon's organization, known as the People's Rally for Progress (RPP). With the shift to a multiparty system in 1992, two major opposition groups, the Party for Democratic Renewal (PRD) and the National Democratic Party (PND), emerged to oppose the RPP in the

Soldiers looking on as protesters rally against the French presence in Djibouti in 1976.   © *Christian Simonpietri/Sygma/Corbis*

approaching elections. The PND soon withdrew, however, leaving the PRD as the sole alternative to the ruling party. Voter turnout in the nation's first multiparty elections was unusually low, and the RPP took all sixty-five seats in the Chamber of Deputies.

Though it did not participate in the elections, a group calling itself the Front for the Restoration of Unity and Democracy, or FRUD, was growing increasingly prominent throughout the country. Dominated by Afars, FRUD began an armed struggle against the government in 1991 in response to what it characterized as systematic discrimination by the Issa majority. After a peace treaty in 1994, the FRUD rebels were integrated into the armed forces, and the group agreed to restrict itself to nonviolent activities. In a remarkable turnaround, FRUD soon became an ally of the RPP, its sworn enemy only a few years before. The latter's dominance has continued, though President Aptidon, the party's founder, retired from office in 1999. He was succeeded by his nephew, Ismail Guelleh (1947–), who won a second term in 2005 when he ran unopposed. In terms of popularity, FRUD represents the most viable alternative to the status quo. Its ties to the RPP, however, have compromised its ability to lead the opposition or even to field its own candidates.

The FRUD-RPP alliance is known as the Union for the Presidential Majority, or UMP, and also includes the PND and the smaller People's Social Democratic Party (PPSD). Opposing it is the Union for Democratic Changeover (UAD), a coalition that includes the Union for Democracy and Justice (UDJ), the Republican Alliance for Democracy (ARD), the Djibouti Development Party (PDD), and the Movement for Democratic Renewal and Development (MRDD). Given the nation's electoral rules, it is unlikely that any of these smaller parties will gain assembly seats in the foreseeable future.

Finally, there exist a number of very small extremist groups. The most prominent of these are probably the FRUD and RPP factions that refused to accept the peace treaty of 1994. In addition, the existence of at least a few Islamic extremists is likely given the nation's proximity to Somalia and Yemen, both of which have seen several attacks by al Qaeda. As the site of the only U.S. military base in Africa, Djibouti is an attractive but relatively difficult target. While the extent of Islamic extremism in Djibouti is unknown, there is no doubt that the government's acceptance of a strong U.S. military presence has earned it enmity from opponents of the United States throughout the region.

Major Events

The dissolution of Somalia into a patchwork of warring fiefdoms in 1991 has had several profound and largely destructive effects on Djibouti. The most visible of these are the squalid refugee camps housing thousands of Somali refugees. The precise number is unknown; recent estimates of ten thousand are probably too low. Though efforts at repatriation are ongoing, they have not been particularly successful. Many of the refugees prefer living illegally in the streets of the capital to repatriation. Among these are children and unmarried women at high risk of abduction, forced labor, and sexual exploitation. Because these crimes are relatively common throughout East Africa and the Middle East, and because Djibouti is a major transit point between those two areas, it has emerged as a center of what is known as human trafficking. The U.S. State Department has placed Djibouti in the second tier of its Human Trafficking Watch List, a classification indicating that the nation's efforts to eliminate these crimes do not meet minimum international standards. It also indicates, however, that the State Department believes local authorities are making significant, good-faith efforts to meet those standards.

Djibouti has recently received considerable attention in the international press in the context of U.S. anti-terror operations. In 2006, for example, Amnesty International released a report naming Djibouti as a center of the U.S. Central Intelligence Agency's so-called "extraordinary rendition" program. Few details are available, but it appears that the CIA has access to a global network of secret prisons in which suspected Islamic extremists have been detained and interrogated without trial. Amnesty International's report named Djibouti, a close U.S. ally, as the site of one of these prisons. While these charges are hotly debated, it is clear that they have focused international attention on Djibouti's own human rights record, which is mixed. Though the nation ratified the International Covenant on Civil and Political Rights in 2002, journalists critical of the government continue to risk detention, and the newspapers that employ them are routinely shut down. In June 2007 the international group Reporters Without Borders drew attention to the government's recent closure of the nation's only remaining privately owned newspaper, *Le Renouveau Djiboutien*, a weekly publication associated with the opposition party MRDD. The newspaper's managing editor was detained four times in 2003 and currently lives abroad. Following this most recent closure, the government controlled all print media in the country.

Twenty-First Century

Many of the problems facing Djibouti in the twenty-first century are related to the chaos in Somalia. In addition to the refugee issue, Djibouti faces a number of difficult foreign policy choices. All of the factions in Somalia have targeted civilians, and none appears able to win. In those circumstances, it is not at all clear which faction to support, or even to recognize. Djibouti recently established a close relationship with the breakaway state of Somaliland, which has rebelled from the internationally recognized but essentially powerless Somali government. Somaliland's success, however, is by no means assured, and many observers have criticized Djibouti's actions as premature and likely to alienate other Somali factions. Should one or more factions in Somalia decide to attempt to crush Somaliland's rebellion, Djibouti may find itself under attack as well.

A similar but slightly less likely scenario exists with regard to the nation's other immediate neighbors, Eritrea and Ethiopia. Armed conflict between the two has been ongoing for decades. Eritrea, though much smaller than Ethiopia, nevertheless possesses one important geographic advantage: it controls landlocked Ethiopia's traditional route to the Red Sea. The best alternative route lies through Djibouti. If the conflict grows more intense, as it has periodically, the rail link between the Ethiopian capital of Addis Ababa and the port of Djibouti will be an attractive target for the Eritreans.

BIBLIOGRAPHY

Battling Terrorism in the Horn of Africa. Robert I. Rotberg, ed. Washington, D.C.: Brookings Institution Press, 2005.

Milas, Seifulaziz. *Prevention of Violent Conflict and the Coherence of EU Policies Towards the Horn of Africa: A Case Study on Demobilisation in Djibouti.* London: InterAfrica Group, 2000.

Woodward, Peter. *The Horn of Africa: Politics and International Relations.* London: I. B. Tauris, 2003.

⊕ Solomon Islands

Type of Government

The Solomon Islands is formally governed by a constitutional monarchy: the British monarch serves as head of state, and the governor-general acts as his or her local representative. In practice, however, the administration of the nation is carried out through a parliamentary democracy. The unicameral (single-chamber) National Parliament is the nation's decision-making body, and the prime minister is head of the government.

Background

The Solomon Islands encompasses two parallel island chains stretching across more than nine hundred miles in the southwestern Pacific Ocean. The nation comprises six main islands—Choiseul, New Georgia, Santa Isabel, Guadalcanal, Malaita, and San Christóbal—and more than nine hundred smaller islands. Two of the largest islands of the Solomon archipelago, Bougainville and

Buka, are politically part of Papua New Guinea. The nation's capital is Honiara, on Guadalcanal Island.

By at least 2000 BC, peoples of Polynesian origin had settled on the Solomon Islands, organizing hunting-and-gathering societies. In 1568 the Spanish explorer Álvaro de Mendaña de Neira (1541–1595) was the first European to have contact with the islands; he believed the islands were the source of the gold that the biblical King Solomon had used to build his temple in Jerusalem. Subsequent Spanish voyages, however, were unable to reach the islands, and it was not until the late eighteenth century that European settlements were established there. Missionaries and traders followed in greater numbers.

During the nineteenth century, tens of thousands of Solomon Islanders were forcibly recruited to work as slave labor on the sugar and cotton plantations of Australia and Fiji, a common practice in the South Pacific known as "blackbirding." The natives fought back against this exploitation, leading to a series of bloody massacres. The British declared a protectorate over the southern Solomon Islands in 1893, partly in response to the labor trade, but also to protect the area from French colonization. The northern islands, which had been under German administration since the 1880s, were transferred to British control throughout the 1890s. The colonial authorities focused on promoting the interests of European planters. Although the labor abuses were halted, the native people reaped few economic or political benefits from the new regime.

At the outset of World War II, the British evacuated the territory's European settlers to Australia, and the Japanese occupied the Solomon Islands in 1942. The islanders saw intense combat between the Allied and Japanese forces, culminating in the pivotal Battle of Guadalcanal from August 1942 to February 1943. At war's end, the British reestablished their protectorate and moved the capital to Honiara on Guadalcanal Island, where the American military had left behind a substantial infrastructure.

The end of the war also marked the beginning of the Solomon Islands' march toward independence. During the late 1940s an independence movement called Maasina Rule (also known as Marching Rule) organized strikes and demonstrations on the islands; the British authorities responded by jailing the movement's leaders, but other groups continued to agitate for self-determination. In 1960 the Solomon Islands was given legislative and executive councils, whose authority grew over the decade. Great Britain granted the protectorate self-governance in 1976, and the Solomon Islands achieved complete independence in 1978.

The Solomon Islands has full membership in the Commonwealth of Nations (also called the British Commonwealth), a voluntary association of more than fifty independent nations that are former colonies or territories of the British Empire.

Government Structure

The structure and functions of government are outlined in the nation's constitution, which was adopted upon independence in 1978. The British monarch Queen Elizabeth II (1926–) is the Solomon Islands' head of state, although the role is purely symbolic. The monarch is represented in the islands by a governor-general, who is chosen by the legislature to serve a five-year term. Although the governor-general is invested with some executive authority—he or she formally appoints members of the cabinet, the chief justice of the Supreme Court, and other judges—the position is largely ceremonial. The governor-general must be a resident of the Solomon Islands.

The head of government is the prime minister, who is elected from among the members of the legislature. The prime minister is advised by a cabinet of twenty members, who are appointed by the governor-general on the recommendation of the prime minister. Cabinet members lead the major departments of government.

The Solomon Islands has a single-chamber legislature called the National Parliament. This body is made up of fifty members who are elected by popular vote from single-member constituencies. Members serve four-year terms. However, the National Parliament has the right to dissolve the government and hold new elections—that is, pass a motion of "no confidence"—before the end of its four-year term with a majority vote. The no-confidence vote has been used frequently in modern Solomon Islands politics, leading to unstable government.

Because politics in the Solomon Islands operates as a multi-party system, seats in the National Parliament may be divided among many parties, giving no single party a clear majority (more than 50 percent). In this case, several parties may join together to form a coalition government, but such administrations are less stable than majority governments and typically have shorter life spans.

The Solomon Islands' legal system is based on English common law. The Court of Appeal is the ultimate judicial authority and the highest appellate court. Lower courts include magistrates' courts and traditional land courts.

At the local level, the Solomon Islands is divided into ten administrative districts: nine provinces governed by elected provincial assemblies, and the capital territory of Honiara, which is administered by a town council.

Political Parties and Factions

The Solomon Islands has a multi-party system—that is, many political parties compete for control of government. Most are based largely on the personality of the leader rather than any cohesive ideology, and there is little party discipline.

The large number of parties in the Solomon Islands ensures that no party can achieve a legislative majority.

Soldiers from New Zealand dispatched to restore order to the Solomon Islands in 2003 after civil unrest. © *Reuters/CORBIS*

In the parliamentary elections of 2006, for example, no single party garnered more than four seats, and thirty members ran as independents. Parties with representation in the legislature in 2006 included the National Party, the Rural Advancement Party, and the People's Alliance Party.

Major Events

At the end of World War II, British authorities moved the Solomon Islands' capital from the small island of Tulagi to Honiara, on Guadalcanal Island. Many Solomon Islanders, including large numbers from the island of Malaita, relocated to Guadalcanal to seek work in the public sector. The influx of settlers caused resentment among some Guadalcanal residents, who began to seek compensation from the government for their lost lands and jobs. In 1998 a group of Guadalcanal natives, feeling their grievances had not been adequately addressed by the government, formed the Isatabu Freedom Movement (also called the Guadalcanal Revolutionary Army) and attempted to drive the newcomers from their homes. In response, the Malaitans formed their own army, the Malaita Eagle Force, and in 2000 kidnapped Prime Minister Bartholomew Ulufa'alu (1950–)—himself a Malaitan—whom they believed had not done enough to protect their interests. Ulufa'alu agreed to resign in exchange for his freedom.

In 2000 the factions signed the Townsville Peace Agreement and agreed to cease fighting. An atmosphere of lawlessness persisted, however, prompting a coalition of Pacific nations led by Australia and New Zealand to form the Regional Assistance Mission to the Solomon Islands (RAMSI) and send troops to the islands. Although RAMSI succeeded in restoring a degree of order, that peace proved short-lived, as rioting continued during the national elections of 2006.

Twenty-First Century

As a result of pervasive political instability and widespread violence, international observers have branded the Solomon Islands a "failed state." The islands saw renewed violence following the parliamentary elections of 2006, when it was alleged that newly elected prime minister Snyder Rini (1949–) had used money obtained from Chinese investors to buy votes. Rini resigned before a no-confidence vote could take place. Although the Australian-led Regional Assistance Mission continues to police the islands, some observers have questioned the mission's success in light of the apparent election fraud and continued lawlessness.

In June 2007 Prime Minister Manasseh Sogavare (1954–) launched a constitutional congress to consider political reform and to draft a new constitution for the Solomon Islands.

BIBLIOGRAPHY

Bennett, Judith A. *Wealth of the Solomons: A History of a Pacific Archipelago, 1800–1978.* Honolulu: University of Hawaii Press, 1987.

Commonwealth Secretariat. "Solomon Islands Country Profile." http://www.thecommonwealth.org/Year bookHomeInternal/139391/ (accessed August 27, 2007).

Moore, Clive. *Happy Isles in Crisis: The Historical Causes for a Failing State in the Solomon Islands, 1998–2004.* Canberra, Australia: Asia Pacific Press, 2005.

⊕ Tuvalu

Type of Government

Tuvalu is formally governed by a constitutional monarchy: the British monarch serves as head of state, and the governor-general acts as his or her local representative. In practice, however, the administration of the nation is carried out through a parliamentary democracy. The single-chamber Fale I Fono (House of Assembly) is the nation's decision-making body, and the prime minister is head of the government.

Background

Tuvalu is located in the Pacific Ocean among the island nations of Polynesia. The nation comprises five atolls

British Queen Elizabeth II, Tuvalu's head of state, is borne aloft by natives in a canoe during her May 2002 visit.   © *Quadrillion/CORBIS*

surrounding a shallow lagoon (Nanumea, Nui, Nukufetau, Funafuti, and Nukulaelae) and four coral reef islands (Nanumanga, Niutao, Vaitupu, and Niulakita). With a total land area of just ten square miles, Tuvalu is the world's fourth-smallest country and one of the least populated. The nation's capital is located on Fongafale Islet on the atoll of Funafuti.

The early settlers of Tuvalu were migrants from Samoa, Tonga, the Cook Islands, and the Gilbert Islands. Early Tuvaluan society was made up of hunter-gatherers who used canoes to travel among the eight islands (the ninth island, Niulakita, was not settled until much later). The name Tuvalu means "cluster of eight" in the Tuvaluan language.

The islands of Tuvalu were first sighted by the Spanish explorer Álvaro de Mendaña de Neira (1541–1595) in 1568, but it was not until the late eighteenth and early nineteenth centuries that Europeans were able to accurately chart and land on the islands. In 1819 Captain Arent Schuyler de Peyster discovered the area around the atoll of Funafuti, calling it "Ellice's Island," after the British member of Parliament who owned his ship. He later discovered other islands to the northwest, which he named for himself. The chain of islands collectively became known as the Ellice Islands.

During the nineteenth century, hundreds of Tuvaluans were forcibly recruited to work as slave labor, a common practice in the South Pacific known as "blackbirding." In 1863 four hundred Tuvaluans (out of a population of 2,500) were kidnapped and sent to work in the guano mines of Peru; others were transported to plantations in Australia, Fiji, Samoa, and Hawaii.

In 1892 the Ellice Islands became a British protectorate, and in 1916 the islands were incorporated into the Gilbert and Ellice Islands Colony. British administration in the region was limited, leaving most governance in the hands of the island governments.

During World War II the islands were occupied by hundreds of thousands of American troops. The Americans built airbases on the atolls of Funafuti, Nanumea, and Nukufetau—infrastructure that is still in use to this day.

In 1974 residents of the Ellice Islands voted to break away from the Gilbert Islands to form a separate colony, Tuvalu. The country achieved complete independence from Great Britain in 1978.

Government Structure

The structure and functions of government are outlined in the nation's constitution, which was adopted upon independence in 1978. The British monarch Queen Elizabeth II (1926–) is Tuvalu's head of state, although the role is purely symbolic. The monarch is represented locally by a governor-general, who is appointed by the monarch on the prime minister's recommendation. Although the governor-general is invested with some executive authority—he or she formally appoints members of the cabinet and gives royal assent to legislation—

the position is largely ceremonial. The governor-general must be a resident of Tuvalu.

The head of government is the prime minister, who is elected from among the members of the legislature. Executive authority is vested in the cabinet, which consists of the prime minister and up to five other ministers of his or her choice. Cabinet members are appointed by the governor-general on the prime minister's recommendation. The cabinet is directly responsible to the legislature.

Tuvalu has a unicameral (single-chamber) legislature called the House of Assembly. This body is made up of fifteen members who are elected by popular vote to serve four-year terms. Seven electoral districts elect two members each; an eighth district elects only one member. The House of Assembly has the right to remove the prime minister from office by passing a motion of "no confidence." In this case, the legislature is dissolved by the governor-general and new elections are held.

As in most parliamentary systems, the House of Assembly controls the introduction and passage of legislation; the assent of the governor-general is merely a formality. However, Tuvalu's government has one notable difference: Before a bill can pass the legislature to become law, it must be presented to the local governments for approval.

Tuvalu has an independent judiciary that comprises the High Court and eight island courts. The High Court is headed by a chief justice who visits the islands twice a year to preside over its sessions. Appeals from the High Court are heard by the Court of Appeals in Fiji.

At the local level, Tuvalu is divided into nine local government districts, many of which encompass several islands.

Political Parties and Factions

Tuvalu has no organized political parties; rather, political affiliations tend to be based on personal or family connections. Members of the legislature often align themselves in informal blocs around a particular issue.

Major Events

By the 1960s ethnic tensions between the Polynesian Ellice Islanders and the Micronesian Gilbert Islanders prompted the British colony to split in two. In 1974 residents of the Ellice Islands passed a referendum to establish themselves as a separate colony. The country was renamed Tuvalu, and the Gilbert Islands became Kiribati.

In 2000 Tuvalu became a full member of the Commonwealth of Nations (also called the British Commonwealth), a voluntary association of more than fifty independent nations that are former colonies or territories of the British Empire. Until that time it had held "special member" status, which afforded it the benefits of membership but limited its capacity for influencing policy.

Twenty-First Century

Tuvalu's most pressing challenge in the twenty-first century is environmental. Because the land is very low-lying, rising to only thirteen to sixteen feet above sea level, Tuvalu is vulnerable to soil erosion and saltwater intrusion. Environmental groups caution that, as a result of global climate change, rising sea levels could make the islands uninhabitable within the next fifty years. Some international observers have proposed that the Tuvaluans be removed to neighboring countries.

BIBLIOGRAPHY

Bennetts, Peter, and Tony Wheeler. *Time and Tide: The Islands of Tuvalu.* Melbourne, Australia: Lonely Planet Press, 2001.

Commonwealth Secretariat. "Tuvalu Country Profile." http://www.thecommonwealth.org/YearbookHome Internal/139407/home/ (accessed August 27, 2007).

Macdonald, Barrie. *Cinderellas of the Empire: Towards a History of Kiribati and Tuvalu.* Suva, Fiji: Institute of Pacific Studies, University of the South Pacific, 2001.

⊕ Dominica

Type of Government

Dominica is a parliamentary democracy whose executive branch comprises a prime minister, cabinet ministers, and a president. Legislative power is wielded by the unicameral House of Assembly, and the independent judicial branch is based on English common law.

Background

Located in the Caribbean island chain known as the Lesser Antilles, Dominica is a mountainous island with unspoiled rain forests. Originally inhabited by the native Arawak people, the island was conquered by Caribs in the fourteenth century. In 1493 Christopher Columbus (1451–1506) landed on the island, claiming it for Spain and giving it its current name. Although Spanish ships often called at the island, the Spanish were prevented from major settlement by the hostile Caribs for more than a century.

After the French claimed the island in 1635, missionaries began arriving. However, the resistance of the Caribs also ended this European incursion, and throughout the rest of the seventeenth century, Dominica remained unsettled by Europeans and declared officially neutral.

The island's rich natural resources attracted both the British and French again in the early eighteenth century, with French planters establishing coffee and banana plantations and the British cutting timber. Throughout the eighteenth century, the island was handed back and forth between France and Britain, with the British establishing hegemony by 1805.

The island has a long history of participatory government. In 1763 the first legislature was established, and by 1831 the British had extended political participation to the non-white population. The British Empire abolished slavery in 1834, and over the following decade Dominica became the only Caribbean colony with a black-controlled legislature. However, the wealthy English planters, fearful of losing their influence, petitioned London, and beginning in 1865, the legislative assembly was no longer directly elected. Instead, half of the members were appointed by the Colonial Office in London, and half were elected. From that time on the power of the black Dominicans waned, and in 1871 Dominica became part of the Leeward Island Federation, a group of British-colonial Caribbean islands that was governed from Barbados. By 1896 the island was governed as a Crown colony, and the political control of the native residents was significantly reduced.

It was not until the years following World War I that local black leaders began agitating for more political power. By 1936 a full half of the members of the legislative assembly were Afro-Dominicans, and in 1951 the British government agreed to allow universal suffrage. Between 1952 and 1958 the classification and administration of the island was in a state of flux: the British transferred the island from the Leeward Island Federation to the Windward Islands and then to the West Indies Federation, with a change in administration at each juncture. In 1967 Dominica became an associated state of the United Kingdom as part of the West Indies Associated States. Though Dominica was internally autonomous from 1967, Britain did not grant full independence until November 3, 1978.

Government Structure

The 1978 constitution established what is known as a Westminster style of parliamentary government, one based in part on the English model. The executive branch comprises a president, prime minister, and cabinet. The president is nominated by the prime minister, in consultation with the leader of the opposition party, and is elected by the unicameral parliament to a five-year term. The prime minister, in turn, is the leader of the majority party in parliament and is appointed by the president. The cabinet ministers, nominated by the prime minister from among members of the majority party in parliament, are also appointed by the president.

Legislative power lies with the House of Assembly, comprising twenty-one regional representatives elected by universal suffrage. These representatives, in turn, determine the selection process for the nine senators in the House of Assembly. The elected representatives can decide to appoint the senators, in which case five are nominated by the prime minister and four by the leader of the opposition party. Conversely, the representatives can also decide to elect the senators, which is done by direct vote of the twenty-one regional representatives. Representatives and senators must be elected every five years; elections can also be called earlier by the prime minister.

The third branch of government, the judiciary, comprises three magistrate's courts, with appeals made to the Trinidad-based Caribbean Court of Justice (CCJ), an itinerant court with oversight over nine member states, one of which is Dominica.

Town Councils elected by universal suffrage govern most municipalities. These councils are supported mostly by property taxation, and are responsible for municipal services, such as roads and sewage. The island is also divided into ten parishes that are governed separately from the town governments. The capital of Dominica is Roseau.

Political Parties and Factions

Dominica has three main political parties: the Dominica Freedom Party (DFP), the Dominica Labour Party (DLP), and the United Workers' Party (UWP).

The DFP is a conservative party. Once the ruling party—under Prime Minister Mary Eugenia Charles (1919–2005), the country's first female prime minister and a co-founder of the party—the DFP has seen a significant decline in support since 1995. In the 2000 elections, the party won only 13.6 percent of the popular vote, earning two seats in the House of Assembly. In the 2005 elections, the party lost even those two seats, though the majority DLP, in order to maintain a coalition with the DFP, gave its leader, Charles Savarin (1943–), a seat on the Senate.

The oldest extant political party in Dominica, the DLP came to power in 1961 under the leadership of Edward Oliver LeBlanc (1923–2004). LeBlanc saw the country to self-ruling status in 1967 before retiring in 1974. Espousing social-democratic policies, the DLP has been the majority party in Dominica since 2000. Despite having two successive prime ministers die in office, the DLP took twelve of the twenty-one seats in the House of Assembly in 2005 and again secured the office of prime minister for the DLP leader, Roosevelt Skerrit (1972–).

The third major party in Dominica is the UWP, a centrist party founded in 1988 by Edison James (1943–). In the 1995 elections, the UWP took eleven seats in the House, thus making it the majority party and its leader, James, the prime minister. In the 2000 elections, though winning the majority of the popular vote, the UWP won only nine seats in the house and became, once again, the opposition party. With the retirement of James in 2005, Earl Williams (1964–) became leader of the party.

Major Events

Dominica was led by an interim government from 1979 to the 1980 election, in which Dame Mary Eugenia Charles, head of the DFP, became the first female head of government in the Caribbean. She took control of a country beset by a poor economy and recently ravaged by hurricanes and set about to establish a degree of

Prime Minister Eugenia Charles of Dominica and President Ronald Reagan of the United States at a press conference regarding the U.S. invasion of Grenada, 1981.   © *Bettmann/CORBIS*

economic stability. She encouraged tourism, but was also determined to preserve the island's ecology and national identity. By the end of the 1980s, the economy of Dominica had made a mild recovery, only to be hurt again by falling banana prices in the 1990s.

Reelected in 1985 and 1990, Dame Charles retired in 1995 at the age of seventy-five. Though the head of a conservative party, Charles pushed through some social welfare measures during her time in office, as well as anti-corruption measures and individual freedom laws. Dominica came to world attention in 1983, when Charles encouraged the U.S. invasion of Grenada to prevent what she saw as Cuban infiltration of that island. With the imposition of austerity measures in 2002, large protests were held throughout the island.

Twenty-First Century

Government corruption and economic underdevelopment have been nagging problems in Dominica. During the administration of Prime Minister Charles, the government initiated policies aimed at balancing tourism with preservation of the island's ecology and native culture, and as a result of government investment, Dominica has become a major destination for ecotourism.

Dominica's primary export is the banana crop, which suffered in 2000, leading to an economic crisis.

In 2005 universal secondary education was introduced in Dominica, enabling all students on the island to attend high school. The ruling DLP took as its next mission the establishment of a post-secondary education system.

BIBLIOGRAPHY

Booth, Robert. "Dominica, Difficult Paradise." *National Geographic* (June 1990): 100–120.

Honeychurch, Lennox. *The Dominica Story: A History of the Island*. Roseau, Dominica: Dominica Institute, 1984.

Myers, Robert A. *Dominica*. Santa Barbara, CA: Clio Press, 1987.

Trouillot, Michel-Rolph. *Peasants and Capital: Dominica in the World Economy*. Baltimore, MD: Johns Hopkins University Press, 1988.

⊕ Iran

Type of Government

As an Islamic republic, Iran has religious clerics who provide oversight to ensure that policies, laws, and

Iran. *Maryland Cartographic*

elected officials operate in accordance with Islamic law. The government, however, functions as a secular republic in its daily operations. Many leaders are elected by the people, and referenda are held to decide important issues.

Background

Iran is in southwest Asia, covering an area slightly larger than Alaska (636,296 square miles). Its land was once part of the Persian Empire, and Iran was known as Persia to Western nations until 1935, when Iran's ruler asked the international community to refer to the country by its native name.

Archaeology identifies Iran as the site of some of the world's oldest civilizations. Southwestern Iran is part of the region known as the Fertile Crescent. Archaeologists

have found sophisticated agricultural centers that raised crops and domestic animals around 6000 BC.

About 1500 BC, Aryan tribes began to enter the region, competing for power and territory. The Medes first established the region as a nation and empire. The Median Empire lasted from 728 to 550 BC, when Cyrus the Great (c. 585–c. 529 BC) unified the Medes and Persians under the Achaemenid Empire (550–330 BC). Cyrus the Great was the first ruler in Iran to be known as shah, and he created humanity's first known declaration of human rights. The Achaemenid Empire evolved into the largest empire known in human history until that time. It was built on a model of tolerance and respect for other cultures and religions.

The Achaemenid Empire began to fall with invasions by Alexander the Great (356–323 BC) in 333

BC. Later the Parthian Empire (247–224 BC) and the Sassanid Empire (224 BC–642 AD) restored order to the Persian region. Much of what later become known as Islamic culture, architecture, and art was created by the Sassanian Persians and carried into the rest of the Muslim world.

Persian Empires embraced the religion of Zoroastrianism until the introduction of Islam around 636 AD, when Arab warriors began overwhelming the Sassanian Empire to spread the teachings of Muhammad (c. 570–632). Various invading dynasties gained and lost control for the next few centuries. Only the religion of Islam established a lasting presence. Persians struggled to maintain their culture and independence, particularly under the invading forces of the Turks and Mongols between the tenth and fifteenth centuries.

The Safavid Empire (1502–1736) was the first native Iranian dynasty to arise after almost one thousand years of invasions. Historians credit it with the revival of Persia and the founding of the modern state of Iran.

Other nations began to take interest in the region during the seventeenth century. Around 1722 the Safavid Empire fell to invading forces from Afghanistan. The subsequent Afsharid, Zand, and Qajar Dynasties were all challenged by outside interests, particularly as European nations established colonial footholds in the region. In 1906 civilians forced Iran's leader, called the shah, to accept a constitution, creating a constitutional monarchy. The discovery of oil in 1908, however, and ensuing meddling by the United Kingdom and Russia limited the efficacy of Iran's ruling state. By 1921 the government had fallen into chaos.

In 1925 a new shah, Reza Shah Pahlavi (1878–1944), took power with British support. The Pahlavi Dynasty held power until 1979, first under Reza Shah and then under his son, Mohammad Reza Pahlavi (1919–1980). During this time the country began to modernize society, secularize politics, and strengthen government control over local tribes and provinces. Particularly during the White Revolution of 1962–1963, Iran experienced broad economic, social, and administrative reforms. As the government's policies embraced Westernization and also became more corrupt, a majority of the population grew dissatisfied. Opposition based in the tenets of Islam grew during this time under the leadership of Ayatollah Ruhollah Khomeini (1902–1989), who was exiled to Iraq in 1964 for his antigovernment activities.

In 1979 the Pahlavi Dynasty came to an end with the Islamic Revolution. After many months of demonstrations, marches, strikes, and violent encounters with the army, the shah left Iran. On February 1, 1979, Khomeini returned from exile. He quickly asserted control and appointed a provisional government. Under his guidance, the nation adopted a constitutional government based on the fundamentals of Shia Islam. The government nationalized industry, re-established Islamic traditions in custom and law, and banned the influence of Western cultures. Khomeini led as Valy-e Faqih (Supreme Spiritual Leader) until his death in 1989.

Government Structure

The Islamic Republic of Iran was created in 1979 by a state constitution. A group of eighty-three clerics formed an Assembly of Experts to write the constitution. They did so based on revolutionary leader Ayatollah Khomeini's vision of a republic run according to the beliefs of Islam. The constitution calls for a supreme leader of Iran plus executive, legislative, and judicial branches.

The leader of Iran is known as the Valy-e Faqih, the Supreme Spiritual Leader. The Valy-e Faqih is appointed by the Assembly of Experts, which is a group of eighty-six clerics elected to eight-year terms. The Valy-e Faqih must meet requirements of both spiritual and political leadership. There is no limit to his term of service, but he may be removed by the Assembly of Experts under certain conditions.

The Valy-e Faqih is responsible for guiding Iran's foreign and domestic policies. He is the commander-in-chief of the armed forces and controls intelligence and security operations. The Valy-e Faqih appoints six of the twelve members of the Council of Guardians, a powerful committee that oversees both elections and the country's legislative body, the Majles. He also has power to appoint and dismiss senior officers of the general military, the specialized Islamic Revolutionary Guards, the judiciary, and the state radio and television networks. An estimated two thousand representatives of the Valy-e Faqih serve as clerical operatives throughout all sectors of government with power to intervene in any matter of state on his behalf.

The constitution originally provided two leaders for the executive branch of government: a president and a prime minister. In 1989 the positions were consolidated and the post of prime minister abolished. The president is elected by universal suffrage. As head of the executive branch, he is responsible for setting the country's economic policies, although his policies are always subordinate to those of the Valy-e Faqih. The president is responsible for the day-to-day administration of government and implementation of law. In this capacity he oversees a wide range of government offices and organizations. Eight vice presidents serve under the president as well as a cabinet of twenty-two ministers, the Council of Ministers, who must be confirmed by the Majles.

The Iranian constitution provides a unicameral legislature known as the Majles, or the Consultative Assembly. Two hundred ninety members are publicly elected for four-year terms. The Majles is responsible for drafting all legislation, ratifying international treaties, and approving the country's budget. It also has power to impeach and remove the president with a two-thirds majority vote.

Iranian leader Ayatollah Khomeini praying in the garden of his villa near Paris while in exile. © *Bettmann/Corbis*

The twelve-member Council of Guardians oversees the Majles. Six members, appointed by the Valy-e Faqih, are specialists in Islamic canon law. The other six are civil jurists nominated by the Supreme Judicial Council (part of the judicial branch) and appointed by the Majles. The Council of Guardians reviews all legislation passed by the Majles to ensure consistency with Islamic law, called sharia, and the Iranian constitution. If a majority of the Council's members find a piece of legislation unlawful, they return it to the Majles with suggested revisions. Disagreements that arise between the Council of Guardians and the Majles are settled by the Expediency Council, an appointed, thirty-four member panel that also serves as an advisory body to the Valy-e Faqih.

The judicial branch consists of the Supreme Court, Supreme Judicial Council, and lower courts. In 1983 the judicial system and the nation's penal code were revised to align with sharia precepts. The courts are organized into three divisions to hear different kinds of cases. Public courts handle civil and criminal cases, the revolutionary courts try cases concerning national security, and the Special Clerical Court hears cases involving crimes committed by clerics.

Elections are held in Iran every four years. All candidates must be approved by the Council of Guardians. It is common for the Council to eliminate many choices. In 2004, for example, 3,605 reformist candidates were banned out of a total of 8,157 candidates. About eighty of those banned were sitting members of the Majles. Important matters are often submitted to referenda votes during elections, and there is universal suffrage starting at age sixteen.

To provide local governance, Iran is divided into twenty-eight provinces (*ostanha*). These are subdivided into counties (*shahrestanha*), districts (*bakhshha*), and townships (*dehestanha*). The Minister of the Interior appoints mayors for cities, officials holding county and district positions, and a governor-general for each province. Some mayors and city councils are elected locally. Villages have a village master advised by elders. Each level of local governance has a council that governs along with the municipal leader. In addition, the councils for the twenty-eight provinces send representatives to the Supreme Council of Provinces.

Political Parties and Factions

Political parties were not allowed in Iran until 1941. Since the Islamic revolution of 1979, hundreds of new political parties have formed representing a wide range of political views. Currently there are more than two hundred political parties with permission to operate in Iran. Many have representatives in the Majles with differing political views, but none of them oppose the religious foundation of Iran's government. While the official stance of the government is to allow any party that is committed to an Islamic system, over fifty political parties have been disbanded and exist in exile. The Islamic Republic Party, which ruled at the outset of the revolution, proved to be volatile and is among those that have been outlawed.

With so many political parties, candidates tend to be defined by their stance on issues rather than by party affiliation alone. Parties occasionally form coalitions based on their political values. Currently the two main coalitions are the Conservative Alliance and the Reformist Coalition.

Major Events

Since the Islamic revolution of 1979, Iran has faced international and regional power struggles that have led to armed conflict. The transition of power from the Pahlavi Dynasty to the Islamic Republic of Iran was marked by economic and social difficulty. In November 1979 political and social unrest provoked a group of student militants to seize the United States embassy, where it held 52 hostages for 444 days despite international protests. Political, social, and economic problems result in periodic outbreaks of protest and violence in Iran.

Iran's most difficult regional issue has been its relationship with Iraq. Hoping to take advantage of a weakened Iran during its transition to an Islamic republic, Iraq revived an old border dispute by invading Iran in September 1980. The Iranian army was stronger than Iraq expected, and the conflict broadened to include attacks on oil shipments in the waters of the Persian

Gulf. The war continued until 1988, when the countries reached a cease-fire agreement.

Iran remained officially neutral in the Persian Gulf War (1990–1991) between Iraq and the United States. In fact, however, it condemned the American invasion and allowed Iraqi aircraft and refugees into its country. In 2002, just months after the terrorist attacks in America on September 11, 2001, U.S. President George W. Bush (1946–) labeled Iran as part of a terrorist "axis of evil" with Iraq and North Korea. Despite this provocation, Iran urged Iraq to cooperate with United Nations resolutions to disarm itself of weapons of mass destruction. When the United States attacked Iraq in March 2003, Iran remained officially uninvolved. The Bush administration, however, accused Iran of training and supplying rebels in Iraq who fought to depose the U.S.-supported regime.

Twenty-First Century

Economic problems for Iran persisted into the twenty-first century. Although the government has worked to improve conditions, unemployment and inflation continue to be challenging. Increases in the price of oil have helped the country, but not enough to make up for population growth, shortages of raw materials, and restrictive labor policies.

Iran's stated intention to develop nuclear technology as a power source has strained its relationships with the United Nations and with leading Western nations, who are concerned that Iran will develop nuclear weapons. These concerns are heightened by the Western perception that Islamic terrorists are using Iran as a base for activity and might have collaborators within the Iranian government.

BIBLIOGRAPHY

Dabashi, Hamid. *Iran: A People Interrupted.* New York: New Press, 2007.

Kamrava, Mehran. *The Political History of Modern Iran: From Tribalism to Theocracy.* Westport, CT: Praeger, 1992.

U.S. State Department, Bureau of Near Eastern Affairs. "Background Note: Iran." http://www.state.gov/r/pa/ei/bgn/5314.htm (accessed August 23, 2007).

⊕ Saint Lucia

Type of Government

Saint Lucia is a parliamentary democracy with separate executive, legislative, and judicial branches. The prime minister is the head of government, while a governor general is the ceremonial head of state. The legislature is bicameral, consisting of the House of Assembly, elected by popular vote, and an appointed Senate. The independent judiciary consists of district and high courts.

Background

Saint Lucia is part of the Lesser Antilles. The island's early inhabitants were the Arawak people, who arrived from South America around 300 AD. The Arawak tribe was later supplanted by the Carib tribe, which settled the island between 600 and 1000. The Carib called the island "Hewanorra," or "where the iguana is found," an appellation that persisted and is now used as the name of the island's international airport.

Saint Lucia was not visited by Europeans until about 1500, during the Spanish exploration of the region. Legend has it, however, that the French survivors of a shipwreck gave the island its current name when they washed up on its shores on December 13, the feast day of Saint Lucia. Legend or not, December 13 remains the country's national day. In the seventeenth century, Dutch, French, and English traders attempted to establish outposts on the island but were prevented by hostile attacks by the Carib tribes. In 1651 the French colonized the island from their nearby colony on Martinique, managing to secure treaties with the Carib tribes to prevent attacks. However, the island fell to a British expedition mounted from Saint Kitts in 1664. Initially a thousand men strong, this attempted British settlement had been reduced to fewer than a hundred men in two years due to disease. Thereafter the island changed hands fourteen times, as the British, based in Barbados, and French, based in Martinique, competed for control by both economic and military means. The ascent of the sugar industry in the late eighteenth century made the island economically as well as strategically important. Through the early eighteenth century the majority of Europeans who had actually established residence on the island were French. Even today, almost every inhabitant of the island speaks a French patois. Many of the names of the island's cities and villages are French. Unlike in most former British colonies, the population is still primarily Roman Catholic.

Following the Napoleonic Wars in Europe, the British finally gained lasting control of the Island in 1814. Until the British abolished slavery, in 1834, the island's economy was based on large-scale importation of slaves from West Africa. Modern-day Saint Lucia is thus inhabited mainly by people of African and mixed African-European descent. For fifty years during the nineteenth century, Saint Lucia was part of Britain's Windward Islands administration; however, by the twentieth century moves toward self-government had begun. Constitutional revisions in 1924 introduced a self-representation system to the island and further revisions in 1951 introduced a universal suffrage system. From 1967 to 1979 the island became an associated state of the United Kingdom, though external affairs and defense were left under the supervision of Great Britain. This arrangement ended on February 22, 1979, when Saint Lucia was granted independence.

Government Structure

Under the 1979 constitution, Saint Lucia became an independent member of the British Commonwealth of Nations, and the British monarch was the titular head of state, represented locally by a governor general. Though this head of state has a largely ceremonial role, the constitution does allow him or her to dissolve parliament and to appoint senators, with the advice of the leader of the opposition and the prime minister. Real executive power, however, is held by the prime minister and the cabinet, whose members are chosen from the majority party in the House of Assembly. Saint Lucia conducts most of its foreign policy cooperatively with other countries in the region, in particular through participation in the Organization of Eastern Caribbean States (OECS).

The bicameral parliament is made up of the House of Assembly, whose seventeen members are chosen through universal suffrage in elections held every five years. The House performs the most important legislative functions—creating laws and regulations and determining the budget. Additionally, there is a Senate, with scant political power, whose eleven members are appointed: six on the advice of the prime minister, three on the advice of the opposition leader, and two after consultation with religious, economic, and social groups. The cabinet and prime minister are determined by the makeup of the House of Assembly.

The legal system is based both on English common law and the French Napoleonic legal code. The constitution guarantees a public trial before an independent and impartial court. In cases involving capital punishment, legal counsel is afforded to defendants who cannot otherwise afford counsel. The lowest court is the district or magistrate's court, and above that is the Court of Summary Jurisdiction. Saint Lucia is also a member of the Eastern Caribbean Supreme Court (based on Saint Lucia), and the Caribbean Court of Justice (CCJ), to which higher appeals are made.

Political Parties and Factions

Saint Lucia is essentially a two-party democracy, with the United Workers Party (UWP) and the Saint Lucia Labour Party (SLP) the primary contestants for political power.

The UWP, the more conservative of the two, has been in power for most of the time since the country was granted internal autonomy in 1967. Led by John Compton (1926–), the UWP maintained power from 1964 to 1979, then from 1982 to 1996, and in 2006 the party was once again returned to power, with Compton returning to the office of prime minister.

The left-of-center social democratic SLP took power following independence and returned to power again in 1997, led by Kenny Anthony (1951–), maintaining majority status until the 2006 elections.

Julian Robert Hunte (left), foreign minister of Saint Lucia and president of the United Nations General Assembly, meeting Japanese prime minister Junichiro Koizumi in Tokyo, 2004. *STR/AFP/Getty Images*

Major Events

The first years of Saint Lucia's independence were marked by political rancor, because independence had been a contested issue. The SLP was in favor of a referendum before cutting ties with the United Kingdom; it took power from the UWP, under Prime Minister Allan Louisy (1916–), in the hotly contested 1980 elections. The SLP, however, was hurt by internal dissension. Several SLP members, including the former Louisy deputy George Odlum (1934–2003), defected to found a new party, the Progressive Labour Party (PLP). New general elections were called for 1982.

Though Compton and the UWP took power once again after that election, the new PLP showed it was a political force, winning 27 percent of the vote. That was the high point of its power, though, and in subsequent elections, the PLP lost ground and disappeared from the political scene, leaving the SLP and UWP to contest political power in the country. Though his party did not ultimately succeed, Odlum, known for his leftist views, is credited with opening relations between Saint Lucia and China.

Twenty-First Century

Like other Caribbean nations whose economies are based largely on agriculture, Saint Lucia has had difficulty competing in the global economy of the twenty-first century. The banana crop, long the island's principal export, has been subject to the ravages of weather. In 2002 Tropical Storm Lili, for example, destroyed half the banana crop; in 2004, Hurricane Ivan ruined 35 percent of the banana crop. The European Union's decision to end its preferential trade agreements for imported bananas from former colonies also dealt the industry a blow in Saint Lucia. The island has turned to tourism in an attempt to make up for lost revenues. Increasingly, Saint Lucia is becoming an eco-tourist destination because of its largely unspoiled natural beauty.

Violent crime is also on the increase on the island, so much so that British police officers were brought in during 2006 to assist local police in training and intelligence gathering. Another challenge to Saint Lucia and many low-lying Caribbean islands is the rising sea levels resulting from global warming, which threaten to flood large parts of the island. A World Bank study was funded in 2006 to investigate possible countermeasures.

BIBLIOGRAPHY

Government of Saint Lucia. http://www.stlucia.gov.lc (accessed on April 27, 2007).

Momsen, Janet Henshall. *St. Lucia*. Santa Barbara, CA: Clio Press, 1996.

Philpott, Don. *St. Lucia*. Lincolnwood, IL: Passport Books, 1996.

⊕ Kiribati

Type of Government

Kiribati is a democratic republic, with legislative representatives chosen in free elections and a president selected from among the legislators. The president serves as both head of state and head of the government. The unicameral Maneaba ni Maungatabu (House of Assembly) is the main decision-making body. Members of the judiciary are appointed by the president and have full independence in court decisions.

Background

The Republic of Kiribati is an island nation located in the central Pacific Ocean. It comprises thirty-two low-lying coral atoll islands (twenty are inhabited) spread over an expanse of more than a million square miles. Kiribati is made up of three major island groupings: the Gilbert Islands, where most of the population is centered; the Phoenix Islands, which are largely uninhabited; and the Line Islands, some of which are U.S. territories. Kiritimati (Christmas Island) is the world's largest coral atoll and accounts for half of Kiribati's land area. Kiribati also controls Banaba (Ocean Island) off the eastern coast of Nauru; however, as a result of environmental damage caused by phosphate mining during the twentieth century, the Banaban community has been relocated to Rabi Island in Fiji. The nation's capital is located on Tarawa Atoll.

The Gilbert Islands were originally settled by Micronesian peoples from Southeast Asia between the eleventh and fourteenth centuries AD (the Phoenix and Line islands were not discovered until much later). Their early society was influenced by subsequent invasions of Tongans and Fijians, who introduced Melanesian and Polynesian elements to the native Gilbertese culture.

The islands were first sighted by Spanish explorers in the sixteenth century, but it was not until the late eighteenth and early nineteenth centuries that Europeans made any meaningful contact there. In 1788 Captain Thomas Gilbert charted many of the islands, naming them after himself. Whaling ships, coconut oil traders, and slave merchants arrived in greater numbers throughout the 1800s. The introduction of European religious ways, diseases, and weapons disrupted native life, exacerbating conflicts among the local tribes. The Europeans forced many native Gilbertese into slave labor on plantations on the larger islands.

Great Britain made the Gilbert Islands a protectorate in 1892 and annexed Banaba, with its rich deposits of phosphate, in 1900. In 1916 these territories became part of the Gilbert and Ellice Islands Colony; the Phoenix and Line islands were incorporated into the colony over the next twenty years. British administration in the region was limited, leaving most governance in the hands of the island governments.

During World War II, the Gilbert Islands were invaded and occupied by the Japanese. In 1943 U.S. forces targeted Japanese fortifications on Tarawa Atoll, leading to some of the bloodiest fighting of the Pacific war. The Japanese were subsequently ejected from the islands by the Americans. Following the war, Great Britain used Kiritimati Island as a nuclear testing site.

The first step toward independence was taken in 1967, when the Gilbert Islands were granted a House of Representatives. In 1974 residents of the Ellice Islands voted to break away from the Gilberts to form a separate colony, becoming the nation of Tuvalu in 1976. The Gilbert Islands, renamed Kiribati (a local variant of "Gilberts"), achieved self-governance in 1977 and became a fully independent nation in 1979.

Kiribati remains a full member of the Commonwealth of Nations (also called the British Commonwealth), a voluntary association of more than fifty independent nations that are former colonies or territories of the British Empire.

Government Structure

The structures and functions of government are outlined in the nation's constitution, which was adopted upon independence in 1979. According to the constitution, Kiribati's national government comprises an elected legislative branch, a president elected from among the legislators, and an appointed judiciary.

Kiribati has a unicameral (single-chamber) legislature called the Maneaba ni Maungatabu, or House of Assembly. This body is made up of forty-two members: Forty members are elected from single-member or multi-seat districts; one member is appointed to represent the Banaban community on Rabi Island in Fiji; and

Kiribati Prime Minister Atone Tong (right) visiting Taiwan in 2004. Kiribati is one of few nations to recognize Taiwan's sovereignty.   © *SIMON KWONG/Reuters/Corbis*

the remaining member is the nation's attorney general, who occupies his seat ex officio (by virtue of his position). All members serve four-year terms. The speaker of the legislature is elected by the House of Assembly from outside its membership; the speaker is not a voting member of the legislature.

The president serves as both head of state and head of the government. He or she is chosen from among the members of the House of Assembly. Following legislative elections, the House nominates at least three but no more than four of its members to stand for the presidency in a nationwide election. The elected president appoints the vice president, attorney general, and up to eight other members of the cabinet. The president serves a four-year term, up to a maximum of three terms; during this time, the president retains his or her seat in the legislature.

The House of Assembly has the right to remove the president from office by passing a motion of "no confidence." In this case, an interim Council of State—consisting of the chief justice of the court, the speaker of the House of Assembly, and the chairman of the Public Service Commission—governs until the next elec-

tions are held. The Council of State has taken over the government four times since independence.

Kiribati has an independent judiciary that comprises the High Court, Court of Appeal, and twenty-six magistrates' courts. All judges are appointed by the president.

At the local level, each of Kiribati's inhabited islands is governed by its own council.

Political Parties and Factions

National politics in Kiribati operates as a multi-party system—that is, many political parties compete for control of government. However, these parties are more accurately described as informal coalitions in that they lack cohesive platforms or ideologies, and there is little party discipline. In practice, most candidates function as independents.

Three political parties had representation in the legislature in 2007: the Boutokanto Koaava (Pillars of Truth), the Maneaban Te Mauri (Protect the Maneaban), and the Maurin Kiribati Pati.

Major Events

At the beginning of the twentieth century, vast deposits of phosphate, a key ingredient in the production of fertilizers, were discovered on Banaba. Between 1900 and 1979, extensive mining operations depleted virtually all of Banaba's phosphate stores, with disastrous environmental consequences—nearly 90 percent of the island's surface was stripped away, and much of the land remains uninhabitable to this day.

Following World War II, British colonial authorities began to relocate the residents of Banaba to Rabi Island in Fiji, more than a thousand miles from their homeland. Today, the Banabans on Rabi Island (approximately 2,400) have dual citizenship in both Fiji and Kiribati, and the Rabi Council of Leaders and Elders appoints a representative of the Banaban community to the Kiribati legislature. However, many Banabans wish to be independent of Kiribati. In 2006 Teitirake Corrie, the Banaban representative to Kiribati's House of Assembly, called for Banaba to secede from Kiribati and become part of Fiji.

Twenty-First Century

One of Kiribati's most pressing challenges in the twenty-first century is environmental. Because much of its land is very low-lying, Kiribati is vulnerable to soil erosion and saltwater intrusion caused by rising sea levels. Environmental groups caution that global climate change could make the islands uninhabitable in the not-too-distant future.

Kiribati also faces serious economic difficulties as it lacks sufficient employment opportunities for its expanding population. In 2007, only 20 percent of the population participated in the formal wage economy. Kiribati's economy depends heavily on income from abroad, including fees for fishing licenses, development assistance, and tourism revenues.

BIBLIOGRAPHY

Commonwealth Secretariat. "Kiribati Country Profile." http://www.thecommonwealth.org/YearbookHome Internal/139195/ (accessed August 28, 2007).

Grimble, Rosemary, ed. *Migrations, Myth, and Magic from the Gilbert Islands: Early Writings of Sir Arthur Grimble*. London: Routledge and Kegan Paul, 1972.

Macdonald, Barrie. *Cinderellas of the Empire: Towards a History of Kiribati and Tuvalu*. Suva, Fiji: Institute of Pacific Studies, University of the South Pacific, 2001.

⊕ Saint Vincent and the Grenadines

Type of Government

Saint Vincent and the Grenadines is a parliamentary democracy. The prime minister is the head of government, while a governor general acts as head of state on behalf of the British Crown. The legislature is unicameral, with both elected and appointed members.

Background

A part of the Lesser Antilles island chain, Saint Vincent and the Grenadines lies about one hundred miles west of Barbados and north of Grenada. The country is made up of the larger island of Saint Vincent, where the capital, Kingstown, is located, and a chain of some six hundred islands and islets of the Grenadines, including Bequia, Petit Saint Vincent, Union Island, and Mayreau.

Though Saint Vincent was originally settled by the Arawak people from South America, by the time the Spanish explorers arrived in 1498, Carib tribes had taken control of the island and prevented European occupation until the eighteenth century. With the advent of the slave trade to the Caribbean, shipwrecked African slaves found their way to the islands, where they blended with the Carib tribes through intermarriage to create a group later known to Europeans as the Black Caribs or "Garifuna." When the French established tobacco, cotton, and sugar plantations on the island in the early eighteenth century, the Garifuna were put to work as laborers.

During the eighteenth century, the islands were handed back and forth between Britain and France several times. Under the 1763 Treaty of Paris, which ended the Seven Years' War, the British gained control of Saint Vincent. The British were initially content to share control of the island but were forced to contend with frequent raids by the Caribs, led by the Black Carib chieftain Joseph Chatoyer (d. 1795). The British finally defeated the Caribs in 1795, with Chatoyer dying in battle. The British deported many of the remaining Black Caribs to an island off of Honduras, and most of those who remained were killed during the eruption of the volcano Mount Soufrière in 1812. Their role as laborers was taken over by African slaves, and when slavery was abolished in the British Empire in 1834, Madeiran Portuguese and East Indians were brought in as indentured laborers to work the sugar cane and later the banana plantations.

The British administered Saint Vincent as a Crown colony within the Windward Islands group from 1833 until 1960. The British slowly implemented reforms that granted increased autonomy to the native population, including universal suffrage in 1951. The first important political party, the People's Political Party (PPP), was founded in 1952. It grew out of the labor union movement and was strong throughout the 1960s, but dissolved in 1984. The rival Saint Vincent Labour Party (SVLP) was founded in 1955, and under the leadership of Robert Milton Cato (1915–1997), it built up a strong middle-class following.

In 1958 Saint Vincent became part of the short-lived West Indies Federation, and that federation's

A coastal village on Saint Vincent covered in volcanic ash after the eruption of the La Soufriere volcano in 1979.   © *Nathan Benn/CORBIS*

dissolution led to Saint Vincent and the Grenadines becoming a self-governing state in association with the United Kingdom in 1969. At that point the country had complete control over internal policies, leaving defense and foreign policy decisions to London. A decade later, on October 27, 1979, Saint Vincent and the Grenadines achieved full independence, one of the last of the Windward Islands to do so.

Government Structure

With the 1979 constitution, Saint Vincent and the Grenadines became a parliamentary democracy within the British Commonwealth of Nations. As such, it recognizes the British monarch as head of state, represented locally by a governor general. This position is largely ceremonial, and real executive power rests with the prime minister and cabinet, whose members are chosen from the majority party in the legislature.

The legislature consists of the unicameral House of Assembly, which has twenty-one members. Fifteen of these are elected by popular vote every five years, though the prime minister can call for earlier elections. A further six senators are appointed by the governor general, four on the advice of the prime minister and two on the advice of the leader of the opposition.

Based on English common law and on laws passed by the House of Assembly, the judicial branch is divided into three judicial or magisterial districts with eleven lower courts and three magisterial courts. The constitution guarantees a public trial before an independent and impartial court. In cases involving capital punishment, legal counsel is provided to defendants who cannot otherwise afford counsel. Appeals are taken to the East Caribbean Supreme Court, based in Saint Lucia, and known on Saint Vincent as the Saint Vincent and the Grenadines Supreme Court. The last court of appeal is the Caribbean Court of Justice, which was inaugurated in 2005.

There is no local government in Saint Vincent and the Grenadines; instead the central government deals with such matters as local taxation, education, and roads. The country is divided into six parishes (five of them on Saint Vincent) and fifteen legislative districts.

Political Parties and Factions

Political life in Saint Vincent and the Grenadines is dominated by two major parties, making it difficult for a third party to win seats in the House of Assembly. The two main parties are the New Democratic Party (NDP) and the Unity Labour Party (ULP).

Founded and led by James F. Mitchell (1931–), the centrist NDP initially came to power in 1972, and held the majority for only two years. Then, in the first election after independence, in 1984, it won nine seats in the House of Assembly, and remained in power until 2000.

The ULP was formed by a coalition of the moderately leftist Movement for National Unity and the Saint Vincent and Grenadines Labour Party (SVGLP). By 1998 it was able to win 55 percent of the popular vote but secured only seven seats in the House of Assembly. However, in the 2001 elections, the ULP won twelve seats, and its leader, Ralph Gonsalves (1946–), became prime minister. The ULP also won the 2005 election, though it was contested by the NDP for alleged irregularities.

Major Events

Saint Vincent and the Grenadines faced a crisis when Mount Soufrière erupted in April 1979. Though there were no fatalities, much of St. Vincent's farmland was destroyed, leading to severe economic hardship that lasted several months after independence was declared and exacerbated old grievances between islands in the new country. On December 8, 1979, a secessionist rebellion broke out on Union Island. Prime Minister Milton Cato's government moved quickly to put down the rebellion, with support from Barbados. Aside from this incident, the political situation on Saint Vincent and the Grenadines has been stable.

The country's economic reliance on banana exports has also led to weather-induced hardship, as hurricanes have seriously damaged the islands and the banana crop in 1980, 1987, 1998, and 1999.

Twenty-First Century

One of the main challenges facing Saint Vincent and the Grenadines in the twenty-first century is diversification of its economy to lessen its reliance on bananas. Currently the government is attempting to develop tourism as a major industry. The islands have begun to attract yachting tourists and can now also accommodate cruise ships. In 2005 Prime Minister Gonsalves also reported that the country had reached its goal of universal high school education.

BIBLIOGRAPHY

Fraser, Adrian. *Chatoyer: The First National Hero of St. Vincent and the Grenadines.* Saint Vincent: Galaxy Print, 2002.

Government of St. Vincent and the Grenadines. "Official Website of the Government of St. Vincent and the Grenadines," http://www.gov.vc/govt/index.asp.

Shephard, Charles. *An Historical Account of the Island of St. Vincent.* Portland, OR: Frank Cass, 1997.

⊕ Zimbabwe

Type of Government

Though technically a constitutional democracy, the southern African nation of Zimbabwe is an autocratic regime dominated by Robert Mugabe (1924–), who has headed the state since its independence in 1980. A democratic framework persists but has been thoroughly compromised by Mugabe's practices of rigging elections and jailing opponents. As a result, street protests and mass demonstrations have become the primary means of expressing dissent. These continue to spread throughout the country, despite the increasingly authoritarian methods by which Mugabe has tried to suppress them.

Background

A landlocked nation of twelve million, Zimbabwe shares borders with Mozambique, to the northeast, east, and southeast; South Africa, to the south; Botswana, to the southwest; and Zambia, to the northwest. Its colonial history began in the late nineteenth century under the British South Africa Company. In 1923 the British government assumed control of the territory, known by that time as Southern Rhodesia. In the early 1960s, preparations for independence were derailed after a dispute between white settlers and the British government in London, which rejected the settlers' draft constitution as unfair to the black majority. The settlers declared independence in 1965 anyway, though most nations refused to grant the new state diplomatic recognition. Shortly thereafter, a violent and protracted guerilla war began as part of the majority's efforts to topple an openly racist and antidemocratic regime. Two major forces led the rebellion: Mugabe's Zimbabwe African National Union (ZANU) and the Zimbabwe African People's Union (ZAPU), under the leadership of Joshua Nkomo (1917–1999). In 1976 the two groups formed a loose alliance called the Popular Front. Ethnic tension between ZANU and ZAPU—the former was dominated by the Shona people, the latter by the Ndebele—persisted, however. A series of military and diplomatic victories, meanwhile, resulted in the international community's formal diplomatic recognition of the independent state of Zimbabwe in 1980. Seven years later, Nkomo and Mugabe agreed to a merger of the parties, under the name of Zimbabwe African National Union—Patriotic Front (ZANU-PF), as part of Mugabe's plan for restructuring the nation's political framework. Despite Nkomo's stature, his political influence declined as Mugabe's rose, and by 1990 he was serving as one of his former rival's two vice presidents.

Government Structure

The office of the president is by far the most powerful component of the government. While this is probably

Robert Mugabe—seen here greeting supporters in 2004—has been Zimbabwe's leader since 1980.　© *Howard Burditt/Reuters/Corbis*

due in part to the force of Mugabe's personality, it is also a result of the constitutionally mandated structure of government. Ratified in December 1979, the constitution identifies the president as both chief of state and head of government. There are two vice presidents, both presidential appointees, as are the members of the cabinet. The office of prime minister has not existed since 1987, when Mugabe, its occupant at the time, declared himself president.

Legislative powers are vested in the bicameral parliament. The upper house, known as the Senate, has sixty-six seats. Fifty of these are filled by direct, popular vote for a five-year term, six by presidential nominees, and ten by nominees of the Council of Chiefs, a group of traditional tribal leaders. Nominees must be endorsed by their peers, though this step is usually just a formality. The lower house, known as the House of Assembly, has one hundred and fifty seats. One hundred and twenty of these are popularly elected for a five-year term. Of the remainder, twelve are allocated to presidential nominees, ten to traditional tribal leaders chosen by the Council of Chiefs, and eight to the nation's provincial governors, all of

whom are presidential appointees. The president thus has effective control over fifty-six of the sixty-six Senate seats and twenty of the one hundred and fifty House seats. In the last parliamentary elections, moreover, there were widespread and well-substantiated reports of fraud by and on behalf of ZANU-PF, the ruling party. President Mugabe, analysts concluded, was determined to increase the already substantial legislative influence granted him by the constitution.

As of June 2007, there was no longer any meaningful separation of executive and judicial powers. Both of Zimbabwe's higher courts—the Supreme Court, theoretically the court of final appeal, and the High Court—have proved unable or unwilling to restrain Mugabe's abuse of power. Many of the lower courts, meanwhile, have ceased to function altogether. The same may be said of local and provincial administrations. Civil servants' salaries are often delayed and always inadequate, as they have failed to keep pace with the nation's staggering inflation rate.

Political Parties and Factions

Mugabe's party, the ZANU-PF, dominates Parliament, holding forty-three of the fifty elected Senate seats and seventy-eight of the one hundred and twenty elected seats in the House of Assembly. The major opposition group, the Movement for Democratic Change (MDC), continues to have a sizeable parliamentary presence (seven Senate seats and forty-one Assembly seats), at least on paper, but relations between the two blocs are so hostile that meaningful debate is essentially impossible. Mugabe's security forces, meanwhile, have subjected the MDC's leaders to unrelenting harassment and intimidation. In the most notorious incident, the MDC's leader, Morgan Tsvangirai (1952–), was badly beaten by police following his arrest at a political rally in March 2007.

Other politically active organizations include the Zimbabwe Congress of Trade Unions (ZCTU) and a broad-based pro-reform group called the Crisis in Zimbabwe Coalition. Human rights issues are a particular focus of the latter.

Major Events

In February 2000 Zimbabwe's voters, blacks and whites alike, firmly rejected Mugabe's proposal to evict the nation's four thousand white farmers from their land without compensation. Frustrated by the results of the referendum, Mugabe chose simply to ignore it and proceed. Within two years, there were very few whites of any occupation left in the country. White-owned farms that had once employed thousands of black Zimbabweans lay in ruins, and many of the poor blacks who had been promised the confiscated land saw their portions diverted to the president's wealthy associates. Of the relatively few families who actually received land, meanwhile, many lacked the equipment to cultivate it or the transportation to reach it. As basic commodities grew scarce, rising prices sparked an inflationary spiral that has only worsened with time. All the consequences of Mugabe's land scheme are not yet known. There is almost universal agreement, however, that it ranks as one of the worst economic decisions in the history of postcolonial Africa.

In April 2005 authorities began demolishing houses in poor neighborhoods of Harare, the capital. The ostensible goal was the restoration of order and beauty to a city disfigured by shoddy and illegal construction. Critics of Mugabe's administration, however, noted that it was in precisely those districts targeted for demolition that opposition to the government was traditionally strongest. In light of the strong-arm tactics Mugabe has used against other opponents, what was presented as a simple beautification project immediately acquired a sinister aspect. To date, more than seven hundred thousand residents have been forcibly relocated, usually to squalid camps on the city's periphery.

Twenty-First Century

Zimbabwe may be as close to collapse as any nation in the world. Mugabe's policies are almost universally acknowledged to have ruined the economy. Eighty percent of the population is unemployed, while even those who have jobs face an inflation rate now approaching 2,000 percent a year. In many areas, barter is the only form of economic exchange that still exists. Store shelves are bare, and thousands of people depend on international food aid to survive. These shortages are especially tragic in light of the country's traditional role as the largest food exporter in Africa. As the country slides further into chaos, the stream of Zimbabwean refugees has become a flood. Three million people, almost a quarter of the population, routinely cross the border into South Africa to obtain food and other necessities, and an increasing number are staying there illegally. Botswana, meanwhile, has erected electric fences along its frontier in an effort to keep refugees out. As all of Zimbabwe's neighbors are ill-equipped to handle thousands of new refugees, they have been forced to prop up Mugabe's regime with deliveries of fuel, electricity, and other essentials. This assistance is unlikely to prevent the eventual collapse of Mugabe's administration, either at his death (he is well over eighty years old) or earlier. Most analysts regard a prolonged humanitarian catastrophe in Zimbabwe as almost inevitable.

BIBLIOGRAPHY

Alexander, Jocelyn. *The Unsettled Land: State-Making & the Politics of Land in Zimbabwe, 1893–2003.* Athens, OH: Ohio University Press, 2006.

Sibanda, Eliakim M. *The Zimbabwe African People's Union, 1961–87: A Political History of Insurgency in Southern Rhodesia.* Trenton, NJ: Africa World Press, 2005.

Zimbabwe: Injustice and Political Reconciliation, Brian Raftopoulos and Tyrone Savage, editors. Cape Town, South Africa: Institute for Justice and Reconciliation, 2005.

⊕ Vanuatu

Type of Government

Vanuatu is a democratic parliamentary republic with a president serving as head of state and a prime minister serving as head of the government. The unicameral Parliament is the main decision-making body. The National Council of Chiefs (Malvatu Mauri) advises the government on language and culture.

Background

Vanuatu is an island nation located in the southwestern Pacific Ocean. It comprises eighty-three islands (sixty-five are inhabited) that form a Y-shaped archipelago; the population is concentrated on fourteen principal islands. The two largest islands, Espíritu Santo (sometimes called Santo) and Malekula, account for nearly half the nation's total land area. Vanuatu's capital is Port-Vila, on the

Vanuatu's Parliament House in Port-Vila.   © *Anders Ryman/CORBIS*

island of Efate. The term "ni-Vanuatu" is used to refer to the residents of the islands.

Vanuatu was settled by peoples of Melanesian origin between 1300 and 1100 BC. Much of what is known about the islands' early culture is derived from oral history and legends. Archeological evidence suggests that the tribes of Vanuatu were united by the great chief Roy Mata, under whom a highly stratified society emerged.

The island of Espíritu Santo was first sighted by the Portuguese explorer Pedro Fernandes de Queirós (c. 1570–1615) in 1606, but Europeans did not return there until the late eighteenth century. In 1768 the French navigator Louis-Antoine de Bougainville (1729–1811) rediscovered the islands, and the English explorer James Cook (known as Captain Cook; 1728–1779) gave them the name "New Hebrides" in 1774. The discovery of sandalwood on the island of Erromango in 1825 brought a rush of European traders and Polynesian immigrant workers to the islands.

Initially, the native ni-Vanuatu had little contact with the Europeans, who tended to remain on the coasts. That changed during the 1860s as many ni-Vanuatu were forcibly recruited to work as slave laborers on plantations in Australia, Samoa, and Fiji, a common practice in the South Pacific known as "blackbirding." When these workers returned home, they found that British and French settlers had arrived on the islands intending to establish cotton plantations; when cotton prices fell, the Europeans began to cultivate coffee, cocoa, bananas, and, most profitably, coconuts. British settlers from Australia dominated the islands at first, but by the turn of the century, the French heavily outnumbered the British.

In order to protect their interests in the region, Great Britain and France signed the Joint Naval Commission in 1887, followed by the Anglo-French Condominium of 1906. According to the terms of the arrangement, the two nations shared control of the New Hebrides islands. Each nation appointed a separate commissioner in the capital and ruled over settlers of their own nationality; the indigenous people were ruled jointly but had no rights to acquire citizenship from either country.

During World War II, Vanuatu served as an Allied military base. Thousands of American military personnel arrived in Vanuatu, loaded with tons of cargo such as weapons, food, and medical supplies. The sight inspired the development of a "cargo cult" known as the John Frum Movement. (Cargo cults are quasi-religious movements that develop among historically isolated tribal groups after their exposure to Western goods and culture.) Local villagers believed the mystical figure of John Frum, whom they worshipped as a god, was responsible for sending the U.S. military—and all its precious cargo—to the islands. Adherents to this cult believed that John Frum urged them to reject the teachings of Christian missionaries and return to their traditional ways of life. In this manner, the movement fostered anti-European sentiment among the ni-Vanuatu, who already resented the large amounts of land owned by European settlers on the islands, and set them on a course toward independence. The John Frum cult remains active in Vanuatu to this day—in 2007, believers celebrated the fiftieth anniversary of the movement's founding.

The first step toward independence was taken in 1974, when the islands were granted an elected legislative assembly. The English- and French-speaking populations remained divided as to the colony's future: English-speakers urged independence, whereas francophones either wished to remain under French control or secede altogether. As a result of the split among French-speakers, the colony's first elections gave a majority to the Vanua'aku Pati political party led by the Anglican priest Walter Lini (1942–1999), a strong advocate of independence. In 1980 the independent Republic of Vanuatu (meaning "Our Land Forever") was established.

Vanuatu remains a full member of the Commonwealth of Nations (also called the British Commonwealth), a voluntary association of more than fifty independent nations that are former colonies or territories of the British Empire.

Government Structure

The structure and functions of the executive, legislative, and judicial branches of government are outlined in the nation's constitution, which was adopted upon independence in 1980. Vanuatu has both a president who serves as head of state and a prime minister who is head of government. The president is elected to a five-year term by an electoral college composed of all members of the legislature and the presidents of the regional councils of chiefs; a two-thirds majority is required in order to win election. The position of the president is largely ceremonial and is not considered part of the executive branch.

Executive authority is vested in the prime minister and Council of Ministers. The prime minister is elected from among the members of the legislature by a majority vote (a quorum of three-quarters must be present). The prime minister chooses a cabinet called the Council of Ministers; the exact number of cabinet members varies from one administration to the next but cannot exceed one-quarter of the number of members of the legislature. As in all parliamentary systems, the prime minister and cabinet members also hold seats in the legislature.

Vanuatu has a unicameral (single-chamber) legislature called the Parliament. This body is made up of fifty-two members who are elected from multi-seat districts. Elections are held every four years. Parliament has the authority to pass a motion of "no confidence" against the governing administration. In this case Parliament can be dissolved before the end of its four-year term by a three-quarters majority vote or by a directive from the president (on the advice of the prime minister). To reduce political instability, electoral reforms were implemented in 2004 to disallow no-confidence votes during the first and last twelve months of a parliamentary term.

An important component of the government is the National Council of Chiefs (Malvatu Mauri), whose members are elected by the regional councils of chiefs. This body advises the government on ni-Vanuatu language and culture and participates in the electoral college that elects the president.

Vanuatu's legal system is based on English common law. The Supreme Court is the ultimate judicial authority in Vanuatu. This court is composed of four members: the chief justice, who is appointed by the president on the recommendation of the prime minister, and up to three other members, who are chosen by the president on the advice of the Judicial Service Commission. Two or more members of the Supreme Court may form a Court of Appeal. Magistrates' courts form the base of the judicial system. Vanuatu's constitution also provides for village and island courts, which are presided over by chiefs and handle matters of customary law.

Political Parties and Factions

National politics in Vanuatu operates as a multi-party system—that is, many political parties (or coalitions of parties) compete for control of government. Since independence, the divide between the English-speaking and French-speaking populations has been the most important political fault line in Vanuatu.

For more than a decade after independence, the anglophone Vanua'aku Pati (Party of Our Land) controlled the government. Although English-speakers were a minority in the early post-independence period, they were able to dominate government because the French-speakers were fragmented politically. In the early 1990s, however, many members of the Vanua'aku Pati defected to start a new party, called the National United Party; nonetheless, the Vanua'aku Pati remains an important force in ni-Vanuatu politics. The chief French-speaking party is the Union of Moderate Parties. In the parliamentary elections of 2004, at least seven other parties had representation in the legislature. Since the breakup of the Vanua'aku Pati, coalition building has been necessary to sustain governments.

Major Events

Economic development and disputes between the anglophone and francophone populations have dominated Vanuatu's political life since independence. The instability created by the ongoing feud between language groups has led to several votes of no-confidence and the replacement of the nation's top leadership at frequent intervals. In addition, Espíritu Santo was the site of a rebellion in 1980 during the transfer from colonial rule to independence, with agitators seeking secession from Vanuatu. Troops from Papua New Guinea re-established order on the island, which remained afterwards peacefully within the country.

Government instability has been a factor hindering economic progress in Vanuatu. It receives development aid from international organizations, Australia, New Zealand, and France and has sought to protect its own industries through targeted embargoes on imported products. In addition, Vanuatu's failure to regulate or tax commercial enterprises encourages foreign investment by those seeking to avoid the government oversight typical in more developed economies.

Twenty-First Century

Although Vanuatu has not experienced the degree of unrest that has plagued other South Pacific nations such as Fiji and Papua New Guinea, political stability is a key challenge in the twenty-first century. Electoral reforms implemented in 2004 attempted to stabilize the government by curtailing incessant no-confidence votes.

BIBLIOGRAPHY

Commonwealth Secretariat. "Vanuatu Country Profile." http://www.thecommonwealth.org/Yearbook HomeInternal/139623/home/ (accessed August 28, 2007).

Allen, Michael, ed. *Vanuatu: Politics, Economics, and Ritual in Island Melanesia.* New York: Academic Press, 1981.

Rodman, Margaret Critchlow. *Houses Far from Home: British Colonial Space in the New Hebrides.* Honolulu: University of Hawaii Press, 2001.

⊕ Belize

Type of Government

The Belize government is a parliamentary democracy with power distributed across three separate branches of government. The executive branch consists of a governor general who acts as head of state and a prime minister who serves as head of government. The bicameral legislature, the National Assembly, comprises an elected House of Representatives and an appointed Senate. Members of the independent judiciary are appointed; English common law forms the basis of judicial decisions.

Background

The least-populated nation in Central America, Belize is located west of Mexico and Guatemala on the Caribbean

Sea. Mayan civilization dominated the region from about 1500 BC to 1000 AD, and the Maya legacy can still be seen in major archaeological sites such as Altun Ha and Xunantunich. The first European contact came in 1502 when Christopher Columbus (1451–1506) sailed along its shore; the first recorded European settlement occurred in 1638, when shipwrecked English sailors built a small colony in the area of what is now Belize City. The region was contested by both the British and Spanish during the seventeenth and eighteenth centuries, but by 1798 it had come under British control. In 1871 the region was reorganized as one of England's Crown colonies.

Wood was the major export of Belize until the twentieth century, including logwood, which was important in the formulation of dyes for the wool industry, and mahogany used for furniture. By the twentieth century indiscriminate logging had taken its toll, and the local economy thereafter focused on renewable agricultural exports such as sugar cane and bananas. While the colonial estate owners prospered, the vast majority of the population was impoverished.

The independence movement was led by Belize's trade and labor groups, most prominently the British Honduras Workers and Tradesmen's Union (later the General Workers Union). Social unrest was stirred in 1950 by British devaluation of the Belize dollar, and as a result of ensuing demonstrations, the People's United Party (PUP) was founded. Unofficially, people began calling their country Belize instead of British Honduras and began demanding separation from England. Universal adult suffrage was granted in 1951, and with the country's first elections in 1954, PUP came to power in the newly constituted Legislative Council.

In 1961 a severe hurricane struck the low-lying capital of Belize City, prompting the country to move its capital inland to Belmopan. When the country was granted internal autonomy and self-government in 1964, George C. Price (1919–) became its first premier. Full independence, however, was delayed by a border dispute with Guatemala. Belize became the official name of the country in 1973, and eight years later, the dispute with Guatemala still unresolved, Belize became an independent member of the British Commonwealth, with Price acting as its first prime minister.

Government Structure

Under the terms of the 1981 constitution, Belize is a parliamentary democracy. It recognizes the British monarch as ceremonial head of state, represented locally by a governor general. Real executive power is wielded by the prime minister and the cabinet, chosen from the majority party in the parliament, or National Assembly.

The bicameral National Assembly consists of a twenty-nine-seat House of Representatives (due to increase to

Belizean Prime Minister George Price (right) with the Duke of Kent, finalizing Belize's independence on September 21, 1981. © *Bettmann/CORBIS*

thirty-one in the 2008 elections), whose members are elected by popular vote via universal adult suffrage every five years. The prime minister can call for earlier elections if needed. Legislative power in the National Assembly favors the House of Representatives over the Senate. Not only can the House of Representatives introduce and pass legislation, but it can do so over the Senate's objections, as long as the Senate receives notice of the legislation introduced. The Senate's role is more advisory—for example, it confirms bills passed by the House, authorizes ratification of treaties, and approves appointments of judges and ambassadors. Its twelve members are appointed to five-year terms: six on the advice of the prime minister, three on the advice of the opposition, and one each on the recommendation of the Belize Council of Churches and Evangelical Association of Churches; the Belize Chamber of Commerce and Industry and the Belize Business Bureau; and the National Trade Union Congress and the Civil Society Steering Committee.

Belize is divided into six administrative districts: Corozal, Orange Walk, Belize, Cayo, Stann Creek, and Toledo. Belize City has an elected city council of nine members; the other districts are each administered by a seven-member elected town board. Village councils govern at the village level.

The independent judiciary, whose members are appointed, consists of local magistrates, the Supreme Court (presided over by a chief justice), and the Court of Appeal. The law of Belize is the common law of England, as supplemented by local legislation. Defendants have rights to presumption of innocence, protection against self-incrimination, counsel, appeal, and public trial. The final court of appeal is the regional Caribbean Court of Justice (CCJ), based in Trinidad.

Political Parties and Factions

Though several political parties operate in Belize, the country essentially has a two-party system. The two major parties are the People's United Party (PUP) and the United Democratic Party (UDP).

Formed in 1950 and led for forty years by George C. Price, the PUP derives its support primarily from conservative voters. It dominated Belize elections from 1954 to 1984 and was instrumental in the country's struggle for independence. Price and the PUP returned to power in 1989 but lost in the 1993 elections. Under the leadership of Said Musa (1944–), the party was returned to power in 1998 and 2003.

The UDP was founded in the 1970s from a merger of several smaller liberal parties. Representing a center-left position on the political spectrum, the UDP first came to power in 1984 under the leadership of Manuel Esquivel (1940–). The party's second electoral victory came in 1993, also under Esquivel.

Other smaller parties with no members in parliament include the We the People Reform Movement (WTP) and the National Reform Party (NRP). Unions also continue to have a strong voice in the country, including the Public Service Union (PSU) and the National Trade Union Congress of Belize (NTUCB).

Major Events

Guatemala refused to recognize Belize's independence in 1981 and severed relations with the United Kingdom over the dispute. Though relations were restored in 1986, the British continued to maintain soldiers in Belize as a preventative measure. After Belize was admitted to the Organization of American States (OAS), Guatemala granted full recognition of Belize's independence in 1992. The following year the two countries signed a non-aggression pact, and in 1994 the United Kingdom withdrew its troops from Belize. Despite this progress, there is still considerable dispute between Belize and Guatemala regarding Belize's southern border and maritime territorial limits.

In the 1980s and 1990s Belize turned from agriculture to tourism as the basis of its economy. The number of tourists grew quickly; from 64,000 tourists in 1980 to 247,000 in 1992. By the mid-1990s the contribution of tourism to GDP outpaced that of the sugar industry.

Twenty-First Century

Challenges to the stability of Belize in the twenty-first century include continuing instability related to the territorial dispute with Guatemala. Talks between Belize and Guatemala have continued amid persistent tensions. In 2000 the Belize ambassador was expelled from Guatemala and talks were broken off, but they were later resumed.

In 2005 Belize was wracked with labor unrest, demonstrations, and strikes by both public and private sector workers as a result of a proposed government budget requiring tax increases. Further strikes were called later in the year as a result of the government's attempt to privatize the telephone system. Labor disputes are complicated by high unemployment rates and low overall wages.

Belize is also experiencing a rise in violent crime—fueled by the South American drug trade and high unemployment—which threatens the continued growth of tourism. In a positive economic development, petroleum was discovered in commercial quantities in 2006.

BIBLIOGRAPHY

Government of Belize. http://www.belize.gov.bz/index.php (accessed May 3, 2007).

Thomson, P. A. B. *Belize: A Concise History.* London: Macmillan Caribbean, 2005.

Twigg, Alan. *Understanding Belize: A Historical Guide.* British Columbia: Harbour Publishing, 2006.

⊕ Antigua and Barbuda

Type of Government

The government of Antigua and Barbuda is a constitutional parliamentary democracy. The executive branch consists of a governor general who is head of state and a prime minister who is head of government. The legislature is bicameral, comprising the House of Representatives and Senate, each with seventeen members. The judicial branch is based on English common law.

Background

Located in the eastern Caribbean, the country of Antigua and Barbuda is made up of those two main islands and the dependency of Redonda, which are all part of the Lesser Antilles archipelago.

In 1493, when Christopher Columbus (1451–1506) sighted the larger island of Antigua on his second voyage, the island was populated by the Carib people. He named it after the church of Santa Maria de la Antigua in Seville. Though the Spanish and French attempted settlement, permanent European settlement did not occur for well over a century, largely because of Antigua's lack of fresh water and determined Carib resistance. In 1632 a group of Englishmen from Saint Kitts established a successful settlement, and Antigua formally became a British colony in 1667; Barbuda was not colonized until 1674.

In 1674 the sugar economy was introduced to Antigua by Christopher Codrington, who came from Barbados and established the first plantation. Cane-processing windmills were soon built all over the island; by the middle of the eighteenth century there were more than 150 of these, each demarking a sizeable plantation. With sugar cane also came traffic in African slaves, a practice which continued until 1834 when slavery was abolished throughout the British Empire. Codrington leased Barbuda to raise slaves and supplies for the sugar cane enterprise. Barbuda's only town is named after him.

In addition to its importance as an exporter of sugar, Antigua also became an important strategic port, and the British Royal Navy headquartered its Caribbean fleet there in the eighteenth century. In 1860 Antigua annexed Barbuda, and in 1871, both islands were placed under the auspices of the Leeward Islands Federation. The island's administration was transferred to the Federation of the West Indies in 1958. Meanwhile, the economy of the islands languished as the sugar industry declined due to increased competition, reduction in world sugar prices, and over-farming.

Antigua and Barbuda remained economically underdeveloped well into the twentieth century. Farmland was

The Governor's House on Antigua. © *Bruce Adams; Eye Ubiquitous/CORBIS*

always scarce on the islands, and former slaves had no access to credit with which to start new businesses. Poor islanders increasingly constructed shantytowns and attempted to provide for their families as occasional laborers. This general impoverishment gave rise to a labor union movement in the late 1930s, which effectively dovetailed with a movement for independence from England.

The Antigua Trades and Labor Union was formed in 1939, and by 1943 it was led by Vere Cornwall Bird (1910–1999), who also founded the Antigua Labour Party (ALP). In the 1951 elections, when universal adult suffrage was first instituted, the ALP became the majority party, a position that it held, with a brief hiatus in the 1970s, for over half a century. Bird established a political dynasty and ultimately led his country to full independence.

Independence came in stages. Antigua became an associated state of the United Kingdom with full internal self-government in 1967. However, residents of Barbuda initially opposed independence until they could be guaranteed a degree of economic and administrative autonomy from Antigua. Antigua and Barbuda became an independent state within the Commonwealth of Nations in 1981, and Bird became the nation's first prime minister.

Government Structure

With its Commonwealth status, the nation of Antigua and Barbuda recognizes the British monarch as its head of state, represented on the islands by a governor general whose role is largely ceremonial. The prime minister and the cabinet, chosen from the majority party in the lower house of parliament, form the actual government and are responsible for conducting affairs of state.

The parliament is bicameral. The lower house, called the House of Representatives, has seventeen members elected every five years by universal adult suffrage, but the prime minister can call for earlier elections if needed. The House holds the bigger share of legislative power in the parliament. The Senate comprises seventeen members who are appointed by the governor general: eleven on the advice of the prime minister (this must include at least one resident of Barbuda); four on the advice of the leader of the opposition; one of the governor general's own choosing; and one on the advice of the Barbuda Council, that island's governing body.

The island of Antigua has six parishes and two dependencies, Barbuda and Redonda. Local government affairs are conducted by twenty-nine community councils, each with nine members, five elected and four appointed.

The judicial system is based on English common law and statutory law, as enacted by the Antigua and Barbuda parliament. The constitution prohibits arbitrary arrest and detention, and suspects must be brought before a court within forty-eight hours of arrest or detention. There are also constitutionally protected rights of privacy, freedom of speech, press, worship, movement, and association. Three magistrates' courts deal with summary offenses and lesser civil cases, while a court of summary jurisdiction on Antigua deals with larger civil cases. The Eastern Caribbean Supreme Court, based in Saint Lucia, provides a High Court and Court of Appeal. Since 2005 final appeals may be made to the Trinidad-based Caribbean Court of Justice (CCJ).

Political Parties and Factions

Antigua and Barbuda functions under a two-party system. The dominant party in the country since the time of independence has been the Antigua Labour Party (ALP). Its main rival for power is the United Progressive Party (UPP). Other minor parties include the Barbuda People's Movement for Change, allied to the ALP, and the Barbuda People's Movement, allied to the UPP.

The ALP, an outgrowth of the trade union movement in Antigua and Barbuda, held power from 1946 to 2004, except for a period from 1971 to 1976. With the retirement of Vere Bird in 1994, his son, Lester Bird (1938–), took over his father's term of office as prime minister. He successfully stood for election that same year, and maintained power until 2004.

Formed in 1992 through the coalition and merger of several smaller political parties, the UPP was the opposition party throughout the 1990s and into the twenty-first century. Led by the labor activist Winston Baldwin Spencer (1948–), the party finally swept into power in 2004, winning 55 percent of the vote and taking twelve of the seventeen seats in the House of Representatives.

Major Events

The Bird political dynasty was the longest-serving elected government in the Caribbean. During the course of their long term in power the country prospered through tourism and the establishment of financial services. However, there were also many allegations of corruption leveled at the government and the country for activities related to drug trafficking, arms smuggling, and money laundering. Lester Bird's brother was arrested for cocaine smuggling, and the country was put on several international watch lists for money laundering. In 2000 Antigua and Barbuda, along with other Caribbean nations, agreed to reforms to aid in the battle against money laundering.

Despite such challenges and difficulties, the ALP remained in power until 2004. Shortly after the UPP took power, income tax, eliminated in 1975, was reintroduced to help reduce the country's deficit. Beginning in 2003, the country also fell into an ongoing dispute with the United States over the legality of Internet gambling, which had become a large part of the Antigua and Barbuda economy.

Twenty-First Century

The main challenges to a stable government in Antigua and Barbuda are corruption and the creation of a strong economic base. In 2000 the government instituted policies to prevent money laundering, which has helped to restore the nation's financial reputation and increase foreign investment. The country's other main source of income is tourism, accounting for more than 50 percent of GDP. The tourism industry has declined since 2000, significantly reducing government revenues and thereby halting development programs. Internet gambling proved for a time to be vital to the country in its attempt to move away from tourism as its main source of foreign currency. With the U.S. ban in 2003, however, such gaming operations were reduced from 100 to 36, and the number of employees in Antigua and Barbuda shrank from 5,000 to 2,500. The outcome of an international court case brought against the United States by Antigua and Barbuda will thus have important long-term effects for the country.

BIBLIOGRAPHY

Berleant-Schiller, Riva, Susan Lowes, and Milton Benjamin. *Antigua and Barbuda*. Oxford: Clio Press, 1995.

Coram, Robert. *Caribbean Time Bomb: The United States' Complicity in the Corruption of Antigua*. New York: William Morrow, 1993.

Gaspar, David. *Bondsmen and Rebels: A Study of Master-Slave Relations in Antigua*. Durham, NC: Duke University Press, 1993.

⊕ Saint Kitts and Nevis

Type of Government

Saint Kitts and Nevis is a parliamentary democracy and an independent state within the British Commonwealth. The executive branch consists of a prime minister, who is head of government, and a governor general, who is head of state and the representative of the British monarch. The prime minister and his or her cabinet is responsible to the unicameral parliament, the National Assembly, three of whose members are appointed and the remaining eleven of which are elected by popular vote. The country's judicial system is modeled on English common law.

Background

Saint Kitts and Nevis is made up of two Caribbean islands separated by just two miles. Christopher Columbus (1451–1506) explored the islands in 1493, but no colonial settlements were established on either island until 1623 when the British founded the colony of Saint Christopher on Saint Kitts under Sir Thomas Warner (d. 1649). Granted a Royal Commission, Warner sent colonists to nearby islands, including Nevis and Anguilla. The French settled on Saint Kitts in 1625, and the following year Warner and his fellow European settlers, fearful of attack by the indigenous inhabitants, the Carib, struck first, killing more than two thousand natives. Thereafter, the English and French divided the island, but tensions grew between the two countries for the next century until a decisive British victory in 1782 ended French presence on both islands.

Meanwhile, the settlers became relatively prosperous cultivating tobacco. Nevis became renowned for its peacefulness and wealth, but did suffer one major setback: in 1690 a huge earthquake and subsequent tsunami completely destroyed the island's capital city, Jamestown. By 1640 tobacco had given way to sugar cane as the major export for the islands, and African slaves were imported to work the crop. Soon the African population far outstripped the number of British settlers. With the abolition of slavery in the British Empire in 1834, sugar profits began to decline, a problem exacerbated by over-farming and by competition from countries such as Brazil and Cuba.

Administratively, the two islands were grouped with Anguilla and the British Virgin Islands in what was called the Leeward Islands; in 1833 this was renamed the Federal Colony of the Leeward Islands, with the separate islands maintaining a degree of independence from London and from one another. However, in 1883, Saint Kitts, Nevis, and Anguilla were united, with a common president. This forced unification caused tensions between the formerly independent islands.

During the twentieth century, as sugar prices and production declined, workers on the islands grew restive. The Great Depression of the 1930s brought worker frustrations to a head, and an organized labor movement was founded as labor riots spread. The Saint Kitts and Nevis Trades and Labour Union was formed in 1940 to tap the growing labor movement, and its political arm, the Saint Kitts and Nevis Labour Party (SKLP), managed to put the union leader Robert Bradshaw (1916–1978) into the local legislature; later he became the first premier of Saint Kitts, Nevis, and Anguilla. For the next three decades, the Labour Party was at the forefront of politics in Saint Kitts and Nevis.

The road to independence was long. The British granted universal adult suffrage in 1952 and allowed for increased local representation. In 1958 Saint Kitts, Nevis, and Anguilla were placed under the auspices of the West Indies Federation and then reclassified again, in 1967, as associated states of the United Kingdom. Anguilla, seeking its own independence, broke away from the state in 1971; final ratification of its secession came in 1980. Saint Kitts and Nevis gained formal independence from Britain in 1983, becoming a fully sovereign and democratic state, though remaining a constitutional monarchy within the Commonwealth.

Government Structure

The country of Saint Kitts and Nevis is a federation of those two islands. According to the 1983 constitution, the British monarch is head of state, represented locally by a governor general at the capital of Basseterre on the larger island of Saint Kitts. A deputy governor general is also delegated for Nevis. However, real power resides in the hands of the parliament and the prime minister.

The prime minister is the leader of the majority party or ruling coalition in the unicameral legislature, the National Assembly. The prime minister is the head of government and rules along with the members of the cabinet, also chosen from members of the majority party or coalition majority. The prime minister can call for elections if they are demanded by the people in a referendum.

The fourteen-member National Assembly is elected every five years (suffrage is universal for all citizens eighteen or older). Eleven members are directly elected from the eleven different constituencies, three of them representing Nevis and eight Saint Kitts. Three additional senators are appointed by the governor general in consultation with the prime minister and the leader of the opposition. By the terms of the 1983 constitution, Nevis has its own legislative assembly, the Nevis Island Assembly, and local administration. The Nevis Island Administration (NIA) is led by the premier and a cabinet. Nevis was also guaranteed in the 1983 constitution the right to secede from the federation if such a motion is approved by three of the five members of the local Nevisian assembly and thereafter by two-thirds of the voters on the island of Nevis.

The judicial branch of the federation operates on the principles of British common law as well as the laws and regulations passed by the National Assembly (also sometimes referred to as the House of Assembly). Magistrates' courts deal with petty criminal and civil cases; legal assistance is provided to indigent criminal defendants. The attorney general, a member of the cabinet, is the government's principal legal adviser. Saint Kitts and Nevis also belongs to the Eastern Caribbean Supreme Court, based in Saint Lucia; there is one judge of this court residing in Saint Kitts. Higher appeals go, since 2005, to the Trinidad-based Caribbean Court of Justice (CCJ).

Political Parties and Factions

Four major parties dominate Saint Kitts and Nevis politics: the SKLP, the People's Action Movement (PAM), the Concerned Citizens Movement (CCM), and the Nevis Reformation Party (NRP).

Independence day parade through Charlestown, on the island of Nevis, 1989. © *Peter Guttman/CORBIS*

The SKLP dominated politics until 1980, led at first by Robert Bradshaw, considered to be the father of independence. With Bradshaw's death in 1978, his deputy took over, only to die a year later. Thereafter, the party floundered for a time, coming back into power in 1995 under Denzil Douglas (1953–). The SKLP also won the 2004 election, taking more than fifty percent of the vote, and keeping Douglas in power as prime minister.

PAM was formed in 1964 by families of the former estate and plantation owners, a conservative reaction to the power of the SKLP. Throughout the 1980s and early 1990s, PAM, alone or in coalition, controlled the government under Kennedy Simmonds (1936–).

CCM is a political party formed in Nevis whose members hold seats both in the National Assembly and in the Nevis Island Assembly. It advocates constitutional reform to give greater autonomy to Nevis in administering its own affairs and in its relationship with Saint Kitts. Another Nevis-based party, NRP, was founded in 1970 and is led by Simeon Daniel (1934–), premier of Nevis from 1983 to 1992.

Major Events

Since independence in 1983, St. Kitts and Nevis has gone through major economic restructuring, as its three-century reliance on sugar was doomed by a worldwide price drop in that product. Accordingly, the government, under various administrations, has pushed for diversification into tourism and financial services. In the financial services sector, the country became embroiled in various forms of illegal or unethical practices, including money laundering, and was blacklisted by some international financial agencies. By 2002, though, such irregularities seemed to have been corrected.

In 1998 residents of the island of Nevis voted on a referendum to secede. The measure, which by the terms of the constitution required a two-thirds majority to pass, achieved about 62 percent of the vote, and thus narrowly failed.

Twenty-First Century

The economy and Nevis secession continue to be the dominant challenges to stability in Saint Kitts and Nevis. In 2005 the government decided to abandon the state-owned sugar industry, which had been suffering since the 1960s. Tourism has become the nation's top industry, but it is not known if that can completely replace revenues formerly derived from sugar exports. Nationalist sentiment on Nevis has not abated since the referendum, and the movement for secession persists despite attempts by the federal government to provide increased constitutional autonomy to lessen tensions.

BIBLIOGRAPHY

Cox, Edward L. *Free Coloreds in the Slave Societies of St. Kitts and Grenada, 1763–1833.* Knoxville, TN: University of Tennessee Press, 1984.

Government of St. Christopher (St. Kitts) and Nevis. http://www.gov.kn/ (accessed April 10, 2007).

Moll, V. P. *St. Kitts-Nevis.* Santa Barbara, CA: Clio Press, 1995.

⊕ State of Brunei Darussalam

Type of Government

Officially known as the State of Brunei Darussalam, Abode of Peace, or Negara Brunei Darussalam, Brunei is an independent and constitutional Islamic sultanate on the northern coast of the island of Borneo. Brunei's ruling monarch, or sultan, serves as head of state. The sultan appoints ministers to serve on five Constitutional Councils, which advise and assist him in governing. An appointed chief minister oversees the work of the councils and exercises the government's executive authority. One of the five councils, the Legislative Council, is designated as Brunei's parliament. The Legislative Council is expected to transition gradually from an appointed to an elected body. Brunei's Supreme Court hears appeals from lower courts and heads the country's judicial branch of government.

Background

Almost an enclave within Eastern Malaysia, Brunei is geographically separated into two parts, both surrounded on three sides by the Malaysian state of Sarawak and on the north by the South China Sea. Situated on Borneo, which is part of a large island grouping called the Malay Archipelago, Brunei has a population that is two-thirds ethnic Malay and approximately one-fifth ethnic Chinese, the latter living in Brunei's urban areas. The balance of the population consists of various groups of indigenous peoples. Islam is Brunei's official religion and is practiced by 67 percent of the population. Buddhism is practiced by 13 percent, Christianity by 10 percent, and indigenous beliefs and practices, such as animism, by the remaining 10 percent.

Brunei has a history shaped by its proximity to maritime trade and the vital shipping lanes leading through the South China Sea and into the Indian and Pacific Oceans. Traces of Hindu influence arrived via trade or conflict with Java. By the early fifteenth century, Muslim traders from India settled in the region and brought with them the religion that shapes Brunei's government and continues to be practiced by the majority of its population.

Brunei covers only some 2,226 square miles (5,765 square kilometers), but in the early sixteenth century, when it was already an Islamic sultanate, its control extended over the entire northwestern area of the island of Borneo, including the present-day Malaysian states of Sabah and Sarawak, and some portions of the Sulu islands in the southern Philippines. Spanish explorers were the first Europeans to visit the sultanate of Brunei, and trade with Europe quickly ensued. Internal strife brought on by conflicts over royal succession, and colonial expansion by European powers, caused a period of decline. By the end of the eighteenth century, Brunei was known as a haven for marauding pirates. Predominant British influence began in 1849, when the British, looking for a way to protect their lucrative trade between Singapore and northwest Borneo, took action against the pirate fleets and disabled them within five years. Previous British influence in the region had come from a British officer, Sir James Brooke (1803–1868), who was instrumental in helping the Sultan of Brunei quell a civil war; in 1841 the grateful sultan ceded to Brooke the state of Sarawak. Brooke and his successors purchased or acquired other territories on Borneo, until Britain controlled all of northern Borneo. In 1888, reduced almost to its present size, the sultanate of Brunei became a British protectorate. A British diplomatic agent administered the state and advised the sultan in all matters except Malay customs, traditions, and Islamic religion.

Much of Brunei's late nineteenth- and early twentieth-century history coincides with that of neighboring Malaysia, including the Japanese invasion and occupation from 1941 to 1945 during World War II. Years after the war, in 1959, Britain granted self-government to Brunei, while remaining in charge of the country's defense and foreign affairs. Also that year, Sultan Omar Ali Saifuddien (1914–1986), the reigning monarch, promulgated Brunei's first constitution. In 1962 the leftist Brunei People's Party, which sought to remove the sultan from power, won all elected seats in elections for the Legislative Council. The sultan dissolved the council, declared an official state of emergency, and began ruling by decree. A subsequent revolt by the Brunei People's Party was quickly put down with British assistance, and as of 2007 the official state of emergency remained in effect.

In 1963 Brunei became the only Malayan state to choose to remain a British dependency rather than join the new Federation of Malaysia. Many believe the ruling sultan feared joining the federation would mean the loss of Brunei's separate identity and the loss of a large portion of the state's oil and gas revenues. Following independence in 1984, Brunei became a member of the British Commonwealth. While the sultan's 1959 constitution remains in effect, important provisions of it were suspended under the 1962 state of emergency, and additional provisions were suspended following Brunei's complete independence from Britain.

Hassanal Bolkiah, Sultan of Brunei, signing a constitutional amendment into law on September 29, 2004. The amendment cleared the way for the country's first elections in more than forty years. © HO/Reuters/Corbis

Government Structure

Brunei's head of state—and its official prime minister—is one of the world's longest reigning monarchs. Hassanal Bolkiah (1946–) became sultan in October 1967 following the abdication of his father, Sultan Omar Ali Saifuddien. Brunei's constitution grants executive authority to the Council of Cabinet Ministers, a body of twelve who are appointed by the sultan and presided over by the sultan and the chief minister, or *mentri besar*. Brunei's present sultan also holds office as defense minister and finance minister. Other cabinet ministries include home affairs; development; industry and primary resources; and culture, youth, and sports. There are three other important national councils whose members are all appointed by the sultan. The Religious Council advises on religious matters; a Privy Council deals with constitutional matters; and the Council of Succession determines succession to the throne when necessary.

The fifth national council called for by Brunei's constitution is its parliamentary body, the Legislative Council. Originally consisting of eleven appointed members and ten elected ones, the council was dissolved in 1962 after one legislative election, which resulted in hostility toward the monarchy. The ruling sultan declared the state of emer-

gency, which would persist into the twenty-first century. The Legislative Council was reconstituted by appointment from time to time. Political parties, outlawed under the state of emergency, reemerged briefly in the 1980s. In what was seen as a rare move toward political reform, the sultan reopened parliament and the Legislative Council met again, for the first time in twenty years, in September 2004. Its twenty-one members were all appointed by the sultan. This Legislative Council passed a constitutional amendment calling for a forty-five-member council with fifteen elected, rather than appointed, members. In September 2005 Sultan Hassanal Bolkiah dissolved this new Legislative Council and appointed one with twenty-nine members. Brunei's last legislative elections were held in March of 1962, and, while new legislative elections are expected, a date for them has yet to be determined.

Brunei's legal system is based on the Indian penal code and English common law. For Brunei's Muslims, the courts of first instance are the courts of Kathis, which handle family matters, such as marriage and divorce, by applying sharia, or Islamic law. There are also sultan's courts, presided over by magistrates, followed by the High Court, which hears appeals in both criminal and civil cases, and the Court of Appeals, which hears appeals from the High Court. Brunei's judiciary is headed by a Supreme Court, whose chief justice and judges are sworn in by the sultan for terms of three years. The Judicial Committee of Privy Council in London remains the final court of appeal for civil cases in Brunei. Final appeal of criminal cases is to Brunei's Supreme Court. In May 2002 a State Judiciary Department was formed to take over administration of Brunei's judicial matters. Brunei declares its judiciary to be an independent branch of government.

Political Parties and Factions

With the same royal dynasty ruling Brunei for six centuries (Sultan Hassanal Bolkiah is the dynasty's twenty-ninth monarch), political parties in Brunei have been minimized. They first appeared with the formation of Brunei's self-government in 1959, but all political parties were outlawed in the wake of the sultan's declaration of a state of emergency following legislative elections in 1962. They reemerged in the 1980s, and in 1984 the government legalized the Brunei National Democratic Party—composed mostly of businessmen loyal to the sultan—and followed with the legalization of the Brunei National Solidarity Party in 1986. In 1988 both were banned. In 1995 the Brunei National Solidarity Party, one of the parties banned in 1962, formally requested authorization and held a convention. In 2005 the National Development Party registered as a political party.

Major Events

In 1984, the year of its independence, Brunei joined the Association of Southeast Asian Nations (ASEAN), which had first been established by Malaysia, Singapore, Indonesia, the Philippines, and Thailand in 1967. Vietnam, Laos, Cambodia, and Myanmar became members in the 1990s. ASEAN seeks to reduce tensions and increase collaboration among its member nations. Accelerating the region's economic growth, cultural development, and social progress are among its most important stated aims. In 1999 ASEAN's member nations agreed to pursue development of a free trade zone in Southeast Asia by eventually eliminating duties on most goods traded in the region. Estimated to take effect in the year 2010 or later, the proposed zone will be the world's largest free trade zone, encompassing some 1.7 billion people and trade valued at $1.2 trillion. In May 2002 ASEAN's ten member countries pledged to form a united front against terrorism in response to the September 11, 2001, terrorist attacks in the United States. They established a regional security framework, including joint training programs, exchange of intelligence information, and the introduction of national laws governing arrest, investigation, and extradition of suspects.

In 1991 Sultan Hassanal Bolkiah introduced a conservative state ideology known as Malay Muslim Monarchy, or Melayu Islam Beraja (MIB). It combined Islamic values with traditional Malay culture and declared the Brunei monarchy to be a defender of the Islamic faith. Thought to have been aimed at preempting calls for a more democratic government, the ideology is said to have alienated Brunei's Chinese and expatriate communities.

Southeast Asian financial markets took a sudden, precipitous decline in 1997 when investors lost confidence in a number of Asian currencies and securities. In Brunei the value of shares and other assets was affected, and oil prices simultaneously declined. As with other economies in the region, Brunei's economy eventually recovered.

In 1998 a financial scandal involving the royal family erupted when Amedeo, a business conglomerate owned by the sultan's younger brother, Prince Jefri Bolkiah, collapsed, leaving massive debts and precipitating a financial scandal. Sultan Hassanal Bolkiah removed his brother as chief of Brunei Investment Agency, over concerns about his stewardship of the agency. In 2000 the government of Brunei filed a civil suit against Prince Jefri for alleged misuse of state funds, and the case was settled out of court. Revealed to have spent more than $2 billion on luxury goods over ten years' time, Prince Jefri agreed to return all assets allegedly taken from the state-owned Brunei Investment Agency.

Twenty-First Century

Most of Brunei's private press is either owned or controlled by the royal family. Those outlets that are not owned by the royal family usually exercise self-censorship in matters of politics and religion, and offer little, if any, criticism of the government. Foreign television is available via cable, and access to the Internet is described as unrestricted.

Concerns unique to a constitutional sultanate also manifest themselves in Brunei's economic situation. While increasing integration into the world marketplace benefits Brunei economically, the country's leadership is concerned that aspects of this integration—especially increasing worldliness and affluence among the country's youth—may end up adversely affecting Brunei's internal social cohesion.

Brunei has benefited enormously from its extensive petroleum and natural gas fields and today has one of the highest per capital gross domestic products (GDPs) in Asia. Crude oil and natural gas production account for just over half of the GDP and more than 90 percent of exports. Throughout the decades, the state has invested much of its oil and gas revenue on modernization and social, educational, and medical services. Reserves of oil and natural gas, however, are dwindling. Future plans in the twenty-first century call for diversifying the country's economic base, including marketing the country as a financial center and a destination for ecotourism. This may require retraining up to 25 percent of the labor force and strengthening the economy's banking and tourist sectors.

In February 2007 Brunei, along with neighboring Malaysia and Indonesia, signed a "Rainforest Declaration" and agreed to conserve a large area of Borneo that is home to rare species.

BIBLIOGRAPHY

Brunei Government. "The Government of Brunei Darussalam Official Website." http://www.brunei.gov.bn (accessed June 28, 2007).

Osborne, Milton. *Southeast Asia: An Illustrated Introductory History.* New South Wales: Allen & Unwin, 1991.

Tarling, Nicholas. *Britain, the Brookes and Brunei.* London: Oxford University Press, 1971.

⊕ Federated States of Micronesia

Type of Government

The Federated States of Micronesia is governed as a democratic federal republic in free association with the United States. Legislative, executive, and judicial powers are divided between the federal government and four state governments. The president serves as both head of state and the head of the government. The unicameral (single-chamber) Congress is the main decision-making body.

Background

The Federated States of Micronesia is an island nation located in the western Pacific Ocean, east of the Philippines. It comprises more than six hundred islands and islets, forming the eastern portion of the Caroline Islands archipelago (the western islands are politically part of Palau). The nation has four constituent states: Chuuk, Kosrae, Pohnpei, and Yap. The capital is Palikir, on the island on Pohnpei. The name Micronesia may be used to refer either to the Federated States or to the region as a whole.

Settlers arrived on the Micronesian islands as early as three thousand to four thousand years ago. In the years before European contact, the hunter-gatherer societies there achieved a high degree of complexity. On the island of Yap, a sophisticated social structure, tribute system, and trade network contributed to the development of a centralized empire that dominated the islands of Micronesia.

Spanish explorers reached the islands in the sixteenth century, naming them the Caroline Islands in honor of Spanish King Charles II (1661–1700), but they would remain uncolonized for nearly three centuries. Throughout the nineteenth century, whaling merchants and traders introduced European weapons, diseases, and religious ways to the islands. The Spanish officially colonized the Caroline Islands in 1886, but their rule lasted little more than three decades. In 1899, suffering losses from the Spanish-American War, Spain sold the islands to Germany.

In 1914 the Caroline Islands were ceded to Japan, which later governed the territory under a mandate from the League of Nations following World War I. Under Japanese colonial administration, the islands' economy grew, and more than one hundred thousand Japanese settled in Micronesia. Following World War II, however, much of the infrastructure developed by the Japanese during the war was left destroyed, and the United States assumed control of the Caroline Islands as part of the Trust Territory of the Pacific Islands created by the United Nations in 1947. (The trust also included the Northern Mariana Islands, the Marshall Islands, and Palau.)

Micronesian leaders began to negotiate with the United States for their independence in 1969, and in 1975 a constitution was drafted for the Federated States of Micronesia. The trust states of Truk (now Chuuk), Kosrae, Ponope (now Pohnpei), and Yap voted to join the federation; the Marshall Islands, the Northern Marianas, and Palau opted to form their own independent states. In 1983 voters in the Federated States of Micronesia approved the Compact of Free Association with the United States, which outlined the two nations' future relationship. The agreement, which became effective in 1986, granted the Federated States of Micronesia independence while assigning responsibility for the islands' external defense to the United States. In addition, the United States agreed to provide significant, ongoing financial assistance to the new nation. In 2003 the compact was renegotiated for an additional twenty years.

Government Structure

A democratic federal republic, the Federated States of Micronesia has a government whose structure and functions are outlined in the nation's constitution, which was adopted in 1979, and in the Compact of Free Association with the United States, which became effective in 1986 (an amended compact took effect in 2004).

According to the constitution, legislative, executive, and judicial powers are divided between the federal government and four state governments. All powers that are not of an "indisputably national character" are reserved to the states. The state governments exercise considerable authority relative to the federal government, particularly over budgetary matters. The composition of the state governments mirrors that of the federal government: Each has its own constitution and maintains three branches of government. Constitutional amendments require a three-fourths majority in at least three of the four states.

The Federated States of Micronesia has a unicameral legislature called the Congress. This body is made up of fourteen senators. Four at-large senators, one from each state, serve four-year terms. The remaining ten members, representing single-member constituencies apportioned by population (as of 2007, Chuuk had five seats, Pohnpei had three seats, and Kosrae and Yap had one each), serve two-year terms.

The president serves as both head of state and head of the government. The president and vice president are elected from among the four-year senators in the legislature. Once chosen, their seats in Congress are filled by special elections. The president and vice president both serve four-year terms, with a two-term limit. Proposals for electoral reform have called for the popular election of the president and vice president, but in 2002 voters rejected a constitutional amendment to do so. The president and vice president are advised by a cabinet of eight ministers who lead the major departments of government. Cabinet ministers are appointed by the president with congressional approval.

The federated nature of the state influences the legislative process. In order to become law, bills must pass two readings on separate days. To pass the first reading, a two-thirds majority in Congress is required. On the second reading, each state's legislative delegation casts one vote; a two-thirds majority among all the delegations is required for the bill to proceed. The president has the right to return approved bills to Congress within ten days of passage; if the president has no objections, the bill becomes law.

The Supreme Court, which has both trial and appellate divisions, is the ultimate judicial authority in the Federated States of Micronesia. The court consists of three judges who are appointed by the president and confirmed by the Congress. Judges serve lifetime appointments.

Political Parties and Factions

There are no organized political parties in the Federated States of Micronesia; rather, candidates align themselves according to family, island, or state allegiances.

Major Events

The adoption of the Compact of Free Association between the Federated States of Micronesia and the United States in 1986 had the unintended consequence of stimulating significant emigration from the Micronesian islands. The provisions of the compact permitted residents of the Federated States of Micronesia to enter the United States without visa requirements, prompting many to leave the country. Emigrants from Micronesia tend to be younger and more educated, sparking fears of a "brain drain" in Micronesia.

Twenty-First Century

Dependent on financial assistance from the United States, the Federated States of Micronesia faces important economic challenges in the twenty-first century. According to the amended Compact of Free Association, the United States will provide $100 million in direct financial assistance each year until 2023. The nation lacks industry and infrastructure that would allow it to become more self-sufficient. One potential area for economic development is tourism, although the area's remote location and lack of commercial air connections are impediments to future growth.

BIBLIOGRAPHY

U.S. Department of State. "Background Note: Micronesia." http://www.state.gov/r/pa/ei/bgn/1839.htm (accessed June 27, 2007).

U.S. Government Accountability Office. *Compacts of Free Association: Trust Funds for Micronesia and the Marshall Islands May Not Provide Sustainable Income.* Washington, DC: Government Printing Office, 2007. http://www.gao.gov/new.items/d07513.pdf (accessed June 26, 2007).

Willens, Howard P., and Deanne C. Siemer. *National Security and Self-Determination: United States Policy in Micronesia, 1961–1972.* Westport, CT: Praeger, 2000.

Republic of the Marshall Islands

Type of Government

The Republic of the Marshall Islands is governed as a democratic republic in free association with the United States. Its government combines elements of the presidential and parliamentary systems of governance. The president serves as both head of state and head of the government. The unicameral (single-chamber) Nitijela carries out legislative functions. The Council of Chiefs advises the legislature on matters of customary law and land tenure.

Background

The Republic of the Marshall Islands is located in the central Pacific Ocean among the island nations of Micronesia. The nation comprises twenty-nine low-lying coral atolls (each made up of many islets) and five islands scattered over 180,000 square miles. The islands and atolls form two parallel groupings: the Ratak, or "Sunrise," chain and the Ralik, or "Sunset," chain. More than two-thirds of the population resides on Ebeye Island and Majuro Atoll, where the nation's capital is located.

Historians and archeologists know little about the early history of the Marshall Islands. It is speculated that the first settlers arrived there from Micronesia two thousand to three thousand years ago and established a hunter-gatherer society. Eventually, a culture based on matrilineal clans (groups of families sharing a common maternal ancestor) took hold on the islands.

In 1529 the Spanish explorer Álvaro Saavedra y Cerón was the first European to sight the islands, but they would remain uncolonized for more than two hundred years. In 1788 English captain John Marshall visited

A mushroom cloud rising as an atomic bomb is exploded off Bikini Atoll in the Marshall Islands in 1946. Between 1946 and 1958 the United States exploded sixty-seven nuclear or atomic bombs in the area. © *CORBIS*

the region during his Pacific voyages with Thomas Gilbert, naming the islands after himself. However, the islands were not fully charted until the early nineteenth century, when navigators Adam Johann von Krusenstern (1770–1846) and Otto von Kotzebue (1787–1846) headed Russian expeditions to the region. Throughout the nineteenth century the islands were frequented by American whaling ships and Protestant missionaries seeking to convert the natives to Christianity.

Although Spain was technically able to claim all of Micronesia according to the Treaty of Tordesillas, negotiated with Portugal in 1494, it had left the Marshall Islands undisturbed for nearly three centuries. In the late nineteenth century Germany also began to lay claim to the islands, signing an agreement with local chiefs to build a coaling station on Jaluit Atoll. In 1885 Spain agreed to cede control of the Marshall Islands to Germany in exchange for hefty compensation. Germany made the islands a protectorate in 1886. The German colonial administration focused on ensuring trade flows, while the indigenous chiefs handled local matters. In 1914 the islands were ceded to Japan, which received a mandate from the League of Nations to govern them following World War I.

During World War II the United States occupied several atolls in the Marshall Islands, and the region saw intense combat between the Allied and Japanese forces.

At the end of the war the United States assumed control of the islands as part of the Trust Territory of the Pacific Islands created by the United Nations. (The trust also included the Northern Mariana Islands and the Caroline Islands.) Under U.S. administration, the Marshall Islands' Bikini and Enewetak atolls became official nuclear testing grounds.

In 1978 the Marshall Islanders separated from the Trust Territory of the Pacific Islands, and a constitution was approved the following year. A year later the United States recognized the constitution and government of the Marshall Islands, and the two nations negotiated the Compact of Free Association to outline their future relationship. The agreement, which became effective in 1986, granted the Marshall Islands independence while assigning responsibility for the islands' external defense to the United States. In addition, the United States agreed to pay the republic for the continued use of a military installation on Kwajalen Atoll, compensate the islands for past nuclear testing, and provide other financial subsidies. In 2003 the compact was renegotiated for an additional twenty years.

Government Structure

The Republic of the Marshall Islands' democratic government combines elements of the presidential and parliamentary systems of governance. The structure and functions of government are outlined in the nation's constitution, which was adopted in 1979, and in the Compact of Free Association with the United States, which became effective in 1986 (an amended compact took effect in 2004).

The Marshall Islands has a unicameral legislature called the Nitijela. This body is made up of thirty-three senators who are elected by popular vote. Nineteen members are chosen from single-seat electoral districts, while the remaining fourteen members are elected from five multi-seat districts. All members serve concurrent four-year terms. In addition, a twelve-member Council of Chiefs advises the Nitijela on matters of customary law and land tenure; this body may also request the reconsideration of a bill in the legislature.

The president serves as both the head of state and the head of government in the Marshall Islands. The president is elected to a four-year term from among the members of the Nitijela. In turn, the president appoints a cabinet of six to ten advisers from among the members of the legislature. Executive authority is vested in the president and the cabinet members, who recommend legislative proposals to the Nitijela and control the flow of legislation. The legislature has the authority to remove the president by passing a motion of no confidence. In this case, the legislature has fourteen days to elect a new president; if a no-confidence vote is carried twice and no new president is elected, the Nitijela is dissolved and new elections are held.

The Republic of the Marshall Islands has an independent judiciary that comprises the Supreme Court, High Court, and district or community courts. Traditional rights courts exist to deal with matters related to land tenure, custom, and traditional practices. At the local level, the Marshall Islands are divided into thirty-three municipal governments.

Political Parties and Factions

There are no organized political parties in the Republic of the Marshall Islands; rather, candidates align themselves in informal factions and interest groups centered on particular issues. As of 2007, all members of the legislature were listed as independents. Two informal political parties have existed since the 1990s: the Aelon Kein Ad Party and the United Democratic Party, both of which have appeared on the ballot in elections.

Major Events

Since its independence in 1986, an issue of great concern to the Marshall Islands has been adequately addressing past nuclear testing in the area by the United States. Following World War II, the United States had relocated residents of the Marshall Islands' Bikini and Enewetak atolls and began using the area as an official

Map used by U.S. President Dwight Eisenhower at a 1954 press conference to demonstrate the "warning area" around the atomic proving grounds in the Marshall Islands. *© Bettmann/CORBIS*

testing ground for nuclear bombs. Between 1946 and 1958 the United States tested sixty-seven nuclear weapons on the atolls and in the surrounding waters, including the first hydrogen bomb dropped by a U.S. airplane. After more than a decade of nuclear testing, the atolls suffered from severe radioactive contamination. During the 1960s the U.S. government attempted to clean up the environmental damage on Bikini Atoll and resettle its residents, but the area was found to be uninhabitable. Enewetak Atoll was declared decontaminated in 1980 and its residents were permitted to return, but after crops showed unsafe levels of contamination, residents were again removed.

The Compact of Free Association between the United States and the Marshall Islands, adopted in 1986 and renegotiated in 2003, provides for the settlement of claims related to nuclear testing conducted from 1946 through 1958. The islands, however, continue to petition the U.S. government for increased compensation.

Twenty-First Century

Like many other South Pacific nations, one of the Marshall Islands' most pressing challenges in the twenty-first century is the environment. Because much of the land is very low-lying, the islands are vulnerable to soil erosion and saltwater intrusion caused by rising sea levels. Environmental groups caution that global climate change could make the islands uninhabitable in the not-too-distant future. In 2007 President Kessai H. Note (1950–)

stated that global climate change represents the single greatest threat to life in the Marshall Islands.

BIBLIOGRAPHY

Bryan, E. H. *Life in the Marshall Islands.* Honolulu: Pacific Scientific Information Center, 1972.

Dibblin, Jane. *Day of Two Suns: U.S. Nuclear Testing and the Pacific Islanders.* New York: New Amsterdam, 1990.

U.S. Department of State. "Background Note: Marshall Islands." http://www.state.gov/r/pa/ei/bgn/ 26551.htm (accessed June 27, 2007).

Introduction to The Post-Communist World (1988–Present)

During the Cold War, the Communist governments of the Soviet Union and Eastern Europe tightly restricted freedom of expression, association, and movement by their citizens. Changes stirred in 1985, when Mikhail Gorbachev (1931–) assumed leadership of the Soviet Union. Gorbachev's political and economic reforms unleashed pent-up demands for freedom that proved impossible to contain.

In 1989 citizens' movements across Eastern Europe swept the Communists from power. Poland, whose Solidarity labor union had defied the authorities, elected a non-Communist parliament. Massive protests brought down the Czechoslovakian and Romanian governments. On November 9, 1989, East Germany's embattled leadership allowed transit into West Berlin across the border marked by the Berlin Wall, which had divided the city and symbolized Communist tyranny, and jubilant citizens tore down the wall. A year later, Germany itself was reunited under democratic rule. By 1991 the Soviet Union's constituent republics were breaking away. Russia declared its sovereignty, and its new president, Boris Yeltsin (1931–2007), took control of the Soviet state apparatus. Gorbachev resigned on December 25, 1991, marking the end of the Soviet Union.

The federation of Yugoslavia was dissolving as well, into nationalist and ethnic rivalries. Croatia, Slovenia, and Macedonia declared independence in 1991. Bosnia plunged into a vicious civil war between ethnic Serbs, Croats, and Muslims. Some regions of Bosnia suffered "ethnic cleansing," systematic rape, and other war crimes. In 1998 Serbian troops attacked ethnic Albanians in the province of Kosovo. The North Atlantic Treaty Organization (NATO) bombed Serbia to halt the violence.

While Yugoslavia and the Soviet Union faced disintegration, a process of integration was underway in Western Europe. Six European states had merged their coal and steel production in the 1950s, and later organized a European common market. In 1993 the Maastricht Treaty created the European Union, an intergovernmental organization to coordinate policies on trade, agriculture, diplomacy, and security. Many former Communist states were admitted to the EU; Bulgaria and Romania joined in 2007, increasing membership to twenty-seven nations.

With state-led communism repudiated, corporate-led capitalism entered a triumphant phase. The worldwide spread of blue jeans, soft drinks, and other Western consumer artifacts symbolized the phenomenon of globalization. Telecommunications made a major advance in the 1990s with the World Wide Web. The advance of free markets, trade, and communications did not eliminate global poverty; in fact, in many countries, the gap between rich and poor widened. A global protest movement arose in the late 1990s, exploiting the Internet's networking potential, to resist global capital's power to dictate the terms of international trade.

Western values also came under attack by radical Islam. A series of terrorist attacks by Muslim radicals against Western targets culminated on September 11, 2001, when hijacked aircraft damaged the Pentagon and destroyed the twin towers of New York's World Trade Center. U.S. president George W. Bush (1946–) responded by declaring a "global war on terror" and toppling the government of Afghanistan, which had provided safe haven for international terrorists, as well as the Iraqi government of Saddam Hussein (1937–2006), who was accused of developing nuclear and biological weapons. After the collapse of Hussein's regime, the situation in Iraq rapidly degenerated into civil war and threatened to escalate into a wider, regional conflict.

The Post-Communist World (1988–Present)

⊕ Republic of Hungary

Type of Government

Hungary is a parliamentary democracy with a legislative branch consisting of a single house, the 386-seat National Assembly, whose members are elected by the people. The National Assembly then elects the country's two executives, a president who serves as the chief of state and a prime minister who is the head of the government. The National Assembly also elects the judges of the Constitutional Court.

Background

The history of Hungary begins in the winter of AD 895–896, when a tribe of horsemen known as the Magyars settled in the Carpathian Basin. (Hungary's name in Hungarian, Magyarország, is taken from this tribe.) The Magyars conquered the earlier inhabitants of the area and launched raids as far away as France and Italy in search of settlements to plunder.

The Magyars' raiding days came to an end in 955, when they were crushed by a German army at the Battle of Augsburg. The tribe, however, was left in possession of a considerable amount of territory. In addition to modern-day Hungary, the Magyars also ruled some or all of modern-day Slovakia, Croatia, Serbia, Ukraine, and Romania. Under King Stephen I (977–1038), Hungary developed into a full-fledged feudal kingdom. Stephen adopted Christianity and ordered the people of his kingdom to do the same. He also established a feudal social order, with Magyar and foreign nobles ruling over a mix of Magyar, Romanian, and Slavic peasants.

Hungary ceased to be an independent kingdom in 1526, when its king died while fighting a Turkish army at the Battle of Mohács. Subsequently much of Hungary was conquered by the Ottoman Turks. The Hungarian lands that did not become part of the Ottoman Empire were absorbed into the territory of the Austrian Empire, which was ruled by the Habsburg family.

By 1697 the Habsburgs had driven the Turks out of Hungary and taken complete control of the country. The Hungarians chafed at being ruled by the Habsburgs, who kept a tight rein over activities in Hungary. Hungarian discontent broke out into a full-fledged revolution in 1848, but the Austrians, with help from Russian troops, defeated the Hungarians in 1849. For eighteen years after this defeat, the Habsburg rule was even harsher than before the revolution. Then, in 1867, the Austrian emperor, Francis Joseph (1830–1916) agreed to allow the Hungarians more autonomy. The Austrian Empire became the Austro-Hungarian Empire, and Hungary was allowed to have its own parliament again.

Hungary entered World War I on the Austrian side in 1914, but when the war degenerated into a bloody stalemate the Hungarian people became restless. By 1917 there were massive demonstrations and strikes to protest the war, and in the fall of 1918 this discontent turned revolutionary. The Hungarian military refused to follow orders to end the protests, and the Hungarian king was forced to appoint a liberal, reformist government, led by Mihály Károlyi (1875–1955), that sued for peace and declared Hungary to be an independent, democratic republic.

Hungary lost a great deal of its territory because of its defeat in the war. It lost Transylvania to Romania; Croatia, Vojvodina (the northern part of modern-day Serbia), and Bosnia and Herzegovina to the newly created Kingdom of the Serbs, Croats, and Slovenes (later to become Yugoslavia); and Slovakia to the newly created country of Czechoslovakia. Overall Hungary lost nearly three-quarters of its land and two-thirds of its inhabitants.

The new, fragile democratic government could not withstand such a defeat. In March 1919 it was overthrown in a Communist coup led by Béla Kun (1886–1937). Kun instituted a Communist dictatorship that promised to empower workers and peasants, but which

Soviet tanks rolling through the heart of Budapest during Hungary's unsuccessful 1956 uprising against Soviet rule. © *Hulton-Deutsch Collection/CORBIS*

also arrested and tortured people who opposed the Communists' plans. Kun promised to restore the lands that Hungary had lost, but when he launched an invasion of Slovakia, his army was defeated and the Communist government fell to the Romanian army. In 1920 the Treaty of Trianon formalized Hungary's loss of territory.

After a brief but violent period known as the "white terror," in which anti-Communist forces arrested and executed Communists and other leftists, Hungary became a democracy in the 1920s, before tending toward fascism in the 1930s. Hungary's friendly relations with Nazi Germany allowed it to temporarily regain some of its lost land, but when the Nazis were defeated Hungary was again forced to give up those territories. Hungary also suffered another period of political terror—its third in thirty years—in the closing days of the war, as German troops and members of Hungary's fascist Arrow Cross Party slaughtered Jews, and the advancing Soviet Army sent a quarter of a million Hungarians to murderous forced labor camps in Siberia.

After World War II Hungary fell under the influence of the Soviet Union, and by 1949 Hungary was a fully Communist country. The government took control of nearly all of the farms and businesses in the country and cracked down on the churches. It also empowered the police and internal intelligence agencies to spy on all of the citizens of the country and to arrest and torture those who were believed to be insufficiently loyal to the government.

In 1956 tens of thousands of people held a protest in Budapest against this Communist dictatorship. Soviet troops, who had been stationed in Hungary since the end of World War II, rushed to suppress the protests. The Hungarian army sided with the protesters, and the Hungarian uprising became a war. The Soviet Union crushed the uprising a few weeks later, with the help of 250,000 troops sent in from outside the country, but thousands of people were killed in the process.

Hungarians became resigned to living under a Communist dictatorship and stopped protesting against it. Because of their quietness, the Soviet Union allowed Hungary's leaders more freedom to experiment than it gave to the leaders of more restless countries such as Czechoslovakia and Poland. From the late 1960s to the late 1980s, Hungary slowly moved toward a more capitalistic and democratic system. By 1989 Hungary was largely a free country, and on October 7, 1989, it became official when Hungary's ruling Communist party, the Socialist Workers' Party, announced that it was abandoning communism and becoming a democratic socialist party. Less than two weeks later Hungary's National Assembly amended the country's constitution to make Hungary a fully democratic republic.

Government Structure

The members of the Hungarian National Assembly are elected under a complex system of varying geographical districts and different methods of voting. One hundred seventy-six of the 386 members of the assembly are elected based on individual constituencies (in which one person represents one district, as in the U.S. House of Representatives). These elections generally occur in two rounds. If no candidate receives a majority of the vote in the first round of voting, the top two finishers in the first round go head-to-head in the second round.

Two different party-list systems determine the remainder of the representatives, with the votes going to parties rather than to individual candidates. In the first party-list system, 152 representatives are elected from 20 electoral districts (one for each of the 19 counties of Hungary and one for the capital, Budapest). Voters in each district vote for the party that they prefer, and each party receives a number of seats in the parliament based on the number of votes that party received. (The exact number of seats is determined using a mathematical formula known as the d'Hondt method.) Each party prepares a ranked list of candidates before the election, and if, for example, the party received ten seats in a given district, those ten seats would go to the people listed one through ten on its list.

In the second party-list system, the remaining 58 seats are filled by nationwide party lists. The voters do not vote directly for the national lists. Instead, all of the votes that went to losing candidates in the individual constituencies' portion of the voting are used to determine how many of these 58 seats a party receives. So, for example, a party that had many candidates finish a close second in the individual constituencies' portion of the voting would receive a large portion of these seats, whereas a party whose candidates generally placed a distant fourth or fifth—or a party whose candidates all won their individual races—would receive few or no seats. A party has to receive at least 5 percent of the total nationwide vote in order for the party to receive any seats in parliament based on the district or the national list portions of the voting.

Once the National Assembly has been elected, it elects people to the other major positions within the government, including the president, the prime minister, the judges of the Constitutional Court, the chairperson of the Supreme Court, and the prosecutor general (similar to the U.S. attorney general). The prime minister is the most powerful official in the government, as is the case in nearly all parliamentary democracies.

The president is supposed to be elected by a two-thirds majority of the National Assembly, but if no candidate wins two-thirds of the vote in the first two rounds of voting, the president may be elected by a simple majority. The president, whose position is largely ceremonial, is elected to a five-year term and is limited to serving no more than two terms.

The Constitutional Court functions much as the Supreme Court does in the United States. Its eleven members, who are elected for nine-year terms, review laws to ensure that they are constitutional. The Hungarian Supreme Court is a separate body that acts as the highest appeals court; that is, defendants who appeal court decisions to a higher court can go no higher than the Supreme Court.

Political Parties and Factions

Hungary is a multiparty democracy in which two parties dominate: the Hungarian Socialist Party (a direct descendant of the Socialist Workers' Party that ruled the country in Communist times) and Fidesz (also known as the Federation of Young Democrats–Hungarian Civic Union). The Hungarian Socialist Party is nominally the left-wing party and Fidesz is nominally on the right, but in reality, the Hungarian Socialist Party has been a strong defender of free markets and privatizing government-owned industries, whereas Fidesz has frequently argued against such reforms.

Smaller parties include the Alliance of Free Democrats (which has traditionally been allied with the Hungarian Socialist Party), the Hungarian Democratic Forum, the Christian Democratic People's Party, and the Independent Smallholders' Party (which was formerly a major party but has since collapsed to the point such that it can no longer earn enough votes to win any seats in parliament).

Since Hungary became a multiparty democracy, power has been handed back and forth between various coalitions in the Hungarian parliament. The first elected post-Communist government, from 1990 to 1994, was run by the Hungarian Democratic Forum, the Independent Smallholders' Party, and the Christian Democratic People's Party. The Hungarian Socialist Party and the Alliance of Free Democrats ruled from 1994 to 1998, and again from 2002 to the present. Between 1998 and 2002 Fidesz, in coalition with the Hungarian Democratic Forum, controlled the government.

Major Events

Hungary's transition from communism to capitalism and democracy was relatively smooth. Post-Communist Hungarian politics have been raucous, with frequently bitter arguments and allegations of corruption between the various factions in the parliament, but elections have been free and fair and many necessary economic reforms have been carried out.

Twenty-First Century

Twenty-first-century Hungary is well on the road to becoming a fully developed country and a full member of Europe. Hungary was one of the first Eastern European countries to join the North Atlantic Treaty Organization, which it did in 1999, and it joined the European Union in 2004. The major problems facing Hungary are economic, as nearly everyone realizes that Hungary cannot afford the generous health, educational, and other benefits that the government continues to provide to all citizens, but there is little political support for making cuts to these popular programs.

BIBLIOGRAPHY

Ake, Anne. *Hungary.* San Diego, CA: Lucent Books, 2003.

Crampton, R. J. *Eastern Europe in the Twentieth Century—And After.* 2nd ed. New York: Routledge, 1997.

Republic of Hungary. "Hungary.hu." http://www.magyarorszag.hu/english (accessed June 14, 2007).

⊕ Poland

Type of Government

Poland is a republic with a parliamentary form of government. The parliament consists of two houses, the 460-seat Sejm (lower house) and the 100-seat Senate (upper house). Both houses are elected by the people. After the parliament is elected, the prime minister is chosen by the coalition of parties that has the most seats in the Sejm. Poland also has a president who is elected by the people and serves as the head of state.

Background

Although the area now known as Poland has been inhabited by various Slavic tribes for thousands of years, there was no Polish nation until the tenth century AD. Around that time one tribe, the Polanie, conquered the other tribes in the area and created a unified government. In 966 the ruler of the Polanie, Prince Mieszko I (ruled c. 963–992), adopted Christianity and forced the religion on his subjects, thereby bringing Poland into what was then considered the "civilized" world. (Traditionally, this event has been viewed as the beginning of Polish history.)

Mieszko's son, Bolesław I (ruled 992–1025), conquered more land for Poland and further unified the country, but the state he built proved to be short-lived. Bolesław's descendants fought over the throne and ended by dividing Poland into an ever-larger number of ever-smaller kingdoms. These tiny, weak kingdoms proved to be no match for Poland's more powerful neighbors, including the German Teutonic Knights, the Czech kingdom of Bohemia, and the invading Tatars from Mongolia. By 1300 the majority of Poland was occupied by foreign countries, mostly Bohemia.

Poland underwent a resurgence in the fourteenth century. Two kings, Władysław the Short (ruled 1306–1333) and Kazimierz the Great (ruled 1333–1370; his name can also be spelled Casimir), reunited Poland into a single kingdom. Poland's strengthening continued under Queen Jadwiga (1374–1399), a Hungarian princess who became queen of Poland at the age of ten. Poland's nobles arranged for a marriage between Jadwiga and the Grand Duke of Lithuania, Władysław II Jagiełło (1351–1434). Jagiełło thus became the king of both Poland and Lithuania, a position that his descendants would hold for the next two hundred years. This joint Polish-Lithuanian state was one of the largest and most powerful countries in Eastern Europe.

Poland was one of the first countries in Europe to have an elected parliament (the Sejm, founded in 1493) and a constitution guaranteeing the rights of the country's citizens (1505). The Sejm had one unusual feature, in that it could pass laws only if its members were unanimous. This system made it very difficult for the Sejm to do anything, because there was almost always at least one member of the Sejm who opposed any proposal. This gridlock, combined with the weak kings who ruled Poland during this period, left Poland without any sort of strong government.

This governmental weakness contributed to Poland's dissolution in the next few centuries. First Poland's Ukrainian provinces successfully fought for their independence in 1648; then in 1655 Sweden seized some of Poland's territory along the Baltic Sea. In 1772 Russia, Austria, and Prussia (a German state) each took a piece of Poland, and in 1793 Russia and Prussia seized even more Polish territory. The Poles rose up in protest of this second partition and tried to win their territory back, but they were quickly defeated. As a result of this defeat, Poland was helpless to prevent Russia, Prussia, and Austria from dividing up the remains of Poland between themselves in 1795.

Poland was reborn after World War I, in large part because of U.S. president Woodrow Wilson's strong support for "national self-determination" (the idea that people who view themselves as a nation should be able to rule themselves, rather than being ruled by a foreign power). Poland was originally given pieces of land taken from Russia, Austria, and Germany, and between 1919 and 1921, in the Russo-Polish War, it conquered more land that had formerly belonged to Russia. This independence, however, lasted only until the outbreak of World War II in 1939.

Poland was devastated by World War II. Although the country had signed nonaggression pacts with both

Nazi Germany to the west and the Soviet Union to the east, those two countries secretly conspired to divide Poland between themselves. On September 1, 1939, Germany invaded Poland, and seventeen days later the Soviet Union followed suit. The following six years of war saw the deaths of six million Poles—over 20 percent of the country's prewar population—and Poland's capital, Warsaw, was completely leveled.

The aftermath of World War II also caused a dramatic shift in Poland's borders. The Soviet Union, which drove out the Germans and occupied Poland in the closing days of the war, took possession of almost half of Poland's prewar territory—over 70,000 square miles in a band along Poland's eastern border. In compensation, Poland was given approximately 40,000 square miles of former German territory on its western and northern borders. Three million Poles who had lived in the lands that were now part of the Soviet Union were forced to move to the new lands that had previously been part of Germany. The end result was to move the country of Poland west by over 100 miles.

The Soviets installed a Communist government, known as the Lublin Committee, as the provisional government of Poland in January 1945. Over the next three years the Polish United Workers' Party, a Soviet-backed Communist party often known by its Polish initials, PZPR, took complete control of Poland. Many Poles opposed this Communist takeover. Around 35,000 Poles joined an underground guerrilla war against the Communists, and other Poles tried to compete with the Communists in elections that were supposed to be free but were actually rigged. The Communists, however, were not afraid to kill, arrest, or otherwise harass the anti-Communist Poles, and in the end the Communists were victorious. Poland became the Polish People's Republic, a one-party state ruled entirely by the Polish United Workers' Party.

In the Polish People's Republic, nearly all aspects of life were controlled by the Communist government. The government owned all of the factories. It took the peasants' farms and combined them into giant "collectives," where the peasants were forced to work as laborers on land owned by the state. The government controlled the ideas that writers and artists were allowed to express. It harassed the Catholic Church (which strongly opposed the atheistic Communist system) and arrested some of the Polish church's top leaders.

These changes were too much for the Poles to bear. In 1956 tens of thousands of people participated in anti-Communist riots in the city of Poznań. The army sent soldiers and tanks to Poznań to stop the rioting. The army succeeded, but more than fifty people were killed in the process. Workers across Poland remained restless, and some of them began banding together to demand changes in the government. Poland's government was worried about more riots and decided to give in to some of the people's demands. They named Władysław Gomułka (1905–1982), a moderate Communist, to be leader of the Polish United Workers' Party (and therefore head of the government); broke up most collective farms and returned the land to the farmers; and allowed Polish Catholics to worship freely. These concessions gave Poles more freedom than the citizens of most other Communist countries in Eastern Europe, but Polish workers were still not completely satisfied. Occasional protests against the Communist government occurred throughout the 1950s, 1960s, and 1970s.

In the summer of 1980, another round of protests began. In Gdańsk (a major port city on the Baltic Sea), workers at the Lenin Shipyard went on strike. The leader of the striking workers was a young electrician named Lech Wałęsa (1943–). These workers had a number of demands, but the primary one was that they be allowed to form a union that would be free from governmental control. As workers across Poland banded together to join in the strike, Solidarity—a nationwide trade union—was born. Soon nearly one-quarter of the Polish population had joined Solidarity.

The Polish government declared martial law (rule by the military) in December 1981 in an attempt to crack down on Solidarity. The government was able to weaken, but not destroy, the independent union. In the late 1980s, when the Soviet Union's grip on Poland began to weaken, Solidarity was able to surge back and win concessions from the government, including the right to run its own candidates in the 1989 parliamentary elections. Solidarity and other non-Communist parties won a majority of seats in the election, and in August 1989, under Prime Minister Tadeusz Mazowiecki (1927–), a new government took office and began transforming Poland into a free and democratic country.

Government Structure

Legislative power in Poland lies with the National Assembly, a bicameral (two-house) parliament consisting of a lower house, the Sejm, and an upper house, the Senate. The 460 members of the Sejm and the 100 members of the Senate are elected under very different systems. The Sejm is elected by proportional representation, whereby voters vote for a party rather than an individual candidate. The parties that receive the most votes get the most seats in the parliament, but all parties that get at least 5 percent of the vote receive at least one seat. The Senate is elected in a first-past-the-post system, which is the system used in the United States. Each district is represented by the single candidate who receives the most votes in that district. Unlike in proportional representation, in a first-past-the-post system the parties whose candidates do not place first in a district receive no representation in that district at all.

Once the parliament has been elected, the members of the Sejm must form a government. If one party has

Polish labor leader Lech Walesa being carried on workers' shoulders during a strike at the shipyards in Gdansk, 1980.   © *Alain Keler/Sygma/ CORBIS*

more than 50 percent of the seats in the Sejm, that party may form a government by itself; that is, the party will choose some of its own members to serve as prime minister and as members of the Council of Ministers (cabinet). If no party has a majority of seats by itself, then two or more parties will form a coalition that controls more than 50 percent of the seats. In that case the prime minister will usually be a member of the largest party, and the seats within the cabinet will be divided between members of all of the parties in the coalition. The prime minister and the Council of Ministers together have executive authority; that is, they have the authority to execute (carry out) the laws passed by the parliament. The prime minister and Council of Ministers are also in charge of Poland's foreign policy and military affairs.

The majority of the political power in Poland lies with the prime minister, the Council of Ministers, and the Sejm, rather than the president. The president can veto legislation passed by the parliament, although the Sejm can override the president's veto if three-fifths of the representatives vote to do so. Other than this veto power, the president's role is largely ceremonial, as in most parliamentary democracies.

Political Parties and Factions

Poland is a multiparty democracy where a number of political parties are represented in the parliament. The most powerful party is the Law and Justice Party (known by its Polish initials, PiS), a conservative Catholic, free-market party that was founded in 2001 by identical twin brothers Lech and Jarosław Kaczyński (1949–). Some Poles have been concerned about the amount of power concentrated in the Kaczyńskis' hands: Lech Kaczyński was elected Poland's president in 2005, and Jarosław became the country's prime minister in 2006.

Other political parties include the Citizens' Platform, a party founded in 2001 to advocate for free-market principles and civil liberties that is popular with businesspeople and entrepreneurs; the Democratic Left Alliance, a social-democratic party born of the 1999 merger of several left-wing groups, including former Communists; the Social Democracy of Poland Party, which broke away from the Democratic Left Alliance in 2004 to protest nepotism and corruption in that party; the League of Polish Families, an extremely conservative, religious, nationalist party; the Self-Defense Party, an anti-Western, left-wing populist party that appeals to the unemployed and disadvantaged workers; the Democratic Party–democrats.pl, a socially liberal party founded in 2005; and the Polish Peasant Party or Polish People's Party, an anti-Western party of farmers and rural residents that was one of the largest and strongest parties in the country in the early 1990s.

Major Events

Poland joined the European Union (EU) in 2004, but the still conservative and overwhelmingly Catholic state of Poland is an uncomfortable fit with the much more liberal states that dominate the EU. Poland has clashed with the rest of the EU over whether or not the Christian God should be mentioned in the EU constitution and the legality of Poland's laws against abortion, among other matters. Poland has also found itself in conflict with the rest of the EU over the EU's goal of closer ties with Russia. The country has even gone so far as to veto an EU-Russia partnership deal in 2006.

Poland is also very concerned about maintaining its power relative to Germany, Poland's historical enemy and one of the largest and most powerful countries in the EU. Poland has had some success on that front—it succeeded in delaying the implementation of a new EU voting system that will decrease Poland's power and increase Germany's until 2014, for example—but Poland's aggressive defense of its own national interest has left it with few friends among European diplomats.

Twenty-First Century

Twenty-first-century Poland is still concerned about its position in the world, trapped as it is between a resurgent Russia and an EU that, the Polish government believes, does not always have Poland's best interests at heart. As a result Poland has closely allied itself with the United States, which it hopes will stand up for Poland against Poland's stronger neighbors should the need arise. Poland was one of the few countries to send soldiers to both Iraq and Afghanistan to fight alongside American troops in those countries. Poland also agreed to allow the United States to place interceptor missiles in Poland that could be used to shoot down missiles carrying nuclear weapons from hostile states such as Iran—a move that led to harsh criticism, and, from Russia, threats to deploy its own missiles on the Polish border.

BIBLIOGRAPHY

Crampton, R. J. *Eastern Europe in the Twentieth Century— And After.* 2nd ed. New York: Routledge, 1997.
Ministry of Foreign Affairs of the Republic of Poland. "Polska," Information Portal of the Republic of Poland. http://www.poland.gov.pl (accessed June 9, 2007).

⊕ Namibia

Type of Government

Namibia is a parliamentary republic with independent executive, legislative, and judicial branches. The executive branch is headed by the president, who is both head of state and head of government, and includes the prime minister and cabinet. The legislative branch is made up of a bicameral (two-house) parliament consisting of the National Council and the National Assembly. The judicial branch is led by the Supreme Court. The president and members of parliament are elected by direct vote; the judges of the Supreme Court are appointed.

Background

Approximately the size of Texas and Louisiana combined, Namibia is located in southwestern Africa. The Atlantic Ocean is its western border, and neighboring countries are South Africa, Botswana, Angola, and Zambia; a thin, northern panhandle, the Caprivi Strip, stretches about three hundred miles eastward toward Zimbabwe. Much of Namibia's landscape is desert, and the climate ranges from arid to subhumid. Drought is common, but the varied topography and climate allows for a wide assortment of plants and wildlife.

The Khoisan-speaking San, or Bushmen, are widely acknowledged to be the earliest people to settle the region. Later arrivals included the Nama and the Damara people, followed by the Bantu-speaking Ovambo and Herero from the north around the fourteenth century. Traditionally, herders and farmers, such as the Ovambo (who would eventually comprise about half of Namibia's population), had little exposure to the more nomadic people, such as the Nama, of the central plains. Further, each ethnicity had a distinct cultural identity and tribal organization.

For a long period, the forbidding Namib Desert along Namibia's coast proved an effective deterrent to European exploration. Indeed, except for a couple of fifteenth-century visits by the Portuguese, the area was left mainly on its own until the late eighteenth century. Its autonomy was finally ended by Germany, which established a protectorate there in 1884 and formally annexed the country, after border treaties with Portugal and England, as German Southwest Africa in 1890. Native uprisings began in 1892 and continued for several years, resulting in the near-complete eradication of the Herero people and devastating losses among the Nama. (Germany issued a formal apology in 2004 for the Herero killings, but declined to compensate descendants of the victims.)

The discovery of diamonds in 1908, in the coastal town of Luderitz, provided a tremendous economic incentive and the Germans increased their presence in Namibia accordingly. In 1915, however, in the midst of World War I, South Africa invaded Namibia and wrested control from Germany. Five years later, the new occupiers received a mandate from the League of Nations (which was succeeded by the United Nations, or UN) to govern what then became known as South-West Africa. The international community came to regret its decision in due time, refusing to allow South Africa to annex the territory in 1946 and officially revoking its mandate in 1966, but the occupier determinedly continued to administer Namibia as a de facto colony for decades.

South African rule was harsh and oppressive. Establishment of the South West African Native Labour Association in 1943, which prevented native inhabitants from relocating from their traditional regions, and the introduction of apartheid practices after 1948 were just two developments that provoked the indigenous people. Among their responses was the 1958 creation of the Ovamboland People's Congress ("Congress" was changed to "Organization" the next year), which became the South West Africa People's Organization (SWAPO) in 1960. That organization, along with its military arm, the People's Liberation Army of Namibia (PLAN), thus began the long, slow march toward Namibian independence.

PLAN's armed struggle began in 1966, and the UN renamed the country "Namibia" in 1968. The efforts toward liberation gained momentum with UN recognition of SWAPO as the only true representative of the Namibian people and, even more importantly, the collapse of Portuguese colonial rule in Angola in 1975. The latter gave the rebels a nearby base from which they could conduct operations. As the conflict escalated, so did international pressure on South Africa to withdraw. A settlement plan was proposed by the UN Security Council in 1978 and agreed to by South Africa, but it was yet another decade before anything came of it.

After years of armed conflict and international negotiation, South Africa finally bowed to the pressure in 1988. In return for Cuban withdrawal from Angola, it agreed to Namibian independence. UN-supervised elections for a Constituent Assembly were held in 1989. That body, which became the nation's first National Assembly, drew up a constitution and elected SWAPO leader Shafiihuna (Sam) Nujoma (1929–) as Namibia's first president. The country's long-awaited formal Independence Day was March 21, 1990, approximately three-quarters of a century after the South African takeover.

Government Structure

Namibia's executive branch includes the president—who is both head of state and of government—prime minister, and cabinet. The president wins office via direct election in which more than 50 percent of the vote must be obtained. According to the constitution, the president is normally eligible to serve two five-year terms. Worth noting, however, is that Namibia's first president, Nujoma, was an exception in that the constitution was amended to allow him to serve a third term of office, which ended in 2005. The prime minister is the president's primary adviser and oversees the government's various offices, ministries, and agencies. There are twenty cabinet ministerial positions; the president fills

Sam Nujoma, who for twenty-four years had led an armed insurgency against South African control of his country, being sworn in as Namibia's first president in March 1990. *Trevor Samson/AFP/Getty Images*

the cabinet positions from among the members of the National Assembly.

The National Council and the National Assembly make up the bicameral parliament of the legislative branch. The National Assembly comprises seventy-two elected members and six nonvoting members nominated by the president, all of whom serve five-year terms. It is considered the principal house of parliament and its elected members win seats through a proportional-representation electoral system. The National Council is the second house of parliament, consisting of two representatives from each of Namibia's thirteen regions. National Council members serve six-year terms.

The Supreme Court is the highest court of Namibia's judicial branch. Its judges are appointed by the president on the recommendation of the Judicial Service Commission. The commission is made up of the chief justice of the Supreme Court, a judge nominated by the president, the attorney general, and two representatives from the legal profession. As a further check and balance, although not strictly part of the judiciary, Chapter 10 of Namibia's constitution provides for a lawyer or judge to be appointed national ombudsman by the president. The ombudsman is charged with guarding against government corruption and protecting basic rights of the citizens, and he or she is provided with wide-ranging powers (subpoena and interrogation, for instance) toward that end. Other important judicial offices are those of the attorney general and the prosecutor general, both of which are political appointments that expire at the end of the appointing government's term.

Namibia has universal suffrage for all people over the age of eighteen. The predominant religion is Christianity (about 80 percent), and about one-half of the total population is Lutheran. Approximately 10 to 20 percent of the population holds indigenous beliefs. The official language is English, although only about 7 percent of the general populace speaks it. Afrikaans is the most common language, with German and such indigenous languages as Oshivambo, Herero, and Nama also in use.

Political Parties and Factions

Namibia's major political parties include the Congress of Democrats (COD), the Democratic Turnhalle Alliance of Namibia, the Monitor Action Group, the National Democratic Movement for Change, the National Unity Democratic Organization, Republican Party, the South West Africa National Union, SWAPO, and the United Democratic Front. Among these, however, SWAPO is the most influential.

SWAPO's founding members included both Nujoma, who went on to serve three terms as the newly independent Namibia's president (1990–2005), and Hifikepunye Pohamba (1935–), who was inaugurated as the country's second president in 2005. In 1991 SWAPO held its first congress, at which it formally transformed itself from a liberation movement to a political party. As such, it dominated all post-independence elections through 2004. Its general platform advocated national reconciliation, economic development, and improved quality of life for the populace. Some found its ruling style overbearing and authoritarian, but SWAPO's ongoing popularity was impossible to deny—in the 2004 presidential election, for instance, Pohamba received 76.4 percent of the vote. His closest competitor, Benjamin Ulenga of the COD, was a distant second with just 7.3 percent.

Major Events

Namibia survived a secessionist challenge by the Caprivi Liberation Army in 1999 amid allegations of government persecution of Caprivi Strip residents, but new upheaval was a possibility as ambitious land reform measures were put into place. That is, the 2005 government was replacing the "willing-seller, willing-buyer" policy as a means of increasing black land ownership with the much more controversial expropriation of white-owned farms to black citizens.

Twenty-First Century

The twenty-first century presents many challenges as Namibia matures as a republic. One prime concern is an HIV/AIDS epidemic that reportedly affects about 25 percent of Namibia's population, constituting one of the highest rates in the world. Nujoma made the disease a national priority during his tenure as president, but more progress is still needed.

How the expropriation policy of increasing ownership of land by blacks will ultimately fare remains to be seen. Yet another worry is the economy. Although the country boasts one of the top gross domestic products (GDP) among developing nations, the wealth is extremely unevenly distributed, leaving the bulk of the population in abject poverty. Further, the economy continues to be inextricably linked with that of South Africa (approximately 80 percent of Namibian trade is with, or through, its former oppressor). Namibia was still one of the world's leading sources of gem-quality diamonds in 2007—making mining a key component of its economy. Economic diversification in such areas as tourism, fisheries, and manufacturing, as well as foreign investment, are being encouraged by the government.

BIBLIOGRAPHY

Government of Namibia. http://www.grnnet.gov.na (accessed June 8, 2007).

Kahn, Owen Ellison, ed. *Disengagement from Southwest Africa: The Prospects for Peace in Angola and Namibia.* New Brunswick, NJ: Transaction, 1991.

Sparks, Donald L., and December Green. *Namibia: The Nation after Independence.* Boulder, CO: Westview Press, 1992.

⊕ Czech Republic

Type of Government

The Czech Republic is a parliamentary democracy with a separation of powers between the three branches of the government. The legislative branch consists of a bicameral (two-house) parliament with the Chamber of Deputies and the Senate. The executive branch includes the prime minister, cabinet, and president. The judicial branch is capped by three separate courts: the Supreme Court, the Supreme Administrative Court, and the Constitutional Court.

Background

The ancestors of today's Czechs settled in Bohemia and Moravia, the two major regions of the modern Czech Republic, around the fifth century AD. The Czechs were and are a Slavic people (related to Russians), but historically the Czechs have been oriented more toward Western than Eastern Europe.

The Czechs joined with other Slavic tribes, including the Slovaks, to form the Great Moravian Empire in the early ninth century AD. That empire collapsed less than one hundred years later, when the Hungarians invaded and took possession of the eastern (Slovak) part of the empire. The Czechs retained their independence and formed the Kingdom of Bohemia.

The Kingdom of Bohemia grew into one of the more powerful kingdoms in Central Europe. From 950 onward it was subordinate to the Holy Roman Empire (which was centered in Germany), but the Germans generally allowed the Bohemians to rule themselves with little interference. One of the greatest Bohemian kings, Charles IV (1316–1378), even became the Holy Roman emperor and moved the capital of the empire to Prague (the Bohemian, and later Czech, capital).

Between approximately 1400 and 1620, Bohemia was torn by religious and nationalistic wars. A dissident Catholic priest, Jan Hus (1372 or 1373–1415), began arguing against the corruption of the Catholic Church in the early fifteenth century. Although Hus's teachings were primarily religious, the movement that formed around him was also nationalistic, as his followers, the Czech Hussites, squared off against their German Catholic rulers. The Germans burned Hus at the stake in 1415, launching twenty-one years of Hussite Wars. The wars ended with the Czechs being granted a certain degree of freedom to practice their own version of Catholicism. This freedom, however, was taken away after Bohemia fell under the rule of the Habsburg Empire (a Catholic empire centered in Austria) in 1526.

Many Bohemians joined the Protestant Reformation, to the dismay of Bohemia's Habsburg king, Ferdinand I (1503–1564). Ferdinand tried to stamp out not only Protestantism in Bohemia, but also the Czech language and the power of the Czech aristocrats. This policy was continued by Ferdinand's successors, and the Czechs continued to resist. In 1618 the Bohemians threw two councilors of the Catholic emperor out of a window in Prague, launching another round of religious wars.

The Bohemians were defeated in 1620, and the Habsburgs harshly punished them for their rebellion. Most of the Czech aristocrats were either killed or forced to emigrate, and all of the non-Catholic clergy were forced out of Bohemia. The Czech language was suppressed in favor of German, and much of Czech culture went up in flames as Catholic priests burned entire libraries of Czech books. Bohemia and Moravia lost all remaining traces of self-rule and became the personal property of the Habsburg emperors.

Czech nationalism was successfully forced underground for the next two hundred years, but in the nineteenth century it began to reemerge. Authors began writing in Czech and schools began teaching in Czech rather than German. Moravian historian František Pal-acký (1798–1876) published a five-volume history of the Czech people (in German, 1836–1867, and in Czech, 1848–1876), which reawakened awareness of the Czech people's centuries-long struggle for independence from the Germans. By the time World War I broke out in 1914 there was strong support for an independent Czech nation.

The Czechs' wish came true in 1918, when they were reunited with their Slovak neighbors in a single, independent country for the first time in over one thousand years. This new country, Czechoslovakia, was one of the freest, most industrialized, and most democratic countries in Central Europe between World War I and World War II, but its independence did not last long: Czechoslovakia was one of the first countries to fall to Nazi Germany during World War II.

After World War II, Czechoslovakia, like most of Eastern Europe, fell under Communist control. Czechoslovakia, however, was different in that Communists were genuinely popular there. The Czechs felt that the Western European democracies had betrayed the country to Nazi Germany in the 1930s, and they appreciated that the Soviet Union had liberated them and allowed Czechoslovakia to become an independent country again. The Communist Party won in free and fair elections in 1946, and by 1949 nearly 20 percent of the population of Czechoslovakia had joined the Communist Party.

Nevertheless, discontent with Communist rule in Czechoslovakia increased during the 1950s and 1960s. In January 1968 a new, reformist Communist ruler, Alexander Dubček (1921–1992) came to power. Dubček rolled back many of the more unpopular aspects of communism: He allowed people to speak and write freely and to operate businesses that were not owned by the government, and he increased trade between Czechoslovakia and non-Communist countries. In August 1968 the Soviet Union, worried that the Czech people would take advantage of their increased freedom to overthrow communism entirely, invaded the country and reimposed a strict Communist dictatorship.

The crushing of the Prague Spring, as this reformist movement was called, ended overt resistance to communism, but it did not end anti-Communist feelings in Czechoslovakia. As the Soviet Union weakened its hold on Eastern Europe in the late 1980s, resistance began bubbling to the surface again. In November 1989 hundreds of thousands of Czechs protested in Prague against their Communist government. The protest movement was led by the Civic Forum, a coalition of pro-democracy groups headed by former playwright Václav Havel (1936–). In the face of these massive protests—on November 25 alone, eight hundred thousand people took to the streets in Prague—the Communist system collapsed peacefully. As a result of this so-called Velvet Revolution, a non-Communist government took power in December 1989 and elected Havel the country's interim president.

Government Structure

The Czech Parliament has two houses, the Chamber of Deputies and the Senate. The two hundred representatives in the Chamber of Deputies are elected to four-year terms via proportional representation. In elections for the Chamber of Deputies, voters in each of the Czech Republic's fourteen regions vote for a slate of candidates prepared by a party, rather than for individual candidates. Parties that receive less than 5 percent of the vote receive no seats in the Chamber; seats are allocated among the remaining parties based on the number of votes that their slates received. Once a party has been allocated a certain number of seats, the top candidates on its list receive those seats. For example, if a party received ten seats from a region, the first ten candidates on its list would be given those seats. Although the lists of candidates are prepared by the parties, the voters can cast "preference votes" to indicate which candidates they want to see at the top of the list.

Elections to the Czech Senate, by contrast, are conducted via a majority voting system. The country is divided into eighty-one districts, each of which elects a single senator. The elections are conducted in two rounds. If a single candidate wins over 50 percent of the votes in his or her district in the first round, that candidate is elected. Otherwise, the top two finishers from the first round go head-to-head in a second round of voting. As in the U.S. Senate, senators are elected to six-year terms, and not all of the senators are elected at once. Instead, the Senate is divided into thirds, with one-third of the Senate seats coming up for election every two years.

The president of the Czech Republic is elected by the parliament rather than by the people. The president serves a five-year term and can be reelected only one time before he or she must step down. The president's role is primarily ceremonial, but he or she is the commander-in-chief of the country's armed forces. The president also has the power to negotiate international treaties and to commute the sentences of convicted criminals.

Most executive power lies with the prime minister and the "government" (cabinet). The prime minister, who is elected by the parliament, oversees the work of the various ministers who make up his or her government. Most of the ministers are in charge of various ministries, such as the Ministry of Transport, the Ministry of Defense, and the Ministry of Agriculture, but the Czech cabinet can also have "ministers without portfolio" who do not oversee any particular agency.

Courts in the Czech Republic are independent from the political process. There are three chief courts: the Constitutional Court, the Supreme Court, and the Supreme Administrative Court. The Constitutional Court is responsible for overturning laws that contradict the constitution, reviewing international treaties to ensure that those treaties would not contradict the constitution if they were signed, and protecting the people's constitutional rights. The fifteen judges of the Constitutional Court, who serve ten-year terms, are appointed by the president and confirmed by the Senate.

The Supreme Administrative Court is a young court: it was created only in 2003. This court is responsible for protecting individuals' legal rights in relation to government agencies. It oversees the decisions of both government agencies and of regional courts when those courts hear cases involving government agencies. The Supreme Administrative Court primarily carries out this duty by hearing appeals from people who believe that they were wronged by a government agency and that their regional court failed to correct this wrong. The Supreme Administrative Court also hears cases relating to elections and referenda.

The Supreme Court is the highest court of appeal for criminal and civil cases. It caps the general legal system, which also includes local courts and regional appellate courts that hear appeals from the local courts. The Supreme Court is divided into two collegia that specialize in specific types of cases: the Civil Law and Commercial Law Collegium and the Criminal Collegium. Most cases that appear before the Supreme Court are heard by a three-judge tribunal called a senate; there are a number of these senates within each collegium.

The Czech government is highly decentralized: Much political power lies with the country's fourteen regions (including the capital city, Prague, which is its own region) and 6,249 municipalities, rather than with the federal government. The highest political official in a municipality is the mayor, while the regions are overseen by marshals. The regions also have local assemblies, with between 45 and 65 representatives in each assembly. Elections for these regional assemblies are held via a proportional representation system that is very similar to the one used for the Chamber of Deputies.

Political Parties and Factions

The two dominant political parties in the Czech Republic are the Civic Democratic Party and the Czech Social Democratic Party. The Civic Democratic Party (often known by its Czech initials, ODS) is a center-right party that is committed to free-market capitalism and limited powers for the government. Currently the most prominent ODS politician is Václav Klaus (1941–), who was prime minister of the Czech Republic from 1993 to 1997 and was elected president of the Czech Republic in 2003. The Czech Social Democratic Party is a very moderately socialist party, along the lines of the Labour Party in the United Kingdom. Although the party's platform claims that it wants a "social market economy," the party favors privatizing government-owned businesses and banks and some other free-market reforms.

The Communist Party of Bohemia and Moravia remains in existence and retains some popularity with

Candles are lit to honor students at the place they were injured during Velvet Revolution protests in Prague, Czechoslovakia, in 1989. © *Peter Turnley/CORBIS*

the voters, particularly the unemployed and older people. Following the 2006 elections the Communist Party was the third-largest party in the Chamber of Deputies, with twenty-six seats. Other minor parties include the Christian and Democratic Union–Czechoslovak People's Party (a conservative Catholic party popular with voters in the rural areas) and the Green Party, which runs on environmental issues such as opposition to nuclear power.

Major Events

Czechoslovakia split into two countries, the Czech Republic and Slovakia, on January 1, 1993. The split resulted from clashes between Czech and Slovak politicians over the level of autonomy that Slovakia should have, and over nearly every other issue that came before the government. Czech and Slovak politicians were unable even to agree on a name for the country after the fall of communism. The Czechs wanted to call it the Czechoslovak Republic, while the Slovaks preferred the Czecho-Slovak Republic. Although the breakup of Czechoslovakia sparked acrimonious debates among Czech politicians, the populations of both halves of the country—the majority of whom did not want to see

Czechoslovakia divided—were less passionate on the subject. As a result, the so-called Velvet Divorce was accomplished without violence.

Twenty-First Century

From the beginning the Czech Republic was expected to be one of Eastern Europe's post-Communist success stories, and it did not disappoint. Under Havel—who remained president of Czechoslovakia until June 1992, and then was president of the Czech Republic from January 1993 until 2003—and Klaus, the Czech Republic turned itself into a free country politically and economically. Although Czech politics are often messy and sometimes corrupt, elections are free and fair and the people have the freedom to speak their minds about political issues and to form political and social organizations. The Czech Republic also successfully privatized most of its state-owned industries and created a stable and well-functioning free-market economy. As a result of these successes, the Czech Republic was one of the first post-Communist countries to be permitted to join the North Atlantic Treaty Organization, which it did in 1999, and it joined the European Union in 2004.

BIBLIOGRAPHY

Czech Republic: The Official Web Site of the Czech Republic. http://www.czech.cz (accessed July 27, 2007).

Press, Petra. *Czech Republic.* San Diego, CA: Lucent Books, 2002.

⊕ Republic of Yemen

Type of Government

Yemen is a parliamentary republic that was created with the unification of the former Yemen Arab Republic (North Yemen) and the former People's Democratic Republic of Yemen (South Yemen) in 1990. The president is the head of state, and the prime minister is the head of government. Together with a cabinet of ministers they form the executive branch of the government. Yemen has a bicameral legislature consisting of the Shura Council and the House of Representatives.

Background

Yemen is located at the southern end of the Arabian Peninsula and borders Oman and Saudi Arabia. It extends to the Arabian Sea and Gulf of Aden to the south, and the Red Sea to the north and west. Within those waters lies Bab el-Mandeb, one of the most active shipping lanes in the world, which links the Gulf of Aden to the Red Sea. Yemen's interior is primarily desert and mountains, with a fairly temperate climate in the western mountains affected by seasonal monsoons, a hot and humid climate on the west coast, and extremely hot and arid conditions throughout the rest of the country. Fresh water resources are very limited, and dwindling supplies are an ongoing concern.

Known to the ancient Romans as "Arabia Felix," Yemen is reputed to have been the home of the legendary Queen of Sheba and is one of the oldest centers of civilization in the Near East. Part of the Minaean, Sabaean, and Himyarite kingdoms between the twelfth century BC and the sixth century AD, it was poised at the crossroads of Africa, the Middle East, and Asia along one of the lucrative spice trading routes of the time. The influence of Islam in the area, especially in the north, dates from the seventh century. Caliphates, or Islamic states, established a theocratic, or religious, political structure that endured well into the modern era. However, the futures of the north and the south of Yemen began to diverge.

North Yemen was controlled by the Ottoman Empire in the sixteenth century and again in the nineteenth. It gained independence from Turkey upon the empire's dissolution in 1918. The country then came under the rule of Imām Yahya (1904–1948), leader of the Zaidi Shiites. The Imām's reign continued through his sons until 1962, when a military coup d'etat created the Yemen Arab Republic (YAR) and ignited a civil war between royalists (backed by Saudi Arabia) and republicans (backed by Egypt).

South Yemen had come under the influence of Great Britain with the capture of the port of Aden in 1839. That administration evolved into the Federation of South Arabia and the Aden Protectorate. The revolution in 1962 and ensuing civil war spawned terrorism and violence that resulted in the withdrawal of both British and Egyptian troops in 1967. However, by that time Yemen's north and south had been divided. The People's Republic of South Yemen was declared independent in 1967. The YAR was recognized as a nation in 1970, the same year the then-Marxist southern state was renamed the People's Democratic Republic of Yemen (PDRY). Yemen remained thus divided for twenty years.

Although the PDRY and YAR agreed as early as 1972 that a union was desirable, it was a long and arduous process to attain that goal. Border skirmishes in the 1970s, a major earthquake in 1982 that killed three thousand people, and violent infighting in the south in 1986 were but a few of the obstacles to peace and unity. Unification was achieved, however, on May 22, 1990, with the declaration of the Republic of Yemen. Ali Abdullah Saleh (1942–), who had been president of the YAR since 1978, became the new nation's first president, and the unity constitution was ratified by the Yemeni people in May 1991.

Government Structure

Yemen is a parliamentary republic with separate executive, legislative, and judicial branches. The executive branch consists of the president (head of state), the prime minister (head of government), and the council of ministers. The president is elected by popular vote from a minimum of two candidates endorsed by parliament. His or her term of office is seven years. The prime minister and the council of ministers are appointed by the president.

A constitutional amendment ratified on February 20, 2001, provides for a bicameral legislative branch of government. This is made up of a House of Representatives with 301 members and a Shura Council of 111. Shura Council members are appointed by the president, and House members are elected by direct vote to six-year terms. Yemen has universal suffrage over the age of eighteen.

The Yemeni constitution calls for an independent judiciary, and the laws of the former PDRY and YAR have been unified for consistency. The Supreme Court is based in the capital city of Sanaa. The general populace, however, appears to be largely unaffected by the modern judiciary, relying instead on more traditional forms of justice.

Political Parties and Factions

The unification and ensuing political liberalization of Yemen led to the establishment of myriad political parties.

Yemeni President Ali Abdullah Saleh during his re-election campaign in September 2006. He has served as president since the unification of North and South Yemen in 1990, and for twelve years before that he was president of North Yemen. *Cris Bouroncle/ AFP/Getty Images*

There were as many as twenty-two at one point, but that number had diminished to approximately twelve by 2007. Of those, the most widely supported were the General People's Congress (GPC), Islamic Reform Grouping (Islah), and the Yemen Socialist Party (YSP).

The General People's Congress was founded in 1982 in the Yemen Arab Republic as a consulting body, rather than a political party. Saleh, who was president in the north before becoming president of the new republic in 1990, served as the GPC's secretary general and maintained prominence in the party after leaving his official position for the presidency. The GPC was criticized by the opposition as not being truly national, a situation that came to a head with a brief civil war in 1994. Saleh attempted to assuage that condemnation by such measures as appointing a prime minister from the south in 2001.

Islah was formed in 1990, with Sheikh Abdullah bin Hussein al-Ahmar (1933–) as its leader. The party won sixty-two seats in parliament in the 1993 elections, and Ahmar was elected speaker of the House of Representatives, a position he still held in 2007. Islah is a conservative proponent of adherence to Islamic law. That conservatism was reported to take a more radical turn around the turn of the century, as certain factions within the party were rumored to cultivate connections to al Qaeda.

The Yemen Socialist Party was established in 1978 in the People's Democratic Republic of Yemen. Marxist in nature, it was the south's sole party until joining with the GPC to manage the transition after unification in 1990.

Major Events

Political tensions exploded into a civil war in 1994, during which YSP leaders tried to secede the south from the new republic. After the secession attempt failed and

order was restored, the YSP had largely lost influence. It was excluded from the new government coalition of October 1994 and boycotted the 1997 elections. By the time it participated in the 2003 parliamentary elections, its power base had been sufficiently eroded that the party only garnered seven seats.

Tensions between north and south and, accordingly, those within their attendant political parties, have calmed in the twenty-first century. Resentments certainly remain, however, as evidenced by the assassination of the secretary general of the YSP by an Islah member in 2002.

Twenty-First Century

Yemen is one of the poorest countries in the Arab world and is heavily dependent on foreign aid. It is working to reduce widespread corruption and modernize the economy. Compounding its economic challenges is a population of almost twenty million people that is expanding rapidly. The increase in population presents a problem of an even more basic nature—water. Potable fresh water supplies, never in abundance in such a dry land, are dwindling rapidly because of increased demand and the effects of soil erosion and overgrazing. The cultivation of khat, a mildly narcotic plant Yemenis like to chew, also depletes the country's limited water resources as large amounts are used for irrigation.

Terrorism is another twenty-first century concern in Yemen. Incidents such as the 2000 attack on the U.S. naval ship *Cole* have given Yemen a reputation as a breeding ground of Islamic extremists. The government has actively combated this image, expelling more than one hundred suspected terrorists in 2002 and prosecuting fifteen alleged terrorists in 2004.

BIBLIOGRAPHY

Halliday, Fred. *Revolution and Foreign Policy: The Case of South Yemen 1967–1987.* New York: Cambridge University Press, 1990.

Ismael, Tareq Y. *The People's Democratic Republic of Yemen: Politics, Economics, and Society; The Politics of Socialist Transformation.* Boulder, CO: L. Rienner, 1986.

Wenner, Manfred W. *The Yemen Arab Republic: Development and Change in an Ancient Land.* Boulder, CO: Westview Press, 1991.

⊕ Germany

Type of Government

Germany is a democratic republic with independent executive, legislative, and judicial branches. The executive branch is made up of the president (head of state), the chancellor (head of government), and the cabinet. The legislative branch comprises a bicameral (two-house) parliament that includes a Bundestag or Federal

Assembly (the lower house) and a Bundesrat or Federal Council (the upper house). The Federal Constitutional Court heads the judicial branch.

Background

Slightly smaller than the state of Montana, Germany lies in Central Europe. It borders the North Sea and the Baltic Sea, as well as Austria, Belgium, the Czech Republic, Denmark, France, Luxembourg, the Netherlands, Poland, and Switzerland. It boasts Europe's largest economy and second-largest population.

For centuries, Germany did not exist as a single entity, but as hundreds of German-speaking kingdoms, fiefdoms, and principalities. It first emerged as a distinct realm as the Holy Roman Empire of the German Nation in the tenth century, but even the empire failed to establish a strong centralized authority. Matters were not improved by the sixteenth-century Reformation, when Germans became divided along religious lines. Those divisions culminated in the Thirty Years' War (1618–1648), which essentially destroyed any pretense of centralized control and reaffirmed the sovereignty of the various local German princes. The empire was officially abolished upon its takeover by Napoléon I (1769–1821) in 1806.

By the early nineteenth century, the strongest German-speaking states, Prussia and Austria, were vying for dominance. Prussia eventually prevailed due to its military, economic, administrative, and technological advantages over its rival. Under Otto von Bismarck (1815–1898), Prussia won wars with Denmark (1864), Austria (1866), and France (1870–1871). These victories resulted in the creation of the German Empire in 1871, with Bismarck as its first chancellor.

The German Empire fell after World War I and was succeeded by the Weimar Republic in 1919. Although that government was broadly democratic, it was hampered by the country's economic troubles and a rise in political extremism. By 1929 global economic depression, rampant unemployment, and social unrest had combined to destabilize the republic sufficiently to make it ripe for takeover by extremists. That happened in 1933 when the National Socialist (Nazi) Party was elected to power and Adolf Hitler (1889–1945) became chancellor. The single-party Third Reich was declared in 1934. Remilitarization and the systematic persecution of Germany's Jewish population soon followed. In 1939 Germany invaded Poland and thereby ignited World War II.

After Germany's defeat in 1945, the country was occupied by the United States, Great Britain, France, and the Soviet Union. That alliance deteriorated with the onset of the Cold War, and Germany once again became a divided nation in 1949. The Soviet-dominated East Germany became the German Democratic Republic (GDR), while the domain of the Western Allies became the Federal Republic of Germany (FRG). For the next forty years, the GDR went the way of communism and the FRG pursued capitalism and democracy. Ultimately, the decline of the Soviet Union allowed for Germany's reunification. East and West came together as the united Federal Republic of Germany on October 3, 1990.

Government Structure

Germany's constitution, known as the Basic Law, was adopted by the FRG on May 23, 1949, and extended to include the GDR upon the country's reunification in 1990. The executive branch comprises the president (head of state), the chancellor (head of government), and the cabinet. The president, whose role is largely ceremonial, is elected to a five-year term by a Federal Convention and is eligible to serve a second term. The Federal Convention includes all the members of the Bundestag (Federal Assembly) and an equal number of delegates from the state parliaments. It is a body formed solely for the purpose of presidential elections. The chancellor is elected by an absolute majority of the Bundestag to a four-year term. Cabinet members, or federal ministers, are appointed by the president upon recommendation of the chancellor.

Legislative power resides in a bicameral parliament comprising the Bundestag and the Bundesrat (Federal Council). The members of the Bundestag are the only federal officers that are directly elected by the German public. The Bundestag has at least twice the number of seats as the number of electoral districts (299) in the country. Its members are elected to four-year terms by a mixed, two-ballot system that combines direct election of one member from each electoral district in single-seat elections known as mandates, and a multi-seat election for the remaining members, who are chosen from the list of each party's top vote-getters by proportional representation (in other words, each party gets seats in the lower house in proportion to their showing in the popular vote). This mixed system creates an oddity of the German electoral process, the overhang seats—if a party has more mandates than seats received in the proportional election, additional seats are added to the Bundestag to make up the difference. In a rule informed by the political chaos and factionalism of the Weimer Republic, a political party is required to win either 5 percent of the popular vote or three direct mandates to gain representation in parliament.

The Bundesrat consists of sixty-nine delegates appointed by the governments of Germany's sixteen states. Each state has three to six votes in the Bundesrat, according to population. Representatives are required to vote as a bloc per the dictates of their state, and the body has the power to veto legislation passed by the Bundestag.

The judiciary is headed by the Federal Constitutional Court. It is empowered with judicial review over national and state legislation and the constitutionality of political parties, as well as ensuring uniform interpretation of the constitution and protection of citizens' rights. Half of its judges are elected by the Bundestag and half by the Bundesrat. Other courts include a high court of justice and those with jurisdictions from finance to labor to social concerns.

German citizens enjoy universal suffrage at the age of eighteen years. The official language is German and more than 90 percent of the populace is ethnic German. There is also a fairly substantial Turkish minority, as well as a smattering of Danes, Serbo-Croatians, Greeks, Italians, Poles, Russians, and Spaniards. Religious affiliation is roughly 70 percent Christian—nearly evenly divided between Protestants and Roman Catholics—with a Muslim population of just over 3.5 percent and the remainder either unaffiliated or "other."

Political Parties and Factions

Germany has several major political parties, the faces of which are often changing because of coalitions and "grand coalitions" formed among or between them. Their complicated nature harkens back to the mid-nineteenth-century revolutions. Since those times, naturally, they have gained sophistication and evolved to better suit the needs of a modern world.

Important contemporary parties include the Social Democratic Party (SPD); the Christian Democratic Union (CDU) and its smaller Bavarian sister the Christian Social Union (CSU); the Free Democratic Party (FDP); the Party of Democratic Socialism (PDS), which became known as the Left Party upon the formation of an alliance in 2005; and the Greens, which aligned with the Eastern German Alliance '90 to form the Alliance '90/The Greens in 1993.

The SPD is one of the oldest political parties in the world. Once committed to Marxism, it moderated its stance in 1959. It continues to advocate social welfare programs and derives much of its support from large cities and industrialized states. In the 2005 parliamentary elections, the SPD came in second to the CDU/CSU, with 34.3 percent of the vote. One notable SPD member was former West Berlin mayor (1957–1966) and German chancellor (1969–1974) Willy Brandt (1913–1992).

The CDU is generally conservative on social and economic issues. An early proponent of the European Economic Community (now the European Union), its support is broadly based among Catholics, Protestants, rural citizens, and all economic classes. The party was badly hurt by a funding scandal in 1999, but had recovered sufficiently by 2005 to allow the election of its leader, Angela Merkel (1954–), as Germany's first female chancellor. Its sister party, the CSU, is solely in Bavaria and is more conservative than the CDU. The two parties maintain their own internal structures but form a joint caucus in the Bundestag.

The FDP's traditional base is among middle- and upper-class Protestants who are liberal in the European sense of the word. That is, the party advocates minimal government interference in both economic policy and social issues. Like the CDU, however, the FDP was also an early backer of participation in European integration. It no longer boasts the dominance it once did, but remains an important force. Former FDP member Theodor Heuss (1884–1963) served as the first president of the FRG from 1949 to 1959.

The PDS was established as the successor to the Socialist Unity Party of Germany after the fall of the Berlin Wall in 1989. It retains its Marxist leanings, although it has abandoned most of its prior extremism, and draws most of its support from Germany's eastern states. In 2005 it teamed up with the WASG (Wahlalternative Arbeit und soziale Gerechtigkeit) to form an alliance called the Left Party. The Left Party won 8.7 percent of the 2005 parliamentary vote.

As the name suggests, the Greens were founded as the political party of environmental activists. Originally focused on the opposition to such things as nuclear power and military enterprise, the party first achieved the requisite 5 percent to enter parliament in 1983. Since then, it has broadened its agenda and become more mainstream, although still left of center. After it joined forces with the Eastern German Alliance '90 to become the Alliance '90/The Greens, the party attained 51 seats in parliament, with 8.1 percent of the vote, in the 2005 elections.

Several other minor parties exist in Germany, many of which appear on state-level ballots but do not meet the benchmark percentage for parliamentary representation.

Major Events

After World War II, two primary concerns of the German people were reunifying the country and eradicating its Nazi past. Although the GDR was considered one of the most prosperous Warsaw Pact countries—the Warsaw Pact was the Soviet counterpart to the western Allies' North Atlantic Treaty Organization—many of the Germans living there longed for the freedom and prosperity enjoyed by their brethren in the FRG. In 1953 Soviet-imposed labor quotas caused mass strikes and protests in East Germany which were violently put down with the assistance of the Soviet Army. By 1961 more than a million East Germans, particularly skilled professionals and scientists, had fled to the west, inciting the GDR to seal its borders, literally building a wall around West Berlin, and adopting repressive policies of internal security and surveillance enforced by the Stasi, or secret police.

The political gulf between East and West Germany narrowed in the 1970s, when FRG chancellor Willy Brandt adopted the policy of *Ostpolitik* (literally, "politics of the east") by which West Germany recorgnized the statehood of territories formerly held by Germany which had become Soviet client states, such as the GDR, Czechoslovakia, and Poland. However, the two nations remained separated, both politically and physically, until 1989. That year Hungary's independence from Soviet

West Germans watching East German border guards demolish a section of the Berlin Wall, which had separated Communist-controlled East Berlin from the western part of the city, in November 1989. © AP/Wide World Photos

influence created a new avenue for East Germans to migrate west. The appearance of holes in the Soviet "Iron Curtain" and the protests that followed showed the East German government that a policy of sealed borders was futile. In November 1989, free transit between east and west was restored, and the Berlin Wall began to be dismantled. Although from that point, Germany's legal reunification was a simple matter, taking less than a full year, the actual re-integration of East and West was a complicated and evolving process. More than a decade after reunification, former East Germans continue to be poorer than their western counterparts, and a significant cultural divide still exists.

In both East and West Germany, the Nazi Party was banned after World War II. In West Germany, an extensive "denazification" program was undertaken between 1946 and 1949 to find and prosecute significant contributors to the Nazi cause. Under German law, despite generally liberal policies toward free speech and political expression, Nazi symbols, propaganda, and any publications denying the Holocaust are illegal. In 2000 the German government negotiated reparations payments to Holocaust survivors to compensate for forced labor performed in support of the Third Reich.

Twenty-First Century

While Germany boasts the largest economy in Europe and the fifth-largest in the world, the costs of modernizing and integrating the economy of the former East Germany continue to be huge. As of 2007, the West was still transferring approximately $80 billion per year to the East. The reunification has also had a social cost, as lower wages and higher unemployment in the East and a heightened tax burden in the West have led to resentment on both sides. Nonetheless, the commitment to a thorough integration of the formerly divided country remains strong.

BIBLIOGRAPHY

Berghahn, Volker Rolf. *Modern Germany: Society, Economy and Politics in the Twentieth Century.* 2nd ed. New York: Cambridge University Press, 1987.

Kitschelt, Herbert, and Wolfgang Streeck, eds. *Germany: Beyond the Stable State.* Portland, OR: Frank Cass, 2004.

Turner, Henry Ashby. *Germany from Partition to Reunification.* New Haven, CT: Yale University Press, 1992.

⊕ Republic of Georgia

Type of Government

The Republic of Georgia was one of the many constituent republics of the Soviet Union that gained its independence in 1991 but subsequently struggled through a dozen years of political turmoil. In 2003 a popular pro-democracy movement known as the Rose Revolution swept through the country and brought several years of autocratic rule to a close. Georgia is a representative democracy with a unicameral parliament and a president who is head of state. Executive power as head of government is divided between the president and the prime minister, with the president having control of the ministries of defense and interior, and the prime minister controlling all other executive functions.

Background

Georgia is a relatively small but strategically located nation of the Caucasus area of Eurasia, with a population of just 4.6 million (about the same as Toronto, Canada). The Georgians are a distinct ethnic group whose language shares no characteristics with other languages outside the Transcaucasus. Linguists theorize that Georgian is one of the oldest living languages, and its endurance combined with Georgia's relative isolation to preserve an unusually high degree of ethnic identity and culture. The area was inhabited as early as 6000 BC, and the ancient Greeks later established trading colonies in the area, but attempts at conquest by the armies of Alexander the Great (356–323 BC), and then by various Persian and other foreign powers, ultimately proved futile. A Roman invasion later led to Georgia's conversion to Christianity in AD 327, when the king proclaimed it the official state religion and made Georgia only the second political entity in the world to do so.

The Georgian kingdom reached its peak in the early twelfth century under the rein of King David IV (1073–1125) but by the mid-thirteenth century the country had been overrun by Mongol armies, and by 1600 nearly all of this formerly Christian outpost was Muslim. For a time, it was divided between Persia and the Ottoman Empire, but by 1802 it came under Imperial Russian rule. This ended briefly in 1917 following the Bolshevik Revolution, when a group of Georgian nationalists proclaimed it the Democratic Republic of Georgia. Local Communist supporters were installed when Soviet Russia's troops returned, and a 1924 anti-Soviet uprising was brutally suppressed by a native Georgian, Joseph Stalin (1879–1953), who was the Communist Party leader in Moscow. During its decades as the Georgian Soviet Socialist Republic, its temperate climate made it a favorite vacation haunt for the Soviet elite, but it remained a hotbed of resistance to Soviet rule.

Soviet leader Mikhail Gorbachev (1931–) came to power in 1985 and ushered in an era of immense reform that would propel the Soviet Union to its ultimate demise six years later. One of Gorbachev's closest advisers was Eduard Shevardnadze (1928–), who had risen to power as head of the Communist Party of Georgia in 1972 by fighting corruption. Following an example set in other Soviet republics, Georgia held its first multiparty elections in October 1990, and five months later voted overwhelmingly for independence in a national referendum. Genuine sovereignty, however, came later, with the end of the Soviet Union in 1991.

Government Structure

Georgia's constitution was adopted on October 17, 1995. An elected president serves as head of state, is elected by direct vote to a five-year term, and is limited to two terms. The president formerly served as head of government, too, until changes in 1999 gave the chief cabinet appointee, the minister of state, powers similar to that of a prime minister. In 2004 the minister of state's title was changed to prime minister.

Georgia's legislative branch is its unicameral (one-house) parliament, the Sakartvelos Parlamenti, or Parliament of Georgia. Its 235 deputies are elected to four-year terms by popular vote.

The electoral system for the parliament combines eighty-five single-seat constituencies—in which individual elections are held for each seat—with a proportional representation vote for the remaining seats. Those one hundred fifty seats are chosen in a single, national election in which each party receives a number of seats in proportion to its total vote count, and those seats are then allocated to the top vote-getters on each party's list of candidates. A party must surpass a threshold of five percent of the vote to receive seats in parliament. Ten seats in parliament are allocated to representatives of persons displaced from the conflict-ridden region of Abkhazia.

Georgia's judiciary is independent in theory, and supervised by separate Council of Justice, but historically the president has been able to exert influence on judges, and at the local level the judges are sometimes subjected to pressure by clan leaders. The Supreme Court is the highest court in the land, and serves as the court of final appeal. The Constitutional Court was established in 1996, and a year later a new Law on Common Courts was enacted, specifying a three-tier system—regional courts of appeal hearing cases from the lowest level (the district courts that hear civil cases and lesser criminal ones), and more serious criminal cases prosecuted at the regional court level. The 1997 law also instituted a test on legal principles for judges, and many judges failed during the first wave of exams.

Georgia is divided into nine administrative districts, plus one for the capital of Tbilisi; there are also two autonomous regions, Abkhazia and Adjara. The districts are further divided into sixty-nine *rayons*. In 1998 elections for local assemblies were held for the first time.

Suffrage (the right to vote) in Georgia is universal for those eighteen and older.

Political Parties and Factions

When Georgians voted in the first multiparty elections in October 1990, a coalition slate called Round Table–Free Georgia won the majority of parliamentary seats. Ethnic tensions, which had long been simmering in Georgia between the majority population and the Russian, Ossetian, and Abkhazian minorities, flared in the first years following independence. Georgia's new leaders claimed that Moscow, which had refused to formally recognize Georgia's declaration of sovereignty, was inciting the unrest, and responded with military action. A coup occurred in Tbilisi in December 1991, aided by a paramilitary group, Mkhedrioni, followed by a bitter and bloody civil war. The Mkhedrioni provided armed support to the new president, Shevardnadze, but was accused of human rights abuses and organized-crime activities and ordered to disband in 1995.

In 1993 Shevardnadze founded a new party, the center-right Citizens' Union of Georgia (also known by its Georgian initials, SMK). It dominated electoral politics following Shevardnadze's first official election to the presidency in 1995, a vote widely believed to have been rigged. During this decade, several credible political figures died under suspicious circumstances, including the first democratically elected president (ousted in the 1991 coup), Zviad Gamsakhurdia (1939–1993), and Giorgi Chanturia (1959–1994), head of the National Democratic Party. But even members of Shevardnadze's SMK began to oppose what had become an intractable separatist conflict and corruption at the highest levels of government. A respected jurist, Nino Burjanadze (1964–), broke from the party and formed a bloc known as the Burjanadze-Democrats in 2003. A longtime ally of Shevardnadze and chair of parliament, Zurab Zhvania (1963–2005), also broke with the SMK and formed a new party, the United Democrats, in 2002; he, too, would die under somewhat suspicious circumstances. Zhvania's protégé was another pro-Western lawyer, Mikhail Saakashvili (1967–), who founded the United National Movement, a center-right organization, in 2001. Burjanadze, Zhvania, and Saakashvili joined forces in November 2003 to protest the blatantly fraudulent results of recent parliamentary elections. Shevardnadze resigned from office, and Saakashvili was elected president in January 2004. His party is an amalgamation of the reformist groups and known as the National Movement–Democrats.

Major Events

Georgia's first free and open presidential elections were held in May 1991, with Gamsakhurdia declared the winner. His victory came at a time of severe troubles in Georgia, however, with Gorbachev firmly opposed to the new parliament's declaration of independence, in addition to a rising tide of separatist violence in the minority enclaves of South Ossetia and Abkhazia. Criticized for his increasingly authoritarian decisions, a rebellion against Gamsakhurdia began in December 1991 that resulted in his ouster in January 1992, and a state of emergency went into effect. Rule by military council continued until March 1992, when Shevardnadze was named head of a provisional government. Gamsakhurdia attempted a return to power in September 1993 from the western city of Zugdidi, and forces loyal to him became involved in a civil war that was raging over Abkhazia, which would end with nearly ten thousand dead. Gamsakhurdia's body was discovered with a single bullet to the head in December 1993, and was officially ruled a suicide.

Shevardnadze's government was finally forced to ask Moscow for military help in quelling the separatist rebellions and the Gamsakhurdia faction, and in return for this aid agreed to join the Commonwealth of Independent States (CIS) in March 1994. In November 1995, presidential elections were held in which Shevardnadze beat out six other candidates with 70 percent of the vote, and was widely hailed—at both home and in the West—as the savior of his nation.

Five years later, however, the April 2000 presidential elections were criticized as fraudulent by the Organization for Security and Cooperation in Europe, which regularly sends observer missions to monitor elections. Shevardnadze won with some 80 percent of the vote, but his popular support was waning and the government faced drastic opposition when the results of the November 2003 parliamentary elections were announced. In that contest, Burjanadze-Democrats and Saakashvili's United National Movement appeared to have won a majority according to exit polls, but Shevardnadze's new party, For a New Georgia, and its ally the Revival Party were declared the winners. Georgians took to the streets in mass demonstrations against the official tallies, and finally on November 23 Shevardnadze announced his resignation. Two days later the Georgian Supreme Court annulled the results of the parliamentary elections. The relatively peaceful change of power was dubbed the Rose Revolution for the roses carried by protesters—a symbol of nonviolence—when they stormed parliament on the opening day of its new session. The following January, Saakashvili was elected president with a stunning 96 percent of the vote.

Twenty-First Century

Despite its years of post-Soviet turmoil, Georgia continues to be a relatively prosperous nation and is poised to become a regional leader in the twenty-first century. Nevertheless, Saakashvili inherited the reins of power in a country struggling under onerous burdens: problems in the breakaway regions of Ossetia and Abkhazia remained unresolved, and the nation's economy was in shambles and heavily reliant on U.S. and Russian aid.

After the Rose Revolution of November 2003 in Georgia, a member of Parliament carries a rose into session of parliament. *© Antoine Gyori/ AGP/Corbis*

Conflicts with Russia under a new hard-liner, President Vladimir Putin (1952–), resumed over various issues, and in January 2006 a pair of natural-gas pipelines and one electricity cable—both running between Georgia and Russia—were bombed. This resulted in serious disruptions of heat and electricity for Georgians during the coldest weeks of the year. The Saakashvili government claimed the strikes were retaliatory moves by Putin for Georgia's continued assertion of power on several fronts: Russia hoped to control those same export pipelines, and the issue with South Ossetia and Abkhazia, because Russian peacekeeping troops were still present in both areas, continued to strain relations between Georgia and Russia. Finally, since taking office Saakashvili had become one of Putin's most challenging foes—a fiercely pro-West politician who had been assiduously cultivating Georgia's entry into the North Atlantic Treaty Organization and, at a future date, the European Union.

BIBLIOGRAPHY

Alaolmolki, Nozar. *Life after the Soviet Union: The Newly Independent Republics of Transcaucasus and Central Asia.* Albany: State University of New York Press, 2001.

Streissguth, Thomas. *The Transcaucasus.* San Diego, CA: Lucent Books, 2001.

Wheatley, Jonathan. *Georgia from National Awakening to Rose Revolution: Delayed Transition in the Former Soviet Union.* Burlington, VT: Ashgate, 2005.

⊕ Somaliland

Type of Government

Somaliland declared its independence from Somalia in 1991. Since that time, its transitional government has worked toward establishing a democracy, although the country is not officially recognized by the international community. Nevertheless, Somaliland adopted a constitution in 2001 and has established a functioning government. Its executive branch comprises a president, vice president, and council of ministers. The legislative branch consists of a bicameral parliament that includes the House of Elders and the House of Representatives. The judiciary is headed by a Supreme Court appointed by the president. The president, vice president, and members of the House of Representatives are elected by popular vote.

Background

Somaliland lies in the eastern Horn of Africa, bordered by Somalia, Ethiopia, Djibouti, and the Gulf of Aden. The climate is tropical with four distinct seasons—rainy spring, dry summer, rainy autumn, and dry winter. The spring rains (April through June) are especially important, as a drought following the arid winter can be disastrous to the livestock, which is the backbone of the economy.

The coastline along the Gulf of Aden was settled by Arab tribes as early as the seventh century and was firmly established as a sultanate by the tenth century. The sultanate fell apart in the sixteenth century, leaving the area to form small states.

European colonization and influence followed in the nineteenth century, with England, France, and Italy all gaining footholds in the region by the late 1800s. The French acquired what would become Djibouti, the Italians took over central Somalia and later consolidated it with territory in the south, and the English established a protectorate over Somaliland in 1884. Although the English largely left Somaliland to its own devices, most importantly as to its traditions and culture, its rule was not without native opposition. The most famous of these militant groups was the Dervish movement led by Sayyid Muḥammad ibn ʾAbd Allāh Hasan (1864–1920). Known as the "Mad Mullah" by the English, Hasan led a twenty-year armed revolt against English, Italian, and Ethiopian colonial forces that was fraught with violence and turmoil. It is estimated that approximately one-third of Somaliland's male population died during this period.

Except for a brief occupation by Italian forces from 1940 to 1941, England retained control of Somaliland until June 26, 1960, when it granted the country independence. Five days later, however, on July 1, the nation joined the former Italian Somalia to form the democratic Somali Republic. The union was not a happy one.

The northern people of the former Somaliland grew quickly dissatisfied with the new republic's divisions of political power and designation of faraway Mogadishu as its capital. This discontent was made worse as it became clear that many clan-based traditions of the Somalis were not easily compatible with Western democracy. Internal conflict came to a head with the assassination of the country's president, and ensuing bloodless military coup d'etat by General Mohamed Siad Barre (1919–1995) in 1969. Barre declared Somalia a socialist state the following year.

Barre's government instituted innovative social policies, such as the introduction of Somali script and a huge literacy campaign, but its popularity began to wane as it grew more iron-fisted and controlling. Crackdowns on everything from traditional social organization to religion soon rendered the populace frustrated and restless. These misgivings were exacerbated by governmental corruption and clan politics. Tensions between north and south also increased, especially after masses of refugees with southern sympathies settled in the north following the 1977–78 Somali-Ethiopian War. Those tensions led to armed resistance to the government by the Somali National Movement (SNM) beginning in 1981. Ten years of civil war and governmental repression followed, finally resulting in the ousting of Barre and collapse of the republic. Somaliland declared itself an independent nation in May 1991, but it did not gain recognition from the international community.

As Somaliland worked toward building a stable state, one of its greatest challenges was to incorporate the various clans into the government by blending traditional and democratic systems of rule. Somaliland citizens overwhelmingly (97 percent) approved a constitution and reaffirmed their independence in 2001. In April 2003 they conducted their first direct vote for president, and in May 2005 the first popular parliamentary election was held. As of 2007, however, Somaliland was still awaiting recognition as an independent state.

Government Structure

Shortly after Somaliland declared its independence, various clans began vying for control. The SNM quickly realized that a transitional national government could not impose order on its own. Thus, it called for a council of clan leaders, the Guurti, to both settle the conflicts of the time and choose a group of elders to resolve future disputes. It proved effective in melding the traditions of old with the aspirations of a new republic, and the council persevered as bloody clashes among rival clans erupted throughout the years. In 1996 the Guurti formally transformed itself into the upper house of a bicameral parliament. It also drafted a transitional national charter, appointed an interim parliament, and established a Supreme Court.

With a referendum in May 2001, Somaliland endorsed a constitution that solidified its democratic intentions. It provides for a division of governmental powers among independent executive, legislative, and judicial branches. A president, vice president, and council of ministers make up the executive branch, of which the president is head of state. The president and vice president are elected to five-year terms on a joint ticket by direct vote of the people. Presidential service is limited to two terms in office. The council of ministers, or cabinet, is appointed by the president and must be confirmed by the House of Representatives by a majority vote. Both men and women may vote and run for office in Somaliland.

The bicameral parliament comprises a House of Representatives and a House of Elders, each with eighty-two members. To serve in the House of Representatives, members must be practicing Muslims at least thirty-five years old and high school graduates. They are elected by popular vote to five-year terms. The House of Elders is, as noted above, essentially the incorporation of the Guurti

Judge Mohamed Farah announcing the results of legislative elections in Somaliland in 2005.   *Ali Musa/AFP/Getty Images*

into the democratic government. Its role is mainly advisory, especially with regard to religion, cultural tradition, and security. Members must be at least forty-five years old and be well versed in either Islam or Somali tradition. They serve six-year terms.

The judicial branch is headed by a Supreme Court of no fewer than four judges, in addition to a chairman of the court. The judges and chairman are appointed by the president in consultation with the Judicial Commission. The chairman's appointment must be confirmed at a joint session of parliament within three months of the nomination. Other courts include Appeals Courts of the Regions, Regional Courts, District Courts, and Courts of the National Armed Forces.

Political Parties and Factions

In an effort to avoid the clan-based rivalries that plagued Somaliland in the past, the constitution makes specific provisions as to political parties. First, it limits the number of parties allowed to just three. This is to encourage party formation based on ideology, as opposed to tribal loyalties. (National elections in the 1960s, for example,

generated over sixty parties, giving way to political inefficiency and fragmentation.) Further, the constitution unequivocally states that parties based on regionalism or clan identification are illegal.

The three political parties competing at the time of the 2003 presidential elections were the Unity of Democrats (UDUB), Solidarity (KULMIYE), and Justice and Welfare (UCID) parties. The UDUB prevailed in both that and in the 2005 parliamentary elections, but only by a slight margin. The Solidarity Party was a close second in both elections, with the UCIC finishing third with nearly 16 percent of the vote in 2003 and 26 percent of the vote in 2005. Thus, there was neither a hugely disproportionately dominant party, nor were loyalties widely scattered among various factions.

Major Events

The British occupation of Somaliland was primarily characterized by inattention, which was a double-edged sword in its consequences. On one hand, Independence Day in 1960 found the country woefully neglected in terms of such things as education and basic services.

There were, for instance, no sealed roads linking the major towns and only one secondary school was operating. On the other hand, England's distant administration also left Somaliland's traditions and culture mainly intact. Although this presented some later problems with clan rivalries, it preserved the fabric of society that likely gave the country a basic stability that allowed it to cope with internal dissension on its own.

The dictatorship of Barre also loomed large in the country's history. The civil war was, of course, paramount among the regime's brutal and repressive effects. However, the corruption, oppression, and ruthlessness of Barre's government was also defined by its 1988 retaliation for SNM rebellion—ground and aerial forces devastated Hargeysa, leaving thousands of civilians dead and causing hundreds of thousands to flee to Ethiopia.

Twenty-First Century

Somaliland maintains its own police force, army, and government institutions, as well as having its own currency, flag, and national anthem. Yet ostensibly because of reluctance to further destabilize Somalia, formal recognition from the international community has not been forthcoming and remains foremost among the goals of the government. Somaliland continues to face the potential for internal conflict, especially resulting from Islamic extremism in the region. The country's Muslims are traditionally moderate, and many are striving to neutralize fundamentalist influences within its borders.

Poverty and unemployment are other concerns. While there is a flourishing private sector, the economy remains dependent on contributions from outside the country, including those who have fled regional violence. Further, the country's vital livestock industry was hard hit in 2007 by embargoes invoked against the possible spread of Rift Valley Fever, a mosquito-borne illness that affects domestic animals and may be transmitted to humans.

BIBLIOGRAPHY

Fatoke, Aderemi Samuel Olumuyiwa. *British Colonial Administration of Somaliland Protectorate, 1920–1960.* Chicago: University of Illinois at Chicago Circle, 1982.

Jacquin-Berdal, Dominique. *Nationalism and Ethnicity in the Horn of Africa: A Critique of the Ethnic Interpretation.* Lewiston, NY: Edwin Mellen Press, c. 2002.

Lawaha, Ahmed Shire. *Political Movements in Somalia.* Washington, DC: American University, 1960.

⊕ Croatia

Type of Government

Croatia is a parliamentary democracy with a unicameral, or one-house, parliament called the Sabor. Its executive branch includes the prime minister, the cabinet (called the "government"), and the president. The judicial branch has four different types of lower courts—all of which are overseen by the Supreme Court—as well as a separate Constitutional Court.

Background

The Croatian people have lived on the Balkan Peninsula since the seventh century AD. In 924 Croatia became an independent nation, but this independence did not last long: Croatia was absorbed into the Hungarian empire in 1091. Croatia, however, retained some rights to self-rule. It had its own parliament, the Sabor, and its own governor. One Croatian city, Dubrovnik, even became nearly independent from the Hungarian empire and developed into a major regional economic power with a high standard of living.

This medieval golden age began to fade in the late fourteenth century. Croatia fell into a civil war, and the neighboring state of Venice took advantage of the chaos to seize many of Croatia's coastal cities. Then, during the fifteenth and early sixteenth centuries, much of Croatia was conquered by the Ottoman Empire. Only a small portion in the northwest of Croatia remained unaffected by the combined forces of the Ottomans and the Venetians. The city of Dubrovnik, which became completely independent at this time, retained much of its former glory and power until 1667, when it was leveled by an earthquake that killed half of its population.

The Croatian lands were all reunited under a single empire—the Austrian Hapsburg Empire—by the end of the eighteenth century. This empire, which ruled Hungary beginning in 1526, succeeded in driving the Ottomans out of much of former Croatian territory in the seventeenth and eighteenth centuries, and it took control of Venice's former Croatian provinces when the Venetian Republic collapsed in 1797. However, parts of Croatia that had formerly been under Ottoman control were ruled by Austria as a military border region, and thousands of Serbs and members of other ethnic groups were settled in these areas to serve as border guards. Even after the Ottoman threat was essentially gone, Austria refused to remove these guards.

Both Austria and Hungary attempted to force their own languages and cultures on the Croatian people, but a backlash against these Germanization and Magyarization policies of the Austrians and Hungarians, respectively, developed in Croatia in the late eighteenth century. By around 1830 this backlash had developed into a full-fledged Croatian nationalist movement, which was called the Illyrian movement. (The Illyrians were the ancient tribe that lived in and around modern-day Croatia before the invasion of Slavic tribes into the area in the sixth century AD.) Croatia's Hungarian rulers cracked down on this movement—even at one point banning the mere use of the word "Illyria" in Croatia—but were unable to eradicate it.

Power struggles between Croatian nationalists and their Hungarian rulers continued until the Austro-Hungarian Empire collapsed in the wake of World War I. Croatia received its independence from the empire, and on December 1, 1918, it joined with two other south Slavic ethnic groups to form the Kingdom of the Serbs, Croats, and Slovenes.

Politics in this new state (which changed its name to Yugoslavia in 1929) were unsettled from the start. The confederation had been conducted hastily in the face of the military pressures of World War I, and many questions about how the new country would be organized and governed remained to be worked out. One of the major questions was whether the government would be centralized—the position favored by Serbia, which was the largest and most powerful of Yugoslavia's ethnic groups—or whether more power would be left with Croatia, Slovenia, and Bosnia, as those three nations wished. This question turned deadly in 1928, when a Serbian member of parliament shot five Croatian representatives. When Croatians responded to the murders with demonstrations, the Serbian authorities dissolved Yugoslavia's democratic institutions and declared a dictatorship. Clashes between Croatians and the Serbian authorities continued throughout the 1930s. During this time a small group of Croatian nationalists formed themselves into a violent separatist organization called the Ustase, and in 1934 a member of this group assassinated the king of Yugoslavia.

Croatia finally won autonomy within Yugoslavia on August 26, 1939, but less than a week later World War II broke out. Yugoslavia wanted to remain neutral, but in April 1941 Germany and its allies invaded and defeated the country. Yugoslavia was carved up into several pieces that were controlled by different countries. Croatia wound up as a nominally independent state—encompassing both Croatia and modern day Bosnia and Herzegovina—that was actually a puppet state of Nazi Germany. Ante Pavelić (1889–1959), the founder of the Ustase, was put in charge of Croatia, and he turned the Ustase loose on Croatia's minorities, which included Serbs, Jews, and Roma (Gypsies). Estimates of the number of people killed by the Ustase vary widely, but a reasonable estimate would be five hundred thousand Serbs, thirty-two thousand Jews (over three-quarters of Croatia's prewar Jewish population) and forty thousand Roma.

The most effective opposition to the German occupation came from the Communist Party, which was led by the Croatian Josip Broz Tito (1892–1980). After the Soviet Union liberated the region in 1944, Yugoslavia was reassembled, and Tito and his Communist Party were left in charge of the country. Under Tito, Yugoslavia was organized as a federation, with each of the six separate republics within the country nominally having a certain degree of autonomy. In reality, though, the country was firmly under the control of the Communist authorities in Belgrade. Tito and the Communist officials managed to suppress the nationalist movement in Croatia during Tito's lifetime, but after he died in 1980 Croatia's nationalist movement strengthened. Other republics within Yugoslavia also began making demands for autonomy, and by the late 1980s it was clear that Yugoslavia was doomed as a unified Communist country. Croatia became a multiparty democracy in 1989, and in free elections held in 1990 Croats elected a nationalist government headed by Franjo Tudjman (1922–1999). On June 25, 1991, Tudjman's government declared Croatia's independence from Yugoslavia.

Government Structure

The legislative branch of the Croatian government consists of the Sabor, a unicameral parliament. The number of representatives in the Sabor can vary from 100 to 160; as of 2007, there were 151 representatives in the Sabor. These representatives are elected directly by the people to four-year terms. Many powers lie with the Sabor, including the power to pass laws, amend the constitution, and declare war and peace.

The highest level of the executive branch consists of the prime minister; the "government," or cabinet; and the president. The majority of executive power lies with the prime minister and the cabinet, who propose laws to the parliament, create a proposed budget for the country, enact regulations, conduct foreign policy, and carry out the laws passed by the Sabor. The prime minister, who is appointed by the president and confirmed by the Sabor, is typically the leader of the largest party or coalition in the parliament. The prime minister chooses the ministers who will serve in his or her cabinet, but these ministers must be confirmed by the Sabor as well.

The president of Croatia is elected by the people to a five-year term of office, with the possibility of being reelected only one time. When Croatia first became independent, the president of Croatia had a great deal of power, but following the death of Croatia's founding president, Tudjman, the constitution was amended to reduce the powers of the presidency to bring them more in line with other parliamentary democracies. Following these constitutional amendments, the president's major duties are serving as commander-in-chief of the country's armed forces, representing Croatia at diplomatic functions, and working with the prime minister to determine the country's foreign policy and oversee its diplomatic corps.

The judicial system in Croatia has four different branches: commercial courts (whose decisions can be appealed to the high commercial court), municipal courts (whose decisions can be appealed to county courts), misdemeanor courts (whose decisions can be appealed to the high misdemeanor court), and an administrative court

The Croatian parliament, or Sabor, in Zagreb. © *Richard Klune/ Corbis*

that can rule on decisions made by various administrative bodies. Decisions of the high commercial court, the county courts, the high misdemeanor court, and the administrative court can be appealed to the Supreme Court, which is the highest court in Croatia. Judges are appointed by the National Judicial Council, an eleven-member body that is appointed by the Sabor. All judges are appointed for life, with a retirement age of seventy.

Croatia also has a separate Constitutional Court that is outside of the normal judicial system. This court, which is composed of thirteen judges who are elected to eight-year terms by the Sabor, has the power to decide whether or not laws passed by the Sabor and regulations enacted by the national and local governments comply with the constitution. The Constitutional Court also oversees elections and referenda and settles disputes between the various branches of the government, and it can hear impeachment cases against the president and decide to ban political parties if those parties are found to threaten either Croatian democracy or the survival of Croatia as a country.

At the local level Croatia is divided into twenty counties, 416 cities and municipalities, and the city of Zagreb, which is considered both a city and a county. The cities and municipalities are run by elected councils, while the counties are run by elected assemblies. Both groups are elected to four-year terms. Many governmen-

tal functions, including maintaining roads, public transportation, and supplying heat, drinking water, and other utilities, are handled by these local governments.

Political Parties and Factions

The dominant political party in Croatia since independence has been the Croatian Democratic Union (often known by its Croatian initials, HDZ). This party was founded in 1989, before the break-up of Yugoslavia, by Croatian nationalists led by Tudjman. It is a nationalist party that is affiliated internationally with the European People's Party.

The Democratic Center (DC) broke away from HDZ in 2000. DC is a centrist party that is more moderate than HDZ, but its three members of parliament have been part of the HDZ-led coalition government since 2003.

As of 2007 the major opposition party was the Social Democratic Party of Croatia (SDP), which in the 2003 elections ran in coalition with three liberal democratic parties: the Party of Liberal Democrats, the Liberal Party, and the Istrian Democratic Assembly. SDP is a pro-Western party that favors Croatia's bids to join the European Union and NATO and opposes Croatian interference in Bosnia and other neighboring countries. SDP is a moderately left-wing party; internationally, it is a member of the Socialist International and the Party of European Socialists.

In the early 1990s the Croatian Social Liberal Party (HSLS) was the major opposition party. HSLS is a centrist party founded in 1989. As of 2007 it advocated for a mix of liberal, democratic, and socialist policies, although in the 1990s it supported Croatian nationalism as well. On the European level, HSLS is a member of the Liberal International.

Splits within HSLS have led to the formation of two other political parties: the Liberal Party (LS), which broke away from HSLS in 1997, and LIBRA, which broke away in 2002. In 2005 LIBRA merged with the Croatian People's Party to form the Croatian People's Party—Liberal Democrats. The merged party is affiliated internationally with the European Liberal Democrat and Reform Party.

The Istrian Democratic Assembly is a liberal party that operates in Istria, an economically prosperous peninsula in extreme western Croatia that historically belonged to Italy rather than to Croatia. The party advocates for more autonomy for Istria and for generally liberal policies. It is a member of the European Liberal Democrat and Reform party.

Other minor parties include the Littoral and Highland Regional Alliance, the Slavonian-Baranian Croatian Party, the Croatian Peasants' Party, the Croatian Party of Rights, the Zagorje Democratic Party, and the Croatian Party of Pensioners.

Major Events

Tensions between Croatian nationalists and Serbian nationalists in Croatia—who were supported by Slobodan Milosevic (1941–2006) and the Yugoslav National Army—were high even before Croatia formally declared independence. Serbs in Croatia's Krajina region (on the border with Bosnia) declared themselves autonomous in March 1991; after Croatia declared independence, guerrilla war broke out between Serbs and Croats in that area. The Serbs succeeded in capturing one-quarter of Croatia's territory and in driving 500,000 non-Serbs out of their homes. In January 1992 a cease-fire was declared that formalized Serbian control over those portions of Croatia. Not until 1995 did the Croatian military succeed in regaining control of Krajina. However, between 130,000 and 200,000 Serbs fled Krajina ahead of the Croatian Army, leading to charges of war crimes, specifically ethnic cleansing, against several of the military figures involved in that campaign.

Twenty-First Century

Following Tudjman's death in 1999, Croatia has made slow but steady progress towards becoming a member-in-good-standing of the European community. After years of refusing to turn over some accused war criminals to the International Criminal Tribunal for the Former Yugoslavia (an international court in The Hague, Netherlands, that was set up to try war criminals on all sides of Yugoslavia's 1992–1995 war), Croatia finally began to fully cooperate with the tribunal in 2005. Once Croatia did so, the European Union (EU) agreed to begin formal talks on Croatia's accession to the EU. As of 2007, those talks were still ongoing, but Croatia is expected to become a full EU member around 2009. Croatia has also asked to become a member of NATO.

BIBLIOGRAPHY

Embassy of the Republic of Croatia in the United States. http://us.mfa.hr/ (accessed August 11, 2007).

Goldstein, Ivo. *Croatia: A History.* Montreal: McGill-Queen's University Press, 1999.

Supreme Court of the Republic of Croatia. http://www.vsrh.hr/ (accessed August 11, 2007).

⊕ Slovenia

Type of Government

Slovenia is a parliamentary republic with a bicameral (two-house) parliament that consists of a ninety-seat National Assembly and a forty-seat National Council. Executive power in Slovenia is exercised by the prime minister and the cabinet; the president, who serves as head of state, holds a largely ceremonial position. Slovenia also has an independent court system composed of thirteen regular courts and a separate Constitutional Court.

Background

The original Slovenes, a Slavic tribe, settled in what is modern-day Slovenia during the sixth century AD. In the seventh century the Slovenes formed an independent state named Caratania, but this state fell to the Frankish empire in 745. From that time until World War I Slovenia was ruled over by one or another of the great empires of central Europe, including the Holy Roman Empire and then, after 1278, the Austrian Empire.

Slovenia participated in the Reformation and the Renaissance to a much greater extent than did many other Eastern European countries. This was largely due to its close political ties with Germany (center of the Reformation) and its physical proximity to Italy (center of the Renaissance). The first book to be printed in the Slovene language was published in 1550, and Slovenia began participating in international trade in the seventeenth century. By the late 1700s Slovenia was a prosperous county in which the children of the upper-classes were sent abroad to attend universities and the population was literate enough to support a Slovenian-language newspaper.

As the Slovenian people became more literate, Slovenia began to develop its own national culture. Slovenian scholars wrote histories of Slovenia, writers began composing poetry in the Slovenian language, and Slovenians began thinking of themselves as a nation for the first time. This nationalism extended to the other so-called "South Slav" nations, including the Croats and Serbs, who beginning in the early nineteenth century began thinking of themselves as a common Yugoslav ("South Slav") people. Throughout the nineteenth century the Slovenes agitated against their Austrian rulers and in favor of political self-determination, either on their own or as part of a union of Yugoslav peoples. When the Austro-Hungarian Empire collapsed in the wake of World War I, the Slovenes got their wish: on December 1, 1918, the Kingdom of the Serbs, Croats, and Slovenes was founded. The country was renamed Yugoslavia in 1929.

Slovenia was always an uncomfortable fit in Yugoslavia, which was dominated by the economically less-developed but more numerous Serbs. Slovenians were also hard-hit by the conversion of Yugoslavia into a Communist state following World War II. As the most economically prosperous region of Yugoslavia, Slovenia had the most to lose when businesses were nationalized, the middle class was persecuted, and investment decisions were made based on politics rather than on sound business principles.

Yugoslavia's central government began to weaken in the 1980s, and in 1990 Slovenia began distancing itself from the central government and moving toward democratization and independence. In a free and democratic referendum held on December 23, 1990, 88 percent of Slovenian voters voted to break away from Yugoslavia. The actual declaration of independence came on June 25, 1991.

Slovenian Prime Minister Janez Janša addressing Parliament in February 2005, at a session in which the governing body ratified the European constitution by an overwhelming majority. *Stringer/AFP/Getty Images*

Government Structure

Slovenia has a bicameral parliament. The lower house of the parliament, the National Assembly, has ninety seats; the upper house, the National Council, has forty seats. The members of the National Assembly, who serve four-year terms, are elected by the people. Two seats are reserved to represent members of Slovenia's ethnic Italian and Hungarian communities, and the remaining seats are elected via proportional representation.

The National Council, whose members serve five-year terms, is elected by an electoral college rather than by the people. The National Council is unique in that eighteen of its members are elected specifically to represent certain social and economic groups, rather than to represent specific geographic areas or the country as a whole. Of the forty members of the National Council, four represent employers; four represent employees; four represent farmers, tradespeople, and independent professionals; and six represent specific not-for-profit professions (research, education, universities, health care, social work, and culture and sports). The remaining twenty-two members of the National Council represent traditional geographically based districts. Most legislative power lies

with the National Assembly, with the National Council holding primarily an advisory role.

The prime minister is the head of government in Slovenia and holds the largest share of executive power. The prime minister is elected by the National Assembly after being nominated by the president. The cabinet, which shares executive power with the prime minister, is nominated by the prime minister and then formally elected by the National Assembly.

The president is elected by the people to a five-year term. Presidential elections are held in two rounds. If a single candidate receives more than 50 percent of the vote in the first round, that person is elected, but if no candidate receives a majority in the first round, then the top two finishers from that round go head-to-head in a second round of voting. Presidents can only be reelected to the position once before they must step down. The president is the commander-in-chief of the country's armed forces, but otherwise the position is largely ceremonial.

Slovenia's regular court system consists of eight trial courts, four appeals courts, and the Supreme Court. This court system hears all criminal and civil cases. Slovenia also has a separate Constitutional Court that reviews laws to confirm that they do not conflict with the country's constitution. The judges of the Supreme Court are nominated by the Judicial Council and the judges of the Constitutional Court are nominated by the president, but both types of judges must be confirmed by the National Assembly.

Political Parties and Factions

As of the 2004 parliamentary elections, the Slovenian Democratic Party (SDS) was the largest party in the National Assembly, with twenty-nine out of ninety seats. SDS is a center-right party that is affiliated internationally with the European People's Party, the Centrist Democrat International (formerly the Christian Democrat and People's Parties International), and the International Democratic Union. It was formed from the merger of two previous parties, the Social-Democratic Union of Slovenia and the Slovenian Democratic Union. SDS governs in coalition with two Christian Democratic parties: New Slovenia (which is affiliated internationally with the Centrist Democrat International) and the Slovene People's Party (which is affiliated internationally with the European People's Party).

The Liberal Democratic Party (LDS), which is also known as Liberal Democracy of Slovenia, was the dominant political party in Slovenia from the country's independence in 1991 until 2004. Although LDS suffered a steep loss of support in the 2004 elections, it is still the second-largest party in the National Assembly, with twenty-three seats. LDS is a center-left party that, in its current form, emerged from the 1994 merger of four previous parties: the Liberal-Democratic Party, the Democratic Party, the Socialist Party, and the Green Party. LDS supports individual freedoms and a free market economy, but it also believes in a strong welfare state. The LDS delegation to the European Parliament has joined the centrist Alliance of Liberals and Democrats for Europe (the ALDE Group), and LDS is also a full member of the Liberal International.

The third-largest party in Slovenia is the Social Democrats, a moderately left-wing party. This party began as a coalition of the Party of Democratic Reforms of Slovenia, the Social Democratic Union, the Workers' Party of Slovenia, and the Democratic Party of Pensioners of Slovenia. This coalition, which was called the United List of Social Democrats (known by its Slovene acronym, ZLSD), ran a combined list of candidates in parliamentary elections from 1992 and became a full-fledged party in 1993. (The Democratic Party of Pensioners of Slovenia, however, declined to join the new party in 1993 and remains independent; as of the 2004 parliamentary elections, it held four seats in the National Assembly.) Internationally, the Social Democrats are a full member of the Socialist International and the Party of European Social Democrats.

Another minor party is the Slovene National Party, a populist party that is skeptical of Slovenian integration with Europe and of international institutions such as NATO. As of the 2004 parliamentary elections, this party held six seats in the National Assembly.

Major Events

In the 1990s Slovenia was the sole success story to emerge from the former Yugoslavia. Slovenia separated from Yugoslavia relatively peacefully: It fought a ten-day-long war (from June 26 to July 6, 1991) against the Yugoslav army immediately after its declaration of independence, but this war resulted in fewer than one hundred deaths and relatively little destruction of Slovenian infrastructure. Slovenia quickly recovered from this war and went on to build a well-functioning government and civil society at a time when most of its former Yugoslavian neighbors were still fighting their own wars.

Twenty-First Century

Slovenia's successes have been recognized and rewarded on the world stage: It has been quickly accepted into international organizations that have been hesitant to admit some of the other former Communist countries. Slovenia joined the North Atlantic Treaty Organization (NATO) and the European Union (EU) in 2004; in both cases it was the first of the former Yugoslav countries to do so. Slovenia was also the first post-Communist country to be permitted to adopt the Euro, which it did on January 1, 2007, and on January 1, 2008, Slovenia will become the first post-Communist country to host the rotating presidency of the EU.

BIBLIOGRAPHY

Benson, Leslie. *Yugoslavia: A Concise History*. New York: Palgrave, 2001.
European Forum for Democracy and Solidarity. "Slovenia Update." http://www.europeanforum.net/country/slovenia (accessed August 5, 2007).
The Republic of Slovenia. http://www.gov.si (accessed August 5, 2007).

⊕ Estonia

Type of Government

The Republic of Estonia returned to independence following the 1991 disintegration of the Soviet Union, of which it was a member. Since then it has operated as a parliamentary republic, and many political parties have flourished in the newly democratic climate. Under a 1992 constitution, Estonia's executive branch is headed by the president, prime minister, and cabinet. The president serves as head of state and is elected by the Riigikogu, or parliament, a 101-member body that is directly elected. Estonia's judiciary, headed by the Riigikohus, or National Court, is independent.

Background

Estonia is one of the three Baltic republics located on the eastern coast of the Baltic Sea in northeastern Europe. The country borders another Baltic nation, Latvia, as well as Russia. Its native population of 1.3 million speaks a language related to both Finnish and Hungarian and makes up about 70 percent of Estonia's ethnic mix; the remaining 30 percent are predominantly Russian, Ukrainian, or Belarussians. Because the Estonian language is part of the Finno-Ugric family, historians believe the original inhabitants may have been part of a migratory wave out of an area further east, perhaps between Scandinavia and Russia's Volga River. Present-day Estonia was settled around eleven thousand years ago, and there is evidence of flourishing farming communities from at least the first century AD. In that same century, the people of the area were mentioned in *Germania*, a book written in AD 98 by Roman historian Cornelius Tacitus (c. 56–c. 120), who referred to them as the Aestii and claimed they spoke a language also heard in Britain.

In addition to engaging in agriculture, early Estonian societies were amber traders and were among Europe's final pagan holdouts, converting to Christianity only as a result of the Estonian Crusade of the early 1200s, an effort by a combined force of missionary soldiers from Germany along with some newly converted Lithuanians and Latvians. The modern-day capital, Tallinn, became an important outpost of the Hanseatic League, a confederation of Baltic and North Sea cities established in 1285 to facilitate Northern European trade and commerce. Estonia's strategic location between Germany, Sweden, and Russia led to conquests by all three powers over the next 450 years, and it remained a part of imperial Russia from 1721 until the end of World War I. By that point a growing Estonian nationalist movement had taken root, and independence was declared in February 1918 following the Bolshevik Revolution of 1917 and the overthrow of the Russian czar.

In 1939 the Soviet Union and Nazi Germany signed a treaty of nonaggression containing a secret protocol that sanctioned a Soviet invasion of the Baltic lands. The invasion, which occurred in June 1940, was accompanied by a concentrated effort to abolish anti-Soviet influences through executions that targeted Estonia's political and military leadership; in addition, thousands of ordinary civilians were also deported. The nonaggression pact proved ineffectual, however, and Nazi Germany's armies marched into Estonia in 1941. As the end of World War II neared, the Soviets returned and installed a puppet government of the Estonian Soviet Socialist Republic. By the late 1980s, however, the Soviet Union was undergoing a period of enormous change under new leader Mikhail Gorbachev (1931–), and his reform program served to accelerate the push for independence in the Baltic republics.

The Estonian Popular Front (EPF) was formed in 1988, but its support for a new, independent Estonian republic consisting of all residents—including the large numbers of Russians encouraged to settle there as part of the Soviet Union's postwar "Russification" policy—resulted in the formation of another group, which argued that the pre-1940 republic still technically existed and that the Soviet annexation was unlawful. This second group coalesced with Estonian Citizens' Committees, which began registering all Estonians who were living in the country at the time of the 1940 invasion or their descendants; it also offered Russians and other minority groups a chance to apply for eventual citizenship. The grassroots movement even elected its own legislature, called the Congress of Estonia, in early 1990, which challenged the Estonian Supreme Soviet for power after that legislature was convened with an EPF majority after the republic's first multiparty elections in March 1990. In the midst of the August 1991 coup attempt in Moscow against Gorbachev, the Estonian Supreme Soviet declared the country's independence, but it only formally came into being as a sovereign state with the subsequent dissolution of the Soviet Union later that year.

Government Structure

Estonia operated under its Constitution of 1920 until passage of a referendum on a new governing document, which took place on June 28, 1992. Under the new constitution's terms, Estonia's executive branch is headed by the president, prime minister, and cabinet. The president serves as head of state and is elected by the Riigikogu, or parliament, to a five-year term; he or she may serve no more than two terms. The president has few actual powers but does command the armed forces, represents the country abroad, serves as a peacemaking leader when partisan bickering erupts in the Riigikogu, and appoints the prime minister. This last decision requires a confirmation vote by the Riigikogu, and the prime minister then becomes head of government with the selection of a cabinet of ministers.

Estonia's legislative power is vested in the Riigikogu, a 101-member body whose name is borrowed from a pair of Estonian terms: *riigi*, meaning "of the state," and *kogu*, or "assembly." Its deputies are elected by direct vote to four-year terms and gain their seats by proportional representation, with the highest number of seats given to the political party that received the most votes. Parties must achieve a 5-percent minimum of votes in the legislative elections in order to win any seats in the Riigikogu. In addition to electing the president, the Riigikogu adopts laws, approves a national budget, and may call national referenda.

The Riigikohus (National Court) is the highest court in the land and serves as the final court of appeal for civil and criminal cases as well as a review body to

Independence demonstration in Tallin, Estonia, 1990.   © *Bob Stern/Liaison Agency/Getty Images*

determine if legislation or other acts violate Estonia's constitution. Its nineteen judges are appointed for life and serve in one of a trio of chambers—criminal, civil, or administrative. A constitutional review chamber consists of the chief justice plus eight other justices of the aforementioned three chambers. The chief justice nominates candidates for vacancies on the bench, who are then subject to Riigikogu approval, and also recommends candidates to the president for appointment to benches on the lower courts. These are the circuit courts of appeal and then the rural, city, and administrative courts.

Estonia is divided into fifteen counties called *maakond*, which are further subdivided into *valds*, or "communes," and then 205 rural and 42 urban municipalities. In national elections, only Estonian citizens age eighteen or older may vote, but for local elections all adult residents of the district may cast votes. The lists created by the Citizens' Committees of 1989–90 were later used to determine citizenship, and the 1992 constitution includes a provision for allowing those who were born elsewhere in the Soviet Union but settled in Estonia to attain citizenship relatively easily. Though noncitizens may not hold public office, the constitution specifically states that "the rights, liberties, and duties of everyone and all persons, as listed in the Constitution, shall be equal for Estonian citizens as well as for citizens of foreign states

and stateless persons who are present in Estonia." Local elections may be conducted via the Internet, and in the March 2007 Riigikogu elections Estonia became the first country in the world to permit voters to cast ballots via e-voting. About 30,000 votes out of the 940,000 eligible voters did so.

Political Parties and Factions

Only Estonian citizens can become members of political parties, a rule designed to prevent the rise of a non-Estonian minority in the country which might oppose Estonian sovereignty. Several parties were created in the late 1980s and in the first few years of independence, but as in any new democracy, significant shifts in the parties' popularity and power have occurred. In the first parliamentary elections under the new constitution, the conservative Fatherland Alliance—some of whose members had been persecuted during the Soviet era—won 29 of the 101 seats in the 1992 elections. Three years later that party's hold was ended by the victory of a coalition slate made up of members of several agrarian parties, but the remainder of the decade would see the merging of several parties as a result of local election losses or corruption scandals. The free-market Reform Party and two "fatherland" parties, Pro Patria Union and Res Publica, came to play a leading role in government, and in 2003 the conservative agrarian Peasants' Party formed the Social Democratic Party (SDP) of Estonia with former members of the Moderates Party and People's Party. The Centre Party was the winner of the largest number of Riigikogu seats in the 2007 legislative elections. There are a few pro-Russian parties, such as the Russian Party of Estonia, made up of naturalized Estonian citizens.

Major Events

The last detachment of Russian troops departed Estonian soil in August 1994. Eight years later Estonia joined the North Atlantic Treaty Organization (NATO), the military alliance between the United States and several western European nations formed in 1949 to discourage Soviet aggression in the rest of Europe. In September 2003 Estonians went to the polls to decide whether to join the European Union (EU), and the measure passed with a 66 percent yes vote. Estonia became an EU member nation on May 1, 2004, a jubilant day for many Estonians, who viewed it as the moment their nation finally ended centuries of Russian domination and joined western Europe's liberal democracies.

Twenty-First Century

Estonia's troubles with Russia, however, did not abate entirely in 2004. In early 2007 the Riigikogu passed a measure to move the Bronze Soldier, an immense statue that had dominated a Tallinn park since 1947 and had been an unwanted reminder of Soviet authority for many Estonians. The statue stood over the remains of fourteen Red Army soldiers who died during the 1944 battle to oust the Nazis from Estonia. The Riigikogu plan involved relocating both statue and remains to a military cemetery, but the act enraged many Estonian Russians and prompted protests in Tallinn as well as in Moscow, where Russian right-wing nationalists tried to attack the Estonian ambassador and sang Red Army songs outside the Estonian Embassy for days. Once the statue was dismantled, irate Russian activists attempted to "stand in" for the statue in the park. The incident took a darker, more high-tech turn when several Estonian government Web sites were inundated with traffic and crashed. Some accused the government of Russian President Vladimir Putin (1952–) of orchestrating the attack, but Internet security experts judged the disruptions of service to be the work of renegade hackers instead.

BIBLIOGRAPHY

Lieven, Anatol. *The Baltic Revolution: Estonia, Latvia, Lithuania and the Path to Independence.* New Haven, CT: Yale University Press, 1994.

Smith, David J. *The Baltic States: Estonia, Latvia and Lithuania.* London: Routledge, 2002.

Subrenat, Jean-Jacques. *Estonia: Identity and Independence.* Translated by David Cousins et al. New York: Rodopi, 2004.

⊕ Latvia

Type of Government

After a period of Soviet rule that began in 1940, Latvians quickly seized the opportunity to reassert their sovereignty when Soviet authority disintegrated in 1991. Since then the country has operated as a parliamentary democracy, with a directly elected Saeima, or National Assembly, which elects the president. The president appoints a prime minister, but the choice must be ratified in the Saeima as well.

Background

Nearly 60 percent of Latvia's population of 2.3 million are Latvians, with Russians constituting the largest minority group at 28 percent; the remainder are members of the two other Baltic groups, Estonians and Lithuanians, along with a smattering of Belorussians, Ukrainians, and Poles. The original indigenous inhabitants of this heavily forested area on the Baltic Sea were originally known as Livs and spoke a branch of the Balto-Finnic language group, which includes Finnish and Estonian. Latvians were relative latecomers to Christianity who remained pagan until the early thirteenth-century arrival of an order of German warrior-monks known as the Livonian Brothers of the Sword. In AD 1282 Latvia's Baltic seaport capital, Riga, became part of the powerful Hanseatic League, a trade confederation of Baltic and North Sea cities that would dominate Northern European commerce for the next four centuries. Latvia was part of the Polish-Lithuanian Commonwealth in later medieval times, then subdued by imperial Sweden, and finally came under Russian control in 1710. At the end of World War I in November 1918, Latvian nationalists proclaimed the Republic of Latvia, and the new nation received international recognition—even from Soviet Russia.

Latvia prospered during this interwar era, but the strategic location of the Baltic lands as a buffer zone between Nazi Germany and Soviet Russia brought an end to independent Latvia in June 1940, when the Soviet Red Army invaded. A secret clause in the previous year's German-Soviet Nonaggression Pact sanctioned a Soviet invasion of the Baltic region. A period of appalling political repression began, including the murder or imprisonment of scores of the Latvian military's officer corps and the deportation of civilians to Soviet forced-labor camps. Under a special directive designed to rid the nation of its "anti-Soviet" element, some fifteen thousand Latvians were deported on one night alone in June 1941. After the war the Latvian Soviet Socialist Republic was established, and a policy of "Russification" went into effect that proclaimed Russian as the official language of all government business; the policy also encouraged thousands of ethnic Russians to settle there.

Despite these efforts, homegrown Latvian resistance to Soviet rule remained strong, and it intensified when a new, reform-minded leader of the Soviet Union, Mikhail

Gorbachev (1931–), came to power in 1985. In the summer of 1987 an estimated five thousand people demonstrated in Riga against Soviet rule on the anniversary of the German-Soviet deal, with a similar number gathering in Vilnius, the capital of neighboring Lithuania. The Latvian National Independence Movement and the Latvian Popular Front (LPF) were founded in 1988 and began agitating in earnest for independence.

In March 1990 the first multiparty elections took place for the Latvian Supreme Council; this was the ruling body dominated entirely by Communist Party members until this point. When results of the election were announced, the LPF had won a two-thirds majority of seats. Two months later the Supreme Council approved a resolution that restored the interwar name, the Republic of Latvia, and declared that it would enter into a transitional period of negotiation with the Soviet Union to return the country to its full, pre-1940 sovereignty. The situation remained locked in a stalemate, however, until an August 1991 coup attempt in Moscow by Communist hardliners seeking to oust Gorbachev. Nearly all of the Soviet republics seized the opportunity to declare their independence.

Government Structure

The May 1990 declaration of independence by the Supreme Council also ordered the restoration of several articles of Latvia's original constitution of 1922. The other articles, which were suspended for the time being, were revised and restored in July 1993 by vote of the newly seated Saeima, or parliament, which replaced the Supreme Council after elections in June 1993.

Latvia's 1922 constitution had been modeled on Great Britain's, and its revised version retained the main feature of that system, with parliament playing a key role in the governance of the country. The Saeima's one hundred representatives are elected by direct vote to four-year terms, and the seats are assigned to political parties by proportional representation. Political parties need to receive a 5 percent majority in legislative elections to win any Saeima seats. The executive branch of Latvia's government is embodied in the president, who is elected by the Saeima and is responsible for representing Latvia in foreign affairs and in meetings with leaders of other nations. The president appoints the prime minister, but the chosen candidate must meet with Saeima approval before taking office. The prime minister also holds executive power and appoints a cabinet, called the Council of Ministers. He or she may fire these ministers or even dismiss members of the Saeima, but only the president can dissolve parliament entirely—though the process is risky and can lead to the end of the president's tenure instead.

Latvia's judiciary has a Constitutional Court that reviews legislation and other acts of government and is made up of seven judges appointed by the Saeima. There is also a Supreme Court, which serves as the highest appellate court in the land, and the justices of this bench as well as judges of district and regional courts are also appointed by parliament. All elements of Latvia's judiciary are considered fully independent and free from interference, and the constitution asserts that judges are beholden only to Latvian law. Civil liberties are fully guaranteed by the revised constitution, including the rights to privacy, travel within and outside the borders, and freedom of thought, conscience and religion.

Suffrage in Latvia is universal at the age of eighteen for citizens of Latvia, but the issue of citizenship has been a source of contention since independence in 1991. In the first 1993 parliamentary elections, only those who were citizens before the 1940 invasion or their descendants were allowed to vote, which effectively disenfranchised 34 percent of the voting-age population who were ethnic Russians. In 1994 the Saeima approved passage of a restrictive new law that made it extremely difficult for the seven hundred thousand non-Latvians without "family connections"—meaning those who had married Latvians—to become naturalized citizens. Even ethnic Russians who had been born in Latvia during the Soviet period and had never left were required to meet a nonretroactive residency requirement of sixteen years. Furthermore, the new law included a cap on the annual quota of naturalizations at two thousand. This meant that most Russians who had chosen to remain in Latvia essentially became stateless persons, and they were further incensed by the phasing-out of their language in official business and education, which prompted protests from Moscow that the government in Riga was engaged in human-rights violations. International pressure forced Latvia's government to reconsider the citizenship law, and it was amended in October 1998 after a national referendum. The new requirements reduced the residency period to five years but still required an oath of loyalty and knowledge of the Latvian language.

Latvia is divided into seven cities, sixty-nine towns, and 492 rural administrative divisions. Residents of each elect a local council, and these officials also represent their constituencies at a council for the next level, which are the twenty-six districts known as *rajons* or *aprinki*. The seven municipal districts have their own county level of government as well.

Political Parties and Factions

In the first Saeima elections in 1993, the centrist Latvian Way Union, made up of former Latvian Popular Front (LPF) leaders and newly returned exiles, won a majority of seats and formed a coalition government with the agrarian Farmers' Union party. During the remaining years of the decade, coalition governments and political parties alike disintegrated over partisan bickering and accusations of corruption. An anticorruption party called New Era was founded in 2001 and won twenty-six Saeima seats out of one hundred in the 2002 parliamentary elections. It formed a coalition government with another new

Latvian President Vaira Vike-Freiberga (left) and Prime Minister Einars Repse signing the Accession Treaty for Latvia's admission to the European Union, 2003.   *Virginia Mayo-Pool/Getty Images*

organization, Latvia's First Party, which emphasized traditional family values in its socially conservative platform. In 2006 legislative elections, another conservative group, the People's Party, won twenty-three seats and continued with the coalition government it had forged with the Latvian Greens and the aforementioned Farmers' Union and Latvia's First Party.

Latvian political partisanship is also divided between two camps: nationalist groups and pro-Russian ones. The first group includes a former youth organization called All For Latvia! and the For Fatherland and Freedom Party, which takes its name from Latvia's official motto. The latter party has occasionally been able to form coalition governments with other parties. Parties that support increased political participation for ethnic Russians and non-Latvians include the For Human Rights in a United Latvia Party, which won six seats in the 2006 Saeima balloting,

Major Events

In 1994 U.S. President Bill Clinton helped broker a deal between Latvia and Russia that ended the presence of

Russian troops in Latvia, the final legacy of Soviet rule. The first female president of Latvia, Vaira Vike-Freiberga (1937–), was elected by the Saeima in June 1999 and reelected for another four-year term in 2003. Vike-Freiberga had fled Latvia as a child with her parents during World War II, and they eventually immigrated to Canada where she became a professor of psychology in Montreal and expert in Latvian culture. An immensely popular figure in Latvia, she is one of the few politicians untouched by scandal.

Latvians went to the polls in September 2003 to vote on an important referendum question regarding membership in the European Union (EU). The measure passed with a 66 percent yes vote. Eight months later Latvia became part of the EU's historic 2004 enlargement, which included the two other Baltic republics, Lithuania and Estonia, and other former Soviet satellite states.

Twenty-First Century

Issues with Latvia's Russian minority remain and have occasionally prompted threats of economic reprisals from Moscow. Some neighborhoods of Riga remain populated by elderly Russians who have spent nearly all of their lives there and still do not speak Latvian—nor have any desire to learn it. On the economic front, Latvia's continued financial uncertainties since independence have led to inflation, and until Latvia curbs this, the nation will be unable to adopt the euro, the common EU currency. The country's 2004 entrance in the EU community also had an unexpected secondary effect: some one hundred thousand Latvians left to seek better-paying jobs in western European countries, and the sudden gap in the job market was filled with an influx of illegal Russian workers.

BIBLIOGRAPHY

Eglitis, Daina Stukuls. *Imagining the Nation: History, Modernity, and Revolution in Latvia.* University Park: Pennsylvania State University Press, 2002.

Lieven, Anatol. *The Baltic Revolution: Estonia, Latvia, Lithuania and the Path to Independence.* New Haven, CT: Yale University Press, 1994.

Pabriks, Artis, and Aldis Purs. *Latvia: The Challenges of Change.* New York: Routledge, 2001.

⊕ Ukraine

Type of Government

After centuries of domination by its powerful neighbors, Ukraine achieved independence in 1991 following the break-up of the Soviet Union. Its 1996 constitution provides for an executive branch centered on the president, who holds relatively broad powers. The prime minister serves as head of the government, but the president can dismiss the prime minister or suspend his or her authority temporarily. The legislative branch in Ukraine comprises a unicameral parliament that proposes and adopts laws, authorizes budgets, and appoints judges.

Background

More than three-quarters of Ukraine's population of forty-six million identify themselves as Ukrainian, with ethnic Russians making up the largest of several minority groups at 17 percent. The country borders Russia, Belarus, Poland, Hungary, Slovakia, Moldavia, and Romania, and its capital of Kiev was once the center of the mighty Kievan Rus empire of the early medieval era. After thirteenth-century Mongol invasions, Ukraine was subjugated by the Poles and Lithuanians, but a strong national identity was forged by the Cossacks, the fearsome horsemen who had fled serfdom in Slavic territories elsewhere and settled on the Ukrainian steppes. Decades of tension in the region, however, between Cossacks and neighboring Poles and Tatars led to an alliance with imperial Russia in the seventeenth century that eventually resulted in full annexation.

After the 1917 Bolshevik Revolution that overthrew the Russian czarist government, an attempt by Ukrainian nationalists to establish an independent state failed, and once again the area was co-opted by Russian masters, this time as the Ukrainian Soviet Socialist Republic. In the early 1930s Ukrainian farmers resisted the Soviet policy of forced collectivization, and the standoff led to a massive famine in which an estimated two to five million Ukrainians starved to death. More casualties were suffered during World War II, when the region became a battlefield between Soviet forces and Nazi German armies.

An explosion at the Chernobyl nuclear power plant, near the city of Pripyat, in April 1986 was a devastating environmental disaster for Ukraine and the worst nuclear accident in world history. The catastrophe intensified the still-active Ukrainian nationalist movement, and independence activism was furthered by the formation of a new organization known by its acronym Rukh, for "People's Movement of Ukraine." This dovetailed with reforms implemented by the Soviet leader Mikhail Gorbachev (1931–) throughout the Soviet Union, and Rukh candidates won several seats in the Ukrainian Supreme Soviet in the first multiparty elections held in Ukraine in March 1990. In July 1990 the newly seated Supreme Soviet issued a Declaration of State Sovereignty of Ukraine, claiming that local authority now superseded that of Moscow. The situation remained at a stalemate until August 1991, when Communist Party hardliners in Moscow attempted to stage a coup against Gorbachev that quickly collapsed and resulted in several of the constituent republics immediately declaring independence. On December 1, 1991, a referendum on Ukrainian independence was overwhelmingly approved with more than 90 percent of votes cast in favor.

Government Structure

Ukraine's constitution was adopted in June 1996, making it the last of the former Soviet republics to implement one; prior to this it abided by the terms of a 1978 constitution to which significant amendments had been made. Ukraine is divided into twenty-four oblasts, or provinces, two urban districts for Kiev and Sevastopol, and the Autonomous Republic of Crimea. Suffrage is universal at the age of eighteen.

The president is the head of state, and elected by direct vote to a five-year term and limited to two of these. A prime minister serves as head of the government, but the president can dismiss the prime minister or suspend his or her authority temporarily. The president also has the power to dissolve parliament under certain conditions.

Ukraine's legislative branch is its parliament, the Verkhovna Rada. Its name is a mix of Russian and Ukrainian: *verkhovna* is an adjective meaning "supreme" in Russian, while *rada* is a Ukrainian term for "council" and related to the Latin term *ratio*. The unicameral body consists of 450 deputies who are elected to four-year terms. An amendment in 2005 altered the system of seat allocation, revising it to assign all of the Rada seats to parties that received more than 3 percent of the vote in the parliamentary elections, and parceled out according to the proportion of votes won by each party. In the previous arrangement, half of the seats were allocated in this way, with the other 225 seats given to the winning candidates in individual constituencies. Duties of the Rada include establishing foreign and domestic policy, introducing constitutional amendments, and approving the state budget; the 2005 amendment package also gave it the power to appoint the prime minister and cabinet.

The judicial branch of Ukraine's government is not entirely independent, and is under the supervision of the Ministry of Justice. At the top is a Supreme Court, which serves as the final court of appeal for the system of local and appellate courts below it; its judges are appointed by the Rada, and there is no fixed number for this bench. A Constitutional Court is charged with reviewing legislation passed by parliament. A third of its eighteen judges are appointed by parliament, another third by the president, and the remaining six by a congress of judges convened for the purpose.

Political Parties and Factions

Ukrainian politics are divided between pro-Western reformers and those who advocate closer ties with Russia, a battle shaped by geography: a palpable enmity exists between the eastern oblasts, where the majority of Russian speakers live, and more fiercely nationalist provinces that border Europe. In the earliest years of independence, the Communist Party dominated politics, but in the 2002 parliamentary elections a new coalition emerged and bypassed them for the majority lead in Rada seats. The newcomer was Nasha Ukrayina (Our Ukraine), an opposition group led by Viktor Yushchenko (1954–), a respected economist and onetime head of the National Bank of Ukraine who had until recently served as prime minister. Yushchenko had been appointed to that post by President Leonid Kuchma (1938–), but Our Ukraine was aimed at unseating the increasingly autocratic president.

On the other side of the political spectrum, the Party of Regions culls its support from ethnic Russians and former Communist Party supporters. It was founded in 2001 by Viktor Yanukovych (1950–), and emerged as the majority leader in 2006 parliamentary elections. In that contest, the second biggest winner was the Yulia Tymoshenko Bloc. Yulia Tymoshenko (1960–) is an entrepreneur often described in international media reports as one of the more compelling personalities of twenty-first century European politics. Famously rich and formidably brilliant, Tymoshenko was head of the Batkivshchina Party, also known as the All-Ukrainian Union "Fatherland" Party, and had earlier allied with Yushchenko and served as prime minister. Her career in government, however, has been dogged by accusations of political maneuvering and conflicts of interest due to her ties to the natural gas industry.

Major Events

Ukrainians went to the polls on December 1, 1991, to vote in the first free presidential elections, and chose Leonid Kravchuk (1934–), a reformed communist who supported independence. He lost his 1994 re-election bid amid a faltering economy and accusations of widespread government corruption. Kuchma, his successor, was reelected in 1999 and won permission to stand for a third term from the Constitutional Court, which agreed with his petition that the two-term limit did not apply because Kuchma's first win came in 1994, two years before Ukraine's constitution went into effect. That was one of several controversial maneuvers by Kuchma, whose government failed to stem corruption among officials and then began to restrict the activities of its political opponents.

In November 2000, Kuchma was accused of orchestrating the murder of journalist Georgiy Gongadze (1969–2000), whose decapitated body had just been found after a two-month-long mystery surrounding his disappearance. Audio recordings made secretly in Kuchma's office seemed to implicate him in the Gongadze case and other criminal activities, and prompted months of public protests in Kiev under the banner of "UBK"— the Ukrainian-language acronym for "Ukraine without Kuchma." Despite the scandal, Kuchma refused to step down, and instead allied with Russian President Vladimir Putin (1952–), but his third term was due to expire at the end of 2004. His heir-apparent in the 2004 presidential race was Yanukovych, the prime minister, a choice said to have been endorsed by Putin. Yushchenko, the Our Ukraine founder, ran as an independent candidate.

On September 21, 2004, Yushchenko spoke before a stunned audience of his Verkhovna Rada colleagues, his face ravaged by cysts. He said he had been poisoned a few weeks earlier, and medical tests conducted outside the country pointed to dioxin, a byproduct of pesticide manufacturing known for its extreme toxicity. He dated the onset of his illness to the hours following a dinner meeting with the chief of the Security Service of Ukraine (SBU), or secret police; Russian secret-police involvement was widely suspected as well, but never proven. On October 31, Yushchenko won 39.87 percent of the vote, with Yanukovych polling 39.32. Because a 50 percent margin was necessary for a candidate to win office, a run-off vote took place on November 21, but was marked by blatant irregularities at polling stations and reports of voter intimidation. The exit polls had

Victor Yushchenko being sworn in as Ukraine's president in January 2005 after leading the Orange Revolution. *Gleb Garanich/ AFP/Getty Images*

predicted a strong margin of victory for Yushchenko, but instead the official results gave Yanukovych the victory by three percentage points.

Pro-Yushchenko groups had already begun gathering in Kiev on Election Day, and as the results were broadcast their numbers swelled and reached 500,000 within two days. Similar demonstrations amassed in other cities, and became known as the Orange Revolution, with supporters of Yushchenko borrowing his campaign advertising color, orange, to show their support. The situation remained deadlocked, with parliament passing a no-confidence vote, which should have forced the resignation of Yanukovych's government but did not. On December 3, the Supreme Court reviewed the election results and found enough evidence of fraud to declare the results null. It ordered another run-off to be held on December 26, which Yushchenko won by eight percentage points in a closely monitored race. He was inaugurated on January 23, 2005. In an unusual twist, the head of the SBU—one of the possible culprits in the Yushchenko dioxin poisoning—was said to have issued a crucial recommendation to restrain government troops

during the heat of the protests, which averted bloodshed. Senior officials in that organization and among the military were allegedly unhappy with Moscow's interference in Ukrainian politics as well as the choice of Yanukovych, who had served time in prison for robbery as a young man.

Twenty-First Century

Ukraine's political drama did not end with Yushchenko's inauguration. Later that year, he dismissed Tymoshenko as prime minister, but she soon emerged as a serious rival to him. Another surprise came in 2006 parliamentary elections, which resulted in a solid win for Yanukovych and his Party of Regions. The Rada then appointed Yanukovych as prime minister, which provoked a months-long power struggle between the president and parliament. Finally, Yushchenko dismissed the Rada in the spring of 2007 and called for new legislative elections. Observers note that Ukraine teeters between two ideological spheres: the rigid authoritarianism of Russia under Putin and the liberal-democratic ideals of the European Union (EU) countries. Yushchenko's 2004 campaign pledges included support for Ukraine's application to join the EU, which forces its member nations to abide by stringent democratic and human-rights principles.

BIBLIOGRAPHY

Åslund, Anders, Michael McFaul, editors. *Revolution in Orange: The Origins of Ukraine's Democratic Breakthrough.* Washington, DC: Carnegie Endowment for International Peace, 2006.

Whitmore, Sarah. *State Building in Ukraine: The Ukrainian Parliament, 1990–2003.* London: Routledge, 2004.

Wilson, Andrew. *The Ukrainians: Unexpected Nation.* New Haven, CT: Yale University Press, 2002.

⊕ Belarus

Type of Government

Belarus, which gained independence from the Soviet Union in 1991, is a republic whose government is structured like many other republics, with an executive branch headed by a president elected by popular vote, a bicameral (two-chamber) legislature, and a judicial branch led by a Supreme Court. Belarus, however, retains many of the characteristics of an authoritarian socialist regime. Its longtime leader, Aleksandr Lukashenko (1954–), has flouted and even altered the Belarus constitution since coming to power in 1994 and is often described as Europe's last dictator.

Background

Situated at the far end of Eastern Europe, Belarus—which means "White Russia" in most of the Slavic languages—shares borders with Poland, Ukraine, Russia,

Lithuania, and Latvia. Just over three-quarters of its population of 9.7 million identify themselves as Belarusian, and another 13 percent are ethnic Russians; most of the remainder are either Poles or Ukrainians. The original inhabitants of Belarus, a mixture of Baltic and Slavic peoples, came under the rule of the princes of Kievan Rus, who conquered what was known as the principality of Polatsk around 980. In the mid-thirteenth century Belarus became part of the Grand Duchy of Lithuania, a sizable empire that included the Baltic territories, part of Poland, and much of Ukraine.

In 1772 Belarus was annexed by Russia, a turn of events aided by a predominantly Russian Orthodox Belarusian population who had long resented the domination of a landowning class of Polish Catholic extraction. Belarusian nationalism surfaced in the latter half of the nineteenth century, propelled by a movement to establish a formal Belarusian-language grammar and literary tradition. In the final months of World War I, Belarusian nationalists proclaimed an independent Republic of Belarus on March 25, 1918, but less than a year later Red Army troops from the new Soviet Russia invaded the Belarus capital, Minsk. The area remained part of the Soviet Union as the Belarusian Soviet Socialist Republic (BSSR) until 1991.

In 1988 a mass grave was uncovered near Minsk containing the remains of some one hundred thousand victims of a Soviet or Nazi atrocity during World War II. The shocking discovery helped renew nationalist fervor, and the Belarusian Popular Front (BPF) came into being in October 1988 under the leadership of Zianon Pazniak (1944–), the researcher who had played a large role in publicizing the grave's discovery. By then a new, reform-minded Soviet leader, Mikhail Gorbachev (1931–), had risen to power in Moscow, and multiparty elections were held for the first time in the Soviet republics in 1990. Belarus's election for deputies to its Supreme Soviet took place in March of that year, and in July 1990 the newly seated Supreme Soviet issued a Declaration of State Sovereignty of the Belarusian Soviet Socialist Republic. Full sovereignty came a year later in the wake of an attempted coup in Moscow by Communist Party hardliners in August 1991.

Government Structure

The Republic of Belarus's constitution was adopted in 1994 and significantly amended twice in referenda that failed to meet international standards for free and fair voting. It provides for an executive branch with a president elected by popular vote to what was originally a five-year term, with a two-term limit imposed. The president serves as head of state and appoints a prime minister who is the head of the government. The president also appoints a cabinet. In 1996 a constitutional referendum was held and its proposed amendments passed; these gave the office of president far greater power and

Belarus President Alexander Lukashenko (right) with Russian President Vladimir Putin in December 2006. *Dmitry Astakhov/AFP/ Getty Images*

extended the term of incumbent Aleksandr Lukashenko until 2001, though the vote was denounced as fraudulent. One of the amendments created an upper house of the legislature and restricted the entire National Assembly to two sessions yearly, not to exceed 170 days in total. Furthermore, the new amendment granted the president the power to rule by decree when the National Assembly was not in session. A 2004 referendum that ended presidential term limits also passed by a wide but suspect margin of yes votes.

The two houses of the Belarus National Assembly are the Council of the Republic, the upper house, and a lower body called the Chamber of Representatives. The upper house has sixty-four members who serve four-year terms. Eight of them are appointed by the president, while regional councils for the country's seven administrative divisions each chose eight deputies. The Council is charged with enacting laws, approving the national budget, and carrying out foreign-policy directives. The lower house of the National Assembly has 110 members who are elected to four-year terms by direct vote from single-member constituencies.

The judiciary of Belarus remains closely allied with the executive branch. A Constitutional Court exists for judicial review of legislation, with half of its judges appointed by the president and the other half by the

Chamber of Representatives; all serve eleven-year terms. After the sham 1996 constitutional referendum, seven of the Constitutional Court judges resigned in protest and were replaced by Lukashenko with political supporters. Belarus also has a Supreme Court, which serves as the highest court of appeal in the land and has consistently sided with the Lukashenko government in its decisions. One example of this has been the president's crackdown on international human rights organizations in Belarus, with the Supreme Court ordering the confiscation of some of these groups' equipment and assets.

Civil liberties in Belarus are virtually nonexistent. Lukashenko's government regularly shuts down independent newspapers, compels journalists to receive state accreditation in order to work, and monitors all religious groups. Criticism of the government is forbidden by law, and arbitrary arrest and detention at the hands of the state security apparatus—which still bears its Soviet-era name, shortened to acronym form as KGB—serves to keep journalists, opposition leaders, and even ordinary citizens fearful. Telephone conversations, both landline and wireless, are monitored, and private mail is opened. Belarusian citizens are required to carry internal passports, and changes of residency are difficult to obtain. Along with Albania, Belarus is one of the two remaining European nations whose statutes still include the death penalty.

Organizing a public protest can be construed as a criminal offense in Belarus, and those convicted face a minimum three-year jail term. Prison conditions are said to be abysmal, and tuberculosis outbreaks have occurred due to overcrowding from an unusually large number of political detainees, who may be held without trial indefinitely. Some of Lukashenko's political opponents have simply vanished, most notably in the 1999 disappearances of Yuryy Zakharanka, once the Minister of Internal Affairs, and Viktar Hanchar, former head of the Central Election Commission.

Political Parties and Factions

Belarus has multiparty elections, but the Central Election Commission, staffed by Lukashenko loyalists, consistently rejects the ballot-registration applications of opposition candidates, and the majority of seats in the National Assembly are held by independent candidates who are Lukashenko supporters. The Belarusian Popular Front (BPF), founded in 1988, renamed itself the Partyja BNF and joined several other political parties to mount an organized opposition to Lukashenko as People's Coalition 5 Plus in the 2004 legislative elections; the group failed to win any seats in a contest denounced as blatantly manipulated by the Lukashenko government.

A year later members of the Coalition 5 Plus became United Democratic Forces of Belarus in preparation for the March 2006 presidential election. In that race Aleksandr Milinkevich (1947–) was Lukashenko's main chal-

lenger, but the incumbent won with 82 percent of the vote in balloting that was marked by fraud once again. Crowds in Minsk jeered in the public square as large-screen televisions broadcast the official results, which gave Milinkevich just six percent of the popular vote. The opposition leader spoke before the crowd and was later arrested for participating in what was termed an unauthorized rally.

There are some active underground groups in Belarus, most notably the youth group Zubr (Bison), which operates under conditions of extreme secrecy. It attempts to stage small protest events on the sixteenth day of every month, which commemorates September 16, 1999, the date of Viktar Hanchar's disappearance. Slavic specialists note, however, that Lukashenko does have a solid support base among rural and older voters, citing the heavy losses the country suffered in World War II that seem to make many older Belarusians uneasy with political change.

Major Events

Three months after Belarus declared its independence in August 1991, it became one of the three founding members of the Commonwealth of Independent States (CIS), along with Russia and Ukraine. At the time, Stanislav Shushkevich (1934–) was chair of the Supreme Soviet and acting president, but a 1993 no-confidence vote forced him out of office after he was accused of corruption. In March 1994 Belarus's new constitution went into effect, which replaced the Supreme Soviet with a National Assembly and provided for a directly elected president. Lukashenko ran as the anticorruption candidate and won by a vote that was judged to be fair. However, he soon began using questionable means to consolidate his power.

The November 1996 referendum marked the most significant turning point for Belarus's young democracy. As controversy flared prior to the vote, Lukashenko fired the head of the until-then independent Central Election Commission, and on the day of the referendum the building that housed its offices was surrounded by government troops. The official results were denounced as fraudulent by Lukashenko's political opponents in the National Assembly, who earlier that year had signed a petition threatening him with impeachment for violating the constitution. After the questionable results of the November balloting, Lukashenko summarily dissolved the Assembly and replaced those who refused to withdraw their name from the impeachment petition with handpicked loyalists. Similarly, the president informed the judges of the Constitutional Court that they could remain on the bench if they refrained from choosing sides in the matter.

Twenty-First Century

Basic human rights and efforts to bring peaceful political change in Belarus are so broadly disregarded by the government that outsiders have given it the dubious place of honor as Europe's last dictatorship. Lukashenko has asserted that he rules with the support of the people, and a superficial addressing of issues takes place every five years at the All-Belarusian People's Assembly, a general meeting similar to the Soviet-era Communist Party congresses in which twenty-five hundred government officials and handpicked supporters discuss the state of the nation. Lukashenko was the keynote speaker at the 2006 People's Assembly; he trumpeted the economic successes of the past few years and urged Belarusians to adopt a healthier lifestyle by exercising regularly and cutting down on evening snacks.

Belarus enjoys occasionally tense but mostly cordial relations with Moscow. In 1999 the nation signed the Treaty of Creation with Russia, a document declaring an official intent to establish a Union of Russia and Belarus. A major obstacle remains Belarus's continued reliance on a Soviet-style centralized economy, despite the urging of Russian president Vladimir Putin (1952–) to adopt free-market reforms. Extreme-right nationalist groups in Russia have even voiced support for Lukashenko's candidacy in the 2008 Russian presidential election.

BIBLIOGRAPHY

Korosteleva, Elena A., Rosalind J. Marsh, and Colin W. Lawson. *Contemporary Belarus: Between Democracy and Dictatorship*. London: Routledge, 2003.

Marples, David R. *Belarus: A Denationalized Nation*. Amsterdam: Harwood Academic, 1999.

White, Stephen, Elena Korosteleva, and John Löwenhardt, editors. *Postcommunist Belarus*. New York: Rowman & Littlefield, 2005.

⊕ Moldova

Type of Government

Moldova is a parliamentary republic with a unicameral (one-house) parliament that is elected by the people. The country also has a president, who is elected by the parliament; a prime minister, who is nominated by the president and confirmed by the parliament; and a cabinet, which is nominated by the prime minister and confirmed by the parliament.

Background

The history of Moldova is closely tied to the history of its western neighbor, Romania. From early in the first century AD, when troops from the Roman Empire occupied what is today Romania and Moldova, until 1947, when Moldova became a part of the Soviet Union, Moldova was almost always considered a part of the Romanian lands. In the twenty-first century, Moldova's approximately four million people are still primarily ethnic Romanians, and they still speak the Romanian language.

Moldova was originally part of Moldavia, one of two Romanian states that broke away from the Hungarian Empire in 1360. However, Moldavia was a small, poor, isolated state that was unable to maintain its independence for long. Late in the fourteenth century the Ottoman Empire, centered in what is modern-day Turkey, began expanding into Europe, and by the late fifteenth century the Ottomans had turned their sights on Moldavia. Stephan IV (1435–1504; known as Stephan the Great) ruled Moldavia at that time, and under his leadership the Moldavians fought fiercely to protect their country. The Ottomans were unable to conquer Moldavia in Stephan's lifetime, but not long after Stephen died, his son, Bogdan III the One-Eyed, was forced to admit defeat and sign an agreement making Moldavia a vassal (subject) of the Ottoman Empire.

In the early eighteenth century Moldavia found itself in an unenviable position, situated between two great empires: the Ottomans to the south and the Russians to the northeast. Moldavia was still subject to the Ottomans, but the strengthening Russian Empire saw the possibility of prying Moldavia away from a weakening Ottoman Empire. The Russians invaded Moldavia for the first time in 1711, returning several more times in the next century. Finally, in 1812, Russia permanently occupied the part of Moldavia then known as Bessarabia (the eastern half of the country, which lay east of the Prut River) and incorporated it into Russia. Bessarabia, along with neighboring territory known as Transnistria, later became known as Moldova.

Romania gained Bessarabia back in 1918, during World War I, but this reunion of ethnic Romanians proved short-lived. The Soviet Union occupied Bessarabia in June 1940, near the beginning of World War II, and renamed it the Moldavian Soviet Socialist Republic. Romania, which was allied with Nazi Germany, briefly managed to win Moldova back, but by 1944 the Romanians had been driven out and Moldova was left in the Soviets' hands.

Moldova's ethnic Romanian population was oppressed under Soviet rule. The Soviet Union forced Moldovans to write their language in the Cyrillic alphabet (which is used for Russian and other Slavic languages), rather than the Latin alphabet. It encouraged ethnic Russians to move into the Moldavian Soviet Socialist Republic (SSR), and then gave those Russians leadership positions over the ethnic Romanians. Moldovans also faced the typical hardships of life under Communist rule. One such hardship was collectivization, in which family farms were taken by the state and turned into large collective farms, with farmers then forced to work for the state. Moldovans also had to worry about being deported to another part of the Soviet Union if they spoke out against collectivization or Soviet rule; tens of thousands of Moldovans were sent to Kazakhstan under this policy.

Russian (left), Moldovan (center), and Transnistrian (right) soldiers guarding the security zone between Moldova and the unrecognized Republic of Transnistria, by the Dniestr River.   *Yoray Liberman/Getty Images*

In the late 1980s the Soviet Union began relaxing some of the restrictions on free speech within its republics. In the Moldovan SSR the people took advantage of this freedom to speak out in favor of greater rights for ethnic Romanians. In 1989 the Moldovan Popular Front was formed to advance this cause, and in 1990 the Popular Front ran in the first democratic elections for the lower house of the Soviet legislature. The Popular Front won. On August 27, 1991, Moldova declared its independence from the collapsing Soviet Union.

Government Structure

Moldova adopted its first post-Communist constitution in 1994 and then passed several amendments changing the structure of the government in 2000. The 1994 constitution created a unicameral parliament with 101 seats. Representatives are elected by the entire country (not a single state or district, as in the U.S. Congress) and are elected via a party-list system. In this type of election, voters vote for parties rather than individual candidates, and seats in the parliament are distributed to the parties based on the percentage of the vote that they received. Before the election each party creates a ranked list of candidates. After the votes are counted and the seats are assigned to the parties, the first candidate

on the list receives the party's first seat in the parliament, the second receives the second seat, and on down the list until all of the party's seats are filled.

Under Moldova's 1994 constitution the president was elected directly by the people, but the 2000 amendments scrapped that system. The president is now elected by the parliament. The president then nominates a prime minister, who assembles a cabinet. The parliament must vote to accept both the prime minister and his or her cabinet before they can take office.

In Moldova the regular court system is separate from the Constitutional Court. The Constitutional Court is responsible for determining if laws contradict the Moldovan constitution and for ensuring that the other branches of the Moldovan government do not take any actions that violate the constitution. The six judges of this court are appointed to six-year terms and are politically independent. The regular judicial system, which is responsible for hearing criminal and civil cases, is capped by a Supreme Court that is the highest appeals court in the country.

Local governments have had little independent power in Moldova since 2002. That year the recently elected Communist-led government passed a law eliminating the existing ten local government districts and replacing them with thirty-two smaller districts, called *raions*, that are largely controlled by the national government. Mayors and local councils are still elected by the people, but they are dependent upon funding from the national government. This method of funding makes it very difficult for local governments to carry out policies of which the national government disapproves.

Political Parties and Factions

The three major political parties in Moldova are the Communists, the Democratic Moldova Bloc, and the Popular Christian Democratic Party. The Communists, who have controlled the government since 2001, are Communist in name only: the party favors closer ties with the European Union and the United States, and it has taken some small steps to free the Moldovan economy. The Democratic Moldova Bloc is a centrist party that wants to improve Moldova's relationships with both Russia and Europe. The Popular Christian Democratic Party is a right-wing party that wants Moldova to strengthen its ties to Romania.

Major Events

When the Soviets created the Moldavian SSR, they combined two territories with very different populations—Bessarabia, populated by ethnic Romanians, and Transnistria, a small strip of land that had formerly belonged to Ukraine and that was populated by ethnic Ukrainians. As the Soviet Union collapsed in the early 1990s, the Ukrainian and Russian residents of the Moldavian SSR feared that they would soon find themselves an oppressed minority in an ethnic Romanian-dominated country. In 1990 they formed their own breakaway country in Transnistria.

The Moldovans and Transnistrians fought a brief civil war in 1992 when Moldova tried to reassert its control over the area. The fighting stopped when the Russian army intervened to drive the Moldovans out of Transnistria. Russia calls these troops—who remain in Transnistria as of 2007—peacekeepers, but Moldovans consider them an occupying force and a serious threat. Transnistria is still technically considered to be a part of Moldova, but in reality the Moldovan government has no control over the area. There have been periodic negotiations between Moldova and Transnistria over the years in an attempt to reach an agreement on the status of Transnistria, but no settlement has yet been reached.

Twenty-First Century

Moldova is still the poorest country in Europe, with a high unemployment rate and a large number of its citizens living and working outside the country. At the beginning of the twenty-first century much of the population of Moldova survived as subsistence farmers, living almost entirely on the food that they grew for themselves and earning little or no cash income. Voters

felt frustrated over the collapse in Moldova's economy between 1991 and 2001: During that period the average Moldovan went from earning around $2,000 per year to around $200 per year. This frustration helped to propel the Moldovan Communist Party to a series of electoral victories, as people longed for a return to the relative prosperity and steady paychecks of Moldova's Communist past. The Communists held 70 percent of the seats in the parliament from 2001 to 2005 and won fifty-six seats in the 2005 elections. However, the twenty-first-century Communist party has evolved into something very different from its twentieth-century ancestor. The Communists came to power in 2001 calling for closer ties with Russia, but they have since become suspicious of Russian interference in Moldova and have worked to develop friendlier relations with the European Union and the United States, both of which are attempting to help Moldova economically and politically.

BIBLIOGRAPHY

Fedor, Helen, ed. *Moldova: A Country Study*. Washington, DC: Federal Research Division, Library of Congress, 1995.

Freedom House. "Country Report: Moldova." http://www.freedomhouse.org/template.cfm?page=22&country=7232&year=2007 (accessed August 8, 2007).

King, Charles *The Moldovans: Romania, Russia, and the Politics of Culture*. Stanford, CA: Hoover Institution Press, 2000.

⊕ Kyrgyzstan

Type of Government

Kyrgyzstan, sometimes referred to as the Kyrgyz Republic, was the first among the Soviet Union's Central Asian republics to establish genuine democratic institutions in its swift transition to independence in the early 1990s. Nevertheless, that hopeful start dissolved into authoritarian rule after the first presidential elections, and each of Kyrgyzstan's two successive leaders quickly abandoned the promises of democratic reforms with which he gained public support, reverting instead to Soviet-style totalitarianism.

Background

Kyrgyzstan's name translates as "the land of forty clans" in the Kyrgyz language. The country shares borders with China, Uzbekistan, Tajikistan, and Kazakhstan, and just over half of its population of 5.2 million are ethnic Kyrgyz; other groups include Russians, Uzbeks, Ukrainians, and Germans. The Kyrgyz were once known as the Kara, or black Kyrgyz, to differentiate them from nearby Kazakhs, who are also a Turkic people. Ancient Kyrgyz are believed to have migrated southward from the Yenisey River area of Siberia, near Mongolia, and

Chinese accounts from the seventh to twelfth centuries described them as having red hair, fair skin, and green eyes. They battled with the Uighurs for domination of an area just east of China's Tian Shan mountain range, were subdued by Mongol invasions in the early thirteenth century, and after 1685 were ruled by another Mongolian group, the Kalmyks. Later the area came under the authority of the Khanate of Qŭqon (or Kokand), along with neighboring Uzbekistan, Tajikistan, and Kazakhstan.

Russian incursions into the area began in the 1850s, and by 1876 present-day Kyrgyzstan was entirely annexed by Imperial Russia. Resistance to European rule continued, however, and peaked with a 1916 uprising against military conscription. After the 1917 Bolshevik Revolution in Russia that overthrew the czar, the Kyrgyz took sides in the civil war that soon erupted, joining the anti-Bolshevik factions. Once Soviet authority was established again in Central Asia by the early 1920s, the Kara-Kirghiz Autonomous Oblast was created inside the Russian Soviet Federated Socialist Republic, and some half-million Kyrgyz died from war-related famine. In 1936 Kyrgyzstan became a constituent Soviet republic and was renamed the Kirghiz Soviet Socialist Republic; it existed as a part of the Soviet Union until 1990.

Like other constituent Soviet republics, Kyrgyzstan seized the opportunities created by internal dissent after Soviet leader Mikhail Gorbachev (1931–) came to power in 1985 and initiated sweeping reforms. The Kyrgyzstan Democratic Movement (KDM) was formed, and the country achieved full independence after the collapse of the Soviet Union following an August 1991 coup attempt in Moscow. The first presidential election took place two months later, but neither of the two candidates received a majority of the vote, and so the deputies of the Supreme Soviet—still the central government authority—selected Askar Akayev (1944–), the president of the Kyrghiz Academy of Sciences, to become the first president of Kyrgyzstan.

Government Structure

Kyrgyzstan's new constitution was signed into law by its president, Kurmanbek Bakiyev (1949–), on January 15, 2007, but does not take effect until 2010. Until then, the Kyrgyzstan Constitution of May 1993 remains in effect.

Under the 1993 constitution, Kyrgyzstan has a semipresidential system with a strong executive branch. The president serves as both head of state and head of government, and appoints the prime minister and a cabinet. The president is elected by direct vote to a five-year term, and is limited to two terms in office. Akayev, however, the country's first postindependence president, was able to remain in power for nearly fifteen years (from October 1990 to March 2005), thanks to constitutional amendments passed by national referenda of questionable legal validity.

From 1996 to 2005 Kyrgyzstan had a bicameral (two-house) legislature, with a seventy-member Assembly of People's Representatives and a thirty-five-member Legislative Assembly, both elected by direct vote to five-year terms. In 2005 the legislature reverted to its original unicameral (one-house) form as the Jogorku Kenesh, or Supreme Council, with 75 deputies still elected by direct vote to five-year terms. Since 2005 the Supreme Council has been engaged in a long and protracted power struggle over presidential power.

Kyrgyzstan's judiciary is not fully independent. Its Supreme Court justices serve ten-year terms and are technically appointed by the legislature, but come from a list of candidates recommended by the president. The judges are said to be easily swayed by cash payments or other forms of bribes, as are the members of the Constitutional Court, who are appointed to fifteen-year terms in similar fashion. The president also has the power to remove regional and municipal judges.

Kyrgyzstan is divided into seven administrative oblasts (political subdivisions) plus one for the capital, Bishkek.

Political Parties and Factions

Despite its authoritarian characteristics, Kyrgyzstan is a multiparty democracy with several active political organizations, but there is a 1999 law that gives the government the right to ban a political party on grounds of national security. Opposition to the president has centered around Feliks Kulov (1948–), founder of the Ar-Namys (Dignity) Party in 1999. Kulov was later jailed on a corruption charge stemming from his stint as minister of the interior, and sentenced to seven years in prison. Bakiyev, a former factory manager who became politically active in the post-Soviet era, served as prime minister in the Akayev government for several months between 2001 and 2002; in 2004 he formed the People's Movement of Kyrgyzstan, a coalition of anti-Akayev groups planning to mount a challenge in the coming 2005 parliamentary elections. Kulov was released by Bakiyev during a 2005 pro-democracy uprising, appointed prime minister, and then resigned in protest in December 2006 over Bakiyev's sudden turn to authoritarianism. Two months later, Kulov founded a new opposition group, the United Front for a Worthy Future for Kyrgyzstan.

Major Events

Kyrgyzstan's political atmosphere since achieving independence has been a troubled one, and while many of its parliamentary, presidential, and constitutional-referenda elections have been flawed, a few have been conducted under relatively fair terms, and in no way is the country blighted by the human rights crimes that take place in other Central Asian countries, most notably those in Turkmenistan. That said, corruption and interference by the government in the democratic process have

Protesters seizing government buildings in Bishkek, Krygyzstan, in the Tulip Revolution of March 2005.   © *Vasily Shaposhnikov/Kommersant/ Zuma/Corbis*

consistently interrupted Kyrgyzstan's path to stability. A 1993 corruption scandal prompted Akayev to dismiss his government, and the battle that ensued culminated in a boycotting of parliament a year later, which resulted in an invalid quorum for its final session. The crisis spurred Akayev into pushing through a constitutional referendum held in October 1994 for two amendments: one that created a bicameral parliament to replace the 350-member chamber that had been unable to come to agreement on several major issues, and a second that allowed for constitutional change by national referendum. Both passed with a nearly 75 percent yes vote.

The 1995 parliamentary elections, and then those in 2000, contained serious irregularities. By 1996 there were calls for Akayev to step down amid charges of widespread government corruption, but instead he pushed for a February 1996 referendum that was in itself considered unconstitutional. The proposed amendments passed, and included one that added to the powers of president—including the right to dissolve parliament—but it also granted parliament some additional powers, which it began to exercise almost immediately, and the resulting power struggle endured for the next decade. Opposition to Akayev grew, especially after a 2000 deci-

sion of the Constitutional Court allowing him to stand for election for a third term on the grounds that his first term technically began in 1995 because Kyrgyzstan's constitution did not go into effect until 1993.

Parliamentary elections held in February 2005 were once again denounced as fraudulent, and this time, just weeks after a successful, peaceful conclusion of protests in Ukraine, many in Kyrgyzstan took to the streets in large numbers to protest the official results. The demonstrations became known as the Tulip Revolution. By late March, protesters controlled two cities in the south, and Bakiyev emerged as the credible opposition leader. When the protesters marched toward Bishkek and were met by pro-government crowds, violence ensued and Akayev fled the country. Bakiyev became acting president and prime minister, and ordered Kulov released from jail. In July 2005 presidential elections, Bakiyev bested five other candidates with 88 percent of the vote, though international observers found some instances of ballot-stuffing and other fraud.

Twenty-First Century

Despite the promise of the Tulip Revolution, Bakiyev and parliament were soon at odds over constitutional reform, much in the same way that Akayev had been with the legislators. Like his predecessor, the new president showed himself unwilling to move forward with the permanent changes he had promised during his campaign. In November 2006 demonstrations erupted in Bishkek in support of the draft of a new constitution then under consideration in parliament; if adopted, it would limit presidential powers by granting parliament the responsibility for appointing the prime minister and cabinet ministers. The protesters also called for Bakiyev's resignation, and in response he claimed the demonstrations were manufactured by his political opponents as a pretense for a planned coup.

The parliament approved the new constitution on November 8, 2006. In mid-December, Kulov and several other ministers resigned, ostensibly in order to force new parliamentary elections sooner, but then the parliament voted to approve revisions to the new constitution, which returned some power to the president. Bakiyev was also given permission to name a new cabinet for the time being, and in return promised that the new constitution would go into effect in 2010. The standoff between the president and his opponents continued, however. In March 2007 Bakiyev appointed a new prime minister, Social Democratic Party chief Almazbek Atambayev (1956–), marking the first instance of an opposition party prime minister taking office in Central Asia. Two months later Atambayev claimed he was the victim of a near-fatal poisoning.

BIBLIOGRAPHY

Anderson, John. *Kyrgyzstan: Central Asia's Island of Democracy?* Amsterdam: Harwood Academic, 1999.

Jones Luong, Pauline. *Institutional Change and Political Continuity in Post-Soviet Central Asia: Power, Perceptions, and Pacts.* New York: Cambridge University Press, 2002.

Olcott, Martha Brill. *Central Asia's Second Chance.* Washington, DC: Carnegie Endowment for International Peace, 2005.

⊕ Uzbekistan

Type of Government

Uzbekistan achieved independence from the Soviet Union in 1991, but since then its government has been dominated by virtually the same key figures that held power during the Communist era. Central Asia's most populous nation, Uzbekistan has a constitution that gives its president broad powers and authority. In this aspect its leadership seems merely a modern-day variation on the clan system by which Uzbeks and other Central Asian ethnic groups lived for centuries, in which a strong executive is considered the protector of his people.

Background

Uzbekistan is situated between Kazakhstan, Kyrgyzstan, Tajikistan, Afghanistan, and Turkmenistan, and has a dry, arid climate thanks to the massive Kyzyl Kum ("red sand") Desert. In 327 BC, the armies of Alexander the Great (356 BC–323 BC) subdued the area for a time, but the Persians returned and were followed by Turks, Arabs, and Mongols. The great Mongol leader Tamerlane (1336–1405) is revered by Uzbeks as the first genuine ruler of an Uzbek nation. He established his Timurid dynasty at Samarqand, and spent lavishly to make the city one of the most impressive centers of learning in western Asia at the time. Waves of Turkic-speaking peoples came later in the fifteenth century, and with this a fixed Uzbek ethnic identity and nation began to take shape.

Over the next four centuries, Uzbekistan existed not as a nation but as part of an area known as Transoxiana. Various khanates held authority from cities like Bukhara and Qŭqon, but were ousted by imperial Russia in the mid-nineteenth century. Resistance to foreign domination was strong throughout Central Asia, however, and erupted into violence in 1916 when draft notices were issued in the region in order to bolster troop numbers for Russian participation in World War I. In 1929 Uzbekistan formally became part of the Soviet Union as the Uzbek Soviet Socialist Republic, and one-party Communist rule lasted until 1991, when the Soviet Union collapsed.

Government Structure

Uzbekistan declared its independence in September 1991, and a new constitution was adopted in December 1992. Although the document enshrines the concept of separation of powers between the branches of government, this principle is only nominally observed in practice. Instead, the greatest concentration of power rests in the executive branch, which consists of the office of the president, who serves as head of state. The president can form a government by appointing a prime minister and a cabinet, and may also dismiss his ministers as well as parliament; even cabinet ministries can be established or abolished merely by executive order. Under the constitution, the president is elected by direct vote and is limited to two five-year terms.

The legislative branch of Uzbekistan's government is the Oliy Majlis, or Supreme Assembly. A constitutional referendum in 2002 changed the structure of the Oliy Majlis from a unicameral to a bicameral one, with an upper house called the Senate consisting of 100 seats, and the lower Legislative Chamber seating 120 legislators. All members are elected to five-year terms, but Uzbekistan's president has consistently silenced genuine political opposition, and only political parties loyal to the status quo are permitted to exist and thus field candidates in legislative elections. The terms of the constitution give the Oliy Majlis some genuine clout, but this has been overwhelmingly ignored in favor of a strong authority figure embodied in the president. Instead, the chambers serve as an advisory body for the president and his appointed government, with a primary function to legitimize the executive branch's decisions by voting their approval in what amounts to a rubber-stamp process in the exercise of presidential will.

Uzbekistan's judiciary is similarly constrained by executive power and is supervised by the Ministry of Justice. A Constitutional Court sits at the apex of the judicial system along with a Supreme Court. The president appoints judges to those benches for five or ten-year terms as well as the procurator-general, or state prosecutor. The Constitutional Court serves as a consultative body in the event the president moves to dismiss parliament, and its appointed judges rarely voice opposition to the executive's wishes. There is also an Arbitrage Court that handles commercial disputes, and a system of local courts with the Supreme Court serving as the final court of appeal. Since 1999 Uzbekistan's largely rural-based population has had their disputes resolved by local councils called *mahallas*, a practice that reflects a long history of clan-based authority.

Uzbekistan is divided into twelve administrative regions called *veliatlar*, or provinces. Each is run by a *hakim*, or governor, appointed by the president. In addition, Uzbekistan includes the Karakalpak Autonomous Republic, consisting of a Turkic-speaking population living near the delta of the Amu Dar'ya river. Overall, some 80 percent of Uzbekistan's population of twenty-six million identify themselves as ethnic Uzbeks. There are also small numbers of Russian, Tajik, and Kazakh groups within its borders as well as a community of Uzbek-speaking Koreans whose ancestors were forcibly removed from Korea in the late 1930s under Soviet leader Joseph Stalin (1878–1953).

Uzbekistan's human rights record is troublesome. Members of opposition groups are targeted by National Security Services, the country's internal police, with arbitrary arrests and indefinite detention used to silence political dissent. The country's prison system is believed to house at least five thousand political detainees. Uzbekistani women, in a country with a nearly 90 percent Muslim majority, are restricted from political and economic life by long-held customs, and reports of violence against women and self-immolation—suicide by setting oneself on fire—still surface. Homosexual acts are subject to criminal prosecution. Religious groups and their activities are closely monitored by the government, which also oversees media outlets that nearly always voice favorable opinions of the president and the ruling government. Uzbekistan's citizens are not free to move from one province to another without government permission, and relocating to a large cities like Samarqand or Tashkent, the capital, is nearly impossible.

Political Parties and Factions

Since independence, political life in Uzbekistan has been dominated by the People's Democratic Party of Uzbekistan (PDP), made up of former members of the Communist Party. The government tightly controls the ability of opposition parties via stringent licensing requirements, and the five parties that are active in the country are loyal to Uzbekistan's longtime president, Islam Karimov (1938–). In the 2004–05 parliamentary elections, these parties—including the Uzbekistan Liberal Democratic Party, Self-Sacrifice National Democratic Party, and Uzbekistan National Revival Democratic Party—won the remainder of seats in the Oliy Majlis after the twenty-eight taken by PDP candidates.

According to Karimov, the most serious threat to the stability of Uzbekistan is the Islamic Party of Turkistan, formerly known as the Islamic Movement for Uzbekistan (IMU). This militant group was formed in 1998 with the intention to overthrow Karimov's nominally democratic government and replace it with an Islamic state. Its founders received support from the Taliban government of hard-line Islamic militants then in control of neighboring Afghanistan. Another outlaw group, Hizb ut-Tahrir (Party of Liberation), also works to foment an Islamic revolution in Uzbekistan and across the predominantly Muslim nations of Central Asia.

Genuine secular-based opposition to former communists and hard-line Islamic militants coalesced in the Birlik (Unity) Party, formed in 1988 during the final years of the Soviet era as an opposition group. In 1989 a faction of its leadership founded the Erk (Freedom) Party, and one of those party chiefs ran against Karimov in 1991 in the country's first presidential election. Muhammad Solih (1949–) received about 12 percent of vote in a contest widely believed to have been conducted unfairly, and he was later forced to give up his seat in the Oliy Majlis and flee the country.

Major Events

Uzbekistan's political sphere has been dominated by one man during its first two decades of independence. Islam Karimov became first secretary of the Uzbekistan Communist Party Central Committee in 1989, and in early 1990 was elected president of the Soviet republic by vote of the Supreme Soviet. Independence was declared on September 1, 1991, and the local Communist Party elected to sever ties with the Communist Party of the Soviet Union after that group was banned following a failed coup attempt in Moscow. Uzbek Communists formed the People's Democratic Party of Uzbekistan in October of that year, and Karimov remained its chief. He was the party's candidate in the country's first popular vote for the presidency in December 1991. He won with 86 percent of the vote, a resounding endorsement that some observers considered suspicious. A year later, citing internal threats that were leading the country to the brink of civil war, Karimov announced a ban on all opposition parties.

International observers have consistently cited Uzbekistan's elections as vulnerable to fraud by Karimov's associates and the incumbent leadership. A referendum held in 1995 on the question of whether or not to extend Karimov's term an extra three years to January 2000 received a resounding 99 percent yes vote. A similar outcome occurred with a 2002 referendum asking voters if they wished to extend Karimov's term by another five years. Presidential elections are tentatively scheduled for January 2008, but Karimov has continued to sound warnings that Islamic extremist groups pose a tremendous threat to Uzbekistan's future and it may be necessary for him to remain in charge until this danger abates.

Twenty-First Century

Karimov and his regime enjoy cordial relations with both Moscow and the West. In October 2001, when the United States launched an effort to oust Afghanistan's Taliban government, Karimov permitted U.S. military aircraft to use Uzbekistan's large, Soviet-built air base at Karshi-Khanabad. In return, Uzbekistan received generous foreign-aid dollars and was praised by U.S. Secretary of Defense Donald H. Rumsfeld (1932–) as a crucial participant in the U.S.-led war on terror. Karimov and his government, however, later balked when the United States attempted to pressure it to enact more democratic reforms and improve its human-rights record. These tensions were exacerbated by a government crackdown on suspected opposition organizers in Uzbekistan following the May 2005 Anjian Massacre, when government troops fired on protesters in that city, and the United States was asked to leave the base.

Uzbekistan has also been singled out for criticism by Britain's former ambassador to the country, Craig Murray (1958–), who served from 2002 until his removal under a storm of controversy two years later. Murray has said that human rights abuses in Uzbekistan are rampant and essentially funded outright by foreign aid from the West, which goes directly to the security services.

BIBLIOGRAPHY

Alaolmolki, Nozar. *Life after the Soviet Union: The Newly Independent Republics of Transcaucasus and Central Asia.* Albany, NY: SUNY Press, 2005.

Melvin, Neil J. *Uzbekistan: Transition to Authoritarianism on the Silk Road.* London: Routledge, 2000.

Yalcin, Resul. *The Rebirth of Uzbekistan: Politics, Economy and Society in the Post-Soviet Era.* Reading, UK: Garnet & Ithaca Press, 2002.

⊕ Lithuania

Type of Government

The Republic of Lithuania reemerged as a parliamentary democracy in 1991 after more than fifty years of Soviet rule. Its constitution provides for a tripartite division of authority among the three branches of government, with a system of checks and balances to prevent abuses of power. The executive branch is headed by the president, who serves as head of state, and the prime minister, who serves as head of government. An independent judiciary serves as a counterweight to potential abuses of authority.

Background

Lithuania is a nation of 3.5 million people located on the eastern shore of the Baltic Sea; it borders Latvia, Belarus, Poland, and Russia. Strategically located, Lithuania possesses an illustrious history dating back to the 1200s, as well as a rebellious streak evident in the equally long pattern of armed struggle against foreign domination. The first ethnically distinct communities in the area were the Balts, who are believed to have been a mix of early Slav and Indo-European tribes. From the Balts emerged a people called the Liths, from whom the nation took its name. By AD 1000, several tribes opposed to German encroachment had united as Litua, which evolved into the Kingdom of Lithuania by the 1200s and then the Grand Duchy of Lithuania. In 1386 Grand Duke Jogaila (c. 1351–1434) entered into an arranged marriage with the eleven-year-old queen of Poland, Jadwiga (1374–1399), contingent upon his conversion to Christianity; with this arrangement, the majority of Lithuanians gave up their pagan faith. They were the last Europeans to abandon a pure form of ancient polytheism.

The Polish-Lithuanian Union resulting from Jogaila and Jadwiga's marriage evolved into the Polish-Lithuanian Commonwealth in 1569, and this regional power endured for another 226 years until successive deals struck between the German kingdom of Prussia and imperial Russia eliminated both Poland and Lithuania from maps entirely by 1795. After repeated uprisings for independence over the next century, in February 1918 an independent Lithuanian nation was declared, but in 1939 Lithuania and the two other Baltic nations, Estonia and Latvia, were invaded by Soviet troops and annexed according to a secret clause in the German-Soviet Nonaggression Pact. After World War II Lithuania existed as a constituent republic of the Soviet Union known as the Lithuanian Soviet Socialist Republic.

Resistance to foreign rule and the Soviets' one-party socialism remained strong, however, and Lithuanian nationalist groups intensified their efforts for independence in the late 1980s. Taking their cue from a new era of reform underway across all the Soviet constituent republics under a new Soviet leader, Mikhail Gorbachev

A statue of Soviet leader Vladimir Ilich Lenin being removed from the Lithuanian capital of Vilnius in 1991 after the Communist Party was banned in this former Soviet republic. *Wojtek Druszcz/ AFP/Getty Images*

(1931–), groups like Sąjūdis (Reform Movement of Lithuania), began to challenge the Communist Party's authority. Sąjūdis grew rapidly in the months following its founding in June 1988, and in May 1989 it issued a proclamation stating that the Soviet occupation had been illegal. In December 1989 the Lithuanian Communist Party broke from the Communist Party of the Soviet Union (CPSU), and in February 1990 the first multiparty elections for the Supreme Council, Lithuania's Communist-controlled governing body, were held. Sąjūdis candidates won a stunning victory, taking seventy-two out of ninety contested seats in the 141-member Council. A few weeks later, run-off elections added more Sąjūdis legislators to that total, and on March 11, 1990, the newly convened Council elected one of the founders of Sąjūdis, Vytautas Landsbergis (1932–), as the first non-Communist premier of Lithuania since 1926.

On that same day, the Supreme Council also voted to secede from the Soviet Union and restore its pre-

1940 independence as the Republic of Lithuania, despite a demand from Gorbachev a few days earlier that Lithuanian sovereignty would require a payment of $33 billion in hard currency as compensation for the Soviet-built infrastructure. More Soviet troops were added to an already strong military presence, and in January 1991 they began seizing government buildings and demanding the resignation of cabinet ministers. After three days of tense confrontation, Soviet tanks advanced on Lithuania's main television and radio tower in Vilnius. This was an attempt to halt the broadcasting of images out of the capital, where thousands of independence supporters had heeded Landsbergis's call to resist the Soviets by sheer numbers. The Soviets succeeded and fourteen Lithuanian civilians lost their lives, but the event proved a debacle for Gorbachev's leadership. Weeks later, Lithuanians voiced their support of secession from the Soviet Union in a referendum that passed with a 91 percent yes vote. The Soviet Union enforced an economic blockade of the breakaway republic, but Lithuania's sovereignty was finally recognized on September 6, 1991, several days after an attempted coup against Gorbachev by Communist Party hardliners in Moscow.

Government Structure

Lithuania's constitution, which was approved by national referendum on October 25, 1992, specifies a division of powers between the executive, legislative, and judicial branches. The executive branch consists of the office of the president, who is elected by direct vote to a five-year term. The president appoints a prime minister with the approval of the legislative branch. The prime minister serves as head of government and recommends candidates for the Cabinet of Ministers for presidential appointment. The president's main responsibilities lie in conducting foreign policy, while the prime minister supervises the administration of government.

Lithuania's parliament is called the Seimas, a variant on an old Polish word for "a meeting of the populace" that dates back to the twelfth century. The 141 deputies of the Seimas are elected to four-year terms by direct vote; seventy-one are elected from single-seat constituencies (in which there is a separate election for each seat), while seventy are chosen in a single multi-seat election under a proportional representation system, whereby each political party receives seats in the Seimas in proportion to the percentage of the total vote they receive. The seats are then allocated to the individuals in that party who received the most votes. For a party to win any seats in the Seimas, it must win a minimum 5 percent of the vote in parliamentary elections. Coalition slates, consisting of multiple parties, must receive at least 7 percent in nationwide balloting in order to gain a presence in the body. The Seimas meets twice yearly for sessions of three and a half months. Its deputies have the power to call new presidential elections when necessary, adopt constitutional amendments, reject international treaties, and declare martial law.

Lithuania's judiciary is independent, and the nation's code of law is based in part on the Casmir Code, named after a grand duke of the fourteenth century who promulgated the first written statutes for the Grand Duchy of Lithuania. The 1992 constitution provides for a Constitutional Court whose function is to review laws. Its nine judges serve nine-year terms, with the president of Lithuania appointing three, the chair of the Seimas chair specifying another three, and the president of the Supreme Court providing the final three. The judges' terms are not renewable. Seimas appoints the presidents of both the Constitutional Court and the Supreme Court. The Supreme Court, the final court of appeal for most civil and criminal cases, consists of thirty-seven justices who are appointed by Seimas upon recommendation from the president. Cases are usually heard before a panel of three justices. Below the Supreme Court is a Court of Appeals, then fifty-four district courts and five regional courts. There is also an administrative courts system with its own Supreme Court for disputes related to government actions and welfare benefits. A Senate of Judges, made up of members of the Supreme Court and Court of Appeals, can overturn decisions of other courts if they agree that there has been a violation of the European Convention on Human Rights.

Lithuania's 25,173 square miles are divided into ten administrative counties called *apskritys*, each headed by appointed governors. The counties are further divided into sixty municipalities. Local elections are held every three years in the municipalities for their governing councils, which then elect a mayor. The sixty municipalities are divided into elderates, which function as community offices that handle public records, such birth certificates and welfare-benefit matters. Suffrage in Lithuania is universal at the age of eighteen. About 83 percent of the population is Lithuanian, with about six percent each of ethnic Poles and Russians. When the country gained its independence in 1991, settling the status of its Russian population did not prove as controversial an issue as it had in Estonia and Latvia: The new government of Lithuania automatically granted citizenship to all residents, even Russians, if they chose it.

Political Parties and Factions

Coalition governments are commonplace in Lithuania because of the sheer number of political parties competing for power. The first group to gain popular support was Sąjūdis, but in the first parliamentary elections held in the autumn of 1992, former Communists won a surprising victory under the leadership of Algirdas Brazauskas (1932–), who had led the Communist Party of Lithuania's break with the Soviet parent organization. United under the newly formed Democratic Labour

Party of Lithuania (LDDP), the former Communists won 79 of the 141 Seimas seats in 1992. Their resurgence was credited to two factors: permitting ethnic Russians to vote in national elections, and the severe economic hardships that had arrived with the transition to a free-market system. Brazauskas was elected president that same year and served a five-year term. Landsbergis returned in 1996 parliamentary elections as head of the conservative new Homeland Union party, which won seventy Seimas seats that November and soundly defeated the LDDP. The LDDP merged with another party in 2001 to form the Social Democratic Party of Lithuania and won twenty seats in the Seimas in 2004 elections. The biggest winner in the 2004 contest, however, was a new Labour Party, which won thirty-nine seats and formed a coalition government with the Social Democrats and another newcomer called New Union (Social Liberals).

Major Events

In February 1998 Valdas Adamkus (1926–) was elected and sworn in as Lithuania's second president of its post-Soviet era. Adamkus had fled the Soviet invasion during World War II and went on to become a senior official with the U.S. Environmental Protection Agency. He lost his bid for reelection bid to Rolandas Paksas (1956–), who was impeached in April 2004 after a corruption scandal surfaced linking him to Russian organized-crime figures. The Seimas vote to oust him marked the first time that a European head of state had been removed from office by the impeachment process. Adamkus was elected president a second time in June 2004, just a month after Lithuania joined the European Union (EU).

Twenty-First Century

Lithuania hoped to become the first of the former Soviet bloc nations to adopt the euro, the EU common currency, but the planned 2007 monetary conversion was delayed by an inability to meet stringent financial regulations imposed by the EU for nations of the so-called "Euro"-zone. Joining the EU spurred an unfortunate wave of migration, with scores of younger Lithuanians moving to Great Britain for better employment opportunities; since 2004 nearly half a million Lithuanians—about a tenth of the population—have left the country to settle in western European cities. Like the other Baltic capitals of Riga and Tallinn, however, Lithuania's leading city, Vilnius, has emerged as a popular tourist destination.

In foreign relations with Russia, Lithuania remains the only Baltic republic to have concluded a border treaty with its powerful neighbor, but Lithuania remains wary of Russian meddling. In 2007 German chancellor Angela Merkel (1954–) attempted to broker a summit between EU representatives and Russian president Vladimir Putin (1952–), but both Lithuania and Poland—

recalling other German-Russian agreements, perhaps—pointedly declined to participate.

BIBLIOGRAPHY

Berglund, Sten, Joakim Ekman, and Frank H. Aarebrot, editors. *The Handbook of Political Change in Eastern Europe.* Cheltenham, UK: Edward Elgar, 2004.

Lane, A. Thomas. *Lithuania: Stepping Westward.* London: Routledge, 2001.

Snyder, Timothy. *The Reconstruction of Nations: Poland, Ukraine, Lithuania, Belarus, 1569–1999.* New Haven, CT: Yale University Press, 2003.

⊕ Tajikistan

Type of Government

Tajikistan is a presidential republic governed under a constitution that went into effect after the country achieved independence from the Soviet Union in 1991. The constitution outlines a strong executive branch, with the president serving as head of state and leader of the bicameral legislature. However, the ruling People's Democratic Party of Tajikistan and Imomali Rakhmonov (1952–), a former Communist Party official who has served as president since 1992, have instituted a repressive, authoritarian regime that has solidified power through several internal conflicts, including civil war.

Background

Tajikistan is bordered by China, Uzbekistan, Kyrgyzstan, and Afghanistan, but its artificially imposed boundaries have spurred serious ethnic tensions between Tajiks, who make up about 65 percent of the population, and Uzbeks, a 20-percent minority. Tajikistan's rough, mountainous terrain was populated in ancient times by eastern Iranians, and came under Persian control before the arrival of armies under Alexander the Great (356 BC–323 BC) in 329 BC. Several other incursions by foreign powers subjugated the nomadic Tajiks over the next millennium, including an Arab one that established Islam in Central Asia and then a Turkic conquest that grew into the powerful Kara-Khanid Khanate. The Mongols arrived in the early thirteenth century, and under their rule the city of Samarqand flourished as a center of medieval Islamic scholarship and art, as did Bukhara. Both cities, however, became part of present-day Uzbekistan, though historically inhabited by Tajiks. The Russians were the final masters of Tajikistan, subduing it by force in the 1860s and later suppressing a nationalist movement toward independence that followed the 1917 Bolshevik Revolution.

In 1924 Tajikistan became the Tajik Autonomous Soviet Socialist Republic within the borders of Uzbekistan, but in 1929 the Tajikistan Soviet Socialist Republic was created as a separate constituent republic. Opposition groups emerged in the late 1980s, leading to the installa-

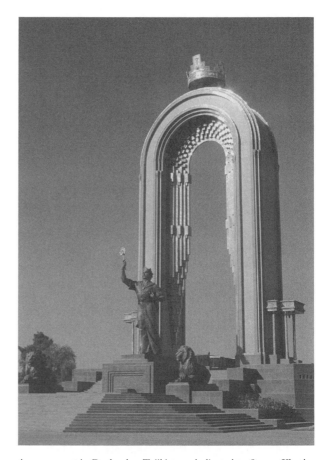

A monument in Dushanbe, Tajikistan, dedicated to Saman Khuda. Khuda was an early hero of the Samanid Empire and a revered figure for the Tajik nationalist movement. *East News/Getty Images*

tion of a former Tajik Communist, Rakhman Nabiyev (1930–1993), in the wake of an attempted coup in Moscow and the ensuing dissolution of the Soviet Union in 1991. Tajikistan declared its independence on September 9 of that year, and held its first presidential elections seven weeks later.

Government Structure

Tajikistan's constitution was adopted on November 6, 1994, and provides for a strong executive branch. The president serves as head of state as well as chair of the bicameral Majlisi Oli (Supreme Assembly), and is elected by direct vote to a seven-year term—though international observers have denounced most of the contests as fraudulent and conducted in an atmosphere that stifles legitimate political discourse. The president may replace his ministers at whim, including the prime minister, who serves as head of the government.

Tajikistan's legislative branch has two chambers. The Majlisi Milliy, or National Assembly, is the upper house and has thirty-three members, with twenty-five of them elected by regional assembly and the remaining eight appointed by the president, all for five-year terms.

The lower house is the Majlisi Namoyandagon, or Assembly of Representatives, with sixty-three deputies elected by direct vote to five-year terms.

The judicial branch of Tajikistan's government is a holdover from the Soviet era. At its apex is the Supreme Court, whose judges are appointed to five-year terms by the president. A Constitutional Court reviews laws, and separate economic and military courts exist. Below these are general courts for regions, districts, and cities. The judiciary is not fully independent, and judges are beholden to the president, political parties, local factions, or even military officials. Judicial appointments are made by the president, with the ostensible input of the Majlisi Oli, but human-rights groups claim judges are poorly trained in the law, and so inadequately compensated that bribery is commonplace.

Administratively, Tajikistan is divided into three regions and the autonomous province of Gorno-Badakhshan. Suffrage is universal at the age of eighteen. The criminal justice system includes a notorious prison system that is used to quell dissent via a statute that prohibits public defamation of any government official, and the government closely monitors the media and all religious organizations.

Political Parties and Factions

Political parties are a relatively new development in Tajikistan. For centuries, traditional clans dominated various regions and competed for hegemony, even during the Soviet era. Communist Party loyalists from the city of Khudzhand held power under the Soviets, but since independence in 1991 their main foes, who come from the Külob area near Dushanbe, have been in power under the guise of the People's Democratic Party of Tajikistan. The PDP has been the ruling party for much of the post-Soviet period, but its legitimate authority has been disputed because of the widespread election fraud its members and supporters are often accused of committing.

During Tajikistan's civil war involving anti-government elements in Garm and Gorno-Badakhshan, opposition parties were banned by order of the Supreme Court but were legalized before the 2000 parliamentary elections. Among the main ones are the Communist Party of Tajikistan and the Islamic Renaissance Party. The latter supports the idea of a secular government and is the only religious party in any of the Central Asian republics to be represented in a parliamentary body. There is also another Muslim party, Hizb-ut-Tahrir, or "Freedom," and a Democratic Party of Tajikistan and Justice Party. In 1999 the head of the Socialist Party, who was predicted to make a run for the presidency later that year, was assassinated in Dushanbe.

Major Events

Tajikistan's first presidential elections were held in October 1991 and resulted in victory for Nabiyev, the former head of the Communist Party of Tajikistan, although the official results were disputed by opposition groups. Among the accusations of election fraud were charges that a filmmaker named Davlat Khudonazarov (1944–) might have bested Nabiyev had the ballot boxes not been stuffed. Demonstrations erupted in Dushanbe over the results, and in August 1992 Nabiyev was kidnapped and forced to resign; he died under suspicious circumstances a year later. Seizing on the political instability, civil war broke out, and the five-year conflict pitted government troops against various militia clans, Communist hardliners, pro-Islamic forces, and a long-persecuted ethnic minority in Gorno-Badakhshan, the Pamiris. This predominantly Shiite group shared strong cultural ties with Pamiris in neighboring Afghanistan; by contrast the majority of Tajikistan's Muslim population are Sunni Muslim.

With Nabiyev forcibly removed from office, Rakhmonov—another former Communist Party official—was installed as acting head of state by the only body with any government authority at the time—the remnants of the Supreme Soviet. Under the 1994 constitution, Rakhmonov ran for the presidency and won, but rampant fraud was said to have been committed by his party, the PDP, to ensure that he remained in power.

Opposition to Rakhmonov and the PDP coalesced around the United Tajik Opposition (UTO), a coalition of pro-democracy groups and Islamic organizations that came to play a key role in the civil war. The terms of a June 1997 peace accord specified that 30 percent of cabinet posts in Rakhmonov's government would go to representatives of opposition groups, and in exchange Rakhmonov would be allowed to remain in power. Two years later, however, the president secured passage of amendments to the constitution by means of a referendum vote whose results were widely denounced as fraudulent. One of these amendments created a bicameral legislature, while the second provided for a seven-year term for Tajikistan's president. Rakhmonov stood for election later in 1999 and won with 97 percent of the vote. Another referendum vote took place in June 2003, again under conditions that do not conform to international standards for legitimacy, which permitted the president to hold two additional seven-year terms. In 2006 he was reelected to the first of those with a 79-percent majority of the vote, and is likely to remain in office until 2020.

Twenty-First Century

Tajikistan is one of the poorest countries in the world, with an export-dependent economy that relies on cotton crops and aluminum mining. It has also been named as a significant participant in international narcotics trafficking. Its Muslim population is predominantly Sunni, and the older generation of Tajiks—accustomed to the atheism of the Soviet era—seem uninterested in attempts by Islamic fundamentalist groups to stir up anti-government opposition. One of these groups is the Islamic Movement of Uzbekistan, a militant organization allied with al Qaeda that advocates the establishment of a Islamic state across Central Asia. Analysts of Central Asian politics warn that a younger generation of unemployed, politically disenfranchised Tajiks is vulnerable to the ideology of such movements. One check on that threat is the presence of Russian troops stationed on Tajikistan's border with Afghanistan, a situation that dates back to the Soviet era. In 1999 Tajikistan and Russia signed an agreement that permitted the troops—largely ethnic Tajik members of the 201st Motorized Rifle Division—to remain there until 2024.

BIBLIOGRAPHY

Alaolmolki, Nozar. *Life after the Soviet Union: The Newly Independent Republics of Transcaucasus and Central Asia.* Albany, NY: SUNY Press, 2005.

Cummings, Sally, editor. *Power and Change in Central Asia.* London: Routledge, 2002.

Olcott, Martha Brill. *Central Asia's Second Chance.* Washington, DC: Carnegie Endowment for International Peace, 2005.

⊕ Armenia

Type of Government

Armenia is a parliamentary republic. The country's executive branch is led by the president (head of state), and includes a prime minister (head of cabinet) and a cabinet, or council of ministers. The legislative branch consists of a unicameral (one-house) parliament called the National Assembly. The judicial branch is headed by the Constitutional Court. The president is elected by popular vote; parliament members are elected by a system that combines direct vote and proportional representation. The prime minister, cabinet, and Constitutional Court members are appointed.

Background

Armenia is a landlocked country on the border of Europe and Asia, in southwestern Asia. Encompassing 11,506 square miles, it is surrounded by Turkey, Iran, Georgia, and Azerbaijan. Its climate is "highland continental," with cold winters and hot summers. Topographical features include mountainous highlands, fertile valleys, fast-flowing rivers, and very little forestland.

Armenia made its historical debut around 800 BC within the Kingdom of Urartu, or Van, which became one of the Near East's most formidable of the time. Its present-day capital of Yerevan stands on the Urartian fortress of Erebuni and still uses one of the irrigation canals built by those ancient forebears. The first Armenian state was founded about 190 BC, and it expanded to encompass all of Caucasus, as well as what is now eastern Turkey, Syria, and Lebanon. It became a part of the Roman Empire in 64 BC and was the most powerful state in the Roman East.

One of the most important events of Armenia's early history is, certainly, its adoption of Christianity around AD 303. It was the first country in the world to do so. The Armenian Apostolic Church became integral to preserving the country's cultural identity throughout many centuries of foreign rule. It also, through a member of its clergy, created the singular Armenian alphabet in AD 405. The alphabet was unique to the Armenian language and the church was independent of both the Roman Catholic and Eastern Orthodox churches, two factors that remain true in the twenty-first century and help give the country its distinct flavor and heritage.

Despite some periods of autonomy, including the 1080 to 1375 Kingdom of Cilicia (or Little Armenia) established near the Mediterranean Sea, Armenia spent much of the time from the fourth to twentieth centuries under the domain of other empires. Those conquerors included the Persians, Byzantines, Arabs, Mongols, and Turks. Turkish rule was especially harsh, resulting in an estimated 600,000 to 1.5 million Armenian deaths starting in 1915.

The end of World War I and defeat of the Ottoman Empire led to a brief Armenian independence from 1918 until 1920. But Soviet Russia moved into the eastern part of the country in late 1920, and Armenia was incorporated into the Union of Soviet Socialist Republics (USSR) in 1922. In 1936 it became the Armenian Soviet Socialist Republic, a constituent republic of the USSR. Perhaps the most defining event of the Soviet era was the 1923 placement of the primarily Armenian region of Nagorno-Karabakh under the jurisdiction of neighboring Azerbaijan. The repercussions of that action have lasted well into the twenty-first century.

As the collapse of the Soviet Union drew near in 1990, Armenia held parliamentary elections and began to form a government. On September 21 of the following year, a referendum was held in which an overwhelming majority of the electorate voted for secession from the Soviets and independence. Its first presidential election was held in October, and a constitution was adopted in 1995, with substantial amendments voted in by nationwide referendum in 2005. The nation's first parliamentary elections were also held in 1995.

Government Structure

Armenia is a parliamentary republic with powers divided among executive, legislative, and judicial branches. The president leads the executive branch, and holds considerably more power than his or her counterpart in comparable European governments. The president, for instance, appoints the prime minister. Elected by popular vote to a five-year term, the president is eligible for a second term of office. Although the prime minister—who presides over the cabinet—is appointed by the

An estimated 600,000 to 1.5 million Armenians were massacred as a result of a 1915 compulsive resettlement policy of the Turkish government. © *Bettmann/CORBIS*

president, that appointment must be confirmed by parliament and is subject to a no-confidence ouster if the appointee's political agenda is not accepted. The cabinet is appointed by the president upon recommendation of the prime minister.

Legislative power rests in a unicameral parliament called the National Assembly. The 131 members are elected through a combination of direct vote and a proportional representation system to four-year terms. Political parties must secure at least 5 percent of the vote to win a seat. The National Assembly has two ordinary sessions—spring, from February to June, and autumn, from September until December. Extraordinary sessions may be convened by the president or the parliamentary chairman if either has the backing of at least one-third of parliament. The chairman is elected by majority vote of the National Assembly members.

The judiciary is headed by the Constitutional Court, first established on February 6, 1996; it rules on the constitutionality of legislation, electoral disputes, and international agreements. Five of its members are appointed by the National Assembly and four by the president. Constitutional Court members are eligible to serve until the age of seventy. Other courts include the Court of Cassation, or Court of Appeals, the highest court. It hears appeals of cases from lower-level courts.

It is worth noting that there is some dissension about the real independence of the branches of Armenia's government. Those concerns have been compounded by allegations of irregularities in elections and outbreaks of political violence, such as gunmen opening fire in parliament in 1999. The government has endeavored to address those worries by such means as the constitutional referendum of 2005, which broadened legislative powers and made provisions for more judicial independence.

Armenia has universal suffrage at the age of eighteen. Over 97 percent of the population is ethnic Armenian, and Armenian is the official language. Other ethnic groups include Yezidi (Kurds), Russians, and Greeks. The majority of the citizenry (more than 94 percent) is at least nominally affiliated with the Armenian Apostolic Church.

Political Parties and Factions

Armenia has myriad political parties, dozens of which are unregistered and become active only during national campaigns. Among the more significant and mainstream parties are the Armenian Revolutionary Federation (ARF/Dashnak), National Democratic Union of Armenia (AZhM), Rule of Law Party, People's Party of Armenia (HZhK), Republican Party of Armenia (HHK), and the United Labor Party (MAK). There is also the Justice Bloc, which unites several parties under one umbrella.

The ARF/Dashnak was founded in 1890 and was the ruling party during Armenia's short-lived independence after World War I. It resurfaced as an opposition party (also known as the Armenian Socialist Party) in 1990 and became a strident critic of the government. In return, the party was "temporarily suspended" by presidential decree amid allegations of terrorism, political assassination, and drug dealing. Thirty party members were convicted of an alleged coup attempt in 1996, but all were released two years later after the resignation of then-president Levon Ter-Petrosyan (1945–) and resulting reinstatement of the party. Its fortunes changed after supporting the successful presidential candidacy of Robert Kocharyan (also spelled Kocharian; 1954–) in 1998. ARF/Dashnak won 12.7 percent of the vote in the 2007 parliamentary elections.

The AZhM was established in 1991 as a right of center party. It garnered 7.5 percent of the vote in the 1995 parliamentary elections, but internal bickering and the consequent defection of senior members had considerably weakened its influence by 2001. The party won no seats in the 2007 National Assembly elections.

The Rule of Law Party came into being in 1998 as a prime supporter of Kocharyan's presidential bid. It subsequently won six seats in the 1999 parliamentary elections. Politically right wing, the party steadily made progress in the next two elections—it won seven seats in 2003 and nine seats in 2007.

The HZhK was launched in 1999 by former Communist Party leader Karen Demirchian (1932–1999). Dedicated to "democratic and popular socialism," it was fueled by the strong showing that Demirchian had made in the previous year's presidential elections (40.5 percent of the vote in the second round). The party had a standout inaugural outing, in alliance with the HHK, by taking 55 National Assembly seats in the 1999 elections. Demirchian was elected speaker of the new parliament. That triumph was cut short on October 27, however, when armed gunmen stormed a parliamentary debate and killed eight political leaders, including Demirchian. The party ended its alliance with the HHK in 2001 and joined the Justice Bloc in 2003 as the main opposition to Kocharyan's government. Demirchian's son, Stepan Demirchian (1959–), succeeded his father as chairman in December 1999 and ran unsuccessfully against Kocharyan in the 2003 presidential election.

The right of center HHK is now the dominant party in Armenia. Its original incarnation was founded in 1991 and the current version is the result of a 1998 merger with the Yerkrapah Union of Veterans. In alliance with the HZhK, the party was the major player in the 1999 parliamentary elections, capturing 55 of the 131 parliamentary slots and landing Yerkrapah leader and former defense minister Vazgen Sarkisyan (1959–1999) in the

prime minister's seat. That victory was short-lived, however, as Sarkisyan was also one of the eight leaders shot dead in parliament on October 27. Since then, internal dissension caused a shake-up in its leadership and the dissolution of the HZhK alliance, but the party has continued to thrive. It picked up 23.5 percent of the vote in the 2003 parliamentary elections and 32.8 percent in 2007.

Founded by successful entrepreneur Gurgen Arsenyan (1959–), the MAK debuted in 2002 and astonished observers by taking six National Assembly seats on its maiden outing in 2003. The party is firmly committed to the Kocharyan administration. Cynics as well as some members of the opposition believe that Arsenian's wealth gave his party an unfair advantage.

Major Events

For all Armenia's ancient and vivid history, two events stand out as fundamental to the nation's psyche in the twenty-first century. One of those is the bloodshed caused by the Ottoman Turks from 1915 to 1917 and the other is Nagorno-Karabakh situation. The former, which many characterize as the first genocide of the twentieth century, stemmed largely from a compulsory resettlement policy instituted by the Turks in 1915. Between 600,000 and 1.5 million Armenians died as they were forced out of their homes and sent into the surrounding deserts to be bayoneted, buried alive, beheaded, or simply left to succumb to starvation and heat exhaustion. Survivors often were abducted and abused. While this was not the first Turkish massacre of Armenians, its scope and scale were staggering. In 2007 the Armenian government was still seeking acknowledgment from Turkey that the devastation was genocide. The Turkish government maintains that the dead were merely victims of World War I. Unsurprisingly, the two countries have no diplomatic relations.

The 1923 placement by the Soviets of the mainly Armenian region of Nagorno-Karabakh under the jurisdiction of neighboring Azerbaijan remains at the forefront of Armenian politics. Fighting there began in 1988 after its inhabitants voted to secede and become part of Armenia. It escalated into full-scale war after the fall of the Soviet Union in 1991. A cease-fire was agreed to in 1994, but resolution of the problem has yet to be reached. Both countries continue to suffer economic impairment and displaced citizenry because of the conflict.

Twenty-First Century

Armenia appears to be making progress as a democracy in the twenty-first century. The 2007 parliamentary elections, for example, were generally regarded as having met international standards. Unemployment and poverty, however, remain tremendous challenges. And the country's enormous diaspora—an estimated quarter of its population has been lost since independence alone—may be the greatest challenge of all. The government has taken steps, such as a dual-citizenship bill passed in February 2007, to address the problem. Clearly, the country can progress only so far without a young and vibrant population to sustain it.

BIBLIOGRAPHY

De Waal, Thomas. *Black Garden: Armenia and Azerbaijan through Peace and War*. New York: New York University Press, 2003.

Hovannisian, Richard G., ed. *The Armenian Genocide in Perspective*. New Brunswick, NJ: Transaction, 1986.

Libaridian, Gerard J. *Modern Armenia: People, Nation, State*. New Brunswick, NJ: Transaction, 2004.

⊕ Turkmenistan

Type of Government

The Republic of Turkmenistan is one of several former constituent republics of the Soviet Union that seized their independence in 1991. Like Central Asia's other new nations, however, Turkmenistan had only a brief interlude of multiparty democracy before a return to one-party rule. The Constitution of Turkmenistan, which was adopted in May 1992, gives the office of the president broad powers. There is also a fifty-member Mejlis, or parliament, and a special Khalk Maslahaty, or People's Council, neither of which has any real authority in practice. Turkmenistan's judicial system is staffed by jurists who are beholden to the ruling party and is not considered independent.

Background

Turkmenistan is located between Uzbekistan, Kazakhstan, Afghanistan, and Iran, and about three-quarters of its population of 5.1 million identify themselves as ethnic Turkmen. The original inhabitants of this harsh desert landscape were thought to be of ancient Iranian origins. The territory came under Persian rule before it was conquered by Alexander III (356 BC–323 BC), also known as Alexander the Great, and it was subsequently ruled by various Iranian entities before Arab conquests in the seventh century AD, which resulted in the adoption of Islam. The area was part of the historic Silk Road traversed by European and African traders buying luxury goods in China and India.

Oghuz Turks, from further east in Central Asia, eventually made incursions into the area, and were later joined by Seljuk Turks in the eleventh century. This mixed population became known as the "Turcomen," a nomadic people renowned for their archery skills and with an economy dependent on horse breeding. Thirteenth-century Mongol invasions did not significantly alter their ancient way of life, and by the nineteenth century what is now Turkmenistan had a reputation as a dangerous place for travelers and traders alike: clan warfare predominated

and foreign caravans were regularly targeted by robbers. As the boundaries of the Russian Empire began to move further south, there were reports that Russians in nearby Kazakhstan were being kidnapped by Turkmen and sold into slavery, which prompted a Russian military invasion. In 1881 imperial Russia won a decisive battle at a legendary fortress called Gok-Tepe, where a reported seven thousand Turkmen died defending it. Not surprisingly, the Turkmen chafed under Russian rule, and after the 1917 Bolshevik Revolution and subsequent civil war, they became ardent participants in anti-Bolshevik actions in the area. A tribal chief named Junaid Khan ascended to power and briefly ruled what was then known as Transcaspia, but Russian military might prevailed and Turkmenistan became part of the Soviet Union in 1924 as the Turkmen Soviet Socialist Republic.

In 1985 a Turkmen named Sapamurad Niyazov (1940–2006) became first secretary of the Communist Party of Turkmenistan, and five years later was elected chairperson of the Turkmenistan Supreme Soviet. At the time, its deputies were all members of the Communist Party of Turkmenistan, but after a failed coup attempt in Moscow in August 1991, they voted to dissolve and regroup as the Democratic Party of Turkmenistan (DPT). Niyazov was the de facto leader when Turkmenistan's independence was declared by the Supreme Soviet in October 1991, and the deputies chose him to become the new republic's first president.

Government Structure

Under the terms of the 1992 constitution, Turkmenistan's president serves as head of state and chief executive officer of the government and appoints eight deputy chairpersons for a Cabinet of Ministers; under them serve the ministers of various departments. Presidential elections are by direct vote and held ever five years, and a president is limited by the constitution to two consecutive terms in office.

The fifty members of the Mejlis, or parliament, also serve five-year terms and are elected by popular vote. The president may dissolve the Mejlis if two no-confidence votes occur within an eighteen-month period. There is also a special Khalk Maslahaty, or People's Council, with as many as 2,500 members. This is not deliberative or lawmaking body, but rather "the highest representative organ of popular power" according to the Turkmenistan Constitution. Its members include the Mejlis deputies, the president, the president's Council of Ministers, the justices of the Supreme Court, ten regional representatives elected by popular vote in their respective provinces, plus local officials who serve as town administrators. The country is divided into five administrative provinces called *velayaty*, plus another one for the capital city, Ashgabad.

Turkmenistan's judiciary is described as independent in its constitution, but all judges are appointed to the bench by the president, without a confirmation vote by either the Mejlis or Khalk Maslahaty. At its apex is the Supreme Court, with twenty-one justices who serve five-year terms. There is also a Supreme Economic Court and separate military courts. The president also appoints the prosecutor-general.

Though Turkmenistan's constitution guarantees the civil liberties of its citizens, these basic rights are not protected in practice. The government owns or controls most media properties, and has shut down cable-television providers when their programming proved too difficult to censor. Print media are subsidized by the government, and criticism of the Democratic Party of Turkmenistan or any member of government is non-existent; even dissent commentary published abroad has resulted in reprisals for the writers' families back home. Political opposition groups are regularly harassed by government agents, and a wide array of human rights abuses are said to be carried out by a powerful internal security force. Citizens of Turkmenistan must carry an internal passport at all times, and moving from one province to another, or to a city, is extremely difficult. Travel advisories for foreigners warn that a woman seen on the street after dark with a male runs a risk of being arrested for prostitution. The government also keeps a close watch on religious groups; only Sunni Islam and Russian Orthodox Christianity are officially permitted to operate, and members of other sects have been detained and reportedly even tortured.

Niyazov, who remained in office until his death in 2006, established a cult of personality for himself. Known as Turkmenbashi, or "head of all Turkmen," he wrote an epic poem, the *Ruhnama* (Book of the Soul), which became required reading in all classrooms in the country and was intended to serve as a document of spiritual guidance for the Turkmen people. Degree examinations featured a section of it, as did civil-service tests; even driver's-license applicants could expect a section of the test to deal with its spurious nationalist legends. In the capital city, a giant automated version of the *Ruhnama* broadcast passages from it daily. Niyazov renamed the months of the calendar after members of his family. His authoritarian rule—said by political analysts to rival only that of Soviet leader Joseph Stalin (1879–1953) at the height of his power—even extended to an oath of allegiance to Niyazov that prohibited any criticism and was uttered at the start of all government meetings and classrooms each morning. The longtime president and his top allies were believed to engage in widespread corruption, and human rights groups claimed the president had spirited an estimated $2 billion out of the country for deposit into secret European and offshore bank accounts.

Political Parties and Factions

Turkmenistan's constitution specifies a multiparty system, but only the Democratic Party of Turkmenistan (DPT) participates in the political process. It describes itself as the "mother party" of Turkmenistan. In the final two years of Soviet rule, a new party called Agzybirlik, or "Unity," emerged, but it was banned by the government. Some of its members went on to establish the Party of Democratic Development in 1991, but that party was also outlawed. There is also the Republican Party of Turkmenistan, whose leaders have been jailed or otherwise harassed, and which operates from abroad. In early 1992 Niyazov's government introduced a plan whereby some of the former Communist Party leadership from the rural base would form a peasant party; a year later the government stated its intention to legalize this party in the future, but this did not happen.

Major Events

Turkmenistan became a sovereign nation in October 1991, and two months later joined the newly formed Commonwealth of Independent States (CIS). The first presidential elections were held in June 1992 with Niyazov as the only candidate. In January 1994 a national referendum was passed to keep Niyazov in office another five years. Another constitutional amendment was approved in December 1999 that granted him life tenure as president. In November 2002 shots were fired at Niyazov's motorcade, and the assassination attempt prompted a harsh crackdown by state security forces on all suspected dissidents.

Elections in Turkmenistan have been conducted in an atmosphere that does not permit genuine political opposition, and impressive voter turnout numbers—typically 95 to 99 percent, according to government figures—are deemed suspect. In Mejlis and parliamentary elections, candidates came from lists personally approved by Niyazov. He justified this one-party rule by claiming that Turkmenistan was not yet ready for full-fledged democracy. In 1999 he asserted that no political parties would be legalized for at least a decade, and that the next presidential election would not take place until 2010.

That plan abruptly changed on December 21, 2006, when Niyazov died of a heart attack. According to law, the chair of the Mejlis was to become acting president, but in a somewhat unsurprising turn of events, the state news agency announced that the country's prosecutor had launched an investigation of corruption charges against the Mejlis chair. Instead Niyazov's deputy prime minister and personal dentist, Gurbanguly Berdymukhammedov (1957–), was named to succeed him. In February 2007 Berdymukhammedov stood for election as president and won with 90 percent of the vote; all six candidates were DPT members.

Twenty-First Century

Under Niyazov, Turkmenistan was an isolated country with an official foreign policy spelling out its "positive neutrality," a strategy that kept it out of regional political alliances or participation in cooperative security exercises. The country sits atop the world's largest reserves of natural gas, but this immense economic potential has yet to be developed. The ascension of Berdymukhammedov to power was viewed as a positive sign for future change in the country. Soon after taking office, the new president abolished a law that permitted him the right to rename landmarks or cities, which had been widely used during his predecessor's era. He also removed the once-powerful head of the presidential security service, signed a deal with Russia to construct a new natural-gas pipeline, and pledged sweeping educational reforms and an end to Turkmenistan's long policy of foreign isolation. Finally, Berdymukhammedov proclaimed that the former oath of allegiance should be reserved only for special state occasions, not recited daily. Within a year of his taking office, Internet cafes began operating in the capital, Ashgabad.

BIBLIOGRAPHY

Alaolmolki, Nozar. *Life after the Soviet Union: The Newly Independent Republics of the Transcaucasus and Central Asia.* Albany, NY: SUNY Press, 2005.

Power and Change in Central Asia, edited by Sally N. Cummings. London: Routledge, 2002.

Olcott, Martha Brill. *Central Asia's Second Chance.* Washington, DC: Carnegie Endowment for International Peace, 2005.

⊕ Republic of Macedonia

Type of Government

The Republic of Macedonia is a parliamentary democracy with a unicameral (one-house) parliament, the Sobranie, whose members are elected by proportional representation. Its prime minister is elected by the parliament, while its president is elected directly by the people. The Macedonian legal system is headed by two courts, a Supreme Court and a Constitutional Court, which are overseen by the Judicial Council of the Republic.

Background

Macedonia's early history is highly contested. In ancient times a Greek kingdom called Macedonia, which was located in and to the southeast of today's Republic of Macedonia, was one of the most powerful states in the region. Alexander III (356 BC–323 BC; known as Alexander the Great) was a Macedonian king. Ancient Macedonians and other Greeks were the original inhabitants of the modern-day Republic of Macedonia, but they were supplanted by Slavic tribes in the sixth century AD. Modern Macedonians are believed to be primarily descended from these Slavs, and they also speak a south Slavic language that is closely related to Bulgarian. Despite this Slavic heritage, modern Macedonians still claim ancient Macedonian history as their own. This claim dismays the residents of Greece, whose Macedonian provinces comprise the majority of the land that made up ancient Macedonia. In fact, Greece is unhappy

about Macedonia's very name: At Greece's insistence, the Republic of Macedonia is referred to internationally as the Former Yugoslav Republic of Macedonia (FYROM) in order to avoid any possible confusion with the Greek region of Macedonia.

After ancient Greece collapsed, the land that is now modern Macedonia was fought over and at times ruled by many different empires, including the Roman, Byzantine, and Bulgar empires. Then, in 1371, Macedonia fell under the control of the Ottoman Empire, which was centered in modern-day Turkey.

In the late nineteenth century, as the Ottoman Empire began to weaken and nationalist sentiments amongst the peoples of the Balkans began to strengthen, the region then known as Macedonia (an area covering both modern Macedonia and the lands to its south and east that were part of ancient Macedonia) became an ideological battleground. Serbs, Bulgars, and Greeks all tried to win over the residents of Macedonia, in hopes of being able to wrest Macedonia away from the Ottomans and to add its land to their own countries. By the 1890s this contest became violent when various militant groups sprang up. One of these groups, the Internal Macedonian Revolutionary Organization (VMRO), launched a revolt in 1903 and declared an independent Macedonian republic. The Ottomans soon crushed the revolt, but modern-day Macedonians continue to honor this first Macedonian republic politically: several current Macedonian political parties use VMRO in their names.

In 1912 and 1913 Serbia, Greece, and Bulgaria joined together to conquer Macedonia and divide it up amongst themselves. Greece took the coastal regions in southern Macedonia, Bulgaria took the northeastern portion of the region, and Serbia took the rest. The land taken by Serbia later became today's Republic of Macedonia.

Even after this war, Serbia's neighbors still coveted Macedonia. Bulgaria occupied Serbia's portion of Macedonia during World War I, although it was defeated and forced to return the land at the end of the war. Bulgaria also provided a base for VMRO, which sent guerrilla groups across the border into Serbian Macedonia to fight against the Serbian authorities in the 1920s. Between 1941 and 1944 Bulgaria again occupied much of Serbian Macedonia, but Bulgaria found itself on the losing side of World War II and was forced to return this territory to Serbia.

Macedonia essentially disappeared within Serbia, and by extension within the newly created country of Yugoslavia (which included Serbia, Croatia, Slovenia, and Bosnia and Herzegovina), between World War I and World War II. Serbia called Macedonia "southern Serbia" and refused to recognize it as a separate nation within the Yugoslav federation. Such treatment only encouraged the continuation of Macedonia's prewar nationalist movement, which continued to fight for Macedonian independence. The Macedonian independence movement, working in partnership with Croatian nationalists, even succeeded in assassinating the king of Yugoslavia in 1934.

The Communist government that took over in Yugoslavia following World War II finally agreed to recognize Macedonia as a separate nation within the Yugoslav federation. The Socialist Republic of Macedonia was formed in 1944, and its people remained loyal to Communism and to Yugoslav leader Josip Broz Tito (1892–1980), the man who had given them their nation.

After Tito's death in 1980, Yugoslavia began to crumble. The various nations within Yugoslavia began jockeying for more autonomy, and by the late 1980s Communist governments were beginning to collapse across Eastern Europe. On September 8, 1991, Macedonia held a referendum about whether to declare independence. The vast majority—95 percent—of the people who voted were in favor of Macedonian independence, although Macedonia's Serbs and Albanians boycotted the vote. Macedonia formally declared its independence two months later.

Government Structure

Macedonia's parliament, the Sobranie, consists of a single house with 120 members who are elected to four-year terms. Elections to the Macedonian parliament are based on proportional representation using an open party list system. In this type of election voters vote for lists of candidates—which are drawn up by political parties or coalitions before the election—as well as for individual candidates on each list. There are six election districts in Macedonia that each elect twenty representatives, so each party can draw up six lists (one for each district) that can have as many as twenty names on each. Then, when the votes are counted, each party is allocated seats based on the number of votes it received in each district. Macedonia uses the D'Hondt method, a complex mathematical process, for allocating the seats, but the end result is that the parties that received the most votes get the most seats. The seats allocated to each party are then filled by the candidates on the party's list who received the most individual votes.

The party or coalition that receives the largest number of seats in the Sobranie has the power to elect a prime minister, who chooses a cabinet of ministers to help him or her exercise executive power. Unlike in most parliamentary democracies, in Macedonia the prime minister and his cabinet are not chosen from the members of the parliament.

The president is elected directly by the people to a five-year term of office. Presidential elections generally take place in two rounds. If no candidate receives a majority of the vote in the first round, the top two finishers from that round go head-to-head in a second round. The president's powers are limited—most executive power lies with the prime minister and the cabinet—but the president is the commander-in-chief of the country's armed forces. A person can serve no more than two terms in a row as president.

Macedonia has two high courts: a Constitutional Court and a Supreme Court. The Constitutional Court protects Macedonians' constitutional rights, including the right to free speech; ensures that Macedonians are not discriminated against based upon their race, religion, or other such factors; and resolves disputes between the legislative, executive, and judicial branches of the government. The Supreme Court is the highest appeals court in the country, with responsibility for hearing cases that have been appealed from the three Courts of Appeal. Beneath the Courts of Appeal are twenty-seven Courts of the First Instance, which is where legal cases are first heard. All of the courts are overseen by the Judicial Council of the Republic, a seven-person committee elected by the Parliament. This council nominates judges, who are then confirmed by Parliament. Most judges are elected for life. The exceptions are the judges of the Constitutional Court, who are permitted to serve only a single nine-year term.

At the local level, Macedonia is divided into eighty-five *opstini* (municipalities) that are self-governing in regards to affairs within each opstina.

Political Parties and Factions

Macedonia has a large number of political parties, but in elections the small parties often band together to form more broadly based coalitions. Three such coalitions dominated the parliament that was elected in 2006: For a Better Macedonia, which won forty-five seats; Together for Macedonia, which won thirty-two seats; and an unnamed coalition made up of the Democratic Union for Integration, the Party for Democratic Prosperity, and the Democratic League of Bosniaks, which won seventeen seats.

The largest party in the For a Better Macedonia coalition is the Internal Macedonian Revolutionary Organization–Democratic Party for Macedonian National Unity (VMRO–DPMNE), a Christian Democratic party. VMRO–DPMNE is an anti-Communist, pro-Western party that was founded in 1990 by Macedonian nationalists. Despite the party's nationalist roots, beginning in the late 1990s it started to concede to some demands made by Macedonia's ethnic Albanian minority. In 2004 the nationalist wing of the party, which was upset about the concessions that the party leaders had made to the Albanians, split off to form the VMRO–People's Party. The mainline VMRO–DPMNE has largely abandoned nationalism and bases its platform on supporting democracy, civil society, and European integration.

Other major participants in the For a Better Macedonia coalition are the Socialist Party of Macedonia (a traditional left-wing party that draws much of its support from the ethnic Macedonian working-class) and the Liberal Party of Macedonia, which campaigns on a platform of free-market reforms and strengthening Macedonia's economy.

Signs in multiple languages on a currency exchange in Skopje. The acceptance of Albanian as a co-official language of the Republic of Macedonia was key to ending a 2001 rebellion by ethnic Albanians in the country. © *Thorne Anderson/Corbis*

The Liberal Party was formed in 1990 as part of the reformist movement within Yugoslavia. In 1997 the Liberal Party merged with the Democratic Party to form the Liberal Democratic Party (LDP). In 2000 dissident former members of the Liberal Party broke away from the LDP and re-formed the Liberal Party of Macedonia (LPM). The LDP also remains in existence and is a major member of the Together for Macedonia coalition. LDP is a socially liberal party that is affiliated internationally with the European Liberal Democrat and Reformist Party and the Liberal International.

The other major party in the Together for Macedonia coalition is the Social Democratic Union of Macedonia (SDSM). SDSM was the successor party to the Macedonian Communist party, and it has remained a large and influential party. SDSM held the most seats in the Sobranie from 1992 to 1998 and from 2002 to 2006; it lost to VMRO–DPMNE in 2006 in large part because the voters blamed SDSM for Macedonia's many economic problems. SDSM is nominally a left-wing party and is a full member of the Socialist International, but it has cooperated with free-market economic reforms that

were enacted to meet European Union entry requirements and to encourage economic growth.

The Democratic Union for Integration (DUI) is the leading ethnic Albanian party; in the 2002 Sobranie elections it was the choice of 70 percent of ethnic Albanian voters. DUI grew out of the Albanian National Liberation Army (NLA), a militant group that fought violent conflicts with the Macedonian government in 2001. After the NLA signed a peace agreement with the government in August 2001, the organization morphed into a democratic political party under the name DUI.

The other major Albanian parties are the Party for Democratic Prosperity (PDP) and the Democratic Party of Albanians (DPA). PDP, which was founded in 1990, is committed to advocating for Albanian rights by peaceful means. Its major issues have included efforts to get more Albanians into Macedonian universities and into government positions.

DPA was formed in 1997 by the merger of the Party for the Democratic Prosperity of Albanians, which split from the PDP in 1994, and the People's Democratic Party. DPA is more radically nationalist than PDP; it advocates for ethnic Albanians to be recognized as a separate national group.

Major Events

Macedonia faced a series of difficult challenges after it declared its independence. International recognition of the new country was delayed by battles over Macedonia's name and flag (which Greece considered to infringe on its own Macedonian heritage and symbols) and Macedonia's constitution, which hinted at Macedonian designs on formerly Macedonian lands that are now part of Greece and Bulgaria. Without international recognition, Macedonia could not receive foreign loans, which were sorely needed. The Macedonian economy, already weak, suffered further when Greece imposed economic sanctions on Macedonia and when Macedonia agreed to participate in international sanctions against Serbia. The dispute between Macedonia and Greece was partially resolved in 1995, but the damage had already been done to the Macedonian economy.

Macedonia also faced unrest in its western regions, which are populated by ethnic Albanians. When Serbia began persecuting its own Albanian minority in Kosovo in 1999, tens of thousands of these ethnic Albanians found refuge in Macedonia, further increasing that country's Albanian minority. (Estimates of the proportion of Macedonians who are ethnic Albanians range from one-quarter to one-third of the nation's population.) The war eventually spilled over into Macedonian territory, with ethnic Albanian guerrillas from both Kosovo and Macedonia launching attacks within Macedonia's borders in 2001. These attacks, which were popular with many Macedonian Albanians, spawned a several-month-long low-grade civil war that was ended by the Ohrid Agreement in August 2001. Under the terms of the Ohrid Agreement, ethnic Albanians in Macedonia were promised that Albanian would be recognized as an official language in Macedonia and that more ethnic Albanians would be given jobs with the Macedonian police.

Twenty-First Century

Despite the dire predictions of many observers in 2001, the Ohrid Agreement has held. In 2004 Macedonia amended its constitution to devolve more power to the local authorities, allowing ethnic Albanians a larger degree of self-rule in areas where they constitute a majority of the population. Although such concessions to the ethnic Albanian community remain unpopular with a significant fraction of ethnic Macedonian voters, the disputes between these two communities are generally being resolved without violence.

Macedonia continues in the twenty-first century to have a very weak economy, with unemployment rates of well over 30 percent, and it also has a high level of corruption, crime, and smuggling. The Macedonian government has been taking steps to confront these prob-

lems, with the support of the European Union and other international organizations, but progress has been slow. Due to this slow progress, Macedonia's application for European Union (EU) membership has been stalled. Macedonia has been recognized as a candidate for EU membership since 2005, but no date has yet been set for formal accession talks to begin.

BIBLIOGRAPHY

Benson, Leslie. *Yugoslavia: A Concise History.* New York: Palgrave, 2001.

European Forum for Democracy and Solidarity. "FYR Macedonia Update." http://www.europeanforum. net/country/fyr_macedonia_update (accessed August 8, 2007).

Macedonia.org. http://www.macedonia.org (accessed August 8, 2007).

⊕ Romania

Type of Government

Romania is a parliamentary republic, with the president serving as head of state and the prime minister serving as head of government. The power to make laws lies with the two-chambered parliament, but unlike in most parliamentary democracies, in Romania the president retains considerable power. Romania also has an independent court system that has undergone reforms since 2000 in an effort to end corruption and conflicts of interest among prosecutors and justice officials.

Background

Between 101 and 105 AD troops from the Roman Empire conquered the tribes who were then living in the area that would later become Romania. The Romans withdrew from the area in 271, but their influence on the area can still be recognized today: Romanians still speak a Romance language (that is, one descended from Latin) that has more in common with Spanish or French than with the languages of their Slavic neighbors.

After the Romans withdrew, Romania was overrun by one invading force after another—first Germanic tribes who plundered the land and left, and then Slavs, who settled in the area. Early in the eleventh century the Hungarian kingdom absorbed Transylvania, the most central region of Romania. The Hungarians and the German nobles they invited to settle in Romania thoroughly dominated Transylvania's Romanian peasantry for the next nine hundred years.

Some of these peasants, along with Romanian nobility who had been dispossessed by the Hungarians, fled south and east into Romania's two other major regions, Walachia and Moldavia. These two regions are separated from Transylvania by the Carpathian Mountains and the Transylvanian Alps, which made it difficult for the Hungarians to extend their control into these territories. As a result both regions were able to declare partial independence from Hungary; Moldavia did so in 1360, and Walachia followed in 1380.

The Ottoman Empire (centered in what is now Turkey) began pressing against the borders of Walachia and Moldavia in the fifteenth century, but the regions fought back. Walachia's resistance was led by Vlad Ţepeş (ruled 1456–62, 1476–77), whose name means "Vlad the Impaler" and who reportedly killed his enemies by impaling them on tall wooden stakes. The Turks defeated Walachia and drove Vlad into exile in 1462.

The Moldavian army fought under Stephan the Great (1435–1504). Stephan and his army won major victories over the Turks in the 1470s, but the Turks surged back. The Moldavians managed to continue their resistance until Stephan's death in 1504, but not long afterward Stephan's son Bogdan the One-Eyed (c. 1470–1517) signed an agreement subjugating Moldavia to the Ottoman Empire.

Transylvania fell under Ottoman domination after the Ottoman Turks crushed the Hungarian army at the Battle of Mohács in 1526, but the region retained a good deal of its freedom. The Ottomans allowed Transylvania's nobles to make their own laws regarding its internal affairs, as long as the Transylvanians paid an annual tribute to the Ottomans and provided soldiers for the Ottoman army. During this time Transylvania was ruled by a prince who was elected by the Transylvanian Diet (parliament), although the Ottomans could veto the Diet's choice of prince.

The Transylvanian Diet voted in 1688 to transfer itself from being a vassal state of the Ottoman Empire to being a vassal of the Austrian Empire. The Ottomans, who had been weakened by a major military defeat at the Battle of Vienna in 1683, were unable to stop Transylvania from defecting. This defeat also weakened the Ottomans' hold on Walachia and Moldavia. The Russian Empire was determined to expand into Ottoman territory, and Walachia and Moldavia were two of the areas that they coveted. The Russians invaded these areas eight times between 1711 and 1853 and frequently occupied the two countries for several years after an invasion. Russia also permanently occupied the part of Moldavia known as Bessarabia—the eastern half of the country, which lay east of the Prut River—and incorporated it into Russia in 1812.

The residents of Walachia and Moldavia originally supported the Russian invaders, hoping that their fellow Orthodox Christians, the Russians, would free them from the Muslim Ottoman Empire. However, the Walachians and Moldavians soon realized that they would be oppressed under the Russian Empire just as much as they had been under the Ottomans. In the nineteenth century the Walachians and Moldavians began demanding complete independence from both the Ottoman and Russian Empires.

Walachia and Moldavia received partial independence in the 1850s. After the Russians invaded Walachia and Moldavia in the 1853 Crimean War, the major European powers—including Great Britain, France, and Austria—sent troops to help the Turks force the Russians out of Ottoman lands. The 1856 Treaty of Paris, which ended the Crimean War, called for Walachia and Moldavia to become an international protectorate which would nominally remain part of the Ottoman Empire, but which would also be overseen by the European powers.

In 1861 Walachia and Moldavia united to form Romania. The country's most famous king, Carol I (1839–1914), took the throne five years later. In a matter of weeks after becoming king, Carol drafted a new constitution that gave Romania a bicameral legislature, whose members were elected by landholders and the clergy. Carol also sought to modernize Romania, which was still nearly as isolated and poverty-stricken as it had been in the fourteenth century.

Romania declared independence from the Ottoman Empire during the Russo-Turkish War of 1877–1878, in which Romania fought on the Russian side. The European powers formally recognized Romania's independence in 1881, making Romania a completely free country for the first time.

Romania gained a great deal of territory in World War I, which it entered on the side of the Triple Entente (Russia, Britain, and France) in 1916. Romania regained Bessarabia from Russia, and in the closing days of the war it occupied Transylvania and some other former Hungarian, Bulgarian, and Serbian lands. Under the terms of the peace treaties that ended World War I, Romania was permitted to keep nearly all of this territory, which meant that Romania's land area and population both more than doubled. It also meant that, for the first time, nearly all of the ethnic Romanians in Europe lived within Romania.

Romania did not fare as well in World War II. In the summer of 1940 Germany and the Soviet Union forced Romania to give up Bessarabia, Transylvania, and some other territory. Despite this, Romania entered the war on the German side in the fall of 1940. Romanian and German troops invaded the Soviet Union in the summer of 1941, but the Soviet Union was able to stop the advance and push the Romanians and Germans back. Soviet troops assumed control of Romania in 1944 and forced the country to switch sides. Although Romania did gain Transylvania back, the Soviet Union maintained control of Bessarabia.

The Soviet Union also installed a Communist government in Romania. However, this government did not remain loyal to the Soviet Union: in 1964 the Romanian Communists declared themselves independent from the Soviet Communist Party. The next year Nicolae Ceausescu (1918–1989) came to power. Within four years

Romanian dictator Nicolae Ceaucescu a month before his execution in December 1989. *Gerard Fouet/AFP/Getty Images*

Ceausescu had eliminated all opposition and become a dictator, a position he held until 1989. He and his secret police, the Securitate, controlled all aspects of life in Romania. Ceausescu was also accused of mismanaging the Romanian economy, and many people resented the expense involved in Ceausescu's building an enormous palace in Bucharest while ordinary citizens endured shortages of utilities and food.

Opposition to Ceausescu escalated in December 1989. The revolution started with protests on December 15 that turned violent when some protesters were killed by the army on December 17. On December 21, a mob broke into the building housing Ceausescu's offices. Ceausescu and his wife briefly escaped, but were soon captured and turned over to the army, which supported the protesters. On December 25, a makeshift tribunal held a brief trial before declaring the Ceausescus guilty of an array of charges and ordering them to be executed. The sentence was carried out minutes later.

Romania's first post-Communist government was led by former Communists. The National Salvation Front, led by Ion Iliescu (1930–), took control of the

country in the days immediately after Ceausescu's execution. Although the National Salvation Front's rule was often thuggish and corrupt, the voters overwhelmingly supported the Front in elections in 1990. After two years of power struggles within the government, and sometimes violent street protests against the government, Romania enacted a new democratic constitution late in 1991.

Government Structure

Romania's 1991 constitution made the country a republic with a modified parliamentary system of government. The parliament consists of two houses: the Chamber of Deputies and the Senate. It has the power to make the laws, and it votes to confirm the prime minister, who is nominated by the president. The parliament also confirms the appointments of cabinet ministers, who are nominated by the prime minister. Representatives are elected to four-year terms in the Romanian parliament on a party list system. Voters select parties rather than individual candidates, and each party is given seats in the parliament based on the percentage of the vote that it received. Parties then assign seats to their members based on a ranked list of candidates prepared before the election: if the party receives, for example, twenty-five seats, then the top twenty-five candidates on the list receive those seats.

The president of Romania functions as the country's head of state. The president's responsibilities include safeguarding the constitution, ensuring that the state functions properly, commanding the armed forces, chairing the Supreme Defense Council, and mediating between groups within the government and between the government and the people. The president also has the power to veto laws, although his veto can be overridden by a two-thirds vote of the parliament. The president is elected by the people to a five-year term and is allowed to serve a maximum of two terms.

The Romanian judiciary is independent from the political process. There are two supreme courts in Romania: the Constitutional Court, which determines whether or not laws are constitutional, and the High Court of Cassation and Justice, which is the highest appeals court in the country. ("Cassation" means "annulment," referring to the court's power to annul decisions by lower courts.)

Political Parties and Factions

Romania has a large number of political parties, but only a few of them are popular enough to have won seats in parliamentary elections. Dominant parties include the Social Democratic Party on the left (a socialist party containing a number of former Communists), and the Justice and Truth Alliance on the right. The Alliance consists of the center-right Democratic Party and the National Liberal Party, which favors free markets, low taxes, and social liberalism. The nationalist Greater Romania Party, the Hungarian Democratic Union of Romania (which represents the Hungarian minority in Romania), and the Romanian Conservative Party are also represented in the parliament.

Major Events

Iliescu remained Romania's president until 1996, despite the dissolution of the National Salvation Front in 1992. (Iliescu went with the breakaway Democratic National Salvation Front, which, after several subsequent mergers and name changes, became the Social Democratic Party.) Iliescu's rule was marked by corruption and slow economic reforms—the majority of economic activity in the country took place in state-owned businesses well into the 1990s—but it also saw a maturation of Romanian politics, as a free press began to take hold and political street riots became a less common occurrence.

In 1996 Iliescu was voted out as president and the Party of Social Democracy in Romania (the Social Democratic Party) lost control of the parliament. For the next four years various reformist governments tried to fight corruption and push through economic and political reforms, but these efforts were largely ineffective. By 2000 the economy had deteriorated, corruption was no better, and Romanians had had enough of the reforms: they returned Iliescu to the presidency and restored power in the parliament to the Social Democratic Party.

Twenty-First Century

Voters elected a government dominated by the Justice and Truth Alliance in 2004. For the presidency they chose Traian Basescu (1951–), a former merchant-marine captain with a reputation for straight talk. Under Basescu and the Justice and Truth Alliance, Romania finally succeeded in tackling corruption, particularly within Romania's judicial system. Progress was so good that the European Union, long reluctant to admit Romania, allowed the country to join on January 1, 2007.

BIBLIOGRAPHY

Crampton, R. J. *Eastern Europe in the Twentieth Century—And After.* New York: Routledge, 1997.
Siani-Davies, Peter. *The Romanian Revolution of December 1989.* Ithaca, NY: Cornell University Press, 2005.

⊕ Bosnia and Herzegovina

Type of Government

Bosnia and Herzegovina (which is often referred to simply as Bosnia) is an emerging federal democratic republic. The country has a weak central government, but most political power lies with the two states that make up the republic: the Federation of Bosnia and Herzegovina and the Republika Srpska.

Background

The ancestors of today's Bosnians are Serbs and Croats who settled in the area in the seventh century AD. Bosnia emerged as a separate country before 1000 AD, but by the end of the twelfth century Hungary had taken over Bosnia.

Bosnia became independent from Hungary in the thirteenth century, and under the leadership of Tvrtko I (c. 1338–1391), Bosnia became one of the most powerful states in the Balkans. Bosnia united with Herzegovina and conquered portions of Croatia, and its king was also crowned king of one of the Serbian states. However, this independent Bosnia lasted only until the fifteenth century, when the Ottoman Turks expanded their empire into Bosnia. The Ottomans were Muslims, and the Bosnian nobility converted to Islam so that they would be allowed to keep their land, their serfs, and their privileges. Some of the serfs converted to Islam as well, but others remained Christians. (All serfs suffered under Ottoman rule, but the Christians were taxed more heavily than the Muslims.)

When the Ottoman Empire began to weaken in the nineteenth century, the Christian peasants rebelled against their local lords, and their local lords rebelled against the Ottomans. One widespread rebellion in 1875 sparked a wider Balkan war that ended with Austria-Hungary occupying Bosnia. However, Serbia wanted Bosnia for itself, and as Serbia grew stronger in the early twentieth century, Austria-Hungary became more and more concerned about Serbia's designs on Bosnia.

The issue came to a head in 1914, when a Bosnian student who was affiliated with a Serbian nationalist group assassinated an Austrian archduke. This event launched World War I, which ended five years later in defeat for Austria-Hungary. In the closing days of World War I, when it seemed likely that Austria-Hungary's Balkan territories would receive their independence, Slovenia, Croatia, and Serbia reached an agreement to create a new country that would unite all of the South Slavic ("Yugoslav") peoples. This new country was at first called the Kingdom of the Serbs, Croats, and Slovenes; it later changed its name to Yugoslavia. Despite the kingdom's name, it also incorporated Bosnia.

In Yugoslavia, Bosnia once again found itself caught in the middle of power struggles between Serbs (who wanted a centralized and unified Yugoslavia) and Croats (who wanted an autonomous Croatian state that included some Bosnian territory). These power struggles took a bloody turn during World War II, when Yugoslavia was occupied by Nazi Germany and split into several different countries. Bosnia was united with Croatia in a nominally independent country that was actually a German puppet state. This country, the Independent State of Croatia, was dominated by Croatian nationalists who wanted an ethnically pure Croatia. Their ethnic cleansing policy was carried out by a Croatian militant group called the Ustase, which killed tens of thousands of Serbs, Jews, and Roma (Gypsies) on Bosnian territory. The Serbs organized another militant group, the Chetniks, to fight against the Nazis and their Ustase allies, but in the end the Chetniks wound up spending much of their effort on butchering the Muslim population of Bosnia. Battles between the Chetniks and the Partisans, a multiethnic Communist-led resistance group, also occurred on Bosnia soil. By the end of the war an estimated one million Yugoslavs had been killed, and a significant portion of these deaths occurred in Bosnia.

After World War II Yugoslavia was reassembled under the leadership of Josip Broz Tito (1892–1980), the leader of the Communist partisans during World War II. Bosnia was a relatively contented member of Tito's Yugoslavia, which lasted until Tito's death in 1980. Tito had successfully repressed nationalist movements in Yugoslavia during his rule, but after his death the ties binding Yugoslavia's six republics (Serbia, Croatia, Bosnia, Slovenia, Macedonia, and Montenegro) began to weaken. In 1991 Croatia, Slovenia, and Macedonia all declared their independences. Bosnia held a referendum on whether to declare independence in the spring of 1992. Bosnia's Serbs, who wanted to remain part of Yugoslavia, boycotted the referendum, but Bosniacs (Bosnian Muslims) and the Bosnian Croats voted overwhelmingly in favor of independence.

Government Structure

Bosnia is two states in one: the Federation of Bosnia and Herzegovina, which is populated primarily by Bosniacs and Croats, and the Republika Srpska, or the Bosnian Serb Republic. Bosnia has an overarching federal government that governs the country as a whole, but both of these entities also have their own constitutions, their own parliaments, their own presidents, and their own Supreme Courts. Under the Dayton Accords (which ended Bosnia's 1992–1995 war), most of the political power in Bosnia was with the Federation of Bosnia and Herzegovina and the Republika Srpska, but since 1995 the federal government has slowly gained more power.

At the federal level Bosnia has a bicameral (two-house) parliament consisting of a House of Representatives and a House of Peoples. The House of Representatives has forty-two seats, twenty-eight for representatives from the Federation of Bosnia and Herzegovina and fourteen for representatives from the Republika Srpska. Members of this house are elected by the people using a proportional representation system. The House of Peoples has fifteen seats, five each for Bosniacs, Croats, and Serbs. The members of this house are elected by the House of Representatives of the Federation of Bosnia and Herzegovina and the National Assembly of the Republika Srpska, respectively. Members of both houses serve four-year terms.

The Federation of Bosnia and Herzegovina has its own bicameral parliament, consisting of a ninety-eight-seat House of Representatives and a fifty-eight-seat House of Peoples. (The House of Peoples has seventeen seats allocated to each of Bosniacs, Croats, and Serbs, and seven seats allocated to other ethnic groups.) In the Republika Srpska, legislative authority resides in an eighty-three-seat National Assembly. The members of the Bosniac/Croat House of Representatives and the Serb National Assembly are elected by the people to four-year terms.

The head of the Bosnian federal government is the Chairman of the Council of Ministers. This position is essentially the same as the position of prime minister in most parliamentary democracies. The Chairman of the Council of Ministers has the power to propose legislation, to prepare the country's budget for the parliament's approval, and to carry out the laws made by the parliament. The Chairman of the Council of Ministers also has the power to appoint other ministers who will serve under him, but these ministers must be confirmed by the House of Representatives.

Bosnia has a president who serves as the head of state, but the presidency in Bosnia is unusual in that it is shared among three people. At any given time only one of these people is the chairman of the presidency, but that position rotates every eight months. These three people are elected directly by the voters to four-year terms. Two of the members, one Croat and one Bosniac, are elected from the Federation of Bosnia and Herzegovina; the third is a Serb who is elected from the Republika Srpska. The presidency's primary powers are in foreign policy: The presidency has the power to appoint ambassadors, to negotiate treaties, and to represent Bosnia in international organizations such as the United Nations.

At the federal level Bosnia has a nine-member Constitutional Court that decides on disputes between or among the federal government, the Federation of Bosnia and Herzegovina, and the Republika Srpska. Four of the court's judges are elected by the Bosniac/Croat House of Representatives, two are elected by the Serb National Assembly, and three are appointed by the president of the European Court of Human Rights. Bosnia also has a Supreme Court that hears cases that have been appealed from the courts in the Federation of Bosnia and Herzegovina and the Republika Srpska. Each of these entities has its own Supreme Court, as well as its own municipal-level courts.

Political Parties and Factions

Bosnia has a plethora of political parties. One of the largest is the Party of Democratic Action, often known by the initials SDA. SDA was founded in 1990, making it one of the first post-Communist parties in the former Yugoslavia. The membership of SDA is primarily ethnic

Bosnia and Herzegovina after the signing of the Dayton Peace Accords in 1995. *XNR Productions, Inc./Gale, a part of Cengage Learning*

Bosniacs, even though the party's charter declares it to be a multiethnic party. SDA is a moderately conservative party that is aligned internationally with the European People's Party. It wants the Bosnian government to continue to be decentralized and for each ethnic group to have political autonomy. As of the 2006 legislative elections, SDA had nine seats in the federal House of Representatives, making it the largest single party in that chamber of parliament.

The next-largest federal party is the Party for Bosnia and Herzegovina, another nominally multiethnic but largely Bosniac party, which as of 2006 had seven seats in the House of Representatives. This party split off from SDA in the mid-1990s. It advocates for the Republika Srpska and the Federation of Bosnia and Herzegovina to be abolished and for Bosnia to be a unified country.

The largest truly multiethnic party is the Social Democratic Party of Bosnia and Herzegovina, which won five seats in the House of Representatives in the 2006 elections. This left-wing party is descended from the former Communist Party and is affiliated with the Socialist International. It encourages a strong federal government, a closer union between the two halves of Bosnia, and more integration with the rest of Europe.

Ethnic Serbs and Croats also have their own parties. For the Serbs, the two largest parties are the Alliance of Independent Social Democrats (also sometimes known as the Party of Independent Social Democrats or the Union of Independent Social Democrats) and the Serbian Democratic Party. The Alliance of Independent Social Democrats is a moderate party that promotes cooperation between all of Bosnia's ethnic groups and closer ties to the rest of Europe. Its politics are somewhat left-wing, and it is a consultative member of the Socialist International. The Serbian Democratic Party (SDS) is a right-wing, ultranationalist party that was founded in 1990 by accused war criminal Radovan Karadzic (1945–). SDS was formerly the dominant party in Republika Srpska, but it has declined in popularity somewhat in recent years. As of the 2006 elections it held only three seats in the House of Representatives, and it was outnumbered by the Alliance of Independent Social Democrats by forty-one to seventeen in the National Assembly of the Republika Srpska.

For Croats, the major parties are the Croatian Democratic Union of Bosnia and Herzegovina and the Croatian Democratic Union 1990. The Croatian Democratic Union of Bosnia and Herzegovina is a conservative nationalist party that is affiliated with the Croatian Democratic Union proper in Croatia. It is also affiliated with the International Democratic Union and the European People's Party. The Croatian Democratic Union 1990 split from the Croatian Democratic Union of Bosnia and Herzegovina in 2006, in part over the issue of constitutional reforms. The Croatian Democratic Union of Bosnia and Herzegovina has supported constitutional reforms that would strengthen Bosnia's federal government but would also, some Croats believe, weaken the position of the Croats relative to Bosnia's Serbs and Bosniacs. The Croatian Democratic Union 1990 opposes these constitutional reforms.

Major Events

Bosnia was torn apart by civil war between 1992 and 1995. After the country declared independence, many of Bosnia's Serbs (supported by the Yugoslav National Army) organized themselves into an army and set out to take possession of as much Bosnian territory as possible. Within a few months Serbs controlled around two-thirds of Bosnia. Ethnic Croats took possession of much of the rest of the country, leaving the Bosnian Muslim government with only a tiny sliver of territory. However, later in the war Croatia and the Bosniacs, with the tacit support of Western countries, joined forces to retake territory from the Serbs. When the war was ended by the Dayton Peace Accords in 1995, the Croatian/Bosniac coalition and the Serbs each controlled around half of Bosnia.

A number of war crimes were committed during the war in Bosnia, primarily but by no means entirely by Serbs. Serbian war crimes included attempting to ethnically cleanse parts of Bosnia of Bosniacs (a goal that was also pursued by some Croats, although with less vigor)

War-ravaged buildings in the city of Mostar, Bosnia and Herzegovinia, in November, 1995. © *David Turnley/CORBIS*

and killing civilians indiscriminately during their siege of the city of Sarajevo. The most notorious war crime took place in the city of Srebrenica, where in the summer of 1995 Bosnian Serb forces overran the United Nations–designated "Safe Area" that had been set up there for Bosniac refugees. The Serbs separated the male refugees from the women and children and executed between seven thousand and eight thousand men and teenage boys. By the time the war ended, more than 5 percent of the population of Bosnia had been killed and half of the country's citizens were refugees.

Twenty-First Century

Bosnia and Herzegovina is still struggling to recover from its civil war. The country is not yet fully sovereign; European Union peacekeepers remain in the country, and the Bosnian government is still overseen by the United Nations–sponsored Office of the High Representative for Bosnia and Herzegovina, an international institution that was created by the Dayton Accords. The High Representative has real power over political affairs in Bosnia, including the final say over the interpretation of the Dayton Accords. Although the Office of the High Representative would like to end its mission, and most Bosnians would like to see it go, this is not likely to

happen until politicians from all three of Bosnia's major ethnic groups reach a stable agreement on the future of their country.

BIBLIOGRAPHY

Benson, Leslie. *Yugoslavia: A Concise History*. New York: Palgrave, 2001.

Domin, Thierry. *History of Bosnia and Herzegovina from the Origins to 1992*. http://www.nato.int/sfor/indexinf/bihistory.htm (accessed August 13, 2007).

European Forum for Democracy and Solidarity. "Bosnia Herzegovina Update." http://www.europeanforum.net/country/bosnia_herzegovina_u (accessed August 13, 2007).

⊕ Serbia

Type of Government

Serbia is a republic with a parliamentary form of government. Its parliament is the unicameral (one-house) National Assembly. The executive branch is headed by the prime minister, the cabinet, and the president, while the court system is headed by both a Supreme Court and a separate Constitutional Court.

Background

The first Serbs settled in what is now Serbia in the seventh century AD. For several centuries these Serbs lived in small clans that were under the rule of the Byzantine Empire, but in the twelfth century the chief of one clan, Stefan Nemanja (1109–1199), began conquering the neighboring clans, declared independence from the Byzantines, and created the first unified Serbia. Nemanja's descendants continued to expand Serbia's territories and to strengthen Serbia's position in relation to its more powerful neighbors, and in the following 150 years Serbia had its "golden age." By 1350 the Serbs ruled not only modern-day Serbia, but also modern-day Albania, Macedonia, and much of modern-day Greece.

This golden age began to decline in the mid-fourteenth century, when the Ottoman Turks began expanding their empire into the Balkan peninsula. It took more than one hundred years—from 1345 to 1459—for the Turks to completely conquer Serbia, but the majority of the Serbian resistance was broken at the Battle of Kosovo in 1389. This battle became the heart of Serbia's national legends in the following years. Serbian writers composed epics about the heroes who died there, and even today Serbia celebrates its national holiday on the anniversary of the battle, on June 28.

Most of modern-day Serbia remained under the Ottoman's harsh rule until the nineteenth century. (The exception was the Vojvodina region, an area settled by ethnic Serbs that was ruled by the Hungarian Empire.) Serbia finally won its independence in 1878, and in 1912 it defeated the Ottoman Empire again and won Kosovo and Macedonia.

Serbia's growing size and power concerned the Austro-Hungarian Empire, which ruled Vojvodina (roughly the northern quarter of modern-day Serbia) and modern-day Bosnia and Croatia. Several secret societies formed in Serbia that were dedicated to promoting Serbian nationalism and expanding Serbian territory, generally at the expense of Austria-Hungary. When a Bosnian student who was affiliated with one of these secret societies assassinated an Austrian archduke in 1914, Austria-Hungary used the provocation as an excuse to declare war on Serbia.

Austria's declaration of war on Serbia sparked World War I, which ultimately resulted in the defeat of the Austro-Hungarian Empire and its allies. As the war was nearing an end in 1918, it seemed likely that Austria-Hungary's Balkan territories would receive their independence, and Serbia convinced the about-to-be-independent Slovenes and Croats to join Serbia in a new country that would unite all of the South Slavic ("Yugoslav") peoples. On December 1, 1918, the Serbian Prince Aleksandar proclaimed the founding of the Kingdom of the Serbs, Croats, and Slovenes. (Despite the country's name, it also included Bosnia.) It changed its name to Yugoslavia in 1929.

Serbian President Slobodan Milosevic in 1990. © *Petar Kujundzic/ Reuters/Corbis*

Politics in Yugoslavia were extremely unsettled between the world wars. Serbia wanted Yugoslavia to be a centralized country where Serbians dominated, but Croats and Slovenes wanted more autonomy. The fighting between Serbs and Croats over the organization of Yugoslavia became bloody after 1928, when a Serbian member of parliament shot five Croatian representatives, and Croatians clashed with the Serbian authorities in the streets.

Ethnic strife in Yugoslavia only worsened during World War II. Yugoslavia was conquered by Nazi Germany and its allies in 1941 and divided up among them. Serbia and Croatia (which absorbed Bosnia) became nominally independent, but both were actually German puppet states. Ethnic Serbs were heavily involved in fighting in both Serbia and Croatia. A Nazi-allied Croatian militant group, the Ustase, set out to ethnically cleanse Croatia by killing the country's ethnic minorities, of which the largest was Serbs. Between three hundred thousand and five hundred thousand ethnic Serbs were killed by the Ustase. At the same time, two separate militant groups were fighting against the Nazis and the Ustase: the purely Serbian Chetniks and the multiethnic Partisans. The Chetniks were fighting to protect ethnic Serbs from the Ustase and to restore the prewar,

Serbian-controlled Yugoslavia, while the Partisans, who were backed by the Communists, wanted to take over Yugoslavia and turn it into a Communist country. Because of their differing goals, the Chetniks and the Partisans wound up fighting against each other, and the Chetniks were also involved in massacring Bosnian Muslims. By the end of the war more than one million Yugoslavs were dead (including more than half a million Serbs) and the Partisans, led by Josip Broz Tito (1892–1980) were in control of a reunited Yugoslavia.

The government of Tito's Yugoslavia was still dominated by ethnic Serbs (much to the displeasure of the other ethnic groups, Croats in particular), but Tito encouraged people to think of themselves as Yugoslav rather than as Serbs or Croats in order to reduce ethnic tensions. This policy had mixed success, but during his lifetime Tito had sufficient control over the country to suppress nationalist movements in Yugoslavia. After Tito died in 1980, however, Yugoslavia began to unravel.

Slobodan Milosevic (1941–2006) became the head of the Serbian Communist Party in 1986. He incorporated a robust Serbian nationalism into the party's platform and cracked down on dissent both inside and outside of the party. When the Communist system collapsed across Eastern Europe in 1989, Milosevic smoothly transformed the Serbian Communist party into a nationalist party, under the name the Socialist Party of Serbia, that was fully loyal to himself.

The other Yugoslav republics, particularly Slovenia and Croatia, were extremely concerned by Milosevic's rhetoric. In the late 1980s they began pushing for more autonomy within Yugoslavia, and in June 1991 both declared independence from Yugoslavia. Macedonia followed that November, and Bosnia and Herzegovina declared its independence the next year. Later in 1992 Serbia and Montenegro also became independent and signed a new constitution, changing Yugoslavia from the Socialist Federal Republic of Yugoslavia to simply the Federal Republic of Yugoslavia. The joint state abandoned the Yugoslavia name in 2003, adopting the name Serbia and Montenegro, but when Montenegro declared its independence from Serbia in 2006, the separate nations were then known by their respective names.

Government Structure

Serbia is a republic with a parliamentary form of government. Legislative authority in the country is vested in the 250-seat National Assembly, whose members are elected by the people to four-year terms. Once the National Assembly has been elected, it elects a prime minister and the "government," or cabinet, which exercises the majority of executive power in Serbia. Serbia also has a president, but this position is largely ceremonial. The president's main duties are to represent Serbia abroad and to serve as commander-in-chief of the armed forces.

The president is elected directly by the people to a five-year term of office.

There are several levels of courts in Serbia, from municipal courts at the lowest level, through district and appellate courts, to the Supreme Court at the highest level. The Supreme Court of Serbia hears appeals from the lower courts, settles jurisdictional disputes between lower courts, and oversees the judges who are employed by the Serbian judicial system. The Supreme Court is a large body with several dozen judges who are divided into four divisions: the case law division, the administrative division, the civil division, and the criminal division. The criminal division is further divided into a war crimes panel, a juvenile delinquency panel, a special division for organized crime-related cases, and a division for cases involving the military. Serbia also has a separate Constitutional Court, which is not part of the regular judicial system, that determines whether or not the laws and actions of the Serbian government contradict the Serbian constitution.

The province of Kosovo within Serbia has its own government that is independent from the Serbian government. Kosovo is also a parliamentary democracy, with a parliament, prime minister, president, and judicial system. The Kosovar parliament is the Assembly, a unicameral parliament with 120 representatives who serve three-year terms. One hundred representatives are elected directly by the people; the remaining twenty are elected to represent minority ethnic groups in Kosovo. The Assembly elects Kosovo's president (who also serves a three-year term), prime minister, and cabinet. The Kosovar judicial system is under the control of UNMIK, the United Nations mission that is currently administering Kosovo. Before December 2004 UNMIK appointed all of the judges in Kosovo. Since December 2004, when the Kosovar Ministry of Justice was created, UNMIK has slowly been transferring oversight of the judicial system to that ministry.

Political Parties and Factions

The three largest political parties in Serbia are the Serbian Radical Party (SRS), the Democratic Party (DS), and the Democratic Party of Serbia (DSS). These three parties won more than three-quarters of the seats in the 2007 parliamentary elections. As of 2007, DS, DSS, and the smaller G17 Plus party governed in coalition.

DS is a moderately nationalistic social democratic party that has been a major player in Serbian politics since 1993. The party and its leader, a former philosophy professor named Zoran Djindjic (1952–2003), were actively involved in bringing down Milosevic as president of Serbia in 2000. Djindjic became prime minister early in 2001, and later that year he agreed to turn Milosevic over to the war crimes tribunal at The Hague, Netherlands. Serbian radicals assassinated Djindjic in 2003 in protest of this decision. Despite this, DS has continued to support a policy of cooperating with the international war crimes tribunal and of strengthening ties with the rest of Europe. In European politics, the party is affiliated with the Socialist International.

DSS is a moderately right-wing, nationalist party that advocates liberal economic policies and conservative social policies. The party is critical of NATO, of Western intervention in the former Yugoslavia, and of DS's cooperation with the war crimes tribunal in The Hague. In addition, some of its members have expressed support for expanding Serbia's borders and creating a Greater Serbia. However, the party firmly supports democracy, and its leader, Vojislav Kostunica (1944–), has a reputation for honesty and integrity that is rare in Serbian politics. Kostunica was president of Serbia from 2000 until 2003 and became prime minister in 2004.

Although SRS is the largest single party in the parliament, with eighty-one seats, it is not part of the governing coalition. This party is extremely nationalistic, advocating for Serbia to reconquer all of the territory it has ever possessed, from the northernmost reaches of Croatia all the way into Greece. SRS also opposes sending accused war criminals from Serbia to The Hague to be tried by the International Criminal Tribunal for the Former Yugoslavia. One of the two cofounders of SRS, Vojislav Seselj (1954–), has been accused of war crimes and is at The Hague awaiting trial.

Notable minor parties include G17 Plus (with nineteen parliamentary seats) and the Socialist Party of Serbia (with sixteen seats). Some minority ethnic groups also have their own political parties. These include the Alliance of Vojvodina Hungarians, with three seats in the parliament, and two parties representing Roma (Gypsies), with one seat apiece.

Major Events

Serbia reacted violently to the dissolution of Yugoslavia. It fought a ten-day-long war with Slovenia immediately after Slovenia declared its independence, but Serbia soon admitted defeat. Serbia was more tenacious with Croatia and Bosnia. When those two republics declared their independences, Milosevic and the Yugoslav National Army (which was heavily dominated by Serbs) threw their support behind ethnic Serbs in those countries who fought to rejoin Serbia. The resulting wars were marked by ethnic cleansing, the indiscriminate shelling of civilian populations, and other war crimes. Although none of the three sides (Serb, Croat, and Bosnian) was completely innocent, the majority of these war crimes were carried out by Serbs. The wars in Croatia and Bosnia were both ended by the Dayton Peace Accords in 1995.

Serbia then fought another war in Kosovo, the majority ethnic Albanian province in southwestern Serbia. The Kosovo Liberation Army (KLA) began fighting for independence for the province in 1997. The Serbian security forces struck back harshly, and international concern began to mount that Serbia planned to repeat the ethnic cleansing of Bosnia in Kosovo. In 1999, after negotiations to end the conflict had failed, NATO began an aerial bombing campaign against Serbia. The bombing continued for seventy-eight days until Serbia was forced to concede defeat. By that time well over half a million Kosovars had become refugees in Albania and Macedonia.

Twenty-First Century

One major issue facing Serbia is the fate of Kosovo. Kosovo has been governed by the United Nations since the end of the war in 1999, and the final status of the province has remained an open question. By 2007 the Kosovars had grown tired of dragged-out negotiations about their future and announced that they would declare independence by the end of the year. The Serbian government has declared an independent Kosovo "unacceptable," but it is unclear what Serbia will do if Kosovo should declare independence unilaterally.

BIBLIOGRAPHY

Benson, Leslie. *Yugoslavia: A Concise History.* New York: Palgrave, 2001.

European Forum for Democracy and Solidarity. "Serbia Update." http://www.europeanforum.net/country/serbia (accessed August 13, 2007).

Supreme Court of Serbia. http://www.vrhovni.sud.srbija.yu/code/navigate.php?Id=32 (accessed August 16, 2007).

⊕ Slovak Republic

Type of Government

The Slovak Republic, also known as Slovakia, is a parliamentary democracy. Its legislature, the National Council, consists of a single house with 150 seats. Most power in the government lies with the prime minister; the country has a president, but that position is largely ceremonial. The Slovak Republic also has four separate court systems: the Constitutional Court, the regular court system, a military court system, and a special court that deals only with cases of corruption.

Background

The first Slovaks arrived in what is today Slovakia around 500 AD, but little is known about Slovak history until the early ninth century. At that time the Slovaks and their neighbors, the Czechs, joined together to form the Great Moravian Empire. The Great Moravian Empire ended when the Magyars (ancestors of modern-day Hungarians) conquered it in 907. Slovakia was then incorporated into the Kingdom of Hungary, and it remained under Hungarian rule for the next one thousand years. When the Kingdom of Hungary was defeated by the Ottoman Turks in 1526, Slovakia became part of the Austrian

Habsburg Empire, but the Hungarian nobles who lived in Slovakia continued to rule over the Slovak peasants.

After World War I the Austro-Hungarian Empire was broken up, and the many nations that had been part of the empire became independent. Slovakia was joined with the Czech lands of Bohemia and Moravia to form a new country, Czechoslovakia. Slovaks generally supported this merger at first, but many of them later came to feel oppressed in Czechoslovakia. The Slovaks were dominated politically and economically by the Czechs, who were more numerous, more educated, more industrialized, and less devoutly Catholic than the Slovaks.

Nazi Germany actively meddled in the affairs of Czechoslovakia in the late 1930s, and some radicals in the Slovak parts of the country allied themselves with the Germans against the Czechs. The Slovaks were briefly rewarded, when under pressure from Germany, the Czechoslovak government permitted Slovakia to form its own autonomous government in October 1938. When the Czechs tried to reassert their control over Slovakia in March 1939, Slovakia, at German urging, declared its independence; the next day, the Germans conquered the Czech portions of the country. Slovakia remained closely allied with, and largely controlled by, Nazi Germany throughout World War II.

The Soviet Union liberated Slovakia from the Germans in 1944. In 1945 Slovakia and the Czech lands were once again reunited into the single country of Czechoslovakia. With the support of many Czechs and Slovaks, the Soviet Union punished the Slovaks who had collaborated with the Germans during World War II and instituted a new government. This government was originally democratic, but in 1948 Czechoslovakia became a Communist dictatorship.

Slovaks had somewhat more power relative to the Czechs in Communist Czechoslovakia than they had had in interwar Czechoslovakia, although the country was still dominated by the Czechs. Two of Czechoslovakia's Communist presidents, Alexander Dubcek (1921–1992) and Gustav Husák (1913–1991), were Slovaks. However, ultimately both Slovaks and Czechs were ruled by the Soviet Union. The Soviet Union even invaded Czechoslovakia in 1968 in order to remove Dubcek as the country's leader and to end the reforms that Dubcek had instituted under the slogan "socialism with a human face."

The Communist government of Czechoslovakia was brought down by popular protests late in 1989. The old tensions between Czechs and Slovaks reemerged almost immediately thereafter. Czech and Slovak politicians were unable to agree on a new constitution, on the speed of economic reform, or even on the country's name. (The Czechs wanted to call it the Czechoslovak Republic; the Slovaks preferred Czecho-Slovak Republic.) By the end of 1992 politicians on both sides had become resigned separation, despite the fact that fewer than 40 percent of both Slovaks and Czechs said in polls that they wanted the country to be dissolved. On January 1, 1993, Slovakia officially became an independent country.

Government Structure

Political power in the Slovak Republic centers on the National Council, a unicameral (one-house) parliament containing 150 seats. Representatives are elected to four-year terms in the National Council based on a nationwide proportional representation system. (Under a proportional representation system, voters vote for parties, rather than for individual candidates, and the seats in the parliament are divided up among the parties based on the percentage of the votes that each party receives.) There are no districts; all voters in the country vote for the same lists of candidates, and all representatives represent the entire country. Parties have to receive a minimum of 5 percent of the vote in elections in order to be assigned seats in the parliament.

Once all of the seats in the parliament have been assigned, the parties negotiate with each other to form a governing coalition—a group of parties that controls (usually) a majority of the seats in the parliament and that agrees to work together to govern the country. The leader of the largest party in this coalition generally becomes the prime minister. The prime minister then selects a group of legislators from the parties in his coalition to form a cabinet, which is officially appointed by the president. Together, the prime minister and the cabinet exercise the majority of executive power in Slovakia.

Before 1998 the president was elected by the parliament, but that year a constitutional amendment was passed calling for the president to be elected directly by the people. These elections take place in two rounds, with the top two finishers in the first round competing head-to-head in the second. The president serves a five-year term as the head of state. He or she has some executive powers, including the power to command the Slovak military, but most power in the government lies with the prime minister, the cabinet, and the parliament.

The Slovak Republic has four separate court systems: a Constitutional Court that determines whether laws contradict the Slovak constitution, the regular court system, a military court system, and a Special Court that deals only with cases of corruption. The regular court system is headed by a Supreme Court, the highest appeals court in the country, whose judges are elected by the National Council. The judges of the Constitutional Court and the Special Court are appointed by the president, but in both cases the president is limited in his or her choices. Constitutional Court judges must be appointed from a list of nominees approved by the National Council, and Special Court judges are elected by other judges before being appointed by the president.

President Ivan Gašporevič of the Slovak Republic (far right) meeting with other Eastern European leaders in 2005. The Slovak Republic is a member of the Visegrad Group, whose other members are Poland, the Czech Republic, and Hungary. © *Andrzej Grygiel/epa/Corbis*

Political Parties and Factions

The Slovak Republic has had a dizzying number of political parties and coalitions since it became independent in 1993. The longest-lasting parties have been the party of former Slovakian Prime Minister Vladimir Meciar (1942–), the People's Party–Movement for a Democratic Slovakia (LS–HZDS, which formerly went by the name Movement for a Democratic Slovakia); the Christian Democratic Movement, a small conservative party; and the Slovak National Party, a far-right party known for its hostility toward Slovakia's Hungarian and Roma (Gypsy) minorities.

As of the 2006 elections, the most popular political party in Slovakia was Smer ("Direction"), a populist ex-Communist party that was founded in 1999 when the original Slovakian ex-Communist party, the Party of the Democratic Left, split. Following this split, most of the Party of the Democratic Left's supporters defected to Smer, and on January 1, 2005, the two parties remerged. The remerged party, which also incorporated the smaller left-wing parties the Social Democratic Alternative and the Social Democratic Party of Slovakia, goes by the full name Smer–Social Democracy.

Other important political parties include the Party of the Hungarian Coalition, which represents the substantial Hungarian minority in Slovakia; the Slovak Democratic and Christian Union–Democratic Party, a right-wing party formed by the 2006 merger of the Slovak Democratic and Christian Union and the Democratic Party; the Alliance of the New Citizen (known by its abbreviation ANO, which means "yes" in the Slovak language), an economically and socially liberal party; and the Communist Party of Slovakia, whose support has hovered between 4 and 6 percent since 2000.

Major Events

For most of the 1990s Slovakia was under the control of Meciar, an ex-Communist who perpetuated some of the worst aspects of Communist rule. During Meciar's time as prime minister, the government controlled television, radio, and theaters; Meciar's political opponents were harassed; and foreigners viewed the government as so corrupt that the European Union and NATO (the North Atlantic Treaty Organization) would not even discuss allowing Slovakia to join those organizations. Meciar, however, was popular with many voters because he provided them with jobs and other economic benefits.

Meciar was finally voted out as prime minister in 1998. His party, the Movement for a Democratic Slovakia, won more seats than any other party in the parliament that year, but five opposition parties united to form a broad coalition of both liberals and conservatives that together controlled 93 out of the 150 seats in the parliament. This coalition's leader, Mikuláš Dzurinda (1955–), became prime minister.

Dzurinda and his allies enacted a number of reforms. They attacked corruption within the police, the intelligence services, and other arms of the government; simplified the tax system; reformed the health care and retirement systems to make them less costly; and ended state control over the prices of goods and services. These changes improved Slovakia's image in the eyes of foreigners. Foreign investment money began to pour into Slovakia, and the country joined both NATO and the European Union in 2004. However, the reforms proved less popular with the voters. Dzurinda's government was forced to cut many expensive but popular programs as it tried to dig the country out of the debts that Meciar had left behind, and by 2003 Dzurinda's popularity rating was a mere 5 percent.

Twenty-First Century

In 2006 Slovaks voted out Dzurinda's reformist government and voted in a populist government led by Smer and also including Meciar's People's Party–Movement for a Democratic Slovakia and the Slovak National Party. During the campaign these parties promised to roll back many of Dzurinda's reforms, to the dismay of the business community and foreign investors in Slovakia, but once in power they did not make any strong moves toward carrying out their promises.

BIBLIOGRAPHY

Crampton, R. J. *Eastern Europe in the Twentieth Century–and After*. New York: Routledge, 1997.
National Council of the Slovak Republic. http://www.nrsr.sk (accessed July 4, 2007).

⊕ Eritrea

Type of Government

The newest nation in Africa, Eritrea is nominally in transition to a constitutional republic; in practice, however, it is an autocratic presidential regime. A multiparty legislature of the sort envisioned in the constitution does not yet exist. A transitional National Assembly does meet, but it is firmly in the hands of the president, who has shown little interest in replacing it. The president also commands the military, chooses cabinet ministers and provincial governors, and appoints judges to the Supreme Court. All media are state-run, and opposition parties are banned.

Background

An arid nation of roughly four and a half million people, Eritrea is bordered by Sudan to the west and north, Ethiopia and Djibouti to the south, and the Red Sea to the east. The population is split fairly evenly between Christians and Muslims, a division that usually, but not always, coincides with ethnic and linguistic differences. Among the most important ethnic groups are the Tigrinya, Tigre, Kunama, Afar, and Saho peoples.

The enormous economic and strategic value of the Red Sea has long attracted foreign powers. From the end of the nineteenth century to World War II, Eritrea, Ethiopia, and most of Somalia were under Italian control. After defeating Italy, the Allied powers stripped it of its colonial possessions, passing the question of the future governance of those possessions on to the United Nations (UN). One of the major issues has always been Eritrea's relationship to Ethiopia, its much larger southern neighbor. Italy had ruled the two as a single region, and Ethiopia is landlocked without Eritrea. These considerations, together with strong U.S. support for Ethiopian Emperor Haile Selassie (1892–1975), prompted the UN in 1952 to designate Eritrea as an autonomous, federated territory within Ethiopia.

The arrangement made some economic and structural sense at the time, because it was not clear that Eritrea's resources alone would be sufficient to create and maintain the infrastructure—schools, roads, telephone lines—necessary for a modern state. But little attention was paid to the opinions of the Eritrean people, many of whom were determined to assert their independence regardless of the practical challenges involved. Tensions mounted steadily, finally flaring into armed rebellion in 1961 with the formation of the Eritrean Liberation Front (ELF). Selassie responded by dissolving the federation and ruling Eritrea directly as an annexed province. The insurgency continued until 1991, when the fall of Selassie's successor, Mengistu Haile Mariam (1937–) enabled the Eritrean People's Liberation Front (EPLF), an ELF offshoot, to drive the remaining Ethiopian forces out of the region. A provisional government dominated by the EPLF and headed by the group's leader, Isaias Afwerki (1946–), then took over, administering a referendum two years later that revealed overwhelming support for independence. Eritrea officially became a nation on April 27, 1993.

Government Structure

After independence, a unicameral, transitional National Assembly replaced the provisional government. The dominance of the EPLF, which became known as the People's Front for Democracy and Justice (PFDJ), continued, however, and one of the first acts of the new body was to elect Afwerki president of the nation. As of 2007 he remained in office. The national assembly contains one hundred and fifty seats, half of which are allocated to members of the PFDJ's Central Committee. Of the remainder, fifteen are held by expatriate Eritreans and sixty by members of the Constituent Assembly, an ad-hoc group organized in 1997 to finalize a constitution. The constitution is finished, but mandated elections have been postponed twice, and as of 2007 none

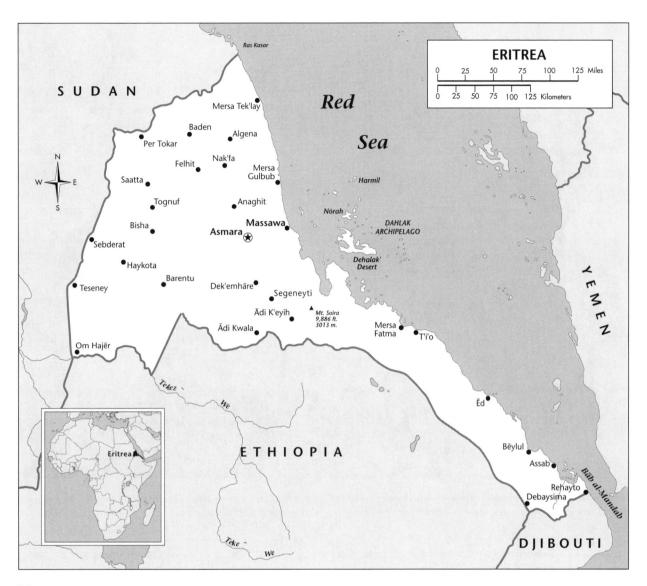

Eritrea. *Maryland Cartographics*

were scheduled. The legislative branch thus remains constrained by an organizational framework that was supposed to be temporary.

Executive power is in the hands of President Afwerki and his handpicked cabinet, also known as the State Council. Six regional governors chosen by the president handle local affairs. At the summit of the judicial branch is the Supreme Court, whose members are also presidential appointees. These appointments are theoretically subject to the National Assembly's approval, but in most cases approval has been granted without serious debate.

Political Parties and Factions

Although the PFDJ is the sole legal party, other groups do exist, often formed along ethnic and regional lines. Some of these are engaged in armed rebellion. The Afar Revolutionary Democratic Unity Front (ARDUF) is

fighting a destructive but low-intensity war to create a separate homeland for the Afar people. Meanwhile a small group of Muslim extremists, the Eritrean Islamic Jihad (EIJ), has been receiving considerable attention in the international press. It is difficult, however, to assess the real strength of these groups and of the opposition as a whole because of Eritrea's widespread practice of detaining dissidents, journalists, and others who speak out against the government.

Major Events

A boundary dispute with Ethiopia sparked a devastating war in 1998. A negotiated ceasefire ended the conflict in 2000, and a UN peacekeeping force was dispatched to enforce a demilitarized zone in the disputed areas. Tensions remained high, however, particularly around the town of Badme, which Ethiopia continues to control in

Eritreans demonstrating outside of the European Parliament in Strasbourg, France, in October 2005. They hoped to convince the European Union to support peace negotiations between Eritrea and Ethiopia. © *VINCENT KESSLER/Reuters/Corbis*

defiance of an international commission's decision. Eritrea expelled the UN force in 2005, and observers have since reported frequent troop movements on both sides of the frontier.

Twenty-First Century

Eritrea faces an array of severe problems. As much as a third of the population must rely on international food aid for survival, and the vast majority lack electricity and clean water. The most pressing problem, however, is probably the deteriorating situation with Ethiopia. Recent reports have suggested that Eritrea may be supporting Islamic militants fighting the Ethiopia-backed Somali government.

BIBLIOGRAPHY

Jacquin-Berdal, Dominique, and Martin Plaut. *Unfinished Business: Eritrea and Ethiopia at War.* Lawrenceville, NJ: Red Sea Press, 2005.

Mengisteab, Kidane, and Yohannes Okbazghi. *Anatomy of the African Tragedy: Political, Economic, and* *Foreign Policy Crisis in Post-Independence Eritrea.* Trenton, NJ: Red Sea Press, 2005.

U.S. Congress, House Committee on International Relations, Subcommittee on Africa, Global Human Rights, and International Operations. *Ethiopia and Eritrea: Promoting Stability, Democracy and Human Rights—Hearing before the Subcommittee on Africa, Global Human Rights, and International Operations of the Committee on International Relations, House of Representatives, One Hundred Ninth Congress, First Session, May 5, 2005.* Washington, DC: U.S. Government Printing Office, 2005.

⊕ Principality of Andorra

Type of Government

Despite its formal name as the Principality of Andorra, this European microstate is actually a parliamentary democracy. Andorra is wedged in the Pyrenees between Spain and France and is one of history's rare examples of a successful duumvirate (a state with two leaders). In this case the French president and the Spanish bishop of Urgell are Andorra's heads of state.

Background

Andorra is the last surviving state of the Marca Hispanica (Spanish March), a line of small buffer states set up by the Frankish king Charlemagne (742–814) to thwart Spain's aggressive tendencies. Charlemagne placed nobles in charge of these small states, and in Andorra's case he named the count of La Seu d'Urgell to serve as overlord in 798. In the eleventh century a dispute arose between the reigning count and his counterpart in France, and its resolution was finally settled in 1278. France and Spain declared that henceforth the bishop of La Seu d'Urgell and the count of Foix would serve as "coprinces" of Andorra. Over time, the French count's duties were assumed by the French sovereign and, later, the French president.

This somewhat unorthodox arrangement endured until the final decade of the twentieth century. Urged by European Union officials, Andorra established a constitutional commission, and its first constitution was approved by referendum in 1993. The document formally established Andorra's 181 square miles as a sovereign parliamentary democracy, and even though the two coprinces remained heads of state, the constitution specified that the head of government would be the *cap de govern* (prime minister).

Government Structure

Before 1993 Andorra had no real executive branch of government, though there was an elected parliament after 1419. Under the 1993 constitution, the cap de govern wields all executive power, legislative power is held by the government and parliament, and the judiciary is independent of both.

All citizens over the age of eighteen can vote for the twenty-eight legislators who sit in the General Council of the Valleys, Andorra's unicameral (one legislative body) parliament. Each of Andorra's seven *comuns* (administrative districts) sends four representatives to it. Fourteen are elected directly by voters in each *comú*, and the other half are chosen to serve at large from a national list. The *sindic* (president of the General Council) and *subsindic* are elected by parliament to serve a three-year term; they carry out legislative decisions.

The twenty-eight General Council members, in turn, select the cap de govern to serve as president of the Executive Council. Technically, the coprinces have approval over this choice. Likewise, the Executive Council president chooses the seven members who serve on the Executive Council, which functions as an executive-branch cabinet.

Andorran law is a mixture of local custom with some elements law from the Roman era and from the Spanish territory of Catalonia. Its judiciary is overseen by the five-member Superior Council of Justice. Each of the coprinces, the cap de govern, the General Council sindic, and the members of the lower courts are allowed to seat a Superior Council panel member to a six-year term. Civil cases in Andorra are heard by a tribunal of four judges and may advance to the Court of Appeals. Final appeals are heard either in Perpignan, France, at the Supreme Court of Andorra, or at the Ecclesiastical Court of the bishop of La Seu d'Urgell in Spain. Criminal cases pass first through the Tribunal des Cortes in Andorra la Vella. There is one jail in the country, and it is used only for defendants awaiting criminal trials; those sentenced to prison terms may choose a French or Spanish facility.

Neither of Andorra's coprinces live in the country. In 2007 they were French president Nicolas Sarkozy (1955–) and Joan Enric Vives i Sicília (1949–), the bishop of La Seu d'Urgell. Their role is considered largely ceremonial, and they have no veto power over government acts. Regardless, Spain and France have a long-standing agreement to provide for the defense of Andorra.

Political Parties and Factions

There were no political parties in Andorra until 1976. In the years since the 1993 constitution, several groups have arisen to supplant the old Andorran families who dominated the political scene for seven centuries. Foremost among them is the Liberal Party of Andorra, a center-right group that emerged as the winner in the 2005 elections with fourteen seats in the General Council. Other leading political parties are the Social Democratic Party, Andorran Democratic Centre, Century 21, Democratic Renewal, and the Greens of Andorra.

Voter turnout is relatively high, with 80 percent casting ballots in the 2005 election. Only Andorran citizens, however, are allowed to vote. Of the country's 71,800 residents, only a third are actual citizens; the rest are French, Spanish, or Portuguese nationals. Some come to Andorra to find work, whereas their wealthier counterparts are lured by Andorra's lack of income tax. Since the 1970s there has been a movement to grant foreigners more rights and open the door to citizenship, and the 1993 constitution provides for this.

Major Events

In 1607 King Henry IV (1553–1610) of France issued the edict specifying that Andorra's coprinces would be the head of the French state and the bishop of La Seu d'Urgell in Spain. Over the next three and a half centuries life in Andorra remained relatively unchanged, save for a brief period in the 1930s, when it was occupied by France because of social unrest, and then the site of a bizarre coup attempt by a Russian con artist and raconteur who declared himself Boris I, the sole prince of Andorra. By the mid-1970s both Spain and France had begun to encourage Andorra to enact some political, economic, and social reforms, which led to the establishment of the Executive Council in 1981. The

Coprinces French president Francois Mitterand (center) and Bishop of La Seu d'Urgell Joan Marti Alanis (right), visiting Andorra in 1993. *© Sygma/Corbis*

microstate remained isolated from the rest of Europe, however, and finally the Council of Europe urged Andorrans to begin the process of drafting a constitution in 1990. A separate body from the European Union, the Council of Europe was created to safeguard the principles of democracy and respect for human rights among its member nations. Andorra's first constitution went into effect in 1993, the same year it became a member of the United Nations.

Twenty-First Century

Andorra has tight banking secrecy laws that are fostering its emergence as a new European financial services center. Tourism also continues to drive the economy, as it has since the 1950s.

BIBLIOGRAPHY

Duursma, Jorri. *Self-determination, Statehood, and International Relations of Micro-states: The Cases of Liechtenstein, San Marino, Monaco, Andorra, and the Vatican City.* New York: Cambridge University Press, 1996.

Eccardt, Thomas M. *Secrets of the Seven Smallest States of Europe: Andorra, Liechtenstein, Luxembourg, Malta, Monaco, San Marino, and Vatican City.* New York: Hippocrene Books, 2005.

Leary, Lewis Gaston. *Andorra: The Hidden Republic.* New York, McBride, Nast, 1912.

⊕ European Union

Type of Government

The European Union (EU) is a hybrid governing entity based on treaties agreed to by its twenty-seven member countries, or states. Its organization is complex and unique, employing a combination of supranational elements (whereby one government body reigns over others) and intergovernmental elements (whereby various sovereign governments come together to cooperate on matters that may fall partially or completely outside of their respective jurisdictions). Its basic structure can be best understood within the framework of traditional executive, legislative, and judicial branches. An appointed European Commission, with representatives from each of the member states, including a president, forms the EU's executive branch. It has a bicameral legislature, with its upper house, the Council of the European Union, being the dominant lawmaking body, composed of government officials from each member state, and a European Parliament, which is directly elected by the citizens of the member states. The judicial branch is headed by the European Court of Justice.

Background

The European Union is made up of twenty-seven independent nations, often referred to as "member states"— Austria, Belgium, Bulgaria, Cyprus, the Czech Republic, Denmark, Estonia, Finland, France, Germany, Greece, Hungary, Ireland, Italy, Latvia, Lithuania, Luxembourg, Malta, the Netherlands, Poland, Portugal, Romania, Slovakia, Slovenia, Spain, Sweden, and the United Kingdom. It encompasses 1.6 million square miles, approximately half of billion people, and more than twenty-three languages. Nearly one-third of the world's gross national product is produced by the union. The EU's official currency, the euro, has been adopted as the sole legal tender in thirteen member states.

The idea of a unified Europe is a very old one and many battles have been fought over it. But the creation of the present-day European Union stemmed from a very different premise than those that had gone before: achieving that integration without force. The actualization of such a concept was almost without precedent.

World War II (1939–1945) left Western Europe physically and economically devastated. Its aftermath also included the advent of the Cold War—a period of heightened tensions between the United States and the Soviet Union—and the Soviet Union's obvious designs on parts of Eastern Europe beyond Poland and Bulgaria. The Western powers thus saw a need to rebuild their economies while protecting themselves from both one another and from the Soviet Union. French statesman and economist Jean Monnet (1888–1979) and foreign minister Robert Schuman (1886–1963) believed that the most effective way to begin the necessary international cooperation was to establish economic ties. This philosophy was reflected in the Schuman Plan, a joint suggestion from the two Frenchmen to pool European coal and steel production under a common authority. In addition to the economic incentive of a more efficient market, the proposal ensured that control over the materials of war was shared by various national governments. Their plan is widely seen as the first step toward a unified Europe.

The European Coal and Steel Community (ECSC) was brought into being by the Treaty of Paris, signed in April 1951 by Belgium, the Federal Republic of Germany (West Germany), France, Italy, Luxembourg, and the Netherlands, a group that came to be known as "the Six." The ECSC worked beautifully, increasing trade by almost 130 percent over five years, so the Six sought other areas that could be unified. Their next successful

efforts were two treaties signed in Rome in 1957 and entered into force the following year—one established the European Economic Community (EEC) and the other the European Atomic Energy Community (EAEC, or EURATOM).

Treaties continued to be key to the integration process. Important agreements leading up to the creation of the EU include the Merger Treaty of 1967, which incorporated the ESCS, EEC, and EAEC into one unit known as the European Communities, and the Single European Act of 1987, which assisted in the formation of a single market. Then came the Treaty on European Union (also known as the Maastricht Treaty), which took effect in November 1993. The Maastricht Treaty formally established the European Union and expanded and enhanced the provisions of the founding three treaties. Among the essential points of this treaty were a timeline to attain Economic and Monetary Union (EMU) and create a single currency, specific eligibility requirements for potential member states, a Common Foreign and Security Policy (CFSP), a Justice and Home Affairs (JHA) policy, a Social Chapter on labor standards and other social issues, and the introduction of EU citizenship. The Maastricht Treaty served as the basis of the current EU.

Government Structure

The European Union (EU) is a hybrid governing entity based on treaties agreed to by its member countries. A comparison to the United States is somewhat apt, as the two bodies do have some characteristics in common. Member countries of the EU, for instance, have relinquished some of their inherent powers in the interest of unity and shared values, as the U.S. states did when forming the federal government. In those instances, such as trade, the EU acts directly on its members' behalf, as the U.S. government does for its states. Like citizens of the United States, EU citizens have the right to free movement from one member state to the others, and can establish residence in other EU states. There are, however, many differences between the two as well. Key among these is that each EU member is a sovereign nation. This means that each retains its own authority in numerous areas, including defense. While there is a single unit of currency, the euro, most member states have not agreed to a joint monetary policy and still circulate their own money. Regardless of these limitations, the EU is the only governmental entity that can, in many cases, enact laws that are directly binding on citizens of different countries.

Thus, similarities to the United States aside, the EU's combination of supranational and intergovernmental elements renders it one of a kind. It is not exactly a federation, nor a mega-state to replace existing nations, yet it is more than a simple cooperative organization among governments—the EU is forging a new governmental template.

The executive role is played by the European Commission (EC), which is made up of an appointed commissioner from each member state and a single president. The Commission is appointed every five years, within six months of the European Parliament (EP) elections. First, member governments agree on new Commission president. A majority of the EP must then approve their choice. Next, the president-elect, in consultation with member governments, selects the twenty-seven commissioners. Finally, the EP interviews each prospective member before issuing a verdict on the entire group. It is important to note that the EP retains supervisory power over the Commission after appointments have been approved—it can, for example, dismiss the entire Commission through a motion of censure, and the Commission must clarify and/or justify its policies to the EP upon request.

The Commission's principal duties include acting as guardian and enforcer of the EU's underlying treaties, initiating legislation, managing policies and the budget, and representing the EU internationally. The Commission can issue guidelines for the implementation of legislation and treaties, initiate infringement proceedings against member states who violate EU directives, impose fines on companies or individuals, and administer the Union's budget appropriations. It also negotiates international agreements on the EU's behalf and retains the sole right of legislative initiative. Note that the Commission acts independently of the underlying individual governments, representing the interests and perspective of the EU instead.

The legislative function is essentially served through the bicameral efforts of the Council of the European Union and the European Parliament (EP). The Council represents the interests of the EU's member states, thus providing a check to the Commission's larger perspective, and is the primary decision-making entity. One minister from each country attends meetings according to the agenda, and so the individual minister varies depending on the subject at hand—an agriculture minister would, for instance, be sent to discuss crop prices. Ministers in attendance must have the authority to commit their government's votes, which are weighted by (but not directly proportional to) each member state's population. The Council presidency rotates among member states every six months (January through June, and July through December). The Council is assisted by a permanent body of member states' ambassadors called the Permanent Representatives Committee (COREPER). Council decisions are made in one of two ways: by the vote of a qualified majority representing a minimum of 73.9 percent of votes and at least 62 percent of the EU population, or, in areas such as taxation or asylum and immigration policy, by unanimous vote. Unanimity is also required when the Council wants to deviate from Commission proposals or reject Commission-accepted EP amendments.

The Council addresses both supranational and intergovernmental issues. Major supranational responsibilities include adopting European laws (often in conjunction with the EP), coordinating economic policies of member states, concluding international agreements, and approving the EU budget (jointly with the EP). Intergovernmental duties include developing the EU's Common Foreign and Security Policy (CFSP) and coordinating national judicial and law enforcement cooperation in criminal matters.

The other half of the legislative branch is the European Parliament (EP). Established in 1979, the EP is directly elected by EU citizens. Each member state holds its own parliamentary elections for the EP—the only requirement is that elections be held on a population-based, proportional representation system. The EP's 785 members serve five-year terms, and the size of each country's delegation is based on overall population. The composition in 2007 was as follows: 99 from Germany; 78 each from France, Italy, and the United Kingdom; 54 each from Spain and Poland; 35 from Romania; 27 from the Netherlands; 24 each from Belgium, the Czech Republic, Greece, Hungary, and Portugal; 19 from Sweden; 18 from Austria and Bulgaria; 14 each from Denmark, the Slovak Republic, and Finland; 13 each from Ireland and Lithuania; 9 from Latvia; 7 from Slovenia; 6 each from Estonia, Cyprus, and Luxembourg; and 5 from Malta. The EP elects its own president, who serves a two-and-a-half year term.

Primary duties of the EP are the passing of European laws (often in conjunction with the Council), supervising other EU institutions (most notably, the Commission), and, jointly with the Council, overseeing the EU budget. The EP serves an important role as a check upon the other governmental bodies. It has the ability to approve or reject Commission members and the right to censure and dismiss the entire Commission; the Council must also obtain the EP's consent as to some crucial decisions, such as those involving international agreements or procedures for parliamentary elections.

The EU's governance also includes the European Council (not to be confused with the Council of the European Union), which was granted legal status in 1974. This entity is made up of the member countries' heads of state or government, along with the president of the European Commission, and meets up to four times a year. Another way of maintaining proper balance between the supranational and intergovernmental, these senior diplomats set broad policy for future action and reconcile issues left unresolved by the Council. On a less formal level, these meetings provide a forum for brainstorming among member nations at the highest political level.

The judicial branch is headed up by the Court of Justice of the European Communities or, as it is commonly known, the European Court of Justice (ECJ). It is composed of twenty-seven justices, one per member

The official seat of the European Parliament, in Strasbourg, France. © *Murat Taner/zefa/Corbis*

state, assisted by eight advocates-general. Judicial appointments are for renewable six-year terms (staggered between thirteen and fourteen members, lest the entire Court be replaced at one time), and are mutually agreed to among member states. The Court selects its own president who serves a three-year, renewable term. Justices rarely sit en masse, given the size of the Court, but instead either convene as a Grand Chamber of thirteen or in panels of three to five.

The ECJ hears cases involving member states, institutions, businesses, and individuals, while ensuring EU legislation is construed and applied consistently in all member nations. The Court generally regards European legislation as prevailing over conflicting national laws. A Court of First Instance was established in 1989 to help ease the ECJ's heavy caseload. Its particular focus is on cases involving individuals and those concerning competition law. The newest addition to the EU's judiciary is the European Civil Service Tribunal. As the name implies, its role is to hear disputes between the EU and its civil service.

The other vital component of the EU judiciary is the European Court of Auditors (ECA). Its function is to monitor and oversee the use of all EU funds. It submits a yearly report to assist in the implementation of the EU's annual budget and has the authority to audit any person or organization handling EU funds, among other duties. The ECA is made up of one member from each EU nation. Members are appointed by the Council for renewable six-year terms and elect a president from within their own ranks to a three-year term.

Although it is not part of the EU's governmental structure, the European Central Bank (ECB) is another significant institution. Founded in 1998, its primary purpose is overseeing the EU's monetary policy. Managing the euro is an important part of that role, and the ECB is charged with maintaining the currency's price stability through such means as controlling the money supply via setting interest rates. The thirteen member states that have adopted the euro, along with their central banks and the ECB, make up what is known as the Eurosystem.

Political Parties and Factions

The political parties of the EU are coalitions of various political parties from the member nations that share common ideologies or goals. The most prominent parties are the European People's Party–European Democrats (EPP–ED), a coalition of conservative and Christian-democratic parties throughout Europe; the Party of European Socialists (PES), which encompasses various national labor and social democratic parties; the Alliance of Liberals and Democrats for Europe (ALDE); the European Greens–European Free Alliance, a coalition of environmentalist "green" parties and parties that represent stateless regions such as the Basque country; and the Union for Europe of the Nations (UEN), a conservative group that espouses national sovereignty within the EU. In the EP, members sit together in these party groups rather than as national contingents.

Major Events

After the Maastricht Treaty formally established the EU in 1993, there were three additional treaties of notable impact. The Treaty of Amsterdam, which took effect in 1999, took a renewed look at EU institutions with an eye toward enhancing economic and security objectives. Preparation for the union's growth, or "enlargement," was also part of the agenda. Among the treaty's more salient provisions were measures extending the scope of qualified majority voting, increasing the EP's powers and responsibilities (this, for example, is where parliament's decision-making role was placed on a more equal footing with the Council), and strengthening the EU's ability to engage in joint foreign policy endeavors. The Treaty of Nice (2003) went even further by setting the conditions for enlargement through more policy revisions. Those revisions included re-weighting votes within the Council, redistributing member country representation with the EP, and re-vamping the European Commission. It also extended the use of "enhanced cooperation," which permits a minimum of eight member states to proceed with policy initiatives on their own, providing those initiatives do not infringe on the rights of other members. All this build-up led to the largest single expansion of the EU when ten new members—Cyprus, the Czech Republic, Estonia, Hungary, Latvia, Lithuania, Malta, Poland, the Slovak Republic, and Slovenia—were admitted on May 1, 2004, bringing its membership to twenty-five. Additional expansion in 2007 brought two more Eastern European nations, Romania and Bulgaria, into the fold.

The EU's next major treaty enterprise was not initially as successful as its predecessors. In February 2002, the Convention of the Future of Europe (also known as the "European Convention"), composed of 105 members representing the governments of the EU's member nations and candidate nations, the parliaments of those states, the EP, and the Commission, began work on a draft treaty to create a European Constitution. The process lasted sixteen months and was open to the public, including the publication of official documents on

the Internet. A draft constitution was completed in the early summer of 2003 and approved via the European Constitutional Treaty on October 29, 2004.

The Constitution for Europe contains many major reforms and innovations. These include creating a five-year presidency for the Council (as opposed to the six-month rotation policy), establishing a foreign minister and foreign service, simplifying voting procedures, providing EU citizens with more opportunity for direct participation in government, and improving overall transparency. However, the document requires ratification by popular referendum or parliamentary vote by every EU member. In this, it has so far failed. French and Dutch voters refused the constitution in 2005. The matter has been put on hold while a report is compiled for the European Council, which is then expected to offer guidance on how to proceed sometime in 2008.

Twenty-First Century

Despite the setback of not gaining ratification of its proposed constitution, the EU appears poised to continue growing and evolving. 2007 saw the admission of Bulgaria and Romania to its ranks, bringing its membership up to twenty-seven. Entrance negotiations with Croatia and Turkey were begun in 2005, and an application from the former Yugoslav Republic of Macedonia were being entertained. Some member states worry that expansion may hamper decision-making as members with less "European" perspectives are brought into the union, while others are concerned about potential economic burdens caused by less-affluent member states or a possible influx of immigrants. Proponents of expansion, on the other hand, welcome the new blood and look forward to continuing to forge economic and political bonds with all the people of Europe. Such integration was, after all, the point of the EU's creation.

BIBLIOGRAPHY

European Union. "Europa–A Gateway to the European Union." http://europa.eu/index_en.htm.

Pinder, John. *The Building of the European Union.* 3rd ed. Oxford: Oxford University Press, 1998.

Shore, Cris. *Building Europe: The Cultural Politics of European Integration.* London: Routledge, 2000.

⊕ Russian Federation

Type of Government

The government of Russia operates under a super-presidential system that grants broad powers to the elected head of state, the president. The president appoints and shares executive powers with the prime minister, who is the head of the government. The legislative branch includes a bicameral assembly, the upper chamber of which comprises a Federation Council made up of representatives from geographical areas. The lower house, the State Duma, holds the authority to confirm the appointment of the prime minister in addition to its legislative functions. Following more than sixty years of Communist rule during the twentieth century, democracy brought stunning changes to Russia in the 1990s, but perhaps none so surprising as a return to an autocratic style of leadership under President Vladimir Putin (1952–), who has taken full advantage of the authorities granted him by the constitution.

Background

Stretching across 6.6 million square miles and eleven time zones, Russia is the world's largest country in area, and ranked sixth in population with 142 million people. Just over 80 percent of its citizens identify themselves as ethnic Russians, with the remaining 20 percent consisting of minorities from the former Soviet republics. Its origins as a state date back to the ninth-century founding of Kievan Rus in nearby Ukraine, the first unified entity of the Eastern Slavic tribes. By the 1400s the center of power had shifted from the city of Kiev to the more heavily fortified settlement in Moscow. Rulers there began using the title of "czar," the Russian-language variant of "caesar," and carried out an ambitious expansion program that established autocratic rule across a vast empire stretching from Europe to the Pacific Ocean.

St. Petersburg, built by Czar Peter the Great (1672–1725), was the opulent capital of imperial Russia after 1712, and it was there that the Romanov dynasty was overthrown in 1917 during World War I. A seizure of power by Communist hardliners known as the Bolsheviks followed later that year, and the new government reestablished Moscow as the capital. The terms "Russia," "Soviet Union," and "USSR" (Union of Soviet Socialist Republics) have often been used interchangeably, but technically Russia (as the Russian Soviet Federated Socialist Republic, or RSFSR), was only the largest of the constituent Soviet republics during the Soviet period. It was also the most powerful, and the Communist Russian elite who ruled it and the rest of the Union enjoyed privileged status. The control maintained by the Communist Party of the Soviet Union (CPSU) began to wane with the introduction of reforms by Soviet leader Mikhail Gorbachev (1931–) after 1985, and the first multiparty elections since 1917 were held in March 1990. Three months later, the RSFSR's new parliament, the Congress of People's Deputies, issued a declaration of sovereignty. A year later, in June 1991, the first presidential elections in the RSFSR took place, and an outspoken, reform-minded former Communist official named Boris Yeltsin (1931–2007) won the office by a landslide.

Yeltsin played a crucial role in the dissolution of the Soviet Union following an attempted coup by Communist Party operatives against Gorbachev in August 1991. With that event, the individual constituent republics began declaring independence, and the economic situation became perilous. Yeltsin responded by transferring Soviet assets, institutions, and authorities to Russian control over the next three months, and outlawed the Communist Party for its role in the failed coup. Citing a 1922 Treaty on the Creation of the Soviet Union, which contained a clause permitting the constituent republics to secede, Yeltsin and the leaders of Ukraine and Belarus signed the Belavezha Accords on December 8, 1991, followed several days later by a meeting with leaders of Soviet republics in Central Asia. The end result of these agreements was the formal dissolution of the Soviet Union and the establishment of the Commonwealth of Independent States (CIS) in its stead. Gorbachev resigned on December 25.

Government Structure

During its first two years in existence, Russia was governed by a 1978 Soviet-era constitution, although this was amended in several sections in order to allow for significant changes to the country's political and economic structure. The new Russian Constitution was approved by referendum on December 12, 1993. Under it the president holds the right to dissolve parliament, has the power to initiate national referenda, and is granted immunity from prosecution. He or she is elected to a four-year term by direct vote and is limited to two terms. The prime minister serves as head of government and is appointed by the president but subject to a confirmation vote by the lower house of the legislature. In theory, impeachment of a president is possible in the event of high treason or other serious crimes, but the stringent process requires actions by both houses of the legislature, the Supreme Court, and the Constitutional Court, making a legal ouster unlikely in practice.

Russia's bicameral parliament is jointly referred to as the Federal Assembly. Its upper chamber is the 178-seat Federation Council, which consists of two deputies from each of Russia's 89 administrative divisions. The 1993 constitution did not specify how the Federation Council was to be chosen, and initially the membership included regional governors and leaders of regional assemblies. When Putin came to power in 2000, however, he overhauled the selection system, providing for the election of the Federation Council deputies by the regional assemblies.

The lower house of Russia's Federal Assembly is the State Duma, with 450 seats. Half of them are allocated to candidates from single-mandate constituencies who won a majority vote in legislative elections, and the other 225 come from party lists of candidates. These latter 225 seats are allocated on a proportional basis according to election tallies, and parties must receive a minimum of 7 percent in the popular vote in order to qualify for seats. The deputies of the State Duma serve four-year terms, and may issue a no-confidence vote in the current

Russia. *Maryland Cartographics*

government, appoint or dismiss the head of the Central Bank, and initiate legislation—although this last power is not exclusively theirs. The Constitution grants deputies of the lower house the right to override decisions of the Federation Council by a two-thirds vote, and presidential vetoes may be nullified with the same percentage in a joint vote of both houses.

The judicial branch in Russia is blighted by pervasive corruption and attempts by elected officials to influence outcomes. Both are a legacy of the Soviet era, when the judiciary functioned as a rubber-stamp body for the policies of the Communist Party. At the top of the post-Soviet judiciary is a Constitutional Court, charged with reviewing legislation, presidential decrees, and international treaties. Its nineteen judges are appointed by the president and confirmed by a vote of the Federation Council, as are the justices of the Supreme Court, which is the final court of appeal for criminal and civil cases. The number of judges on the Supreme Court is not fixed by the constitution, but they are appointed in the same manner as the Constitutional Court. This

appointment process also applies to the High Court of Arbitration, which hears commercial disputes. Russian law does not recognize the principle of judicial precedent (abiding by previous court decisions) in issuing rulings. Criminal-case conviction rates in Russia are abnormally high, generally estimated above 95 percent, and judges who acquit defendants are often targeted for review or dismissal. Jury trials have been introduced in some regions and have a slightly higher acquittal rate than trials decided from the bench; however, jury trials comprise only a small percentage of criminal trials in Russia and have been more likely to be overturned on appeal by the state.

Russia is divided into eighty-nine administrative regions, covering six territories known as *kraya*; ten *okruga*, or autonomous districts; twenty-one ethnic enclaves; fifty *oblasts*, or provinces; and two municipal districts, St. Petersburg and Moscow. These regions have historically battled with the Moscow government over certain governance issues. During the early years of the Russian Federation, Yeltsin bested his political opponents in Moscow by

Chechen rebels hope to separate Chechnya from Russia. © *David Turnley/CORBIS*

winning support from regional politicians, to whom he granted greater autonomy in return for their help. However, this policy eventually intensified separatist sentiments in some of the eighty-nine regions. When Putin came to power he reasserted federal authority by establishing seven super-regions, called *federalnyye okruga*, which are Northwest, Central, Volga, North Caucasus, Ural, Siberia, and Far East. A plenipotentiary representative, or presidential envoy, is appointed by Putin to oversee each of them, and these loyalists wield a great deal of administrative power over locally elected officials.

Political Parties and Factions

Political parties have failed to achieve any genuine status in Russia, which observers link to the country's long history of absolute monarchy and then one-party rule. New parties are usually formed before legislative elections, but then dissolve. For the 1993 elections, the Russia's Choice Party was created, followed two years later by the Our Home Is Russia Party. The Unity Party won eighty-two seats in the State Duma in 1999, and was the bloc that backed Putin's ascension to power. It evolved into the United Russia Party in 2003 in time for parliamentary elections, in which it won 222 seats. The Communist Party has continued to win a substantial number of seats in each election since independence.

In the mid 1990s a group of newly rich entrepreneurs began to influence Russian politics. They had typically accrued their fortunes from privatization deals in which Yeltsin's government sold off the formerly state-run industries during Russia's transition to a free-market economy. Accordingly, they backed Yeltsin in his 1996 presidential re-election bid. They did the same for Putin in the 2000 race, but once elected the new president swiftly moved to end their influence. Some of the oligarchs were arrested, and others fled the country. Russia's wealthiest citizen, Mikhail Khodorkovsky (1963–), who was chair of the Yukos petroleum company is the best-known example. Khodorkovsky had publicly stated his support for increased transparency and democracy in Russia, and had strong connections to financial powers outside the country. He was arrested in 2003, put on trial, and sentenced to nine years in prison for fraud and tax evasion. Meanwhile, Yukos's assets were frozen by Putin's government, and the company was later declared by authorities to be bankrupt.

Major Events

Russia's fragile democracy has faced threats on several fronts since Communist rule ended in the early 1990s. Yeltsin's reform program met with serious opposition from Communists in the Russian Supreme Soviet, and in September 1993 he ordered that body dissolved. When the deputies refused to budge, troops were sent in to oust them. In 1994 a separatist war broke out in Chechnya, a predominantly Muslim area of the Caucasus that had declared its independence from Russia, and Chechen rebels battled Russian troops over the next two years.

In 1996 Yeltsin was reelected, but he suffered a heart attack between the first round of balloting and a run-off election—a perilous situation kept secret from the public for a time, which left the government essentially rudderless. A year later, a recovered Yeltsin concluded a peace treaty with the Chechen rebels specifying that a decision on Chechnya's status would be delayed until 2002. In 1998 Russia teetered on the brink of financial disaster with the collapse of the ruble, but a serious economic crisis was averted. Yeltsin still faced major opposition and resigned on December 31, 1999, in a surprise announcement. Putin was prime minister at the time and automatically became acting president. He was elected by direct vote in March 2000.

Putin's government resumed the war in Chechnya, despite the terms of the 1997 peace accord, after an apartment building in Moscow was the target of a supposed Chechen terrorist attack in 1999. The war escalated in October 2002 after the seizure of a Moscow theater during a performance; 850 audience members and theater personnel were held hostage, and more than 150 people died in the incident. In September 2004 nearly four hundred people were killed in an attack by Chechen separatists on a school in Beslan, a city in the autonomous republic of North Ossetia. Most of the fatalities in the incident resulted when Russian special forces took action against the hostage-takers, who were holding about twelve hundred adults and children at gunpoint in the school gymnasium. Putin's tough tactics against Chechen rebels in these crises prompted concern that he was reestablishing a dictatorial-style regime in Russia. One outspoken critic of his policies was the journalist Anna Politkovskaya (1958–2006), who was fatally shot in the elevator of her Moscow apartment building in October 2006 in what appeared to be a contract killing. Weeks later, Alexander Litvinenko (1962–2006), a former officer in the Russian state security service, died in London, England, where he had been living. Litvinenko had publicly accused Putin of responsibility for Politkovskaya's death, and British authorities launched a massive investigation that tied his death to poisoning by radiation after he met with a Russian operative linked to the Federal Security Service, known by its Russian-language acronym FSB.

Twenty-First Century

The Russian economy was growing at a pace of more than 6 percent annually in 2007 due in large part to its natural resources industries, including exports of oil, gas, timber, and metals. Because of the rapid economic growth, observers warned that the country's low birth rate and demographic shifts may result in a shortage of workers within the next decade. In addition, labor migration within Russia has led to ethnic tensions and was blamed for an increase in hate crimes. As of 2007, in an effort to entice workers to affected areas, the government was offering housing, relocation allowances, and cash incentives to returning ethnic Germans who had been forced out of Russia during Communist rule.

During his two terms in office Putin had consolidated power at the federal level and silenced his liberal opponents. While some of his policies, such as tight control of the media, were considered antidemocratic by Western standards, they received broad support within Russia, and his approval rating was among the highest in the world for a national leader. The 1993 constitution limits Putin to two terms in office, and the next presidential elections are scheduled for March 2008. Several politicians close to him, including FSB officers and the female governor of St. Petersburg, Valentina Matviyenko (1949–), are believed to be the most likely successors to the office.

BIBLIOGRAPHY

Fish, Michael Steven. *Democracy Derailed in Russia: The Failure of Open Politics.* New York: Cambridge University Press, 2005.

Jack, Andrew. *Inside Putin's Russia.* New York: Oxford University Press, 2004.

Remnick, David. *Resurrection: The Struggle for a New Russia.* New York: Random House, 1997.

⊕ Palau

Type of Government

Palau is a parliamentary republic in free association with the United States. The executive branch of government is led by the president, who serves as both chief of state and head of the government. In addition, the vice president and an appointed cabinet participate in executive functions. The legislative branch is made up of a bicameral parliament consisting of the Senate and the House of Delegates. The Supreme Court leads the judicial division. The executive and legislative branches are elected by popular vote, while Supreme Court justices are appointed.

Background

Palau is the westernmost archipelago of the Caroline Islands, lying about five hundred miles southeast of the Philippines. It consists of six island groups that total more than three hundred islands. The topography ranges from the mountainous main island of Babelthuap

Palau's capitol complex on Babeldaob.   © *Bob Krist/Corbis*

to low, coral islands. The climate is tropical, and includes a typhoon season from June to December.

Palau is thought to have been first settled sometime between 1000 and 2500 BC. Those early inhabitants likely migrated from what is now Indonesia, and the current populace indicates an ancestral mix of Indonesian Malays, New Guinea Melanesians, and Polynesians. Fishing and farming were the primary subsistence activities.

Extensive European contact started with the shipwreck of the British vessel *Antelope* in 1783. The captain and crew stayed in Palau for three months, rebuilding the ship with local assistance, and an active trading relationship between England and Palau soon followed. Foreign rule began with Spain in 1885, continuing with Germany in 1899 and Japan in 1914. Each of those countries left its mark on the culture and society of Palau. Spain introduced the still-dominant Roman Catholic Church and Latin alphabet, for example, as well as helping to eliminate traditional inter-village conflict. Germany instigated a program to utilize the country's natural resources, including mining phosphate and establishing coconut plantations. Japan's influence was perhaps the greatest. The Japanese created a market economy and shifted the customary clan ownership of property to that of individuals. The onset of World War II made Palau a target for

Allied attacks because of Japan's military and naval facilities there—some islands, especially Peleliu, were sites of intense fighting.

In 1947 Palau became part of the UN Trust Territory of the Pacific, under the administration of the United States. It chose not to join a single, federal Micronesian state in 1979, opting instead to form its own republic. A constitution was adopted in 1980, and Palau's first president took office the following year. A Compact of Free Association with the United States, which provided for Palau's sovereignty and economic assistance in return for U.S. management of its defense, was subsequently signed. Palau's constitution, however, hindered ratification of the Compact, as it included a nuclear-free clause. Repeated referendums to override the constitutional ban failed to achieve the required three-quarter majority approval of the population. In 1992 a constitutional amendment lowering the approval requirement to a simple majority was passed, which led to approval of the Compact in 1993. Thus, the Compact took effect in 1994, and Palau became an independent state on October 1 of that year.

Before independence, Palau's political agenda was dominated by debate over approving the Compact. This either caused, or was compounded by, acrimony and scandal within the government that led to the assassination of the territory's first president in 1985 and the apparent suicide of the second in 1988. The situation stabilized after 1994.

Government Structure

Palau is a parliamentary republic led by the president, who is both chief of state and head of the government. The president is elected to a four-year term of office by popular vote, as is the vice president, and both executives are eligible for second terms. The cabinet, called the Council of Chiefs, is made up of prominent traditional chiefs from each of Palau's sixteen states, and advises the president on matters of traditional law and custom.

Legislative power rests in a bicameral parliament called the Olbiil Era Kelulau (Palau National Congress). The two houses of parliament are the Senate and the House of Delegates. The nine senators are elected to four-year terms by nationwide direct vote on a population basis. The sixteen members of the House of Delegates are elected to four-year terms by popular vote from each of Palau's states. Each of the individual states also elects its own governor and legislature. Palau citizens enjoy universal suffrage at age eighteen.

The Supreme Court leads the judicial branch. It includes both trial and appellate divisions and is headed by the chief justice. Other courts are the Court of Common Pleas and the Land Court. Palau's constitution also provides for a National Court, but one was not active as of mid 2007. Judges are appointed for life by the president, with approval by parliament.

Political Parties and Factions

Palau has no formal political parties. All parliamentary members elected in the 2004 elections, for instance, were considered independents. During the pre-independence Compact dispute, there were two broad factions in evidence: the Coalition for Open, Honest, and Just Government, which opposed the Compact, and the Te Belau Party, which defended it. However, those groups did not continue once the issue had been resolved.

Major Events

The debate surrounding the Compact of Free Association has been the most important issue defining Palau's status and direction. The Compact provides for financial and other aid from the United States in return for Palau's allowing U.S. defense and military operations, as well as an option on one-third of Palau's land for fifty years. The financial aid consists of up to $700 million over a period of fifteen years, and the Compact also created a trust fund to provide budget assistance after direct support was withdrawn. It was ratified in 1994.

Twenty-First Century

The direct financial support of the United States is scheduled to end in 2009, and that embodies Palau's greatest challenge in the twenty-first century: how to prosper in the absence of foreign aid. Palau's best means to address this challenge lies in its tropical island beauty and pristine marine environment, which make it a prime tourist destination. In order to bolster its tourism industry, the government is making environmental preservation a priority and taking strides to position itself as an exclusive destination. The cushion provided by the Compact's trust fund will help Palau continue to prosper after U.S. financial aid is withdrawn, but the country is actively repositioning itself to achieve financial independence.

BIBLIOGRAPHY

Republic of Palau. "National Government." http://www.palaugov.net/ (accessed September 12, 2007).

Smith, Roy H. *The Nuclear Free and Independent Pacific Movement: After Mururoa.* New York: I. B. Tauris, 1997.

Tamanaha, Brian Z. *Understanding Law in Micronesia: An Interpretive Approach to Transplanted Law.* Boston: BRILL, 1993.

⊕ Hong Kong

Type of Government

Hong Kong is a limited democracy under the control of the People's Republic of China, as one of its special administrative regions. That control is largely hands-off, as the former British colony has been governed via the principle of "one country, two systems" since 1997. The government has its own constitution called the Basic Law, which outlines the functions of the executive, legislative, and judicial branches. The executive branch consists of the nominal president (chief of state), chief executive (head of government), and cabinet. The legislative branch comprises a unicameral Legislative Council, and the judiciary is led by the Court of Final Appeal.

Background

Hong Kong is bordered by China to its north and is otherwise surrounded by the South China Sea. It includes Hong Kong Island, Lantau Island, the Kowloon Peninsula, the New Territories, and 262 outlying islands. It also boasts Victoria Harbor, one of the world's most noted natural deepwater harbors. Archeological evidence suggests human habitation of Hong Kong dating back to the Stone Age. It was settled by Han Chinese during the seventh century, and a major migration from northern China occurred during the Sung Dynasty (960–1279). European contact was first made in the late seventeenth century with the British East India Company and, while trade was established, Western influence was fairly inconsequential until the nineteenth century. That changed when China was defeated in the first Opium War and ceded Hong Kong to the British in 1842.

The British accumulated additional land in the area, including a perpetual lease on the Kowloon Peninsula in 1860 and a ninety-nine-year lease on the New Territories in 1898. The latter acquisition increased the size of the Hong Kong colony by more than 90 percent.

Hong Kong prospered during the late nineteenth and early twentieth centuries, as it became a hub of British trade with China. Population exploded, reaching 1.6 million by 1941. World War II and the harsh Japanese occupation of the colony temporarily reversed this trend however, with only 650,000 people left in residence at war's end. England re-established its control in 1946, and prosperity soon returned. Assisted by an increase of hundreds of thousands of new residents fleeing Mainland China after the Communist takeover there in 1949, Hong Kong's citizenship had risen to 2.2 million by 1950. This influx of talent and labor fueled an economic success that began with manufacturing and progressed to finance and technology. By the 1970s Hong Kong was an economic "Asian Tiger," and China had begun to cast covetous eyes in its direction.

After China opened its doors to international trade and investment in 1978, Hong Kong's potential value to it became clear, and the Chinese government declined an extension of British rule. Talks between the two countries about the colony's future began in 1982. In 1984 they signed an agreement that provided for Hong Kong's timely return (per the New Territories lease of 1898) to Chinese rule in 1997. The conditions of handover included the concept of "one country, two systems," through which Hong Kong's economic, political, and social systems would remain largely intact and autonomous (except for defense and foreign affairs) for fifty years.

Despite misgivings on both sides, Hong Kong was duly returned to the Chinese on July 1, 1997. It thus became the Hong Kong Special Administrative Region, and more than 150 years of British rule came to an end.

Government Structure

As a limited democracy under the control of China, Hong Kong is necessarily something of a hybrid. An open and free society on one hand, its ultimate master is Communist China, so the ability to change government policy or effect democratic development is restricted. Nonetheless, the terms of the handover agreement provide for a level of independence otherwise unheard of in China. Those terms are codified in Hong Kong's Basic Law, which was approved by China's National People's Congress in April 1990.

The Basic Law outlines the functions and responsibilities of the executive, legislative, and judicial branches. The executive branch consists of the president (chief of state), chief executive (head of government), and cabinet. The presidency is nominal in that it is a Chinese government role and thus not literally part of the government of Hong Kong. The chief executive is elected to

a five-year term by an eight-hundred-member Election Committee made up of a spectrum of Hong Kong residents and representatives from Mainland China. The cabinet is called the Executive Council and is composed of fourteen official and fifteen unofficial members. All Council members serve by appointment of the chief executive and hold office only until the term of the chief executive expires.

The legislative branch includes a unicameral Legislative Council, or LEGCO. The Council has sixty members, half of whom are elected by popular vote and half of whom are indirectly elected through functional constituencies. All members serve four-year terms. Suffrage is universal for Hong Kong residents over the age of eighteen who have lived in the territory for at least seven years. A more truly universal suffrage is sought by pro-democracy factions.

The Legislative Council illustrates the unusual situation of the Hong Kong government. For example, there is a complicated system of checks and balances between the executive and legislative branch that allows the chief executive to return an unacceptable bill to Council for reconsideration. If the Council passes the bill again by a two-thirds majority, the chief executive may either sign it or dismiss the Council. If the chief executive opts for the latter and the same bill is passed by the new Council by the same margin, the chief executive must either sign it or resign. For all that potential democratic tension however, the Council is also obliged to report any enacted laws to the Standing Committee of the Chinese National People's Congress. If the Standing Committee disapproves, the law is returned for prompt invalidation.

Hong Kong's independent judiciary is headed by the Court of Final Appeal. Citizens have the right to a fair and speedy trial, and are presumed innocent until proven guilty. The Legislative Council endorses appointments and removals of all justices attached to the Court of Final Appeal, including the chief judge.

Political Parties and Factions

Because of the atypical nature of Hong Kong's government, political parties have little power to do much more than agitate. There are, nonetheless, competing factions.

The largest party in the LEGCO is the Democratic Alliance for the Betterment and Progress of Hong Kong, a generally pro-China group that won twelve Council seats in the 2004 elections. The second most dominant is the conservative, pro-business Liberal Party, which garnered ten seats. The Democratic Party (DP) is adamantly pro-democracy and enjoys a great deal of popular support, although it only won nine seats in the 2004 Council elections. The newest entrant is the Civic Party, which was established in 2006. It is also pro-democracy, but less stridently than the DP in hopes of reaching a broader base of citizens. Overall, the pro-democracy

The ceremony at which Hong Kong's sovereignty reverted to the Chinese government after 156 years as a British Crown Colony, 1997. © *AP/Wide World Photos*

parties won 63 percent of votes in the 2004 Council election, while the pro-China parties received 37 percent.

Major Events

Although colonization by the British had lasting repercussions for Hong Kong, the colonial period itself could not really be characterized as harsh. Compared to the communist regime in China, many considered British rule preferable, which partially explains the pains England went through to ensure Hong Kong's previous way of life remained mainly intact after the 1997 handover. Much bleaker, for instance, was the territory's occupation by Japan during World War II, when severe conditions and food shortages forced hundreds of thousands to flee to Mainland China.

Since the administrative handover in 1997, the reconciliation of democratic and communist systems has brought forward numerous practical issues with political repercussions, particularly regarding the rights of citizens of Hong Kong and the extension of those rights to others, including their dependents. For example,

because the status of permanent residency in Hong Kong is desirable for the higher standard of living enjoyed in comparison with that of the mainland, there is controversy over who qualifies for residency. Recognized classes of people include Chinese citizens who were born in or lived in Hong Kong for a period of at least seven years before the transfer of power, the children of qualified citizens who were born elsewhere, and children born in Hong Kong to parents who attain residency status before the children reach twenty-one years of age.

Twenty-First Century

As the government of Hong Kong explores its limited democracy in the twenty-first century, its primary challenge will be in reconciling its dual loyalties. China is almost certainly unwilling to relinquish further control over its prosperous territory, yet much of the citizenry of Hong Kong continues to demand a more democratic society. How those conflicting interests are addressed and resolved will dictate the path of Hong Kong's future. Even so, the agreement that allows Hong Kong near-autonomy expires in 2047, and at that time the Hong Kong government will be required to transition to full incorporation within China.

BIBLIOGRAPHY

Government of Hong Kong. "Government, Law & Order." http://www.gov.hk/en/residents/government/ index.htm (accessed September 11, 2007).

Wang, Gungwu and Siu-lun Wong, eds. *Hong Kong's Transition: A Decade after the Deal.* New York: Oxford University Press, 1995.

Yahuda, Michael B. *Hong Kong: China's Challenge.* New York: Routledge, 1996.

⊕ Macao

Type of Government

Macao is governed as a special administrative region of the People's Republic of China. It is directly under the authority of the Chinese central government but has a high degree of independence in its economic and political affairs.

Background

Macao is one of two special administrative regions of the People's Republic of China (the other is Hong Kong). It is located on the southeastern coast of China on the Pearl River estuary. The Macao Special Administrative Region comprises the Macao Peninsula, which extends from Guangdong province to the islands of Taipa and Colôane; the islands are connected to the mainland by bridges.

Because of its strategic location, Macao became a stopping point for international merchants early on. The area was first settled in the mid-sixteenth century by the Portuguese, who established a trading post there for commerce between Lisbon, Portugal, and Nagasaki, Japan. Beginning in 1670 Portugal leased the Macao Peninsula from China and appointed a governor to oversee its operations, though the Chinese retained official sovereignty over the territory. Macao thrived as a center of trade until the mid-nineteenth century, when it was eclipsed by Hong Kong, which became a free port under British control in the 1840s.

Portugal stopped making lease payments to China in 1849 and declared Macao independent of Chinese rule. According to the Treaty of Tianjin (1862), Macao became a Portuguese colony; however, the Chinese never ratified the treaty, so the territory was never officially ceded to the Portuguese. Macao's status was resolved by the Protocol of Lisbon (1887), which stipulated that China would recognize Portugal's right to occupy and govern Macao; in exchange Portugal agreed that it would not transfer the territory to another country without China's approval.

Following a military coup d'état (sudden overthrow of a government) in Portugal in 1974, the Portuguese government granted independence to Macao and recognized the region as a Chinese territory. The Chinese, however, did not accept the territory until 1979, when diplomatic relations were established between Portugal and the People's Republic of China. The two nations finally reached an agreement to return Macao to Chinese rule in 1987. According to the Sino-Portuguese Joint Declaration, Macao was declared a special administrative region within China, effective on December 20, 1999.

Government Structure

Macao is governed as a special administrative region of the People's Republic of China. It is directly under the authority of China's central government, which controls defense and foreign policy matters, but has a high degree of independence in its economic and political affairs. Macao's relationship with China and its governmental structure are outlined in the Basic Law of the Macao Special Administrative Region, which was adopted in 1999.

The president of the People's Republic of China serves as Macao's head of state. The chief executive serves as the head of government and is appointed to a five-year term by China's central government on the recommendation of a three-hundred-member election committee. The chief executive is advised by the ten-person Executive Council.

Macao's legislature, the Assembleia Legislativa da Região Administrativa (Legislative Assembly of the Macao Special Administrative Region), is unicameral—that is, it has only one chamber. The Legislative Assembly consists of twenty-nine members serving four-year terms: twelve members are directly elected by popular vote, ten members are appointed to represent the region's main constituencies, and seven members are chosen by the chief executive.

The Macanese legal system is based on Portuguese law. The judiciary was administered from Portugal until 1993, when an independent court system was established. The Tribunal de Ultima Instancia (Court of Final Appeal), headed by a chief justice, is the ultimate judicial authority. All judges are appointed by the chief executive on the recommendation of a selection committee.

Political Parties and Factions

Macao has no formal political parties, but several political associations are represented in the legislature, including the Associação de Novo Macau Democrático (New Democratic Macao Association), the Associação dos Cidadãos Unidos de Macau (United Citizens Association of Macao), the União para o Desenvolvimento (Union for Development), and the União Promotora para o Progresso (Union for Promoting Progress).

Major Events

After more than four centuries of Portuguese rule Macao was returned to Chinese rule in 1999. The Sino-Portuguese Joint Declaration, which was approved by the National People's Congress of China in 1993 and became effective in 1999, gave the Macanese the right to elect local leaders, to travel freely within China, and to preserve their unique cultural heritage; in turn, the Chinese government assumed responsibility for Macao's defense and foreign policy. The Basic Law of the Macao Special Administrative Region, which also took effect in 1999, serves as Macao's constitution. The treaty and the Basic Law are to remain in effect until 2049.

Twenty-First Century

In 2000 Macao held its first elections under Chinese rule, turning out a record number of voters and electing a Chinese-majority legislature. The region's key challenge in the twenty-first century is the preservation of its independence and unique heritage under Chinese authority.

BIBLIOGRAPHY

Gunn, Geoffrey C. *Encountering Macau: A Portuguese City-State on the Periphery of China, 1557–1999.* Boulder, Colo.: Westview Press, 1996.

Shipp, Steve. *Macau, China: A Political History of the Portuguese Colony's Transition to Chinese Rule.* Jefferson, N.C.: McFarland, 1997.

Yee, Herbert S. *Macau in Transition: From Colony to Autonomous Region.* New York: Palgrave, 2001.

⊕ East Timor

Type of Government

The government of East Timor is a parliamentary republic with the president serving as head of state and the prime minister serving as head of government; together with an appointed cabinet they make up the executive branch. The legislative branch comprises the Parlamento Nacional (National Parliament), a unicameral assembly with sixty-five members. The president and members of parliament are elected by popular vote, while the judges of the Supreme Court of Justice are appointed.

Background

East Timor is located in Southeast Asia, northwest of Australia at the edge of the Indonesian archipelago. The country includes the eastern half of the island of Timor, as well as the islands of Pulau Atauro and Pulau Jaco and the Oé-Cusse region of Indonesian West Timor. Its climate is tropical, with dry and rainy seasons, and its coastal areas are separated by a mountainous interior that rises nearly ten thousand feet above sea level at its highest point.

Portuguese and Dutch traders in search of sandalwood and spices first arrived in East Timor in the early sixteenth century. Colonization by Portugal followed, although the Portuguese tussled with the Dutch for influence until a treaty signed in 1859 ceded the western part of the island to the Netherlands. Except for a three-year occupation by Japan during World War II, the Portuguese remained in control of East Timor until the mid 1970s. After a coup ended fascist rule in Portugal in 1974, the new, democratic administration began transitioning the country's colonial territories to independence. Political parties were sanctioned in East Timor at that time and with them came an increase in political tension. A short but brutal civil war caused by hostilities between the two major parties—the Timorese Democratic Union Party (UDT) and the Revolutionary Front for an Independent East Timor (FRETILIN)—resulted in 1975. FRETILIN prevailed, and declared East Timor an independent state on November 28, 1975. Independence was short-lived, however, as Indonesia invaded East Timor ten days later.

Despite UN condemnation of the takeover and subsequent annexation of East Timor, Indonesia was largely unchallenged in its control of the region for two decades. The early years of the occupation were especially harsh, resulting in approximately sixty thousand Timorese deaths—a number that grew to an estimated two hundred thousand before the occupation ended. In addition, although Indonesian tactics became slightly more conciliatory during the 1980s and few disputed that its introduction of a universal education system to East Timor was a positive development, political repression remained in full force and human rights violations continued. The Timorese, anxious to preserve their culture and national identity, struggled for independence through the armed resistance movement FALINTIL (National Liberation Forces of East Timor). Finally, in 1999 Indonesia agreed to hold a referendum in which the citizens of East Timor could choose between Indonesian autonomy and independence. The UN-supervised vote was held on August 30, 1999, and 98.6 percent of the electorate took part to vote overwhelmingly (78 percent) for independence.

The 1999 vote for freedom led to yet another round of bloodshed in East Timor. Anti-independence Timorese militias and the Indonesian military launched a retribution campaign that killed an estimated fourteen hundred people and forced as many as three hundred thousand into refugee camps. Additionally, the country's infrastructure, including homes, irrigation systems, water supply systems, schools, and nearly all of its electrical grid, was left in ruins. The violence prompted the intervention of an international peacekeeping force to take control of the country, and the UN Transitional Administration in East Timor (UNTAET) was established on October 25, 1999. Elections for representatives to draft a constitution

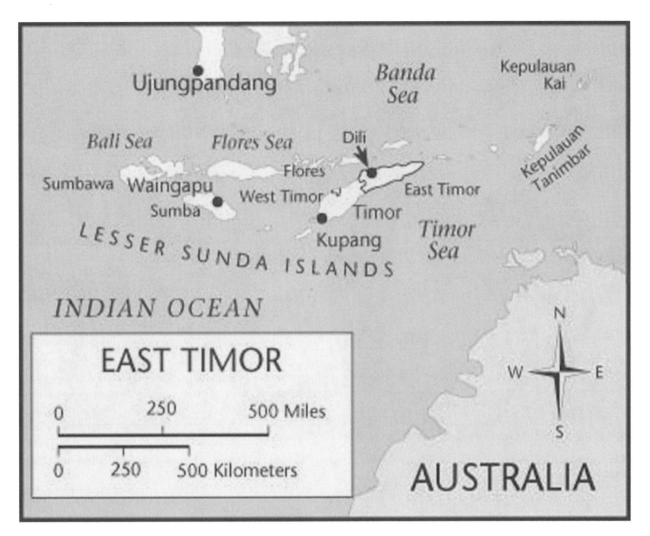

East Timor. *Maryland Cartographics*

were held on August 30, 2001, and the constitution was approved on March 24, 2002. East Timor was internationally recognized as an independent state on May 20, 2002.

Government Structure

East Timor was established as a parliamentary republic with powers divided among executive, legislative, and judicial branches. The executive branch is made up of the president (head of state), the prime minister (head of government), and the cabinet, or council of ministers. The president serves a primarily ceremonial role but retains the power to veto legislation, dissolve parliament, and call national elections. The president is elected by popular vote to a five-year term and is eligible for a second term of office. The prime minister is the leader of the prevailing political party and is formally appointed by the president after the elections. There are fourteen ministerial positions in the cabinet, in addition to an evolving number under the purview of the prime minister.

The legislative branch of government is the unicameral National Parliament. The minimum number of seats is fifty-two and the maximum is sixty-five, with members chosen by direct election to five-year terms. The parliament's initial term, however, was exceptional in that the eighty-eight delegates elected in 2001 to adopt a constitution named themselves legislators in 2002. Elections for the first regular term under the new constitution were held in June 2007, with universal suffrage for all people at least seventeen years old.

As outlined in the constitution, the judicial branch is headed by the Supreme Court of Justice. The chief judge of the court is appointed to a four-year term by the nation's president; in addition, one court member is elected by parliament, and the rest are selected by the Superior Council for Judiciary. However, as of mid 2007 the constitutional directives pertaining to the judiciary had not been fully implemented, and the Supreme Court had not yet been formed. The Court of Appeals, composed of one East Timorese and two international

East Timor President Xanana Gusmao (second from left) at the signing of a treaty establishing diplomatic relations with Indonesia, July 2, 2002. © *Reuters/CORBIS*

judges, was serving on an interim basis in its stead, while East Timor continued the difficult task of constructing a judiciary from the ground up. Judicial mentoring and training programs were instituted in 2001 in an effort to give the country's inexperienced legal pool the necessary tools to serve. The ongoing process was being overseen by the Ministry of Justice.

Political Parties and Factions

Sixteen political parties participated in East Timor's first elections in 2001, and their numbers continued to change during the country's early years. Major parties include FRETILIN, the Democratic Party, the Social Democratic Party, the Timorese Social Democratic Association, and the UDT.

FRETILIN was founded on September 11, 1974, in the wake of the coup in Portugal. One of its founding members was José Ramos-Horta (1949–), who became a leader in East Timor's struggle for independence and won the 1996 Nobel Peace Prize for his efforts. Another early member was Xanana Gusmao (1946–), who later became a national hero as leader of FALINTIL and was elected East Timor's first president in 2002. The party was formed with an aim toward immediate and complete

independence (FALINTIL was its military arm), and espoused a radical, left-wing agenda that especially resonated with the rural population.

By the twenty-first century, after East Timorese liberation had been achieved, FRETILIN still enjoyed popularity as evidenced by its strong performance in parliamentary elections. However, its two most legendary members, Ramos-Horta and Gusmao, had left the fold. Ramos-Horta, who was named foreign minister in 2002 and prime minister in 2006, was elected president of East Timor in May 2007 as an independent candidate. Gusmao, who headed a new party—the Congress for the National Reconstruction of East Timor—was named prime minister in August 2007 when a coalition government was formed following a narrow victory for FRETILIN in parliamentary elections.

Major Events

Although colonization by Portugal unquestionably had a major impact on East Timor—the Portuguese language and the Roman Catholic religion being but two important legacies from that time—other events were perhaps even more notable for their brutal devastation. One of these was the Japanese occupation from

February 1942 until September 1945. An estimated fifty-thousand East Timorese died during that time.

The Indonesian annexation also brought about its share of misery, including the 1999 retribution campaign and overall deaths of approximately two hundred thousand people. Also important was the Santa Cruz Massacre of 1991, in which more than two hundred East Timorese civilians were killed by the Indonesian military. That episode, as well as the 1992 imprisonment of Gusmao by the Indonesian government (he was released on September 7, 1999), helped place the predicament of East Timor in a world spotlight. International attention grew when the Nobel Peace Prize was awarded to Ramos-Horta and compatriot Bishop Ximenes Belo (1948–) in 1996.

Twenty-First Century

East Timor's young democracy faces several challenges. The rebuilding of the infrastructure destroyed in 1999 is an ongoing project. Unemployment and poverty are rampant, leading to such problems as gang violence that necessitated another UN peacekeeping force being deployed to the country in 2006. The government itself appears stable, but it faces challenges in developing basic administrative and criminal justice components, such as the judiciary. Efforts, for instance, to bring the persons responsible for the 1999 violence to justice in cooperation with Indonesia largely failed, and the majority of the suspects were acquitted.

Prospects for an improved economy primarily rest on the huge oil and gas fields in the Timor Sea. In June 2005 parliament unanimously approved the formation of a Petroleum Fund for all potential and future revenues from such sources, but the country remained hampered by a lack of internal production facilities or a technology-proficient workforce. However, East Timor and Australia, where the oil and gas is piped, have reached an agreement to work together and share revenues. Using that prospective wealth to bring growth and prosperity to the general populace is yet another challenge of the twenty-first century.

BIBLIOGRAPHY

Government of Timor-Leste. http://www.timor-leste. gov.tl/ (accessed September 12, 2007).

Kingsbury, Daniel, ed. *Guns and Ballot Boxes: East Timor's Vote for Independence*. Clayton, Australia: Monash Asia Institute, 2000.

Human Rights Watch/Asia. "The Limits of Openness: Human Rights in Indonesia and East Timor." New York: Human Rights Watch, 1994.

⊕ Montenegro

Type of Government

Montenegro is a republic with a parliamentary form of government. It has a unicameral parliament with eighty-one members; a prime minister and cabinet with executive authority; a largely ceremonial presidency; and an independent judiciary.

Background

Montenegro is one of the smallest countries in Europe, with a population of approximately 680,000 (about the same size as Memphis, Tennessee). The Montenegrin people are closely related to the Serbs, their neighbors to the northeast. Montenegrin territory became part of the first Serbian nation late in the twelfth century, when Stefan Nemanja (ruled 1167–1196), the founder of Serbia, conquered Montenegro and other surrounding lands and declared Serbia' independence from the Byzantine Empire.

Montenegro emerged as an independent country in the second half of the fourteenth century, as the Serbian empire was crumbling in the face of the invading Ottoman Turks. The rugged mountains and dense forests of Montenegro made the area an ideal refuge for Serbs who were fleeing from the Turks, and a group of Serbian refugees set up their own small state there. Although Montenegro fought an almost continuous war with the Ottoman Turks, the Turks never succeeded in conquering Montenegro.

Montenegro remained an independent country until 1918, when it joined with Serbia, Macedonia, Croatia, Vojvodina, and Bosnia and Herzegovina to form the Kingdom of the Serbs, Croats, and Slovenes. The country changed its name to the Kingdom of Yugoslavia in 1929.

Montenegro was an integral part of Yugoslavia until the 1990s. Even when Yugoslavia began to collapse in the late 1980s, and when Croatia, Slovenia, Macedonia, and Bosnia-Herzegovina each declared independence in 1991 and 1992, Montenegro remained loyal to Serbia and to what remained of Yugoslavia.

Montenegrins' attachment to Serbia began to fade during the late 1990s. In 2002 Serbia and Montenegro signed a new agreement dissolving Yugoslavia and creating the Union of Serbia and Montenegro, a loose federation in which both countries had a great deal of independence. The Montenegrin government agreed to this new union reluctantly, and only on the condition that it could hold a referendum on complete independence in three years. This referendum was held on May 21, 2006, and in it just over 55 percent of Montenegrins voted to sever all remaining ties with Serbia and become an independent state.

Government Structure

Montenegro is a parliamentary republic with a unicameral parliament containing eighty-one seats. Representatives are elected to parliament for four-year terms based on a party list proportional representation system. In this type of election voters endorse a list of candidates prepared by a political party or coalition, rather than individual candidates. Seats in the parliament are divided among the parties and coalitions based on the number

Montenegrin nationalists in Podgorica celebrating the success of a May 2006 referendum in which the Balkan nation decided to separate from Serbia. © *KOCA SULEJMANOVIC/Corbis*

of votes received by each list. All of Montenegro is considered to be a single election district, so every voter in the country chooses from the same lists of candidates. Seventy-six of the eighty-one seats in the parliament are allocated based on the results of this nationwide voting. The remaining five representatives are elected under a different set of rules by voters in parts of Montenegro where the population is primarily Albanian.

Once the parliament has been elected its membership selects a prime minister and cabinet. Together the prime minister and cabinet hold executive power, including the authority to conduct the country's foreign policy. The president, who is elected by the people to a five-year term, has little practical power; his position as head of state is largely ceremonial.

The Montenegrin court system is separate from the political process. There are two top-level courts in the country: the Constitutional Court, which determines whether the laws and other actions of the government are constitutional; and the Supreme Court, which is the highest appeals court in the country. Judges on the Constitutional Court have nine-year terms, while the judges of the Supreme Court are appointed for life.

Political Parties and Factions

A number of political parties are represented in the Montenegrin parliament. As of the 2006 elections the largest group in parliament was the Coalition for a European Montenegro, which includes the Democratic Party of Socialists and the left-wing Social Democratic Party. The Democratic Party of Socialists is directly descended from the League of Communists of Montenegro, which ruled the country from 1945 until 1991. The leader of the Democratic Party of Socialists, Milo Djukanovic (1962–), ruled Montenegro for fifteen years, first as its prime minister (a position that he assumed on his twenty-ninth birthday), then as its president from 1998 to 2002, and then as prime minister again from 2002 to 2006. Although the membership of the Democratic Party of Socialists is largely made up of former communists, it is now a relatively liberal, center-left party that favored independence from Serbia and that favors closer integration with the European Union.

The major opposition to the Democratic Party of Socialists has come from parties dominated by ethnic Serbians, including the Socialist Peoples Party, the Peoples Party, the Democratic Serbian Party, and the Serbian List coalition, which includes the Serbian Peoples Party and some other, smaller parties. Prior to the 2006 referendum on Montenegrin independence these parties campaigned primarily on their desire to maintain Montenegro's union with Serbia; it is unclear as yet whether the parties will disband or transform now that the issue of Montenegrin independence is settled.

The other major opposition party in Montenegro is the Movement for Change. This group was founded in 2002 by several economists and university professors as a nonpartisan civic organization. The Group for Change, as it was then called, was designed to encourage economic and political reform. In 2006 the organization transformed itself into a full-fledged political party. Competing in its first parliamentary elections, it won eleven seats that year.

Major Events

Djukanovic surprised many Montenegrins when he announced that he was stepping down as prime minister and retiring from politics in October 2006. However, as of 2007 he continued to head the ruling Democratic Party of Socialists and maintained a great deal of influence with high-level politicians from that party.

Twenty-First Century

Political and judicial corruption have continued to plague Montenegro, but the country is well on its way to becoming a full member of the European community. Montenegro joined the Organization for Security and Cooperation in Europe and the United Nations in June 2006, and entered negotiations with the European Union and the North Atlantic Treaty Organization about joining those bodies.

BIBLIOGRAPHY

BBC News. "Q & A: Montenegro Votes." http://news. bbc.co.uk/2/hi/europe/5328428.stm (accessed September 12, 2007).

Benson, Leslie. *Yugoslavia: A Concise History.* New York: Palgrave, 2001.

Country Updates: Montenegro. Amsterdam, Netherlands: European Forum for Democracy and Solidarity, 2006.

Further Reading

Banyard, Peter. *The Rise of the Dictators, 1919–1939.* Edited by John Pimlott. New York: Watts, 1986.

Bentley, Jerry H., and Herbert F. Ziegler. *Traditions and Encounters: A Global Perspective on the Past.* 3rd ed. Boston: McGraw-Hill, 2006.

Berger, Mark T., and Douglas A. Borer, eds. *The Rise of East Asia: Critical Visions of the Pacific Century.* London: Routledge, 1997.

Berman, Bruce, Dickson Eyoh, and Will Kymlicka, eds. *Ethnicity and Democracy in Africa.* Athens: Ohio University Press, 2004.

Bertman, Stephen. *Handbook to Life in Ancient Mesopotamia.* New York: Facts on File, 2003.

Black, Jeremy, ed. *Revolutions in the Western World, 1775–1825.* Burlington, VT: Ashgate, 2006.

Boquérat, Gilles, and Frédéric Grare, eds. *India, China, Russia: Intricacies of an Asian Triangle.* Singapore: Marshall Cavendish Academic, 2004.

Chidester, David. *Christianity: A Global History.* San Francisco: HarperSanFrancisco, 2000.

Clavin, Patricia. *The Great Depression in Europe, 1929–1939.* New York: St. Martin's Press, 2000.

Coleman, Fred. *The Decline and Fall of the Soviet Empire: Forty Years That Shook the World, from Stalin to Yeltsin.* New York: St. Martin's Press, 1996.

Collins, Robert O. *Africa: A Short History.* Princeton, NJ: Markus Wiener, 2006.

Connelly, Owen. *The Wars of the French Revolution and Napoleon, 1792–1815.* London: Routledge, 2005.

Cotterell, Yong Yap, and Arthur Cotterell. *The Early Civilization of China.* New York: Putnam, 1975.

David, René, and John E. C. Brierley. *Major Legal Systems in the World Today: An Introduction to the Comparative Study of Law.* 3rd ed. London: Stevens, 1985.

Des Forges, Roger, and John S. Major. *The Asian World, 600–1500.* New York: Oxford University Press, 2005.

Esposito, John, ed. *The Oxford History of Islam.* New York: Oxford University Press, 1999.

Falola, Toyin, ed. *Africa.* Durham, NC: Carolina Academic Press, 2000–2003.

Farr, James R., ed. *The Industrial Revolution in Europe, 1750–1914.* Detroit: Thomson Gale, 2003.

Fitzpatrick, Martin, et al., eds. *The Enlightenment World.* London: Routledge, 2004.

Flynn, Matthew J. *China Contested: Western Powers in East Asia.* New York: Chelsea House, 2006.

Frankel, Benjamin, ed. *History in Dispute.* 21 vols. Detroit: St. James Press, 2000–2005.

Freeman, Charles. *Egypt, Greece and Rome: Civilizations of the Ancient Mediterranean.* 2nd ed. Oxford: Oxford University Press, 2004.

Furet, François. *The Passing of an Illusion: The Idea of Communism in the Twentieth Century.* Translated by Deborah Furet. Chicago: University of Chicago Press, 1999.

Gaddis, John Lewis. *The Cold War: A New History.* New York: Penguin Press, 2005.

Ganshof, François Louis. *Feudalism.* Translated by Philip Grierson. 3rd English ed. London: Longmans, 1964.

Goodwin, Jason. *Lords of the Horizons: A History of the Ottoman Empire.* New York: Holt, 1999.

Hillman, Richard S., ed. *Understanding Contemporary Latin America.* 3rd ed. Boulder, CO: Lynne Rienner Publishers, 2005.

Hillstrom, Kevin, and Laurie Collier Hillstrom, eds. *The Industrial Revolution in America.* Santa Barbara, Calif.: ABC-CLIO, 2005.

Hodge, Mary G., and Michael E. Smith, eds. *Economies and Polities in the Aztec Realm.* Albany: Institute for Mesoamerican Studies, University at Albany, State University of New York, 1994.

Hydén, Göran, Dele Olowu, and Hastings W. O. Okoth-Ogendo, eds. *African Perspectives on Governance.* Trenton, NJ: Africa World Press, 2000.

Iliffe, John. *Africans: The History of a Continent.* 2nd ed. New York: Cambridge University Press, 2007.

James, Lawrence. *Raj: The Making and Unmaking of British India.* New York: St. Martin's Press, 1998.

Jones, Philip. *The Italian City-State: From Commune to Signoria.* Oxford: Clarendon Press, 1997.

Keen, Benjamin, Robert Buffington, and Lila M. Caimari, eds. *Keen's Latin American Civilization: History and Society, 1492 to the Present.* 8th ed. Boulder, CO: Westview Press, 2004.

Laqueur, Walter. *Fascism: Past, Present, Future.* New York: Oxford University Press, 1996.

Lieberthal, Kenneth. *Governing China: From Revolution through Reform.* 2nd ed. New York: Norton, 2004.

Lorge, Peter. *War, Politics and Society in Early Modern China, 900–1795.* London: Routledge, 2005.

MacMillan, Margaret. *Paris 1919: Six Months That Changed the World.* New York: Random House, 2002.

Mann, Michael. *The Dark Side of Democracy: Explaining Ethnic Cleansing.* New York: Cambridge University Press, 2005.

Norton, Augustus Richard, ed. *Civil Society in the Middle East.* 2 vols. Boston: Brill, 1995–1996.

Parry, J. H. *The Age of Reconnaissance: Discovery, Exploration, and Settlement, 1450 to 1650.* New York: Praeger, 1969.

Parry, J. H. *Trade and Dominion: The European Oversea Empires in the Eighteenth Century.* London: Phoenix Press, 2000.

Peloso, Vincent C., and Barbara A. Tenenbaum, eds. *Liberals, Politics, and Power: State Formation in Nineteenth-Century Latin America.* Athens: University of Georgia Press, 1996.

Postman, Neil. *Building a Bridge to the 18th Century: How the Past Can Improve Our Future.* New York: Knopf, 1999.

Ringrose, David R. *Expansion and Global Interaction, 1200–1700.* New York: Longman, 2001.

Salih, M. A. Mohamed, ed. *African Parliaments: Between Governance and Government.* Cape Town, South Africa: HSRC Press, 2006.

Scarborough, Vernon L., and John E. Clark, eds. *The Political Economy of Ancient Mesoamerica: Transformations during the Formative and Classic Periods.* Albuquerque: University of New Mexico Press, 2007.

Schirokauer, Conrad, et al. *A Brief History of Chinese and Japanese Civilizations.* 3rd ed. Australia: Thomson/Wadsworth, 2006.

Shankman, Steven, and Stephen W. Durrant, eds. *Early China/Ancient Greece: Thinking through Comparisons.* Albany: State University of New York Press, 2002.

Sternhell, Zeev. *The Founding Myths of Israel: Nationalism, Socialism, and the Making of the Jewish State.* Translated by David Maisel. Princeton, NJ: Princeton University Press, 1998.

Strachan, Hew. *The First World War.* New York: Viking, 2004.

Tuchman, Barbara Wertheim. *The Guns of August.* New York: Macmillan, 1962.

Udovitch, A. L., ed. *The Islamic Middle East, 700–1900: Studies in Economic and Social History.* Princeton, NJ: Darwin Press, 1981.

VerSteeg, Russ. *Law in the Ancient World.* Durham, NC: Carolina Academic Press, 2002.

Watkins, T. H. *The Great Depression: America in the 1930s.* Boston: Little, Brown, 1993.

Weaver, John C. *The Great Land Rush and the Making of the Modern World, 1650–1900.* Montreal, Canada: McGill-Queen's University Press, 2003.

Weinberg, Gerhard L. *A World at Arms: A Global History of World War II.* 2nd ed. New York: Cambridge University Press, 2005.

Wilson, Henry S. *African Decolonization.* London: E. Arnold, 1994.

Wolffe, John, ed. *Religion in History: Conflict, Conversion and Coexistence.* Manchester, U.K.: Open University, 2004.

Zeff, Eleanor E., and Ellen B. Pirro, eds. *The European Union and the Member States: Cooperation, Coordination, and Compromise.* Boulder, CO: Lynne Rienner Publishers, 2001.

Index

A

’Abbāsid Empire, 1:49, **67–69**, 2:399

’Abd al-’Aziz ibn ’Abd ar-Rahman (Saudi prince), 1:307

Abdallah, Ahmed (Union of Comoros president), 2:554–555

Abdullah (Saudi king), 1:307

Abdullah I (Jordanian king), 2:339

Abdullah II (Jordanian king), 2:339, 340–341

Aborigines, Australian, 1:249, *252*

Abū al-’Abbās as-Saffāh (’Abbāsid caliph), 1:67

Abu Dhabi, 2:534

Abu Ja’far al-Mansūr (’Abbāsid caliph), 1:67

Acamapichtli (Aztec emperor), 1:103

Achaemenid Empire, 1:62, 2:350, 587

Adamkus, Valdas (Lithuania president), 2:665

Adams, Sir Grantley (Barbados prime minister), 2:512, 513

Adams, Tom (Barbados prime minister), 2:513

Afar tribe, 2:578

Afghanistan, **1:282–286**

Africa
  Carthage, 1:20–21
  Cush, 1:16–17
  exploration of, 1:151
  independence of nations of, 2:415
  map of kingdoms of, *1:105*

African National Congress (ANC), 1:319–320

Afrikaners, 1:318–319

Afwerki, Isaias (Eritrea president), 2:688, 689

Agade, city of Empire of Akkad, 1:4

Agboyibo, Yawovi, 2:420

Age of Settlement, 1:321

Agesilaus II (Sparta king), 1:27, 29

Agricultural revolution, 1:1

Agriculture, Empire of Ghana, 1:72

Aguda, Wanyan (Jin emperor), 1:89, 132

Aguinaldo, Emilio, 2:341–342

Ahidjo, Amadou (Cameroon president), 2:417–418

Ahmad bin Said (imam of Oman), 2:386

Ahmad ibn Fadhlan, 1:65

Ahmar, Sheikh Abdullah bin Hussein al-, 2:631

Ahmed, Abdullahi Yusuf (Somalia president), 2:427

Ahtisaari, Martti (Finland president), 1:282

AIM (American Indian Movement), 1:131

Aja people, 2:429

Akayev, Askar (Kyrgyzstan president), 2:659, 660, 661

Akbar (Mughal emperor), 1:107, 122

Akhenaton (ancient Egypt pharaoh), 1:8

Akkad, Empire of. *See* Empire of Akkad

Akkadians, 1:1, 3–5

Aksumite Kingdom, **1:45–46**

Al-Andalus, 2:564

Al-Azhar (mosque), *1:79*

Al-Azhari, Ismail (Sudan prime minister), 2:396

Al-Bashir, Omar Hassan Ahmed (Sudan president), 2:393–394, 395, 396

Al-Jazeera satellite television network, 2:532

Al-Khalifa, Sheikh Isa bin Sulman (Bahrain prime minister), 2:529

Al-Khalifa, Khalifa bin Salman (Bahrain prime minister), 2:528

Al Qaeda
  in Afghanistan, 1:285
  Mauritius, money laundering in, 2:518
  in Morocco, 2:399
  in Saudi Arabia, 1:310
  Spain, bombing in, 2:566
  in Tunisia, 2:401
  U.S. embassy bombings, 2:488, 490

Al-Zubayr, Rabih (Sudanese warlord), 2:437, 440

’Ālamgīr (Mughal shah), 1:123, 124

Alanis, Joan Marti (Bishop of La Seu d’Urgell), *2:692*

Alans, 1:66

Alaric I (Visigoth king), 1:55, 56

Alash Orda, 1:286

Albania, Republic of, 1:270–273

Albanians, 2:675, 676

Alberoni, Giulio, 1:98

Albuquerque, Afonso de (Portuguese explorer), 1:112

Alesana, Tofilau Eti (Samoa prime minister), *2:468*

Alevi people, 1:299

Alexander II (Russian czar), 1:148

Alexander IV (Macedonian king), 1:32

Alexander the Great (Macedonian king)
Egypt and, 1:8
empire of, *1:32*
Persian Empire and, 1:23
Persian Empire, conquest of, 1:33

Alexius I Comnenus (Byzantine emperor), 1:52–53, 54, 81

Alexius II Comnenus (Byzantine emperor), 1:84

Algeria, Democratic and Popular Republic of, 2:401, **475–478**

Algerian War of Independence, 1:162

Al-Hākim (Fātimid caliph), 1:79–80

'Alī ibn Abī Tālib (Umayyad caliph), 1:64, 78

Aliyev, Heydar (Azerbaijan president), 1:274, 275

Aliyev, Ilham (Azerbaijan president), 1:275

Allende, Salvador (Chile president), 1:176

Al-Mu'izz (Fātimid caliph), 1:78

Alphabet, Armenian, 2:668

Amalings, 1:56

American Colonization Society, 1:226

American Indian Movement (AIM), 1:131

Americas
European contact with, 1:107
Spanish colonies in, map of, *1:115*
Spanish Empire conquest of, 1:118
Spanish Empire discovery of, 1:116

Amin Dada, Idi (Uganda president), 2:483–484

Ammianus Marcellinus, 1:61

Amorites, 1:5

Amritsar, Punjab, 2:351

Amundsen, Roald (Norwegian explorer), 1:258

Anatolia, 1:9–10, 297

ANC (African National Congress), 1:319–320

Ancient Egypt. *See* Egypt, ancient

Andorra, Principality of, **2:690–692**

Angkor Thom (Khmer capital), 1:73, *74*

Anglo-Irish War, 1:289

Angola, 1:112, **2:561–564**

Animism, 2:569

Anjian Massacre, 2:663

Anjouan Island, *2:555*

Annan, Kofi (UN secretary general), 2:335

Antarctic Treaty Summary, **2:411–413**

Anthony, Kenny, 2:591

Antigua and Barbuda, **2:603–605**

Anuradhapura, Sri Lanka, 2:361

Anziani, 1:86

Apartheid, *1:320*, 2:625

Aptidon, Hassan Gouled (Djibouti president), 2:578

Aquino, Benigno, Jr. (Philippines senator), 2:344

Aquino, Corazon (Philippines president), 2:344

Arab League, 2:461, 547

Arab Republic of Egypt, **1:291–293**

Arabia Felix, 2:630

Arabian American Oil Company (Aramco), 1:309

Arabic language, 1:64

Arabs
in Algeria, 2:475
invasion of Libya, 2:388
in Palestine, 2:547
resistance to Jewish state, 2:366

Arafat, Yasser (Palestine president), 2:547, *548*

Arawak people, 2:590

Ardashīr I (Sassanid emperor), 1:62

Argead dynasty, 1:32

Argentine Republic, **1:232–236**

Arias Madrid, Arnulfo (Panama president), 1:255

Arias Sánchez, Oscar (Costa Rica president), 1:213

Aristide, Jean-Bertrand (Haiti president), 1:164–165

Aristotle, 1:20

Arjun (Sikh religious leader), 1:122

Armenia, **2:668–671**

Armenian Apostolic Church, 2:668

Arnarson, Ingólfur (Iceland king), 1:321, *322*

Arsaces (Parthian king), 1:38

Artabanus V (Parthian king), 1:39

Articles of Confederation, 1:155–156

Artigas, José, 1:195

Aryan tribes, 2:350

Asantehene, 1:134–135

Ashanti Empire, **1:134–137**

Ashikaga clan, 1:128

Ashurbanipal (Assyrian king), 1:19

Aśoka (Magadha king), 1:34, 35

Assamese separatist movement, 2:377

Assemblée Nationale (France), 1:161

Assembly
of Macedon, 1:32
of Roman Republic, 1:37
of Sparta, 1:27–28

Association of Southeast Asian Nations (ASEAN)
Brunei, 2:610
Laos, 2:571
Malaysia, 2:405
Singapore, 2:504
Vietnam, 2:577

Assoumani, Azali (Union of Comoros president), 2:555–556

Assyrian Empire, **1:17–19**

Atahuallpa (Inca emperor), 1:109, 180, 190

Atatürk, Mustafa Kemal (Turkey president), 1:297, *298*

Ateas (Scythia king), 1:29

Athens
democratic government of, 1:1
overview of, **1:24–26**
Parthenon, *1:26*
in Peloponnesian Wars, 1:28–29
Thebes and, 1:31

Attila (Hun ruler), 1:60–61

Auckland, New Zealand, 2:346

Augustus (emperor of Rome), 1:42

Aung San (Burmese leader), 2:359, 360

Australia, Commonwealth of, **1:249–253**, 2:559

Austria, 1:232, 275–278

Austria-Hungary, 2:683

Austro-Hungarian Empire, **1:236–238**

Autocracy, 1:42

Aviz (Portuguese dynasty), 1:111, 263

Azerbaijan, Republic of, 1:273–275

Azeri people, 1:273

Aztec Empire, 1:81, **101–103**

B

Baath Party (Iraq), 1:310–313

Ba'ath Party (Syrian Arab Republic), 2:335–337

Bab el-Mandeb, 2:630

Babeldoab, *2:701*

Babur (Mughal emperor), 1:122

Babylon (city), 1:5

Babylonian Empire, 1:5–6
Assyrian Empire and, 1:17
Code of Hammurabi, 1:1
overview of, **1:5–6**

Badr al-Jamālī (Fātimid vizier), 1:79

Bagan society, 2:358

Baganda ethnic group, 2:483

Baghdad, Iraq, 2:335

Bagiri people, 2:437

Bahamas, Commonwealth of the, **2:538–540**

Bahrain, **2:527–530**

Bainimarama, Frank, 2:525, 527

Bakiyev, Kurmanbek (Kyrgyzstan president), 2:659, 660–661

Baku Pygmies, 2:416, 423, 442

Bakufu, 1:128, 129, 2:347

Balance of power, United Nations, 2:333

Balance of power, U.S. government, 1:156–157

Balboa, Vasco Núñez de (Spanish explorer), 1:253

Balthings, 1:56

Banaba (Ocean Island), 2:592

Banda, Hastings (Malawi president), 2:491, *492*

Bangkok, Thailand, *1:306*

Bangladesh, 2:357, **535–538**

Banking
    in Andorra, 2:692
    in Bahamas, 2:540
    in Grenada, 2:542
    in Luxembourg, 1:239
    in San Marino, 1:98

Banny, Charles Konan (Côte d'Ivoire prime minister), 2:436

Barbados, **2:511–513**

Barbuda, Antigua and, **2:603–605**

Baré, Ibrahim (Niger president), 2:431, 432

Barre, Mohamed Siad (Somaliland leader), 2:638, 640

Barrow, Errol Walton (Barbados premier), 2:512

Basescu, Traian (Romania president), 2:679

Basil II, 1:*52*, 53–54

Basothok people, 2:509–510

Basques, 2:566

Basutoland, 2:509

Batista, Fulgencio, 2:409

Battenberg, Alexander (Bulgarian prince), 1:259

Battle of Lepanto, *1:85*

Battle of Thermopylae, 1:28

Batu Khan (Mongol ruler), 1:78)

Baudouin I (Belgian king), 1:*203*, 206

Bay of Pigs invasion, 2:410

Bayezid I (Ottoman sultan), 1:121

Beaver Wars, 1:125

Bédié, Henri Konan (Côte d'Ivoire president), 2:435–436

Belacázar, Sebastián, 1:209

Belarus, **2:653–656**

Belavezha Accords, 2:697

Belgian Congo, 1:206
    See also Democratic Republic of the Congo

Belgian Free State, 2:424

Belgium
    administration of Rwanda, 2:469
    annexation of Congo, 2:423–424
    overview of, **1:203–206**

Belize, **2:601–603**

Ben Ali, Zine El Abidine (Tunisia president), 2:399–401

Bendjedid, Chadli (Algeria president), 2:477

Benedict XVI (Catholic pope), 1:304

Benelux Economic Union, 1:174

Benin, **2:428–430**

Benin Kingdom, 2:457

Berbers, 2:460, 475

Berdymukhammedov, Gurbanguly (Turkmenistan president), 2:672

Berisha, Sali (Albania president), 1:272

Berlin Wall, 2:633, *634*

Bhumibol Adulyadej (Thai king), 1:305–306

Bhutan, **2:375–378**

Bhutto, Benazir (Pakistan prime minister), 2:356

Biafra, 2:458

Bikini atoll, *2:613*

Bill of Rights, 1:156

Bimbisāra (Magadha king), 1:34

Bin Laden, Osama, 1:292, 310, 532

Bioko, 2:521

Bird, Lester (Antigua and Barbuda prime minister), 2:605

Bird, Vere Cornwall (Antigua and Barbuda prime minister), 2:604, 605

Bishop, Maurice (Bahamas prime minister), 2:541

Bismarck, Otto von (German chancellor), 1: 138, 140, 151, 2:416, 632

Bissau, *2:545*

Biya, Paul (Cameroon president), 2:418

Black Death
    effect on Europe, 1:81
    in Florence, 1:91
    in Norway, 1:256

Black September, 2:340

Blackbeard, 2:538

Blackbirding, 2:581

Boeotia, 1:30–31

Boeotian League, 1:30, 31

Boer War, battles of, *1:318*

Boganda, Barthélemy, 2:440

Bogdo Khan (Mongol ruler), 1:300

Bohemians, 2:627

Boiro Camp, 2:408

Bokassa, Jean-Bédel (Central African Republic emperor), 2:441

Bol, 1:197

Bolívar, Simón (Bolivia/Colombia president)
    defeat of Spanish, 1:190
    in Ecuador, 1:197–198
    illustration of, *1:191*
    Venezuelan independence and, 1:200–201

Bolivia, **1:190–192**

Bolkiah, Hassanal (Brunei sultan), 2:609, 610

Bolkiah, Jefri (Brunei prince), 2:610

Bolsheviks, 1:293, 2:697

Bonaparte, Napoléon (French emperor)
    Haiti and, 1:164
    occupation of Italy, 1:243
    overview of, 1:151, 160–161
    Russian invasion by, 1:149
    war with Portugal, 1:263
    war with Prussia, 1:139

Bongo, Albert-Bernard "Omar" (Gabon president), 2:446, 447

Bonifacio, Andres, 2:341

Borgia, Cesare, 1:98

Borneo, 2:404, 608–611

Borsellino, Paolo, 1:246

Bosch, Juan (Dominican Republic president), 1:225

Bosnia and Herzegovina, **2:679–682**

Botswana, **2:507–509**

Boudiaf, Muhammad (Algeria president), 2:477

Bougainville Province (Papua New Guinea), 2:560–561

Boule (Council of Five Hundred), 1:24, 25

Boumédienne, Houari (Algeria president), 2:477

Bourguiba, Habib (Tunisia president), 2:399, *400*

Bouteflika, Abdelaziz (Algeria president), 2:477–478

Bouterse, Désiré, 2:568

Boxer Rebellion, 1:133

Boyar class, 1:100–101

Boyer, Jean-Pierre (Haiti president), 1:165, 223–224

Bozizé, François (Central African Republic president), 2:441, 442

Bradshaw, Robert, 2:606

Bragança (Portuguese dynasty), 1:111

Brahmans, 1:59

Brandt, Willy (Federal Republic of Germany chancellor), 2:633

Brant, Joseph (Mohawk captain), 1:126

Brazil, 1:112

Brazil, Federative Republic of, **1:187–190**

Breviarium Alaricianun, 1:55

Britain
    Australia, colonization of, 1:249
    Australia, monarchy in, 1:250
    Bahamas, colonization of, 2:539
    Bahrain, protectorate, 2:527–528
    in Belize, 2:601
    Brunei, action against pirates, 2:608
    Burma, domination of, 2:359
    Cameroon, colonization of, 2:416–417
    Canada, colonization of, 1:240
    Cherokee and, 1:193
    China, export of opium to, 2:380
    Cyprus, annexation of, 2:448
    Dahomey, colonization of, 2:429
    Dominica, colonization of, 2:584
    Fiji, colonization of, 2:526
    Gambia, slave trade in, 2:498
    Ghana, colonization of, 2:402
    Guyana, colonization of, 2:505
    Haiti, settlements in, 1:163
    Haiti, slave rebellion in, 1:164
    Hong Kong, rule in, 2:702–703
    India, colonization of, 2:350
    Iraq, invasion of, 1:312
    Iraq, rule in, 1:310
    Ireland, 1:289, 290
    Ireland, rule of, 1:288
    Jamaica rule of, 2:479
    Jewish state, support for, 2:365–366
    Jordan, administration of, 2:339
    Kenya, colonization of, 2:485
    Kuwait, British protection of, 2:464
    Malaysia, influence in, 2:404
    Malta, colonization of, 2:493
    Malta, withdrawal from, 2:495
    New Zealand, colonization of, 2:344
    Nigeria, disruption of slave trade in, 2:457
    North America, colonization by, 1:155
    Nyasaland Districts Protectorate, 2:491
    Oman, rule in, 2:386
    Palestine, withdrawal from, 2:366

Saint Kitts, 2:605
    Saint Vincent, colonization of, 2:594
    Seychelles, 2:572
    Sierra Leone, 2:462
    Singapore, colonization of, 2:502–503
    Solomon Islands, 2:581
    Somaliland, occupation of, 2:638, 639
    South Yemen, influence in, 2:630
    Sri Lanka, annexation of, 2:363
    Strait of Malacca, control of, 2:404
    Swaziland, administration of, 2:519
    Togo, 2:419
    Tonga, 2:524
    Trinidad and Tobago, 2:481
    Zambia, colonization of, 2:496
    Zulu, defeat of, 1:179–180
    See also The United Kingdom

British East India Company, 2:502, 702

British Honduras. *See* Belize

British North Borneo, 2:404

British Phosphate Commission, 2:514

Brooke, Sir James, 2:404

Brunei Darussalam, State of, 1:325, 2:404, **608–611**

Brunswijk, Ronnie, *2:568*

Buck, Pearl S., *1:168*

Budapest, Hungary, *2:619*

Buddhism
    in Bhutan, 2:375
    in Goguryeo Kingdom, 1:58
    in India, 2:350
    in Japan, Tokugawa period, 1:129
    in Khmer Empire, 1:75
    in Laos, 2:569
    in Mongolia, 1:300, 301
    in Myanmar, 2:358, 360–361
    in Sri Lanka, 2:361
    in Tibet, 1:98–99

Bulgaria, Republic of, **1:258–262**

Bundehaus (Swiss Confederation), 1:228

Bureau of Indian Affairs (U.S.), 1:195

Bureau of Military Affairs (Sung Dynasty), 1:88

Burgundy, dukes of, 1:172, 203

Burkina Faso, **2:432–434**

Burma (Myanmar), **2:358–361**

Burnham, Forbes (Guyana president), 2:506

Burundi, **2:472–475**

Buscetta, Tommaso, 1:246

Bush, George, H. W. (U.S. president), 1:256

Bush, George W. (U.S. president), 1:145, 158–159, 203, 211, 2:590, 617

Bustamante, Sir Alexander (Jamaica prime minister), 2:479, *480*

Byzantine Empire
    Fātimid dynasty and, 1:80
    Khazars and, 1:67
    overview of, 1:49, **51–54**
    in premodern world, 1:81
    Republic of Venice and, 1:82

Byzantion, 1:52

Byzas (Byzantion king), 1:52

C

Cabot, John (Italian navigator), 1:240

Cabral, Amilcar, 2:543

Cabral, Luis (Guinea-Bissau president), 2:543, 544

Cacao, 1:197, 198

Caesar, Julius, 1:35

Caetano, Marcello (Portugal prime minister), 1:265

Caldera, Rafael (Venezuela president), 1:202

Calendar, Mayan, 1:47

Caliphates, Islamic
    'Abbāsid Empire, 1:68–69
    abolition of in Turkey, 1:297
    Fātimid dynasty, 1:78

Caliphs, 1:63, 64

Cámara de Diputados (Argentina), 1:235

Cambodia, **2:390–393**
    See also Khmer Empire

Cambyses II (Persian king), 1:8, 21, 23

Cameroon, Republic of **2:416–419**

Camp David Peace Accords, 2:367

Canada, 1:130, **240–242**

Canada Act, 1:242

Canal Hotel, 2:335

Canberrra, Australia, *1:250*

Candra Gupta I (Gupta king), 1:58

Candra Gupta II (Gupta king), 1:60, 2:350

Candragupta (Magadha king), 1:34–35

Cão, Diogo (Portuguese explorer), 1:111, 2:561

Cape Verde, **2:552–553**

Captain's Regent (San Marino), **2:552–553**

CAR (Central African Republic), **2:439–442**

Caracas, Venezuela, 1:200

Cargo cult, 2:599

Carib tribes, 2:594

Caribbean Islands, 2:415

Caroline Islands, **2:611–612**

Carranza, Venustiano (Mexico president), 1:184–185

Carrera, Rafael, 1:216

Carter, Jimmy, 2:367, *548*

Carthage, 1:**20–21**, 35, 37, 2:399

Casa di San Giorgio, 1:87

Caste system
Gupta Empire, 1:59
imperial China, 1:89
Qing Dynasty, 1:133
Songhai Empire, 1:114
Tibet, 1:99
Tokugawa Shogunate, 1:128–129

Castro, Fidel (Cuba president), 2:408, 409–410

Catherine II (Russian empress), 1:147–148

Catholic Church
in Argentina, 1:233
in Mexico, 1:186
in premodern world, 1:81
during World War II, 1:303

Catholicism
in Dominican Republic, 1:224–225
in East Timor, 2:708
in Ireland, 1:289, 290
in Palau, 2:701
in Portugal, 1:264
in Saint Lucia, 2:590
in Trinidad and Tobago, 2:481
in United Kingdom, 1:141, 142

Caucasus, 2:635

Caudillos (Dominican Republic), 1:224

Ceausescu, Nicolae (Romania dictator), 2:677–678

Celts, 1:288

Central African Republic (CAR), **2:439–442**

Central Tibetan Administration (CTA), 1:99

Chaco War, 1:169, *171*

Chad, 2:389, **437–439**

Chambre des Deputes, 1:239

Chandragupta II (ruler of India), 2:350

Chao K'uang-yin (Sung Dynasty emperor), 1:88

Charlemagne (Frank king)
crowning of, 1:71
Genoa and, 1:86

Holy Roman Empire founding and, 1:69
illustration of, 1:70

Charles I (Austro-Hungarian emperor), 1:238

Charles I (British ruler), 1:141–142

Charles I (Portuguese king), 1:263

Charles I (Spain emperor), 1:116

Charles II (British ruler), 1:141, 142

Charles IV (Bohemian king), 2:627

Charles, Mary Eugenia (Dominica prime minister), 2:585, *586*

Chávez, Hugo (Venezuela president), 1:201, 202, 203

Chechnya, 2:*699*, 700

Cheng (Ch'in dynasty king), 1:15–16

Ch'eng T'ang (Shang dynasty king), 1:10, *11*

Chenla era, 1:73

Chernobyl nuclear power plant, 2:651

Cherokee, **1:192–195**

Chetniks, 2:680, 683

Chiang Ching-kuo, 2:386

Chiang Kai-shek, 2:380, 383

Chiefs, Chippewa, 1:130

Chikura, Wadyambeu (Great Zimbabwe ruler), 1:105

Chile, **1:174–178**

Chiluba, Frederick (Zambia president), 2:497

Chimú, 1:110

Ch'in dynasty, 1:40

Ch'in Shi Huang Ti (Qin king), 2:378
See also Quin Shi Huang-Di

China
Chou dynasty, 1:14–16
Goguryeo Kingdom, influence on, 1:56–57
Han dynasty, 1:40–41
Hong Kong, control of, 2:703, *704*
Hong Kong, leasing of, 2:702–703
immigration to Taiwan from, 2:383
Korea, influence in, 2:369
Macao, rule of, 2:705–706
Mongolia and, 1:300
Shang dynasty, 1:10–12
Singapore, immigration to, 2:503
Tibet and, 1:99–100
Tokugawa period Japan, relations with, 1:127
Vietnam, rule of, 2:574
World War II, 2:327

China, People's Republic of, **2:378–382**, 705

Chionites (tribal group), 1:61

Chippewa, **1:130–132**

Chou dynasty
description of, 2:378
King Wu Wang, *1:14*
overview of, **1:14–16**

Chou En-lai (China premier), 2:382

Chou Hsin (Shang dynasty king), 1:11

Christianity
in Armenia, 2:668
in Bulgaria, 1:259
in Byzantine Empire, 1:53
in Fātimïd dynasty, 1:79
in Georgia, 2:635
in Iceland, 1:322
in Estonia, 2:646
in Ireland, 1:288
in Japan, Tokugawa period, 1:129
in Norway, 1:256
in Poland, 2:621
in Spain, 2:564
in Spanish Empire, 1:116
in Sudan, 2:393
in Turkmenistan, 2:672
Visigoths and, 1:56

Christmas Island. *See* Kiribati

Chrysargyron, 1:53

Chulalongkorn (Thai king), 1:304

Cicero, *1:36*

Citadel (Teotihuacán palace), 1:50–51

City-states, Mayan, 1:47

Civil liberties, Kazakhstan, 1:286–287

Civil liberties, Saudi Arabia, 1:308–309

Civil service system, Sung Dynasty, 1:89

Cleisthenes (Athenian statesman), 1:25, 26

Coalition Provisional Authority (CPA), 1:312

Cocaine trade in Colombia, 1:211

Code of Hammurabi, 1:1, 5

Codex Euricianus, 1:55

Codex Justinianus, 1:53, 54

Codrington, Christopher, 2:603

Coffee, El Salvador production of, 1:220

Cold War
communist governments during, 2:617
Korean War, 2:370
overview of, 2:415

College of Cardinals, 1:302

College of Electors, 1:69

Collor de Mello, Fernando (Brazil president), *1:189*

Colombia, **1:208–211**

Colombo, Sri Lanka, 2:364

Colosseum, Roman, *1:43*

Columbus, Christopher (explorer), 1:107, 116, 200

Comitatus, 1:53

Committee of Union and Progress (CUP), 1:121

Commodus (emperor of Rome), 1:42

Commonwealth of Australia, **1:249–253**, 2:559

Commonwealth of Nations
  Barbados, 2:512
  Fiji, 2:526
  Grenada, 2:541
  Nauru, 2:515
  Saint Lucia, 2:591
  Saint Vincent and the Grenadines, 2:595
  Samoa, 2:467
  Solomon Islands, 2:581
  Tonga, 2:524
  Vanuatu, 2:600

Commonwealth of the Bahamas, **2:538–540**

Communism
  in Czechoslovakia, 2:627
  in Hungary, 2:619
  in Laos, 2:571
  in Lithuania, 2:663–664, 665
  in Moldova, 2:658
  in Poland, 2:622
  repudiation of, 2:617
  Slovenia, effects on, 2:643
  in Tajikistan, 2:667

Communist Party
  in Albania, 1:272
  in Bulgaria, 1:261–262
  in China, 2:380–381
  German disbanding of, 1:314
  Soviet Union, control of by, 2:697
  in USSR, *1:294*
  in Vietnam, 2:576

Communist rebellion, Malaysia, 2:405

Comoros, Union of, **2:553–556**

Compact of Free Association, 2:702

Companionate of Macedon, 1:32

Compaoré, Blaise (Côte d'Ivoire president), 2:433

Compton, John (Saint Lucia prime minister), 2:591

Comune government of Genoa, 1:86

Concentration camps, Nazi Germany, 1:317

Confederation of Senegambia, 2:453

Confucian legalism, 1:87

Confucianism
  description of, 1:15
  in Goguryeo Kingdom, 1:58
  in Han dynasty, 1:41
  in Laos, 2:569

Confucius, 1:15

Congo, Democratic Republic of the (DRC), 2:**423–426**, 485

Congo, Republic of the, **2:442–445**

Congo-Brazzaville, **2:443–445**

Congo-Ocean Railway, 2:442

Congreso de la Unión (Mexico), 1:185

Congresso Nacional (Brazil), 1:188

Constantine (Byzantine scholar), 1:75

Constantine I (Byzantine emperor), 1:52, 70

Constantine VII, 1:52

Constantinople, 1:45, 54
  See also Byzantion

Constitution for Europe, 2:696

Consuls, Roman Republic, 1:36

Conté, Lansana (Guinea president), 2:407

Convention of the Future of Europe, 2:696

Convention on the Regulation of Antarctic Mineral Resource Activities (CRAMA), 2:412

Coprinces of Andorra, 2:691, *692*

Corpus Juris Civilis, 1:53

Cortés, Hernán (Spanish explorer), 1:116, 118, 183

Cosa Nostra, 1:245–246

Cossacks, 1:149

Costa Rica, **1:211–214**

Côte d'Ivoire, Republic of, **2:434–437**

Council of State (Netherlands), 1:173

Council of Ten (Republic of Venice), 1:83

Council of the Indies, 1:117

CPA (Coalition Provisional Authority), 1:312

Crassus, Marcus Licinius, 1:35, 39

Credenza, Milan, 1:92

Creoles
  independence in Colombia, 1:209
  in Mauritius, 2:516, 517–518
  returned to Sierra Leone, 2:462
  in Suriname, 2:567

Crimean War, 2:677

Croatia, **2:640–643**

Croats, 2:679–681, 683–684

Cromwell, Oliver, 1:142

Cromwell, William Nelson, 1:253

Crusades, 1:54, 71, 81, 87

Crystal Night, 1:317

CTA (Central Tibetan Administration), 1:99

Cuba
  Angola civil war, involvement in, 2:563
  relations with Barbados, 2:513
  revolution of, 2:327

Cuba, Republic of, **2:408–411**

Cuban Missile Crisis, 2:410

Cubas, Raúl (Paraguay president), 1:170

Cuneiform script, 1:2

CUP (Committee of Union and Progress), 1:121

Cush, 1:*16*, **16–17**

Cuzco (Incan city), 1:180

Cyaxares (Median king), 1:19

Cyprus, 1:208, **2:447–451**

Cyril (Byzantine missionary), *1:76*

Cyrillic alphabet, 1:75

Cyrus II (Persian king), 1:20, 21, 22

Czech Republic, **2:626–629**

Czechoslovakia, 2:686

D

Da Costa, Manuel Pinto (São Tomé and Príncipe president), 2:557–558

Da Silva, Luiz Inácio Lula (Brazil president), *2:558*

Dacko, David (Central African Republic president), 2:441

Daddah, Moktar Ould (Mauritania president), 2:460

Dahomey, 2:429

Dáil Éireann, *1:288*

Daimyos, 1:128, 129

Dakar, Senegal, 2:451, 454

Dalai Lama, 1:98–99

Damascus, Syria, 2:335

Daniel, Simeon (Nevis premier), 2:607

Darfur, 2:395, 396

Darius I (Persian king)
  invasion of Greece, 1:23
  invasion of Scythia, 1:30
  Judeans and, 1:22
  rule of, 1:21

Darius II Ochus (Persian emperor), 1:8

D'Aubuisson, Roberto (El Salvador politician), 1:222

David (Israel king), 1:12, 13

Dayaukku (Mede Empire ruler), 1:19

Dayton Peace Accords, 2:681, 682, 685

De Administrando Imperio (Constantine VII), 1:52

De Menezes, Fradique (São Tomé and Príncipe president), 2:557, *558*

Débat, Alphonse Massamba, 2:443–444

Déby, Idris (Chad president), 2:438, 439

Decembrist Uprising, 1:149

Declaration of Independence, 1:155

Deioces (Mede Empire ruler), 1:19

Della Torre, Martino, 1:93

Democracy, 1:272, 2:620

Democratic Kampuchea, 2:393

Democratic People's Republic of Korea
    invasion of Republic of Korea, 2:370
    overview of, **2:372–375**
    relations with Republic of Korea, 2:371–372

Democratic and Popular Republic of Algeria, 2:401, **475–478**

Democratic reforms, Athens, 1:24–25

Democratic Republic of the Congo (DRC), 2:**423–426**, 485

Denard, Bob, 2:555

Denmark, **1:230–232**

Derg, 1:247

DeRoburt, Hammer (Nauru president), 2:515

Dge-lugs-pa sect (Tibet), 1:99

Dhofar, 2:388

Dia, Mamadou, 2:453

Diamonds, 2:333, 624

Dias, Bartolomeu (Portuguese explorer), 1:111

Díaz, Porfirio (Mexico president), 1:184

Didi, Amir (Maldives president), 2:500

Dikasteria, 1:25

Diocletian (Roman emperor), 1:42

Diogo, Luisa (Mozambique prime minister), 2:550

Diori, Hamani (Niger president), 2:431

Diouf, Abdou (Senegal president), 2:452

Djibouti, **2:578–580**

Djohar, Said Mohamed (Union of Comoros president), 2:554, 555

Djukanovic, Milo (Montenegro president), 2:710–711

Doe, Samuel K. (Liberia dictator), 1:227

Doge, 1:82, 86

Dollfuss, Engelbert (Austria chancellor), 1:276

Dome of the Rock (mosque), 1:64–65

Dominica, **2:584–586**

Dominican Republic, **1:222–226**

Dominion of Pakistan, 2:354

Doria, Andrea, 1:87

Dorji, Jigme Palden (Bhutan prime minister), 2:377

Dos Santos, José Eduardo, 2:563

Dos Santos, Monso, 2:558

Draco (archon), 1:25

DRC (Democratic Republic of the Congo), 2:**423–426**, 485

Drought
    in Cape Verde, 2:553
    in Malawi, 2:493
    in Mali, 2:456
    in Sudan, 2:396

Drug trade
    in Bahamas, 2:540
    Colombian, 1:211
    Tajikistan, trafficking in, 2:667
    in Vietnam, 2:577

Drystone, 1:104

Duar War, 2:375

Dutch
    Guyana, colonization of, 2:505
    Indonesia, colonization of, 1:324
    Papua New Guinea, interests in, 2:559
    Suriname, colonization of, 2:567
    Taiwan, colonization of, 2:383

Durrāni, Ahmad Shāh (Afghanistan king), 1:283

Duvalier, François (Haiti president), 1:165

Dzurinda, Mikuláš (Slovak Republic prime minister), 2:688

E

Early Byzantine era, 1:52

East Francia, 1:75

East Germany, 2:617

East Timor, **2:706–709**

Easter Uprising, 1:289

Eastern Chou dynasty, 1:14, 15

Eastern Orthodox Christianity, 1:259

Eboué, Félix, 2:442

Ecclesia (Assembly), 1:24, 25

Economic and Social Council (ESC), 2:333

Economy
    Albania, 1:272
    Argentina crisis, 1:235
    Bahamas, 2:540
    Barbados, 2:513
    Belize, 2:603
    Bolivia, 1:192
    Brazil, 1:189–190
    Bulgaria, 1:262
    Cambodia, 2:393
    Cameroon, 2:419
    Cape Verde, 2:553
    China, 2:382
    Cuba, 2:411
    Denmark, 1:232
    East Timor, 2:709
    Ecuador, 1:199
    Finland, 1:282
    Gabon, 2:447
    Germany, 2:634
    Guatemala, 1:217
    India, 2:354
    Iran, 2:590
    Ireland, 1:290
    Italy, 1:246
    Japan, 2:349
    Kiribati, 2:594
    Laos, 2:571
    Lesotho, 2:511
    Liberian, 1:227
    Malaysia, 2:406
    Mauritius, 2:518
    Micronesia, 2:612
    Nazi Germany, 1:316
    New Zealand, 2:346
    Nicaragua, 1:215
    Niger, 2:432
    North Korea, 2:375
    Norway, 1:256
    Portugal, 1:265
    Qatar, 2:530
    Republic of Korea, 2:371
    Russia, 2:700
    Salvadoran challenges, 1:222
    Sudan, 2:396
    Syria, 2:338
    Tanzania, 2:490
    Thailand, 1:306
    Vietnam, 2:577
    Zimbabwe, 2:598

Ecotourism
    Dominica, 2:586
    Palau, 2:702
    Saint Lucia, 2:592

Ecuador, **1:197–200**

Edo period. *See* Tokugawa Shogunate

Egypt
    Fātimid dynasty and, 1:78
    merger with Syria, *2:336*
    Suez Crisis, 2:367

Egypt, ancient
    Assyrian Empire and, 1:19
    Cush and, 1:16–17
    Hittites and, 1:9–10
    overview of, **1:6–8**
    Sphinx, pyramid in Giza, *1:7*

Egypt, Arab Republic of, **1:291–293**

El Dorado, 1:209
El Salvador, 1:219, **220–222**
Elamites, 1:6
Eleutherian Adventurers, 2:538
Elizabeth II (Britain queen), *2:583*
Ellice Islands, 2:583, 584, 592
Emperors, Roman, 1:42–44
Empire of Akkad
    Iraq and, 1:310
    overview of, **1:3–5**
    sculpture of Akkadian king, *1:4*
    Ur and, 1:2
Empire of Ghana, **1:71–73**
Ensi (temple priest), 1:2
Environmental issues
    Australia, 1:252
    Brazil, 1:190
    Chernobyl power plant, 2:651
    Denmark, 1:232
    Greece, 1:208
    Guinea, 2:408
    Honduras, 1:220
    Kiribati, 2:594
    Malaysia, 2:406
    Marshall Islands, 2:614
    Norway, 1:258
    Portugal, 1:265
    Republic of Korea, 2:371
    Suriname, 2:568
    Tuvalu, 2:584
Epaminondas (Theban general), 1:31
Ephors, 1:27
EPRDF (Ethiopian People's Revolutionary Democratic Front), 1:247
Equatorial Guinea, **2:521–523**
Erik II Magnusson (Norwegian king), 1:322
Eritrea, 2:580, **688–690**
Ershad, Hussain Mohammad, 2:537
Escobar, Pablo, *1:209*
Esquivel, Manuel, 2:602
Estonia, **2:645–647**
Estrada, Joseph (Philippines president), 2:344
ETA (Euskadi Ta Askatasuna), 2:566
Ethiopia
    Djibouti, conflict with, 2:580
    Eritrea, relationship with, 2:688–689, *690*
    overview of, **1:246–249**
Ethiopian People's Revolutionary Democratic Front (EPRDF), 1:247
Ethnic cleansing. *See* Genocide
Etruscan civilization, **1:23–24**
Euric (Visigoth king), 1:55
Europe
    exploration of Americas, 1:107
    twentieth century, 1:269
    USSR influence on, 1:295–296

European Commission, 2:694
European Constitutional Treaty, 2:696
European Convention, 2:696
European Parliament, 2:694, *695*
European Union
    Bulgaria, 1:262
    creation of, 2:617
    Cyprus, 2:450
    Estonia, 2:648
    Finland, 1:281, 282
    Hungary, 2:621
    Lithuania, 2:665
    Luxembourg participation, 1:239
    Macedonia's application to, 2:676
    Malta, 2:495
    overview of, **2:692–696**
    Poland, conflicts with, 2:624
    Slovak Republic, denial of entrance, 2:687
    Slovenia, 2:645
    Spain, 2:566
    Turkey, 1:299
Euskadi Ta Askatasuna (ETA), 2:566
Events. *See* Major events
Extraordinary rendition program, 2:580
Eyadéma, Gnassingbé (Togo president), 2:420

F

Fahd (Saudi king), 1:307
Fa-hsien, 1:59
Faisal (Saudi Arabia king), *1:309*
Faisal I (Iraq king), 1:310
Falcone, Giovanni, 1:246
Falklands War, 1:234
Fang kingdom, 2:445
Farah, Mohamed (Somaliland judge), 2:639
Fascism, 1:269
Fāṭimid dynasty, **1:77–78**
Federal Republic of Germany (FRG), 2:632
Federal Republic of Nigeria, **2:456–459**
Federated States of Micronesia, **2:611–612**
Federative Republic of Brazil, **1:187–190**
Ferdinand I (Bulgaria king), *1:261*
Ferdinand II (Spain king), 1:116, *117*, 2:564
Ferrer, José Figueres (Costa Rica president), 1:212, *213*
Fifth Republic (French), 1:161
Fiji, **2:525–527**

Final solution, 1:315
Finboni Accord, 2:556
Finland, **1:278–282**
First Continental Congress, 1:155
First Crusade, 1:54
First Grand National Assembly of Bulgaria, 1:259
First Indochina War, 2:574, 576
First Mexican Empire, 1:183
First Partition of Poland, 1:139
First Republic (French), 1:160
Floor Crossing amendment (South Africa), 1:320
Florence (city-state), **1:89–91**
Folketinget (Denmark), 1:230–231
Former Yugoslav Republic of Macedonia, 2:673
Fortress of the Golden Religion, *2:377*
Fourth Crusade, 1:54
Fourth Republic (French), 1:161
Fox, Vicente (Mexico president), 1:186
France
    Algiers, occupation of, 2:475, *478*
    in Andorra, 2:691
    annexation of Central African Republic, 2:440
    Belgium and, 1:203
    bombing of Greenpeace vessel, 2:346
    Cambodia, control of, 2:391
    in Cameroon, 2:416
    Canada, colonization of, 1:240
    Chad, colonization of, 2:437
    Comoros, colonization of, 2:554
    Congo, control of, 2:442
    Côte d'Ivoire, control of, 2:434–435
    Côte d'Ivoire, peacekeeping in, 2:436
    Dahomey, colonization of, 2:429
    Djibouti, presence in, *2:579*
    Dominica, colonization of, 2:584
    in Dominican Republic, 1:223
    Gabon, colonization of, 2:445
    Guinea, colonization of, 2:407
    Haiti settlements, 1:163
    Iroquois Confederation and, 1:125
    Madagascar, colonization of, 2:421
    Mauritania, colonization of, 2:460
    Mexico, war with, 1:183–184
    Niger, colonization of, 2:431
    overview of, **1:159–163**
    Saint Kitts, 2:605
    Saint Lucia, colonization of, 2:590
    Saint Vincent, 2:594
    Senegal, occupation of, 2:454
    Seychelles, colonization of, 2:572
    Syria, occupation of, 2:336
    Togo, 2:419

Upper Volta, control of, 2:433
Venice, conquest of, 1:84
Vietnam, colonization of, 2:574–575

Francis Joseph I (Austrian emperor), 1:236–237, 276

Franco, Francisco (Spain prime minister), 2:565, *566*

Franz Ferdinand (Austrian archduke), 1:276

Franz Joseph I (Austrian emperor), 1:276
See also Francis Joseph I

Frederick I (Prussian king), 1:137, *139*

Frederick II (Prussian king), 1:137, 138, 139

Frederick III (Danish king), 1:230

Frederick IX (Danish king), 1:*231*, 232

Frederick William (Brandenburg ruler), 1:137

Frederick William I (Prussian king), 1:137

Frederick William II (Prussian king), 1:137–138

Frederick William III (Prussian king), 1:139

Frederick William IV (Prussian king), 1:140

Free France Movement, 2:437, 440, 443

Free trade zone, Southeast Asia, 2:577

FRELIMO (Mozambique Liberation Front), 2:549

French Equatorial Africa, 2:437, 440, 442

French Revolution, 1:151

FRG (Federal Republic of Germany), 2:632

Frum, John, 2:599–600

Frumentius (Aksum king), 1:46

Fujimori, Alberto (Peru president), 1:182

Fujiware clan, 1:127

Funan era, 1:73

Funan Kingdom, 2:391

Fyodor I Ivanovich (Russia czar), 1:78

G

Gabonese Republic, **2:445–447**

Gacumbitsi, Sylvestre, 2:472

Gairy, Eric Matthew (Grenada prime minister), 2:541

Gama, Vasco da (Portuguese explorer), 1:112

Gambia, Republic of the, **2:498–500**

Gamsakhurdia, Zviad (Georgia president), 2:636

Gandhi, Indira (India prime minister), 2:352, 353–354

Gandhi, Mohandas, 2:350, 353, 354

Gang of Four, 2:382

Garang, John, 2:393, 394

García Moreno, Gabriel (Ecuador ruler), 1:198

García Pérez, Alan (Peru president), 1:182–183

Garibaldi, Giuseppe, 1:243, *244*

Gašporevič, Ivan (Slovak Republic president), *2:687*

Gaudalcanal, 2:582

Gaul, 1:54

Gayoom, Maumoon Abdul (Maldives president), 2:500, 501, 502

Gaza Strip, 2:367, 548

Gbagbo, Laurent, 2:435, 436

GDR (German Democratic Republic), 2:632

General Assembly (GA), United Nations, 2:332–333

Geneva Conventions, 2:332

Genghis Khan (Mongol ruler)
    conquest of Eurasia, 1:81
    overview of, 1:94
    unification of Mongolia, 1:300

Genoa, Republic of, **1:85–86**

Genoa harbor, *1:86*

Genocide
    of Armenians in Turkey, 2:669, 670
    in Bosnia, 2:681–682, 685
    in East Timor, 2:706
    of Nazi Germany, 1:317
    in Rwanda, 2:469
    Soviet/Nazi atrocities, Minsk victims of, 2:654

George Tupou V (Tonga king), 2:524

Georgia (U.S. state), 1:193–195

Georgia, Republic of, **2:635–637**

German Confederation, 1:236

German Democratic Republic (GDR), 2:632

Germany
    Cameroon, occupation of, 2:416
    Great Moravia, conquest of, 1:77
    Kenya, colonization of, 2:485
    Luxembourg occupation of, 1:239
    Maji Maji uprising, 2:490
    Marshall Islands, colonization of, 2:613
    Namibia, annexation by, 2:624
    overview of, **2:631–634**
    Poland, power struggle with, 2:624
    Prussia, relations with, 1:140
    reunification of, 2:617
    in Samoa, 2:467
    Venezuela, colonization of, 1:200
    World War II alliance with Italy, 1:245
    Zanzibar, annexation of, 2:488–489
    See also Nazi Germany

Gerousia (Council of Elders), 1:26, 27

Ghana, **2:401–403**

Ghana, Empire of, **1:71–73**

Ghana, Empire of, ancient
    Mali and, 1:96
    overview of, 1:49
    Senegal region, 2:454

Ghedi, Ali Mohammed (Somalia prime minister), 2:427

Gilbert Islands, 2:583, 584, 592

Glagolithic alphabet, 1:75

Glasnost, 1:295

Global warming, 2:502, 592

Gnassingbé, Faure (Togo president), 2:420

Go-Daigo (Japanese emperor), 2:347

Goguryeo Kingdom, 1:49, **56–58**

Gokomere, 1:103

Golan Heights, 2:337

Gold
    in Colombia, 1:209
    Empire of Ghana trade in, 1:72–73
    in Ghana, 2:402
    in Great Zimbabwe, 1:104
    in Mali, 1:96–97

Gold Coast, 1:134, *135*, 136
    See also Ghana

Golden Bull (decree), 1:69

Golden Stool, 1:134

Golden Triangle, 2:571

Gomułka, Władysław, 2:622

Gongadze, Georgiy, 2:652

Gonsalves, Ralph (Saint Vincent and the Grenadines prime minister), 2:596

Gonzi, Lawrence (Malta prime minister), 2:494

Gorbachev, Mikhail (Russia president), 1:295, 296, 2:651, 697

Goths. *See* Visigoths

Governors, provincial, 1:44

Gowon, Yakubu, 2:458

Grand Duchy of Luxembourg,
1:238–240

Grand Embassy, 1:149

Great Depression, 1:269, 314

Great Enclosure (Zimbabwe), 1:*104*,
104–105

Great Fatherland War, 1:295

Great King, 1:9

Great Leap Forward, 2:381

Great Moravia, **1:75–77**, 2:685

Great Proletariat Cultural Revolution,
2:381

Great Schism, 1:53

Great Socialist People's Libyan Arab
Jamahiriya, **2:388–390**

Great Wall of China, 2:378

Great Zimbabwe, **1:103–106**

Greece
Athens, 1:24–26
Cyprus, control of, 2:448
India, invasion of, 2:350
Kingdom of Macedonia, 2:673
Macedon, 1:31–33
Macedonia, disputes with, 2:676
overview of, **1:206–208**
Persian invasions against, 1:23
Scythians and, 1:29
Sparta, 1:26–29
Thebes, 1:30–31

Greek Cypriots, 2:448

Green March, 2:398

Greenpeace, 2:346

Grenada, **2:541–543**

Grenadines. *See* Saint Vincent and the
Grenadines

Grimaldi, François, 1:266

Grimaldi dynasty, 1:266–267

Guatemala, **1:215–217**, 2:601, 603

Guei, Robert, 2:435–436

Guelleh, Ismail (Djibouti president),
2:579

Guelphs, 1:90, 91

Guerra de Fútbol, 1:219

Guevara, Ernesto "Che," 2:409

Guilds, Florence, 1:90

Guinea, **2:406–408**
See also Equatorial Guinea; Papua
New Guinea

Guinea-Bissau, **2:543–545**

Gulf War, 2:529

Gupta Empire, 1:34–35, **58–60**,
2:350

Gurkha Kingdom, 1:152

Gusenbauer, Alfred (Austria
chancellor), 1:278

Gusmao, Xanana (East Timor
president), *2:708*

Gustav (Swedish king), *1:168*

Gutenberg, Johannes, 1:71

Gutiérrez, Lucio (Ecuador
president), 1:199–200

Guyana, **2:505–507**

H

Habré, Hissène (Chad prime
minister), 2:439

Habsburgs
in Austria, 1:276
Bohemia domination by, 2:627
Hungary, rule of, 2:618
Liechtenstein and, 1:146
Netherlands and, 1:172

Habyarimana, Juvénal (Rwanda
president), 2:469

The Hague, 2:334, 643

Haiti, **1:163–166**

Halonen, Tarja (Finland president),
1:282

Hamad bin Isa al-Khalifa (Bahrain
king), 2:528, 529

Hammurabi (Babylonian Empire
king), 1:5–6

Han dynasty, **1:40–41**, 2:378–379

Hans Adam II (Liechtenstein prince),
1:147

Hariri, Rafiq (Lebanon prime
minister), 2:330

Hārūn ar-Rashīd ('Abbāsid caliph),
1:68

Hasan, Sayyid Muhammad ibn 'Abd
Allāh, 2:638

Hashemite Kingdom of Jordan,
2:339–341

Hassan II (Morocco king), *2:397*

Hatshepsut (ancient Egypt queen),
1:8

Havel, Václav (Czech Republic
president), 2:627, 629

Haya de la Torre, Victor Raúl, 1:182

Heian period, 1:127, 2:347

Hejaz, 1:307

Henry IV (Holy Roman emperor),
1:70–71

Henry the Navigator, 1:263

Hephthalites, 1:61

Heraclius (Byzantine emperor), 1:52,
53

Herodotus (Greek historian), 1:19,
23

Herzegovina, Bosnia and,
2:679–682

Herzl, Theodore, 2:365

Heuss, Theodor (FRG president),
2:633

Hezbollah movement, 2:329, 330,
368, 517, 518

Hindenburg, Paul von (Germany
president), 1:314

Hinduism, 1:59, 2:350

Hindus
in Bhutan, 2:377
in Mauritius, 2:516
migration of, 2:355

HIPC (Highly Indebted Poor
Countries) initiative, 2:551

Hirohito (Japanese emperor), *2:349*

Hispaniola, 1:222–223

Hitler, Adolf (German chancellor)
Beer Hall Putsch, 1:314
election of, 1:314–315
laws of, 1:313
and Nazi Germany, 313–317
rise of, 1:71, 269

Hittite Empire, **1:9–10**

Hittites of Anatolia, 1:8

HIV/AIDS epidemic
Botswana, 2:509
Burundi, 2:474
Lesotho, 2:511
Malawi, 2:493
Namibia, 2:626
Swaziland, 2:521
Thailand, 1:306–307
Zambia, 2:497

Ho Chi Minh, 2:415, 574, 576,
577

Holy Roman Empire
founding of, 1:49
map of, *1:71*
Milan, defeat of, 1:92
overview of, **1:69–71**

Honduras, **1:217–220**

Hong Kong, **2:702–705**

Horsemen, Hunnic, 1:61

Houphouët-Boigny, Félix
(Côte d'Ivoire president), 2:435

House of Representatives, U.S.,
1:157–158

House of Saud, 1:309

House of Trade (Spanish Empire),
1:117

Howard, John (Australia prime
minister), 1:252

Hoxha, Enver (Albania premier),
1:270, 272

Hoyte, Hugh Desmond (Guyana
prime minister), 2:506

Huáscar, 1:109, 180

Huayna Capac, 1:108–109, 180

Huitzilopochtli (Aztec god), 1:101,
102

Hukbalahap, 2:342

Humāyūn (Mughal emperor), 1:122

Human rights
Afghanistan, abuses in, 1:285
Belarus, abuses in, 2:655–656
Bosnia, war crimes in, 2:681–682
Cambodia, abuses in, 2:393
Colombia, abuses in, 1:211
Costa Rica, abuses in, 1:213
Djibouti, abuses in, 2:580
Dominican Republic, abuses in, 1:224, 225
East Timor, abuses in, 2:706
El Salvador, abuses in, 1:221
Guinea, abuses in, 2:407–408
Honduras, abuses in, 1:218
Malaysia, abuses in, 2:406
Mauritania, abuses in, 2:461
Nazi Germany, abuses in, 1:315–316
South Africa, abuses in, 1:319, 320
Sudan, abuses in, 2:395
Tunisia, abuses in, 2:401
Turkmenistan, abuses in, 2:672
Uzbekistan, abuses in, 2:663
Vietnam, abuses in, 2:577–578
Human trafficking
in Djibouti, 2:580
in Laos, 2:572
in UAE, 2:534
Hundred Schools of Thought, 2:378
Hungary, 2:640–641
See also Austro-Hungarian Empire
Hungary, Republic of, **2:618–621**
Hunnic Empire
Gupta Empire and, 1:60
overview of, 1:60–61
Visigoths and, 1:54
Hunte, Julian Robert, *2:591*
Hurricane Emily, 2:542–543
Hurricane Ivan, 2:542
Hurricane Mitch, 1:219
Hurricanes, Saint Lucia, 2:591
Husayn ibn 'Alī (Umayyad ruler), 1:64
Hussein (Jordan king), 2:340
Hussein, Saddam (Iraq president), 1:310, 311–313, *312*
Hutu ethnic group, 2:468–469, 472, 473–474

I

Ibn Sa'ūd (Saudi prince), 1:307, 309
Iceland, **1:321–323**
Idris I (Libya king), 2:388
Iliescu, Ion (Romania president), 2:678–679
Illiteracy, Guinea, 2:408
Illyrian movement, 2:640
Imām Yahya (Yemen ruler), 2:630

Immigration
in Andorra, 2:691
in Kuwait, 2:464
Malta, illegal, 2:495
in New Zealand, 2:346
Imperial Circles, 1:70
Imperial government, Roman Empire, 1:42, 44
The Imperial Reform, 1:69–70
Inca Empire, **1:108–110**
India
Assamese separatists, attacks on, 2:377–378
independence of, 2:327
Indians in Fiji, 2:527
Indians in Malaysia, 2:404
Magadha, 1:33–35
Pakistan, border dispute with, 2:356–357
India, Republic of, **2:349–354**
Indo-Bhutan Treaty, 2:375
Indonesia, invasion of East Timor, 2:706
Indonesia, Republic of, 1:323–325
Indo-Pakistani Wars, 2:356
Indus Valley society, 2:350
Industrial Revolution, 1:151
Industry privatization, Bolivia, 1:192
Industry privatization, Uruguay, 1:197
Ingraham, Hubert (Bahamas prime minister), 2:540
Internal Macedonian Revolutionary Organization (VMRO), 2:673
International Court of Justice (ICJ), 2:334
International Criminal Court (ICC), 2:334
International Criminal Tribunal for Rwanda (ICTR), 2:471
Internet gambling, 2:605
Intifada, 2:368
Ionian Revolt, 1:22–23
IRA (Irish Republican Army), 1:289
Iran
Islamic revolution in, 2:415
Mede Empire, 1:19–20
overview of, **2:586–590**
Persian Empire, 1:21–23
See also Sassanid Empire
Iraq
Assyrian Empire, 1:17–18
Canal Hotel bombing, 2:335
Iran, relations with, 2:589–590
Jordan, refugees in, 2:341
Kuwait, invasion of, 2:465–466
overview of, 1:310–313
Ireland, 1:142–143, 145, 287–290
Irene (Byzantine empress), 1:53

Irish Republican Army (IRA), 1:289
Iron Curtain, 2:634
Iroquois, war with Cherokee, 1:193
Iroquois Confederation, **1:124–127**
Isabella I (Spanish queen), 1:116, *117*, 2:564
Islam
in Afghanistan, 1:283
in Bahrain, 2:529
in Brunei Darussalam, 2:608
in Comoros, 2:554
criticism of Western values, 2:617
Djibouti, extremism in, 2:579
establishment of, 1:49
in Gambia, 2:499
in Indonesia, 1:324, 325
in Iran, 2:588
Iran revolution, 2:415
in Maldives, 2:500
in Oman, 2:386, 388
in Persian Empire, 2:588
in Republic of Yemen, 2:631
in Saudi Arabia, 1:309–310
in Senegal, 2:452
in Spain, 2:564
in Tajikistan, 2:666, 667–668
in Turkmenistan, 2:672
in Uzbekistan, 2:662
Vatican City diplomacy with, 1:304
Islamic caliphates, 1:63–65, 68–69
Islamic Party of Turkistan, 2:662
Islamic Republic of Mauritania
Morocco, conflict with, 2:398–399
overview of, **2:459–462**
Senegal, conflict with, 2:453–454
Islamic Republic of Pakistan, **2:354–358**
Israel
Egypt, defeat of, 1:292
Golan Heights, annexation of, 2:337
Lebanon, attacks on, 2:330
Palestine and, 2:547
Saudi Arabia and, 1:309
Israel, kingdom of, **1:12–13**
Israel, State of, **2:365–369**
Israelites, 1:12–13
Issa tribe, 2:578
Istanbul, 1:43, 49, 121
See also Byzantine Empire; Turkey
Italian Renaissance, 1:91
Italo-Ethiopian War, 1:247
Italy
Albania, 1:270
Ethiopia control of, 1:246
Etruscan civilization in, 1:23–24
Florence, conflict with, 1:90
Libya, occupation of, 2:388
overview of, **1:242–246**

Republic of Genoa recognition by, 1:87
San Marino and, 1:98
Ivan IV Vasilyevich (Russian ruler), 1:78
Ivan the Terrible (Russian ruler), 1:78
Ivory Coast. *See* Côte d'Ivoire, Republic of

J

Jagan, Cheddi (Guyana president), 2:505
Jagan, Janet (Guyana president), 2:507
Jahūngīr (Mughal emperor), 1:122
Jamaica, **2:478–481**
James II (British ruler), 1:142
Jammeh, Yahya (Gambia president), 2:498–499
Jangsu (Goguryeo king), 1:58
Janjaweed, 2:394, 395
Janša, Janez (Slovenia prime minister), *2:644*
Japan
  Caroline Islands, colonization of, 2:611
  Korea, annexation of, 2:372
  Korea, occupation of, 2:369
  Laos, occupation of, 2:569
  Malaysia, occupation of, 2:404
  Nauru, occupation of, 2:514
  overview of, **2:346–349**
  Palau, influence in, 2:701
  Philippines, occupation of, 2:342
  Qing Dynasty and, 1:133
  Solomons, occupation of, 2:581
  Taiwan, colonization of, 2:383
  Vietnam, occupation of, 2:574
Jawara, Dawda Kairaba (Gambia president), 2:498–499
Jayasthiti Malla (Nepal king), 1:152
Jayavarman II (Khmer Empire king), 1:73, 74
Jayavarman VII (Khmer Empire king), 1:74, 2:391
Jemaah Islamiyah, 1:325
Jeroboam (Israel king), 1:13
Jews
  in Fātimid dynasty, 1:79
  in Nazi Germany, 1:317
  statehood movement, 2:546–547
Jiang Qing, 2:382
Jie (Hsia ruler), 1:10
Jiménez de Quesada, Gonzalo, 1:209
Jin Dynasty
  overview of, 1:87–88
  Sung Dynasty and, 1:89
  Sung wars, 1:132

Jinnah, Muhammed Ali (Pakistan governor general), 2:354–355
John I (Portugal king), 1:263
John II (Portugal king), 1:111–112
John Paul II (Catholic pope), 1:303
Johnson-Sirleaf, Ellen (Liberia president), 1:227
Jomon period, 1:127, 2:346
Jonathan, Joseph Leabua (Lesotho prime minister), 2:509–510
Jonestown, Guyana, 2:507
Jordan, Hashemite Kingdom of, **2:339–341**
Juan Carlos I (Spain king), 2:565
Juárez, Benito (Mexico president), 1:183–184, *185*
Judah (Israel), 1:13
Judaism, Khazars conversion to, 1:66–67
Jumblatt, Walid, *2:329*, 330
Jurchen tribe, 1:132
Justinian I (Byzantine emperor), 1:53

K

Kabbah, Ahmad Tejan (Sierra Leone president), 2:463, 464
Kabila, Joseph (Congo president), 2:426
Kabila, Laurent-Désiré, 2:426
Kaczyński, Jarosław (Poland prime minister), 2:623
Kaczyński, Lech (Poland president), 2:623
Kagan (Khazar ruler), 1:65
Kagyu sect (Tibet), 1:99
The Kalevalaa, 1:279
Kāmandakīya, 1:59
Kambuja Kingdom, 2:391
Kandyan dynasty, 2:363
Kanem-Bornu kingdom, 2:437, 457
Karamanlis, Konstantinos (Greece prime minister), 1:208
Kargil War, 2:357
Karimov, Islam (Uzbekistan president), 2:662–663
Karume, Abeid (Tanganyika president), 2:489
Kasavubu, Joseph (Democratic Republic of the Congo president), 2:424, 425
Kashka, 1:9
Kashmir, 2:356
Kassites, 1:6
Kathmandu, *1:154*
Katipuneros, 2:341

Kaunda, Kenneth (Zambia president), 2:495, 496, 497
Kaya (Creole singer), 2:517
Kazakhstan, Republic of, **1:286–287**
Keita, Modibo (Mali president), 2:455
Kekkonen, Urho (Finland president), 1:282
Kelly, Grace, 1:*266*, 267
Kennedy, John F. (U.S. president), 2:410, *444*
Kenya, **2:485–488**
Kenyatta, Jomo (Kenya president), 2:485, *486*
Kérékou, Mathieu (Benin president), 2:429, 430
KGB (Committee for State Security, USSR), 1:294
Khalifa bin Zayed al-Nahyan, Sheikh (United Arab Emirates president), 2:533
Khama, Seretse (Botswana president), 2:508
Khans, Mongol, 1:94
Kharji, 1:64
Khazars, **1:65–67**
Khmer Empire, 1:49, **73–75**, 2:391
Khmer independence movement, 2:391
Khmer Rouge, 1:75, 2:392–393
Khomeini, Ayatollah Ruhollah (Iran Valy-e Faqih), 2:415, 588, *589*
Khorāsān, 1:65, 68
Khosrow I (Sassanid ruler), 1:63
Khuda, Saman, *2:666*
Kiev (Kievan city), 1:77
Kievan Rus'
  Byzantine Empire and, 1:53–54
  Novgorod Republic and, 1:100
  overview of, 1:49, **77–78**
Kifaya movement, 1:292
Kikuyu people, 2:485
Kim Il Sung (North Korea president), 2:374–375
Kim Jong Il (North Korea president), 2:*374*, 375
Kindia graves, 2:408
Kingdom of Bohemia, 2:627
Kingdom of Hormuz, 2:532
Kingdom of Israel, **1:12–14**
Kingdom of Kongo, 2:423, 442
Kingdom of Prussia, 1:**137–140**, 232
Kingdom of Saudi Arabia, **1:307–310**
Kingdom of Tonga, **5:23–25**
Kingdom of Urartu, 2:668
Kingdom of Van Lang, 2:574

Kiribati, **2:592–594**

Klaus, Václav (Czech Republic prime minister/president), 2:628

Kocharyan, Robert (Armenia president), 2:670

Kofun period, 1:127

Koizumi, Junichiro (Japan prime minister), 2:347, *591*

Kolhufushi Island, *2:501*

Kolingba, André (Central African Republic president), 2:441

Konaré, Oumar (Mali president), 2:455–456

Konbuang Dynasty, 2:359

Kongo Kingdom, 2:561

Korea, 1:133
    See also Democratic People's Republic of Korea; Goguryeo Kingdom; Republic of Korea

Korean War, 2:370, 374

Kosovo, 1:272, 2:685

Kountché, Seyni (Niger president), 2:431

Kouroukan Fouga, 1:96

Krajina, Croatia, 2:643

Kraprayoon, Suchinda (Thai general), 1:305

Kravchuk, Leonid (Ukraine president), 2:652

Krios, 2:462

Kristallnacht, 1:317

Kublai Khan, 1:94, *95*

Kuchma, Leonid (Ukraine president), 2:652

Kufuor, John (Ghana president), 2:403

Kulov, Feliks, 2:659

Kumāra Gupta II (Gupta king), 1:60

Kumasi (Ashanti city), *1:136*

Kun, Béla, 2:618–619

Kuomintang, 2:380, 383, 385

Kurdish people, 1:299, 310

Kush, 1:8

Kuwait, **2:464–466**

KwaZulu-Natal, 1:180

Kyrgyzstan, **2:658–661**

L

La Seu d'Urgell, Bishop of, 2:691–692

La Soufriere volcano, *2:595*

La Violencia, 1:211

Labarnas I (Hittite Empire king), 1:9

Labor, imported, 2:505

Labor movement, Saint Kitts, 2:606

Labour Party (United Kingdom), 1:144, 145

Lahoud, Émile (Lebanon president), 2:329

Lamaseries, 1:98–99

Lamizana, Sangoulé (Upper Volta president), 2:433

Land grants, Gupta Empire, 1:59–60

Landsbergis, Vytautas (Lithuania president), 2:664

Lao People's Democratic Republic, **2:569–572**

Las Casas, Bartolomé de, 1:117–118

Late Byzantine era, 1:52

Later Zhao Kingdom, 1:88

Lateran Treaty, 1:302

Latvia, **2:648–651**

Laws
    French, 1:161–162
    Gupta Empire, 1:59
    Holy Roman Empire, 1:70
    Iceland, 1:321
    Israeli, 2:366–367
    Liberia, 1:226
    Oman, 2:387
    Ottoman Empire, 1:120
    Qing Dynasty, 1:132–133
    Saudi Arabia, 1:308
    Sung Dynasty, 1:88
    Tibetan, 1:99
    Turkey, 1:298
    United Kingdom, 1:143
    Visigoths, 1:55

League of Arab States, 2:547
    See also Arab League

League of Corinth, 1:32

League of Nations, 1:314, 2:332

Lebanese civil war, *2:329*

Lebanon, **2:328–332**, 368

LeBlanc, Edward Oliver, 2:585

Lee Kuan Yew (Singapore prime minister), *2:503*, 504

Legalism
    in Ch'in dynasty, 1:40
    description of, 1:15
    in Han dynasty, 1:41

Lekhanya, Justin, 2:510–511

Lenin, Vladimir (Russia president), 1:293, 295, 2:664

Leonidas (Sparta king), 1:28

Leopold I (Belgium king), 1:205

Leopold II (Belgium king), 1:205, 2:423–424

Lesotho, **2:509–511**

Levant, 2:328

Liao Dynasty, 1:89

Liberal Democrat Party (United Kingdom), 1:144

Liberia, **1:226–227**, 2:333

Libyan Arab Jamahiriya, Great Socialist People's, **2:388–390**

Liechtenstein, Principality of, **1:145–147**

Lima, Peru, 1:180

Linas-Marcoussis Accord, 2:436

List of Sumerian Kings, 1:2

Lithuania, **2:663–666**

Litvinenko, Alexander, 2:700

Liu Ch'e (Han dynasty emperor), 1:40, 41

Liu Hsiu (Han dynasty emperor), 1:41

Liu Pang (Han dynasty emperor), 1:40, 41, 87

Locke, John, 1:107

Lockerbie bombing, 2:389–390

Lombard League, 1:92

Lon Nol (Cambodia prime minister), 2:392–393

Louis II (East Francia ruler), 1:69

Louverture, Toussaint, 1:164

Lugals (kings), 1:2

Lukashenko, Alexander (Belarus president), 2:*654*, 655–656

Lumumba, Patrice (Democratic Republic of the Congo prime minister), 2:424, 425

Lusaka Peace Accords, 2:564

Lutheran Church, 1:230

Luxembourg, Grand Duchy of, **1:238–240**

M

Maastricht Treaty, 2:693, 696

Macao, **2:705–706**

Macapagal-Arroyo, Gloria (Philippines president), 2:344

MacArthur, Douglas, *2:349*

MacDonald, John A. (Canada prime minister), 1:240, *241*

Macedon, **1:31–33**

Macedonia, Republic of, **2:673–676**

Machel, Samora (Mozambique president), *2:550*

Machiavelli, Niccolò, 1:91

Machi-bugyo, 1:128

Machu Picchu, 1:110

Mad Mullah, 2:638

Madagascar, **2:421–423**

Madison, James (U.S. president), 1:156

Madrid bombing, 2:566

Mafia, Italian, 1:245–246

Magadha, **1:33–35**

Magellan, Ferdinand (Spanish explorer), 2:341, 564

Magi, 1:19, 23

Magna Carta, 1:140–141

Magyars, 1:66, 2:618

Mahabharata, 1:59

Maine (U.S. battleship), 2:409

Maji Maji uprising, 2:490

Makarios III (Cypriot archbishop), 2:448, *451*

Maktoum, Sheikh Muhammad bin Rashid al- (United Arab Emirates prime minister), 2:533

Malawi, **2:491–492**

Malay Muslim Monarchy, 2:610

Malaysia, **2:403–406**, 502

Maldives, **2:500–502**

Malagasy people, 2:421

Mali, 2:434, **454–456**

Mali Empire, 1:**95–97**, 113

Malietoa Tanumafili II (Samoa chief), 2:467

Malla period (Nepal), 1:152

Malloum, Félix (Chad president), 2:439

Malta, **2:493–495**

Mambos, 1:104

Mancham, James (Seychelles president), 2:572, 573

Manchuria, 1:89, 132

Manco Capac (Inca emperor), 1:108

Manco Inca Yupanqui (Inca emperor), 1:109

Mandela, Nelson (South Africa president), 1:321

Mansa Mūsā (Mali ruler), 1:96–97

Mansabdari, 1:123–124

Mao Tse-tung (Chinese statesman), 2:380, 381–382

Maoists, 1:152–153

Maoris, 2:344–345, 346

Mapuche people, 1:175

Marāthās, 1:124

Marca Hispanica, 2:691

Marcos, Ferdinand (Philippines president), 2:*342*, 343–344

Marcos, Subcomandante, 1:*186*, 187

Marduk (Babylon's patron god), 1:6

Marino (Croatian stonecarver), 1:97

Maroons, 2:567

Marshall Islands, Republic of the, **2:612–614**

Martí, José, 2:409

Martínez, Maximiliano H. (El Salvador president), 1:220, *221*

Marwān II (Umayyad caliph), 1:67

Masire, Quett Ketumile (Botswana president), 2:508

Mata, Roy (Vanuatu chief), 2:599

Matabele tribe, 2:507

Mau Mau revolution, 2:468, 487, 488

Mauritania, Islamic Republic of
  Morocco, conflict with, 2:398–399
  overview of, **2:459–462**
  Senegal, conflict with, 2:453–454

Mauritius, Republic of, **2:516–518**

Mauryan dynasty, 1:33, 34–35, 2:350

Maximian (Roman soldier), 1:42–43

Mayan civilization, 1:1, **47–48**, 2:601

Mayotte, 2:554

Mayta Capac (Inca emperor), 1:108

Mazdak (Zoroastrian priest), 1:63

Mazowiecki, Tadeusz (Poland prime minister), 2:622

Mazzini, Giuseppe, 1:243

Mba, León (Gabon president), 2:445, 447

Mea'ole, Tupua Tamasese (Samoa chief), 2:467

Mecca (city-state), 1:64

Meciar, Vladimir (Slovak Republic prime minister), 2:687

Mede Empire, 1:**19–20**, 22

Media
  in Brunei, 2:610
  in Djibouti, 2:580
  Vietnam, control of in, 2:577–578

Median Empire, 2:587

Medici, Lorenzo de, *1:91*

Medici family, 1:90

Medina, Saudi Arabia, 1:64

Megali Idea, 1:207

Mehmed I (Ottoman sultan), 1:121

Mehmed II (Ottoman sultan), 1:121

Meiji (Japan emperor), 1:129

Meiji Restoration, 2:347

Mein Kampf (Hitler), 1:314

Mencius, 1:15

Menes (ancient Egypt king), 1:7

Mengistu Haile Mariam (Ethiopia president), 1:247

Merchants, premodern Europe, 1:81

Merina kingdom, 2:421

Merneptah (ancient Egypt pharaoh), 1:8

Mesoamerica. *See* Mayan civilization

Mesopotamia
  Babylonian Empire, 1:5–6
  early civilizations in, 1:1
  Empire of Akkad, 1:3–5
  Sassanid Empire and, 1:61
  Ur, 1:2–3

The Mespot Commission, *1:144*

Messenia, 1:27, 28

Methodius (Byzantine missionary), *1:76*

Metternich, Klemens von (Austria ruler), 1:276

Mexìcâ people, 1:101

Mexican Revolution, 1:184

Mexico, 1:50, **183–187**

Mfecane, 1:178

Michel, James (Seychelles president), 2:572–573

Micronesia, Federated States of, **2:611–612**

Middle Atlantic Kingdom, 2:561

Middle Byzantine era, 1:52

Middle East, conflict in, 2:415

Midewiwin Society, 1:130–131

Milan, **1:91–93**

Military kingship, 1:55

Milli Mejlis, 1:273, 274

Milosevic, Slobodan (Serbia president), 1: 273, 2:643, *683*, 684

Minamoto clan, 1:127

Minamoto Yoritomo (Japanese shogun), 1:127–128

Ming Dynasty, 2:380

Mining
  in Colombia, 1:209
  Mozambique, de-mining efforts in, 2:551
  on Nauru, *2:514*
  in Zambia, 2:496

Misericórdia, 1:111

Mithradates I (Parthian king), 1:38, 39

Mitterrand, Francois, *2:692*

Mobutu Sese Seko (Democratic Republic of the Congo president), 2:425

Mogadishu, 2:427–428

Mogae, Festus (Botswana president), 2:508

Mohammad ibn Hauqal (historian), 1:65

Mohammed I Askia (Songhai emperor), 1:114

Mohammed V (Morocco king), 2:397

Mohammed VI (Morocco king), 2:397

Mohammed, Khalid Sheikh, 2:401

Mohawk tribe, 1:125–126

Mohéli, 2:554

Moisiu, Alfred Spiro (Albania president), 1:272

Mojmír (Great Moravia king), 1:75

Mokhehle, Ntsu, 2:510–511

Moldavia, 2:656, 677

Moldova, **2:656–658**

Momoh, Joseph Saidu (Sierra Leone prime minister), 2:463

Mon people, 2:358

Monaco, **1:265–267**

Mongkut (Thai king), 1:304

Mongol Empire
  invasion of China, 2:380
  overview of, 1:81, **93–95**
  sacking of Baghdad, 1:310
  Tibet and, 1:99

Mongolia, 1:89, **299–301**

Mongolian People's Revolutionary Party (MPRP), 1:300–301

Mon-Khmer, 1:73, 2:569

Monnet, Jean (French statesman), 2:693

Monte Carlo, 1:267

Montenegro, **2:709–711**

Moors, 1:110, 263

Morales, Evo (Bolivia president), 1:192

Moravia, Great, **1:75–77**, 2:685

Morgan, John Pierpont (U.S. financier), 1:253

Moro, Aldo (Italy prime minister), 1:245

Morocco, **2:397–399**

Moscow, 1:101

Moshoeshoe II (Lesotho king), 2:509, *510*

Mossi people, 2:432

Mostar, Bosnia and Herzegovina, *2:682*

Mount Titano, 1:97

Mouvement Démocrate (MoDem), 1:162

Movement of Democratic Forces of the Casamance (MFDC), 2:454

Mozambique, **2:549–551**

Mozambique Liberation Front (FRELIMO), 2:549

Mswati III (Swaziland king), 2:518, 519

Mu'āwiyah I (Umayyad caliph), 1:64

Mubarak, Hosni (Egypt president), 1:292

Mugabe, Robert (Zimbabwe president), 2:596, *597*, 598

Mughal Empire, **1:122–124**, 2:350

Muhammad, 1:49, 64, 307

Muhammad ibn 'Abd al-Wahhāb, 1:307

Muhammad, Murtala, 2:458

Mukāta'a, 1:120

Murad V (Ottoman sultan), *1:121*

Murray, Craig (British ambassador), 2:663

Musa, Said (Belize political leader), 2:602

Muscat, Oman, 2:386

Museveni, Yoweri (Uganda president), 2:483–484

Musharraf, Pervez (Pakistan president), 2:356, 357–358

Muslim Brotherhood, 2:337

Muslims
  Afghani, 1:282
  in Comoros, 2:554
  India, invasion of, 2:350
  India/Pakistan partition and, 2:356–357
  in Indonesia, 1:323
  in Iraq, 1:313
  in Israel, 2:365
  in Mauritius, 2:517
  Morocco, extremism in, 2:399
  in Spain, 2:564
  in Spanish Empire, 1:116
  Tunisia, invasion of, 2:399
  in Zanzibar, 2:489

Mussolini, Benito (Italy dictator), 1:243–247, 269

Mütalibov, Ayaz (Azerbaijan president), 1:274–275

Mwanawasa, Levy (Zambia president), 2:497

Myanmar, **2:358–361**

N

Nabiyev, Rakhman (Tajikistan president), 2:667

Nabopolassar (Chaldean leader), 1:6

NAFTA (North American Free Trade Agreement), 1:187

Nagorno-Karabakh, 1:274, 2:670

Naguib, Mohammed (Egypt president), 1:291

Namgyal, Lama Ngawang, 2:375

Namibia, **2:624–626**

Nara period, 1:127

Naram-Sin (Akkadian king), 1:4

Nasir, Ibrahim (Maldives president), 2:500, 501

Nasrallah, Sheikh Hassan *2:330*

Nassau, Bahamas, *2:538*

Nasser, Gamal Abdel (Egypt president), 1:291, 2:367

Nation-states, 1:151

National Assembly (French), 1:160

National Assembly (Haitian), 1:164

National Security Council (NSC), 1:299

National Socialist (Nazi) Party, 2:632, 634

National Union for the Total Independence of Angola (UNITA), 2:562, *563*

Native American peoples
  in Argentina, 1:233
  in Brazil, 1:187
  in Canada, 1:240
  in Chile, 1:175
  Colombian, 1:209
  in El Salvador, 1:220
  map of, *1:130*
  in Panama, 1:253
  See also Chippewa

NATO (North Atlantic Treaty Organization), 1:174

Nauru, **2:513–515**

Nazarbayev, Nursultan (Kazakhstan president), 1:286, 287

Nazi Germany
  occupation of Czechoslovakia, 2:627
  occupation of Poland, 2:622
  overview of, 1:313–317
  Slovakia, control of by, 2:686
  World War II, 2:327

Nazi Party, 2:632, 634

Ndadaye, Melchior (Burundi president), 2:473–474

Ne Win, Bo (Myanmar president), 2:359, 360

Nebuchadrezzar II, 1:6

Nehru, Jawaharlal (India prime minister), 2:352, 353

Nemanja, Stefan, 2:683

Nepal, **1:152–154**

Netherlands, **1:172–174**

Nevis, Saint Kitts and, **2:605–608**

Nevsky, Alexander, *1:100*, 101

New Deal, 1:159

New Granada, 1:209, 253

New Zealand, **2:344–346**, 467, *582*

Ngouabi, Marien (Republic of the Congo president), 2:444

Nicaragua, **1:214–215**

Nicholas II (Russian czar), *1:148*, 149, 293

Niger, **2:430–432**

Nigeria, Federal Republic of, **2:456–459**

Night of the Generals, 1:324

Nimeiri, Gaafar, 2:394

Niyazov, Sapamurad (Turkmenistan president), 2:671, 672

Nkomo, Joshua, 2:596

Nkrumah, Kwame (Ghana prime minister), 2:402

No-confidence votes, 2:560–561, 601

Nobel, Alfred, 1:168–169

Noriega, Manuel (Panama general), 1:255

Normans, 1:140

North American Free Trade Agreement (NAFTA), 1:187

North Atlantic Treaty Organization (NATO), 1:174

North Field, 2:530

North Yemen, 2:630

Norway, 1:168, **256–258**

Note, Kessai H. (Marshall Islands president), 2:614–615

Novgorod Republic, **1:100–101**

Nubia, 1:16–17

Nuclear accident, Chernobyl, 2:651

Nuclear disarmament, 2:348

Nuclear program
Bikini atoll tests, *2:613*
of India, 2:353, 354
of Iran, 2:590
Marshall Islands tests, 2:614
of North Korea, 2:375
of Pakistan, 2:357

Nujoma, Sam (Namibia president), 2:*625*, 626

Nuremberg Laws, 1:316

Nyasaland Districts Protectorate, 2:491

Nyatsimba Mutota (Great Zimbabwe ruler), 1:105–106

Nyerere, Julius K., 2:489, 490

Nyingma sect (Tibet), 1:99

O

Obasanjo, Olusegun (Nigeria president), 2:458–459

Obiang Nguema Mbasogo, Teodoro (Equatorial Guinea president), 2:522–523

Obote, Milton (Uganda prime minister), 2:483–484

Odoacer (king of Germany), 1:43

Ohrid Agreement, 2:676

Oil
in Azerbaijan, 1:274
in Bahrain, 2:527, 529
in Brunei, 2:610
in Ecuador, 1:199

in Equatorial Guinea, 2:523
in Iraq, 1:313
in Kuwait, 2:464–465
Kuwait fields, burning of, *2:466*
Libyan reserves, 2:388
in Norway, 1:258
Oman reserves, 2:388
in Qatar, 2:530
in São Tomé and Príncipe, 2:558
Sudan, discovery in, 2:394
in Trinidad and Tobago, 2:482
in United Arab Emirates, 2:533, 534
in Venezuela, 1:202

Oil embargo of 1973, 1:309

Olmert, Ehud (Israel prime minster), 2:330, 367

Olympio, Sylvanus (Togo president), 2:419–420

Oman, **2:386–388**

One Thousand and One Nights, 1:68

OPEC (Organization of Petroleum Exporting Countries), 1:309

Opium War, 1:133, 2:380

Oracle bone divination, 1:10

Ordinances of Justice, 1:90

Organization of Petroleum Exporting Countries (OPEC), 1:309

Osei Tutu (Ashanti ruler), 1:134

Oslo Accords, 2:366

Osman I (Ottoman chieftain), 1:119

Ostrogoths, 1:54

Otto I (Greece king), 1:206–207

Otto I (Holy Roman emperor), 1:69, 71

Ottoman Empire
Albania, 1:270
Bulgaria, occupation of, 1:259
Constantinople and, 1:54
Cyprus, control of, 2:448
Greece and, 1:206
Hungary, rule of, 2:618
Libya, control of, 2:388
map of, *1:120*
Moldavia, rule of, 2:656, 677
North Yemen, control of, 2:630
overview of, **1:119–122**
Syria, 2:336
Tunisia, occupation of, 2:399
Venice, conflict with, 1:84

Ottoman Turks
Armenians, massacre of, 2:670
Bosnia, expansion into, 2:679
Serbia, expansion into, 2:683

Ouattara, Alassane (Côte d'Ivoire prime minister), 2:435–436

Ouédraogo, Jean-Baptiste (Upper Volta president), 2:433

Ousmane, Mahamane (Niger president), 2:431

Oviedo, Lino (Paraguay general), 1:170

P

Pachacuti (Inca emperor), 1:108, 109

Pacific Islands, 2:415

Padmasambhava, 2:375

Pahlavi, Reza Shah (Iran shah), 2:588

Pahlavi Dynasty, 2:588–589

Pakistan
Bangladesh independence, 2:535
establishment of, 2:352
India, territorial dispute with, 2:353, 354

Pakistan, Islamic Republic of, **2:354–358**

Palau, **2:700–702**

Palazzo Ducale, 1:82

Palestine
Britain and, 2:339
Jewish immigration to, 2:366
Kingdom of Israel, 1:12–13
Lebanon, refugees in, 2:330
overview of, **2:545–549**
Saudi Arabia and, 1:309

Palestine Liberation Organization (PLO), 2:546, 547

Palestinian Authority, 2:548

Palestinians, 2:340, 366

Pamir people, 1:304

Panama, **1:253–256**

Panama Canal, *1:254*

Pangeng (Shang dynasty king), 1:10

Papadopoulos, George (Greece prime minister), 1:208

Papadopoulos, Tassos (Cyprus president), 2:451

Papal States, 1:302

Papua New Guinea, **2:559–561**

Paraguay, 1:**169–171**, 192

Parakramabahu I (Pollanaruwa king), 2:361

Park Chung Hee (Republic of Korea president), 2:370–371

Parliamentarians, 1:142

Parthenon (Athens), *1:26*

Parthian Empire, **1:37–39**

Pass Law (South Africa), 1:320–321

Patassé, Ange-Félix (Central African Republic president), 2:441, 442

Patricians, Roman Republic, 1:37

Patriotic Union (Liechtenstein), 1:146–147

Pax Mongolica, 1:95

Pax Romana, 1:42, 45

Paz Estenssoro, Victor (Bolivia president), 1:192

Peace of Augsburg, 1:71

Peace of Lodi, 1:93

Peace of Westphalia, 1:71

Pedro I, Dom (emperor of Brazil), 1:188

Pedro II, Dom (emperor of Brazil), 1:188, *189*

Peisistratus (Athens ruler), 1:25–26

Peloponnesian Wars, 1:28–29, 30

People of the Long House, 1:124–125

People's Republic of China, **2:378–382,** 705

Perdiccas I (Macedonia king), 1:31

Pereira, Aristedes (Cape Verde president), 2:553

Perestroika, 1:295

Pérez, Carlos Andrés (Venezuela president), 1:202

Pericles (Athenian statesman), 1:25

Perón, Juan (Argentina president), 1:233, *234*

Perón, María Eva, 1:233, *234*

Perónism, 1:233

Perpetual Diet, 1:70

Perry, Matthew (U.S. Navy commodore), 1:129, 2:347

Persian Empire, 1:6
    Aksum and, 1:46
    Mede Empire and, 1:20
    overview of, 1:1, **21–23**
    tombs of, *1:22*
    See also Iran; Sassanid Empire

Persian Gulf War, 2:337, 590

Persian Wars, 1:30

Personal Rule, 1:141

Peru, **1:180–183**

Peter I (Russia czar), 1:147–148, 2:697

Petroleum industry. *See* Oil

'Phags-pa, 1:98

Pharaoh, 1:7–8

Philip II (king of Macedonia), 1:31, 32

Phillip, Arthur (British explorer), 1:249

Phoenicia, 2:448

Phomvihan, Kaysone, 2:571

Phosphate mining, 2:515, 593–594

Piankhi (Cush king), 1:17

Pietro II Orseolo (Venice doge), 1:82

Pinelli, Giuseppe, 1:245

Pinochet, Augusto (Chile president), 1:176–177

Piracy, 2:504, 608

Pirate Coast, 2:532

Pires, Pedro Verona (Cape Verde president), 2:553

Pizarro, Francisco (Spanish navigator), 1:109, 118, 180

Plague, 1:138, 256

Plebeians, 1:37

PLO (Palestine Liberation Organization), 2:546, 547

Pol Pot (Khmer Rouge leader), 2:393, 415

Poland
    Lithuania, union with, 2:663
    overview of, **2:621–624**
    Partition of Poland, 1:149
    Solidarity movement, 2:617

Polanie tribe, 2:621

Polder district, 1:174

Political authority, 1:1

Political parties and factions
    'Abbāsid Empire, 1:68
    Afghanistan, 1:284
    Aksumite Kingdom, 1:46
    ancient Egypt, 1:8
    Angola, 2:562–563
    Antarctic Treaty Summary, 2:413
    Antigua and Barbuda, 2:605
    Arab Republic of Egypt, 1:292
    Argentine Republic, 1:231–232
    Armenia, 2:669–670
    Ashanti Empire, 1:135–136
    Assyrian Empire, 1:17–18
    Athens, 1:25
    Australia, Commonwealth of, 1:251
    Austria, 1:277–278
    Austro-Hungarian Empire, 1:237
    Aztec Empire, 1:103
    Babylonian Empire, 1:6
    Bahrain, 2:529
    Bangladesh, 2:537
    Barbados, 2:512–513
    Belarus, 2:655
    Belgium, 1:205
    Belize, 2:602–603
    Benin, 2:429–430
    Bhutan, 2:376
    Bolivia, 1:191
    Bosnia and Herzegovina, 2:680–681
    Botswana, 2:508
    Brazil, Federative Republic of, 1:189
    Bulgaria, Republic of, 1:260–261
    Burkina Faso, 2:433–434
    Burundi, 2:474
    Byzantine Empire, 1:53
    Cambodia, 2:392
    Canada, 1:242
    Cape Verde, 2:552–553
    Central African Republic, 2:441

Chad, 2:438

Cherokee, 1:194

Chile, 1:176

Chippewa, 1:130–131

Chou dynasty, 1:15

Colombia, 1:210–211

Commonwealth of the Bahamas, 2:540

Costa Rica, 1:213

Croatia, 2:642–643

Cush, 1:17

Cyprus, 2:450

Czech Republic, 2:628–629

Democratic and Popular Republic of Algeria, 2:477

Democratic People's Republic of Korea, 2:374

Democratic Republic of the Congo, 2:424–425

Denmark, 1:231–232

Djibouti, 2:578–579

Dominica, 2:585

Dominican Republic, 1:225

East Timor, 2:708

Ecuador, 1:199

El Salvador, 1:222

Empire of Akkad, 1:4

Empire of Ghana, 1:72

Equatorial Guinea, 2:522

Eritrea, 2:689

Estonia, 2:647–648

Ethiopia, 1:247

Etruscan civilization, 1:24

European Union, 2:695–696

Fātimid dynasty, 1:79

Federal Republic of Nigeria, 2:458

Federated States of Micronesia, 2:612

Fiji, 2:526–527

Finland, 1:281

Florence, 1:91

France, 1:162

Gabonese Republic, 2:446–447

Germany, 2:633

Ghana, 2:402

Goguryeo Kingdom, 1:57–58

Great Moravia, 1:75

Great Socialist People's Libyan Arab Jamahiriya, 2:389

Great Zimbabwe, 1:105–106

Greece, 1:207

Grenada, 2:541–542

Guatemala, 1:217

Guinea, 2:407

Guinea-Bissau, 2:544

Gupta Empire, 1:59–60

Guyana, 2:506–507

Haiti, 1:164–165

Han dynasty, 1:41

Hashemite Kingdom of Jordan, 2:340

Hittite Empire, 1:9

Holy Roman Empire, 1:70–71

Honduras, 1:219

Hong Kong, 2:703–704
Iceland, 1:322
Inca Empire, 1:110
Iran, 2:589
Iraq, 1:313
Ireland, 1:290
Islamic Republic of Mauritania, 2:460–461
Islamic Republic of Pakistan, 2:356
Italy, 1:244–245
Jamaica, 2:480
Japan, 2:348
Kenya, 2:486–488
Khazars, 1:66–67
Khmer Empire, 1:74
Kievan Rus', 1:78
Kingdom of Israel, 1:13
Kingdom of Saudi Arabia, 1:309
Kiribati, 2:593
Kuwait, 2:465
Kyrgyzstan, 2:659
Lao People's Democratic Republic, 2:571
Latvia, 2:649–650
Lebanon, 2:329–330
Lesotho, 2:510
Liberia, 1:226–227
Liechtenstein, Principality of, 1:146–147
Lithuania, 2:665
Luxembourg, Grand Duchy of, 1:239
Macao, 2:705
Macedon, 1:32
Madagascar, 2:421–422
Magadha, 1:34
Malawi, 2:492
Malaysia, 2:405
Maldives, 2:501
Mali, 2:455–456
Mali Empire, 1:96
Malta, 2:495
Mayan, 1:48
of Mede Empire, 1:19–20
Mexico, 1:185–186
Milan, 1:93
Moldova, 2:658
Monaco, 1:267
Mongol Empire, 1:94
Mongolia, 1:301
Montenegro, 2:710–711
Morocco, 2:398
Mozambique, 2:550
Mughal Empire, 1:124
Myanmar, 2:359–360
Namibia, 2:626
Nauru, 2:515
Nazi Germany, 1:315
Nepal, 1:152–153
Netherlands, 1:173
New Zealand, 2:345–346
Nicaragua, 1:215
Niger, 2:431–432
Norway, 1:257–258

Novgorod Republic, 1:101
Oman, 2:387
Ottoman Empire, 1:121
Palau, 2:702
Palestine, 2:547–548
Panama, 1:255
Papua New Guinea, 2:560
Paraguay, 1:170
Parthian Empire, 1:39
People's Republic of China, 2:381
Persian Empire, 1:23
Peru, 1:182
Poland, 2:623–624
Portugal, 1:263–264
Portuguese Empire, 1:111
Principality of Andorra, 2:691
Prussia, Kingdom of, 1:138
Qatar, 2:531
Qing Dynasty, 1:133
Republic of Albania, 1:272, 274
Republic of Cameroon, 2:417
Republic of Côte d'Ivoire, 2:435
Republic of Cuba, 2:410
Republic of Genoa, 1:87
Republic of Georgia, 2:636
Republic of Hungary, 2:620
Republic of India, 2:352–353
Republic of Indonesia, 1:324
Republic of Kazakhstan, 1:287
Republic of Korea, 2:370
Republic of Macedonia, 2:674–676
Republic of Mauritius, 2:516–517
Republic of South Africa, 1:319–320
Republic of Sudan, 2:394
Republic of the Congo, 2:443
Republic of the Gambia, 2:498–499
Republic of the Marshall Islands, 2:614
Republic of the Philippines, 2:343
Republic of Venice, 1:84
Republic of Yemen, 2:630–631
Roman Empire, 1:45
Roman Republic, 1:37
Romania, 2:678–679
Russian Empire, 1:148–149
Russian Federation, 2:699
Rwanda, 2:471
Saint Kitts and Nevis, 2:606–607
Saint Lucia, 2:591
Saint Vincent and the Grenadines, 2:595–596
Samoa, 2:468
San Marino, 1:98
São Tomé and Príncipe, 2:557
Sassanid Empire, 1:63
Scythia, 1:29–30
Senegal, 2:452–453
Serbia, 2:684–685
Seychelles, 2:573
Shang dynasty, 1:11
Sierra Leone, 2:462–463
Singapore, 2:504

Slovak Republic, 2:687
Slovenia, 2:645
Socialist Republic of Vietnam, 2:576–577
Solomon Islands, 2:581–582
Somalia, 2:427
Somaliland, 2:639
Songhai Empire, 1:114
Spain, 2:565–566
Spanish Empire, 1:117–118
Sparta, 1:28
Sri Lanka, 2:363–364
State of Brunei Darussalam, 2:610
State of Israel, 2:367
Sung Dynasty, 1:89
Suriname, 2:567–568
Swaziland, 2:520
Sweden, 1:167–168
Swiss Confederation, 1:229
Syrian Arab Republic, 2:337
Taiwan, 2:385
Tajikistan, 2:667
Thailand, 1:305–306
Thebes, 1:31
Tibet, 1:99
Togo, 2:419–420
Tokugawa Shogunate, 1:128–129
Tonga, 2:524–525
Trinidad and Tobago, 2:482
Tunisia, 2:401
Turkey, 1:298–299
Turkmenistan, 2:672
Tuvalu, 2:584
Uganda, 2:484
Ukraine, 2:652
Umayyad Empire, 1:64
Union of Comoros, 2:554–555
Union of Soviet Socialist Republics, 1:295
United Arab Emirates, 2:533
United Kingdom, 1:143–144
United Nations, 2:334–335
United Republic of Tanzania, 2:490
United States, 1:158
Ur, 1:2
Uruguay, 1:196–197
Uzbekistan, 2:662
Vanuatu, 2:600
Venezuela, 1:202
Visigoths, 1:56
Zambia, 2:497
Zimbabwe, 2:597–598
Zulu Empire, 1:179
Political turmoil
  in Burkina Faso, 2:434
  in Guinea-Bissau, 2:545
  in Jamaica, 2:481
  in Kyrgyzstan, 2:659–660
  in Madagascar, 2:423
  in Solomon Islands, 2:582
Politkovskaya, Anna, 2:700
Pollanaruwa era, 2:361
Polo, Marco, *1:95*

Pompey the Great, 1:35

Pope, Roman Catholic, 1:49, 301–302

Popular Front for the Liberation of Oman, 2:388

Port Louis, Mauritius, *2:517*

Portugal
Angola, control of, 2:562
Brazil, colonization of, 1:187–188
in Cameroon, 2:416
Cape Verde, colonization of, 2:552
in Congo, 2:423, 442
East Timor, colonization of, 2:706
Ghana, interests in, 2:402
Guinea-Bissau, occupation of, 2:543
Kongo, trade in, 2:561
Macao, interests in, 2:705
Oman, rule in, 2:386
overview of, **1:262–265**
São Tomé and Príncipe, slave trading in, 2:556
Sri Lanka, domination of, 2:363
Strait of Malacca, control of, 2:404

Portuguese Empire, 1:**110–112**

Portuguese Guinea. *See* Guinea-Bissau

Poverty
Angola, 2:564
Burkina Faso, 2:434
Burundi, 2:474
Central African Republic, 2:441
East Timor, 2:709
Ecuador, 1:199
Ghana, 2:403
Guyana, 2:507
Jordan, 2:340
Kenya, 2:488
Madagascar, 2:423
Malawi, 2:493
Mauritius, 2:518
Moldova, 2:658
Myanmar, 2:361
Nauru, 2:515
Philippines, 2:344
Republic of the Congo, 2:445
Republic of Yemen, 2:631
Sierra Leone, 2:464
Somaliland, 2:640
Tajikistan, 2:667
Zambia, 2:497–498

Powell, Colin, 2:395

Prague Spring, 2:627

Prajadhipok (Thai king), 1:305

Pre-Columbian era, 1:183

Prefectures, Sung Dynasty, 1:88

Préval, René (Haiti president), 1:164–165

Price, George C. (Belize president), 2:601, *602*

Priesthoods, Babylonian Empire, 1:6

Priests of Amon, 1:8, 16, 17

The Prince (Machiavelli), 1:91

Principality of Andorra, **2:690–692**

Principality of Liechtenstein, **1:145–147**

Principate, 1:43

Príncipe, São Tomé and, **2:556–559**

Prithvi Narayan Shah (Nepal ruler), 1:152

Privatization, industry, 1:192, 197

Protestantism, 1:141, 289

Prussia, Kingdom of, 1:**137–140**, 232

Psamtik III (ancient Egypt pharaoh), 1:8

Ptolemy I (Egypt ruler), 1:8

Pugachev Rebellion, 1:149

Punic Wars, 1:37

Puntland, 2:427

Puranas, 1:59

Putin, Vladimir (Russian Federation president), 2:*654*, 700

Pyramid of the Sun, *1:51*

Q

Qabus bin Said (Oman imam), 2:386–387

Qadhafi, Muammar al- (Libya dictator), 2:388–390

Qatar, 2:529, **530–532**

Qin Dynasty, 2:378

Qing Dynasty
conquest of Mongolia, 1:300
description of, 2:380
overview of, **1:132–134**

Quarantia, 1:83

Quebec, Canada, 1:242

Quin Shi Huang-Di (Qin Empire king), 1:87
See also Ch'in Shi Huang Ti

Quito, Ecuador, 1:197

R

Rabi Island, Fiji, 2:594

Rabuka, Sitiveni (Fiji leader), 2:527

Racial discrimination
in Guyana, 2:507
in Mauritania, 2:461
in New Zealand, 2:346
in Suriname, 2:567

Rahman, Khaleda Zia-ur, 2:537

Rahman, Mujibur (Bangladesh president/prime minister), 537, *2:538*

Rahman, Tunku Abdul (Malayan ruler), *2:406*

Rahman, Ziaur (Bangladesh general), 2:537

Rainforest Declaration, 2:406, 611

Rainier III (Monaco prince), 1:*266*, 267

Rainsy, Sam, 2:392

Rakhmonov, Imomali (Tajikistan president), 2:666, 667

Rama IV (Thai king), 1:304

Rama V (Thai king), 1:304

Ramanantsoa, Gabriel, 2:422

Ramayana, 1:59

Ramgoolam, Sir Seewoosagur (Mauritius prime minister), 2:516

Ramos-Horta, José, 2:708

Ratislav (Great Moravia king), 1:75, 77

Ratsirahonana, Norbert (Madagascar president), 2:422–423

Ratsiraka, Didier (Madagascar president), 2:422–423

Ratzinger, Joseph (Catholic pope), 1:304

Ravalomanana, Marc (Madagascar president), 2:421, 423

Rawlings, Jerry (Ghana president), 2:403

Reagan, Ronald (U.S. president), 1:256, 2:*586*

Rebellion, in Haiti, 1:164

Rebellion, Prussia, 1:140

Red Brigade, 1:245

Red Guards, 2:381

Referendum procedures, 1:196

Reformation, German, 2:632

Reformation, Slovenia, 2:643

Refugees
Albanian in Macedonia, 2:676
Burundian, *2:473*
in Guinea, 2:408
Kosovars in Albania/Macedonia, 2:685
Laotian in Thailand, 2:571
Senagalese in Gambia, 2:500
Somalia in Djibouti, 2:580
in Uganda, 2:485

Reichstag, 1:314

Reign of Terror, 1:160

Religion
ancient Egypt, 1:8
Babylonian Empire, 1:5, 6
Bangladesh, 2:535
Belarus, 2:654
Bohemia, 2:627
Bosnia, 2:679

Brunei Darussalam, 2:608
Bulgaria, 1:262
Cambodia, 2:391
Chou dynasty, 1:14–15
Cush, 1:16–17
Empire of Akkad, 1:4
Etruscan civilization, 1:24
India, 2:350
Jordan, 2:339
Khmer Empire, 1:74
Kingdom of Israel, 1:12–13
Laos, 2:569
Lebanon, 2:328
Lithuania, 2:663
Malaysia, 2:404
Maldives, 2:500
Myanmar, 2:358
Oman, 2:387
Ottoman Empire, 1:120
Persian Empire, 1:23
political authority and, 1:1
Shang dynasty, 1:10–11
Singapore, 2:505
Spain, 2:564
Sudan, 2:393, 394
Switzerland, 1:229
Syria, 2:335–336
Tanzania, 2:489
Tibet, 1:98
Tokugawa Shogunate, 1:129
Turkey, 1:297
Turkmenistan, 2:672
United Kingdom, 1:141
Zoroastrianism in Azerbaijan,
1:273
René, Albert (Seychelles prime minister), 2:572, *573*
Repse, Einars (Latvia prime minister),
2:650
Republic of Albania, 1:270–273
Republic of Azerbaijan, 1:273–275
Republic of Bulgaria, **1:258–262**
Republic of Cameroon, **2:416–419**
Republic of the Congo, **2:442–445**
Republic of Côte d'Ivoire,
2:434–437
Republic of Cuba, **2:408–411**
Republic of the Gambia, **2:498–500**
Republic of Genoa, **1:85–86**
Republic of Georgia, **2:635–637**
Republic of Hungary, **2:618–621**
Republic of India, **2:349–354**
Republic of Indonesia, **1:323–325**
Republic of Kazakhstan, **1:286–287**
Republic of Korea, 2:**369–372**
Republic of Liguria, 1:87
Republic of Macedonia, **2:673–676**
Republic of the Marshall Islands,
2:612–614
Republic of Mauritius, **2:516–518**

Republic of the Philippines,
2:341–344
Republic of South Africa
Angola civil war, involvement in,
2:563
Botswana, relations with, 2:509
Namibia, invasion of, 2:624–625
overview of, 1:317–321
Republic of the Sudan, **2:393–397**
Republic of Venice, **1:82–85**
Republic of Yemen, **2:630–631**
Republican Party (U.S.), 1:158–159
Revolt of the Ciompi, 1:91
Revolution
American, 1:155–156
Burkina Faso, 2:434
French, 1:151
Mexican, 1:184–185
Portuguese, *1:264*
Russian, 1:293
Revolutionary United Front (Sierra
Leone), 2:463
Reyes Católicos, 1:116
Reykjavík, 1:321
Rhodes, Cecil, 1:106
Rhodesia, 1:106
See also Zambia; Zimbabwe
Rigsraadet, 1:230
Riksdag, 1:167
Rini, Snyder (Solomon Islands prime
minister), 2:582
Rizal, Jose, 2:341
Roberts, Joseph Jenkins (Liberia
governor), 1:226
Robespierre, Maximilien de, 1:160
Roh Moo Hyun (Republic of Korea
president), 2:370
Roman Catholic Church, 1:70–71,
302–303
See also Catholicism
Roman Empire
Corpus Juris Civilis, 1:53
Etruscans and, 1:24
Florence and, 1:90
Hunnic Empire and, 1:60
map of, *1:44*
overview of, **1:1, 42–45**
in Portugal, 1:262
Visigoths and, 1:54, 55
Roman Republic, 1:35–37, 1:42
Romania
conquest by Roman Empire, 2:676
Moldova, common history with,
2:656
overview of, **2:676–679**
Rome
Carthage and, 1:20, 21
Etruscans and, 1:24
Roman Republic, 1:35–37
Vatican City, 1:301–304

Romero, Óscar (El Salvador
archbishop), 1:221
Romanov dynasty, 1:78, 147, 149,
2:697
Romulus Augustus (emperor of
Rome), 1:42
Roosevelt, Franklin D.
(U.S. president), 1:159
Roosevelt, Theodore
(U.S. president), 1:253
Rose Revolution, 2:636, *637*
Ross, John (Cherokee chief), 1:194
Roxas, Manuel (Philippines president), 2:342
Royal Scyths, 1:29–30
Royalists, 1:142
RPF (Rwandan Patriotic Front),
2:469
Rudolf I (Holy Roman emperor),
1:71
Rurik (Kievan Rus' ruler), 1:77
Russia
Azerbaijan, rule in, 1:273–274
Belarus, annexation of, 2:654
Belarus, relations with, 2:656
Estonia, conflict with, 2:648
Finland, rule of, 1:279, 280
Kazakhstan, and, 1:286
Korea, support of, 2:369
Kyrgyzstan, annexation of, 2:659
Latvia and, 2:650–651
map of, *2:698*
Moldavia/Walachia, invasion of,
2:677
Mongolia and, 1:300
post-WWI, 1:269
Turkmenistan, rule of, 2:671
Russian Empire, **1:147–150**
Russian Federation, 2:637,
696–700
Russian Orthodox Church, 1:49
Russification
in Estonia, 2:646
of Finland, 1:280
in Latvia, 2:648
Russkaya Pravda, 1:78
Russo-Polish War, 2:621
Rutli, oath of, *1:229*
Rwanda, **2:468–472**
Rwandan Patriotic Front (RPF),
2:469

S

Saakashvili, Mikhail
(Georgia president), 2:636
Sabah, Sabah al-Ahmad al-Jabir al-
(Kuwait emir), 2:465

Sadat, Anwar as- (Egypt president), 1:291, 292, 2:367

Safavid Empire, 2:588

Sahara, 2:398

Saint Kitts and Nevis, **2:605–608**

Saint Lucia, **2:590–592**

Saint Mark, 1:84

St. Petersburg, Russia, 2:697

Saint Vincent and the Grenadines, **2:594–596**

Sakyapa sect (Tibet), 1:99

Salazar, António de Oliveira (Portugal prime minister), 1:265

Saleh, Ali Abdullah (Republic of Yemen president), *2:631*

Salote Tupou III (Tonga queen), 2:524

Samandar (Khazar city), 1:65

Samandra Gupta, 1:58–59

Sambi, Ahmed Abdallah Mohamed (Union of Comoros president), 2:554

Sami people, 1:167, 257

Samoa, **2:467–468**

Samsu-Ilena (king of Babylonian Empire), 1:6

Samuel (Bulgar king), 1:53

San Marino, **1:97–98**

Sanguinetti, Julio María (Uruguay president), *1:196*

Sankara, Thomas (Upper Volta prime minister), 2:433

Santa Anna, Antonio López, 1:183

Santa Cruz, Andrés (Bolivia president), 1:191

Santo Domingo, Dominican Republic, 1:223

Sao Kingdom, 2:416

São Tomé and Príncipe, **2:556–559**

Sarajevo, Bosnia, 2:682

Sargon (Akkadia king), 1:4

Sargon II (Assyria king), 1:17–19

Sarmatians, 1:30

SARS (severe acute respiratory syndrome), 2:504

Sarsenbayev, Altynbek, 1:287

Sassanid Empire, **1:61–63**

Sassou-Nguesso, Denis (Republic of the Congo president), 2:443, 444–445

Sato, Eisaku (Japan prime minister), 2:348

Satraps (provincial governors), 1:21

Saudi Arabia, Kingdom of, 1:307–310

Saul (Israel king), 1:12

Savang Vatthana (Laos king), *2:570*

Savimbi, Jonas, 2:563

Saw Maung, 2:361

Scholars, 'Abbāsid Empire, 1:68–69

Schuman, Robert (French foreign minister), 2:693

Scientific revolution, 1:151

Scotland, 1:141–143

Scythia, **1:29–30**

Sea Peoples, 1:8, 10

Second Congolese War, 2:485

Second Mexican Empire, 1:184

Second Republic (French), 1:161

Seita clan (Mali), 1:96

Selassie, Haile (Ethiopia emperor), 1:247, *248*

Seleucids, 1:38

Seljuk Turks, 1:119, 273

Seneca tribe, 1:125–126

Senegal, **2:451–454**

Senghor, Léopold Sédar (Senegal president), 2:452

Sennacherib (Assyria king), 1:*18*, 19

Sepúlveda, Juan Ginés de, 1:117–118

Serbia
Croatia, conflict with, 2:643
Macedonia, occupation of, 2:673
Montenegro, separation from, 2:709, *710*
overview of, **2:679–682**

Serbs
Bosnian, power struggle with Croats, 2:679–681
Yugoslavian, power struggle with Croats, 2:683–684

Serf class
Novgorod Republic, 1:101
Russia, 1:148–149
Tibet, 1:99

Serrano, Jorge (Guatemala president), 1:217

Sesostris (Egypt pharaoh), 1:16

Severe acute respiratory syndrome (SARS), 2:504

Seybou, Ali (Niger president), 2:431

Seychelles, **2:572–574**

Sforza family (Milan), 1:93

Shāh Jahān (Mughal emperor), 1:123, 2:350

Shahenshah, 1:62

Shahjahan. *See* Shāh Jahān

Shaka (Zulu chief), 1:178

Shakespeare, William, 1:*85*

Shang dynasty
description of, 2:378
overthrow of, 1:14
overview of, **1:10–12**

Shāpūr I (Sassanid ruler), 1:63

Shar-kali-sharri (Akkadia king), 1:4

Sharon, Ariel (Israel prime minster), 2:367

Shevardnadze, Eduard (Georgia president), 2:636

Shia Islam
Fātimid dynasty, 1:78
in Iran, 2:588
Umayyad dynasty, 1:64

Shiite Muslims, 1:310

Shinzo Abe (Japan prime minister), 2:349

Shogunate. *See* Tokugawa Shogunate

Shulgi (Ur king), 1:3

Siad Barre, Mohammed, 2:426

Siam. *See* Thailand

Sicily, 1:21

Sidonius, Apollinaris, 1:55

Sierra Leone, **2:462–464**

Signoria, 1:90

Sihanouk, Norodom (Cambodia king), 2:392

Sikhs, 1:123, 124

Silk Road trade routes, 1:87, 95

Simmonds, Kennedy, 2:607

Singapore, 2:404, **502–505**

Sinhalese people, 2:361, 364

Sinn Féin, 1:289

Sisavang Vong (Laos king), 2:569–570

The Six, 2:693

Six Day War
Egypt, 1:292
Israel, victory of, 2:367
Palestinians under Israeli control, 2:548
United Nations resolution concerning, 2:333

Six Nations, 1:124, 126

SLA (South Lebanon Army), 2:330

Slave trade
Central African Republic, 2:440
Chad, 2:437
Congo, 2:423–424
Gabon, 2:445
Gambia, 2:498
Nigeria, 2:457
São Tomé and Príncipe, 2:556
Sierra Leone, 2:462
Tuvalu, 2:583

Slavery
abolition of in Danish colonies, 1:230
Barbados, 2:511
Empire of Ghana, 1:72
Equatorial Guinea, 2:521
Guyana, 2:505
Haiti, 1:163–164
Jamaica, 2:479

Solomon Islands, 2:581
   United States, 1:156
   Vanuatu, 2:599
Slavic tribes, 2:673
Slovak Republic, **2:685–688**
Slovak territories, 1:75
Slovakia
   Czech Republic split from, 2:629
   Hungary's loss of, 2:618–619
Slovenia, **2:643–645**
Sobhuza II (Swaziland king), 2:519
Soccer, World Cup, in Honduras, 1:219
Social order
   Aztec Empire, 1:102
   France, 1:159–160
   Great Zimbabwe, 1:104–105
   Incan, 1:109
   Khmer Empire, 1:74
   Roman Empire, 1:45
Social unrest
   Belize, 2:603
   Gambia, 2:499
   Jamaica, 2:480
Socialist Republic of Vietnam, **2:574–578**
Soga clan (Japan), 1:127
Sogavare, Manasseh (Solomon Islands prime minister), 2:582
Soglo, Nicephore (Benin president), 2:430
Solomon (Israel king), 1:12, 13, 106
Solomon Islands, **2:580–582**
Solon (Athenia lawmaker), 1:25
Somalia
   anarchy in, 2:335
   Djibouti, effects of dissolution on, 2:580
   overview of, **2:426–428**
   Somaliland independence from, 2:638
Somaliland, 2:427, **637–640**
Somare, Michael (Papua New Guinea prime minister), 2:560
Somoza family, 1:214, 215
Songhai Empire
   control of Niger region, 2:431
   overview of, **1:113–114**
Songstan Gampo (Tibet king), 1:98
Soninkes (Empire of Ghana tribe), 1:72
Sonni 'Ali (Songhai emperor), 1:113
Sosurium (Goguryeo king), 1:58
Souphanouvong (Laos prince), 2:571
South Africa, Republic of
   Angola civil war, involvement in, 2:563
   Botswana, relations with, 2:509
   Namibia, invasion of, 2:624–625
   overview of, 1:317–321

South Korea. *See* Republic of Korea
South Lebanon Army (SLA), 2:330
South Yemen, 2:630
Soviet Union. *See* Union of Soviet Socialist Republics (USSR)
Soweto massacre, 1:321
Spain
   Argentina, colonization of, 1:233
   Aztec Empire conquest of, 1:103
   Belgium, 1:203
   Caribbean, colonization of, 2:408
   Chile, colonization of, 1:175
   Colombia, colonization of, 1:209
   Dominican Republic, colonization of, 1:223
   Ecuador, colonization of, 1:197
   El Salvador, colonization of, 1:220
   Equatorial Guinea, administration of, 2:521–522
   Inca Empire, conquest of, 1:109
   Jamaica, colonization of, 2:479
   Mexico and, 1:183
   Morocco, invasion of, 2:397
   Nicaragua, conquest of, 1:214
   overview of, **2:564–566**
   Panama, colonization of, 1:253
   Paraguay, colonization of, 1:169–170
   Peru, colonization of, 1:180
   Philippines, occupation of, 2:341
   rule of Bolivia, 1:190
   Sahara, concession of, 2:398
   Uruguay revolt, 1:195
   Venezuela, colonization of, 1:200
   Visigoths and, 1:54
Spanish-American War, 2:409
Spanish Empire, **1:114–119**
Sparta, 1:1, **26–29**, 31
Sposalizio del Mar, 1:82
Spring and Autumn period, 2:378
Srebrenica, Bosnia, 2:682
Sri Lanka, 2:354, **361–365**
Stalin, Joseph (Russia president), 1:295
Stambolov, Stefan, 1:259
Standard Oil, 1:309
State of Brunei Darussalam, 1:325, 2:404, **608–611**
State of Israel, **2:365–369**
Staten General, 1:172
Stele of Aksum, 1:46
Stevens, Siaka (Sierra Leone prime minister), 2:463
Stock market, 1929 crash, 1:269
Strait of Malacca, 2:404
Straits Settlements, 2:503
Stroessner, Alfredo (Paraguay dictator), 1:170
Suárez González, Adolfo (Spain prime minister), 2:565

Sucre, Antonio José de (Bolivia president), 1:190, 198
Sudan, Republic of the, **2:393–397**
Suez Canal, 1:292
Suez Crisis, 2:367
Sugar, 2:603
Suharto (Indonesia president), 1:323, 324–325
Sui Dynasty, 1:88, 2:379
Sukarno, Ahmed (Indonesia president), 1:323–324
Sukarnoputri, Megawati (Indonesia president), 1:325
Süleyman I (Ottoman emperor), 1:107, 121–122
Sultanates, Ottoman Empire, 1:119
Sumerians, 1:1, 2–3
Sumu-Abum (Babylonian Empire king), 1:5
Sun Yat-sen, 2:380
Sundiata (Mali chief), 1:96
Sung Dynasty
   description of, 2:379–380
   Jin wars, 1:132
   overview of, **1:87–89**
Sunni Islam, 1:80
Sunni Muslims, 1:310, 2:554
Suppiluliumas I (Hittite Empire king), 1:9
Supreme Soviet, 1:294
Suriname, **2:567–569**
Suryavarman I (Khmer Empire king), 1:74
Suryavarman II (Khmer Empire king), 1:74
Suu Kyi, Aung San, 2:360, 361
Svatopluk (Great Moravia king), 1:77
Svyatoslav I (Kievan prince), 1:78
Swaziland, **2:518–521**
Sweden
   Norway and, 1:256
   overview of, **1:167–169**
   rule of Finland, 1:279
Swiss Confederation, **1:227–230**
Syrian Arab Republic, 2:329–330, **335–339**

T

Tabinshwehti (Burma king), 2:358
Taffe, Eduard von (Austria prime minister), 1:236–237
Tai people, 2:569
Taif Accord, 2:328, 337
Taika Reforms, 1:127
Taiwan, 2:**382–386**, *593*
Taj Mahal, *1:123*

Tajikistan, **2:666–668**

Taki, Mohammed (Union of Comoros president), *2:555*

Taliban, 1:283–284

Tallinn, Estonia, 2:*647*, 648

Tamerlane (Mongol leader), 2:661

Tamil ethnic group, 2:364

Tamil Tigers, *2:365*

Tandja, Mamadou (Niger president), 2:431, 432

Tang Dynasty, 1:88, 2:379

Tanzania, United Republic of, **2:488–491**

Taoism, 1:15

Tarawa atoll, 2:592

Tarquinius Superbus, Lucius (Etruscan king), 1:24, 35

Tatik Papik, *1:273*

TaungNgoo Dynasty, 2:358

Taxation
Aztec Empire, 1:103
Byzantine Empire, 1:53
Empire of Ghana, 1:72
France, 1:160
Gupta Empire, 1:59
Khazars, 1:66
Kievan Rus', 1:77
Mughal Empire, 1:122
Ottoman Empire, 1:121
Republic of Genoa, 1:87
Umayyad Empire, 1:67
United Kingdom, 1:141
Visigoths, 1:56

Taya, Maaouya Ould Sid'Ahmed, 2:460, 461

Taylor, Charles G. (Liberia president), 1:227

Teach, Edwin (Blackbeard), 2:538

Temple of Solomon (Jerusalem), 1:12, 13

Temüjin, 1:94

Ten Years' War, 2:409

Tenochtitlán (Aztec city)
founding of, 1:101
map of, *1:118*
overview of, 1:81
Spanish siege of, 1:103

Tenzin Gyatso, 1:99

Teotihuacán (Mayan city), 1:47–48, 49, **50–51**

Terrorism
Bangladesh, 2:538
Chechen rebel attacks, 2:700
Indonesia, 1:325
Italy, domestic, 1:245
Libya, sponsored by, 2:389–390
Morocco, 2:399
Tunisia, 2:401
Yemen, 2:631

Textile manufacturing, Ecuador, 1:197

Thailand, **1:304–307**

Thaksin Shinawatra (Thailand prime minister), 1:306

Thammana Kingdom, 2:361

Thani, Sheikh Ahmad bin 'Ali al- (Qatar emir), 2:530, 531

Thani, Sheik 'Ali bin Abdulla al- (Qatar emir), *2:531*

Thani, Sheikh Hamad bin Khalifa al- (Qatar emir), 2:530, 531–532

Thani, Sheikh Khalifa bin Hamad al- (Qatar prime minister), 2:530, 531–532

Thani, Sheikh Muhammad bin, 2:530

Thebes, **1:30–31**

Themata system (Byzantine Empire), 1:52

Theodora (Byzantine empress), 1:53

Theravada Buddhism, 1:75

Third Reich. *See* Nazi Germany

Third Republic (French), 1:161

Thorkelsson, Thorgeir, 1:322

Three Kingdoms, 1:58
See also Goguryeo Kingdom

Thutmose III, 1:8

Tibet, **1:98–100**, 2:375

Timbuktu (Songhai Empire city), 1:113

Timor (island), 1:324

Timurid dynasty, 1:95

Tito, Josip Broz (Yugoslavia leader), 2:641, 684

Tlaxcala, 1:103

Tobago. *See* Trinidad and Tobago

Togo, **2:419–421**

Tokugawa Shogunate, **1:127–129**, 2:347

Toledo, 1:54, 56

Tombalbaye, François (Chad president), 2:*438*, 439

Tong, Atone (Kiribati prime minister), *2:593*

Tonga, **2:523–525**

Touré, Amadou Toumani (Mali president), 2:455, 456

Touré, Sékou (Guinea president), 2:407

Tourism
Bahamas, 2:540
Grenada, 2:542–543
Jamaica, 2:481
Maldives, 2:502
Mauritius, 2:518
Morocco, 2:399
New Zealand, 2:346
Palau, 2:702

Portugal, 1:265

Tunisia, 2:401

Trade
Aksum, 1:45
Argentina, 1:233
Belgium, 1:203
Burma, 2:358
Djibouti, 2:578
Empire of Ghana, 1:72–73
with Khazars, 1:65
Macao, 2:705
Myanmar, sanctions against, 2:361
Portuguese Empire, 1:112
Silk Road trade routes, 1:87, 95
Spanish Empire, 1:117
Tokugawa Shogunate, 1:129

Trail of Tears, 1:195

Transnistria, 2:658

Transylvania, 2:677

Traoré, Moussa (Mali president), 2:455, 456

Treaties, European Union, 2:693

Treaty of Amsterdam, 2:696

Treaty of Constance, 1:92

Treaty of Montevideo, 1:195

Treaty of Nanjing, 2:380

Treaty of New Echota, 1:194–195

Treaty of Paris, 2:342

Treaty of Seeb, 2:386

Treaty of Verdun, 1:71

Treaty of Versailles, 2:332

Tribunes, 1:36

Trinidad and Tobago, **2:481–482**

Trovoada, Miguel (São Tomé and Príncipe president), 2:557, 558

Trujillo, Rafael Leónidas (Dominican Republic dictator), 1:224, *225*

Trusteeship Council, 2:333–334

Truth and Reconciliation Commission (TRC), 1:321

Tsiranana, Philibert (Madagascar president), 2:422

Tsong-kha-pa, 1:99

Tsunami
devastation to Indonesia, 1:325
devastation to Thailand, 1:306
Maldives destruction, *2:501*

Tsvangirai, Morgan, 2:598

Tubman, William (Liberia president), 1:227

Tudjman, Franjo (Croatia president), 2:641

Tulip Revolution, *2:660*

Tunisia, **2:399–401**

Turkey
Cyprus, conflict in, 2:448
overview of, 1:297–299
Turkish Republic of North Cyprus, 1:208

Yemen's independence from, 2:630
See also Ottoman Empire
Turkish Cypriots, 2:448
Turkish Grand National Assembly (TGNA), 1:297
Turkmenistan, **2:671–673**
Turks
in 'Abbāsid Empire, 1:68
in Bulgaria, 1:261
Ottoman Empire, 1:119
See also Ottoman Turks
Tutsi ethnic group, 2:469, *471,* 472–474
Tuvalu, **2:582–584**
Twelve Doors of Mali, 1:96
Tydings-Duffie Act, 2:342

U

UAE (United Arab Emirates), **2:532–535**
Uganda, **2:482–485**
Ukraine, **2:651–653**
Ulfilas (Gothic bishop), 1:56
Ulufa'alu, Bartholomew (Solomon Islands prime minister), 2:582
Umayyad dynasty, 1:49
Umayyad Empire, **1:63–65**
Union Island, 2:596
Union of Comoros, **2:553–556**
Union of Soviet Socialist Republics (USSR)
Armenia, incorporation into, 2:668
Cuban Missile Crisis, 2:410
dissolution of, 2:617, 697
Estonia, control of, 2:646
Finland, 1:281
Hungary, relations with, 2:619
Kazakhstan, 1:287
Korea, interests in, 2:372, 374
Kyrgyzstan, 2:659
Lithuania, annexation of, 2:663–664
Mongolia, 1:300
Nazi Germany, war with, 1:316
overview of, 1:293–297
Poland, post-WWII control of, 2:622
rule of Latvia, 2:648–649
Uzbekistan, independence from, 2:661
World War II, 2:327
United Arab Emirates (UAE), **2:532–535**
The United Kingdom
Ashanti Empire and, 1:136
Chippewa and, 1:131
Iroquois Confederation, 1:126
Mughal Empire, 1:124

overview of, **1:140–145**
Qing Dynasty and, 1:133
See also Britain
United Nations
Jewish state, support for, 2:366
Korean War response, 2:370
overview of, **2:332–335**
Suez Crisis, 1:292
United Nations Security Council (UNSC), 2:333
United Republic of Tanzania, **2:488–491**
United States of America (USA)
Antigua and Barbuda, dispute over Internet gambling, 2:605
Cherokee Nation and, 1:193–195
Chippewa bands in, 1:130
Colombia, aid to, 1:211
Cuba, occupation of, 2:409
Cuba, relations with, 2:410
Cuba, sanctions against, 2:410
Cuban Missile Crisis, 2:410
Djibouti, presence in, 2:579–580
Dominican Republic, influence in, 1:224–225
El Salvador, influence in, 1:221
European Union comparison, 2:693
Grenada, U.S. military intervention in, *2:542*
Guatemalan coup, backing of, 1:216
Haiti, 1:165
Honduras, influence in, 1:218–219
Iran, seizure of embassy in, 2:589
Iraq, conflict in, 1:310, 312, 313
Japan, opening for trade, 2:347
Kenya/Tanzania embassy bombings, 2:488, 490
Korea, interests in, 2:369, 372
Kuomintang, ties with, 2:380
Kuwait, use of for Iraq invasion, 2:466
Mexican War, 1:183
Micronesia, immigrants from, 2:612
military, Qatar support of, 2:532
Mozambique, aid to, 2:551
Nicaragua, intervention in, 1:214
Operation Enduring Freedom, 1:285
overview of, **1:154–159**
Palau, aid to, 2:702
Palau, presence in, 2:701
Panama, interests in, 1:253
Panama Canal, 1:253, 255–256
Philippines, influence in, 2:342
Samoa, presence in, 2:467
Saudi Arabia, relations with, 1:309–310

Somalia, troops in, 2:427
Taiwan, support of, 2:385–386
United Arab Emirates and, 2:533–534
United Kingdom and, 1:145
Uzbekistan, relations with, 2:663
Vietnam, conflict in, 2:576
World War II, 1:317, 2:327
Universal Postal Union, 2:332
Upper Volta, 2:433
Ur, **1:2–3**
Ur III dynasty, 1:3
Urban planning, Teotihuacán, 1:50
Uribe Vélez, Álvaro (Colombia president), 1:210, 211
Ur-Nammu (Ur king), 1:3
Uruguay, **1:195–197**
'Uthmān ibn 'Affān (Umayyad caliph), 1:64
Uzbekistan, **2:661–663**

V

Vajiravudh (Thai king), 1:304
Valdivia culture, 1:197
Valy-e Faqih, 2:588
Vanuatu, **2:598–601**
Vargas, Getúlio (Brazil dictator), 1:188
Vatican City, 1:301–304
Veche, 1:100
Velasco Ibarra, José María (Ecuador president), 1:198
Velvet Revolution protests, *2:629*
Venetiaan, Runaldo Ronald (Suriname president), 2:568
Venezuela, **1:200–203**
Venice. *See* Republic of Venice
Vernet, Claude-Joseph (painter), 1:86
Viceregal system, 1:117
Victor Emmanuel II (Italy king), 1:302
Vieira, João Bernardo (Guinea-Bissau president), 2:544, 545
Vienna, Austria, *1:277*
Vienna International Exhibition, 1:237
Vietnam, Socialist Republic of, **2:574–578**
Vietnam War, *2:575*
Vike-Freiberga, Vaira (Latvia president), 2:650
Viking Age, 1:230, 256, 288
Visconti, Azzo, 1:93
Visconti, Gian Galeazzo (Duke of Milan), 1:93

Visconti, Ottone, 1:93

Visigoths, **1:54–56**, 263

Vizier (chief administrator)
  of ancient Egypt, 1:6
  of Fātimid dynasty, 1:79
  power of, 1:7

Vladimir I (Kievan prince), 1:49,
  53–54, 78

Vladimir II (Kievan prince), 1:78

VMRO (Internal Macedonian Revolutionary Organization), 2:673

Voltaire, 1:69

Vouli ton Ellinon, 1:207

Vsevolodovich, Mikhail (Kievan
  prince), 1:78

W

Wadai people, 2:437

Wade, Abdulaye (Senegal president),
  2:451–452, 454

Wahhābism, 1:307

Walachia, 2:677

Wałęsa, Lech (Poland president),
  2:622, *623*

Walker, William, 1:214

Wang Anshi, 1:88

Wang Mang (Hsin dynasty emperor),
  1:41

Wangchuck, Jigme Dorji (Bhutan
  king), 2:376–377

Wangchuck, Jigme Singye (Bhutan
  king), 2:377

Wangchuck, Ugyen (Bhutan king),
  2:375

Wanké, Daouda Mallam, 2:432

War crimes, Bosnia, 2:681–682

War of the League of Cambrai, 1:93

War of the Triple Alliance, 1:196

War on terror
  George W. Bush, 2:617
  Mauritius participation, 2:518
  Pakistani support of, 2:358

Warsaw Pact, 2:633

Warsaw Treaty Organization, 1:262

Washington, George (U.S. president),
  1:157

Water shortages, 2:388, 631

Waverly, John, *2:524*

Weimar Republic, 1:314, 2:632

West Bank, 1:292, 2:367, 368, 548

Western Chou dynasty, 1:14, 15

Western Sahara, 2:398

Western Samoa, 2:467

Westminster Statute of 1931, 1:251

Westphalian system, 1:71

William of Normandy (British king),
  1:140

William the Conqueror. *See* William
  of Normandy (British king)

Williams, Eric Eustace (Jamaica prime
  minister), 2:482

Wilson, Woodrow (U.S. president),
  2:332

Women
  in Ashanti Empire, 1:134
  in Indian society, 2:354
  in Oman politics, 2:387
  in Tunisia, 2:401

World Court, 2:334

World War I
  aftermath, 1:269
  Albania, 1:270
  Austria, 1:276
  Austro-Hungarian war declaration
    on Serbia, 1:238
  Belgium, 1:205
  France, 1:162
  Germany, aftermath in, 1:314
  Hungary, 2:618
  Lebanon, 2:328
  New Zealand, 2:346
  Romania's territory gain from, 2:677
  Sweden, 1:168
  Togoland, 2:419
  Yugoslavia, 2:679

World War II
  Antarctica, 2:412
  Austria, 1:276
  Bulgaria, 1:261
  Burma, 2:359
  China, 2:380
  Denmark, 1:232
  Finland, 1:281
  France, 1:162
  Gambia, 2:498
  Gilbert Islands, 2:592
  Indonesia, 1:323
  Italy, 1:245
  Japan, 1:129, 2:347
  Korea after, 2:372
  Malaysia, 2:404
  Marshall Islands, 2:613
  Mongolia, 1:301
  Norway, 1:258
  overview of, 1:269, 2:327
  Palau, 2:701
  Poland, 2:621–622
  Prussian, 1:140
  Romania invasion of Russia, 2:677
  Soviet Union, 1:295
  Sri Lanka, 2:363
  Sweden and, 1:168
  Tuvalu, 2:583
  Ukraine, 2:651
  United Kingdom, effects on, 1:145
  United Nations in aftermath of,
    2:332

Vanuatu, 2:599

Western Europe, effects on, 2:693

Yugoslavia, 2:641, 683

Written language, 1:1, 2

Wu Wang (Chou dynasty king), 1:1,
  11–12, 14

X

Xerxes I (Persian king), 1:21, 23

Xia Dynasty, 2:378

Xiongnu tribe, 1:60

Y

Ya qūb ibn Killis (Fātimid prime
  minister), 1:79

Yahweh, 1:12

Yala, Kumba (Guinea-Bissau
  president), 2:544

Yaméogo, Maurice (Upper Volta
  president), 2:433

Yamoto clan (Japan), 1:127

Yandarbiyev, Zelimkhan (Chechnya
  president), 2:532

Yanukovych, Viktor (Ukraine
  president), 2:652–653

Yarlung Dynasty (Tibet), 1:98

Yaroslav (Kievan prince), 1:78

Yasodharapura, 2:391

Yasovarman I (Khmer Empire king),
  1:74

Yassa, 1:94

Yayi Boni, Thomas (Benin president),
  2:430

Yayoi period, 1:127

Yazdegerd III (Sassanid ruler), 1:63

Yeltsin, Boris (Russian Federation
  president), 2:617, 697, 698–700

Yemen, Republic of, **2:630–631**

Yin dynasty, 1:10, 11

Yom Kippur War, 1:309, 313, 2:367,
  415

Yoshida, Shigeru, 2:348

You (Chou dynasty king), 1:15

Youlou, Fulbert (Republic of the
  Congo president), 2:443, *444*

Yugoslavia
  Croatian/Serbian conflict, 2:641
  dissolution of, 2:617
  formation of, 2:643, 679, 683
  Macedonia, occupation of,
    2:673–674
  Montenegro, separation from, 2:709
  post-WWII reformation of, 2:680
  Serbia, reaction to dissolution of,
    2:685
  Slovenia, separation from, 2:645

Yupanqui, Tupac (Inca emperor), 1:108
Yushchenko, Viktor (Ukraine president), 2:652–653
Yushin Constitution, 2:371

Z

Zagreb, Croatia, *2:642*
Zahīr-ud-Dīn Muhammad (Mughal emperor) 1:122
Zambia, **2:495–498**

Zanzibar, 2:488
Zarqawi, Abu Musab al-, 2:335, 341
Zayed bin Sultan al-Nahyan, Sheikh (United Arab Emirates president), 2:533
Zelaya, José Manuel (Honduras president), 1:219
Zerbo, Saye, 2:433
Zheng Chenggong, 2:383
Zia, Khaleda (Bangladesh prime minister), 2:537, 538

Ziggurat, 1:2, *3*
Zimbabwe, 2:551, **596–598**
Zimbabwe, Great, **1:103–106**
Zoroaster (Persian prophet), 1:62
Zoroastrianism
    in Azerbaijan, 1:273
    in Persia, 2:588
    in Sassanid Empire, 1:61, 62–63
Zulu Empire
    Botswana, attacks on, 2:507
    overview of, **1:178–180**
    Swaziland, attacks on, 2:518–519